Quick Guide

S0-AXI-772

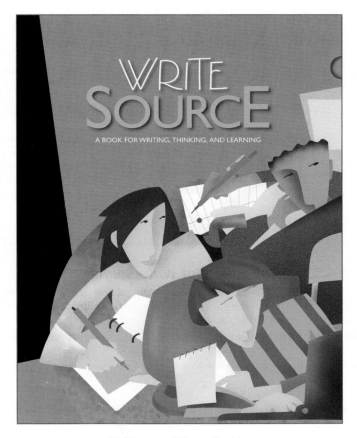

WRITE SOURCE

A BOOK FOR WRITING, THINKING, AND LEARNING

Written and Compiled by

**Dave Kemper, Patrick Sebranek,
and Verne Meyer**

Illustrated by

Chris Krenzke

WRITE SOURCE®

GREAT SOURCE EDUCATION GROUP
a division of Houghton Mifflin Company
Wilmington, Massachusetts

Reviewers

Technology Connection for *Write Source*

Visit our Web site for additional student models, writing prompts, updates for citing sources, multimedia reports, information about submitting your writing, and more.

The Write Source Web site . . . . **www.thewritesource.com**

Using *Write Source*

Your ***Write Source*** book is loaded with information to help you learn about writing. One section that will be especially helpful is the "Proofreader's Guide" at the back of the book. This section covers the rules for language and grammar.

The book also includes main units covering research writing as well as the types of writing that you may have to complete on district or state tests. In addition, a special section provides samples and tips for writing in science, social studies, math, the applied sciences, the arts, and the workplace.

Write Source will help you with other learning skills, too—test taking, note taking, and making oral presentations. This makes *Write Source* a valuable writing and learning guide in all of your classes. (The **Quick Tour** on the next two pages highlights many of the key features in the book.)

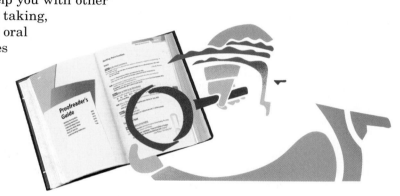

Your *Write Source* guide . . .

With practice, you will be able to find information in this book quickly using the guides explained below.

- The **Table of Contents** (starting on page **vi**) lists the five major sections in the book and the chapters found in each section.
- The **Index** (starting on page **765**) lists the topics covered in the book in alphabetical order. Use the index when you are interested in a specific topic.
- The **Color Coding** used for the "Proofreader's Guide" (yellow) makes this important section easy to find. Colorful side tabs also provide a handy reference.
- **Page References** in the book tell you where to turn for additional information about a specific topic. *Example:* (See page **350**.)

> If, at first, you're not sure how to find something in *Write Source,* ask your teacher for help. With a little practice, you will find everything quickly and easily.

A Quick Tour of *Write Source*

Write Source contains many key features that will help you improve your writing and language skills. Once you become familiar with this book, you will begin to understand how helpful these features can be.

Checklists serve as effective revising and editing guides within the writing units.

Writing guidelines help you, step-by-step, to complete different forms of writing.

Rubrics help you evaluate your finished pieces of writing. They also help to keep you on track during your writing.

204

Essay of Speculation

In the following essay, Carla predicts what might happen if an invasive plant called crown vetch is left unchecked.

Uncontrollable Invasion

Beginning
The writer introduces the topic and states her thesis (underlined).

Fifty years ago, road crews began planting crown vetch along newly constructed highways to prevent soil erosion. Crown vetch is an aggressive ground-cover plant with appealing foliage and flowers. Road improvement scars were quickly covered and erosion was no longer a concern. Then planners discovered an alarming problem. Crown vetch didn't like staying in one place. Instead, it started taking root in land adjacent to the roadsides. As a result, it became clear that crown vetch could not be planted carelessly or left unchecked. What would happen if this plant were left alone to grow and spread? If left unchecked, crown vetch could change the nation's landscape as we know it.

Middle
Each middle paragraph addresses a main point.

Most people pay little attention to this plant along the nation's highways and freeways. Motorists use these roadways to get to a destination quickly. However, crown vetch matures into an 18-inch-high creeping, competitive plant that grows in all climates—wet or dry, hot or cold. It can literally begin to take over a roadside and nearby land, overwhelming any vegetation in its path, including small trees (Fernald). If this would happen, even the most unobservant driver would begin to notice a sameness in the vegetation mile after mile after mile. Eventually, motorists would complain, demanding that the government do something about the problem.

An authority is cited.

If crown vetch really took hold in an area, local crops and gardens could be at risk. According to Art Gover of Pennsylvania State University, crown vetch sprouts from rhizomes (underground root runners) and seeds, which makes it fast growing and difficult to eradicate. The rhizomes can be up to 10 feet in length. As a result, crown vetch could easily overwhelm backyard gardens or croplands near roadsides. To eliminate the problem, strong chemicals may have to be applied to an infested area. Unfortunately, chemicals could kill any nearby desirable plants or contaminate the soil. Otherwise, fires would have to be set in these areas year after year.

Writing an Essay of Speculation **205**

Each middle paragraph begins with a topic sentence, followed by supporting details.

The greatest danger posed by crown vetch is its potential to invade, and destroy, native prairie habitats. Native prairie land is unique to interior parts of the United States, primarily in the Plains states. Most of the original prairie is gone, and crown vetch could threaten what remains (Heim). A prairie needs to maintain a special balance of native plants and animals to thrive, and the introduction of crown vetch into the area would certainly destroy that balance. Fires, historically caused by lightning storms, help maintain the health and vitality of the prairies. However, if crown vetch were in the area, the plant burns too quickly and without the necessary heat to aid in prairie regeneration. It would be a tragedy to lose what remains of the nation's prairie lands because of an invasive plant such as crown vetch.

Ending
The ending summarizes the writer's thesis.

Crown vetch has helped control erosion along U.S. roadways, but if left unchecked, it has the potential to do as much harm as good. Croplands, gardens, and prairies are the areas where an infestation of crown vetch could be the most harmful. Most plants in their rightful place benefit the landscape or ecosystem; but in the wrong place, without the proper restraint, they may cause serious, long-term problems.

Expository

? **Respond to the reading.** Answer the following questions about the sample essay of speculation.

Ideas (1) What is the thesis or focus of this essay? (2) What main points does the writer include to support the thesis? Name at least two.

Organization (3) How does the writer organize the essay—spatially, chronologically, or by order of importance?

Voice & Word Choice (4) Does the writer sound interested in and knowledgeable about the topic? Explain.

The **writing samples** will stimulate you to write your own effective essays.

Graphic organizers show you how to organize your ideas for writing.

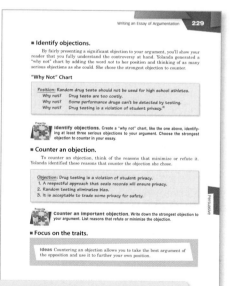

Writing an Essay of Argumentation **229**

■ **Identify objections.**

By fairly presenting a significant objection to your argument, you'll show your reader that you fully understand the controversy at hand. Yolanda generated a "why not" chart by adding the word *not* to her position and thinking of as many serious objections as she could. She chose the strongest objection to counter.

"Why Not" Chart

Position: Random drug tests should not be used for high school athletes.
Why not? Drug tests are too costly.
Why not? Some performance drugs can't be detected by testing.
Why not? Drug testing is a violation of student privacy.

 Identify objections. Create a "why not" chart, like the one above, identifying at least three serious objections to your argument. Choose the strongest objection to counter in your essay.

■ **Counter an objection.**

To counter an objection, think of the reasons that minimize or refute it. Yolanda identified these reasons that counter the objection she chose.

Objection: Drug testing is a violation of student privacy.
1. A respectful approach that seals records will ensure privacy.
2. Random testing eliminates bias.
3. It is acceptable to trade some privacy for safety.

 Counter an important objection. Write down the strongest objection to your argument. List reasons that refute or minimize the objection.

■ **Focus on the traits.**

Ideas Countering an objection allows you to take the best argument of the opposition and use it for your own position.

Persuasive

Links to the traits help you appreciate the importance of different traits at different points in the writing process.

Writing Stories **347**

■ **Develop a symbol.**

A symbol is a person, a place, a thing, or an event that represents something else. You can use a symbol to make ideas concrete and to unify your writing. Jordan used a thought map to think about symbols. He wrote important characters and ideas in the center, and then thought of concrete symbols to represent them.

Thought Map

football helmet   macaroni   hot bath   driver's license   textbooks
   Marcus   His mother   Responsibility
bedroom   trophy   Reader's Digest   desk

Create a thought map. Write down important characters and ideas for your story. Then write possible symbols of each, connecting them. Choose one main symbol for your story, but also keep the other symbols in mind.

■ **Use dialogue.**

Dialogue lets characters speak for themselves. Jordan's story uses regular dialogue, set off with quotation marks (""), and internal dialogue, indicated with *italics*, which lets the reader hear the conflict inside the main character.

"I love you, son." *How long has it been since he said that to me?*

Note: Use internal dialogue only with the main character so that your point of view does not shift.

Try It!

Experiment with dialogue. Answer each of the following questions the way your main character would. Use regular dialogue to let the person speak and use internal dialogue to show what the person is thinking.

1. What's your least favorite thing to do?
   Example answer: "Algebra homework," Marcus said. *Though cleaning my room would be a close second.*

2. What's your favorite thing to do?
3. What's the biggest challenge that you face?
4. Do you think you'll overcome the challenge? Why or why not?

Creative Writing

contents

The Writing Process

contents

The Forms of Writing

NARRATIVE WRITING

EXPOSITORY WRITING

contents

PERSUASIVE WRITING

RESPONSE TO LITERATURE

CREATIVE WRITING

RESEARCH WRITING

contents

WRITING ACROSS THE CURRICULUM

The Tools of Learning

A Writer's Resource

contents

Proofreader's Guide

Why Write?

You write essays, develop research papers, and respond to writing prompts. These are important *practical* types of writing that you do in school. Be prepared. You'll continue to do a lot of practical writing when your schooling is completed. As writer Patricia T. O'Conner states, "Because of computers, we're suddenly a nation of writers." Engineers, mechanics, lawyers, health-care workers, fitness trainers—everyone is "wired in" and writing reports, requests, proposals, news briefs, and so on.

You may also keep a writer's notebook, write about your course work in a learning log, and e-mail your friends and family members. These are important *personal* types of writing that help you figure things out and determine where you fit in. Writer Natalie Goldberg says that personal writing "allows you to penetrate your life and learn to trust your own mind." If you don't already do any personal writing, get started as soon as possible.

- ■ **Using a Writer's Notebook**
- ■ **Writing in Action**

"It is by sitting down to write every morning that one becomes a writer."

—Gerald Brenan

Using a Writer's Notebook

A writer's notebook (also called a journal) is a place to record your thoughts on any topic. As you do so, you will make countless discoveries about your world. You may also find yourself inspired to create more polished forms of writing—stories, poems, and narratives.

Getting started may not be easy for you, but if you keep at it, you will find that writing in a notebook will become part of your regular routine. As writer Thomas Mallon states, "There comes a point when, like a marathon runner, you get through some sort of 'wall' and start running on automatic." To find out if this is true, write every day—no excuses!

Ensure success.

To make sure that your writer's notebook is a success, consider the approach, quality, and variety of your entries.

- **Approach:** Begin each entry with a high level of enthusiasm. Write about things that matter to you and develop your ideas fully.
- **Quality:** Focus on exploring and developing your ideas, not on producing perfect copy. Your notebook is your place to experiment, take risks, and make mistakes.
- **Variety:** Write some of your entries from different points of view. For example, after a disagreement with a family member, write about the experience from the other person's point of view, or from the perspective of someone who overheard the discussion.

Rules for Notebook Writing

1. Date each entry. The date on an entry helps you find it later and places it in a context with other entries and experiences.

2. Write freely. Push to keep your pen moving or your fingers keyboarding. Continuous writing helps you make discoveries.

3. Write regularly. Develop the habit of writing daily. Then reread your entries to consider what you've discovered. Those ideas may prompt additional writing.

> "Have fun. Your sense of freedom and play will infuse your writing with energy, and that energy will make your words enjoyable to read."
>
> —Jack Heffron

Write about anything—and everything.

There are no limits to what you can write about—just as long as each of your entries connects with you personally. Write about people, places, and things; delve into your hopes, dreams, and memories; explore snippets of conversations that you overhear. Your notebook is the perfect place to explore these topics and form new understandings in the process.

When you can't think of something to write about, refer to the following questions for ideas.

- **Observations:** What is happening around you right now? What are your thoughts and feelings about what's happening?

- **Memories:** What was the best moment of your day? The week? The year? What was the worst moment?

- **Hopes and dreams:** What do you want in life? What do you hope for in the future?

- **People:** What person means the most to you? What person do you most admire? What sort of person do you think you are or wish you were?

- **Places:** Where are you right now? Where do you wish you were? Where do you never want to be again?

- **Things:** What is your favorite possession? Your least favorite? What one thing most closely links you to your past?

- **Thoughts:** What is the most peculiar thing you've learned recently? What is the best piece of advice you've given or received?

Try It!

Find inspiration. Write freely for 8 to 10 minutes. The topic is you. Begin with *I wish I were . . .* and see where your writing takes you. Afterward, underline at least two discoveries that you made in this writing.

Take it personally.

Here is a page from a student writer's notebook. This powerful entry focuses on the writer's future and does several important things. It . . .

- shows the depth of the writer's feelings,
- captures a time in her life,
- describes a place, and
- makes colorful comparisons.

Sample Notebook Entry

> April 3, 2006
>   When I came home from school I headed right down to the lakefront. It had been a rough day, and it's always been easier to think when I'm looking at that big, blank expanse of water.
>   My guidance counselor was really upset with me when I told him I wasn't going to college next year. He kept going on about my good science grades, my potential, my future. But that's just it. It's my future, and I just don't see college as part of it—at least not right now. My parents aren't thrilled about my decision, either, but it's too late to do anything about it now. I missed all the application deadlines.
>   Tomorrow I'm going down to enlist in the navy. I know it's kind of weird for a girl, but I want to experience those big ships, to spend time out on the ocean. I can study oceanography and meteorology in the navy better than at any school. There's always been something pulling me to the water. My biology teacher used to talk about how we all came from the sea, and I laughed and said I always thought I had seawater in my veins. I just know this is the right decision, and that I am finally steering the right course.

Note: Keeping a writer's notebook lets you look at ordinary things in new ways, describe your feelings, choose good descriptive words, and practice writing until you feel confident.

Try It!

Write freely for 5 to 10 minutes about an obstacle in your life. Reflect on how you felt as you faced it.

Writing in Action

A notebook can be a useful tool for sorting out your thoughts. Below are passages that show how three different students use their notebooks.

Examining Feelings

This student uses her notebook to sort out her feelings about her aunt.

> I still can't believe Aunt Tanya is gone, even though I was right there when she slipped away. It's not fair! She wasn't that old! That cancer worked so fast, and she was suffering so much, but at least she was fighting! She was so brave. Two weeks ago, she joked that she'd found a foolproof way to lose weight! Then the regression, and today she's gone. But she's out of pain now. Mom's a basket case, and I guess I can be strong for her. Strong like Aunt Tanya.

Reliving an Experience

Here a student reflects on a memorable time.

> Visiting New York with the choir was the best! I've never seen so many people or so much traffic! When Alex and I asked directions from a pushcart owner, he gave us free hot dogs and said, "See, New Yorkers aren't so unfriendly!" We even got to sing on the steps of Lincoln Center. My favorite part was riding the ferry to see the Statue of Liberty. Suddenly someone started singing "America the Beautiful," and we all joined in. What an awesome moment! I'll always remember that feeling.

Questioning/Solidifying a Belief

This student explores her mistaken impression about a classmate.

> I don't know why I didn't like Luke. I guess I just figured he was this big popular jock. Then we got paired for this calculus lab. I thought I'd end up doing everything, but surprise! He really worked hard. He's actually had to help me with stuff I didn't understand, but he's been really nice about it. I liked working with him, and I think we can even be friends. I guess I shouldn't have judged him so quickly.

6

Using the Writing Process

Understanding Writing

Writing is mind traveling, destination unknown. Let this statement be a reminder that when you write, you may be engaged in uncharted thinking, mind traveling, so to speak. As you go along, you may stumble upon old memories, face realities of the present, and speculate on what might be. You won't necessarily know where your writing will take you, at least not at the beginning. Your destination will only become clear as you travel further and further into your writing.

This is why writing may frustrate you. You feel you must know exactly where you are going before you start each journey. But effective writing seldom works that way. Instead, writing often works best when it is the product of an unexpected detour, a surprising thought burst, an ordinary idea gone haywire. That is why writing is thought of as a process; it can't be rushed, and it can't be fully scripted beforehand. In other words, it requires some mind traveling.

- ■ **Becoming a Good Writer**
- ■ **Understanding the Writing Process**
- ■ **The Process in Action**
- ■ **Learning from the Pros**

"There's a sureness to good writing . . . it comes only after writing every day, sometimes for years."

—Anne Bernays

> "The way around writer's block is to write every day and to give up judging. Just write the novel or story or essay or poem and keep writing."
>
> —Ron Koertge

Becoming a Good Writer

To become a good writer, you should act like one, which means that you should follow this advice:

- **Make reading an important part of your life.** Read anything and everything—books, magazines, and newspapers. Reading helps you internalize the traits of effective writing. Unless you become a regular reader, you can't expect to do your best as a writer.
- **Make writing an important part of your life.** Get into a regular writing routine, and stick to it! When writing becomes something that you want to do, rather than something that you have to do, you will begin to see improvement. (See pages **2–5** for more information.)
- **Explore meaningful topics.** In your personal writing, address your foremost thoughts, feelings, and experiences. In your assignments, write about topics that have special meaning to you. You will do your best work if you write about topics that truly interest you.
- **Set high standards.** If a first draft does not seem inviting, add more detail or voice to the writing. If the nouns and verbs in your writing are too general, replace them with more specific ones. Writer William Zinsser says, "Quality is its own reward." In other words, you will feel good about your writing if it is the result of a strong effort.
- **Try different forms.** Write essays, articles, stories, poems, and plays. Each form can teach you something about writing.
- **Become a student of writing.** Learn about the traits of writing (see pages **47–50**) and build your writing vocabulary. For example, you should know what is meant by *focus, specific details,* and *transitions.* You should also know the difference between *narrative, descriptive, expository,* and *persuasive* writing.

FYI

Each writer's process is different. Some writers do a lot of planning in their heads, while others need to put everything on paper. In addition, some writers find it helpful to talk about their work throughout the process.

Try It!

Find one quotation that says something inspirational or insightful about writing. Share it with your classmates and explain its significance.

Understanding the Writing Process

You should develop a piece of writing through a series of steps called the *writing process* before you share it. This page briefly describes these steps.

The Steps in the Writing Process

Prewriting

The first step in the writing process involves selecting a specific topic, gathering details about it, and organizing those details into a writing plan.

Writing

During this step, the writer completes the first draft using the prewriting plan as a guide. This draft is a writer's *first* chance to get everything on paper.

Revising

During revising, the writer reviews the draft for five key traits: ***ideas, organization, voice, word choice,*** and ***sentence fluency.*** After deciding what changes to make, the writer deletes, moves, adds to, and rewrites parts of the text.

Editing

Then the writer edits the revised draft for the ***conventions*** of punctuation, capitalization, spelling, and grammar and proofreads the final copy before sharing it.

Publishing

Finally, the writer publishes the work by preparing a final copy and sharing it with others.

Analyze your own process. Are you a slow writer or a fast one? Do you do a lot of planning? Do you make many changes to a first draft? Explain.

The Process in Action

The next two pages give a detailed description of each step in the writing process. The graphic below reminds you that, at any time, you can move back and forth between the steps in the process. Also remember that carefully attending to the first steps in the writing process will make the final steps much easier.

Prewriting ■ Select a topic.

- Search for topics that meet the requirements of the assignment.
- Select a specific topic that appeals to you.

■ Gather and organize details.

- Gather as many ideas and details as you can about the topic.
- With the purpose of the assignment in mind, find one point to emphasize about the topic—either an interesting part or your personal feeling about it. This will be the focus, or thesis, of your writing.
- Decide which details fit your topic.
- Organize your details into a writing plan using an outline, a chart, or some other method.

Writing ■ Develop the first draft.

- When writing the first draft, concentrate on getting your ideas on paper. Don't try to produce a perfect piece of writing.
- Use your prewriting plan as a guide and include the details you collected, but feel free to add new ideas that occur to you as you go along.
- Be sure your writing has a beginning, a middle, and an ending.

Tip

Write on every other line and on only one side of the paper when using pen or pencil and paper. Double-space on a computer. This will give you room for revising, the next step in the process.

Revising ▪ Improve your writing.

- Set aside your first draft for a while so you can return to it with a fresh perspective.
- Read your first draft slowly and critically.
- Use these questions as a revising guide:
  - Is my topic interesting for the reader?
  - Does the beginning catch the reader's attention?
  - Are the ideas in order and easy to understand?
  - Have I included enough details to support my central idea?
  - Does the ending leave the reader with something to think about?
  - Do I sound interested in and knowledgeable about the topic?
  - Are the nouns specific and the verbs active?
  - Are the modifiers (adjectives and adverbs) clear and descriptive?
  - Does the whole piece read smoothly?

- Ask at least one person to review your writing and offer suggestions.
- Make as many changes as necessary to improve your writing.

Editing ▪ Check for conventions.

- Check for errors in punctuation, capitalization, spelling, and grammar.
- Have another person check your writing for errors.
- Prepare a neat final copy.
- Proofread the final copy before publishing it.

Publishing ▪ Share your writing.

- Share your writing with friends, classmates, and family.
- Consider submitting your writing to a newspaper or other publication.
- Include the writing in your portfolio.

Tip

For assignments, save all your work. Refer to the earlier drafts and to the teacher's comments on the graded piece for ideas and inspiration for future writing projects.

 Consider the process. Some experts say that revising is the most important step in the writing process. Explain why this may be true.

Learning from the Pros

Keep the following thoughts in mind as you develop your writing. They come from experienced authors who appreciate writing as a process of discovery.

"I don't pick subjects so much as they pick me."
—Andy Rooney

"When I speak to students about writing, I hold myself up as an example of that ancient axiom—write about what you know."
—Robert Cormier

"The inspiration comes while you write."
—Madeleine L'Engle

"Writing comes more easily if you have something to say."
—Sholem Asch

"I think one is constantly startled by the things that appear before you on the page while you write."
—Shirley Hazzard

"By the time I reach a fifth version, my writing begins to have its own voice."
—Ashley Bryan

"Half of my life is an act of revision."
—John Irving

"I am an obsessive rewriter, doing one draft and then another and another, usually five. In a way, I have nothing to say but a great deal to add."
—Gore Vidal

"I believe in impulse and naturalness, but followed by discipline in the cutting."
—Anaïs Nin

"Write visually, write clearly, and make every word count."
—Gloria D. Miklowitz

Try It!

Create two of your own quotations that reflect your own experience as a writer. Share those quotations with your classmates, explaining their significance.

One Writer's Process

At your age, you probably know quite a lot about the steps in the writing process: prewriting, writing, revising, editing, and publishing. You also probably know that using the process helps you to produce your best work, an effective finished piece of writing. Since you already understand this, there's no real need to read further, is there?

Well, yes—in fact, refamiliarizing yourself with the steps in the writing process is always a good idea. As you become a better writer, it may be tempting to slack off, take it easy, skip a step or two. But *every* step in the process is essential to doing your best work. This chapter, which chronicles student writer Roberto Salazar's process for a persuasive essay, will serve as a simple reminder of that fact.

- **Previewing the Goals**
- **Prewriting**
- **Writing**
- **Revising**
- **Editing**
- **Publishing**
- **Assessing the Final Copy**
- **Reflecting on Your Writing**

"If you want to write, or really to create anything, you have to risk falling on your face."

—Allegra Goodman

Previewing the Goals

Before Roberto Salazar began writing his essay, he previewed the goals for persuasive writing, which are shown below. He also looked over the rubric for persuasive writing on pages **254–255**. Both of these activities helped him get started.

Traits of Persuasive Writing

- ### Ideas
  Select a timely topic, a controversial issue that you care about. Form your opinion and use specific reasons and details to defend your position.

- ### Organization
  State your opinion in the beginning, use facts and examples to support your opinion in the middle, and end with a call for action.

- ### Voice
  Use a confident voice that balances facts and feelings, and maintain an appropriate tone for your topic and audience.

- ### Word Choice
  Choose fair and precise words to state and defend your position. Explain important terms that may be unfamiliar to your audience.

- ### Sentence Fluency
  Write clear, complete sentences with varied beginnings and transitions that guide the reader smoothly through your argument.

- ### Conventions
  Follow rules of punctuation, capitalization, spelling, and grammar.

Try It!

List two or three topics that would be suitable for a persuasive essay. What tone of voice would be appropriate for each? What important terms would you need to explain for each?

Prewriting ■ Select a topic.

Roberto's economics teacher assigned the following topic.

> Recently we've discussed the government's obligations in a market economy—providing for national defense, overseeing health-care initiatives, addressing environmental concerns, among others. Based on what you've learned about the federal budget process, do you support reductions in defense spending or is the current spending level necessary? Support your position in a persuasive essay.

■ Reflect on the topic.

Roberto made a list of pros and cons on the issue.

YES to reductions	NO to reductions
• Other issues that affect our citizens should be addressed before spending more on defense.	• Our military should be the best in the world.
• Another country won't attack us on our soil, so why worry about defense?	• We need to keep up with other countries.
• Having a strong military may lead to unwise involvement in conflicts.	• Lots of industries provide for defense and have a big effect on the economy.
• One day, armed conflict will be a thing of the past.	• There will always be conflict in the world; we have to be ready.

Roberto found that he still had some questions. He wrote them down and researched them before forming his opinion.

- How much does our military spend, especially in relation to other countries?
- What do we spend on the nation's health and education?
- Is there public support for reducing defense spending?

Try It!

Which of Roberto's reasons (pro or con) is strongest? Weakest? Which of the opposing viewpoints would *you* address in a persuasive essay? Explain.

Prewriting ▪ Gather details.

Roberto went to the library and looked for information about defense spending; he also looked on the Internet. He recorded his source information on note cards.

Sources of Information

Stockholm International Peace Research Institute. SIPRI Yearbook 2005: Armaments, Disarmament and International Security. Oxford: Oxford UP, 2005.

Kouri, Jim. "The New Pentagon Papers." The National Ledger. Feb. 10, 2006.

"Department of Defense." Office of Management and Budget. Feb. 27, 2006. http://www. whitehouse.gov/omb/budget/ fy2005/defense.html

Quotations and Paraphrases

Roberto used note cards to record quotations and paraphrases, too. He was sure to include the source for each.

Quotation

"Leveraging rapidly changing technology with flexible organizations and adaptable doctrine, the U.S. military aims to become lighter, faster, and more lethal."

Source: Dept. of Defense

Paraphrase

Worldwide military spending reached a trillion dollars in 2004, and the United States was responsible for a large portion of that amount.

Source: Stockholm

Try It!

Look at the questions Roberto still had (on the previous page). Find some sources that would answer his questions.

Writing

■ Form a thesis statement.

Once Roberto had formed his opinion and had enough information to support it, he was ready to write the *thesis statement* for his essay. An effective thesis statement consists of two parts: a specific topic plus a particular feeling or opinion about it. Roberto wrote this thesis statement:

specific topic		particular opinion about it		thesis statement
this country's spending for national defense	**+**	is excessive and should be reduced	**=**	This country's spending for national defense is excessive and should be reduced.

■ Organize the essay.

Next, Roberto wrote a topic outline for his essay. This step organized the details that supported his thesis.

I. Introduction
II. Background
   A. Explanation of how federal budget is distributed
   B. National defense as half of discretionary budget
   C. Comparison to budgets for education and health
III. Key Supporting Points
   A. Other countries' spending on defense far less than U.S.
   B. U.S. current level of preparedness
   C. Widespread public support to reduce defense spending
IV. Concession
   A. Defense contractors benefitting from large budget
   B. Economic impact of losing some defense contracts not great
V. Conclusion

Try It!

Imagine that you had taken the opposite side of the issue. Write a thesis statement that supports that opinion, and then create an outline like the one above.

Writing ■ Develop your first draft.

Roberto referred to his outline as he wrote his first draft. At this point, he wanted to get all his ideas down on paper without worrying about writing the perfect essay.

The first paragraph states the issue and ends with the thesis statement.

The first middle paragraph covers the background.

Sources are identified throughout.

The next three paragraphs support the thesis.

It sure takes a lot of cash to make a country feel secure. The defense budget for China was $62.5 billion. The defense budget for 11 countries in the European Union totaled $185.8 billion. But the United States spent $420.7 billion ("U.S. Military Spending"). That's 43 percent of the world's total. Worldwide military spending had reached a trillion dollars by 2004, with the United States responsible for a lopsided amount. It's obvious that this country's spending for national defense is excessive and should be reduced.

In the United States, the federal budget is classified in two ways. National defense falls under a category of the federal budget called "discretionary" spending. Congress decides on the level of resources set aside for any specific area. Congress decides where to increase or decrease funds. Congress earmarks the other two-thirds of the budget for programs where the level of funding is decided by the number of people who is qualified for entitlements. Funding for the Department of Defense currently accounts for fully half of the federal discretionary budget. The president's request for 2007 was $439.3 billion for the Department of Defense ("Dept. of Defense"). Besides this, the departments' budget does not include ongoing military costs in the Middle East. The Department of Education meritted a request of $56.8 billion—about an eighth of the defense budget; and the amount budgeted for health was $53.1 billion ("FY '07"). Also, the 2007 defense budget had increased 14 percent over the 2005 budget ("Dept. of Defense"), while the education and health budgets decreased 9 and 5 percent ("Education Dept.," "Budget"). Priorities seam a bit skewed here.

As the U.S. military gobbles up more and more of the world's military spending pie, here is a logicle thought: decreasing the amount spent on national defense would have little affect on U.S. military capability. Especially relative to other countries' military power. Even if the defense budget were cut in half, the next 2 big spenders combined wouldn't come near our level.

Further, the U.S. doesn't need the level of military preparedness it currently has. We're surrounded by friendly neighbors! An attack by another country on our soil is unlikely. Second, in the words of Charles Peña, "The real threat to the United States no longer consists of nation states, but the terrorist threat represented by al-Qaeda, which is relatively undeterred by the U.S. military" ("More"). In other words, continuously increasing military funding will do little to prevent terrorism. A change in terrorist thinking will come only with international cooperation to address poor conditions.

For another thing, there are lots of public support to reduce military spending. A 2005 poll by the University of Maryland's Program on International Policy Attitudes showed 65 percent of the respondents cutting defense spending (Soto). And another 2005 poll, conducted by the Pew Research Center, showed that 36% of respondents think lowering defense and military spending is a top priority in reducing the budget deficit ("Federal"). And there are dozens of organizations and Web sites that support decreased defense spending. Congress's leaders should take note.

While it is true that the current level of spending benefits many defense contractors and other businesses to the tune of $230 billion (Borgen), their impact on the economy isn't important. If these businesses could no longer rely on government contracts, they could evolve to the market (convert their production to non-military use). This is exactly what many defense contractors did following WWII.

It is not crazy to believe that huge military budgets are outdated. Humanitarian efforts make a huge difference. And contrary to "hawkish" thinking, when conflict does arise, peaceful resolutions are possible. It's time to start taking apart the military machine and spend that money better.

Sources are identified throughout.

An opposing argument is addressed.

The closing paragraph restates the thesis and ends with a call to action.

Revising ▪ Focus on ideas, organization, and voice.

Roberto set his essay aside for a while before giving it a fresh look. When he did review it, he rechecked the goals on page 14. Then he wrote down some changes he planned to make in terms of ideas, organization, and voice.

Ideas

"I should make the opening sentence more interesting. I need to beef up details in some places and delete one or two details that aren't really necessary."

Organization

"I should separate the second paragraph into two paragraphs to improve the organization. I need to be sure my ending is a strong finish for this essay."

Voice

"I should add more precise words to show how strongly I feel about this topic."

▪ Roberto's First Revision

Here are some of the revisions that Roberto made in his essay.

The opening sentence is made into a question to increase interest.

An explanation emphasizes an important point.

How much cash does it take
∧ It sure takes a lot of cash to make a country feel
secure. ? The defense budget for China was $62.5 billion.
The defense budget for 11 countries in the European Union
totaled $185.8 billion. But the United States spent $420.7
—close to half—
billion ("U.S. Military Spending"). That's 43 percent ∧ of the
world's total. Worldwide military spending had reached a
trillion dollars by 2004, with the United States responsible

for a lopsided amount. It's obvious that this country's spending for national defense is excessive and should be reduced.

An unnecessary idea is deleted.

In the United States, ~~the federal budget is classified in two ways,~~ National defense falls under a category of the federal budget called "discretionary" spending. Congress decides on the level of resources set aside for any specific area. Congress decides where to increase or decrease funds.

An added detail completes the explanation.

Congress earmarks the other two-thirds of the budget for "mandatory" spending: programs where the level of funding is decided by the number of people who is qualified for entitlements. ¶ Funding for the

A new paragraph improves the organization.

Department of Defense currently accounts for fully half of the federal discretionary budget. The president's request for 2007 was $439.3 billion for the Department of Defense ("Dept. of Defense"). Besides this, the departments' budget does not include ~~outlays for~~ ongoing military costs ~~operations~~ in

A few well-placed words intensify the voice and clarify the statistics.

the Middle East. The Department of Education meritted a request of just $56.8 billion—about an eighth of the defense budget; and the amount budgeted for health was even less: $53.1 billion ("FY '07"). Also, the 2007 . . .

Try It!

Review the changes Roberto made to the first few paragraphs of his essay. Make similar revisions to the rest of the essay, suggesting at least one revision in the area of ideas, one in organization, and one in voice.

Revising ▪ Use a peer response sheet.

Kinsey evaluated Roberto's essay using a rubric like the one on pages 254–255. Her suggestions on the response sheet below showed Roberto where he could make additional improvements.

Peer Response Sheet

Writer: <u>Roberto</u>   Responder: <u>Kinsey</u>

Title: <u>Cut Defense Spending</u>

What I liked about your writing:

<u>I'm glad you included lots of facts and figures to support your</u>

<u>thesis.</u>

<u>I can tell you really believe your opinion is right!</u>

Changes I would suggest:

<u>More details are needed in some areas (for instance, the year of</u>

<u>the budgets you mention in the first paragraph). Also, it's hard</u>

<u>to imagine how much $439 billion really is. Could you clarify that</u>

<u>somehow?</u>

Try It!

Review Kinsey's suggestions for improvement above. Which suggestion seems to be the most important? Explain why. Add at least one new suggestion to improve Roberto's writing. (Look at the explanations of ideas, organization, and voice on page **14** to refresh your memory.)

■ Roberto's Revision Using a Peer Response

Here are some revisions Roberto made, using Kinsey's comments.

The year of the budget is added.

A statistic is placed earlier in the paragraph for more impact, and the source of the figure is stated.

An example that improves the definition of the term is added.

A comparison helps the reader understand the enormity of a figure.

How much cash does it take to make a country feel secure? The defense budget for China was $62.5 billion. The [2005] defense budget for 11 countries in the European Union totaled $185.8 billion. But the United States spent $420.7 billion ("U.S. Military Spending"). That's 43 percent—close to half—of the world's total. Worldwide military spending had reached a trillion dollars by 2004, with the United States responsible for a lopsided amount. (Stockholm) It's obvious that this country's spending for national defense is excessive and should be reduced.

In the United States, national defense falls under a category of the federal budget called "discretionary" spending. Congress decides on the level of resources set aside for any specific area. Congress decides where to increase or decrease funds. Congress earmarks the other two-thirds of the budget for "mandatory" spending: programs (such as social security) where the level of funding is decided by the number of people who is qualified for entitlements.

Funding for the Department of Defense currently accounts for fully half of the federal discretionary budget. The president's request for 2007 was $439.3 billion for the Department of Defense ("Dept. of Defense"). To give some perspective on how much $439.3 billion is, a mere four percent of that budget, or $19 billion, could cut global poverty by half in just 10 years (Borgen.) Besides this, the departments' budget does not include ongoing military costs in the Middle East. . . .

Revising ▪ Focus on style.

Roberto also reviewed his writing for its flow and style. His thoughts below tell you what changes he planned to make.

Word Choice

"I can use more formal language in some spots. I need to change some words that might have the wrong connotations. These changes will help me better defend my position."

Sentence Fluency

"I could combine related sentences to improve the flow. The reader will then be able to follow my argument from one point to the next. I could also expand a sentence here and there."

Try It!

Review the second revision of Roberto's essay (page **23**). What two or three changes would you make in his word choice? Name two ways in which you would improve his sentence fluency. Compare your ideas to Roberto's revisions on the next page.

"Learn to evaluate your own work with a dispassionate eye . . . The lessons you acquire will be all the more valuable because you've mastered your craft from within.

—Sue Grafton

■ Roberto's Revisions for Style

After reviewing the style and sound of his writing, Roberto focused on improving his word choice and sentence structure.

> **Sentences are combined to improve sentence fluency.**
>
> **A phrase is added to further support the writer's thesis.**
>
> **Sentence beginnings are varied.**
>
> **Word choice is improved throughout the essay.**

How much ~~cash~~ *money* does it take to make a country feel secure? Worldwide military spending had reached a trillion dollars by 2004, with the United States responsible for a ~~lopsided~~ *disproportionate* amount (Stockholm). *While* The 2005 defense budget for China was $62.5 billion, *and* The defense budget for 11 countries in the European Union totaled $185.8 billion, ~~But~~ the United States spent $420.7 billion ("U.S. Military Spending"). That's 43 percent—close to half—of the world's total. *With the numbers telling the story,* It's obvious that this country's spending for national defense is excessive and should be reduced.

In the United States, national defense falls under a category of the federal budget called "discretionary" spending. Congress decides on the level of resources *allocated to* ~~set aside for~~ any specific area, *and* ~~Congress decides~~ where to increase or decrease funds. ~~Congress earmarks~~ *is earmarked* the other two-thirds of the budget for "mandatory" spending: programs (such as social security) where the level of funding *determined* ~~is decided~~ by the number of people who ~~is~~ *eligible* ~~qualified~~ for *benefits* ~~entitlements~~.

Funding for the Department of Defense currently accounts for fully half of the federal discretionary budget. The president's request for 2007 was $439.3 billion for the Department of Defense. To give some perspective . . .

Editing ■ Check for conventions.

Roberto's last step in the process was to check for punctuation, capitalization, spelling, and grammar errors. He used the "Proofreader's Guide" in the back of his *Write Source* textbook and the checklist below.

Conventions

"I'll look carefully at my essay for punctuation, capitalization, spelling, and grammar errors."

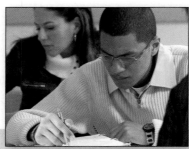

PUNCTUATION

_____ **1.** Do I use end punctuation correctly?

_____ **2.** Do I use commas correctly?

_____ **3.** Do I correctly italicize or use quotation marks for titles?

_____ **4.** Do I use apostrophes correctly?

MECHANICS (CAPITALIZATION AND SPELLING)

_____ **5.** Have I capitalized all the proper nouns and adjectives?

_____ **6.** Have I spelled words correctly?

_____ **7.** Have I used the spell-checker on my computer?

_____ **8.** Have I used abbreviations correctly?

GRAMMAR

_____ **9.** Do I use the proper tense and voice for my verbs?

_____ **10.** Do my subjects and verbs agree in number?

_____ **11.** Do my pronouns clearly agree with their antecedents?

_____ **12.** Do I use the right words (*there, their, they're*)?

DOCUMENTATION

_____ **13.** Are sources properly presented and documented?

Try It!

Find two errors in Roberto's revised draft on page **25**. Did you find the same errors as he found (on page **27**)?

Roberto's Editing

Here is a sample of Roberto's editing. (See the inside back cover of this textbook for common editing and proofreading marks.)

> . . . Congress decides on the level of resources allocated to any specific area and where to increase or decrease funds. The other two-thirds of the budget is earmarked for "mandatory" spending: programs (such as social security) where the level of funding is determined by the number of people who ~~is~~ *are* eligible for benefits.
>
> Funding for the Department of Defense currently accounts for fully half of the federal discretionary budget. The president's request for 2007 was $439.3 billion for the Department of Defense ("Dept. of Defense"). To give some perspective on how much $439.3 billion is, a mere ~~four~~ *4* percent of that budget, or $19 billion, could cut global poverty by half in just 10 years (Borgen). Besides this, the department's budget does not include ongoing military costs in the Middle East. The Department of Education ~~meritted~~ *merited* a request of just $56.8 billion—about an eighth of the defense budget; and the amount budgeted for health was even less: $53.1 billion ("FY '07"). Moreover, the 2007 defense budget had increased 14 percent over the 2005 budget ("Dept. of Defense"), while the education and health budgets decreased 9 and 5 percent respectively ("Education Dept.," "Budget"). Priorities ~~seam~~ *seem* a bit skewed here.

A proper noun is capitalized, and subject-verb agreement is corrected.

A numeric expression is corrected, and a misplaced apostrophe is fixed.

Misspelled and misused words are corrected.

Publishing ▪ Share your writing.

Roberto used the information below to produce a clean and effective copy of his final essay. Then he shared his essay with his class.

Tips for Handwritten Copies

- Use blue or black ink and write clearly.
- Write your name according to your teacher's instructions.
- Skip a line and center your title on the first page; skip another line and begin your essay.
- Indent each paragraph and leave a one-inch margin on all four sides.

Tips for Computer Copies

- Use an easy-to-read font set at 12-point type size.
- Double-space the text and set your margins so that you have a one-inch space around the outside of each page.
- For more tips on using a computer, see pages **91–95**.

■ Roberto's Final Copy

Roberto submitted his final essay with confidence. He felt that his writing met his goals and satisfied the terms of the assignment.

Roberto Salazar
Ms. Whalley
Economics
March 8, 2006

Cut Defense Spending Now!

How much money does it take to make a country feel secure? Worldwide military spending had reached a trillion dollars by 2004, with the United States responsible for a disproportionate amount (Stockholm). While the 2005 defense budget for China was $62.5 billion, and the defense budget for 11 countries in the European Union totaled $185.8 billion, the United States spent $420.7 billion ("U.S. Military Spending"). That's 43 percent—close to half—of the world's total. With the numbers telling the story, it's obvious that this country's spending for national defense is excessive and should be reduced.

In the United States, national defense falls under a category of the federal budget called "discretionary" spending. Congress decides on the level of resources allocated to any specific area and where to increase or decrease funds. The other two-thirds of the budget is earmarked for "mandatory" spending: programs (such as Social Security) where the level of funding is determined by the number of people who are eligible for benefits.

Funding for the Department of Defense currently accounts for fully half of the federal discretionary budget. The president's request for 2007 was $439.3 billion for the Department of Defense ("Dept. of Defense"). To give some perspective on how much $439.3 billion is, a mere 4 percent of that budget, or $19 billion, could cut global poverty by half in just 10 years (Borgen). Besides this, the department's budget does not include ongoing military costs in the Middle East. The Department of Education merited a request of just $56.8 billion—about an eighth of the defense budget; and the amount budgeted for health was even less: $53.1 billion ("FY '07"). Moreover, the 2007 defense budget had increased 14 percent over the 2005 budget ("Dept. of Defense"), while the education and health budgets decreased 9 and 5 percent respectively ("Education Dept.," "Budget"). Priorities seem a bit skewed here.

As the U.S. military devours more and more of the world's military spending pie, it is clear that decreasing our defense budget would have little effect on our military capability relative to that of other countries. Even if the defense budget were cut in half, the next two big spenders—China and Russia—combined wouldn't come near our level of spending. The U.S. would still have the richest military in the world.

Further, the need for our current level of military preparedness is questionable. First, the U.S. is surrounded by friendly neighbors. The likelihood of being attacked on our soil is slim. Second, Charles Peña, of the Coalition for a Realistic Foreign Policy and an analyst for MSNBC television says, "The real threat to the United States no longer consists of nation states, but the terrorist threat represented by al-Qaeda, which is relatively undeterred by the U.S. military" ("More"). In other words, increased military funding will not prevent terrorism. The terrorist legacy will change only as the world addresses conditions that generate unrest.

Additionally, the public widely supports reduced military spending. A 2005 poll by the University of Maryland showed 65 percent of respondents would cut defense spending (Soto). Another 2005 poll by the Pew Research Center showed that 36 percent of respondents strongly favor lower military spending as a way to reduce the budget deficit ("Federal"). There are also many organizations and Web sites that support decreased defense spending. Congress should take note. Although defense spending benefits the defense contractors and other

Salazar 3

businesses to the tune of $230 billion (Borgen), these businesses do not make or break the economy. If they lost some government contracts, they could adapt to the market (convert their production to nonmilitary use). Many defense contractors had to do this after WWII.

It is not idealistic to believe that huge military budgets are an antiquated way of dealing with potential conflict. Humanitarian efforts can make a huge difference in the very need for defense. And contrary to "hawkish" thinking, when conflict does arise, peaceful resolutions are possible. It's time to dismantle the military behemoth and put those funds to better use.

Assessing the Final Copy

The teacher used a rubric like the one found on pages **254–255** to assess Roberto's final copy. (A **6** is the best score for each trait.) The teacher wrote comments under each trait.

Rubric Checklist

4 **Ideas**
Your reasoning is clear, and your choice of details makes your argument very convincing. The answer to an opposing argument could be stronger.

5 **Organization**
You clearly state your position in the beginning, in each middle paragraph you offer background and support your opinion, and you make a call to action in the ending.

5 **Voice**
You obviously care about this issue. Your voice conveys a sense of urgency that fits the topic.

5 **Word Choice**
You use precise, formal language and explain unfamiliar terms.

5 **Sentence Fluency**
You use a wide variety of sentences. Your sentences read smoothly from one idea to the next.

6 **Conventions**
Your writing follows the rules of writing and is free of careless errors.

Reflecting on Your Writing

Roberto filled out a reflection sheet after he completed his essay. This helped him think about the assignment and plan for future writing tasks.

Roberto Salazar

Ms. Whalley

Economics

March 13, 2006

Persuasive Essay: Cut Defense Spending Now!

1. **The best part of my essay is . . .**

   the ending. It expresses my feelings concisely and powerfully.

2. **The part that still needs work is . . .**

   the opposing argument. It's a little weak.

3. **The most important part of my prewriting and planning was . . .**

   my fact finding. I was alarmed at what I found, and I think this came through in my voice.

4. **During revising, I spent a lot of time dealing with . . .**

   adding details and refining word choice.

5. **What I've learned about this type of essay is . . .**

   that it's important to care about my topic. Without that, it would be difficult to convince others to support my position.

6. **Here is one question I still have . . .**

   Do I cite a source for a figure I came up with based on that source's statistics?

Using a Rubric

The rubrics in this book are graphic representations of accepted standards in the six traits of good writing (ideas, organization, voice, word choice, sentence fluency, and conventions). In other words, they help writers evaluate their writing according to a given scale.

Using a rubric throughout the process of your formal writing will result in a better paragraph, essay, or report. During prewriting, review the rubric so you know what's expected. During writing and revising, compare your writing to the ratings in the rubric. When you finish writing, check the rubric once more. Use a rubric throughout the process, and your writing will be the best it can be.

- **Understanding Rubrics**
- **Reading a Rubric**
- **Getting Started with a Rubric**
- **Revising and Editing with a Rubric**
- **Assessing with a Rubric**
- **Assessing in Action**
- **Assessing a Persuasive Essay**

"It is only through evaluation that value exists: and without evaluation the nut of existence would be hollow."

—Friedrich Nietzsche

Understanding Rubrics

A **rubric** is simply a rating scale. Have you ever rated the popularity of something on a scale of 1 (terrible) to 10 (fantastic)? With rubrics, you can rate your writing—in this case, on a scale of 6 (amazing) to 1 (incomplete).

6	5	4	3	2	1
Amazing	Strong	Good	Okay	Poor	Incomplete

The quality of any piece of writing can be rated on the basis of six traits: *ideas, organization, voice, word choice, sentence fluency,* and *conventions.* (For an introduction to these traits, see pages **46–90**.) An essay may be well organized (score of 5) but have repetitive, general word choice (score of 3).

Rating Guide

Here's a brief description of the rating scale.

A **6** means that the writing is **amazing**.
It far exceeds expectations for a certain trait.

A **5** means that the writing is very **strong**.
It clearly meets the requirements for a trait.

A **4** means that the writing is **good**.
It meets most of the requirements for a trait.

A **3** means that the writing is **okay**.
It needs work to meet the main requirements for a trait.

A **2** means that the writing is **poor**.
It needs a lot of work to meet the requirements of a trait.

A **1** means that the writing is **incomplete**.
The writing is not yet ready to be assessed for a trait.

Reading a Rubric

Rubrics in this book are color coded according to the trait. *Idea* ratings appear in a green strip, *organization* in a pink strip, and so forth. There is a description for each rating to help you assess your writing for a particular trait.

Rubric for Persuasive Writing

6 Ideas	**5**	**4**
The position is convincingly presented and supported; it compels the reader to act.	The position is supported with logical reasons; an important objection is countered.	Most of the reasons support the writer's position. An objection is addressed.
Organization		
All parts of the essay work together to build a very thoughtful, convincing position.	The opening states the position, the middle provides clear support, and the ending reinforces the position.	Most parts of the essay are organized adequately except for one part.
Voice		
The writer's voice is completely confident, knowledgeable, and convincing.	The writer's voice is persuasive, knowledgeable, and respectful.	The writer respects the audience but needs to sound more persuasive or knowledgeable.

Guide your writing.

A rubric helps you . . .

- **plan your work**—knowing what is expected;
- **create a strong first draft**—focusing on *ideas, organization,* and *voice;*
- **revise and edit your work**—considering each trait; and
- **assess your final draft**—rating the traits throughout the whole piece of writing.

Think about the rubric. Read the level-5 descriptions above and consider what they have to say about ideas, organization, and voice. What should the essay include? What should each part of the writing do? How should a writer's voice sound?

Getting Started with a Rubric

Each of the writing units in this book includes a page like the one below. This page, which is arranged according to the traits of writing, explains the main requirements for developing the essay in the unit. Studying the "goals" page will help you get started with your planning.

222

Understanding Your Goal

Your goal in this chapter is to write a persuasive essay that states a position about an ethical issue and argues logically to defend the position. The traits listed in the chart below will help you plan and write your essay of argumentation.

Traits of Persuasive Writing

■ **Ideas**
Select a topic that involves an ethical controversy, write a clear position statement, and include reasons that support the position.

■ **Organization**
Create a beginning that states your position, a middle that provides support and answers an objection, and an ending that restates your position. Use transition words and phrases to connect your ideas.

■ **Voice**
Use a voice that shows understanding of the controversy and commitment to a specific position about it.

■ **Word Choice**
Choose fair and precise words to state and defend your position.

■ **Sentence Fluency**
Write clear, complete sentences with varied beginnings and lengths.

■ **Conventions**
Eliminate errors in punctuation, capitalization, spelling, and grammar.

Get the big picture. Look at the rubric on pages 254–255. You can use it to assess your progress as you write. Your goal is to write an essay that takes a position on an ethical issue and defends the position with a logically organized persuasive argument.

A Closer Look at Understanding Your Goal

The following steps will help you get an overview of the assignment in each writing unit.

1. **Read through the traits chart** to familiarize yourself with the unit's goals.
2. **Focus on ideas, organization, and voice** at the start of the project, when you are prewriting and writing. These traits form the foundation of good writing.
3. **Identify specific requirements** for each trait (such as using "reasons and supporting facts" and "a confident, positive, and convincing voice").
4. **Ask questions** if you aren't sure about any part of the assignment.

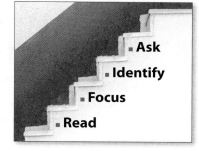

A Special Note About the Traits

Different traits are important at different stages of the writing process. The following chart shows when the specific traits are important.

> During **prewriting** and **writing**, focus on the *ideas, organization,* and *voice* in your work.
>
> During **revising**, focus on *ideas, organization, voice, word choice,* and *sentence fluency.* (For some assignments, your teacher may ask you to pay particular attention to one or two of these traits.)
>
> During **editing** and proofreading, concentrate on *conventions*— spelling, punctuation, capitalization, and grammar.
>
> When you are **assessing** your final copy, consider all six traits. (For some assignments, your teacher may ask you to assess the writing for just a few of the traits.)

Exercise

Review the goals on page 36. Then write a persuasive paragraph defending a position. Keep the traits in mind as you write.

Revising and Editing with a Rubric

6 The position is convincingly presented and supported; it compels the reader to act.

5 The position is supported with logical reasons; an important objection is countered.

4 Most of the reasons support the writer's position. An objection is addressed.

In this book, the pages that deal with revising and editing begin with a rubric strip. Each strip focuses on one trait of writing and will help you improve your first draft. The strip on these two pages focuses on the *ideas* for an essay of argumentation.

How do I use these rubric strips?

A rubric strip can help you look objectively at your writing. Focus on one trait (or "strip") at a time.

- Begin by reading the goal for that specific trait, and then read your writing with that in mind.
- Look at the description for writing that rates a 5 ("strong"). Does your writing match the description? If not, check the other rating descriptions until you find a match.
- If you're not satisfied with that rating, try to strengthen that trait in your writing.

Try It!

Review the persuasive paragraph below. Rate it for the trait of "ideas," using the rubric strip above, and give reasons for your rating.

There are a lot of benefits to be realized if more people used E85, a blend of 85 percent ethanol and 15 percent gasoline, in their vehicles. Ethanol is a fuel made from corn, a renewable resource. We could grow our fuel here instead of drilling for it in other countries. Farmers would certainly benefit if demand for ethanol increased; their corn feeds animals, too. Finally, ethanol burns cleaner than gas, so it benefits the environment, as well. Some people think that it takes more energy to produce ethanol than it saves, but recent studies have refuted that notion. It's clear that ethanol is a winner all around.

3 More supporting reasons and a more convincing response to an objection are needed.

2 A clearer position statement is needed. Better support for the position must be provided.

1 A new position statement and reasons are needed.

How can rubric strips help me revise and edit?

Once you have rated your writing for a given trait, you will see ways to improve your score. The writer of the paragraph on page **38** gave his ideas a score of 4, meaning that the writing meets *most* of the requirements for the trait. The score description told him just what he needed to do to improve his work: make *every* reason support his position. (Scores of 4 or lower offer suggestions for improving your writing.)

In the main writing units, each rubric strip is followed by brief lessons that will help you revise or edit your writing to improve that trait. There are separate rubric strips and lessons for each trait—ideas, organization, voice, word choice, sentence fluency, and conventions.

Make changes.

The writer decided to delete a reason that didn't really support his position and add another that did. He made the following changes.

An idea that doesn't support the writer's position is replaced with one that does.

. . . Farmers would certainly benefit if demand for ethanol
increased; ~~their corn feeds animals, too.~~ Finally, ethanol
burns cleaner than gas, so it benefits the environment, as
well. Some people think that it takes more energy to produce
ethanol than it saves, . . .

consumers would benefit, too, because ethanol blends
are less expensive than pure gasoline.

Revise your paragraph for ideas. Revise the paragraph you wrote for the exercise on page 37, using the strip on these two pages as a guide.

Assessing with a Rubric

Follow these four steps when you use a rubric to assess a piece of writing.

1. **Create an assessment sheet.** On your own paper, write each of the key traits from the rubric, preceded by a short line. Under each trait, leave two or three lines to allow for comments.

2. **Read the final copy.** First, get an overall feeling for the writing. Then read more carefully, paying attention to each trait.

3. **Assess the writing.** Use the rubric to rate each trait. Check the level-5 rubric description first and then go up or down the scale until you find the correct rating. Write the score next to the trait on your assessment sheet.

4. **Provide comments.** Under each trait, make whatever comments would be helpful for improving the writing.

Assessment Sheet   Title: _____

_____ Ideas

_____ Organization

_____ Voice

_____ Word Choice

_____ Sentence Fluency

_____ Conventions

                          Evaluator: _____

Exercise

Assess your persuasive paragraph. Make an assessment sheet like the one above. Evaluate your paragraph using the rubric on pages **254–255**. For each trait, write a comment about something you did well and something you'd like to improve. (See the sample on page **43**.)

254

Rubric for Persuasive Writing

Use this rubric to assess your persuasive writing using the six traits.

...ay of Argumentation 255

Each rubric addresses all six traits of writing.

	6	5	4		1
Ideas	The position is convincingly presented and supported; it compels the reader to act.	The position is supported with logical reasons; an important objection is countered.	Most of the reasons support the writer's position. An objection is addressed.		A new position statement and reasons are needed.
Organization	All parts of the essay work together to build a very thoughtful, convincing position.	The opening states the position, the middle provides clear support, and the ending reinforces the position.	Most parts of the essay are organized adequately except for one part.		The organization is unclear and incomplete.
Voice	The writer's voice is completely confident, knowledgeable, and convincing.	The writer's voice is persuasive, knowledgeable, and respectful.	The writer respects the audience but needs to sound more persuasive or knowledgeable.		The writer needs to learn about voice in persuasive writing.
Word Choice	The writer's choice of words makes a powerful case.	The writer's word choice helps persuade the reader.	The writer avoids unneeded modifiers but removes some repetition.	The writer needs to change modifiers and remove some repetition.	The words do not create a clear message. Some words are repeated.	Word choice for persuasive writing has not been considered.
Sentence Fluency	The sentences flow smoothly throughout the strong essay.	Variety is seen in the types of sentences used and in their beginnings.	Variety is seen in most of the sentences.	More variety is needed in the beginnings or kinds of sentences used.	Too many sentences are worded in the same way.	Sentence fluency has not been considered.
Conventions	The writing is error free.	Grammar and punctuation errors are few. The reader is not distracted by the errors.	Distracting grammar and punctuation errors are seen in a few sentences.	There are a number of errors that will confuse the reader.	Frequent errors make the essay difficult to read.	Nearly every sentence contains errors.

The rubrics provide a scale in which 6 is the highest rating, and 1 is the lowest.

Persuasive

Assessing in Action

In the following persuasive essay, the writer shares information about a type of technology. Read the essay, paying attention to its strengths and weaknesses. Then read the student self-assessment on the following page. (**The essay contains some errors.**)

Psssst: Don't Pass It On!

During history class this morning, I heard several kids coughing and sniffling. A student seated at the desk next to mine sneezed. In my direction, without covering her mouth. This scene repeated itself in classes throughout the day. I just know I'm going to catch something from these sickos. People who have contagious illnesses should stay home and get better instead of "toughing it out" by attending school or going to work.

In the first place, sick people should stay away from healthy people to prevent spreading their sickness. Every winter, different people are sick all season long, and you could probably trace their exposure back to one or two people. The circle of infected people gets bigger and bigger. Even though everyone's not sick at the same time, the bug eventually affects everyone.

Second, someone who's sick is not going to be doing their best work. Work at school or on the job doesn't get done as well as it should be. In most cases, it would be better to wait and do the work when it can be done right.

Last, I can't understand why someone who is ill would place their health at a lower priority than school or work. If he or she doesn't take a break and let the body heal itself, the illness will linger or get worse. Taking off a day or two to get better is much better than working through it, taking much longer to get better, and infecting others.

Some people are afraid of getting behind in their work if they take time off to get better. But if they try to work when their sick, they'll probably get behind anyway. *And* they'll have extra work to do if they end up getting other people sick!

People who are not feeling well need to listen to their bodies instead of the little voice in their heads that says "it's nothing." They need to think of how their actions will affect others, too. Sick people should stay home—so they *don't* pass it on!

Sample Self-Assessment

The student who wrote "Psssst: Don't Pass It On!" created the following assessment sheet to evaluate his essay. He used the persuasive rubric on pages 254–255 as his assessment guide. Under each trait, he wrote comments about the strengths and weaknesses of his writing.

Assessment Sheet   **Title:** Psssst: Don't Pass It On!

5   Ideas
My position is clear.
The essay could use a few more supporting facts.

4   Organization
My essay provides support for my position
in each middle paragraph.
The last reason might not be too convincing.

4   Voice
I sound interested.
The voice should probably be a little more formal.

4   Word Choice
My words help support my position.
I could have used more powerful words.

4   Sentence Fluency
I used different sentence structures.
I need to correct a fragment.

5   Conventions
I caught most errors.
I used "their" instead of "they're" in one sentence.

Evaluator: Rueben

Exercise

Review the assessment. On your own paper, explain why you agree with the responses above (or why you don't). Consider each trait carefully.

Assessing a Persuasive Essay

Read the essay below, focusing on its strengths and weaknesses. Then follow the directions at the bottom of the following page. **(The essay contains errors.)**

Naomi Badalamenti
Ms. Sharp
English III
February 24, 2006

A few months ago, my friend Damon got a job at a local grocery store. He gets paid only through a direct deposit to a bank account, so he had to open one. He got a checkbook and a debit card when he opened his checking account. Within a month, Damon got a notice in the mail that he had overdrawn his account and the bank was charging him $29. Obviously, Damon mismanaged his money, but this really isn't a surprise since he was never taught how to plan a budget or use money from a bank account. His education, as well as that of all the other juniors and seniors here at Arlington High, would be better if it included a mandatory course in money management.

Students should be taught how to plan their spending to help control expenses. We should develop 'practice' budgets that account for food, clothing, transportation, entertainment, computer, and communications expenses. This would help us understand that our income must cover our outlays (or cuts must be made!) We also need to know what will happen if we don't pay our bills on time.

Teachers could help us understand the maze of bank accounts. We need to learn not only how to balance a checkbook, but to record every single transaction in order to do so. If someone doesn't tell us that an unpaid bounced check will result in our names being placed in a national database, preventing us from opening another checking account for five years ("Talking"), how will we know? And we might think we're being smart and thrifty to hang on to a paycheck for months—but we'd certainly be disappointed to find that we

Badalamenti 2

couldn't cash it after only three or six months.

And what about those offers for credit cards that we're already getting? Young adults don't understand how interest compounds. They are falling deep into debt because of credit cards, according to figures such as the following from Nellie Mae. Of undergraduate college students in 2004, 76% had at least one card; nearly half of those carried balances more than $1,000; and only 21% paid their balances in full each month ("Undergraduate"). High school is a good time for students to learn that although good credit is important to many aspects of their later lives, they have to manage their first credit card accounts well. Otherwise, they risk damaged credit or even bankruptcy.

Is financial literacy something that students should learn from their parents? Perhaps, and many parents are able to provide that education. Some, however, don't know enough about it themselves. Some don't have time. Some think it's a school's responsibility. In any case, a teacher, it seems, could devote more time to these important issues than parents or other adults could. High school students also may be more inclined to listen to a teacher.

A good number of us will be leaving home after high school, and we don't want to be dependent on our parents. There are many reasons why young people get in financial trouble; it would be great to know something about budgets and credit before we're faced with it head-on. Arlington should develop such a course to help us better prepare for our real-world futures.

Exercise

Assess this persuasive essay, using the rubric on pages **254–255** as your guide. To get started, create an assessment sheet like the one on page **40**. *Remember:* After each trait, try to write one comment about a strength and one about a weakness.

Understanding the Traits

Understanding the Traits of Writing

When a doctor does a physical examination, he or she checks a patient's blood pressure, height, weight, posture, circulation, breathing, and so on. When someone is in good health, all of these elements are in good working order. If, on the other hand, any of the elements are "out of order," the patient's health will suffer.

Similarly, a piece of writing can be evaluated by reviewing six key traits: *ideas, organization, voice, word choice, sentence fluency,* and *conventions.* If all six of these traits are strong, then the piece of writing will be effective. However, if there are problems with any of these traits, then the essay or article will not be as effective as it could be.

In this chapter, you'll get a quick overview of the six traits of writing, and you'll see how these traits fit into the writing process.

- **Understanding the Six Traits**
- **Using the Traits**
- **Checklist for Effective Writing**

"What is written without effort is in general read without pleasure."
—Samuel Johnson

Understanding the Six Traits

Throughout this book, you'll use the six traits to make your writing the best it can be. Here is a brief description of each trait.

Ideas

The **ideas** in your writing include the topic, the focus (thesis), and the main supporting points and details. Ideas are the heart of writing—the message you want to communicate to your reader.

Organization

Organization refers to the way your writing begins, the order of the ideas in the middle, and the way your writing ends. By using logic and transitions, you can lead your reader step-by-step through your ideas.

Voice

Your writing **voice** reflects your personality, your feelings about the topic, your purpose in writing, and your relationship with the reader. Voice can be bubbly or angry, hopeful or sarcastic, formal or casual.

Word Choice

Word choice considers the quality of the nouns, verbs, and modifiers in your writing. Writers work with words the way jewelers work with gems.

Sentence Fluency

Sentence fluency refers to the flow of sentences and the rhythm of phrases and clauses. Some sentences meander like a melody. Others crack like a rim shot. Fluid sentences can make your writing memorable.

Conventions

Conventions are the rules of punctuation, capitalization, spelling, and grammar. Once upon a time, the rules of writing were taught as writing itself. Now, the rules are a separate consideration, especially important near the end of the writing process.

Try It!

Reflect on the traits by answering the following questions:

1. Which trait challenges me the most? Explain.
2. Which trait is strongest in my writing? Explain.

Using the Traits

Since no one can focus on all six traits at once, different traits are important at different stages in the writing process.

Prewriting	
Ideas	Select a topic, gather details, choose your focus (thesis), and decide on main points.
Organization	Write your thesis statement and topic sentences, decide on a method of organization, and create a list or an outline.

Writing	
Ideas	Connect all your ideas and details.
Organization	Write a beginning, a middle, and an ending, using the plan you have made.
Voice	Use a voice appropriate to your personality, topic, purpose, and reader.

Revising	
Ideas	Revise your focus, main points, and details.
Organization	Check the order and unity of your paragraphs.
Voice	Adjust your voice as needed.
Word Choice	Make sure you use precise nouns, active verbs, and appropriate modifiers.
Sentence Fluency	Check your sentences for varied beginnings and lengths.

Editing, Proofreading, and Publishing	
Conventions	Edit your work for punctuation, capitalization, spelling, grammar, and format.

Try It!

Write a notebook entry explaining which traits are most important early in the writing process and which are most important toward the end.

Checklist for Effective Writing

If a piece of writing meets the following standards, it exhibits the traits of effective writing. Check your work using these standards.

Traits Checklist

Ideas

_____ **1.** Is the topic interesting?

_____ **2.** Is there a specific focus and purpose?

_____ **3.** Do a variety of details support the focus?

Organization

_____ **4.** Is there a clear beginning, middle, and ending?

_____ **5.** Are the details arranged in the best order to support the focus?

_____ **6.** Do transitions and key words connect the ideas?

Voice

_____ **7.** Does the writing sound natural?

_____ **8.** Does the voice fit the topic and the purpose?

_____ **9.** Is the voice appropriate for the audience?

Word Choice

_____ **10.** Are the nouns specific and the verbs active?

_____ **11.** Are the modifiers colorful and necessary?

Sentence Fluency

_____ **12.** Do the sentences have rhythm and flow?

_____ **13.** Do the sentence beginnings and lengths vary?

Conventions

_____ **14.** Does the work follow the rules of punctuation, capitalization, spelling, and grammar?

_____ **15.** Is the work presented in a clear, correct format?

Ideas

When writing, there is nothing more intimidating than staring at a blank piece of paper or an empty computer screen and waiting for an idea to come along. "Every writer I know has trouble writing," said Joseph Heller, author of *Catch-22*. Finding ideas is often the hardest part of the writing process. You need not only a topic and a main idea but also a number of supporting details.

Selecting a topic that interests you is the key to effective writing. "Write what you care about and understand," said writer Richard North Patterson. Being passionate about a topic creates stronger and more dynamic writing.

If, after staring at the computer screen for hours, an idea doesn't materialize, some creative thinking can often supply one. This chapter will help you generate ideas by developing a thinking attitude. You will also learn about the different types of supporting details and about using crots in writing.

- **Developing a Thinking Attitude**
- **The Creative Mind in Action**
- **Reviewing Possible Starting Points**
- **Using Effective Supporting Details**
- **Using Crots in Writing**

"Writing became such a process of discovery that I couldn't wait to get to work in the morning: I wanted to know what I was going to say."

—Sharon O'Brien

"Always make room for the unexpected in yourself."
—Steve Martin

Developing a Thinking Attitude

It's a common myth that people use only 10 percent of their brains. In fact, you use 100 percent of your brain throughout the day, whether you're studying physics, writing an essay, watching TV, or eating a bowl of cereal. Thinking takes place even when you are asleep, and in both halves of your brain.

While some people may use one half of their brain more than the other, to be a complete thinker, you need to be "whole-brained." The more balanced your thinking, the easier it is to develop effective ideas.

Learn about the brain.

Here is a short comparison of how the left and right parts of the brain operate.

Left Part	Right Part
■ processes information logically	■ processes information randomly
■ sees parts and arranges them into big picture	■ sees big picture first, then the details
■ completes tasks in order	■ jumps from one task to another
■ understands symbols easily	■ understands real objects easily
■ prefers using words	■ prefers using visuals
■ likes to make lists and schedules	■ *has to* make lists and schedules

Think to write.

There is no magic formula for forming and developing writing ideas. Whether you are a student writer or a professional writer, you use the same thinking skills. You observe, compare, analyze, evaluate, and solve.

Part of developing a thinking attitude is simply to have an open mind. Writer Robertson Davies said, "I don't get my ideas, they get me." This thought has been expressed by other writers who believe that ideas find them by chance instead of through any systematic thinking process.

Try It!

Try to become a balanced thinker. Decide which part of the brain you use more. Then find someone in class who uses the other half of his or her brain more. Discuss how each of you thinks as you carry out a big project like a research paper. How are your processes similar or different?

Consider the traits of good thinking.

Having a thinking attitude will help you think more consistently and thoroughly. It will also help you complete any type of writing that you may be assigned. To develop a thinking attitude, you need to consider the following traits.

Thinking Traits

Endurance

Thinking can be a sprint or a marathon. If a good idea pops up right away, great. If it doesn't, be prepared to go the distance. Don't worry about time.

Curiosity

Curiosity may have killed the cat, but a lack of curiosity kills great ideas. Be curious, explore, and ask "Why" and "What if."

Concentration

Pick a comfortable place that is conducive to thinking. Noise and distractions often can't be avoided. Learn how to tune them out and stay focused on your goal.

Support

Look for detailed, accurate evidence to support an idea. Don't be satisfied with generalizations. The more support an idea has, the stronger it is.

Skepticism

Having a bit of skepticism is healthy when thinking. Look at an idea from all sides to test its validity. Question evidence and sources.

Openness

Be open to new or opposing viewpoints. Use them to test your own idea for weaknesses. Also be ready to change your ideas if research or discussion changes your opinion.

Try It!

Practice your thinking in a small group. Think of a problem at school or in your community and suggest a solution. Be sure to use all of the qualities described above. Have one member of the group record any examples of the thinking traits employed in the discussion.

The Creative Mind in Action

When confronted with the word *creative*, many people panic, saying, "I'm not creative." Being creative doesn't mean you have to write a novel or develop something from nothing. "Creative" means *being imaginative*, and when applied to thinking, it means looking at something in a new way.

Use your mind creatively by making sensory observations: see, hear, taste, smell, and touch. Examining an object with your senses can get the creative process started. The resulting perceptions can trigger memories, which may develop into creative ideas. As the process continues, you explore, gather, shape, and fine-tune your ideas.

Think creatively.

Imagine you find a baseball cap. Notice the cap's parts: bill, crown, logo, and button. Then look closely at each part by asking yourself these questions.

A Creative Look at a Baseball Hat

- Has the bill been bent into a curve? Is it short, long, a different color than the crown?
- Is the crown striped or multicolored? Does it have a furry animal, cheese, or spinning propeller attached to it? Does it have a saying on it? Is the sweatband stained? Are there holes in it?
- Does the cap adjust with Velcro, a metal buckle, or plastic band? Is it sized small, medium, or large?
- Does its logo represent a college, a professional sports team, a special event, or an attraction? Is it custom printed?
- Does the cap smell new? Can you smell hair products, sweat, or oil?
- Rub the bill or wave the cap in the air. What sounds does it make?
- Bite the bill and crown. What does it taste like?
- Feel the fabric. Is it soft, stiff, scratchy? Wool or cotton?
- In which country was it made? What comes to mind when you think of that country?
- Imagine the process of how the cap was made, from raw materials to finished product.
- If the cap could tell you its story, what would it be?
- Imagine the cap was a gift. What was the occasion?
- What other creative ways are there to look at a cap?

 ## Try It!

Put your creative mind in action. Focus on another common object and look at it in a variety of new ways. Record all of the questions that come to mind about it.

Reviewing Possible Starting Points

During the year, you encounter a number of people, places, experiences, activities, trends, and beliefs. By applying a thinking attitude, many could be turned into writing topics. Listed below are a number of starting points organized according to the basic modes of writing. Just reviewing these ideas should prompt you to uncover interesting starting points for your own writing.

Expository

- Discuss one impact of 9/11 on society in the United States.
- Explain how to make the perfect pizza.
- Explore the evolution of the personal computer.
- Explain the popularity of a particular novel or movie.
- Compare the presidencies of George H. W. Bush and George W. Bush.
- Discuss global warming.

Persuasive

- Convince your school board to initiate an open-campus policy.
- Persuade a doubter of the reasons your favorite sports team will win.
- Identify the country's biggest problem and convince Congress to solve it using your recommendations.
- Argue for or against the increased use of public transportation.
- Persuade the postsecondary school of your choice to accept you.
- Persuade your state's governor to ban cell phone use while driving.

Narrative

- Write about the worst day of work you have ever had.
- Recall the first day you met a good friend.
- Tell about an unforgettable family gathering.
- Write about a vacation horror story.
- Tell about a favorite concert you attended.

Descriptive

- Describe a place you go to get away from it all.
- Describe an influential teacher.
- Describe a popular music style.
- Describe a national park, forest, or monument.
- Describe your perfect job or career.

Try It!

Uncover four writing ideas that interest you by examining the people, experiences, and activities you come across each day. Try to find an idea for each of the writing modes listed above.

Using Effective Supporting Details

There are many types of details you can use when writing about your topic. Your main idea, along with the purpose of your writing, determines which details are most effective. The key types of details are explained below and on the next page.

Facts are *details* that can be proven.

> In 1966, for the first time ever, five African Americans started for the Texas Western Miners in the NCAA basketball championship.
>
> When faced with impeachment as a result of his role in Watergate, President Richard Nixon resigned on August 9, 1974.

Statistics present *numerical information* about a specific topic.

> Making the *Lord of the Rings* films was an epic filmmaking process that included shooting more than 600 million feet of film, using 2,700 special-effects shots, and creating 1,600 pairs of Hobbit feet.
>
> With more than 900 wins and a winning percentage over .800, Tennessee coach Pat Summitt is the winningest coach in college basketball history.

Examples are statements that *illustrate a main point.*

> During the Victorian period of architecture, the Stick style was often overshadowed by other styles, but it had its own unique characteristics (main point). As its name suggests, the Stick style is known for its stickwork, the decorative patterns of boards on a house's exterior. Stick houses were always clad with wood siding. The stickwork created horizontal, vertical, or diagonal patterns on the siding, which imitated architecture from medieval Europe.

Anecdotes are *brief stories* that help to make a point about an idea. They are usually interesting and entertaining and can be more effective than a static list of details.

> Sometimes people's minds play tricks on them, and they need to take the time to look up information that they think they know. Explaining his embarrassing "potatoe" spelling incident, former vice president Dan Quayle admitted, "I should have caught the mistake on that spelling bee card, but as Mark Twain once said, 'You should never trust a man who has only one way to spell a word.' " When told that it was actually President Andrew Jackson and not Mark Twain he quoted, Quayle said, "I should have remembered that was Andrew Jackson who said that since he got his nickname 'Stonewall' by vetoing bills passed by Congress." Quayle was wrong again. He had confused Andrew Jackson with the Confederate general Thomas Jackson, who received the nickname "Stonewall" during the Civil War.

Quotations are *people's statements* repeated word for word. They usually offer powerful supporting evidence.

> Sometimes a comic observation can make you think about an important topic. For example, comedian Jay London observed, "I told my therapist I was having nightmares about nuclear explosions. He said, 'Don't worry, it's not the end of the world.' " We laugh at the idea, but when we actually think about it, the statement does remind us that we live in the nuclear age.

Definitions present the *meaning* of unfamiliar terms. Defining technical terms can be beneficial for the reader and clarify your writing.

> Greener vehicles may run on biodiesel, a renewable fuel derived from vegetable oil or animal fat.

Reasons answer *why* and can explain or justify ideas.

> Filmmakers should not be allowed to make sequels, especially ones with successive numbers in the titles. Producers should know that sequels lose money. Although these movies are made to capitalize on the success of the first film, no sequel has topped an original at the box office. With few exceptions, such as *Godfather II* and *Godfather III*, sequels almost never approach the quality of the original film. With each increasing title number, the film's originality decreases. Did we really need *Jason X* when *Friday the 13th* was enough? Most importantly, for each sequel, you lose one or more "A" stars from the one before it. This clearly makes each movie less watchable.

Comparisons address the similarities or differences between two ideas or things. It is especially helpful to compare something new or unknown to something your reader understands.

> Although they were fought about 40 years apart, the war in Iraq is still similar to the Vietnam War. Most United States citizens did not know where Vietnam was in 1966. In 2006, after three years of war, 63 percent of U.S. citizens ages 18–24 could not find Iraq on a map. The U.S. entered both wars because of a perceived threat: Vietnam because of Communism and Iraq because of terrorism. Both wars were fought against a stubborn enemy that used guerrilla tactics. Early in each war, both Lyndon Johnson and George W. Bush declared that the mission was accomplished. They then saw their approval ratings plummet as the wars continued.

Try It!

Find an article that shows four of the detail types explained on this page and the previous one. On your own paper, write the examples that you find.

"As each crot breaks off, it tends to make one's mind search for some point that has just been made—presque vu!—almost seen!"

—Tom Wolfe

Using Crots in Writing

Crot is an obsolete, odd-sounding word that means *"bit"* or *"fragment."* Writer Tom Wolfe revitalized crots as a writing technique during the 1970s. According to writer and teacher Winston Weathers, a crot "is fundamentally an autonomous unit characterized by the absence of any transitional devices that might relate it to preceding or subsequent crots." An entire essay can be a series of crots that are connected almost randomly. The ideas can be fragments, sentences, or paragraphs, and they are presented without traditional order or transitions.

Reading an essay that includes crots is like viewing the slides of a computer-generated presentation out of order and without graphics. "It will have you making crazy leaps of logic, leaps you never dreamed of before," Wolfe said. An effective series of crots can be a powerful form of writing that jolts the reader from one idea or image to the next.

Sample Essay

Read the following brief essay containing a series of crots and see if you can make the "crazy leaps of logic."

The Big Easy

Riding on the City of New Orleans. This train has got the disappearing railroad blues.

Mardis Gras 2002. Tons of plastic beads, green, gold, purple. Too heavy to carry, dropped and broken, lying in the road.

Long line for Mother's mountain-sized po' boy piled high with debris. Debris floating after the levees broke. Drove my Chevy to the levee, but the levee was dry.

Preservation Hall, dirty and small. Old gentlemanly trombonist with gnarled hands, lips permanently indented from mouthpiece, spit flying. When the saints go marching in. It's hard to be a saint in the city.

Now the boss singing—them who's got out of town, and them who ain't got left to drown, tell me, how can a poor man stand such times and live?

 ## Try It!

Think about your time in high school and write a brief essay of crots about it. Don't worry about trying to connect or explain your ideas too deeply. Leave that to the imagination of the reader.

Organization

Once you have discovered an interesting writing idea and gathered supporting details, you must decide on an organizational pattern. Without clear organization, great ideas just get lost.

Often a topic fits easily into a particular pattern. For example, writing about the first time you met a friend would naturally fall into a narrative or storytelling pattern with a chronological order. Describing how to make the perfect pizza would fit the process pattern. A topic may fit more than one pattern, and it is up to you to determine the best method for presenting your ideas.

At times, an idea deserves a more creative approach. (See "Using Crots in Writing" on page 58.) Writing that breaks out of an organizational pattern and takes its own path is often more exciting and dynamic. Do not be afraid to experiment.

This chapter provides background information about organizing ideas effectively. It will help you learn different ways to structure your writing.

- **Understanding the Big Picture**
- **Following the Thesis Statement's Lead**
- **Organizing Deductively**
- **Organizing Inductively**
- **Using Graphic Organizers**
- **Using the Question-and-Answer Format**

"Complicated outlines tempt you to think too much about the fine points of organization, at a time when you should be blocking out the overall structure."

—Donald Hall

Understanding the Big Picture

The basic structure of informational writing is simple. Essays, articles, and reports contain three main parts: the beginning, the middle, and the ending. Each part plays an equally important role in an effective piece of writing.

Beginning The opening paragraph should capture the reader's attention and state your thesis. Here are some ways to capture your reader's attention:

- Tell a dramatic or exciting story (anecdote) about the topic.
- Ask an intriguing question or two.
- Provide a few surprising facts or statistics.
- Provide an interesting quotation.
- Explain your personal experiences or involvement with the topic.

> **Beginning**
> Middle
> Ending

Middle The middle paragraphs should support your thesis statement. For example, in an essay about improved safety in NASCAR racing, each middle paragraph would focus on one main aspect of improved safety. (An outline can help you write this section.)

> Beginning
> **Middle**
> Ending

Ending The closing paragraph should summarize your thesis and leave the reader with a final thought. Here are some strategies for creating a strong closing:

- Review your main points.
- Emphasize the special importance of one main point.
- Answer any questions the reader may still have.
- Draw a conclusion and put the information in perspective.
- Provide a final significant thought for the reader.

> Beginning
> Middle
> **Ending**

Try It!

Select an essay from this book or an article from a magazine. Outline the three parts of the essay or article to show how it is organized.

Following the Thesis Statement's Lead

An organizing pattern may be built into your essay assignment. For example, you may be asked specifically to develop an argument or to write a process paper. When a pattern is not assigned, one may still evolve quite naturally during your initial thinking and planning. If this doesn't happen, take a careful look at your thesis statement (and supporting information). An effective thesis will almost always suggest an organizing pattern; if it doesn't provide this "controlling vision," consider rewriting it.

Review the following thesis statements and notice how they present the writer's focus and tell how the topic will be developed.

Sample Thesis

Frodo Baggins and Harry Potter are both called upon to save their worlds but have different attitudes toward magic, friendship, and battling evil.

Discussion: This thesis shows how the writer will compare two literary characters on three points: magic, friendship, and battling evil. The middle of the essay will discuss each point in a separate paragraph.

Sample Thesis

Applying for college has become a complicated, stressful process.

Discussion: This thesis indicates that the writer will explain a process. Information must be presented in a logical order, describing each step from beginning to end. The statement also suggests that besides describing each step in this complicated process, the writer will discuss the stress involved.

Sample Thesis

The National Parks Service can reduce damage to Yellowstone National Park by limiting automobile traffic, increasing fees, and hiring additional staff.

Discussion: The writer of this thesis presents a problem and suggests ways to solve it. The statement suggests that after describing the problem the writer will explain each solution.

Try It!

List the thesis statements for two different essays in this book. Explain how each thesis suggests an organizing pattern for the essay. Discuss your findings with your classmates.

"It is a capital mistake to theorize before one has data."
—Sherlock Holmes

Organizing Deductively

Most people are familiar with Sherlock Holmes and his extraordinary powers of deduction. Holmes would make a surprising statement, back it up with many supporting details, and leave Dr. Watson in awe of his conclusion. For example, here is how Holmes deduced Watson had returned from Afghanistan at their first meeting in *A Study in Scarlet*:

> "I *knew* you came from Afghanistan. . . . The train of reasoning ran, 'Here is a gentleman of a medical type, but with the air of a military man. Clearly an army doctor, then. He has just come from the tropics, for his face is dark, and that is not the natural tint of his skin, for his wrists are fair. He has undergone hardship and sickness, as his haggard face says clearly. His left arm has been injured. He holds it in a stiff and unnatural manner. Where in the tropics could an English army doctor have seen much hardship and got his arm wounded? Clearly in Afghanistan.'"

Confronted with all that evidence, Watson can only say, "It is simple enough as you explain it." That is the same reaction you want from your readers, especially when you are trying to persuade them with your ideas.

Most of your academic writing should be organized deductively. *Induction* and *deduction* come from a Latin word meaning "to lead." When writing deductively, you lead the reader to your conclusion by presenting a main idea, or thesis, and then supporting it with specific details. The organizational pattern looks like this:

Deductive Arrangement
- Start with the main idea or thesis.
- Present supporting details and examples.
- Conclude by restating the thesis and/or summarizing the key support.

Deductive writing presents an idea and leads the reader smoothly through the evidence. Supporting details either define the idea, expand it, or illustrate it.

Try It!

Study a building, house, or vehicle. Write down your observations and see what you can deduce from them. *When was it built? What was it used for previously? What condition is it in?* Then write a deductive paragraph about your findings.

Organizing Inductively

Inductive organization—providing details that lead up to the thesis—is not as common in academic writing as deductive organization. However, inductive organization works well in problem-solution essays and in essays of argumentation.

> **Inductive Arrangement**
> - Set the scene.
> - Provide examples and details.
> - Conclude with the main point or thesis.

Review excerpts from an inductive essay.

In excerpts from this sample essay, the main point is stated in the closing paragraph. (The middle of the essay is represented here by topic sentences alone.)

Sardine School

Let's explore a typical school day for the 1,250 students that attend Harding High School.

At this urban school, most students arrive at the same time and enter through one main set of doors. . . .

If you survive entering the building, you must then navigate the crowded halls. . . .

Some classrooms, especially those in the old wing, are packed. . . .

It's almost impossible to move in the crowded physical education classes. . . .

The overcrowded conditions make Harding High School uncomfortable and unsafe. Harding is an older school that should serve 800 students, but it is 25 percent over capacity. The school needs to be remodeled and expanded by next year if the school population remains at its current level. More importantly, plans should be in process to construct a new high school to facilitate learning.

Using Graphic Organizers

Graphic organizers can help you gather and organize details for your writing. Clustering is one method (see page **98**); the next two pages list and model other useful organizers. (Re-create the organizer on your own paper to gather details for an essay.)

Cause-Effect Organizer

Use to collect and organize details for cause-effect essays.

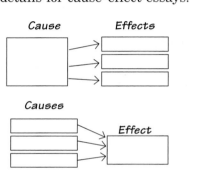

Problem-Solution Web

Use to map out problem-solution essays.

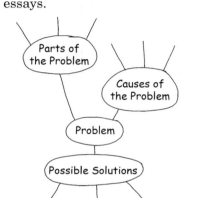

Time Line

Use for personal narratives to list actions or events in the order they occurred.

Subject: _____

(Chronological Order)

① _____
② _____
③ _____
④ _____
⑤ _____

Evaluation Collection Grid

Use to collect supporting details for essays of evaluation.

Subject: _____

Points to Evaluate	Supporting Details
1.	
2.	
3.	
4.	

Traits

Venn Diagram

Use to collect details to compare and contrast two topics.

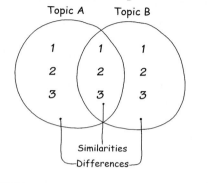

Line Diagram

Use to collect and organize details for academic essays.

Process (Cycle) Diagram

Use to collect details for science-related writing, such as how a process or cycle works.

5 W's Chart

Use to collect the *Who? What? When? Where?* and *Why?* details for personal narratives and news stories.

Subject: _____

Who?	What?	When?	Where?	Why?

Definition Diagram

Use to gather information for extended-definition essays.

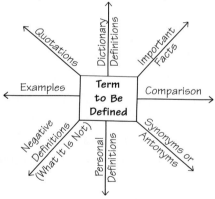

Sensory Chart

Use to collect details for descriptive essays and observation reports.

Subject: _____

Sights	Sounds	Smells	Tastes	Textures

"Start with something interesting and promising; wind up with something the reader will remember."

—Rudolf Flesch

Using the Question-and-Answer Format

In general, you can organize your writing deductively or inductively (see pages **62–63**). More specifically, you can employ one of these methods: classification, cause-effect, comparison and contrast, problem-solution, and so on. (See pages **584–588**.)

There will also be times that your ideas will not fit logically into one of the common methods of organization. Then you must try something different. One unique organization pattern is the question-and-answer format.

Review a question-and-answer essay.

Here is a portion of a humorous essay about a well-known figure.

Poor Richard

Q: Mr. Franklin, why did you call your book of essays <u>Poor Richard's Almanack</u>?

A: People were tired of the headlines I was getting, especially Tom Jefferson. Anyway, "Ben Franklin Invents Electricity," "Ben Franklin Invents Stove," "Ben Franklin Signs Declaration of Independence" all sound too self-serving.

Q: As an inventor, a printer, and a statesman, you weren't poor. So why did you use the name Poor Richard?

A: No one likes to listen to rich people. Besides, who would believe that a wealthy gentleman would say, "A penny saved is a penny earned"?

Q: What was your favorite invention?

A: I do like the armonica, which is Italian for "harmony." I can play really sweet tunes on the armonica, which I invented after noting the sounds produced by rubbing the rims of glasses filled with water.

Voice

Voice is what distinguishes one writer from another. It is how your writing expresses your personality; it is who the reader hears. Everyone's speaking voice is unique and almost instantly recognizable. Writers try to make their writing voice distinct as well.

A reader only has a writer's words to react to, which is why a writer's voice is so important. When you use your own natural voice, the reader senses this, and your words feel real and connect with the reader. Developing a writing voice takes time, but it will make your writing more effective. "Voice separates writing that is not read from writing that is read," says writing teacher Donald Murray. This chapter suggests ways to develop and adjust your voice. It also explains how to use dialogue, understand diction, and write like your favorite author.

- **Developing Voice**
- **Adjusting Voice**
- **Using Dialogue**
- **Understanding Diction**
- **Learning from the Masters**

"Writers should use their own voices as much as possible, for their own voices have power, control, and courage."

—Peter Elbow

Developing Voice

Your speaking voice is filled with your personality, and your writing voice should reflect your true self as well. Writing often, whether in a notebook or in class assignments, will help you develop your voice. Here are some other tips for developing your voice:

- **Write about a topic that interests you.** Your interests help make you the person you are.
- **Be passionate.** If you feel strongly about your writing, these feelings will permeate your voice.
- **Be honest and genuine.** Don't try to be someone else to impress readers.
- **Write freely.** Don't edit your voice out of your writing.
- **Read your writing out loud.** Does it sound like you?

Read the following notebook entry. The thoughts and feelings reflect the writer's personality.

Sample Notebook Entry

I don't know why cops got such a bad rap around here. Jaci and I were walking home yesterday, and a cop car zipped by, flashers and siren and all, and Jaci said, "Yeah, they must need donuts pretty bad." She laughed, but I didn't think it was funny. I mean, they were probably going to help someone. I didn't tell Jaci, but I think I want to be a cop. When my little brother Luis wandered away from Mom, a cop helped find him, and he was really nice. When Tia Bonita got hit by the cab and broke her leg, a cop got to her in a couple of minutes, and he sat and talked to her until the paramedics got there. And I've seen cops working at fires and accidents. I mean, they don't just hand out tickets and arrest people. They help people, and I think that must feel pretty good.

Try It!

Becoming familiar with other writers' voices may help you discover your own voice. Read the following quotation and then rewrite it in your voice, trying to express a comparable thought.

"The sun escaping from the breaking clouds, as it sank toward the hills they had left, was now shining brightly again. Their fear left them, though they still felt uneasy."

—J. R. R. Tolkien, *The Fellowship of the Ring*

Adjusting Voice

You adjust your speaking voice to the audience you are addressing and to your purpose. The same is true of your writing voice.

Adjust for audience.

A personal, informal writing voice is closest to your usual way of talking. You should use it for writing narratives, sending e-mail to friends, or writing personal letters. It is often colorful and visual. To the reader, it is friendly and familiar.

On the other hand, you wouldn't use this voice when you are applying for a job, writing a research paper, or petitioning your senator. For those readers, you would adopt a more formal voice, but without losing your personality.

Adjust for purpose.

You can adjust your writing voice to match your purpose—to relate experience, to share information, or to persuade a reader.

- **Relating an experience:** When you describe an experience, your writing voice should be engaging, animated, and personal, similar to the way you sound when talking to a group of friends.

    Jack Smith gave a speech at our school yesterday that really got us pumped up. I would like to see him elected, but he's a third-party candidate, with about as much chance of winning as I have of being named captain of the football team.

- **Sharing information:** Writing to inform demands an interested, knowledgeable voice that tells the reader you know your topic well.

    The electoral college favors a two-party system, as shown by Ross Perot's receiving 18 percent of the popular vote, but not a single electoral vote, in the 1992 presidential election.

- **Persuading a reader:** Think of how you tried to persuade your parents to let you use the family car, or a teacher to extend an assignment deadline. To persuade the reader, your writing voice must be convincing and informed.

    With the death-hold grip the electoral college has on elections, third-party candidates should not throw their candidates into the ring with the two main parties.

 Try It!

Select a topic, choose one of the purposes above, and write a sentence or two that fits this purpose. Then adjust your voice and rewrite the passage to fit each of the other two purposes.

Traits

Using Dialogue

In creative writing, dialogue is used to give the reader information and to advance the story. Dialogue also breaks up the wall of text, making a story easier to read.

Writing realistic dialogue requires more than just copying what people say. Real speech is not planned or precise. People repeat phrases, add unnecessary words, contract words, and leave out words. They talk at the same time and interrupt each other. As a writer, you need to make use of these characteristics while keeping dialogue interesting and to the point.

When writing dialogue . . .

- mix in some narrative description to help describe a speaker's tone,
- be sure every line has a purpose, and
- read it out loud to be sure it sounds realistic.

Read the following sample. See how the dialogue adds information and develops the personalities of the speakers.

Sample Dialogue

While waiting in line to audition for The Last Great Average American Survival Race, Jack hands Dana the application. "Here. We have to pretend to be a couple for a few minutes. All you have to do is memorize these answers. I made a few changes to fit your . . . "

"Favorite food, spaghetti?" Shaking her head, Dana scowled. "No way, I hate spaghetti. It's a disgusting mess of slimy . . . "

"You don't have to eat any. You just have to say you like it. We need to show them that we're a happy, average, compatible couple."

"Why?"

"Why? Because that's what they're looking for," Jack replied, jabbing the clipboard with his finger. "It's in the name of the show. It's in the contest guidelines."

"Well, if the producers followed my guidelines, then I would be the next great pop diva," Dana said hotly.

Try It!

Record a conversation between yourself and one or more friends. Write it down as accurately as you can. Then rewrite the conversation as if it were dialogue for a story. Add descriptive phrases, keep it real, and give every line a purpose.

Understanding Diction

Diction is the level of language you use based on your purpose and intended audience. Knowing about levels of diction will help you better understand your options for voice. You will use two basic levels of diction for most of your writing.

Formal English

Your essays, research papers, and business letters should meet the standards of formal English. This level of language pays careful attention to word choice, follows the conventions for grammar and usage, and maintains a serious, objective (factual) tone throughout.

> Researchers are developing alternative fuels to decrease the world's dependency on fossil fuels. Automakers believe that re-forming ethanol into hydrogen will create the fuel of the future for flexible-fuel vehicles. Currently, one experimental ethanol re-former is able to produce 110 pounds of hydrogen per day, with its only by-product being one ounce of carbon dioxide per every four ounces of hydrogen.

Informal English

You may write many other pieces, such as personal narratives and feature articles, using a more informal level of language. Informal English usually includes some personal references, a few popular expressions, and shorter sentences.

> Almost two years ago, I passed my driver's test. I was so excited that day. Now, looking ahead, I wonder how much driving I will do. Gas prices are skyrocketing, and each trip I take pollutes the world a little more. Our government must help scientists find new sources of fuel that are less harmful.

Other Forms of Diction

- **Colloquial language** refers to the expressions that are accepted in informal situations and certain locations.

  > You wanna shoot hoops or just hang?

- **Slang** is language used by a particular group of people among themselves; it is also language that is used in fiction to lend color and feeling. It may become dated quickly.

  > During rehearsal, I really got ticked off.

- **Jargon** (technical diction) is the specialized language used by a specific group, such as those who use computers.

  > Hypertext, which is built in to HTML, can retrieve files over the Internet as long as a computer has the proper software that interacts with imported files, usually added through plug-ins.

Learning from the Masters

Each of your favorite writers has a distinct writing voice. In all likelihood, this unique voice is one reason that you enjoy reading his or her books. When you come across sentences that have a voice, write them down. Then practice writing sentences of your own that follow the author's pattern of writing. This process is sometimes called modeling, and it can help you develop your own writing voice.

Model your favorite authors.

Follow these guidelines when you practice sentence modeling. You can also practice writing longer passages modeled after works by your favorite authors.

- **Copy the sentence** (or passage) in your writing notebook.
- **Think of a topic** for your practice writing.
- **Follow the pattern** of the sentence as you write about your own topic. (You don't have to follow the pattern exactly.)
- **Build each sentence** one small part at a time.
- **Save your writing.** Share it with your classmates.

Sample Sentences

Here are sentences by professional writers that exhibit an interesting voice.

"It was one of those days with which September is repeatedly cursed; hot and glaring, with slivers of dust in the wind."
—Dorothy Parker, "The Standard of Living"

"You squirrel away old stuff on the principle of its being useful and interesting someday; it's wonderful when the day finally arrives."
—Garrison Keillor, "Something from the Sixties"

"The winter we'd been waiting for arrived on New Year's Eve—a hard freeze followed by an enormous fall of snow the next day."
—Margaret Atwood, *The Blind Assassin*

"The master met him on the after-deck, looming up in the fog amongst the blurred shapes of the usual ship's fittings."
—Joseph Conrad, "The Tale"

 Try It!

Reserve part of your writer's notebook for sentence modeling. To get started, try writing your own sentences modeled after any two of the sentences listed above.

Word Choice

Your choice of words is where your writing style begins. Word choice can make your writing clear or obscure, lighthearted or hard-hitting, simple or challenging. Which words you select, and how you arrange them, will depend upon your writing task, your audience, and the effect you want to achieve.

As one famous example, when George Orwell was revising his novel *1984,* he decided that many of the words were too colorful, creating the wrong feeling. As a result, Orwell toned down the words and used more passive constructions to make the text less literary.

In this chapter, you will learn how to choose the best words for your writing. The best words are the ones that effectively add meaning, feeling, and sound to your writing.

- **Using General and Specific Nouns**
- **Understanding Action and Linking Verbs**
- **Working with Metaphors**
- **Using Other Figures of Speech**
- **Recognizing Problems with Adjectives**
- **Identifying Other Problems with Word Choice**
- **Considering Polysyndeton and Asyndeton**

"Words—so innocent and powerless as they are, as standing in a dictionary, how potent for good and evil they become in the hands of one who knows how to combine them."

—Nathanial Hawthorne

Using General and Specific Nouns

Your choice of nouns is your primary focusing tool. If all of your nouns are general, your message will be vague and unclear. On the other hand, if every noun is specific, some of them may actually compete against each other and weaken your paper. It is important, then, to understand the levels of specificity and to use them wisely.

General to Specific Nouns			
person	*place*	*thing*	*idea*
man	intersection	food	belief
humanitarian	landmark intersection	fruit	principle
Bono	Times Square	banana	honor

Try It!

Create your own chart showing four sets of nouns *(person, place, thing, and idea)* that become progressively more specific. Use the chart above as a guide.

Be noun smart.

When developing a piece of writing, make sure you have used the best nouns throughout. Use general nouns when giving a broad overview and more specific nouns where detail is important. In the following paragraph, notice how the nouns help to establish a broad idea, discuss its details, and then return to a broad conclusion.

> While art may shape history, it is even more certain that history shapes art. Consider the evolution of landscape painting in China. During the Tang dynasty (618–936 C.E.), landscape served merely as a sketchy background for human figures. At the cultural height of the Song dynasty (960–1279 C.E.), landscape itself became a symbol of order and unity in art. When intellectuals were barred from government service during the Yuan dynasty (1279–1368 C.E.), their landscape paintings became expressions of self-contemplation. The Ming dynasty (1368–1644 C.E.) brought a return of landscapes as images of cultured rule. Thus, historians can gauge a painting's place in history by its use of landscape.

Try It!

Write a brief narrative, recalling how you spent your last weekend. Afterward, circle any nouns that seem too general and underline any specific nouns that seem to compete with each other. Replace some of the nouns you have marked.

Understanding Action and Linking Verbs

Verbs are among the most versatile words in our language. **Action** verbs—like *leap* and *snicker* and *negotiate*—convey the energy of a sentence. **Linking** verbs—like *be* and *seem* and *become*—serve as equal signs, equating the subject with its complement. Both types of verbs have their uses: Action verbs make a sentence dynamic; linking verbs convey certainty.

Use action verbs to . . .

- Write active, forward-moving sentences.
  At the snap of the ball, their lineman charged forward, trying to crack the wall.

- Add energy to your writing.
  Stan vibrated with excitement.

Use linking verbs to . . .

- State a definition.
  Physics is the science of matter and energy.

- Express a condition.
  The lake was frozen.

- Link an adjective to the subject.
  Curried chicken tastes delicious.

Use the appropriate verbs.

Be sure you use the most appropriate verbs in your writing. In the revised version of the passage below, the writer changes the first three verbs to give the writing more energy. The linking verb *remains* works effectively, so she keeps it.

Original: **Consumer bankruptcy grew during the past two decades. It was nearly 92 percent in 1990. By 2000, it was over 97 percent. Unfortunately, consumer bankruptcy remains a critical problem in 2007.**

Revision: **Consumer bankruptcy swelled during the past two decades. It reached nearly 92 percent by 1990. By 2000, it topped 97 percent. Unfortunately, consumer bankruptcy remains a critical problem in 2007.**

Try It!

Review the verbs in an essay that you have recently completed. Improve at least three verbs in the writing using the information and examples above as a guide.

Working with Metaphors

A metaphor is a figure of speech comparing two things without using the words *like* or *as*. Metaphors invite new ways of thinking about key ideas, and they do so in a very stylistic way. There are many ways to develop metaphors, including the three explained below.

Create metaphors with nouns.

The usual way to develop a metaphor is to compare two nouns: **A conversation with Ignacio is a meaty stew of politics, philosophy, and history.** In this example, the reader understands that a conversation with Ignacio is stimulating and challenging.

Create metaphors with verbs.

Another way to develop a metaphor is by means of a verb: **My brain boiled over with competing ideas.** In this example, the verb *boiled over* metaphorically compares an agitated mind (brain) to a boiling pot of liquid.

It is also possible to enhance a comparison of two nouns with a participial phrase. A participial phrase begins with a participle, a verb form ending in *ing* or *ed*. (See page **742**.) Note the following example: **My brain was a boiling teakettle, shrieking with competing ideas.**

Use extended metaphors.

A metaphor doesn't have to be expressed in a single sentence. Sometimes it can serve as a unifying element throughout a series of sentences. Extending a metaphor in this way helps you expand or clarify an idea in your writing.

The whole of human understanding **is an intricate spider's web of thought.** Each filament of insight **connects discrete bits of knowledge. Where much knowledge has been accumulated,** the dense netting **snags increasingly finer details and adds to the richness of our understanding. But oh, the gaps remaining in that web!**

Note: Be careful with extended metaphors. Your writing may sound forced or unnatural if you extend a metaphor through too many sentences.

Try It!

Find two or three effective metaphors in an article or a novel. Then write your own metaphors modeled after the examples that you have found. Be original! Afterward, share your work with your classmates.

Using Other Figures of Speech

Have you ever assembled something from a kit? If so, you know that clear, exact instructions make the job easier to complete. You wouldn't necessarily expect the same level of exactness in more imaginative forms of writing. Fiction and personal essays often include *figures of speech,* which are used to communicate ideas more indirectly or symbolically. The information below covers three common figures of speech.

Personification

Personification is a figure of speech in which an animal, object, or idea is given human characteristics. (This makes personification a form of metaphor.) When used effectively, personification can create a powerful image and help establish the voice in a piece of writing.

> Example: **That car had it in for her. It always waited to break down until she absolutely had to be somewhere important, and whenever she worked on it, it always managed to draw blood. Even when she filled the gas tank, it would be sure to spit some back on her shoes.**

Hyperbole

Hyperbole is an extreme form of exaggeration used to make a point by drawing special attention to the subject. Often, the result is humorous.

> Example: **You think you have a lot of brothers and sisters? I have so many siblings that when we were growing up, the U.S. government gave our house its own ZIP code.**

Understatement

Like hyperbole, understatement draws special attention to a subject in order to make a point. But whereas hyperbole exaggerates, understatement does the opposite, using overly restrained language. Its effect is typically ironic or sarcastic.

> Example: **He [our new dog] turned out to be a good traveler, and except for an interruption caused by my wife's falling out of the car, the journey went very well.**
>
> **—E. B. White, "A Report in Spring"**

Try It!

Write one brief passage about a topic of interest using personification, another passage about the topic using hyperbole, and a last passage about the topic using understatement.

Recognizing Problems with Adjectives

Mark Twain wrote, "When you catch an adjective, kill it. No, I don't mean utterly, but kill most of them—then the rest will be valuable." Obviously, adjectives have their purpose, and when used properly, they can clarify the nouns that they modify. But used carelessly, adjectives can bloat a text, muddying its meaning and effectiveness.

Know what to look for.

Watch for the following types of problems in your writing.

- **Unnecessary adjectives:** Don't add an adjective to modify a noun when a more specific noun would serve.

  Original: An awful smell **rose from the pit.**

  Improved: A stench **rose from the pit.**

- **Empty adjectives:** Remove adjectives that add no real meaning to your sentence.

  Original: The slow turtle **crept across the sidewalk.**

  Improved: The turtle **crept across the sidewalk.**

- **Overused adjectives:** At times, the first adjective that comes to mind will be overused. Replace these worn-out adjectives with fresh ones.

  Original: **We strained to see in the** pitch-black **darkness.**

  Improved: **We strained to see in the** relentless **darkness.**

Note: These overused adjectives contain little meaning: *neat, big, pretty, small, cute, fun, bad, nice, good, funny,* and so on.

- **Multiple adjectives:** Avoid stringing together multiple adjectives before a noun; very often a single adjective can effectively express the meaning that you are looking for.

  Original: **Dionne bit into a** juicy, runny, soggy **barbecue sandwich.**

  Improved: **Dionne bit into a** sloppy **barbecue sandwich.**

Try It!

Rewrite the following passage addressing any problems with the use of adjectives. Consider unnecessary, empty, overused, and multiple adjectives. Use the information above as a guide.

> **Our adorable, cute, cuddly kitten rubbed its downy fur against my cheek. Its little cries reminded me it was hungry. I poured some creamy milk into a bowl and watched as the tiny feline happily lapped it up. I marveled at the beauty of its brown, tortoiseshell coat.**

Identifying Other Problems with Word Choice

The best writing is always clear and interesting. It avoids clumsiness and confusion by showing care in its word choice. When you revise and edit your writing, it is important to evaluate your words for clarity and freshness.

Check for these problems.

Listed below are common problems related to word choice. Check with your teacher for other problems to address.

- **Redundancy** occurs when words or phrases are used together but mean the same thing.

  Original version: **My grandfather stood more than six feet tall in height.**

  Revised version: **My grandfather stood more than six feet tall.**

- **Repetition** occurs when words or phrases are unnecessarily repeated.

  Original version: **When it comes to intelligent people, Louetta is just about the most intelligent person I know.**

  Revised version: **Louetta is just about the most intelligent person I know.**

- **Jargon** refers to specialized words that are not adequately explained.

  Original version: **The enlarged photo was too pixelated to use in our yearbook.**

  Revised version: **The enlarged photo was too pixelated—broken into large dots—to use in our yearbook.**

- **Cliches** are overused phrases that give the reader nothing new.

  Original version: **Advice for freshman: Put your best foot forward!**

  Revised version: **Advice for freshman: Have confidence that you can succeed!**

Try It!

Identify and correct the word problem in each of the following sentences. (Corrections may vary.)

1. A bird-rescue organization in California made a mint by auctioning bird prints.

2. In Spain, a Spanish court recently ruled that divorced couples in Spain cannot demand visitation rights with their dogs.

3. A teenage spelunker in Israel has discovered eight new species including four new crustaceans.

4. Don't drive through the construction site, and be sure to pick a different route if you want to avoid driving over nails.

Considering Polysyndeton and Asyndeton

Writing style is more than just which words you choose. It is also the way you put those words together. Consider, for instance, the use of conjunctions in a series of items. In a normal series, commas separate the individual items, and a conjunction signals the last one. *Benny's "emergency kit" contained a flashlight, an old comic book, and a box of raisins.* There are other ways of presenting a series, however, which can dramatically affect the style of your writing.

Polysyndeton

When a series of words is linked together by multiple conjunctions, this is called *polysyndeton (pŏl ē-sĭn´dĭ-tŏn)*. Here are three reasons to use this technique.

- **Emphasize each item** in a series.
  Example: Their ace pitcher can throw curveballs and sliders and cutters; he will be tough to hit.

- **Slow the pace** of a sentence by methodical attention to detail.
  Example: Sylvia came home from the factory every day and fixed dinner and helped the kids and straightened the apartment before falling exhausted into bed.

- **Or quicken the pace** of a sentence by building a sense of momentum.
  Example: She squeezed the clutch and downshifted and leaned hard into the curve before flying out of the corner like a stone from a sling.

Asyndeton

A different effect is achieved by *asyndeton (ə-sĭn´dĭ-tŏn)*, which means presenting a series with no conjunctions at all. Here are three reasons to use this technique.

- **Suggest incompletion,** that something more should follow
  Example: Jonathan blinked, coughed, wheezed, trembled.

- **Suggest simultaneous or random action.**
  Example: Like windup toys, the dancers spun, dipped, leapt, twirled.

- **Emphasize the finality** of the last item.
  Example: One last chord wavered in the night air, faded, died.

 ## Try It!

Write one example each of polysyndeton and asyndeton. Use the information above as a guide.

Sentence Fluency

Walking is easy. Dancing, on the other hand, takes equal parts of practice and passion. Similarly, it's easy to put a subject and a verb together with a few other words to make a basic sentence. However, it's a challenge to write a sentence that dances, carrying a reader effortlessly along.

In this chapter, you will learn many techniques for improving your sentence style—including expanding main clauses with various types of modifiers, varying the placement of sentence modifiers, and inverting the order of sentence parts. You will also review common sentence problems.

Follow the advice in this chapter, and your sentences will gain a liveliness that makes them a pleasure to read.

- **Varying Sentences**
- **Expanding Sentences**
- **Placing Modifiers**
- **Using Inverted and Periodic Sentences**
- **Checking for Sentence Problems**
- **Checking for Additional Problems**

"Writing is a negative game. Very few sentences come out right the first time, or even the second or third time."

—William Zinsser

Varying Sentences

If all of your sentences follow the same basic pattern, your writing will be lifeless. By varying your sentences in different ways, you can spice up your writing and increase your reader's enjoyment.

Vary sentence beginnings.

Sentences that begin the same way start to plod along. To avoid this problem, vary the way you start them.

Starting with the Main Subject

Original version: Many European countries have megalithic stone monuments. England has the famous Stonehenge circle. France has the Cordon des Druides. Italy has the Fossa in Abruzzo. Europe also has many more examples.

Varied Beginnings

Revised version: Megalithic stone monuments can be found in many places in Europe. The famous Stonehenge circle stands in England. In France, there is the Cordon des Druides. Italy has the Fossa in Abruzzo. These are only three examples of Europe's many ancient stone structures.

Vary sentence lengths.

To avoid plodding sentences, combine some of them to vary their lengths.

Similar Length

Original version: Today, we take the electronic calculator for granted. Until about 50 years ago, there was no such thing. Before then, people used pencil and paper or a slide rule. A slide rule helps a person multiply and divide large numbers. It adds or subtracts logarithmic distances to do this.

Varied Lengths

Revised version: Today, we take the electronic calculator for granted, but it was not invented until about 50 years ago. Before then, people used pencil and paper or a slide rule. A slide rule helps people to multiply and divide large numbers by adding or subtracting logarithmic distances.

 ## Try It!

Find a passage in one of your essays in which many sentences begin in the same way or are close in length. Rewrite the passage, varying the sentences.

"A good writer can express an extremely complicated
idea clearly and make the job look effortless."
—Patricia T. O'Conner

Expanding Sentences

Details seen to spill out of accomplished writers' minds naturally. Readers marvel at how effectively these authors can expand a basic idea with engaging details. Maybe you envy good writers because of this special ability and wish you could write in the same way. The truth is you can by writing *cumulative sentences,* or sentences with modifying clauses and phrases coming before and after the main clause. (See page **750**.) In the following cumulative sentence, the main clause (in blue) precedes the modifying phrases.

Tony is laughing, **halfheartedly, with his hands on his face, looking puzzled.**

In the cumulative sentence below, modifiers are placed both before and after the main clause (in blue).

As the storm continued, the river rose, **rapidly overflowing its banks and sending waves of dirty water over the field.**

FYI

Below are six ways to expand your sentences.

1. with **individual words**: *halfheartedly*

2. with **prepositional phrases**: *with his hands on his face*

3. with **participial (-ing or -ed) phrases**: *looking puzzled*

4. with **infinitive phrases**: *to hide his embarrassment*

5. with **subordinate clauses**: *while his friend talks*

6. with **relative clauses**: *who isn't laughing at all*

Try It!

Expand each of these main clauses by adding at least two modifying words, phrases, or clauses.

1. A dog howled.

2. Junie started the car.

3. The moon cast an eerie glow.

4. My father tried to fix the bike.

5. The leaves blew.

Traits

Placing Modifiers

Sentence modifiers add information to the sentence. One way to vary the rhythm of your writing is to vary the placement of sentence modifiers.

Use trailing modifiers.

The most common placement for a sentence modifier is after the main clause. In this pattern, the main clause provides basic information, and the sentence modifiers add detail. In the following sentence, the main clause (in blue) is followed by a long modifying phrase.

Some people take high doses of vitamin E, **hoping to combat free radicals (molecules) that have been blamed for damaging cells and promoting illnesses.**

Note: The main clause in the sentence above serves as a foundation for the information that follows it.

Try sentence anticipators.

It is also possible to place sentence modifiers before the main clause, in which case the modifiers lead up to the main point of the sentence. In the following sentence, the modifying phrases are in black.

Having reexamined studies of 136,000 people and finding no evidence of beneficial effects, scientists now warn against taking megadoses of any vitamin.

Note: The introductory modifiers in the sentence above build support for the concluding thought in the main clause.

Include sentence interrupters.

Finally, sentence modifiers can interrupt the main clause, giving additional information and adding emphasis or drama to the second part of the clause. Consider the phrases in black in the following example.

Vitamin C, vitamin E, selenium, and beta carotene, **the four most popular antioxidants that many people have assumed to be life extenders,** can cause severe illness in megadoses.

Try It!

Review one of your textbooks for examples of sentences with trailing modifiers, sentence anticipators, and sentence interrupters. (Find at least one of each.) Then rewrite each sentence by placing the modifier or modifiers in a different position. Notice the effect this has on the meaning.

Using Inverted and Periodic Sentences

Another way to add style to your writing is to include inverted and periodic sentences. These types of sentences delay the main information until the end, giving it added emphasis. Like spices in cooking, however, it is best to use inverted and periodic sentences *sparingly* for effect.

Use inverted sentences.

Usually, in English, the subject of a sentence comes before the verb. In an inverted sentence, however, the subject comes after the verb. (Inverted sentences sometimes begin with *there is*.) Compare these sample sentences:

Normal: **Traffic is lighter in a gated community.**

Inverted: **In a gated community, there is less traffic.**

Note: The second sentence above ends with the subject to give added emphasis to the main point: *less traffic.*

Normal: **A nervous Ray Brown stood on the free throw line with two seconds left.**

Inverted: **On the free throw line, with two seconds left, stood Ray Brown.**

Note: The second sentence above gives emphasis to the subject: *Ray Brown.*

Include periodic sentences.

In most sentences, the main clause comes first. Once the reader has this information, additional clauses and phrases add detail. In a periodic sentence, however, the main clause is delayed until the end. This helps to build a sense of suspense and expectation. Consider the following example sentences.

Normal: **A gated community may bring more harm than good to a city, restricting public access to parks, depressing adjacent property values, and shifting crime to other neighborhoods.**

Periodic: **By restricting public access to parks, depressing adjacent property values, and shifting crime to other neighborhoods,** a gated community may bring more harm than good to a city.

Note: In the second sentence, the main clause (in blue) becomes a summation to the argument, rather than an introduction.

Try It!

Review an essay you have recently written and mark sentences that could be revised as inverted or periodic sentences. Change a few of these sentences and evaluate the overall effect on the essay.

Traits

Checking for Sentence Problems

Complete, correct sentences may be made up of several ideas. The trick is getting those ideas to work together to carry your intended meaning. Presenting sentence elements incorrectly disrupts the flow and continuity of ideas in your writing. The most common errors are fragments, comma splices, run-ons, and rambling sentences.

Watch for fragments.

A sentence fragment lacks a subject, a verb, or some other essential part. Because of the missing part, the thought is incomplete.

Fragment: Business transactions in colonial America. (This fragment lacks a verb.)

Sentence: Business transactions in colonial America often did not involve actual money.

Fragment: Because so many dealings were recorded as "book debt." (This fragment does not express a complete thought. We need to know the significance of recording transactions as book debt.)

Sentence: Because so many dealings were recorded as "book debt," colonial courts had to evaluate accounting records when disputes occurred.

FYI

Sometimes writers use fragments for a good reason. For instance, you can use fragments when you write dialogue. It is also okay to use single words or phrases as sentences for dramatic effect. Note the following example from an article about the Stone Age.

What's the main difference between the Mesolithic and Neolithic lifestyles? Farming. Without a doubt.

Try It!

Rewrite the following passage, correcting any fragments that you find.

Last weekend, my mom asked me to clean out the closet. This huge walk-in closet in our living room. Reaches under our attic stairs. We have been storing many boxes in there. In one of the boxes, I found a bunch of old videocassette tapes. Because we always watch DVD's. I forgot we even owned any VCR tapes. Someday, even DVD's will seem old-fashioned.

Check for comma splices.

A comma splice results when two independent clauses are connected with only a comma. A period, semicolon, or conjunction is needed to correct this error.

Comma splice: Countless writers and artists since Aristotle's time have believed that creativity and madness are linked, experts today say that isn't quite the case.

Corrected: Countless writers and artists since Aristotle's time have believed that creativity and madness are linked, **but** experts today say that isn't quite the case. (A coordinating conjunction has been added.)

Corrected: Countless writers and artists since Aristotle's time have believed that creativity and madness are linked; experts today say that isn't quite the case. (A semicolon replaces the comma.)

Watch for run-on sentences.

A run-on is two (or more) sentences joined without adequate punctuation or a connecting word. To correct this error, turn the run-on into two sentences or into a compound sentence.

Run-on: A creative mind-set and bipolar disorder share certain characteristics such as independence and nonconformity both lead to thinking "outside the box."

Corrected: A creative mind-set and bipolar disorder share certain characteristics such as independence and nonconformity. Both lead to thinking "outside the box."

Corrected: A creative mind-set and bipolar disorder share certain characteristics such as independence and nonconformity, **and** both lead to thinking "outside the box."

Try It!

Rewrite the following sentences, correcting the comma splices and run-ons.

1. The commuters had been bottlenecked on the freeway for two hours, some of the commuters had a crazed look in their eyes, the others were napping.

2. I thought the test would never end I had a classic case of finger cramps. In addition, I had severe brain-drain complications only a long nap would restore me.

Note: Be on the alert for a related sentence error—rambling sentence, or sentences that go on and on because they contain too many *and*'s.

Checking for Additional Problems

The errors that follow could confuse a reader. Avoid them to make your sentences clear and readable.

Check for misplaced modifiers.

Misplaced modifiers are modifiers that have been placed incorrectly, leaving the meaning of the sentence unclear.

Misplaced: **The clown entertained the child with a balloon poodle.**
(Who has the balloon poodle, the child or the clown?)

Corrected: **The clown used a balloon poodle to entertain the child.**

Look for dangling modifiers.

Dangling modifiers are modifiers that appear to modify the wrong word or a word that isn't in the sentence.

Dangling: **Having unexpectedly turned red, I had to brake suddenly for the stoplight.**
(Who or what turned red?)

Corrected: **I had to brake suddenly for the stoplight, which had unexpectedly turned red.**

Correct any double negatives.

A double negative is the improper use of two negative words to perform the same function in a sentence. (Using *hardly, barely,* or *scarcely* with *no* or *not* also results in a double negative.)

Double negative: **There were hardly no mistakes on her paper.**
Corrected: **There were almost no mistakes on her paper.**

Try It!

Rewrite each of the following sentences, correcting the misplaced modifier, the dangling modifier, or the double negative.

1. The pool staff offers towels to the students marked with ID numbers.
2. The chef did not mean to sprinkle no pepper on your potatoes.
3. Positioning himself to make the winning goal, Jacque's father yelled from the sideline.
4. Still confused about the concept, the physics teacher gave the students a special study guide.
5. After finishing the drill, Coach James met with the team.

Conventions

A piece of writing with errors in grammar, punctuation, or spelling is like a news commentator with a piece of spinach stuck between his or her teeth. No matter how interesting the subject, the reader or listener has difficulty concentrating. Careless errors, in particular, can rob your message of its impact, suggesting to the reader that the quality of ideas may be less than trustworthy. Before you present your work, it is important, then, for you and a trusted classmate to check for conventions. Professional writers rely on editors and proofreaders for just these reasons.

There are many ways to improve your mastery of the conventions. One is to review the rules from time to time. For example, you can browse the "Proofreader's Guide" in the back of this book to remind yourself of the rules for using punctuation. It also helps to keep a list of errors that you commonly make. Then refer to this list whenever you are editing a piece of writing. The next page serves as a helpful guide for checking the conventions in your writing.

■ **A Quick Guide to Conventions**

"Ignorant people think it is the noise which fighting cats make that is so aggravating, but it ain't so; it is the sickening grammar that they use."

—Mark Twain

"I work on a word processor for the first draft, but for revisions, I always print out a copy and do my corrections by hand."

—Betsy Byars

A Quick Guide to Conventions

Checking to be sure that your work is free of errors becomes especially important near the end of a writing project.

Starting Point: You're ready to check for conventions once you . . .

- complete your major revisions—adding, cutting, rewriting, or rearranging the ideas in your writing;
- make a clean copy of your revised writing; and
- set your writing aside for a day or two (if time permits).

When you check for conventions, try to focus on one type of error at a time. This will help you edit more carefully and thoroughly. (See page **128** for a checklist.)

Tip

Have someone else check your work as well. You're too close to your writing to spot everything that needs to be changed.

Form: If you're working with pen and paper, do your editing with a different color of ink on a neat copy of your revised writing. Then complete a final copy of your work.

If you're working on a computer, do your editing on a printed copy of your writing and key in the changes. Save the edited copy so you have a record of your changes.

The Big Picture: When you check for conventions, remember that you are looking for punctuation, mechanics, spelling, or grammar errors.

- **Punctuation:** Review your work for all forms of punctuation; however, the most common errors involve commas and apostrophes. (See pages **130–131**, **608–617**, and **628–631**.)
- **Mechanics and spelling:** Check your writing for capitalization, the use of numbers, and spelling. (See pages **648–653** and **656–668**.)
- **Grammar:** Review your work for grammar errors. Pay special attention to subject-verb agreement, pronoun-antecedent agreement, and usage errors. (See pages **130–131** and **678–763**.)

Presentation

What's the main difference between a banquet and a picnic? It isn't just the food or the setting. A banquet may serve chicken in a tent, and a picnic may include candlelight and caviar. The main difference is a matter of presentation: A banquet usually involves formal place settings, linen tablecloths and napkins, and silver utensils, while a picnic requires little more than a basket and some paper plates. When it comes to food, presentation plays a very important role, adding dignity or fun to what is otherwise just a necessity of life.

Presentation is important for writing, too. Your choice of typestyle and layout makes an immediate impression on your reader, before he or she reads a word. Taking care with your document design shows that you value your writing and respect your reader. Through effective use of headings, graphics, and white space, you can help your reader follow your ideas. This chapter will help you to understand the elements of good document design.

- **Designing Your Writing**
- **Effective Design in Action**
- **Adding Graphics**

"Writing well is at one and the same time good thinking, good feeling, and good expression; it is having wit, soul, and taste, all together."

—George-Louis Leclerc de Buffon

Designing Your Writing

The test of a good page design is that your writing is clear and easy to follow. Consider these guidelines for creating clean, attractive essays and articles.

Select an appropriate font.

- **Choose an easy-to-read font for the main text.** In most cases, a serif typestyle is best for the text, and a sans serif style works for any headings. For most forms of writing, use a 12-point type size. Use **boldface** for headings if they seem to get lost on the paper.

  The letters of serif fonts have "tails"—as in this sentence.

  The letters of sans serif fonts are plain, without tails—as in this sentence.

- **Make titles and headings short and to the point.** Headings of equal importance should be stated in the same way. Follow the basic rules for capitalizing titles and headings. (See page **650**.)

Use consistent spacing and margins.

- **Set clear margins.** Use a one-inch margin around each page (top, bottom, left, and right).
- **Hit the tab key to indent the first line of each paragraph.** This key should be set at five spaces.
- **Leave one space after every period.** This will improve the readability of your paper.
- **Avoid placing headings, hyphenated words, and first lines of new paragraphs at the bottom of a page.** Also avoid single-word lines at either the bottom or the top of a page.

Include graphic elements.

- **Use lists if appropriate.** Use numbered lists if your points have a clear number order. Otherwise, use bulleted lists (like the ones on this page).
- **Include graphics.** Use tables, charts, or illustrations to help make a point. Keep graphics small within the text. If a graphic is complex and needs to be large, display it on its own page. (See page **95**.)

 Try It!

Compare an article from a newsmagazine like *Time* or *Newsweek* with a chapter in your history text. Which design elements are the same? Which are different? Explain how the design of each piece of writing fits the intended audience.

Effective Design in Action

The following essay by Terence Hatcher demonstrates effective design elements. The side notes highlight important design features.

Terence Hatcher
Ms. Brackett
Economics
May 9, 2006

Avoiding the Crunch

Let's say that you decide to buy three CD's that are $10 each, and the cashier says, "That will be $30, please. If you don't have $30, just pay a little each month for the next 17 years." Sound ridiculous? Teenagers do it every day, creating credit card debt that will follow them into adulthood.

Credit card companies are hoping to cash in by targeting students. Plush toys, T-shirts, and snacks are "freebies" intended to lure potential card users. Sociologist Robert Manning states, "The credit card marketers sign high school kids at college fairs. They get paid by the number of applications they turn in." Many students sign up without considering the fine print. For example, while most cards offer an introductory rate of 0 percent, the rate rises to 15 percent after the six-month promotional period. And if you default or fail to pay, the rate skyrockets to 30 percent!

Doing the Math

What does this mean to you? Let's say you spend $2,000 during the first six months. Then the interest rate zooms up to 15 percent. You decide to start paying off the balance, but you don't have enough money to pay the whole thing. So you pay the monthly minimum of 2 percent or at least $25 a month. How long do you think it would take to pay off the original $2,000 balance? Not only would it take almost 12 years, but you would also end up spending about $4,000! As radio talk show host Clark Howard says, " . . . what you really need to know is that you are ripping yourself off because you are not paying off that balance."

The chart that follows illustrates the problem with making minimum monthly payments.

The title is 18-point sans serif type.

The main text is 12-point serif type.

Subheadings are 14-point sans serif.

Traits

Hatcher 2

$2000 Credit Card Debt, Paid Off at Minimums

A chart adds impact and visual appeal.

Keeping a Clean Record

"Your credit report is often called your second résumé," according to Dr. Flora Williams in her book *Climbing the Steps to Financial Success*. A credit report covers your history of borrowing, bill payment, and debt owed. If you use your credit card irresponsibly, your credit card company will make negative comments on your credit report. Banks, college loan officers, employers, and landlords can request your credit report.

So how do you maintain a positive credit report? Here are four key guidelines:

- Use your credit card wisely. Keep track of what you are buying. Know how long it will take you to pay for each item. Don't be tempted by the latest laptop or video game system that you can't afford.
- Know your credit limit. Going over the limit may result in fines or even cancellation of your account.
- Pay off the balance, or at least more than the minimum.
- Pay on time. This is the simplest way to avoid late fees, increased interest rates, and credit damage.

A bulleted list adds clarity to important points.

What is the lesson here? It takes common sense and hard work to avoid the pitfalls of credit card debt. If you read the fine print, spend wisely, and pay promptly, you'll be on your way to building a solid financial foundation.

Traits

Adding Graphics

When adding graphics to your writing, make sure you aren't simply "dressing up" the words. Instead, include graphics to add information or enhance the reader's understanding. Follow these guidelines:

Use tables to provide statistics in a compact form. Clearly label rows and columns so that the reader can quickly grasp the information.

COMPARING COUNTRIES			
	Canada	Mexico	United States
Size (Sq. Miles)	3.85 million	759,000	3.8 million
Type of Government	Parliamentary	Republic	Republic
Voting Age	18	18	18
Literacy	99%	87%	98%

Use graphs to show statistics visually. Line graphs show how quantities change over time. Bar graphs compare and contrast amounts. Pie graphs show the parts of a whole. Be sure to provide a clear title, labels, and a legend (if needed).

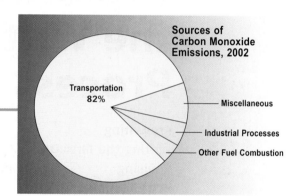

Sources of Carbon Monoxide Emissions, 2002

Transportation 82%

Miscellaneous

Industrial Processes

Other Fuel Combustion

Use diagrams to show the parts of something. Include labels or arrows to inform the reader about the parts being shown.

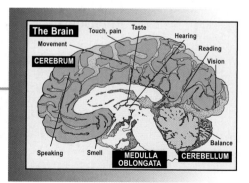

The Brain

Movement

CEREBRUM

Touch, pain

Taste

Hearing

Reading

Vision

Speaking

Smell

MEDULLA OBLONGATA

CEREBELLUM

Balance

Try It!

Review essays you have written and select one that could include a table, graph, or diagram. Create a graphic that demonstrates important ideas or statistics in the essay.

Exploring the Writing Process

Prewriting

Author Barry Lane says writers "continually move back and forth between the sea and the mountain" during a writing project. As Lane explains it, writing begins in the "sea of experience," which contains the memories, experiences, and information that writers work with. When they actually write, writers begin to climb the "mountain of perception," forming new understandings, linking ideas, and drawing conclusions. If they need more details, they head back to the sea.

Prewriting refers to the beginning of a writing project—when you're still at sea—selecting a topic, gathering information about it, and so on. Prewriting also refers to trips back to the sea—when you need to carry out additional research and planning in the middle of a writing project. If you give prewriting the proper attention, you've laid a solid foundation for all of the other steps in the writing process.

- Selecting a Topic
- Gathering Details
- Finding Additional Information
- A Closer Look at Prewriting
- Forming Your Thesis Statement
- Organizing Your Details

"Writing is an exploration. You start from nothing and learn as you go."

—E. L. Doctorow

Selecting a Topic

Your teacher may provide you with a general subject and ask that you narrow it to a specific topic.

General Subject: The Endocrine System

Specific Topic: Glands and Hormones of the Endocrine System

Depending on the assignment, use one of the following strategies to select an effective, specific writing topic.

Keep a writer's notebook.

Write on a regular basis in a personal notebook (journal), exploring your experiences and thoughts. Review your entries on occasion and underline ideas that you could explore in writing assignments. (See pages **1–5** for more information.)

Develop a cluster.

Begin a cluster with a nucleus word, usually a general term or idea related to your writing assignment. Then cluster related words around it.

Sample Cluster

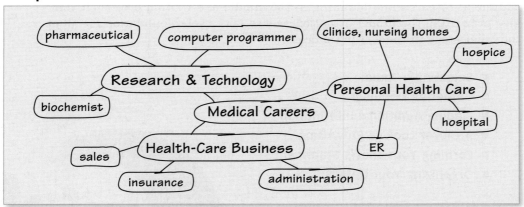

Note: After 3 or 4 minutes, scan your cluster for a word or an idea that interests you. Write nonstop about that idea for 5 to 8 minutes. A few writing topics should begin to occur to you.

Make a list.

Begin with a thought or a key word related to your assignment and simply start listing words and ideas. Listing ideas with a group of classmates (brainstorming) is also an effective way to search for writing topics.

Try freewriting.

Begin writing with a particular focus in mind—one that is related to your assignment. Write nonstop for 5 to 10 minutes to discover possible writing topics.

- Don't stop to judge, edit, or correct your writing.
- Keep writing even when you seem to be drawing a blank. If necessary, write "I'm drawing a blank" until a new idea comes to mind.
- Review your writing and underline ideas you like.
- Continue freewriting about ideas you want to explore further.

Sample Freewriting

Most people think of doctors and nurses when they hear you're interested in a medical career. It's really amazing, the kinds of jobs there are in health care. With some medical careers, people don't even have to see or touch another human being. In others, that's what they do all day. And think about how important computers are to health care now!...

Consider the "Basics of Life" list.

Below you will find a list of the essential elements in our lives. The list provides an endless variety of topic possibilities. For example, the category *education* led to the following writing ideas:

- internships for high school students
- community service requirements
- open campus vs. closed campus

Basics of Life

clothing	education	love	entertainment
communication	machines	rules/laws	health/medicine
exercise/training	faith/religion	science/technology	recreation
housing	family	energy	literature/books
community	trade/money	land/property	tools/utensils
food	agriculture	work/occupation	freedom/rights
arts/music	heat/fuel		

Try It!

List four or five possible writing ideas for any two categories in the "Basics of Life" list. (For your next writing assignment, use one of the strategies above to identify possible topics.)

Gathering Details

In most cases, it's a good idea to first collect your initial thoughts about the topic you've selected, including personal experience and past knowledge. Then, if necessary, do research to find more information.

Gather your thoughts.

These strategies will help you to recall what you already know and establish how you feel about your topic.

- **Freewriting:** Approach freewriting in one of two ways. (1) Do a focused freewriting, exploring your topic from a number of different angles. (2) Approach freewriting as if it were a quick version of the actual paper.
- **Audience appeal:** Address a specific audience as you write. Consider a group of parents, a television audience, or the readers of a popular teen magazine.
- **Questioning:** Ask questions to gather information about your topic. If your topic falls into the categories of *problems*, *policies*, or *concepts*, you can use the questions in this chart.

	Description	Function	History	Value
Problems	What is the problem?	Who or what is affected by it?	What is the current status of the problem?	Why is it important?
Policies	What type of policy is it? What are its features?	What is the policy designed to do?	What brought this policy about?	Is the policy working? Why or why not?
Concepts	What type of concept is it? Who or what is related to it?	Who has been influenced by this concept?	When did it originate? How has it changed?	What value does it hold? What is its social worth?

 Try It!

Gather your thoughts. Use one of these strategies to collect your own thoughts about a writing topic.

Finding Additional Information

For most writing assignments, it won't suffice to simply gather your own thoughts about a topic. Expository and persuasive essays, for example, will almost always require that you consult other sources for information. These sources can be divided into two categories—*primary* and *secondary*.

Explore a variety of sources.

- **Primary sources** include interviews, personal observations, firsthand experiences, surveys, experiments, and so on. A primary source informs you directly, not through another person's explanation or interpretation.
- **Secondary sources** include periodicals, books, references, Web sites, and so on. A secondary source is one that contains information other people have gathered and interpreted. It is at least once removed from the original.

Researching Tips

Follow these guidelines when gathering information:

- Whenever possible, use both primary and secondary sources to get a thorough understanding of your topic.
- Read secondary sources with a critical eye, always evaluating the quality and the purpose of the information. (See page **373**.)
- Take careful notes, writing down important facts, opinions, and quotations. Record any source information you will need to cite. (See page **399**.)
- Consider using a graphic organizer such as a gathering grid (page **396**) to keep track of the facts and details your research uncovers.
- Consult librarians and teachers if you have trouble finding information.

Try It!

Imagine that you've been assigned to write an essay about immigration in the United States. Identify each of the following sources of information as primary and secondary.

1. An e-mail message from a member of the National Immigration Forum, responding to your questions from a previous e-mail

2. An interview concerning immigration in *In Motion*, an online magazine

3. Your participation in an immigration-rights rally

4. A newspaper report, reviewing new immigration legislation

"As soon as you connect with your true subject, you will write."
—Rachel Carson

A Closer Look at Prewriting

After you've selected a topic and gathered details about it, you can plan and write your first draft, or you can consider how well you match up with your topic before you go any further.

Take inventory of your thoughts.

After carefully considering the questions that follow, you will be ready to (1) move ahead with your writing or (2) change your topic.

Purpose

- Does my topic meet the requirements of the assignment?
- Am I writing to explain, persuade, describe, entertain, or retell?

Self

- How do I feel about the topic? Have I made a personal connection with it?
- Do I have enough time to develop it?

Topic

- How much more do I need to know about this topic?
- Has my research changed my thinking about the topic?
- What part of the topic will I focus on?

Audience

- Who are my readers?
- How much do they already know about my topic?
- How can I keep them interested in my ideas?

Form

- How should I present my ideas—in a story, an essay, a report, a multimedia presentation?
- What form of writing should I use—narrative, descriptive, persuasive, expository?

Forming Your Thesis Statement

After you have explored the topic and collected information, you should begin to develop a more focused interest in your topic. If all goes well, this interest will become the thesis of your writing. **A thesis statement identifies the focus of an academic essay.** It usually highlights a particular condition, feature, or feeling about the topic or takes a stand.

Specific topic		**a particular feature**		**an effective thesis statement**
use of indoor tanning beds	**+**	is not safer than tanning in the sun	**=**	The use of indoor tanning beds is not safer than tanning in the sun.

Sample Thesis Statements

Writing Assignment: Essay on some aspect of the '60s generation
Specific Topic: Social issues of the decade
Thesis Statement: The social issues of the 1960s (**specific topic**) continue to play a role in our current culture (**particular feature**).

Writing Assignment: Essay about the introduction of new species into the ecosystem
Specific Topic: The Asian carp in the Great Lakes
Thesis Statement: The introduction of the Asian carp into the Great Lakes (**specific topic**) could lead to a radical change in the lakes' ecosystem (**particular feature**).

Try It!

Write thesis statements. Listed below are specific topics students have used for essays. For two of them, write a thesis statement that focuses on a particular feature of the topic.

General Subject:	**Specific Topic:**
the Internet	peer-to-peer sharing programs
a nineteenth-century author	Edgar Allan Poe
"helpful" insects	butterflies and dragonflies
a natural disaster	the 2005 earthquake in northern Pakistan

Organizing Your Details

After forming a thesis statement, you may need to design a writing plan before you start your first draft. Your plan can be anything from a brief list of ideas to a detailed sentence outline. Use the guidelines that follow to help organize your details for writing.

1. Study your thesis statement. It may suggest a logical method of organization for your essay.
2. Review the details you have gathered.
3. Decide which basic pattern of organization fits your essay topic.

Sample Brief List

Topic: Hunger in Africa

- Natural resources
- India as an example
- The "Harare Declaration"

Sample Sentence Outline

Topic: Hunger in Africa

I. Africa is a land of many valuable resources.
  A. It contains great areas of unused land, water, and minerals.
  B. There are enough resources to feed all of Africa.
  C. Developing these resources will take time and cooperation.
II. India should give African countries hope.
  A. It experienced a similar hunger problem.
  B. The government began producing enough food for its people.
  C. Today, India is in much better shape than it was 25 years ago.

Writing the First Draft

Once you have chosen your topic, gathered details, and organized your details, you're ready to write your first draft. This is your first attempt at developing your prewriting into a complete, cohesive unit of writing.

Writing a first draft can be exciting and satisfying as you see your initial thinking about a topic take shape. Try to write your first draft freely without being overly concerned about correctness. Your goal is to get all your ideas on paper in a form that is easy to follow. Use the planning you've done (outline) as a basic guide, but be open to new ideas that come to mind as you write.

If you are writing an essay or a research paper, develop each of your main points in a separate paragraph. Also connect the paragraphs with linking words or transitions. The information in this chapter provides additional drafting tips and strategies for writing your first draft.

- **Considering the Big Picture**
- **Writing the Beginning**
- **Developing the Middle**
- **Writing the Ending**

"The first draft is the down draft—
you just get it down. The second
draft is the up draft—you fix it up."

—Ann Lamont

Considering the Big Picture

As you prepare to write a first draft, keep in mind these three traits of good writing: *ideas, organization,* and *voice.*

Ideas Start with a specific focus. Then develop the main supporting points you gathered in your prewriting. Write freely and add new ideas as they come to you.

Organization Use your planning as a guide and try to get all of your thoughts on paper. Be sure to include a beginning, a middle, and an ending. (See below.)

Voice Let your words flow naturally and freely, as if you were in a conversation with the reader.

Drafting Hints

- *Review your prewriting materials before you begin. This will help you get started.*
- *If you are drafting by hand, write on every other line; if you are using a computer, double-space your work so you will have room to revise.*
- *Focus on the writing and don't be overly concerned about being neat and avoiding errors. You can make corrections later on.*

Remember to organize your writing.

As you write, keep in mind the three parts of any piece of writing: the beginning, the middle, and the ending.

The Beginning

- Gets the reader's attention.
- Identifies the thesis or purpose of your writing.

The Middle

- Presents the main points that support the thesis.
- Includes details that develop the main points.

The Ending

- Restates the thesis.
- Presents a final insight about the topic.

Try It!

Be sure to review this page before you write your next first draft. Afterward, assess your results. *Did you write naturally and freely? Did you get all of your ideas on paper? Did you include all three parts— beginning, middle, and ending.*

Writing the Beginning

Your opening paragraph, informative and interesting, must hook the reader.

Grab your reader's attention.

Develop an opening statement that reflects the focus and tone of your writing. Here are some ways to attract the reader's interest.

- Give a surprising fact or statement.
  Although the wild dogs called dingoes are generally considered Australian natives, they originated in and still roam Southeast Asia.

- Ask a question.
  When is a dog not a dog? When it is a dingo: part wolf, part dog, and all danger.

- Use a relevant quotation.
  "They're the devil in fur, that's what they are." That's how an angry sheep rancher refers to dingoes, the wild dogs of the Australian outback.

- Present an interesting detail about the topic.
  Dingoes, often considered pests, play an important role in Australia's ecosystem.

Shape your beginning paragraph.

The first part of your opening paragraph should identify your topic and hook the reader. Follow with any necessary background information. End with your thesis statement, identifying the specific part of the topic you plan to emphasize.

Attention-getting opening	*"They're the devil in fur, that's what they are!" That's how an angry sheep rancher refers to dingoes, the wild dogs of the Australian outback.* **Descended from wolves, these lean, shrewd creatures roam Northern Australia, living off their wits and whatever small animals they can find. Farmers who suffer the loss of chickens or sheep to these predators consider dingoes little more than a headache. Yet these long-legged interlopers are actually an important part of the Australian ecosystem.**
Background information	
Thesis statement	

Try It!

Analyze the beginning paragraph you are writing for a current assignment. Experiment with different openings to grab the reader's attention.

Developing the Middle

Your middle paragraphs should provide the details that support your thesis. Use your planning materials to arrange your support in a logical order. Here are some ways to support your thesis:

Explain: Provide important facts, details, and examples.

Narrate: Share a brief story (anecdote) to illustrate or clarify an idea.

Describe: Tell how someone appears or how something works.

Summarize: Present only the most important ideas.

Define: Identify or clarify the meaning of a specific term or idea.

Argue: Use logic and evidence to prove something is true.

Compare: Show how two things are alike or different.

Analyze: Examine the parts of something to better understand the whole.

Reflect: Express your thoughts or feelings about something.

FYI

Most essays, articles, and research papers require a number of these methods to thoroughly develop their theses. For example, an essay of definition may contain two or more definitions, a comparison, a brief story, and so on.

Use various types of support.

Below and on the next page are some examples of how one student used various types of support in his paper about dingoes, wild dogs of Australia.

Explain: Provide important facts, details, and examples.

> Dingoes have proven a real menace to Australian sheep and cattle farmers, who have gone to great lengths to protect their animals by building the Dingo Fence. Built in the 1880s, the fence stretches across New South Wales and southern Queensland, the country's major farming area. It effectively separates the cattle and sheep areas from dingoes. At six feet high, it is also sunk nearly a foot below ground to prevent the predators from digging underneath. At the time this 3,000-mile-long fence was built, it was the longest man-made structure in the world, showing just how far some people will go to protect their investments.

Describe: Create a mental picture of your subject.

> Although dingoes look somewhat like dogs, they have physical characteristics that link them to wolves. Their coats are generally ginger colored, but may vary in color from sandy to dark red to black, with white markings on their feet, throats, and bushy tails. There

are even white dingoes found in the Australian Alps. Dingoes stand about one and a half to two feet high at the shoulder, and are about five feet long. They are long legged and lean, with long, pointed muzzles and pointed ears that stick straight up at the tops of their heads. Although related to dogs, dingoes have larger teeth and do not bark, but howl instead, much like wolves and coyotes. Once considered close relatives to domestic dogs *(Canus familiaris),* dingoes have been given feral status and their own scientific name, *Canus dingo.*

Argue: Present a case for or against a topic.

Ironically, the Dingo Fence has shown that although dingoes may seem like pests, they are an important part of the Australian ecosystem. As predators, dingoes help control the rabbit population. An unchecked rabbit population decimates grazing lands, negatively affecting sheep and cattle ranching. In fact, on the protected side of the Dingo Fence, rabbit and kangaroo populations have depleted grass and water. On the dingo side of the fence, these populations have been effectively reduced, allowing for more luxuriant grasslands. This indicates that dingoes help maintain an ecological balance.

Reflect: Consider the impact of your topic.

Dingoes have been considered pests, ostracized by special fences and overcome by poison, traps, and shooting. Scientists worry about the possible extinction of these animals, so they have set up conservation areas. However, a threat that is less easily controlled is that of dingoes interbreeding with domestic dogs. Scientists fear that in the not-too-distant future, the pure dingo strain may disappear forever.

Analyze: Examine the parts of something to better understand the whole.

Ever since the cry "Dingoes ate my baby!" appeared in a sensationalist tabloid newspaper, people have been concerned about dingo attacks. Scientists exploring the phenomena suggest that attacks on humans are not characteristic of purebred dingoes. The problem comes from offspring of dingoes and domestic dogs. The resulting hybrid pups are larger and more aggressive, with characteristics of a dog and a dingo. Whereas a pure dingo might eat whatever bugs or lizards it finds, a hybrid craves meat, leading to more and more attacks on sheep, cattle, and even humans.

Try It!

Analyze the middle paragraphs in one of the essays in this book. Tell which method of support is used to develop each main point (explaining, comparing, analyzing, and so on).

Developing the Middle ▪ Use different levels of detail.

In most cases each main point is developed in a separate paragraph. Remember that specific details add meaning to your writing and make it worth reading, while writing that lacks effective detail leaves the reader with an incomplete picture and questions about the topic. A well-written paragraph often contains three levels of detail.

Level 1: A controlling sentence names the topic.

> Ironically, the Dingo Fence has shown that although dingoes may seem like pests, they are an important part of the Australian ecosystem.

Level 2: Clarifying sentences provide supporting points.

> As predators, dingoes help control the rabbit population. An unchecked rabbit population decimates grazing lands, negatively affecting sheep and cattle ranching. In fact, on the protected side of the Dingo Fence, rabbit and kangaroo populations have depleted grass and water. On the dingo side of the fence, these populations have been effectively reduced, allowing for more luxuriant grasslands.

Level 3: A completing sentence adds details to conclude the idea.

> This indicates that dingoes help maintain an ecological balance.

Try It!

Identify one set of sentences that show the three levels of detail in the paragraph below. Label each sentence after writing it down. (The topic sentence is the one controlling sentence in the paragraph.)

1 Until a few years ago, dingo watching was a popular tourist attraction
2 on Fraser Island, Australia's top vacation spot. Dingoes have traditionally
3 displayed a mild temperament around humans, but aggressive behaviors
4 began appearing in 2001, with a fatal attack on a child. Since that time,
5 another 20 attacks have been documented. It appears that through continued
6 contact with tourists, the dingoes have lost their innate fear of humans.
7 Because the animals are by nature
8 carnivores, this newfound aggression
9 poses obvious dangers. While dingo
10 watching is not discouraged, it now
11 comes with governmental warnings
12 and regulations.

■ Integrate quotations.

Always choose quotations that are appropriate for your writing. Quotations should support your ideas, not replace them.

Strategies for Using Quotations

Use the strategies below to make the most effective use of quoted material in your writing.

- ■ **Use quotations to support your own thoughts and ideas.**
  Effective quotations can back up your main points or support your arguments.

  Even in the early twentieth century, pollution was a growing concern, as shown in this comment by Franklin D. Roosevelt: "Government cannot close its eyes to the pollution of waters, to the erosion of soil, to the slashing of forests any more than it can close its eyes to the need for slum clearance and schools."

- ■ **Use quotations to lend authority to your writing.**
  Quoting an expert shows that you have researched your topic and understand its significance.

  Despite vociferous opposition to the arms race, the development of the bomb was an important part of world peace. As nuclear physicist Edward Teller explained, "We had a wonderful record on the hydrogen bomb. We tested it, perfected it, and never used it—and that served to win the Cold War."

- ■ **Use quotations that are succinct and powerful.**
  Distinctive quotations add value to your writing.

  Country music's power doesn't come from complicated structures or deep political undertones; it is popular simply because it touches people's lives. As legendary songwriter Harlan Howard once put it, "Country music is three chords and the truth."

Common Quotation Problems to Avoid

Avoid these problems as you choose quotations.

- ■ **Plagiarism**
  Cite sources for all quotations (and paraphrases).
- ■ **Long quotations**
  Keep quotations brief and to the point.
- ■ **Overused quotations**
  Use a quotation only when you cannot share its message as powerfully or effectively in another way.

Process

Writing the Ending

Your ending paragraph allows you to tie together the most important ideas in your essay. Your ending should do at least two of the following things:

- Restate or revisit the thesis of your paper.
- Review the main points.
- Leave the reader with something to think about.

Connecting with the thesis	The dingoes of Australia provide an interesting quandary for the government. The animals have been important to maintaining an ecological balance even though they pose an
Reviewing the main points	increasing threat to domestic animals, and, more recently, to humans. Tourists still love watching dingoes, and scientists still worry about the pure dingo strain dying out due to mixed
A final thought	breeding. The dilemma remains: Will preserving the species be worth the growing danger?

Form a final thought.

Here are three different ways to form a final thought.

A call to action directs the reader to do something.

> Only the city council can save Heathrow Park from the bulldozers. Call, e-mail, or write your representative to ask that our beautiful city park be preserved.

A lingering question encourages the reader to further examine the subject.

> Help save unwanted dogs and cats by having your pet spayed or neutered. Thousands of animals are put to death each year because people didn't take action. Don't you want to do your part to avoid these unnecessary deaths?

A good-or-bad conclusion suggests that your topic poses a possible benefit or threat the reader should be aware of.

> The Starlight Players is the only community theater group in the area. If people don't support it, the company could disband. That would give people another reason to find entertainment elsewhere, and a valuable family activity would be lost. It's your choice.

Try It!

Write an ending for a current writing assignment. Try reworking it using the suggestions above. Select the one you like best.

Revising

In a first draft, you communicate your initial sense of a topic. You do your best to connect all of your ideas. When you revisit a first draft, after setting it aside for a day or two, you will see different parts that you would like to change.

You may spot redundant information, which you need to cut. You may note places that would benefit from more details. You may detect weak arguments, which you can strengthen. You may also decide to reorder ideas to improve the logical flow. These are all the basic revising moves.

Revising may be the most important step in the writing process. It helps you improve the thoughts and details that carry your message. This chapter will give you a better understanding of this step, covering everything from a review of basic revising guidelines to an explanation of a valuable revising strategy.

- Basic Revising Guidelines
- A Revising Strategy That Works
- A Closer Look at Revising
- Revising Checklist
- Revising in Action
- Checking for Depth

"To the confident [change] is inspiring because the challenge exists to make things better."

—King Whitney, Jr.

Basic Revising Guidelines

No writer gets it right the first time. Few writers even get it right the second time. In fact, professional writers almost always carry out many revisions before they are satisfied with their work. As writer Virginia Hamilton says, "The real work comes in the rewriting stage." The following guidelines will help you make the best revising moves.

- **Set your writing aside.** Get away from it for a day or two. This will help you see your first draft more clearly when you are ready to revise.
- **Carefully review your draft.** Read it at least two times: once silently and once aloud. Also ask another person to react to your writing—someone whose opinion you trust.
- **Consider the big picture.** Decide if you've effectively developed your thesis.
- **Look at the specific parts.** Rewrite any parts that aren't clear or effective. Cut information that doesn't support your thesis and add ideas if you think your reader needs more information.
- **Assess your opening and closing paragraphs.** Be sure that they effectively introduce and wrap up your writing.

Revise a timed writing.

When you have little time to make changes, writer Peter Elbow recommends "cut and paste revising." For example, if you are responding to a writing prompt on a test or for an in-class assignment, you may have just 10 to 15 minutes to revise your writing. The steps that follow describe this quick revising strategy.

1. Don't add any new information.
2. Cut unnecessary details.
3. Check for basic organization.
4. Do whatever rewriting is necessary.

Try It!

Find an essay you wrote but haven't read in a while. Read it aloud, either alone or to someone else, paying careful attention to every word, every punctuation mark. *What trouble spots do you notice? Why do you notice them more when reading your work aloud? How would you fix these parts?*

A Revising Strategy That Works

The strategy below covers everything from reading the first draft to improving specific ideas. Use this strategy when you have time for in-depth revising.

Read: Sometimes it's hard to keep an open mind when you read your first draft. It's good to put some distance between yourself and your writing.

- Whenever possible, put your writing aside for a day or two.
- When you return to it, read your first draft aloud.
- Ask others (peers, family members) to read it aloud to you.
- Listen to your writing: What does it say? How does it sound?

React: Use these questions to help you react to your writing:

- What parts of my writing work for me?
- Do all of these parts work together?
- Have I arranged the parts in the best possible order?
- What other revising should I do?

Rework: Make changes until all parts of your writing work equally well. There is usually plenty of reworking to do in the early stages of revising, when you are still trying to bring a clear focus to a topic and share it effectively.

Reflect: Write comments in the margins of your paper (or in a notebook) as you revise. Here are some guidelines for reflecting:

- Explore your reactions freely. Be honest about your writing.
- Note what you plan to cut, move, explain further, and so on.
- Reflect on the changes you make. (How do they work?)
- If you are unsure of what to do, write down a question to answer later.

Refine: Refining is checking specific ideas for logic, readability, and balance. Use these questions to help you refine your ideas:

- Will the reader be able to follow my train of thought from idea to idea?
- Do I use transitional words or phrases to link ideas?
- Have I overdeveloped or underdeveloped certain points?

Tip

Remember that revising is the process of improving the ideas and the details that carry the message in your writing. Don't pay undue attention to conventions too early in the process; just concentrate on improving your message.

A Closer Look at Revising

The later stage of revising allows you to deal with those aspects of your writing that may make it seem boring. Use the questions that follow to check for any uninspired "badlands" in your writing.

- **Is your topic worn out?** An essay entitled "Lead Poisoning" sounds uninteresting. With a new twist, you can enliven it: "Get the Lead Out!"
- **Is your approach stale?** If you are writing primarily to please your teacher, start again. Try writing to learn something or to trigger a particular emotion within the reader.
- **Do you sound uninterested or unnatural?** If you do ("A good time was had by all"), try another approach. This time, be honest. Be real.
- **Do parts of your writing seem boring?** Maybe those parts are boring because they don't say enough, or they say too much. To rework these parts, think of them as a series of snapshots. Each picture needs the proper balance between its main idea and the supporting details.
- **Is your writing constrained by overly tight organization?** The structure of an essay provides you with a frame to build on. However, if the frame is followed too closely, your writing may become predictable. If the "formula" is obvious when you read your draft, change the structure in order to more freely present your ideas.

Try It!

As a class (or in a small group) evaluate these two paragraphs using the questions above as a guide.

Adventures in Cairo

Cairo is a sprawling city of 15 million people. Bazaars, small stalls or storefronts selling various goods, cater mostly to tourists. The prices are quite reasonable, but the vendors are pushy to the point of actually grabbing some people and pulling them into their shops. Adding to the commotion, many poor people beg for "bakshish" or tips (essentially for doing an unrequested "favor").

Traffic is just incredible—but it moves! Drivers are absolutely obsessed about getting where they want to go. There are no lanes; drivers just squeeze in and out of traffic however they can. The few traffic lights seem not to work. If there is too much traffic on one side of a divided highway, well, drivers go the wrong way on the other side. They make left turns from the middle lanes. There is a LOT of honking going on at all times. Also sharing the road are donkey-drawn carts. It's crazy! And although there are police everywhere, they do not seem very concerned about any of this.

"Any activity becomes creative when the doer cares about doing it right or doing it better."
—John Updike

Revising Checklist

Use this checklist as a guide when you revise your writing. Remember: When you revise, you improve the thoughts and details that carry your message.

Process

Ideas

_____ **1.** Is my topic important and relevant?
_____ **2.** Have I developed a specific focus or thesis statement?
_____ **3.** Does each paragraph support my thesis?
_____ **4.** Have I included enough details to make my ideas clear?

Organization

_____ **5.** Does my writing follow a clear pattern of organization?
_____ **6.** Have I developed effective beginning, middle, and ending parts?
_____ **7.** Do I need to reorder any parts?

Voice

_____ **8.** Does my voice fit the purpose of my writing?
_____ **9.** Do I sound interested in and knowledgeable about my topic?

Word Choice

_____ **10.** Have I used an appropriate level of formality?
_____ **11.** Do I use specific nouns and vivid verbs?
_____ **12.** Do I avoid repetition and redundancy?

Sentence Fluency

_____ **13.** Are my sentences complete and clearly written?
_____ **14.** Do my sentences flow smoothly?
_____ **15.** Have I varied my sentence beginnings and lengths?

Revising in Action

When you revise a first draft, focus on improving the writing overall. You can improve a piece by adding, deleting, moving, or reworking information. (See the next page for examples.)

Adding Information

Add information to your writing if you need to . . .

- share more details to make a point,
- clarify or complete an interesting idea, or
- link sentences or paragraphs to improve clarity and flow.

Deleting Information

Delete material from your draft when the ideas . . .

- do not support your focus or
- are redundant or repetitious.

Moving Material

Move material in your writing in order to . . .

- create a clear flow of ideas,
- present points in order, or
- make a dramatic impact.

Reworking Material

Rework material in your writing if it . . .

- is confusing or unclear,
- does not maintain the proper voice, or
- needs to be simplified.

Be your own critic.

When revising, try to anticipate your reader's concerns. Doing so will help you determine what changes to make. Here are some questions and concerns a reader may have:

- What is the main point of this essay?
- Is the writer's voice interested and authoritative?
- Can I follow the writer's ideas smoothly?
- Does the ending wrap up the essay in a clear way?

Process

Sample Revision

The writer of this essay improved it by moving, adding, deleting, and reworking parts. (See the inside back cover of this text for editing and proofreading marks.)

The Sky's Not the Limit

Ever since movies began, filmmakers have tried to put

imaginary things on film. Still, the effects never seemed real

enough. People used model building, hand-drawn cartoons,

or stop-motion animation. In the last 20 years, however,

computer-generated imagery (CGI) has made it possible

Anything that can be imagined can be put on-screen and look real.

to create believable special effects in movies. CGI allows

filmmakers to show things realistically on-screen that people

could only imagine before.

CGI can create totally imaginary characters that look

real. An early example is a knight leaping out of a stained-

glass window in *Young Sherlock Holmes* (1985). ~~Dinosaurs are~~

~~the most popular creatures for special effects over the years,~~

~~starting with the stop-motion puppets of The Lost World~~

~~(1925).~~ Later on, CGI showed us believable dinosaurs in *Jurassic*

Park (1993). More recently, CGI and the voice and acting of

Andy Serkis created the incredible character of Gollum (*Lord*

Today, CGI even replaces older special effects technologies

of the Rings: The Two Towers, 2002). ~~Even though I loved and~~

like the Yoda puppet from *The Empire Strikes Back* (1980).

~~believed in Yoda as a puppet in The Empire Strikes Back (1980),~~

~~the technology is outmoded and too limited.~~ Many of the aliens

in the newer *Star Wars* films are all CGI creations (*Revenge of*

the Sith, 2005). Now, even the most fantastic creatures from

folklore to science fiction can seem real on-screen.

A sentence is moved for clarity.

An interesting detail is added.

An unnecessary detail is deleted.

An important idea is reworded for appropriate voice.

Checking for Depth

One important consideration when revising an essay is to determine whether or not the level of detail is appropriate. Some ideas can be expressed perfectly well without a lot of specifics (and, in fact, may suffer from too many details). If, however, you realize during revision that a particular passage needs more support, the addition of specific details will help the reader better understand your writing.

Different types of writing require different types of details. For instance, facts, statistics, and examples support expository and persuasive writing, while narrative and creative writing benefit from sensory and memory details.

Add depth.

As Alahandra was reviewing her essay about the process of digestion, she came upon these two sentences:

> In the mouth, saliva helps break down food. When someone swallows, a movement called peristalsis pushes the food down into the stomach.

Alahandra then added details to better explain the process.

> In the mouth, the chewing of food causes the exocrine glands to release saliva. Enzymes in saliva help break down food. Saliva also helps condense the chewed-up food into small balls that can pass into the esophagus when swallowed. In the esophagus, peristalsis, or contraction of the smooth muscle tissues, pushes the food down toward the stomach, where it enters through a one-way "gate" called the cardiac sphincter.

Try It!

The following passage is from a student essay about the body's healing process. Explain why the writer should or should not add details.

As soon as you receive a minor cut, your body's healing process begins. Blood from tiny blood vessels fills the wound and begins to clot. Then a scab forms.

Peer Responding

If you had some poppy seeds stuck between your teeth, surely you'd want someone to politely and discreetly point out your little *faux pas.* Similarly, if there is a problem in your writing, you would appreciate a friend or classmate directing your attention to it. That's what peer responding is all about. When you ask your peers for their honest opinions about your writing, they can show you things you don't see yourself—good and bad. Once you have this feedback, you can decide on the best way to address any problem areas.

Feedback from your fellow writers is valuable throughout the writing process, but it is especially helpful during the early stages of revising when you are evaluating your first draft. Some experts go so far as to say that talking about your work will help you more than anything else you do during the writing process.

- **Peer-Responding Guidelines**
- **Using the Traits to Respond**
- **Trying a New Strategy**

"Criticism, like rain, should be gentle enough to nourish a man's growth without destroying his roots."

—Frank A. Clark

"The first rule in listening to comments about your work is 'Never defend yourself' unless you can tell that your critic has misunderstood something."

—Ken Macrorie

Peer-Responding Guidelines

The guidelines below will help you participate in peer-response sessions. (If you're just starting out, work in small groups of two or three classmates.)

Consider the writer's role.

Come to the session with a meaningful piece of your writing—perhaps a recently completed first draft. Make a copy for each member of the group (if this is what the group usually does).

- **Introduce your writing.** Give a brief explanation of what your piece is about without going into too much detail.
- **Read your writing aloud.** If you don't feel comfortable reading aloud, ask group members to read your piece silently.
- **Ask for feedback.** Listen carefully and consider all suggestions. Don't be defensive, because this may stop some members from commenting honestly.
- **Take notes.** Record your classmates' comments on your copy so you can decide later what to change.
- **Answer questions.** If you're unsure of an answer, it's okay to say, "I don't know" or "I'll look into that."
- **Seek assistance.** If you have trouble with a specific part of your writing, ask for help.

Seeking Constructive Criticism

To get constructive criticism, you may need to ask the responders some direct questions. Consider your purpose, your intended audience, and the focus of your writing. Knowing these three things will help you form your questions.

Try It!

Practice your role as the writer in a peer-responding session with a classmate, friend, or family member. First, share the information on the next page about the responder's role. Then follow the guidelines for the writer listed above. Afterward, assess the effectiveness of the session: *Did the session help you see parts of your writing that could be improved? Did the responder answer any questions that you had? Did he or she make any other helpful suggestions?*

Consider the responder's role.

You need to be honest in your feedback without hurting the writer's feelings. Your comments should always be polite and constructive.

Giving Constructive Criticism	
Don't make demands . . . "Change the ending so the reader has something to think about."	**DO make suggestions . . .** "The ending could be stronger if you leave the reader with a question to think about."
Don't focus on the writer . . . "Nobody understands what you're trying to say in the middle part."	**DO focus on the writing . . .** "Don't you think your ideas would be easier to follow if you switched paragraphs two and three?"
Don't focus on the problem . . . "The beginning paragraph is boring."	**DO focus on the solution . . .** "Descriptive details might make the beginning more interesting."
Don't give general comments . . . "Your sentences aren't very interesting."	**DO give specific advice . . .** "Changing from passive to active voice in a few places could liven things up."

Responding Tips

- Listen carefully to the writer's reading and questions.
- Take notes in the margins of your copy.
- Ask questions. If you are not sure of something, ask for clarification.

Try It!

Using the tips above, write three strong criticisms about this paragraph.

In the northwest part of Utah lie the remnants of a sizable lake from the Ice Age. All that remains of the ancient Lake Bonneville is salt—up to six feet deep in some areas. The Bonneville Salt Flats, which occupy approximately 160 square miles, are extremely flat and devoid of plant life. As such, the area is well suited for motor sports, and the state's highway department now maintains a part of the Flats known as the Bonneville Speedway. It was here that numerous land speed records were set, beginning in 1935 when Malcolm Campbell, driving a specially designed Rolls-Royce, passed the 300-mph mark for the first time. For the next 35 years, each of the world's land speed records was broken at the Bonneville Speedway, culminating in Gary Gabelich's rocket-powered record of 622 mph in October 1970.

Process

Using the Traits to Respond

Responders help writers rethink, refocus, and revise their writing. As a responder, you may find it helpful to base your responses on the traits of writing.

Address ideas, organization, and voice early in the process.

Ideas: Help the author focus on ideas.

- Can you tell us the main idea of your writing?
- It seems like you're trying to say . . . Is that right?
- Are these points the main ideas in your writing?
- The most convincing details are . . .
- A few details like . . . may make this part more interesting.
- In my opinion, details like . . . may distract from your main idea.
- Your writing left me thinking . . . Is that what you intended?

Organization: Help the author focus on organization.

- You got my attention in the beginning by . . .
- This sentence seems to state your focus. Is that correct?
- Are the middle paragraphs organized according to . . . ?
- Why did you place the information about . . . in the fourth paragraph?
- Is the purpose of your ending to . . . ?
- I wonder if a transition is needed between the second and third paragraphs.

Voice: Help the author focus on voice.

- The sentences that most clearly show your personality are . . .
- How would you describe your attitude about this topic?
- What audience did you have in mind when you wrote this?
- The third paragraph sounds too formal to me. Do you think it fits in with the rest of your writing?
- The overall feeling I get from your writing is . . .
- The middle part of your essay might be too subjective.

Try It!

Find and read any student writer's paragraph in this book. Afterward, write two constructive criticisms based on the *ideas, organization,* and *voice* in the writing.

Address word choice and fluency later in the process.

Word Choice: Help the author focus on the nouns, verbs, and modifiers.

- The most powerful verbs in the writing are . . .
- I found these general nouns: . . . What specific nouns could you use instead?
- Do you think there are too many modifiers in the first paragraph?
- I'm confused by the meaning of . . . Can you define it, please?
- The words . . . feel wrong to me. You could use . . . instead.
- Have you used . . . too often in the first part of your writing?

Sentence Fluency: Help the author focus on the sentences.

- I like the flow of the sentences in the beginning paragraph.
- Check your sentences in the middle part. Do you think too many of them begin the same way?
- It might add interest to vary the sentences in the closing paragraph.
- Could some of the sentences in the second paragraph be combined?
- For the most part, your sentences have a nice rhythm.

Try It!

Read the following paragraph. Then write a few constructive criticisms about the *word choice* and *sentence fluency* in the writing.

> When I was about six years old, my friend Barbie and I happily spent our summer afternoons exploring the world of our neighborhood. Venturing a block or two away, we'd find an orchard in someone's backyard and help ourselves to a fresh pear. Or we'd hunt for fossils in the stone landscaping near the church parking lot down the street. One afternoon Barbie and I found a caterpillar and brought it home to put in a jar with a branch. We let the caterpillar crawl up and down our little arms. Gradually I became aware that I wasn't feeling well, so I went home. When I reported to my mom, she lifted my shirt and looked at my back, proclaiming that I had chicken pox. For years after that, I believed there was a link between handling a caterpillar and feeling sick.

React to criticism.

You don't have to incorporate all of your classmates' suggestions. The following tips will help you get the most out of response sessions.

- Trust your own judgment about your writing.
- Determine which issues are most important.
- Pay attention to comments made by more than one responder.
- Get another opinion if you are not sure about something.

Process

Trying a New Strategy

Provided on this page are two strategies for evaluating a piece of writing.

React to writing.

Peter Elbow, in *Writing Without Teachers,* offers four types of reactions peer responders might have to a piece of writing:

- **Pointing** refers to a reaction in which a group member "points out" words, phrases, or ideas that impress him or her.
- **Summarizing** is a list of main ideas or a single sentence that sums up the work. It's a reader's general reaction to the writing.
- **Telling** involves the reader describing what happens in a piece of writing: first this happens, then that happens, and so on.
- **Showing** refers to speaking metaphorically about the piece. A reader might speak of a quality as if it were a voice, color, shape, or piece of clothing ("Your writing has a neat, tailored quality").

Critique a paper.

Use this checklist as a guide when you assess a piece of writing in progress.

_____ **Purpose:** Is it clear what the writer is trying to do—entertain, inform, persuade, describe? Explain.

_____ **Audience:** Does the writing address a specific audience? Will the reader understand and appreciate the subject? Why?

_____ **Ideas:** Does the writer develop the topic with enough information?

_____ **Organization:** Are the ideas arranged in the best way?

_____ **Voice:** Does the writer sound sincere and honest? Does the writer speak to his or her audience? Explain.

_____ **Word Choice:** Does the writer include any technical terms? Are these terms defined? Does the level of language fit the audience?

_____ **Sentence Fluency:** Do the sentences read smoothly?

_____ **Purpose Again:** Does the writing succeed in making the reader smile, nod, or react in some other way?

Try It!

Try one of these strategies the next time you respond to one of your peer's essays or papers. Afterward, assess the effectiveness of the strategy.

Editing

Editing is the final step before publishing anything you've written. When you edit, you check your revised writing for errors in spelling, punctuation, and grammar. Your goal is to produce a clean, correct final draft—a necessity if you want the reader to take you seriously as a writer. Errors not only interrupt the reading; they also reduce the reader's confidence in your message.

Editing is most easily accomplished with the appropriate tools: a dictionary, a thesaurus, spell- and grammar-checkers, and the "Proofreader's Guide" in this book (pages **605–763**). These resources will help as you prepare your writing for publication. The information in this chapter will help you improve your editing and proofreading skills.

- **Checklist for Editing and Proofreading**
- **Editing in Action**
- **Errors to Watch For**
- **Special Editing Problems**

"When something can be read without effort, great effort has gone into its writing."

—Enrique Jardiel Poncela

"Grammar is a tricky, inconsistent thing. Being the backbone of speech and writing, it should, we think, be eminently logical, make perfect sense, like the human skeleton. But, of course, the skeleton is arbitrary, too."

—John Simon

Checklist for Editing and Proofreading

Use this checklist as a guide when you edit and proofread your revised writing. Also refer to "Errors to Watch For" on pages **130–131**.

Tip

Always have a trusted friend or peer serve as a second editor. You're too close to your work to catch every error.

Conventions

PUNCTUATION (See pages 605–647.)

_____ Do my sentences end with the proper punctuation?

_____ Do I use commas correctly in compound sentences?

_____ Do I use commas correctly in a series and after long introductory phrases or clauses?

_____ Do I use apostrophes correctly?

MECHANICS (CAPITALIZATION AND SPELLING) (See pages 648–671.)

_____ Do I start my sentences with capital letters?

_____ Do I capitalize proper nouns?

_____ Have I checked for spelling errors (including those the spell-checker may have missed)?

GRAMMAR (See pages 700–756.)

_____ Do the subjects and verbs agree in my sentences?

_____ Do my sentences use correct and consistent verb tenses?

_____ Do my pronouns agree with their antecedents?

_____ Have I avoided any other usage errors?

PRESENTATION (See pages 91–95.)

_____ Does the title effectively lead into the writing?

_____ Are sources of information properly presented and documented?

_____ Does my writing meet the requirements for final presentation?

Process

Editing in Action

Note the editing corrections made in these paragraphs from a student essay. See the inside back cover of this book for an explanation of the editing symbols used.

A comma is inserted after a long introductory phrase.

Apostrophe and spelling mistakes are corrected.

Abbreviations are spelled out.

Placement of punctuation with quotation marks is corrected.

The name of the ship is marked for italics.

Usage errors are corrected.

About 450 miles off the coast of Newfoundland in 12,000 feet of water, scientists discovered the remains of the great ocean liner, the R.M.S. Titanic. The 73-year search for the Titanic, which went down in what is considered the worlds' greatest sea disaster, was a challenging one. It concluded finally in September 1985.

When it was first launched in 1912, the British steamer was the largest ship in the world. An incredible 882 feet long and 175 feet high, the Titanic was proclaimed the most expensive and luxurious ship ever built. It was said to be "unsinkable." It was equipped with a double bottom, and the hull was divided into 16 separate watertight compartments.

Despite its reputation, the mighty Titanic did sink—on its maiden voyage. Carrying approximately 2,200 passengers and over $420,000 worth of cargo, the Titanic set sail from England in April 1912, bound for New York. Just a few days out of port, however, on the night of April 14, the Titanic collided with an iceberg in the north Atlantic Ocean, damaging steel plates along its starboard side. The great "floating palace" sunk in a matter of 2 1/2 hours, taking with it all of it's cargo and 1,522 of it's passengers and crew.

Errors to Watch For

These two pages show 10 common errors to check for in your writing.

1. **Problem: Missing Comma After Long Introductory Phrase**
   Solution: Place a comma after a long introductory phrase.

   > Growing up in suburban Chicago,I longed for a dog of my own.

2. **Problem: Confusing Pronoun Reference**
   Solution: Be sure the reader knows whom or what your pronoun refers to.

   > Although Ty pointed out the error to Hakeem, ~~he~~ Ty didn't fix it.

3. **Problem: Missing Comma in Compound Sentence**
   Solution: Use a comma between two independent clauses joined by a coordinating conjunction—*and, but, or, nor, so, for,* or *yet.*

   > Myra just turned 16 years old,yet she is starting her senior year.

4. **Problem: Missing Comma(s) with Nonrestrictive Phrases or Clauses**
   Solution: Use commas to set off a phrase or clause that is not needed to understand the sentence. (See page **612**.)

   > I ordered a tostada,which is my favorite Mexican food.

5. **Problem: Comma Splice**
   Solution: When only a comma separates two independent clauses, add a conjunction, replace the comma with a semicolon, or create two sentences.

   > First water the vegetable garden; then cut the front lawn.

6. **Problem: Subject-Verb Agreement Error**
   Solution: Verbs must agree in number with their subjects.

   > Tomatoes from the farmers' market ~~tastes~~ taste the best.

7. Problem: **Missing Comma in a Series**
   Solution: Use commas to separate individual words, phrases, or clauses in a series.

> Mr. Taneka was loaded down with balloons gifts and games.

8. Problem: **Pronoun-Antecedent Agreement Error**
   Solution: A pronoun must agree in number with the word that the pronoun refers to. (See page **756**.)

> Either Tracy or her girlfriends left her books on the bus.
> *their*

9. Problem: **Missing Apostrophe to Show Ownership**
   Solution: Use an apostrophe after a noun to show possession.

> Our school's mascot is a bulldog.

10. Problem: **Misusing *Its* and *It's***
   Solution: *Its* is a possessive pronoun meaning "belonging to it." *It's* is a contraction of "it is" or "it has."

> The cute little sports car was missing one of it's taillights.
> *its*

Try It!

Find the errors in the passage below. Write the paragraph correctly on your paper.

Kent wants to attend a four-year college but his family can't afford it. His parents who both work for the telephone company haven't been able to maintain a college savings fund. None of Kents cousins have attended college, either. Maybe Kent will get one or more of the scholarships he applied for, he deserves a chance to continue his education. Its not an easy time of life for him.

Special Editing Problems

The spell-checker and grammar-checker on your computer are great—but they're not foolproof. You still have to look for errors that they may not recognize. For example, a grammar-checker is not likely to catch the following kinds of errors.

Use of a Comma with "Who" Clauses

A dependent clause that begins with the relative pronoun *who* can be a nonrestrictive clause, which requires one or more commas to set it off, or it can be restrictive, requiring no commas. (See page **612**.)

My neighbor who retired from the workforce several years ago **volunteers at the local senior day-care center**. (This "who" clause **is not** needed to understand the point of the sentence. Commas should set off the clause.)

Joel and Marcus are juniors, who often practice their guitars together. (This "who" clause is needed to understand the point of the sentence. Commas should not set off the clause.)

Apostrophes to Show Possession

When two people individually own things, an apostrophe is needed with both names. For joint ownership, however, the apostrophe belongs only with the last owner listed.

Freddy suspiciously eyed Pete's **and Tayshaun's snowboards**. (Since Pete and Tayshaun each own a snowboard, both names need apostrophes.)

We can ride in Carl's **and Carol's car**. (Carl and Carol own the car **together**, so only one apostrophe and *s* is needed.)

Object Pronouns

Trouble sometimes arises when a prepositional phrase contains a pronoun as part of the compound object.

Dane wants to go to the beach with Mom and *me*. ("I" is a subject pronoun and shouldn't be used in a prepositional phrase. The correct pronoun to use is "me," an object pronoun.)

Try It!

Write your own sample sentences that illustrate the rules explained above. Afterward, exchange your sentences with a classmate, and make sure each other's examples are correct.

Publishing

According to *The American Heritage Dictionary*, the word *publish* means "to prepare and issue (printed material) for public distribution." What better destiny for your writing? This chapter offers guidelines for preparing to publish as well as suggestions on where you might submit your work.

This chapter also explains how to prepare a writing portfolio. A writing portfolio shows your teacher (and other readers of your work) your progress as a writer. It gives you yet another reason to put forth your best effort on writing assignments.

- **Preparing to Publish**
- **Places to Publish**
- **Preparing a Portfolio**
- **Parts of a Portfolio**
- **Creating Your Own Web Site**

"To write well, express yourself
like the common people,
but think like a wise man."

—Aristotle

"An essential element for good writing is a good ear. One must listen to the sound of one's prose."
—Barbara Tuchman

Preparing to Publish

Publishing is the final step in the writing process, offering that "other audience"—your readers—a chance to enjoy your writing. The following guidelines will help you prepare your writing for publishing.

Complete these tasks.

- **Work with your writing** until you feel good about it from start to finish. If any parts still need work, then it isn't ready to publish.

- **Ask for input and advice** during the writing process. Your writing should answer any questions the reader may have about your topic. Confusing parts must be made clear.

- **Save all drafts for each writing project** so you can keep track of the changes you have made. If you are preparing a portfolio, you may be required to include early drafts as well as finished pieces. (See pages **136–138**.)

- **Check for the traits of writing** to be sure that you have effectively addressed ideas, organization, voice, word choice, and sentence fluency in your work. (See pages **51–88**.)

- **Carefully edit and proofread for conventions** after you have completed all of your revisions.

- **Prepare a neat final copy** to share with the reader. Use pen (blue or black ink) and one side of the paper if you are writing by hand. If you are using a computer, avoid fancy, hard-to-read fonts and odd margins. (See pages **91–95**.)

- **Know your publishing options** since there are many ways to publish. (See page **135**.)

- **Follow the requirements** indicated by the publisher. Each publisher has its own set of requirements, which must be followed exactly.

Try It!

Use these guidelines once you decide to publish a piece of writing. Be sure to ask your teacher for help if you have any questions about the publishing process.

Process

Places to Publish

Listed below are five well-respected publications that accept student submissions and three writing contests to enter. You can also look in the *Writer's Market*—available in most libraries—for more places to publish.

Publications	Writing Contests
Kids Byline: A Magazine for Kids by Kids (Grades 2-12) FORMS: Fiction, nonfiction, poetry SEND TO: P.O. Box 1838 Frederick, MD 21702	**Read Writing Contests** (Grades 2-12) FORMS: Short stories, personal essays SEND TO: *Read* Writing and Art Awards Weekly Reader Corporation 200 First Stamford Place P.O. Box 120023 Stamford, CT 06912-0023
Teen Ink (Grades 6-12) FORMS: Articles, art, photos, reviews, poems, fiction SEND TO: P.O. Box 30 Newton, MA 02461	**The American Library of Poetry: Student Poetry Contest** (Grades 8-9 and 10-12) FORMS: One poem of no more than 20 lines on any subject, and in any form SEND TO: Student Poetry Contest P.O. Box 978 Houlton, ME 04730
The 21st Century (Grades 9-12) FORMS: Fiction, poetry, nonfiction SEND TO: P.O. Box 30 Newton, MA 02461	
The High School Writer (Grades 9-12) FORMS: Fiction, poetry, nonfiction SEND TO: Senior High Edition P.O. Box 718 Grand Rapids, MN 55744	**Scholastic Writing Awards** (Grades 9-12) FORMS: Short story, essay, dramatic script, poetry, humor, science fiction, fantasy, writing portfolio SEND TO: The Scholastic Art and Writing Awards 557 Broadway New York, NY 10012
Skipping Stones: A Multicultural Children's Magazine (Ages 8-16) FORMS: Stories, articles, art (any language) SEND TO: P.O. Box 3939 Eugene, OR 97403	

Tip

Check with the publication or contest and with your teacher about the submission guidelines. Always include a self-addressed stamped envelope (SASE) when submitting written work to an outside publisher.

Preparing a Portfolio

A writing portfolio is a collection of your work that shows your skill as a writer. Your teacher will probably ask you to compile a *showcase portfolio*—a collection of your best writing for a quarter or a semester. Compiling a showcase portfolio allows you to participate in the assessment process. You decide which writing samples to include, and you reflect upon your writing progress.

Work smart.

Use the following information as a guide when you compile a showcase portfolio. There are no shortcuts when it comes to putting together an effective portfolio, so don't skip any of these suggestions.

1. Organize and keep track of your writing (including planning notes and drafts).

2. Be sure that you understand all of the requirements for your portfolio. If you have any questions, ask your teacher for help.

3. Keep your work in a safe place. Use a good-quality, expandable folder for your portfolio to avoid dog-eared or ripped pages.

4. Maintain a regular writing/compiling schedule. It will be impossible to create an effective portfolio if you approach it as a last-minute project.

5. Develop a feeling of pride in your portfolio. Make sure that it reflects a positive image of yourself. Look your best! (Remember that your teacher will be reviewing your portfolio for assessment.)

Try It!

Create a chart—similar to the one below—to help you keep track of writing you may want to include in a portfolio. For each piece, put a check next to each step you complete.

	Social Studies: "Urban Sprawl"	Literature: Great Gatsby
Prewriting Notes	✓	✓
First Draft	✓	✓
Revision	✓	
Edited Copy		
Final Draft	✓	
Cover Sheet		

Process

Parts of a Portfolio

Check with your teacher about specific requirements for your portfolio. Most showcase portfolios contain the following parts.

- **A table of contents** listing the pieces included in the portfolio.
- **An opening essay or letter** detailing the story behind your portfolio (how you organized it, what it represents to you, and so on).
- **Specific finished pieces** representing your best writing. (Your teacher may ask you to include all of the planning, drafting, and revising for one or more of your writing samples.)
- **A best "other" piece** related to your work in another content area.
- **A cover sheet** attached to each piece of writing, discussing the reason for its selection, the work that went into it, and so on.
- **Evaluation sheets or checklists** charting the basic skills you have mastered as well as the skills you still need to work on. (Your teacher will supply these sheets.)

Write your opening pages.

The first two pages of a showcase portfolio are shown here.

Table of Contents

Showcase Portfolio
Jenna Bosworth

Table of Contents

Opening Letter

Dear Ms. _____

I first thought compiling a portfolio was just another assignment. However, as the semester progressed, I realized that I wanted to "show off" my writing. As a result, I put a lot of effort into the enclosed pieces of writing. You will be able to see that by looking at the different steps I took in writing them.

The first piece—"The U.S. Department of Peace: Why Not?"—is a persuasive essay that I wrote for my current events class. The essay stems from a resolution by Senator Mark Dayton, who proposed that the United States have a Department of Peace. Writing about this resolution helped me feel more connected to the affairs of government. I paid careful attention to both sides of the argument when I crafted this essay. I am pleased to include it in my portfolio for all to read.

The second selection—"Misery in Missouri"—is a feature article I wrote in Honors Composition. It depicts a few summer days in hot, humid St. Louis and how various people cope with the heat. I enjoyed profiling the different personalities. Developing this piece certainly improved my interviewing skills.

My third piece is a letter to the editor that I submitted to the *Bugle-Call.* I was both surprised and happy when it was published. The letter expresses my displeasure with the new rules regarding Senior Prom. I discovered my civil-but-angry voice while writing this letter. This experience gave me new confidence in my writing ability.

Sincerely,
Jenna Bosworth

Create a cover sheet.

When you create your showcase portfolio, you should attach a cover sheet to each writing project you include. (See the sample below written for a student's persuasive essay.) Your cover sheet should do one or more of the following things:

- Explain why you chose the piece for your portfolio.
- Tell about the process of writing you used, including problems you encountered.
- Describe the strong points and the weak points in the writing.
- Reflect on the writing's importance to you.

Sample Cover Sheet

I chose this essay because I am proud of how I expressed myself about an important issue. Our assignment was to write a persuasive essay based on any of the issues we'd been discussing in Current Events. One issue, a resolution by Senator Mark Dayton to create a federal Department of Peace and Nonviolence, really struck me as a commonsense approach to preventing conflict. The resolution, unfortunately, never went anywhere in Congress, but I decided I would write an essay in support of it.

An article from *Time* magazine provided some background information. I researched the issue further using congressional sites on the Internet and the senator's own Web site. I did some personal research, as well, getting the opinions of friends and family members. Then I organized my information using a line diagram before writing my first draft.

The strongest point in this paper is my confident voice. I'm sure it's because I felt so strongly about the topic. The weakest point is probably the flow of my ideas. I was more concerned with presenting my thought than with sentence fluency.

Writing this essay helped me see that persuading someone to accept my viewpoint is more than being passionate about a particular issue. Being persuasive requires a logical presentation of an argument and paying careful attention to opposing points of view.

Try It!

Write a cover sheet for a piece of writing that you would like to include in your portfolio.

Creating Your Own Web Site

Creating a Web site is one way to showcase your work. Check with your Internet service provider to find out how to get started. If you are designing your page at school, ask your teacher for help. The questions and answers below will help you get started.

Q. How do I begin planning my site?

A. Think about the number of pages you want on your site. Do you want just one page to showcase a piece of your work, or do you want multiple pages (a home page, a page of poetry, a short story page, a page of favorite links, and so on)? Check out other students' Web pages for ideas. Then sketch out your pages. Note how the pages will be linked by marking the "hot spots" on your sketches.

Q. How do I make the pages?

A. Each page is created as a separate file. Many word-processing programs let you save a file as a Web page. Otherwise, you may have to learn HTML (hypertext markup language). This is a code that allows you to add text and graphics to a page. Your teacher may be able to help you with it. If not, you can find instructions on the Internet. (See the "Web Design" page on our Web site at *www.thewritesource.com* for help.)

Q. How do I know if my pages work?

A. You should always test your pages. Using your browser, open your first page. Then follow the links to make sure they work correctly.

Q. How do I get my pages on the Web?

A. You must upload your finished pages to your Internet provider's computer. Ask your provider how to do this. (If you're working on your home computer, get a parent's approval. If you're using a school computer, work with your teacher.) Your provider will tell you how to access the pages later, in case you want to make changes. After you upload a page, visit your site and make sure it still works.

Try It!

Get the word out about your site. E-mail your friends and ask them to visit your site. Your service provider can offer tips on how to get your site listed on various Web browsers.

Narrative Writing

Narrative Writing
Writing a Personal Narrative

In his book *Writing About Your Life*, William Zinsser says, "Be surprised by the crazy wonderful events that will come dancing out of your past when you stir the pot of memory." Writing personal narratives provides a perfect opportunity "to stir the pot of memory" in order to recall memorable experiences. No other form of writing connects you with your life in such a meaningful way.

In this chapter, you will read a personal narrative in which the writer recalls charming his grandmother for selfish reasons. Despite his less than honorable intentions, he ends up making the right decision. Then you will learn how to write your own narrative in which you acted appropriately, but for the wrong reason. Special attention is given to creating an effective story line and to considering the value of or need for background information.

Writing Guidelines

Subject: Making the right decision for the wrong reason

Form: Personal narrative

Purpose: To share a meaningful experience

Audience: Classmates

"Wrong reasoning sometimes lands poor mortals in right conclusions."
—George Eliot

Sample Essay

In the following personal narrative, Kenny writes about a time he did the right thing for the wrong reason.

A Greater Wealth

Beginning
The writer draws the reader into the narrative.

Middle
Background information prepares the reader for the story.

The writer's "wrongful" reason is revealed.

Most young kids are very self-centered most of the time. It's like their brain meters are stuck on "Selfish." In just about any situation in which they have a choice, first they wonder what's in it for them. This certainly described me until I met my dear grandmother.

My father had been born in Japan, and he had many old, old photographs of the palatial estate that had belonged to his family through many generations. He told me stories of gorgeous homes full of lacquered furniture, silk wall panels, and polished cedar platforms. He also described magnificent gardens, full of the sweet scents of exotic flowers and the gentle trickle of graceful fountains.

From all this, I figured my grandmother must be rich. I had never met her before she came from Japan, but at eight, I reasoned that if I were nice to her, she would take me back to Japan to live in luxury. It was a good plan, I thought, and I vowed to spend time with my grandmother so she would grow to love me and want me to accompany her upon her return.

"There she is!" my father called. I expected to see some regal kimono-clad creature riding in a satin litter like I'd seen in pictures. Instead, I saw a tiny woman with silver hair, wearing a modern blue suit. She did not look wealthy to me. Still, I vowed to be attentive, to make myself indispensable to her during her stay.

To get closer to her, I flattered her into telling me stories about old Japan. She enjoyed making Temari, fabric balls wound tightly with delicate designs, and as she worked, she wove tales of Japanese legends and history as intricate and beautiful as the designs she created. I listened, fascinated. Her words were a mix of the two languages so I didn't completely understand everything at first. Interestingly, as her English improved, so did my understanding of Japanese.

Narrative

No one spoke of her going back, and I was anxious to commence my life of Japanese luxury, so one evening I worked up my courage to ask.

Dialogue builds suspense.

"Obasan?" I began timidly. She looked up from her embroidery, her amber eyes peeking lovingly over her half-glasses.

"Yes, Kenny-Chan?" She always added the traditional endearment to my name.

"When you go back to Japan, will you take me?"

She seemed surprised by the question, and she stopped her winding and rested her hands on her lap.

The narrative builds to a moment of discovery.

"Kenny-chan, I am no going back. I live here now. But why you want to leave? Here is so wonderful."

"But aren't you rich in Japan? Don't you have beautiful things there?"

"Why you think that?" she asked, surprised.

I told her about my father's stories.

"Yes," she smiled. "I told those stories to your father when he little. My father told them me. Once they all true, and my family had great wealth. But then war came, and it all disappeared. Your sohu—your grandfather—and I worked very hard make good life. Not rich life, but good life. Now he gone, and I wish to remain here with family."

Ending
The writer reveals his new understanding.

My dreams of a luxurious life had been dashed. At first I was disappointed. Then I remembered that she was staying with us, and my sadness disappeared. I had tried to make her love me so that I could join her in Japan. I quickly understood that I didn't need the wealth of Japan. My grandmother had given me great riches right here at home.

 Respond to the reading. Answer the following questions about the sample narrative.

Ideas (1) What is the writer's initial reason for interacting with his grandmother? (2) What does he discover?

Organization (3) Where is time order used in the narrative?

Voice & Word Choice (4) What does the dialogue reveal about the grandmother's character?

Prewriting ■ Select a topic.

To get started, Kenny listed a few times when he did the right thing, but not for the right reason. He then put an asterisk next to the one time he would write about.

Topics List

- gaining my grandmother's attention so she would take me to Japan *
- mowing Mrs. Havel's lawn so I could use her swimming pool
- practicing the guitar to become famous
- befriending a certain classmate to help me in calculus

Prewrite

Select a topic. List at least three personal experiences in which you did the right thing, but not for the right reason. Put an asterisk next to the one experience that you would like to write about.

■ Gather details.

Kenny then completed a Q-and-A chart to gather his initial thoughts.

Q-and-A Chart

Questions	Answers
What did I want?	I wanted to have my grandmother take me to Japan.
Why did I want this?	I wanted to live in luxury.
What did I do?	I was especially nice to her.
What was the result?	I really grew to love her.
What did I learn?	I learned that real wealth comes from love.

Prewrite

Learn about your experience. Complete a Q-and-A chart about your experience.

■ Focus on the traits.

Ideas When you plan and write your narrative, keep in mind the element of surprise. Work in ideas and details that build suspense into your story and lead up to a turning point—a moment of realization.

Narrative

■ Consider the story line.

Since a personal narrative is essentially a true story, it should contain the basic elements that create an effective story or plot line, including a problem to get things started, complications, a moment of truth, and so on. Here's how Kenny's narrative develops according to the base elements of a story or plot. (Also see page **342**.)

Determine the problem.

Kenny believes he would live a life of luxury in Japan, so he needs to convince his grandmother to take him back with her.

Work in complications.

Kenny learns a great deal about life in Japan from his father and his grandmother. No one talks about the grandmother going back, yet Kenny is anxious to start his new life. A conversation between Kenny and his grandmother builds to the moment of truth.

Identify the climax or moment of truth.

Kenny discovers that his grandmother isn't rich and that she isn't returning to Japan.

Bring the story to a close.

In the resolution, Kenny discovers that living without luxury will be okay, and interacting with his grandmother is its own reward—one that is much more valuable than material wealth.

Prewrite

Develop your story line. Identify the main parts for your narrative: problem, complications, climax, and resolution. (During the actual writing, change or add to any part as needed.)

■ Focus on the traits.

Voice Dialogue is an essential feature in narratives. It has three main functions: (1) It helps develop the personalities of the participants. (2) It furthers the action and builds suspense. (3) It serves as a transitional device to move from one part of the experience to the next. See if you can find at least one example of each of these functions in the sample narrative.

"Your opening has to be good—or the rest of the story won't have a chance because nobody'll stick around to read it."
—Lawrence Block

Writing ■ Create a beginning, a middle, and an ending.

A personal narrative relates and reflects upon a pivotal moment in the writer's life. All narratives have a beginning, a middle, and an ending.

The Beginning Draw the reader in. The beginning must hook the reader and introduce the situation. You can gain the reader's interest in several ways:

- Start with an interesting or surprising statement.
- Begin with dialogue to pull the reader into the action.
- Make a statement that piques the reader's curiosity.
- Share information that sets the scene.

Kenny selected the fourth technique. In his introduction, he discusses a common childhood condition—self-centeredness—that every reader can identify with.

The Middle Build suspense through action, dialogue, and details. The middle develops the story line and supports the main idea of your narrative. In the sample narrative, Kenny works to make his grandmother love him; and at the moment of truth, he discovers that his grandmother is not returning to Japan.

The Ending Explain what you learned from the situation. Wrap up your story and explain what you have learned. Remember that the purpose of your narrative is to explore a time when you made the right decision for the wrong reason. In conclusion, Kenny explains that great wealth is not limited to money and luxury.

Write

Develop your first draft. Catch your reader's interest, build suspense through actions and details, and reveal the lesson you learned.

Revising ■ Include background information.

In a personal narrative, be sure that your audience has enough background information to understand the significance of your experience. This is sometimes called the *backstory,* events that occurred before the experience begins.

Kenny's first middle paragraph helps the reader appreciate the importance of the experience.

Sample "Backstory"

My father had been born in Japan, and he had many old, old photographs of the palatial estate that had belonged to his family through many generations. He told me stories of gorgeous homes full of lacquered furniture, silk wall panels, and polished cedar platforms. He also described magnificent gardens, full of the sweet scents of exotic flowers and the gentle trickle of graceful fountains.

Tip

You may find that in your own narrative you will need little, if any, background information. It all depends on the nature of your experience.

Revise

Check for background information. As you review your first draft, determine if you have included, or need, background information. Be sure that you present this information in an engaging way.

■ Assess your ending.

The closing paragraph in your narrative should reveal that you have reflected on the experience. Sentences that show reflection begin with "I remembered," "I realized," "I understood," and so on. In the sample narrative, Kenny reflects on his discovery in the closing paragraph.

Sample Reflective Closing

My dreams of a luxurious life had been dashed. At first I was disappointed. Then I remembered that she was staying with us, and my sadness disappeared. I had begun trying to make her love me so that I could join her in Japan. I quickly understood that I didn't need the wealth of Japan. My grandmother had given me great riches right here at home.

Revise

Check your ending. Be sure that you have reflected on your experience in the closing paragraph.

Narrative

Revising ▪ Improve your writing.

Revise

Use a checklist. On your own paper, write the numbers 1 to 12. Put a check next to the number if you can answer "yes" to that question. If not, go back and revise that part of your personal narrative.

Revising Checklist

Ideas

_____ **1.** Do I identify the reason for my actions?

_____ **2.** Do I include essential background information?

_____ **3.** Do I include specific details and dialogue?

Organization

_____ **4.** Do I include an interesting opening that draws in the reader?

_____ **5.** Does the narrative build to a climax?

_____ **6.** Does my ending reflect on the experience?

Voice

_____ **7.** Does my dialogue sound realistic?

_____ **8.** Does my voice reflect my feelings about the event?

Word Choice

_____ **9.** Do I use specific nouns and active verbs?

_____ **10.** Do I use descriptive modifiers?

Sentence Fluency

_____ **11.** Do my sentences read smoothly throughout the narrative?

_____ **12.** Do I use a variety of sentence lengths?

Revise

Make a clean copy. After you've finished your revisions, make a fresh copy of your writing to edit.

Editing ■ Check your writing.

Edit

Use a checklist. On your own paper, write the numbers 1 to 12. For each of the questions below, put a check by the number if you can answer "yes" to that question. If not, go back and edit your narrative for that convention.

Editing Checklist

Conventions

PUNCTUATION

_____ **1.** Do I use punctuation after all my sentences?

_____ **2.** Do I use commas after long introductory word groups?

_____ **3.** Do I use commas correctly in compound and complex sentences?

_____ **4.** Do I punctuate dialogue correctly?

_____ **5.** Do I use apostrophes correctly?

CAPITALIZATION

_____ **6.** Do I begin all my sentences with capital letters?

_____ **7.** Do I capitalize all proper nouns?

SPELLING

_____ **8.** Have I spelled all my words correctly?

_____ **9.** Have I doubled-checked the words my spell-checker may have missed?

GRAMMAR

_____ **10.** Do I use correct forms of verbs?

_____ **11.** Do my pronouns agree with their antecedents?

_____ **12.** Do my verbs agree with their subjects?

Narrative

Publishing ■ Share your writing.

There are several ways to publish your personal narrative.

■ Read your story out loud to the class.

■ Submit the story to your school's creative writing magazine.

■ Send your story to a student-writing magazine. (See page **135**.)

■ For more ideas, look at the Write Source Web site at <*www.thewritesource.com*> and click on the "Publish It!" link.

Rubric for Narrative Writing

Use the following rubric as a guide for assessing your personal narrative. Refer to it whenever you want to improve your writing.

6 Ideas	**5**	**4**
The narrative shares a memorable event. Details bring the essay to life.	The writer shares an interesting experience. Specific details help maintain interest.	The writer tells about an interesting experience. Details should show, not tell.
Organization		
The structure of the narrative makes it enjoyable and easy to read.	The narrative has a clear beginning, middle, and ending. Transitions are helpful.	For the most part, the narrative is organized. Most of the transitions are helpful.
Voice		
The writer's voice captures the experience for the reader.	The writer's voice sounds natural. Dialogue helps hold the reader's interest.	The writer's voice creates interest in the essay, but dialogue should sound more natural.
Word Choice		
The writer's excellent word choice creates a vivid picture of the event.	Specific nouns, verbs, and modifiers create clear images and feelings.	Some stronger nouns, verbs, and/or modifiers would create a clearer picture.
Sentence Fluency		
The sentences are skillfully written to hold the reader's interest.	The sentences show variety and are easy to understand.	The sentences are varied, but some should flow more smoothly.
Conventions		
The narrative has no errors in spelling, grammar, or punctuation.	The narrative has a few minor errors in punctuation, grammar, or spelling.	The narrative has some errors that may distract the reader.

3	**2**	**1**
The writer should focus on one event. Some details do not relate to the essay.	The writer should focus on one experience. More details are needed.	The writer should select an experience and provide details.
The order of events must be corrected. More transitions are needed.	The beginning, middle, and ending all run together. The order is unclear.	The narrative must be better organized.
The writer's voice usually can be heard. More dialogue is needed.	The voice is weak. Dialogue is needed.	The writer sounds uninvolved or disinterested in the essay.
More specific nouns, verbs, and modifiers would paint a clearer picture of the event.	Better words are needed. Many are overused or too general to paint a clear picture.	The writer has not considered word choice or has used words incorrectly.
A better variety of sentences is needed. Sentences do not flow smoothly.	Many incomplete or short sentences make the writing choppy.	Few sentences are written well. Help is needed.
The narrative has several errors.	Numerous errors make the narrative hard to read and confusing.	Help is needed to find errors and make corrections.

Evaluating a Personal Narrative

As you read the narrative below, focus on the strengths and weaknesses in the writing. (**The essay may contain errors.**) Then read the self-assessment on page **153**.

Girls' Night Out

"I'll pick you up at 6:30!" Greg's voice on the phone was excited.

"Great! I can't wait!" I said and hung up.

I lied. It wasn't great. I wanted to go to a new chick flick with the girls, not sit in the bleachers watching bulky guys getting their faces smooshed into a wrestling mat. The things we do for our boyfriends! I sighed and called my friend Carly.

"What do you mean, you can't go?" Carly nearly shrieked, and I held the phone away from my ear. She did tend to be a little hyper sometimes. "What about me and Shandra and Kate? Friday night is always Girls' Night Out!" I explained that I felt I had to support Greg during his tournament.

"Well, I suppose that's noble of you," she admitted. "But really, Jan, you must become your own person."

"I'm sorry. I'll make it next week!" I said.

"Yeah, unless Mr. Wonderful wants to drag you to a fly-fishing festival or something!"

I hung up, mentally kicking myself. It had been a rough week. I had really been looking forward to our weekly evening of girly giggles. Not a gym that reeked of sweat and testosterone.

At the gym, Greg and I parted; he disappeared into the locker room. I picked my way up through the crowded bleachers to get a good spot. I settled onto a hard wooden seat. I was glad I had brought along a novel to read in between matches.

The meet began. I cheered when Greg won his match with a late takedown, even though I winced at the painful-looking contortions he had to go through to do it. The team did pretty well, coming in second, and the coach announced a pizza party at his house. I must have looked pretty unhappy because Greg hugged me.

"You don't have to go, Jan!" he said. "It's just the guys, and I know it won't be much fun for you."

"You mean you'd go without me? Greg, I gave up Girls' Night Out for you!" He seemed genuinely surprised.

"Jan, you didn't have to do that!"

"I wanted to show you how much I support your stuff!" I blinked hard to stop the stinging in my eyes.

"Look, I know that sometimes my 'stuff' is boring for you, and that's okay! We don't have to do everything together. Sometimes you need your friends, just like I need mine."

He was right. We liked each other for who we are. Not who we might try to be. I, in fact, felt even closer to Greg after what he said. I realized that he had a very mature attitude about our relationship, far more mature than my own attitude.

Student Self-Assessment

Narrative Rubric Checklist

Title: Girls' Night Out

Writer: Jan Harrison

__5__ **Ideas**
- Is the narrative about making the right decision for the wrong reason?
- Is background information provided?
- Does the narrative include specific details and dialogue?

__5__ **Organization**
- Does the beginning interest the reader?
- Does the middle include a series of actions that build to the climax?
- Does the ending show what was learned?

__5__ **Voice**
- Does the writing sound natural?
- Does the dialogue sound realistic?

__4__ **Word Choice**
- Does the writing contain vivid verbs and specific nouns?
- Does it contain descriptive modifiers?

__3__ **Sentence Fluency**
- Do the sentences flow smoothly?
- Is the writing free of fragments and rambling sentences?

__6__ **Conventions**
- Does the narrative avoid careless errors?
- Is the dialogue correctly punctuated?

OVERALL COMMENTS:

I like how I started right in the middle of the action. I also think that my dialogue sounds very real.

My closing paragraph could show more thought and reflection.

Some of my sentences sound choppy. I also have to watch for sentence fragments.

Review your narrative.
Rate your narrative and write comments that explain why you gave yourself the scores you did.

Narrative

Reflecting on Your Writing

You've worked hard to write a personal narrative that your classmates will enjoy. Now take some time to think about your writing. Finish each of the sentence starters below on your own paper. Thinking about your writing will help you see how you are growing as a writer.

My Narrative

1. The strongest part of my personal narrative is . . .

2. The part that still needs work is . . .

3. The main thing I learned about writing a personal narrative is . . .

4. In my next personal narrative, I would like to . . .

5. One question I still have about writing personal narratives is . . .

Writing the College Entrance Essay

For some college applications, you will be asked to write a personal essay in response to a given prompt. Your goal in this essay is to address the prompt specifically, while at the same time telling something about yourself—how you think and why you are drawn to the particular school or program.

Before you begin your essay, be sure that you understand what you are being asked to write about and why. Remember that the reader is trying to gain a better understanding of you, the student and the person; so be sure to present your ideas honestly and sincerely.

This chapter includes a sample entrance essay, writing guidelines, and a list of typical writing prompts you might see on applications. Also refer to online sources that provide additional tips for writing entrance essays.

Writing Guidelines

Subject: Application prompt
Form: Personal essay
Purpose: To reveal something about you as a student and as a person
Audience: School admissions officer

"Be honest with yourself and your readers. Don't try to write only what you think readers want to hear."

—Verne Meyer

Sample College Entrance Essay

As part of his college application, David Schaap was asked to write a personal essay in response to this prompt: "In 500 words or less, explain what you want to study at Burnley College and why."

In his response, David uses an anecdote from his own experience to introduce his goals, and then relates those goals to a particular program at the college. Margin notes point out important features in his essay.

Beginning
The writer uses a personal experience to get the reader's attention.

Middle
The writer explains the point of the experience.

Introductory phrases link the paragraphs.

A New World of Cinema

As one of my duties as a student council member, I help new students learn about our school. Earlier this year, I was doing this by introducing Anastasia Korkoff (a foreign-exchange student from Moscow) to other students. As we talked, a picture of a woman taped on the inside of a locker door caught Anastasia's eye. "Rachel McAdams!" she said. "I loved *The Notebook!*"

"You saw that?" I replied. I was shocked. This girl from Russia had seen a movie that was not a blockbuster, liked it, and even knew the name of the actress—not even a major celebrity. That conversation stuck in my mind for days.

From events like this, I came to realize that film is a major source of shared experience—not just with my friends or with others in this country, but also with people throughout the world. While I had always enjoyed movies as a form of entertainment, I had never realized before how broadly they shape culture—from Miami to Moscow.

A few weeks later, I explained these ideas to Ms. Crane, my English teacher. She listened, smiled, and suggested that I read the essay "Cinema Is the New Cathedral." As I read the piece, suddenly everything clicked. The writer argued that movies have replaced many other forms of communal experience, and even serve a religious-like function. At that point, I knew that understanding film was critical to understanding culture— both culture in this country and in others.

Ever since then, understanding film and filmmaking has been my goal. Entering the film program at Burnley

The writer offers details that explain his educational goal.

Ending
In closing, the writer links the college with the career path he has chosen.

College will help me achieve that goal. I particularly want to study international film and the relationship between a film and its national culture. Also, because films have such a broad international audience, I want to study how Hollywood movies affect cultures outside the United States.

While I'm not sure yet where my film study might lead, I am sure that the trip will be interesting and worth the effort. For example, my mom suggests that I combine film study with communication and think about a career in journalism. My counselor says that the film-study program could be a springboard into the filmmaking industry. But Ms. Crane suggests that I study film and culture—and then teach the subject either in high school or in college. Wherever the film-study path leads, I'd like to start the journey at Burnley College.

Narrative

 Respond to the reading. Answer the following questions about the sample college entrance essay.

Ideas (1) What field of study does the writer want to pursue? (2) Why does he find this field of study appealing?

Organization (3) In which paragraph does the author explain his goal? (4) What purpose is served by the paragraphs before that?

Voice & Word Choice (5) How would you describe the author's voice in this essay—enthusiastic, sincere, negative, confident? Explain. (6) What words or phrases stand out in the essay? Name two or three.

Prewriting ■ Focus your efforts.

The first step in writing your college application essay is to establish a clear focus for your work. To begin, consider the following questions:

- **What does the prompt ask for?** Try restating the prompt in your own words.
- **How does the topic relate to your own experience and goals?** The main purpose of a college application essay is to help the admissions official get to know you.
- **How does the prompt relate to the college or program?** Admission decisions are partly based upon how well an applicant's abilities and goals match those of the institution.
- **What specific instructions are given in the prompt?** Note specifically what the prompt asks you to do (*analyze, explain, describe, evaluate*, and so on.) and how long your response should be.

Once you can answer these questions, draft a **focus statement** to guide your writing. A strong focus statement should clearly state the main point of your response.

Sample Focus Statements

- After studying computer graphics at Norrid College (the program), I hope to expand what can be achieved in Internet films (personal goal).

- I believe that Waterworth University (the college) can help me to become the sort of leader who inspires others to greatness (personal goal).

- I want to learn as much as I can about creative nonfiction writing (personal goal), and Northern University (the college) will certainly help me meet this goal.

■ Gather details.

Experts agree that these strategies will help you prepare a strong essay.

1. **List your strengths and weaknesses with the prompt clearly in mind.** Be honest with yourself in this evaluation.
2. **Select a positive quality related to your goal.** An upbeat essay that focuses on positive, hopeful results has the best chance of catching the attention of admissions officers.
3. **Choose a story that illustrates that quality and goal.** Think of personal experiences that say something about you as a person and a student. Then choose one (or more) experiences to work with.

Writing ▪ Create your first draft.

Admissions personnel face a staggering number of application essays each year. For yours to get the attention it deserves, it must be compelling, honest, and personal. As you write your first draft, be sure each section does its job well.

Write your beginning part.

The beginning part should catch the reader's interest and smoothly lead up to your focus. Here are different ways to begin your essay.

- **Open with a personal anecdote.** This is the approach that we recommend. Be sure that the anecdote reveals something positive about you and relates to the prompt. (Use dialogue to bring the anecdote to life.)
- **Start with a revealing quotation.** Select a quotation that truly reflects your thoughts and feelings about your goal and the school in question.
- **Begin with an eye-catching fact or statistic.** Of course, this statement should effectively introduce the rest of your essay.

Develop the middle part.

As you develop the main part of your essay, use an honest, sincere voice. Also keep these tips in mind.

- **Develop your focus.** Each paragraph in your essay should advance or develop the main point of your response.
- **Include specific details.** Instead of stating *I grew up in the country near a medium-sized city,* write *I grew up on a huge dairy farm near Muncie, Indiana, a medium-sized city northeast of Indianapolis.*
- **Use transitional words and phrases.** To ensure that your essay flows smoothly, link paragraphs with connecting words or phrases such as "From events like this" and "A few weeks later."

Conclude your essay.

The ending part should bring the reader to a satisfying sense of closure and leave him or her with a favorable impression of you. Here are two ways to conclude your essay.

- **Revisit your focus.** Bring your reader back to the main point of your essay.
- **End positively.** State politely but confidently that you look forward to attending the college in question.

Narrative

Revising ■ Improve your first draft.

Once the first draft of your application essay is complete, review and revise it using the following questions as a guide:

- **Ideas** Is your main idea clear, fully developed, and well supported? Is the connection clear between your goal and the school or program?

- **Organization** Does your essay grab the reader's attention right from the beginning? Does the middle of your essay develop your focus? Does the ending revisit the focus statement and end on a positive note? Do you use transitions to lead the reader from idea to idea and from paragraph to paragraph?

- **Voice** Does your essay sound personal, sincere, and positive? Does it help the reader gain a sense of your personality? Does the dialogue, if you've used it, sound realistic?

- **Word Choice** Have you avoided cliches in your writing? Do you use specific nouns and verbs?

- **Sentence Fluency** Do your sentences flow smoothly?

Editing ■ Check for conventions.

With an application essay, first impressions are critical. As a result, careful attention to punctuation, capitalization, spelling, and grammar is also critical. Take time to check your essay for errors, and ask a trusted friend, teacher, or parent to check it as well. Then prepare a clean final copy to submit with your application.

FYI

The Most Important Rule

The most important rule for a college application essay is this: **Be yourself.** Admissions readers must judge whether your goals, experiences, and abilities match well with their school. Your best chance of success overall is in letting them see who you really are. So don't try to impress them with words borrowed from a thesaurus or with grandiose statements. Instead, **focus on yourself and your goals.**

Example Prompts

The following types of writing prompts are typically found on college applications. Most college application prompts also include the words "in one page or less" or a similar instruction about the length of your response.

Open-Ended Prompts

Prompts such as these leave a lot of leeway for possible answers. This means you will have to work extra hard to shape a focused response.

- Please include a personal statement with your application.
- Why is our college a good choice for you?
- Tell us your goals after college. How might our program contribute to those goals?

Influences in Your Life

Prompts like these ask you to write about people, places, and things that are important to you. Remember to relate their influence to your goals and to how the school can help you meet those goals.

- Describe a creative work in literature, art, music, or science that has had an effect on you, and explain that effect.
- Identify a person who has had a significant influence on your life, and describe that influence.

General Subject Prompts

These types of general subject prompts ask you to reflect on your thoughts, feelings, and beliefs.

- What is the value of community service in our society? Tell us how it relates to your life and plans.
- Do you believe there is a "generation gap"? Describe the differences between your generation and others.
- Think of a time when you have taken a risk: What was the effect (whether positive or negative) on your life?

Try It!

Choose one of the prompts above and write a one-page application essay in response. Carefully follow the steps outlined in this chapter. When you are finished, ask a friend, teacher, or parent for feedback. Then try again, using a prompt from a different category.

Narrative

Expository Writing

Expository Writing

Writing an Essay of Opposing Ideas

The world of politics is filled with strong opinions and vigorous debates. Much writing about politics presents ideas persuasively: The writer chooses one side of a political argument and uses facts and ideas to defend it. But in a world full of strong opinions and opposing ideas, it's often helpful to know both sides of an argument.

An essay of opposing ideas thoroughly examines a controversial situation by presenting both sides of an argument without favoring either. In order to present both sides fairly, you'll need to research each position and represent its strengths and weaknesses.

In this chapter, you'll learn the steps necessary to write a thoroughly researched, well-organized, and fairly presented essay of opposing ideas. Your explanation of a controversy should be suitable for publication in a local or school newspaper.

Writing Guidelines

Subject: A controversy with two sides
Form: Essay of opposing ideas
Purpose: To examine both positions fairly
Audience: Local or school newspapers

"A lot of good arguments are spoiled by some fool who knows what he is talking about."

—Miguel de Unamuno

Expository Writing Warm-Up ■ Map a controversy.

Controversies take place around you every day—in classroom debates, lunchroom conversations, or hallway arguments. To understand a controversy, you must understand both sides. A controversy map can help you. Kyreesha created the following map to understand a book-banning controversy at her high school.

Controversy Map

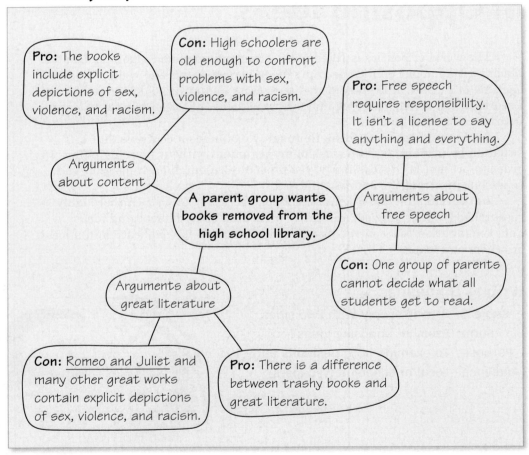

Pro: The books include explicit depictions of sex, violence, and racism.

Con: High schoolers are old enough to confront problems with sex, violence, and racism.

Pro: Free speech requires responsibility. It isn't a license to say anything and everything.

Arguments about content

A parent group wants books removed from the high school library.

Arguments about free speech

Con: One group of parents cannot decide what all students get to read.

Arguments about great literature

Con: Romeo and Juliet and many other great works contain explicit depictions of sex, violence, and racism.

Pro: There is a difference between trashy books and great literature.

Try It!

Think of a controversy that you can be objective about. Create a map or cluster, writing the controversy in the center and creating branches for different arguments. Write down both sides of the argument and try to be fair to each position.

Writing an Expository Paragraph

An expository paragraph explains a controversy in an objective way. Kyreesha used her controversy map (page **164**) to write the following expository paragraph. Her paragraph has three parts.

- The **topic sentence** introduces the main point of the paragraph.
- The **body sentences** use a variety of details to support the main point.
- The **closing sentence** restates the main point in an interesting way.

A Battle over Books

Topic Sentence

Wilson High faces a battle over seven books that some parents feel are offensive—and that others feel are essential. The list of books includes Kurt Vonnegut's *Slaughterhouse Five* and Toni Morrison's *Beloved,* deemed to have explicit depictions of sex, violence, and racism. Other parents disagree, citing explicit material in more than 100 classics including *Romeo and Juliet* and *The Scarlet Letter.* This group argues that high schoolers are old enough to wrestle with such issues, and that their rights to free speech cannot be denied by one group of parents. The parents who are calling for the ban draw a distinction, however, between great literature and books they consider "trash." They also indicate that free speech requires responsibility.

Body Sentences

Closing Sentence

Both groups of parents plan to make their positions clear at the next meeting of the Wilson High School Board.

Expository

Write

Write your own expository paragraph. Write about the controversy you chose on page **164**. Create a topic sentence that focuses on the issue, include body sentences that fairly represent both sides, and write a closing sentence that completes the paragraph.

"You don't notice the referee during the game unless he makes a bad call."
—Drew Curtis

Understanding Your Goal

Your goal in this chapter is to write a well-organized essay of opposing ideas that fairly examines both sides of an argument. The traits listed in the chart below will help you plan and write your essay of opposing ideas.

Traits of an Essay of Opposing Ideas

- ### Ideas
  Choose a topic that will interest the reader, write a clear thesis statement, and include a variety of details that support your topic sentences.

- ### Organization
  Start with a hook that captures your reader's attention. Use middle paragraphs to fairly present both sides of the argument. End with a paragraph that puts the debate in perspective.

- ### Voice
  Use an informative voice that shows respect for both sides of the argument.

- ### Word Choice
  Choose words that explain your topic clearly, that have the right denotation (meaning), and that have an appropriate connotation (feeling).

- ### Sentence Fluency
  Write clear, complete sentences with varied beginnings and lengths.

- ### Conventions
  Eliminate errors in punctuation, capitalization, spelling, and grammar.

Get the big picture. Look at the rubric on pages 198–199. You can use this rubric to assess your progress as you write. Your goal is to write an essay of opposing ideas that fairly explains both sides of a controversy.

Essay of Opposing Ideas

An essay of opposing ideas fairly presents both sides of an argument. It uses facts, statistics, examples, and quotations to support each side. In this article, a student writer presents both sides of the argument about "third parties."

Beginning
The beginning introduces the topic and presents the thesis statement (underlined).

Middle
The first middle paragraphs present one side of the argument.

Expository

Are Third Parties Viable in U.S. Politics?

Since the Republican Party gained major party status in the 1850s, candidates from the Democratic or Republican parties have won the vast majority of United States elections ("Political"). Yet candidates from much smaller "third parties" have participated in many elections, and have even won local and state contests. Often, third-party platforms differ widely from the platforms of the two major parties. Perhaps for this reason, third parties have played a controversial role in U.S. politics. While proponents of third parties laud them for the new ideas they bring to the political arena, critics consider third parties an insignificant or damaging influence on U.S. politics.

Those who support third parties insist that the two-party system is one of the main reasons that new ideas are never tried. In an effort to win a majority vote, proponents say, the Democratic and Republican parties have often adopted watered-down platforms that will attract the necessary number of voters but won't solve society's problems. As long as Democrats and Republicans enjoy an unshakable hold on power, this situation is likely to continue. Third parties such as the Green Party, however, have offered bold solutions to society's problems, and their participation in the electoral system is invaluable ("Fresh Look").

Proponents also argue that the two major parties have created a system of money politics in which politicians are beholden to corporations and other wealthy donors instead of to the average citizen. Since third parties are generally more dependent on grassroots support, they are more likely to be responsive to the concerns of the voters. Third-party supporters also cite the success of third-party candidates in state, local, and even national elections as evidence that a significant number of U.S. voters want fresh ideas and grassroots activism.

Those who oppose third parties insist that the participation of such parties more often results in skewed election results than in any kind of meaningful reform. Often, they cite the "spoiler" role of third-party candidates. In the 2000 presidential election, for example, Green Party candidate Ralph Nader received only 2.74% of the vote ("Election"). Yet many analysts believe that Nader's participation drew enough votes from Democrat Al Gore to deliver a victory to Republican George W. Bush.

In addition to the "spoiler" argument, those who oppose third-party candidacies insist that when people abandon major parties for third parties, they only reinforce the major parties' fear of new ideas. Without new ideas, these partisans argue, the major parties will remain stagnant, and the problem of an unresponsive, money-driven political system will remain.

Although both sides disagree on the effectiveness of third parties, they tend to agree that the U.S. political system needs an influx of new ideas. Chronic problems such as the health-care crisis, the national debt, poverty, and homelessness have resisted solution, despite a range of attempts by the major parties. People on both sides of the third-party debate hope that new ideas capable of solving these problems will be brought to the forefront of our political process.

As major-party politics and pressing social problems remain a focus in U.S. politics, it's likely that third parties will also remain a part of the political system. But whether they will be able to effect meaningful change remains to be seen. Much of their effectiveness—or lack of effectiveness—results from the ability of those on either side of the debate to convince voters to either support or abandon third parties.

Respond to the reading. Answer the following questions.

Ideas (1) What are the two positions about third parties? (2) What are the points of agreement between the two sides?

Organization (3) How do the middle paragraphs work to fairly present both sides of the argument?

Voice & Word Choice (4) How does the writer help the reader understand the terms "third party" and "spoiler"?

Prewriting

In the prewriting stage, you'll identify a controversial issue, explore both sides of the argument, and create an organizational structure for your essay.

Keys to Effective Prewriting

1. Choose a political controversy in which two major positions are in opposition.

2. Gather details that clearly present and support both sides of the argument.

3. Identify areas of agreement between the two positions.

4. Write a thesis statement that summarizes the controversy.

5. Plan your essay using a sentence outline, a topic outline, or an organized list.

Expository

Prewriting ■ Select a controversy.

To create an effective essay of opposing ideas, you need to find a current controversial issue that will interest you and your classmates. Think of controversies at your school, in your community, in the nation, and in the world.

A student named Lin gathered topics by reading local and national newspapers and watching news shows. He made a controversies chart and put an asterisk next to the topic he wanted to write about.

Controversies Chart

School	Community	Nation	World
– funding for new gymnasium	– city council resignations	– congressional redistricting	– how to stop genocides in Africa
– MySpace.com limits	– community service requirement	– electronic voting *	– globalization and free trade
– special education overhaul	– subsidy for Klement Manufacturing	– Congressional ethics reform	– third-world debt relief
			– global warming

Prewrite

Create a controversies chart. Write "School," "Community," "Nation," and "World" at the top of a piece of paper. Then read local and national newspapers, looking for current controversies that interest you. Place an asterisk (*) next to the controversy you choose to write about.

VOTING PRECINCT 75

■ Focus on the traits.

Ideas Select a controversy (1) that has strong support from both sides and (2) you can be objective about. Keep an open mind as you research, doing your best to understand each side of the argument. Think of yourself as a referee, watching closely, noting the strengths and weaknesses of both sides, but not favoring either one.

■ Research the controversy.

Once you have selected a controversy to write about, you need to conduct research to make sure you fully understand the issue. Solid research includes a variety of sources:

- **Print media** such as newspapers and newsmagazines provide in-depth articles on current crises and controversies. Current books can provide even more information. These resources tend to be well edited and reliable, though some publications have a bias.
- **Online media** can provide either authoritative and current information (government or university Web sites) or biased and outdated information (blogs and message threads). All online sources should be carefully double-checked to be sure the information is accurate, up-to-date, and nonbiased.
- **Primary sources** such as surveys and interviews allow you to ask questions and gather opinions from the "person in the street." Of course, the information you receive depends on your interviewing and surveying skills as well as the knowledge of the people you approach.

Lin created the following list to be sure that he could research a variety of sources on his topic: electronic voting.

Sources List

Print Media:
    "36 Days: The Complete Chronicle
      of the 2000 Election Crisis,"
    The New York Times.
    "Is E-Voting Safe?" PC World
    Overtime! The Election 2000 Thriller,
      Larry J. Sabato

Online Media:
    Electronic Frontier Foundation Web site
    "Electronic Voting Raises New Issues," washingtonpost.com

Primary Sources:
    Betty Parks, District 7 voting coordinator

Expository

Prewrite

Create a sources list. Look for a variety of sources—print media, online media, and primary sources.

Prewriting ■ Gather details.

As you conduct research, you need to keep track of many different facts, statistics, examples, and quotations. Note cards are a convenient way to record details and their source. Here are sample note cards that Lin prepared during his research.

Note Cards

Why are people thinking about electronic voting?
In 2000, problems with the Florida elections held up the decision for 36 days.

"36 Days," The New York Times

What problems happened in Florida?
"Butterfly" ballots were confusing and some were miscounted or not counted because of "hanging chads."

Overtime! The Election 2000 Thriller

What are the benefits of electronic voting?
• Quicker and easier
• Can check results before submitting
• Totaled faster
• Counted more accurately
"Electronic Voting Raises New Issues" washingtonpost.com

What are the problems with electronic voting?
• Errors occur
• A power loss means data loss
• No paper trail
• Hacking

"Is E-Voting Safe?" PC World

Prewrite

Research your controversy. Take notes on cards or in a notebook. Write questions you have, answers you find, and the sources that provide the answers.

▪ Organize your essay.

Once you have completed your research, it is time to write a thesis statement.

controversy	+	**pro and con**	=	**a strong thesis statement**
electronic voting machines		some say they are more reliable and efficient, others say that they are less so		Some people say electronic voting machines are more reliable and efficient than paper ballots, and others say they are less so.

Prewrite

Write your thesis statement. Use the model above to create a thesis statement for your essay. Try different versions until you are satisfied.

▪ Write topic sentences.

Write topic sentences first for the "pro" side, then for the "con" side, and last for common ground. Here are Lin's topic sentences.

Topic Sentences

Pro (convenience): Proponents of electronic voting systems say they allow people to vote quickly and easily.

Pro (accuracy): Proponents also point out that electronic voting makes vote counting faster and easier.

Con (unreliability): Opponents of electronic voting insist that such systems are unreliable.

Con (tampering): Opponents of electronic voting also fear that computer hackers could tamper with election results.

Common ground: While people disagree about the effectiveness of electronic voting, they agree that the fiasco of 2000 should not be repeated.

Prewrite

Write topic sentences. Focus first on the "pro" argument, then on the "con" argument, and finally on the common ground.

Expository

Prewriting ▪ Outline your essay.

Before writing your essay of opposing ideas, organize your ideas and details. Lin created a sentence outline, but your instructor may prefer a topic outline (using phrases) or an organized list.

Sentence Outline

THESIS STATEMENT: Some people say electronic voting machines are more reliable and efficient than paper ballots, and others say they are less so.

  I. Proponents of electronic voting systems say they allow people to vote quickly and easily.
    A. Voters simply touch a certain candidate's name.
    B. Voters can review choices before submitting the ballot.

  II. Proponents also point out that electronic voting makes vote counting faster and easier.
    A. The computer keeps a running tally.
    B. Election results are available sooner.

  III. Opponents of electronic voting insist that such systems are unreliable.
    A. In 2004, electronic machines caused many errors.
    B. Some machines failed completely, losing votes forever.

  IV. Opponents of electronic voting also fear that computer hackers could tamper with election results.
    A. Users can fool the machines to allow multiple votes.
    B. Hackers could cause skewed results.

  V. While people disagree about the effectiveness of electronic voting, they agree that the fiasco of 2000 should not be repeated.
    A. The country endured 36 days of "hanging chads."
    B. Castro offered to send "election monitors" to sort out the chaos.

Prewrite

Organize your ideas. Create a sentence outline (as above), a topic outline (using phrases), or an organized list, whichever your instructor prefers.

Writing

Now that you have gathered and organized your ideas and details, you can begin writing the first draft of your essay.

Keys to Effective Writing

1. Use your outline or list as a writing guide.

2. Write on every other line or double-space if you are using a computer. This will allow room for changes.

3. Introduce the topic and state your thesis in the first paragraph.

4. Include your topic sentences in the middle paragraphs.

5. Use a variety of details to support each main idea (topic sentence).

6. End by putting the two opposing arguments in perspective.

Writing ■ See how the parts fit together.

The graphic below shows how the elements of an essay of opposing ideas work together to present a clear picture of a controversy. Use this graphic as a guide when preparing to write your first draft. (The examples are from the student essay on pages 177–180.)

BEGINNING

The **beginning** introduces the controversy and states the writer's thesis.

Thesis Statement
Some people say electronic voting machines are more reliable and efficient than paper ballots, and others say they are less so.

MIDDLE

The **middle** paragraphs clearly explain both sides of the controversy.

Topic Sentences
Proponents of electronic voting systems say they allow people to vote quickly and easily.

Proponents also point out that electronic voting makes vote counting faster and easier.

Opponents of electronic voting insist that such systems are unreliable.

Opponents of electronic voting also fear that computer hackers could tamper with election results.

While people disagree about the effectiveness of electronic voting, they agree that the fiasco of 2000 should not be repeated.

ENDING

The **ending** puts the controversy in perspective.

Closing Sentences
As the population of the United States and its dependence on technology grow, the debate over electronic voting will continue. But many observers envision an eventual compromise between the parties on either side of the electronic voting debate.

■ Start your essay.

The beginning paragraph of your essay of opposing ideas should engage your reader, introduce your topic, and provide your thesis statement.

- **Engage your reader.** Open by capturing your reader's attention and introducing the controversy.

  In the 2000 presidential election, difficulties with counting votes in the state of Florida caused a bruising legal battle between the Democratic and Republican parties.

- **Introduce your topic.** Be sure to include details that expand on your opening sentence and provide necessary background information.

  A major cause of the controversy was unclear markings on traditional paper voting ballots, which muddled election results. . . . Another political battle has ensued.

- **End with a thesis statement.** Summarize the controversy in a sentence that broadly states both sides of the argument.

  Some people say electronic voting machines are more reliable and efficient than paper ballots, and others say they are less so.

Beginning Paragraph

Lin starts his essay by focusing on the fiasco of the 2000 elections. Then he provides background information that leads to his thesis statement.

Expository

> The writer engages the reader, introduces the topic, and states his thesis (underlined).

> In the 2000 presidential election, difficulties with counting votes in the state of Florida caused a bruising legal battle between the Democratic and Republican parties. A major cause of the controversy was unclear markings on traditional paper voting ballots, which muddled election results ("36 Days"). In response to the problem, technology companies and government agencies proposed a radical solution—the use of direct recording electronic (DRE) voting machines. Another political battle has ensued. Some people say electronic voting machines are more reliable and efficient than paper ballots, and others say they are less so.

Write

Write a beginning paragraph. Use the guidelines above as you begin your essay of opposing ideas. (Also refer to the beginning of the essay on page 167.)

Writing ■ Develop the middle.

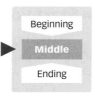

The middle part of your essay of opposing ideas should present each side of the argument fairly. The first middle paragraphs deal with the "pro" position, the next deal with the "con" position, and the last with common ground.

As you write your middle paragraphs, use transitions to connect your ideas. Lin used a variety of transitions to show different relationships between ideas.

Time	Extra Information	Compare/Contrast	Cause and Effect
after	in fact	both	thus
sometimes	also	even	as a result
during	in addition	while	consequently

Middle Paragraphs

Notice how Lin uses topic sentences, facts, statistics, examples, and quotations to build his middle paragraphs.

> The first middle paragraphs present the "pro" side of the argument.

Proponents of electronic voting systems say they allow people to vote quickly and easily. Most DRE systems use touch-screen computer monitors, which are now common across the United States. After choosing a slate of candidates, the user of a DRE machine can review and even change choices before submitting a final ballot—something that is possible but sometimes difficult with paper ballots.

> Each paragraph begins with a topic sentence.

Proponents also point out that electronic voting makes vote counting faster and easier. Most DRE machines are capable of compiling both ongoing and final vote counts immediately, thus eliminating human error from the vote count and allowing faster reporting of election results ("Electronic"). In the 2000 elections, many news anchors "called" state results when only a small percentage of the votes were tabulated—and reported inaccurate information. As a result, voters went to bed one night thinking that a specific candidate had won but woke up the next morning to discover something else—no one had won. Electronic voting machines would eliminate these errors.

Next, the writer explains the "con" side of the argument.

Opponents of electronic voting insist that such systems are unreliable. Studies have shown that in a number of elections, DRE machines produced errors in vote counts ("Accessibility"). In the presidential election of 2004, DRE machines in Ohio gave George W. Bush nearly 4,000 extra votes. In North Carolina, some machines failed totally: One county lost 4,500 votes ("Computer"). In addition, detractors point to another major factor in muddled elections—human error. Many of the same Floridians who found the paper "butterfly" ballot confusing would be even less comfortable poking a screen to indicate their choice. Consequently, voters would make errors in their selections, though this time there would be no paper trail for a recount.

Opponents of electronic voting also fear that computer hackers could tamper with election results. A skilled computer programmer could rewrite the code that controls electronic voting machines to skew the results toward a particular candidate. Since DRE machines do not offer a paper record of a voter's choices, there is no way to prove the validity of vote counts ("Is E-Voting Safe?").

The last middle paragraph covers the common ground between the two positions.

While people disagree about the effectiveness of electronic voting, they agree that the fiasco of 2000 should not be repeated. For 36 days, the outcome of the election was disputed, and the nation received an education in "butterfly ballots" and "hanging chads." In a particularly low point for democracy, Fidel Castro offered to send "election monitors" to Florida to help with the recount ("Stolen Elections"). No one, except perhaps Mr. Castro, would like a repeat of the 2000 debacle, and both sides recognize the problems with the butterfly and punch-card systems. They simply disagree about what should take their place.

Expository

Write

Write your middle paragraphs. Create middle paragraphs that fairly present both sides of the controversy and explain the common ground. Use facts, statistics, examples, and quotations to support your main points.

Writing ■ End your essay.

Beginning

Middle

Ending

You have presented both sides of the political controversy, as well as outlined points on which both sides agree. Now that you have explained the controversy in detail, you are ready to write your ending paragraph. Follow these guidelines:

- Put the controversy in perspective.
- Summarize the current situation.
- Include an insight that makes the reader think.

Ending Paragraph

In his final paragraph, Lin connects the ideas in his essay with current developments and predictions about the future of the controversy.

> The writer creates a thoughtful ending for his essay.

As the population of the United States and its dependence on technology grows, the debate over electronic voting will continue. However, many observers envision an eventual compromise between the parties on either side of the electronic voting debate. Such a compromise would allow electronic voting systems to be employed, but would produce paper "receipts" showing a voter's choices. This innovation would satisfy both parties by enabling rapid, accurate vote counts and ensuring accountability of results. Until then, though, a candidate's best defense against voting irregularities is to win not by a few percentage points, but by a landslide.

Write

Write your ending paragraph. Put the controversy in perspective, summarize current ideas about the controversy, and leave your reader with something to think about.

Write

Prepare a complete first draft. Double-space if you use a computer, or write on every other line if you write by hand. This makes the draft easier to review and gives you room to make revisions.

Revising

Thorough revision helps ensure that the controversy you chose has been clearly explained. When you revise, you check your logic, rearrange parts of your writing, and create a more engaging, informative voice. You also check your word choice and improve sentence structure and variety.

Keys to Effective Revising

1. Read your essay aloud to yourself or to a friend.

2. Be sure you have thoroughly analyzed the controversy.

3. Check your topic sentences and details to confirm that you have followed your outline.

4. Locate and eliminate any errors in logic.

5. Check your draft for strong word choice and variety in sentence length and structure.

6. To mark revisions on your draft copy, use the editing and proofreading marks found on the inside back cover of this book.

Expository

Revising ▪ for Ideas

| **6** My essay brims with fascinating details that engage the reader. | **5** I have effectively used a variety of details to support my main points. | **4** I have used a variety of details, but some details do not support my main points. |

When you revise for *ideas,* you make sure you have used details effectively. The rubric strip above will help you revise.

▪ Have I used different types of details effectively?

You have used different types of details effectively if you have used each for a specific purpose:

- ▪ **Facts** are details that can be proven. Use facts to clearly explain your topic and create a knowledgeable voice.
- ▪ **Statistics** are facts that include a numerical amount. Use statistics to make your information precise.
- ▪ **Examples** are specific events or situations that illustrate a general idea. Use examples to make your writing concrete.
- ▪ **Quotations** are the exact words of a speaker. Use quotations to share an expert's knowledge.

Exercise

Find different types of details in this paragraph and tell what effect each type has.

> For more than a decade, Congress has debated the issue of funding for the Corporation for Public Broadcasting (CPB). In 2006, a House budgetary subcommittee recommended 25-percent cuts to the 400-million-dollar budget of the CPB. Proponents of the cuts argue that the money would be better spent elsewhere, that the Public Broadcasting System has a liberal agenda, and that it is time for the stations to respond to market pressures. Opponents perceive a different agenda: Representative David Obey of Wisconsin said, "Americans overwhelmingly see public broadcasting as an unbiased information source. . . . [Conservatives] are trying to put their ideological stamp on public broadcasting." The next few years will determine whether viewer-supported television and radio are "voter supported" as well.

Revise

Check your details. Read your essay to review how you have used facts, statistics, examples, and quotations. Use each type of detail effectively.

3 I need to use a better variety of details and make sure they support my main points.

2 I need a variety of details and should remove many unneeded details.

1 I need help understanding how to effectively use details to support my main points.

■ Do my details support my main points?

Your details support your main points if you can answer "yes" to the following question about each one: *Does this detail pertain to the topic sentence?*

Exercise

Read the following paragraph and check each detail by answering the question *Does this detail pertain to the topic sentence?* Indicate which details are not needed.

> **The debate over federal funding of the CPB dates back more than 10 years. In 1994, Speaker of the House Newt Gingrich announced a plan to "zero out" funding for the CPB. Gingrich was born in 1943 in Harrisburg, Pennsylvania. Citing conservative grievances with the Corporation for Public Broadcasting and the National Endowment for the Arts and Humanities, Newt Gingrich said, "I personally would privatize them all." He felt conservatives should not have to pay tax money to support "liberal institutions" ("Gingrich"). Gingrich left office in 1998. His budget cuts were unsuccessful, but now, cuts are once again being considered.**

Revise

Check your support. Be sure each detail pertains to the topic sentence of the paragraph in which it appears. If a detail does not, consider cutting it.

Ideas
Statistics make information more precise.

In the presidential election of 2004, DRE machines in Ohio *gave George W. Bush nearly 4,000 extra votes.* ~~made mistakes.~~ In North Carolina, some machines failed ^ *One county lost 4,500 votes* ("Computer"). totally. In addition, detractors point to another major

factor in muddled elections—human error. Many of the

same Floridians who found the paper "butterfly" ballot . . .

Revising ■ for Organization

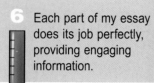
6 Each part of my essay does its job perfectly, providing engaging information.

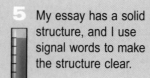
5 My essay has a solid structure, and I use signal words to make the structure clear.

4 My essay has a solid structure, although I could use more signal words to make the structure clear.

When you revise for *organization,* you check the overall structure of your essay to be sure that you have effectively arranged and connected your ideas. The rubric strip above can guide you.

■ How can I check the overall structure of my essay?

You can check the overall structure of your essay by using the essay structure checklist below.

Essay Structure Checklist

BEGINNING PARAGRAPH

_____ **1.** Does my first sentence capture the reader's interest?

_____ **2.** Do I provide background information that leads to my thesis statement?

MIDDLE PARAGRAPHS

_____ **3.** Do my first middle paragraphs explain the "pro" position?

_____ **4.** Do my next middle paragraphs explain the "con" position?

_____ **5.** Does my last middle paragraph address the common ground?

_____ **6.** Does each middle paragraph include a topic sentence?

_____ **7.** Does each paragraph include details that support the topic sentence?

ENDING PARAGRAPH

_____ **8.** Does my ending sum up my analysis?

_____ **9.** Do I leave the reader with a final thought?

Revise

Check your overall structure. Write numbers 1 to 9 on a piece of paper. Then ask yourself the questions above. If you can answer "yes" to a question, check off the number. If not, revise until you can answer the question with a "yes."

My essay's structure is uncertain, and I should use signal words to connect the parts.

 My essay has no clear structure and needs signal words.

 I need to learn basic essay structure and how to use signal words.

■ How can signal words make my structure clear?

Signal words make your structure clear by reminding the reader where he or she is in your argument. Here are some sample signal words:

Proponents say . . .   **Many people argue . . .**   **Those who favor . . .**

Opponents contend . . .   **Both sides agree . . .**   **Those who oppose . . .**

Exercise

Read the following thesis statement and main points for an essay of opposing ideas. Add signal words to make the structure of the essay clear.

Thesis Statement: The proposal to drill for oil in the Arctic National Wildlife Refuge has inspired heated debate on Capitol Hill.

1. Drilling for oil would help alleviate U.S. dependence on foreign oil.
2. Drilling would create new jobs in Alaska and new revenue for the country.
3. The Arctic National Wildlife Refuge is meant for wildlife, not big oil companies.
4. The United States should search for alternative energies to decrease its oil dependence.
5. The question is, "What is right for Alaska and for the nation?"

Revise

Check your topic sentences. Use signal words to help the reader know where she or he is in your argument.

Expository

Organization
Signal words help the reader keep track of the argument.

       Proponents of   *say they*

      ∧Electronic voting systems∧allow people to vote quickly

and easily. Most DRE systems use touch-screen computer

monitors, which are now common across the United States. . . .

Revising ■ for Voice

6 My voice sounds professional and polished from start to finish.

5 I use active voice in most sentences and remain in third-person point of view.

4 I use active voice in most sentences but sometimes shift out of third-person point of view.

When you revise for *voice,* you make sure that most of your sentences are active and that you maintain the third-person point of view. The rubric strip will guide your revision.

■ How can I make a passive sentence active?

You can make a passive sentence active by rewriting it so that the subject of the sentence is doing the action of the verb. Active sentences are clearer, shorter, and more energetic than passive sentences. (See **722.2.**)

Passive Voice
All public schools have been affected by No Child Left Behind.
(The subject, *schools,* is not doing the action.)

Active Voice
No Child Left Behind has affected all public schools.
(The subject, *No Child Left Behind,* is doing the action.)

Exercise

Rewrite the passive sentences below to make them active.

1. The system for federal funding of schools was reformed by the No Child Left Behind law.
2. Schools are required by the law to meet certain standards and show improvement.
3. The legislation has been praised by conservatives.
4. The law has been criticized by liberals.
5. Since its creation, public education has been reformed almost continuously by the government.
6. The public school system was created by the government to educate students and prepare them to be citizens.

Revise

Check for active voice. Read your essay and watch for sentences in which the subject does not do the action of the verb. Rewrite these passive sentences to make them active.

Some of my sentences should be made active, and I need to be consistent in person.

 Many passive sentences and shifts in person make my essay difficult to read.

 I need help understanding active voice and third-person point of view.

■ How can I maintain the third-person point of view?

You can maintain the third-person point of view by using third-person pronouns and avoiding first- and second-person pronouns. (See **708.2**.)

Use: he, she, it, him, her, his, hers, its, they, them, their, theirs
Avoid: I, me, my, we, us, our, ours, you, your, yours

Exercise

Rewrite the following paragraph so that it maintains the third-person point of view.

> Students may feel that you take enough tests already, but the creators of No Child Left Behind legislation disagree. The law mandates tests that demonstrate basic proficiency and yearly advancement. These tests decide not only whether we move up to the next grade but also whether our school gets the federal funding it needs to keep going. You need to do your best on these tests because they will determine the quality of your school in the future.

Revise

Check for third-person point of view. Read your essay and make sure you avoid using first- or second-person pronouns. If you find shifts in person, rewrite the material to remain consistently in third-person point of view.

Expository *(side tab)*

Voice
Changes correct point of view to third person.

As a result, ~~you~~ [voters] went to bed one night~~, and you thought~~ [thinking] that a specific candidate had won but ~~you~~ [they] woke up the next morning to discover something else—no one had won. Electronic voting machines would eliminate these errors. . . .

Revising ■ for Word Choice

6 Precise word choice makes my essay informative and enjoyable to read.

5 I use words with appropriate connotations and correct denotations throughout my essay.

4 Most of my connotations are appropriate, but I should check the denotation of some words.

When you revise for *word choice,* you check the connotation and denotation of your words. The rubric strip above can guide you.

■ How can I check the connotation of my words?

You can check the connotation of your words by making sure each word creates the right feeling in the reader. Not all synonyms are created equal. Note how the feeling of the following sentence changes as different synonyms are inserted:

Congress passed the immigration reform bill.

approved	rubber-stamped	pushed through	mandated
(friendly)	*(jaded)*	*(aggressive)*	*(dictatorial)*

Exercise

In the following sentences, choose a synonym for the italicized words, noting each synonym's connotation or feeling. Write down an adjective that describes the feeling of each word.

1. Protesters *gathered* outside the Capitol building.
2. Police *monitored* the *crowd.*
3. Security forces *detained* any unruly protestors.
4. Inside the Capitol, legislators *discussed* amendments to the bill.
5. The president welcomes the *reform.*
6. Some critics say the bill is costly without yielding many *results.*
7. Others feel that the bill is *unfair* to those who have already immigrated.
8. The new legislation faces an *uncertain* future.

Revise

Check your connotation. Read your essay and weigh the feeling created by each word. If you find a word that creates the wrong feeling, search for a synonym that has a more appropriate connotation.

3 I use some words with the wrong connotation and others with the wrong denotation.

2 Many of my words have the wrong connotation and denotation.

1 I need help understanding how to use connotation and denotation effectively.

■ How can I check the denotation of my words?

You can check your denotation by making sure that you understand the precise dictionary definition for each technical term you use. Note the incorrect denotation of the words in blue:

National Guard troops enforce the new immigration bill.
(Troops enforce *laws,* not *bills.*)

They ticket illegal immigrants crossing the border.
(Troops *arrest* or *detain* illegal immigrants; they don't *ticket* them.)

Exercise

Replace each word in italics with a word that has the correct denotation. Use a dictionary if you need to.

1. Despite patrols, hundred of immigrants cross the *state line* every day.
2. Many of them find work, though they don't have a *license.*
3. The new law allows some resident aliens to apply for *membership.*
4. Critics say the law lets illegal aliens remain, granting them *sanctuary.*

Revise

Check your denotation. Read your essay and look up each technical term in a dictionary, making sure it has the right denotation. If you find words that have the wrong denotation, replace them with correct terms.

Word Choice
Changes improve connotation and correct denotation.

> Opponents of electronic voting also fear that computer
> ~~technicians~~ hackers could ~~change~~ tamper with election results. A skilled computer
> ~~designer~~ programmer could rewrite the ~~language~~ code that controls electronic
> voting machines to skew the results toward a particular . . .

Expository

Revising ■ for Sentence Fluency

6 My sentences are skillfully written and easy to follow.	**5** I use clear comparisons and parallel series.	**4** My comparisons are clear, but I should make a few of my series more parallel.

When you revise for *sentence fluency,* you make sure your comparisons are clear and your series are parallel. The rubric strip above can guide you.

■ How can I fix unclear comparisons?

You can fix unclear comparisons by making sure you indicate what is being compared to what:

Unclear: Doctors care more about antibiotic overuse than patients.

Clear: Doctors care more about antibiotic overuse than patients do.

Clear: More doctors than patients care about antibiotic overuse.

Unclear: Doctors should prescribe antibiotics less.

Clear: Doctors should prescribe antibiotics less often than they currently do.

Exercise

Rewrite the unclear comparisons below to make them clear.

1. It is more dangerous to overprescribe antibiotics.
2. "Superbugs"—or antibiotic-resistant bacteria created by overprescription—pose more threat to patients than viruses.
3. More hospital patients get superbugs than homebound patients.
4. Doctors consider superbugs more dangerous than patients.
5. Scientific studies show more concern about superbugs than opinion polls.

Revise

Check for clear comparisons. Review your essay and make sure all of your comparisons are clear. Rewrite any that are not.

3 I need to make some comparisons clearer and some series parallel.

 2 My comparisons are unclear, and my series aren't parallel.

 1 I need help understanding how to create clear comparisons and parallel series.

■ How can I create parallel series?

You can create parallel series by making sure that each item in a group of three or more is the same kind of grammatical element: three present-tense verbs or three past-tense verbs or three participles, and so on.

> **Not Parallel:** **Superbugs are** adapting, spreading, **and kill thousands.**

> **Parallel:** **Superbugs are** adapting, spreading, **and killing thousands.**

 ## Exercise

Rewrite each series below to make it parallel.

1. Researchers study superbugs, probe their weaknesses, and they hope to find new treatments.
2. The threat of superbugs is serious, a growing problem, and global.
3. Not prescribing antibiotics for viral infections, remaining watchful for hospital infections, and to wash hands are the best policies.

Revise

Check for parallel series. Make sure that each item in a series of three or more has the same grammatical structure.

Expository

Sentence Fluency
A comparison is made clear.

Many of the same Floridians who found the paper "butterfly" ballot confusing would be even less comfortable. poking a screen to indicate their choice

Consequently, voters would make errors in their selections,

though this time there would be no paper trail for a recount. . . .

Revising ▪ Use a checklist.

Check your revising. On a piece of paper, write the numbers 1 to 12. If you answer "yes" to a question, put a check mark next to that number. If not, continue to work on that part of your essay.

Revising Checklist

Ideas

_____ **1.** Do I state my thesis clearly?

_____ **2.** Have I included a variety of details to support each topic sentence?

_____ **3.** Have I fairly represented each side of the argument?

Organization

_____ **4.** Does the overall structure of my essay work well?

_____ **5.** Have I used transitions to connect my ideas?

_____ **6.** Have I also used signal words to help my reader understand the argument?

Voice

_____ **7.** Have I used an active voice?

_____ **8.** Do I use third-person point of view consistently?

Word Choice

_____ **9.** Have I used words with the appropriate connotation?

_____ **10.** Have I used words with the correct denotation?

Sentence Fluency

_____ **11.** Have I fixed any unclear comparisons?

_____ **12.** Are all of my series parallel?

Make a clean copy. When you are finished with your revision, make a clean copy of your essay for editing.

Editing

Now that you have finished revising your essay of opposing ideas, you are ready to edit for conventions: punctuation, capitalization, spelling, and grammar.

Keys to Effective Editing

1. Use a dictionary, a thesaurus, and the "Proofreader's Guide" in the back of this book as editing resources.

2. Check your writing for correctness of punctuation, capitalization, spelling, and grammar.

3. Edit on a clean revised copy of your essay. Then either enter the corrections on your computer file or write a new handwritten copy that includes the corrections.

4. Use the editing and proofreading marks on the inside the back cover of this book.

Expository

Editing ▪ for Conventions

6 My grammar and punctuation are correct, and the copy is free of spelling errors.

5 I have a few minor errors in grammar, spelling, or punctuation, but they won't distract the reader.

4 I must correct some errors in punctuation, spelling, or grammar that may distract the reader.

When you edit for *conventions,* you correct errors in punctuation, capitalization, spelling, and grammar. The rubric strip above will guide you.

▪ How can I check the case of my pronouns?

You can check the case of your pronouns by paying attention to how each pronoun is used in the sentence. (See **710.1.**)

- ▪ Use **nominative case** for subjects and predicate nouns.

  he   she   it   they

  He told the secretary of state to refuse to negotiate with North Korea, but it was she **who gave the reason for the denial.**

- ▪ Use **possessive case** to show ownership.

  Before the noun: his   her   their   its
  After the noun: his   hers   theirs   its

  His **policy prevented the meeting, but the language expressing that policy was** hers**.**

- ▪ Use **objective case** for any objects (direct or indirect objects; objects of prepositions or infinitives).

  him   her   it   them

  The president told her **that multilateral talks were acceptable to** him**.**

Exercise

Replace each underlined pronoun with a pronoun of the correct case.

1. Kim Jong-il said that <u>him</u> wanted Condoleezza Rice to pay <u>his</u> a visit.
2. The purpose of the visit was to let <u>they</u> discuss North Korea's defense and <u>it</u> nuclear weapons program.
3. Secretary of State Rice restated <u>hers</u> desire to enter multilateral discussions, holding <u>they</u> in the company of other nations.

Edit

Check the case of your pronouns. Follow the rules above to check your pronoun use.

3 I need to correct a number of errors that will confuse my reader.

2 I need to fix many errors that make my writing hard to read and understand.

1 I need help finding errors and making corrections.

What adjectives should I capitalize?

Capitalize proper adjectives, which are created from proper nouns:

Britain ⟶ British   Arthur ⟶ Arthurian

Islam ⟶ Islamic   Newton ⟶ Newtonian

Capitalize geographic directions only if they are part of a proper name, unit, or regional term.

South Carolina	**South Pole**	**the East Coast (but the eastern U.S.)**
North Dakota	**Western Hemisphere**	**the Northwest Passage (but northwestern states)**

Exercise

In the following paragraph, correct any errors in capitalizing adjectives.

> The people of north Korea live under totalitarian rule, while the people of south Korea live in a democracy. The korean War was fought because the Northern part of the country had fallen under a stalinist model of government, while the southern part aspired to a jeffersonian democracy.

Edit

Check your adjectives. Be sure your writing follows the capitalization rules above. Make any changes necessary to correct your work.

Conventions
An error in pronoun case is corrected.

> While people disagree about the effectiveness of electronic voting, ~~them~~ they agree that the fiasco of 2000 should not be repeated. For 36 days, the outcome of the . . .

Expository

Editing ■ Use a checklist.

Edit

Check your editing. On a piece of paper, write the numbers 1 to 11. If you can answer "yes," put a check mark after that number. If you can't, continue to edit for that convention.

Editing Checklist

Conventions

PUNCTUATION

_____ **1.** Do I use end punctuation after all my sentences?

_____ **2.** Do I use commas after long introductory phrases and clauses?

_____ **3.** Have I used quotation marks correctly for quotations?

CAPITALIZATION

_____ **4.** Do I start all of my sentences with capital letters?

_____ **5.** Do I capitalize all proper adjectives and nouns?

SPELLING

_____ **6.** Have I spelled all words correctly?

_____ **7.** Have I double-checked for errors my spell-checker may have missed?

GRAMMAR

_____ **8.** Have I checked the case of my pronouns?

_____ **9.** Do my pronouns agree with their antecedents?

_____ **10.** Do my subjects and verbs agree?

_____ **11.** Have I used the right words *(there, their, they're)*?

■ Add a title.

After your editing is complete, add a title that engages your reader and sums up the content of your essay. Here are a few ways to create an effective title for your essay.

■ Use a hook: **A Closer Look at Electronic Voting**
■ Ask a question: **Does Electronic Voting Get the Job Done?**
■ Identify the controversy: **The Battle over Electronic Voting**

Publishing ■ Share your essay.

The purpose of your essay of opposing ideas is to present a clear, evenhanded examination of a political controversy. Now that you've completed your essay, share your ideas in a public forum. The following guidelines will help you publish your work.

Publish

Format your final copy. To format a handwritten essay, use the guidelines below or follow your teacher's instructions. (If you are using a computer, see pages 91–95.) Make a clean copy and carefully proofread it.

■ Focus on presentation.

- Write neatly using blue or black ink.
- Place your name in the upper left corner of page 1.
- Skip a line and center your title; skip another line and start your essay.
- Indent every paragraph and leave a one-inch margin on all four sides.
- Write your last name and the page number in the upper right corner of every page after page 1.

Publish Your Essay

School and local newspapers often welcome writing that clearly examines political controversies. Send your article to a local or school-based newspaper using e-mail or postal mail. Before sending your article, make sure it conforms to the publication's submission guidelines and would interest the publication's audience.

Expository

Add It to a Blog

Many students have created Web logs, or blogs, to share their ideas in online forums. If you have a blog, consider publishing your article on it. You may also invite comments from your readers.

Post It in Public

If you are using a computer to format your essay, add photographs, charts, and other visual elements to support your ideas. Then post a printed copy of your essay on a school bulletin board or other prominent site. (Be sure to get permission first.)

Rubric for Expository Writing

The following rubric will help you assess your expository writing. Use it to improve your writing using the six traits.

6 Ideas   5   4

6 Ideas	5	4
The ideas in the essay are compelling from start to finish.	The essay shows a clear relationship between thesis and supporting evidence.	The essay presents a clear topic and thesis. More support is needed.

Organization

6	5	4
The essay shows thoughtful use of an organizational pattern. Transitions are strong.	The essay uses an effective organizational pattern. Transitions are appropriate.	The essay follows an organizational pattern. Transitions could be stronger.

Voice

6	5	4
The writing voice is lively, engaging, and memorable.	Voice is appropriate for the topic, purpose, and audience and sounds knowledgeable.	Voice fits the audience and sounds knowledgeable in most places.

Word Choice

6	5	4
Word choice is vivid and precise. Special terms are defined or explained.	Word choice is effective. Words are not repeated, and special terms are defined.	Word choice is adequate. Some overused words could be replaced.

Sentence Fluency

6	5	4
Sentences are carefully crafted. Sentences flow naturally and vary in type and length.	Sentences flow well and are varied in type and length.	Sentences could use more variety in type and length.

Conventions

6	5	4
Editing shows mastery of conventions. The essay is error free.	Editing is effective, but a few errors in grammar, spelling, or punctuation remain.	A few too many errors remain.

3	**2**	**1**
The essay shows some understanding of the topic and thesis. More support is needed.	The topic and thesis should be more focused. The essay needs specific support that relates to the topic.	The topic should be reworked and a new thesis formed.
The essay does not follow an organizational pattern. Key points need separate paragraphs and transitions.	The beginning, middle, and ending parts need to be made clear.	The essay must be rewritten using an organizational plan.
Voice sounds uneven. It should match topic, purpose, and audience.	Voice sounds as if the writer does not have a good understanding of the subject.	Voice does not show confidence.
Word choice needs to be more precise, and overused words need to be replaced.	A thesaurus is needed to find more expressive words in many places.	The writer needs help choosing stronger words throughout.
Sentences are basic. More variety is needed in sentence type and length.	Too many sentences are simple and begin the same way.	Most sentences need to be rewritten.
Control of conventions is basic. Errors sometimes get in the way of understanding.	Many corrections are needed to make the essay less confusing.	The writer needs help to understand and edit conventions.

Expository

Evaluating an Essay of Opposing Ideas

Read the essay below and focus on its strengths and weaknesses. **(The essay contains some errors.)** Then read the student self-assessment on the next page.

The Best Route to the Presidency?

Every four years, a president is elected by U.S. voters—or at least most voters think this is the case. In fact, the President of the United States is chosen not by voters but by the roughly 530 members of the electoral college. In each state, members of the college agree to cast their ballots for the candidate who receives the most votes statewide ("Electoral"). While this system has been largely successful, it has created controversy. Some citizens support the Electoral College, but others feel that it should be replaced by a popular vote for the presidency.

Supporters of the electoral college point out that it was created to ensure the survival of U.S. democracy. As the founding fathers worked to create a plan for presidential elections, they worried that a charismatic and dishonest candidate might manipulate the public into voting against its best interests and then impose a dictatorship. So the framers of the Constitution created the electoral college to serve as a buffer against poor choices by the voters. Supporters of the college feel this is still necessary.

Supporters argue the electoral college provides stability by giving influence to sparsely populated states. In order to win the presidency, a candidate must show broad popularity, not just popularity in states with large populations. And for more than 200 years the electoral college has provided stability, resulting in elections decided within the rule of law—no small achievement for any government, democratic or otherwise.

Those who favor a direct election of the president insist that the electoral college system unfairly takes power from voters. They argue that citizens now directly elect every official in the nation except the president and vice president, and are capable of directly electing those officials as well. Supporters of direct election also cite numerous polls of voters, which universally favor election of the president by popular vote.

Another argument against the electoral college is the historical one. Under the electoral college system, three American presidents have won election despite losing the popular vote. This most recently happened in 2000, when George W. Bush was elected president despite losing the popular vote by a small margin ("Popular"). Third party candidates also tend to fare poorly in the electoral college. In the 1992 election, Ross Perot won 19 percent of the popular vote but did not get a single electoral vote ("1992"). Finally, say opponents, the electoral College tends to depress turnout in states in which one party enjoys clear dominance, because people who support the opposing party feel their votes don't count.

With voters largely split between the Democratic and Republican parties, it's likely that presidential elections in the near future will be decided by a relatively small margin. That means the debate over the Electoral College is likely to continue. No matter what turn the debate takes, the decision will just as likely be made using the democratic process—just as the founding fathers intended.

Student Self-Assessment

Expository Rubric Checklist

Title: <u>The Best Route to the Presidency?</u>
Writer: <u>Garret Honnecker</u>

5   **Ideas**
- Does my essay include a clear thesis statement?
- Do I support my thesis with a variety of details?

4   **Organization**
- Does my overall structure work well?
- Have I used signal words to make my structure clear?

4   **Voice**
- Are most of my sentences active?
- Do I use third-person point of view consistently?

5   **Word Choice**
- Do I use words with the appropriate connotation?
- Do I use words with the correct denotation?

5   **Sentence Fluency**
- Are all my series parallel?
- Are my comparisons clear and complete?

4   **Conventions**
- Do I use correct punctuation, capitalization, spelling, and grammar?

OVERALL COMMENTS:

My essay does a good job addressing the controversy.

I forgot to write a paragraph about the common ground between the two positions.

I had a few problems with capitalization and should proofread more closely.

Expository

Review your essay. Rate your essay and write comments that explain why you gave yourself the scores you did.

Reflecting on Your Writing

Now that you have completed your essay of opposing ideas, take some time to reflect on the process of writing it. On a separate sheet of paper, complete each sentence below. This personal reflection will help reinforce what you've learned about writing an essay of opposing ideas.

My Essay of Opposing Ideas

1. The strongest part of my essay is . . .

2. The part that still needs work is . . .

3. The prewriting activity that worked best for me was . . .

4. The main thing I learned about writing an essay of opposing ideas is . . .

5. In my next essay of opposing ideas, I would like to . . .

6. One question I still have about writing an essay of opposing ideas is . . .

Expository Writing
Writing an Essay of Speculation

No one can prove what will happen in the future. The best anyone can do is to speculate on what the world might be like. By definition, *speculate* means "to engage in a course of reasoning based on inconclusive evidence." Effective speculation is far different from wild guessing. It involves careful research, logical thinking, common sense, and a touch of imagination.

In this chapter, you will read an essay of speculation about an invasive ground cover—crown vetch—that could cause serious problems in the future. Then you will be guided through the process of developing your own essay of speculation. *Remember:* For this type of essay, you must think carefully about something in the present and make an educated guess (speculate) about its future.

Writing Guidelines

    Subject: **A timely topic**
      Form: **Essay of speculation**
  Purpose: **To speculate on the future of the topic**
 Audience: **Classmates**

"Common sense in an uncommon degree is what the world calls wisdom."
—Samuel Taylor Coleridge

Essay of Speculation

In the following essay, Carla predicts what might happen if an invasive plant called crown vetch is left unchecked.

Uncontrollable Invasion

Beginning
The writer introduces the topic and states her thesis (underlined).

Fifty years ago, road crews began planting crown vetch along newly constructed highways to prevent soil erosion. Crown vetch is an aggressive ground-cover plant with appealing foliage and flowers. Road improvement scars were quickly covered and erosion was no longer a concern. Then planners discovered an alarming problem. Crown vetch didn't like staying in one place. Instead, it started taking root in land adjacent to the roadsides. As a result, it became clear that crown vetch could not be planted carelessly or left unchecked. What would happen if this plant were left alone to grow and spread? If left unchecked, crown vetch could change the nation's landscape as we know it.

Middle
Each middle paragraph addressees a main point.

Most people pay little attention to this plant along the nation's highways and freeways. Motorists use these roadways to get to a destination quickly. However, crown vetch matures into an 18-inch-high creeping, competitive plant that grows in all climates—wet or dry, hot or cold. It can literally begin to take over a roadside and nearby land, overwhelming any vegetation in its path, including small trees (Fernald). If this would happen, even the most unobservant driver would begin to notice a sameness in the vegetation mile after mile after mile. Eventually, motorists would complain, demanding that the government do something about the problem.

An authority is cited.

If crown vetch really took hold in an area, local crops and gardens could be at risk. According to Art Gover of Pennsylvania State University, crown vetch sprouts from rhizomes (underground root runners) and seeds, which makes it fast growing and difficult to eradicate. The rhizomes can be up to 10 feet in length. As a result, crown vetch could easily overwhelm backyard gardens or croplands near roadsides. To eliminate the problem, strong chemicals may have to be applied to an infested area. Unfortunately, chemicals could kill any nearby desirable plants or contaminate the soil. Otherwise, fires would have to be set in these areas year after year.

Each middle
paragraph
begins with a
topic sentence,
followed by
supporting
details.

Ending
The ending
summarizes the
writer's thesis.

The greatest danger posed by crown vetch is its potential to invade, and destroy, native prairie habitats. Native prairie land is unique to interior parts of the United States, primarily in the Plains states. Most of the original prairie is gone, and crown vetch could threaten what remains (Heim). A prairie needs to maintain a special balance of native plants and animals to thrive, and the introduction of crown vetch into the area would certainly destroy that balance. Fires, historically caused by lightning storms, help maintain the health and vitality of the prairies. However, if crown vetch were in the area, the plant burns too quickly and without the necessary heat to aid in prairie regeneration. It would be a tragedy to lose what remains of the nation's prairie lands because of an invasive plant such as crown vetch.

Crown vetch has helped control erosion along U.S. roadways, but if left unchecked, it has the potential to do as much harm as good. Croplands, gardens, and prairies are the areas where an infestation of crown vetch could be the most harmful. Most plants in their rightful place benefit the landscape or ecosystem; but in the wrong place, without the proper restraint, they may cause serious, long-term problems.

Expository

 Respond to the reading. Answer the following questions about the sample essay of speculation.

Ideas (1) What is the thesis or focus of this essay? (2) What main points does the writer include to support the thesis? Name at least two.

Organization (3) How does the writer organize the essay—spatially, chronologically, or by order of importance?

Voice & Word Choice (4) Does the writer sound interested in and knowledgeable about the topic? Explain.

Prewriting ■ Consider current issues.

The purpose of an essay of speculation is to make an informed prediction about a specific aspect of life. To get started, Carla made a list of current issues—national and global—that will affect life in the future.

Current-Issues List

technology in education	oil resources
urban sprawl	invasive plant species *
fresh water	global warming
voting apathy	the two-party system

Prewrite

Think of current issues. Make a list of current issues that might affect life in the future. Then choose one to explore further for this assignment. Place an asterisk (*) next to the issue you choose.

■ Select a specific topic.

Carla had discussed issues about invasive plant species in her botany class. She decided it would be interesting to investigate one of these species and speculate what effect it might have on future life. After reviewing her class notes and checking on the Internet, she came up with this list. Then she put an asterisk next to the species of plant she wanted to write about.

Topics List

Invasive Plants

pepper trees	hydrilla	kudzu
crown vetch *	leafy spurge	garlic mustard

Prewrite

Choose a topic. List specific topics related to the current issue that you chose above. Then put an asterisk (*) next to the topic that you would like to write about.

Ideas The goal of an essay of speculation is to make an informed prediction. In order to do that, you will need to research your topic so that you can base your speculations on solid information. If you can't find enough information about your topic, switch to another one.

■ Write a thesis statement.

Once you have gained a thorough understanding of your topic, write a thesis statement expressing your topic's potential effect in the future. Here is Carla's thesis statement.

topic		future effect		thesis statement
crown vetch	**+**	could change the nation's landscape	**=**	Crown vetch could change the nation's landscape as we know it.

Prewrite

Learn about your topic. Research your topic to learn as much as you can about it. Then write a thesis statement that expresses its potential effect in the future. (Use the example above as a guide.)

■ Organize your information.

Organizing the facts and details that support your thesis statement is the next important step in the essay-writing process. Carla used a two-column chart to organize her main points and related details.

Two-Column Chart

Main Points	Related Details
dominates roadsides	• grows into dense cover • creates a disturbing sameness • overwhelms other vegetation
could put local crops and gardens at risk	• grows fast • needs strong chemicals or annual fires to eradicate
could destroy native prairie habitats	• destroys prairie unique to U.S. • upsets balance of native plants and animals • hinders prairie regeneration

Prewrite

Organize your support. Complete a two-column chart like the one above in which you list the main points and related details that support your thesis. List main points in the order that you will write about them.

Writing ▪ Create your first draft.

The following tips will help you develop your first draft. Be sure to use your prewriting to guide your drafting.

Beginning Paragraph

The beginning paragraph should introduce your topic and clearly state your thesis.

- Open with interesting information that introduces your topic.
  Fifty years ago, road crews began planting crown vetch along newly constructed highways to prevent soil erosion. Crown vetch is an aggressive ground-cover plant with appealing foliage and flowers.

  Then planners discovered an alarming problem. Crown vetch didn't like staying in one place. Instead, it started taking root in land adjacent to the roadsides.

- End with your thesis statement.
  If left unchecked, crown vetch could change the nation's landscape as we know it.

Middle Paragraphs

The middle paragraphs explain the main points that support the thesis.

- Use an effective topic sentence at the start of each paragraph to state the paragraph's main idea.
  Most people pay little attention to this plant along the nation's highways and freeways.

- Include details to support each topic sentence.
  Motorists use these roadways to get to a destination quickly. However, crown vetch matures into an 18-inch-high creeping, competitive plant that grows in all climates—wet or dry, hot or cold. It can literally take over a roadside and nearby land, overwhelming any vegetation in its path, including . . .

Ending Paragraph

The ending paragraph should restate the thesis and summarize the main supporting points.

- Restate your thesis.
  Crown vetch has helped control erosion along the U.S. roadways, but if left unchecked, it has the potential to do as much harm as good.

Write

Write your first draft. Write an initial draft of your essay, using the sample essay, your prewriting work, and the information above as a guide.

Revising ▪ Improve your first draft.

As you revise, use the checklist below as a guide.

Revising Checklist

Ideas

_____ **1.** Do I clearly introduce my issue?

_____ **2.** Do I make an informed prediction about its future?

_____ **3.** Do I support my thesis with compelling main points?

_____ **4.** Do I effectively develop each middle paragraph?

Organization

_____ **5.** Does my essay have a strong beginning, middle, and ending?

_____ **6.** Have I presented my points in a logical order?

Voice

_____ **7.** Does my voice sound confident and knowledgeable?

_____ **8.** Does my voice show interest in the topic?

Word Choice

_____ **9.** Have I chosen words that clearly explain my ideas?

Sentence Fluency

_____ **10.** Are my sentences varied in type and length?

Revise

Revise your first draft. Read your essay carefully. Then use the checklist above to improve your first draft.

▪ Add a title.

- ▪ Draw on your thesis: **Uncontrollable Invasion**
- ▪ Ask a question: **Can Crown Vetch Be Contained?**
- ▪ Use your imagination: **A "Vetching" Problem**

Expository

Editing ■ Check for conventions.

After revising your essay, use the following checklist to edit your writing for punctuation, capitalization, spelling, and grammar errors.

Editing Checklist

Conventions

PUNCTUATION

_____ **1.** Have I ended my sentences with the correct punctuation?

_____ **2.** Have I used commas, semicolons, and colons correctly?

_____ **3.** Have I punctuated quotations correctly?

CAPITALIZATION

_____ **4.** Do I capitalize the first word in every sentence?

_____ **5.** Do I capitalize all proper nouns and adjectives?

SPELLING

_____ **6.** Have I spelled all my words correctly?

_____ **7.** Have I double-checked for easily confused words that my spell-checker would miss?

GRAMMAR

_____ **8.** Have I used the correct forms of verbs?

_____ **9.** Do my subjects and verbs agree in number?

_____ **10.** Do my pronouns agree with their antecedents?

Edit your essay. Use the checklist above to edit for conventions. Also ask a partner to check your work for errors. Then prepare a final copy and proofread it.

Publishing ■ Share your work.

This final step accomplishes the purpose of sharing information with your audience.

Publish your essay. Share your writing by reading it aloud in the classroom, followed by a question-and-answer session, or by posting it on a bulletin board. Also consider presenting it as a speech or uploading it to a Web site.

Writing for Assessment
Responding to Expository Prompts

Expository writing is basically informational writing. Depending on the topic, you might summarize, illustrate, analyze, explain, classify, or compare. For most expository assignments, you will be given plenty of time to complete your work. However, when you are asked to respond to an expository prompt on an assessment test, you will have to complete your work within a set period of time.

When responding to an expository prompt, you will need to plan, write, and revise your writing quickly. In this chapter, you will learn how to analyze an expository prompt and create an effective, well-organized response—all within specific time constraints. Having the ability to write on demand is a valuable skill that you will use now and later—when you go on to college or enter the work world.

Writing Guidelines

Subject: **An expository prompt**
Form: **Response essay**
Purpose: **To demonstrate competence**
Audience: **Instructor**

"I see only one rule: to be clear. If I am not clear, then my entire world crumbles into nothing."

—Stendhal

Prewriting ▪ Analyze an expository prompt.

To respond effectively to an expository prompt, you will first need to analyze it. If you do a thorough job of analyzing the prompt, you'll have a much better chance of producing a successful essay. To analyze a prompt, use the STRAP questions:

> **Subject:** What topic should I write about?
>
> **Type:** What form of writing should I create (essay, letter, editorial, article, report)?
>
> **Role:** What role should I assume as the writer (student, son or daughter, friend, employee, citizen)?
>
> **Audience:** Who (teacher, parents, classmates, employer, official) is the intended audience?
>
> **Purpose:** What is the goal of my writing (inform, summarize, illustrate, analyze, classify, compare)?

<u>Subject</u>
<u>Type</u>
Role
Audience
Purpose

Some people always stand out as individuals. These people don't follow trends; they set them. *Assuming the role of a historian,* write a brief <u>essay</u> for your classmates about <u>someone you admire for individuality</u>. Explain what makes the person stand out in the crowd and how the person's unique traits make you admire him or her.

Note: One of the following key words or phrases is often found in an expository prompt: *outline, analyze, inform, compare and contrast, explain,* or *define.*

Try It!

Analyze this prompt by answering the STRAP questions. (Some answers may be implied or left open. Use your best judgment.)

According to Mark Twain, "We find not much in ourselves to admire; we are always privately wanting to be like somebody else. If everybody was satisfied with himself there would be no heroes." Write a letter to Twain explaining your own definition of a hero, including examples of people you consider heroic.

■ Plan your response.

After you have analyzed the prompt using the STRAP questions, it's time to start planning and organizing your response. One good way to do this is to use a graphic organizer. The organizers below all provide ways to organize an effective response to an expository prompt.

Quick List (Any Essay)

1. First Point
   —Detail 1
   —Detail 2
2. Second Point
   —Detail 1
   —Detail 2
3. Third Point
   —Detail 1
   —Detail 2

Time Line (How-To/Process)

First
Next
Then
After
Last

T-Chart (Two-Part Essay)

Topic:

Part A	Part B
*	*
*	*
*	*
*	*

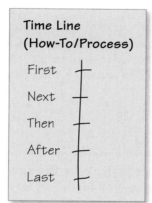

Venn Diagram (Compare-Contrast)

Topic A   Topic B

Similarities
Differences

Cluster (Definition/Classification)

Topic

Prewrite

Use a graphic organizer. Reread the expository prompt on page 212. Use a graphic organizer to plan and organize your response to the prompt. Keep the STRAP questions in mind as you work.

Tip

When it comes to responding to a prompt, good time management is critical. If you have 45 minutes to respond to a prompt, use the first 5 to 10 minutes to analyze the prompt and plan your response, the last 5 to 10 minutes to revise and edit your response, and the time in between for the actual writing.

Expository

Writing ■ Respond to a prompt.

Once you have answered the STRAP questions and planned your response using a graphic organizer, you can begin writing.

Sample Expository Prompt

People under the age of 20 have grown up with computers and are sometimes called "digital natives." Computer technology is their native language. Write an essay that explains to the older generation the role of computers in the lives of today's teens. Be sure to consider the positive and negative effects of computer use.

Try It!

Answer the STRAP questions for the sample expository prompt above. Refer to page **212** for a sample.

Sample Response

Beginning
The beginning paragraph gives the thesis statement (underlined).

> Just as some generations were raised listening to radio and others were raised watching television, my generation was raised using computers. These people are "digital natives" who speak the language of computers and use them throughout life. <u>Computers provide young people many tools for schoolwork, for communication, and for entertainment; they also present a few dangers along the way.</u>

Middle
Each middle paragraph explains part of the thesis.

> To begin with, computers have become indispensable tools for processing information. Word-processing programs allow students to write more quickly, revise more thoroughly, and edit more accurately than ever before. With the use of Internet search engines, students can find exactly the information they need with only a few mouse clicks. However, not every piece of information from the Internet is reliable, and an unwary researcher can end up with material that is biased or downright wrong. Also, computers make it more tempting to plagiarize. Teens have to be conscientious to avoid bad information and plagiarism, recognizing the responsibility that comes with the computer's power.

Modern teens also use computers for communication. Through instant messaging, online games, chat rooms, and group sites like MySpace, teens connect with old friends and meet new ones. Many young people also write their own blogs or create their own Web casts, sharing their ideas with the world. But while communicating online, teens must beware of "stranger danger." Spammers clog up e-mail boxes, hackers develop viruses, and predators lurk on group sites. Even if a computer user can avoid these dangers, having a friend online is no substitute for having one in person. Teens must learn to use computers to enhance friendships, not replace them.

Today's teens also use computers as a source of music and movies. Instead of going to a store, most teens buy music and movies online, either to be delivered or downloaded. They also prefer to buy one or two songs at a time rather than a whole album. Some sites even allow teens to share their files. This can cause problems. Illegal file sharing and downloads might seem a cheap way to get entertainment until the person is caught and fined—or even sent to prison. An illegal download also cheats the person's favorite artist out of the chance to make a living. If teens can steer clear of illegal music and movies, though, there is plenty of listening and watching to do.

For teens today, computers shape everyday life. The question is whether teens can manage the power of these great tools. When handled well, a computer provides homework help, connects people to friends, and even sets the world to music. On the other hand, unwise computer use can result in plagiarized documents, dangerous predators, and even fines and jail time. Most teens avoid these pitfalls almost instinctively. After all, these "digital natives" grew up understanding computers and speaking their language.

Transitions connect the middle paragraphs.

Ending The ending sums up the essay and provides a final thought.

Expository

Write

Respond to an expository prompt. Review the prompt on page 212. Then use your answers to the STRAP questions to plan and write a response within the time limit set by your teacher.

Revising ■ Improve your response.

Most writing tests allow you to make corrections to improve your work, though you should find out ahead of time how many changes are allowed. If changes are allowed, make them as neatly as possible. Use the STRAP questions to guide you.

Subject: Does my response focus on the prompt topic?
Do my main points support my thesis statement?

Type: Have I followed the correct form (essay, letter, article)?

Role: Have I assumed the role called for in the prompt?

Audience: Have I effectively addressed my audience?

Purpose: Does my response accomplish the goal of the prompt?

Revise

Improve your work. Using the STRAP questions above as your guide, revise your response within the allowed time period.

Editing ■ Check your response.

Check your expository response for punctuation, capitalization, spelling, and grammar. You don't want any careless errors that confuse the reader.

Editing Checklist

Conventions

_____ **1.** Have I used end punctuation for every sentence?
_____ **2.** Have I capitalized all proper nouns and first words of sentences?
_____ **3.** Have I checked my spelling?
_____ **4.** Have I made sure my subjects and verbs agree?
_____ **5.** Have I used the right words (*their, they're, there*)?

Edit

Check for conventions. Review your response for any errors in punctuation, capitalization, spelling, and grammar. Make neat corrections.

Expository Writing on Tests

Use the following tips as a guide to help you respond effectively to an expository writing prompt.

Before you write . . .

- **Study the prompt.**
  Use the STRAP question listed on page 212. Remember that an expository response asks you to explain or inform.
- **Budget your time carefully.**
  Spend several minutes planning and organizing your response. Use the last few minutes to read over what you have written.

As you write . . .

- **Choose a clear focus or thesis for your response.**
  Keep your main idea or purpose in mind as you write.
- **Be selective.**
  Use examples that support your focus.
- **End in a meaningful way.**
  Remind the reader about the importance of the topic.

After you've written a first draft . . .

- **Check for completeness.**
  Use the STRAP questions on page 216 to revise your work.
- **Check for correctness.**
  Check your punctuation, capitalization, spelling, and grammar.

Try It!

Analyze one of the prompts below using the STRAP questions. Then plan and write a response. Complete your work within the time your teacher gives you.

- In recent years, political debate has often taken a negative, even angry tone. As someone concerned with the tone of political debate, write a set of guidelines to keep debates civil and focused on solving problems at hand.
- People spend their leisure time in a variety of ways. Some play team sports while others pursue pastimes such as cooking and playing music. Write a brief essay explaining one leisure-time activity that you find rewarding. Include details that provide a clear explanation for your classmates.

Expository

Persuasive Writing

Persuasive Writing

Writing an Essay of Argumentation

Perhaps more than any other leader in American history, Abraham Lincoln understood the value of a logical argument. As president, he led the nation during many fierce debates over the ethics of slavery. Lincoln observed, "I am a firm believer in the people. If given the truth, they can be depended upon to meet any national crises. The great point is to bring them the real facts."

Today, the people of our country are engaging in debate and making decisions about any number of issues. Many of these issues involve ethics, or moral controversies.

One way to participate in these ethical debates is to write an essay of argumentation. An essay of argumentation takes a position on one side of a controversy and defends the position with logical, well-organized reasons and details. In this chapter, you'll learn the steps necessary to create an effective essay of argumentation.

Writing Guidelines

Subject: An ethical issue
Form: Essay of argumentation
Purpose: To argue for a position
Audience: Classmates, readers of a local newspaper

"Let me give you a definition of ethics: It is good to maintain and further life; it is bad to damage and destroy life."

—Albert Schweitzer

Persuasive Writing Warm-Up ▪ Take a stand.

When you take a stand, you give your position (opinion) on a controversial issue and support your position with solid reasons. Most current newspapers and magazines will present several issues to choose from. Once you have found a controversy, filling in a pro-con chart is one way to record facts that support each side.

Pro-Con Chart

Issue: Some people are getting microchip implants beneath their skin to provide identification, medical history, and even global tracking.

Pro	Con
– Microchip implants make photo ID's unnecessary.	– Microchip implants could be faked, just like photo ID's. ("Cybertalk")
– "By carrying complete medical history, an implant can save the person's life." (Cybertalk)	– People with medical problems like diabetes can wear bracelets that identify the disease.
– Implants can give GPS locations, helping to foil kidnappings. ("Chips to Fight")	– GPS tracking can also allow governments and businesses to track anyone.
– Implants could hold credit card numbers, preventing theft and ensuring payment.	– "Companies will use implants to keep vast databases, trafficking in consumer profiles." ("Dangers")
– Different types of information could have different access codes.	– No laws exist about who can access the information.
– Each member of the Jacobs family was implanted because the son was interested in technology and the father requires 10 cancer medications. ("Chips to Keep")	– "The intimacy between technology and the flesh crosses a line. My instinct tells me this is an entirely unnecessary and dangerous technology." ("Chips to Fight")

My Position: Microchip implants may lead to some terrible abuses.

Try It!

Check out newspapers and magazines, looking for controversial issues. Select an issue, write it down, and create a pro-con chart to list arguments for each side. Then write your position.

Writing a Persuasive Paragraph

A persuasive paragraph states a position about a controversial topic and uses reasons to defend the position. A persuasive paragraph has three main parts:

- The **topic sentence** states the position.
- The **body sentences** support the position and respond to an objection.
- The **closing sentence** restates the position.

Sample Persuasive Paragraph

In the following persuasive paragraph, a writer expresses her position about microchip implants. She uses facts, statistics, examples, and quotations she has gathered in her pro-con chart.

The **topic sentence** (underlined) states the opinion.

The **body sentences** use facts, statistics, examples, and quotations.

The **closing sentence** states the opinion in a new way.

A Chip in the Old Block

<u>Microchip implants that carry crucial information about a person may lead to some terrible abuses.</u> Already implants are used in some places in Europe to provide identification, medical information, and credit card numbers. Supporters point to the security, convenience, and foolproof nature of the implants. However, no laws currently exist to prevent unscrupulous people and companies from accessing this information. Imagine a chair arm with a hidden scanner, or a doorway that "knows" who enters at what time. Futurist Tom Dormant foresees a world in which "companies will use implants to keep vast databases, trafficking in consumer profiles" ("Dangers"). Implants with global positioning technology can foil kidnappers, but they can also allow governments to track wearers at all times. These privacy issues deeply concern Simon Davies of Privacy International, who calls microchip implants "an entirely unnecessary and dangerous technology" ("Chips to Fight"). People who voluntarily get a microchip implant should be aware of the risks, and people who don't want to get one should make sure these little pieces of technology never become mandatory.

Persuasive

Write

Write a persuasive paragraph. State your position about the controversy you chose (page 220), provide reasons from your pro-con chart, and end by restating or reinforcing your position.

Understanding Your Goal

Your goal in this chapter is to write a persuasive essay that states a position about an ethical issue and argues logically to defend the position. The traits listed in the chart below will help you plan and write your essay of argumentation.

Traits of Persuasive Writing

- **Ideas**
  Select a topic that involves an ethical controversy, write a clear position statement, and include reasons that support the position.

- **Organization**
  Create a beginning that states your position, a middle that provides support and answers an objection, and an ending that restates your position. Use transition words and phrases to connect your ideas.

- **Voice**
  Use a voice that shows understanding of the controversy and commitment to a specific position about it.

- **Word Choice**
  Choose fair and precise words to state and defend your position.

- **Sentence Fluency**
  Write clear, complete sentences with varied beginnings and lengths.

- **Conventions**
  Eliminate errors in punctuation, capitalization, spelling, and grammar.

Get the big picture. Look at the rubric on pages 254–255. You can use it to assess your progress as you write. Your goal is to write an essay that takes a position on an ethical issue and defends the position with a logically organized persuasive argument.

Essay of Argumentation

An essay of argumentation states a position on a controversy and defends the position with logically organized reasons and details. In this sample essay, a student writer takes a position on lobbyists giving gifts to members of Congress.

Ban Gifts from Lobbyists

Since the invention of political systems, people have tried to use money and other gifts to influence the actions of politicians. In New York City in the 1800s, for example, a political group led by William "Boss" Tweed used bribery to corrupt the operations of city agencies and rob the city taxpayers of millions (Martin 434). Tweed died in prison, but the specter of political corruption is alive and well in the United States. Our system allows lobbyists to give gifts and provide favors to members of Congress, a practice that creates a conflict of interest. Do senators and representatives owe more to their constituents or to lobbyists? The best way to remove this conflict from our political system is to ban lobbyists from giving gifts to politicians.

First of all, banning gifts from lobbyists will eliminate long-standing relationships in which gifts are used to purchase political access and influence. Under current lobbying regulations, lobbyists can offer members of Congress the services of a corporate jet, a weekend golf getaway, or even tickets to sports events. In return, lobbyists often get the opportunity to speak with and even develop personal relationships with senators and representatives. This access may sound harmless, but lobbyists often use these relationships to obtain political favors. In some cases, lobbyists even assist directly in writing legislation, adding passages favorable to their corporate clients ("Great Giveaway").

Banning gifts from lobbyists will restore Americans' trust in Congress. Again and again, members of Congress must defend their actions after taking positions favorable to lobbyists who gave them gifts. In a recent survey, 83 percent of voters indicated that they distrusted lawmakers who accepted gifts from lobbyists (Jones). In the same survey, 64 percent of voters approved an outright ban on all such gift giving. Distrust in public officials has become an epidemic in this country, and gifts from lobbyists to members of Congress contribute greatly to that distrust. Banning such gifts would create an honest, open environment in which respect for our leaders can grow.

The third middle paragraph presents the writer's most important reason.

Perhaps most important, banning gifts will give typical citizens of the United States more opportunity to be heard in Washington. In the 2004 presidential elections, more than one-third of eligible voters chose not to vote (FEC). When surveyed, many nonvoters explained that they felt their votes didn't count, and that the government did not consider their input. With lobbyists using gifts to influence the political process, it's little wonder. Because many lobbyists are former politicians, they already have much more access than common people. Making gifts from lobbyists illegal can help level the playing field in Washington so that regular voters can be heard.

The final middle paragraph defends the position against a significant objection.

Some people might argue that banning gifts from lobbyists will do little to reduce the buying of influence since such gifts can easily be hidden. However, the same could be said for any number of illegal activities. Banning such gifts forces those who wish to buy influence to break the law, and sets up a system of punishment for those who do. An outright ban would be a deterrent and help to prevent corruption.

Ending
The ending restates the writer's position and adds perspective.

When many voters look at Congress, they see an institution in which lobbyists are able to buy power and favorable treatment. Sometimes this is true, and sometimes it isn't. In either case, the ability of lobbyists to give gifts to politicians stirs controversy and contributes to an environment of mistrust that makes it easy for citizens to turn their backs on the political process. Banning these gifts will not only reduce the undue influence of lobbyists, but it will also bring ordinary citizens back into the political process—and that might improve life for everyone.

Respond to the reading. Answer the following questions.

Ideas (1) What is the writer's position on gift giving by lobbyists? (2) What are the three main reasons that support the writer's position?

Organization (3) What is the purpose of the first three middle paragraphs? (4) What is the purpose of the final middle paragraph?

Voice & Word Choice (5) Find two or three examples of specific words that illustrate the author's unfavorable view of lobbyists.

Prewriting

Prewriting begins when you are still deciding what to write about and ends when you are ready to write your first draft. By breaking an essay project into small steps, you'll be well prepared to begin writing.

Keys to Effective Prewriting

1. Choose an ethical controversy that will be of interest to your audience.

2. Gather reasons and details to help form and support your position.

3. Write a position statement that focuses your thoughts.

4. Choose a significant objection to address in the middle part of your essay.

5. Create an outline or organized list to plan your essay.

Persuasive

Prewriting ■ Select a controversy.

To find an ethical controversy, Yolanda searched newspapers, magazines, and news shows. She listed controversies and put an asterisk beside her choice.

List of Political Controversies

Newspapers and Magazines	News Shows
right to privacy for criminals	wiretapping without warrants
drug testing for student athletes *	free speech for student newspapers
universal Internet access	mandatory sentencing laws
animal testing for cosmetics	high cost of prescription drugs
federal budget cuts for housing	carbon emissions laws

Prewrite

Select a controversy. Read national newspapers and magazines and watch news broadcasts, making a list of ethical controversies. Put an asterisk (*) next to the controversy you'd like to write about.

■ Consider sources.

Once you have selected a controversy to write about, you need to research it. Yolanda listed her own experiences and then primary (firsthand) and secondary (secondhand) sources.

Sources List

Personal Experiences	Primary Sources	Secondary Sources
My cousin had to do drug testing to join track.	Interview with Coach Colton	Steroids: Silent Danger, Steven Smith
There was a creatine problem at the high school five years ago.	Interview with school nurse	Major League Baseball Web site (mlb.com)
	Survey of student athletes at Millard Fillmore	"School Tackles Alarming Subject: Steroids Use," USA Today

Prewrite

List research sources. Make a sources list like the one above. Then choose three or four sources to use as you research your controversy.

■ Conduct research.

A well-written essay of argumentation uses a variety of details.

■ **Facts** are bits of information that can be proven to be true. Use facts to lay the foundation of the controversy.

> **Major League Baseball has instituted strict standards for testing pro baseball players for the use of steroids. (mlb.com)**

■ **Statistics** are facts that include a numerical value. Use statistics to provide examples that help to illustrate the controversy.

> **Over a five-year period, steroid use among high school athletes in New Jersey rose from 3 percent to 6.2 percent. (USA Today)**

■ **Quotations** are the exact words of people involved in the topic. Use quotations to let experts and authorities speak for themselves.

> **"Pro sports have, for a long while, forgotten the reason for competition—the love of the game, the pursuit of excellence. Instead of our high school athletes learning from drug-using pros, the pros ought to learn from our kids." (Coach Colton)**

■ **Anecdotes** are brief stories that make a point. Use anecdotes to demonstrate an abstract idea in a concrete way.

> **When the high school had trouble with creatine use five years ago, strict school policies were implemented. At first athletes and parents complained about the invasion of privacy, but now they support the policy for healthy, fair competition.**

■ Use note cards.

Yolanda used note cards to gather her details. She wrote questions at the top and answers below, making sure to note the source.

> What are potential side effects of
> steroid use?
>   – acne
>   – liver damage
>   – heart attacks
>   – increased aggression
>   – dependency and depression
> (sportsci.org/encyc/anabstereff/anabstereff)

Persuasive

Prewrite

Conduct research. Gather facts, statistics, quotations, and anecdotes. Write them down on note cards or in a notebook and be sure to keep track of sources.

Prewriting ■ State your position.

The next step is writing a preliminary position statement. An effective position statement names the controversy and gives a specific stand or opinion about it.

controversy		specific stand		an effective position statement
random testing for performance-enhancing drugs in high school athletes	**+**	testing is the best way to prevent the use of these drugs	**=**	The best way to prevent the use of performance-enhancing drugs in our schools is to institute random drug tests for all high school athletes.

Prewrite

Write a position statement. Use the formula above to create a position statement for your essay. Try two or three versions until you are satisfied.

■ Support your position.

After taking a position, you need to offer reasons and supporting details from your research. Yolanda created the "why" chart below to list her support.

"Why" Chart

Position: Random drug tests should be used for high school athletes.		
Why?	Testing is the only sure way to detect steroids.	Muscles can be built naturally. Steroid use is illegal and secretive. Peer pressure makes people keep silent.
Why?	Testing makes it easy to resist steroids.	Athletes won't risk getting benched. Testing gives an excuse to say "no."
Why?	Athletes' health and well being are at risk.	Drugs damage internal organs. Drugs cause mental-health issues.

Prewrite

Organize support for your position. Create a "why" chart of your own. Write your position and three reasons that answer the question "why?". Then add details that support each reason.

▪ Identify objections.

By fairly presenting a significant objection to your argument, you'll show your reader that you fully understand the controversy at hand. Yolanda generated a "why not" chart by adding the word *not* to her position and thinking of as many serious objections as she could. She chose the strongest objection to counter.

"Why Not" Chart

Position: Random drug tests should not be used for high school athletes.
Why not?   Drug tests are too costly.
Why not?   Some performance drugs can't be detected by testing.
Why not?   Drug testing is a violation of student privacy.*

Prewrite

Identify objections. Create a "why not" chart, like the one above, identifying at least three serious objections to your argument. Choose the strongest objection to counter in your essay.

▪ Counter an objection.

To counter an objection, think of the reasons that minimize or refute it. Yolanda identified these reasons that counter the objection she chose.

Objection: Drug testing is a violation of student privacy.
1. A respectful approach that seals records will ensure privacy.
2. Random testing eliminates bias.
3. It is acceptable to trade some privacy for safety.

Prewrite

Counter an important objection. Write down the strongest objection to your argument. List reasons that refute or minimize the objection.

▪ Focus on the traits.

Ideas Countering an objection allows you to take the best argument of the opposition and use it to further your own position.

Persuasive

Prewriting ■ Outline your essay.

Before actually writing your essay, it is a good idea to organize your reasons and supporting details in an outline or a list. Yolanda created a sentence outline, but your teacher may prefer a topic outline (using phrases).

Yolanda's Outline

<u>Position Statement:</u> The best way to prevent the use of performance-enhancing drugs in our schools is to institute random drug testing for all high school athletes.

I. Random testing is needed because performance drug use can be hard to detect.
   A. Big muscles don't always prove drug use.
   B. Student athletes hide their drug use.
   C. Drug tests can quickly and easily detect steroids.
II. Random testing makes it easier for young athletes to resist the temptation of performance-enhancing drugs.
   A. Athletes love their sports—and want the chance to play.
   B. Tests give students an incentive to not use drugs and an excuse to say "no."
III. Instituting testing can protect young athletes from physical and mental harm.
   A. Performance drugs can lead to major health problems.
   B. The drugs also affect mental health.
   C. Some effects can be reversed if drug use is stopped.
IV. Some civil rights advocates believe that random testing for performance-enhancing drugs violates student privacy rights.
   A. If testing is administered carefully, rights can be respected.
   B. Random testing will prevent bias against certain athletes.
   C. Testing tells kids that adults care about their private lives—and want to help them make good decisions.

Prewrite

Create an outline. Organize your reasons and supporting details in an outline or a list. (Follow your teacher's instructions.)

Writing

After selecting a topic, performing research, writing a position statement, and organizing your essay, you are ready to write your first draft.

Keys to Effective Writing

1. Use your outline or list as a writing guide, closely following it as you work.

2. Write on every other line, or double-space if you are using a computer. This will allow room for changes.

3. In the first paragraph, introduce the ethical controversy and state your position.

4. Include topic sentences in each middle paragraph.

5. In the last middle paragraph, answer a significant objection.

6. End by restating your position and sharing an insight with the reader.

Persuasive

Writing ▪ Get the big picture.

The graphic below shows how the elements of an essay of argumentation work together. Use this graphic as a guide to help you write your first draft. (The examples are from the student essay on pages **233–236**.)

BEGINNING

The **beginning** introduces the controversy and states the writer's position.

Position Statement
The best way to prevent the use of performance-enhancing drugs in our schools is to institute random drug tests for all high school athletes.

MIDDLE

Each **middle** paragraph supports the writer's position.

The last middle paragraph answers a major objection.

Topic Sentences
To begin, random testing is needed because steroid use can be hard to detect.

Random testing also makes it easier for young athletes to resist the temptation of performance-enhancing drugs.

Most importantly, instituting testing can protect young athletes from physical and mental harm.

Of course, some civil rights advocates believe that random testing for performance-enhancing drugs violates student privacy rights.

ENDING

The **ending** puts the controversy in perspective.

Closing Sentence
It's time to level the playing fields again, *without* steroids in the balance.

■ Start your essay.

The beginning paragraph of your essay should engage your reader, introduce your topic, and provide your position statement.

> Beginning
>
> Middle
>
> Ending

- **Engage your reader.** Begin with a sentence that will capture your reader's interest and keep him or her reading.

  In 2005, scandal rocked the world of professional baseball as allegations of the use of steroids and other performance-enhancing drugs hit the headlines.

- **Introduce your topic.** Include details that expand on your opening.

  Steroids and other drugs that quickly build muscle mass and make athletes stronger and faster have permeated virtually all levels of athletics.

- **Provide your position statement.** The thesis statement clearly and concisely states your position on the controversy.

  The best way to prevent the use of performance-enhancing drugs in our schools is to institute random drug tests for all high school athletes.

Beginning Paragraph

> **The controversy is introduced.**
>
> In 2005, scandal rocked the world of professional baseball as allegations of the use of steroids and other performance-enhancing drugs hit the headlines. Responding to pressure by Congress, Major League Baseball instituted standards for testing players for the use of these drugs ("Baseball Battles"). However, the controversy extends far beyond the baseball diamond. Steroids and other drugs that quickly build muscle mass and make athletes stronger and faster have permeated virtually all levels of athletics. For example, in the last five years, steroid use among high school athletes in New Jersey has doubled to 6 percent ("School Tackles"). That means a typical high school football team includes several users. <u>The best way to prevent the use of performance-enhancing drugs in our schools is to institute random drug tests for all high school athletes.</u>
>
> **The position statement is given (underlined).**

Persuasive

Write

Write a beginning paragraph. Be sure to engage your reader, introduce your topic, and provide a clear position statement.

Writing ■ Develop the middle part.

The middle part of your essay supports your position with reasons and details. It also answers a significant objection to your position. Remember to refer to your outline or list (page **230**) as you write.

Beginning
Middle
Ending

■ Link your ideas.

Transition words and phrases help you connect your ideas. You can use transitions to connect your paragraphs, showing the order of importance of your reasons and signaling your answer to an objection.

Reason 1	Reason 2	Reason 3	Answer to Objection
First of all, To begin, For starters,	Secondly, In addition, Also,	Most importantly, The biggest reason The main issue	Even so, some people . . . Granted, opponents say . . . Of course, critics allege . . .

You can also use transitions to show other relationships between ideas, such as time, cause and effect, comparison and contrast, and added information.

Time	Cause	Contrast	More Information
When	Consequently	Although	For example
After	As a result	However	Besides
At first	Because	Nevertheless	In addition

Middle Paragraphs

A topic sentence (underlined) introduces the main idea of each middle paragraph.

To begin, random testing is needed because steroid use can be hard to detect. When young people participate in sports, they build muscle mass naturally, so large muscles are not always recognized as a symptom. Also, because steroids and other performance-enhancing drugs are illegal, most student athletes realize that getting caught with them would mean immediate expulsion from sports. As a result, students will do everything they can to cover up their use. Peer pressure only reinforces the silence (Smith 26). However, drug tests can quickly and easily detect steroids in a minimally intrusive fashion. Once a student is identified as a user of performance-enhancing drugs, he or she can receive treatment and put an end to steroid use.

The body of each paragraph supports the paragraph's topic sentence.

Random testing also makes it easier for young athletes to resist the temptation of performance-enhancing drugs. Most student athletes participate in sports because they love them. If athletes know that testing positive could put them on the sidelines, they are more likely to resist the pressure to bulk up with performance-enhancing drugs. By acting as a deterrent, testing makes it easy for student athletes to resist peer pressure to use steroids and other enhancers. Athletes who do not want to risk their school sports careers are more likely to say "no" because of the random testing.

The middle paragraphs build to the most important reason.

Most importantly, instituting testing can protect young athletes from physical and mental harm. Performance-enhancing drugs can cause a broad range of serious health issues, from liver damage and heart attack to certain types of cancer. In addition, these drugs can affect mental health, causing unprovoked rage and violence among users. Sometimes the mood swings lead to depression and even suicide. That fact makes these drugs doubly deadly. Fortunately, if treatment is provided soon enough, most of these health issues can be avoided or reversed—another reason for supporting mandatory testing ("Anabolic").

The last middle paragraph responds to a significant objection.

Of course, some civil rights advocates believe that random testing for performance-enhancing drugs violates student privacy rights. However, if testing is conducted in a careful manner, students' rights can be respected. Furthermore, random testing eliminates potential bias against students. In a recent survey of track athletes at Fillmore High, 78 percent said they were not bothered by the privacy issues of drug testing. "It makes the sport fair for everyone," said junior Megan Krupinski. Random drug testing is a way of publicly telling athletes that adults care about what students do in their private lives and want to see them make good decisions.

Persuasive

Write the middle. Write middle paragraphs that effectively support your position and counter an objection.

Writing ■ End your essay.

You have stated your position, supported it with reasons and details, and responded to an objection. Now you are ready to write your ending paragraph. To do the job effectively, use the following guidelines:

Beginning

Middle

Ending

- Restate your position clearly and concisely.
- Sum up the main reasons for supporting your position.
- Summarize your response to the significant objection.
- Include an insight for your reader.

Ending Paragraph

The position is restated.

The paragraph sums up the support and ends with a final thought.

Random testing for high school athletes is the best way to prevent kids from using steroids. Right now, all across the United States, thousands of kids are risking their lives for the sake of bigger muscles. Carl Colton, coach of the Fillmore High School wrestling team, said, "Pro sports have, for a long while, forgotten the reason for competition—the love of the game, the pursuit of excellence. Instead of our high school athletes learning from drug-using pros, the pros ought to learn from our kids." The best way to reverse the current trend is to make random drug testing of high school athletes—done in a way that protects civil rights—mandatory. It's time to level the playing fields again, without steroids in the balance.

Write

Write your ending. Write an ending paragraph to summarize your position and your answer to an objection. Include a final thought or an insight for the reader.

Write

Prepare a complete first draft. Write a copy of your entire essay. Double-space if you use a computer, or write on every other line if you write by hand, so that you have room to make revision notes.

Revising

The revision process makes your initial draft better. When you revise, you add or delete details, reorganize parts of your writing, and improve your writing voice. You also check word choice and sentence style.

Keys to Effective Revising

1. Read your essay aloud and note parts that sound unclear or unconvincing.

2. Make sure you have clearly stated your position.

3. Check the order and unity of your middle paragraphs.

4. Be sure you use an informed, confident, and persuasive voice.

5. Check your essay for strong word choice and sentence variety.

6. Use the editing and proofreading marks inside the back cover of this book.

Persuasive

Revising ■ for Ideas

6 My position is clear and compelling, supported by a wide array of details.

5 My essay states and supports my position fairly and is fair to opposing positions.

4 I am fair when stating my position, but I'm sometimes unfair to opposing views.

When you revise for *ideas,* you make sure you have dealt fairly with your own position as well as with opposing views. The rubric strip above can guide you.

■ Have I presented my ideas fairly?

You have presented your ideas fairly if you avoided these logical fallacies:

- **Bandwagoning** implies that the reader should agree because most other people do.
  Most Europeans oppose testing cosmetics on animals, so we should, too.
  (A better argument would state why we should oppose it.)

- **Appeals to ignorance** use a lack of evidence to try to prove something.
  Animal testing facilities don't advertise, so there could be thousands of them.
  (A little research would tell how many facilities exist.)

- **Oversimplification** reduces complex situations to overly simple ones.
  Scientists should be curing cancer, not putting lipstick on rats.
  (Scientists who specialize in cosmetics are probably not experts on cancer.)

Exercise

Read the sentences below and identify the logical fallacy in each one.

1. If the government banned animal testing of cosmetics and drugs, all that would happen is that people wouldn't have such nice mascara.
2. Whenever you buy blush, imagine how many animals were tortured for it.
3. If you're like most attractive people, you won't mind giving up your makeup until animal testing is stopped.
4. Millions of caring people reject cosmetic testing on animals, and you should, too!
5. You don't put eyeliner on your cat, and neither should scientists.
6. Who knows how many animals die each year from testing.

Revise

Present your position fairly. As you present your views, avoid bandwagoning, appeals to ignorance, and oversimplification. If necessary, rewrite statements to eliminate errors in logic.

3 Sometimes logical fallacies make my essay unfair.

2 I need to remove many logical fallacies that make my essay unfair and confusing.

1 I need help recognizing and correcting logical fallacies.

■ Have I presented opposing ideas fairly?

You have presented opposing ideas fairly if you avoided these logical fallacies:

- **Either-or thinking** allows for no other viewpoints.
  Either we end all testing of cosmetics on animals, or we have no compassion.
  (It's unfair to assume opponents have no compassion.)

- **Slanted language** insults the person or position instead of arguing against it.
  Of course, the animal haters see no problem with cosmetics testing.
  (It's unfair to call opponents "animal haters.")

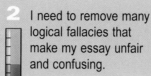

Exercise

Read the sentences below and identify the logical fallacy in each one.

1. People who support animal testing must love seeing chimps with rouge.
2. Either we ban cosmetics testing, or every animal in the world will be in danger.
3. If we don't stop animal testing right now, we'll face a "gorilla" war.
4. Heartless scientists should try to remember their childhoods—if they ever were children.

Revise

Be fair to opposing views. Read your essay and watch for either-or thinking and slanted language. Remove any you find.

Persuasive

Ideas
Slanted language is removed.

civil rights advocates
Of course, some ~~knee-jerk liberals~~ believe that random

testing for performance-enhancing drugs violates student

privacy rights. ~~These people care more about freedom than~~

~~about the health of the young people~~ However, if testing . . .

Revising ▪ for Organization

6 All of the parts of my essay work together to build a thoughtful, convincing position.	**5** My beginning and ending work together, and my middle paragraphs are in the best order.	**4** My beginning and ending work together, but my middle paragraphs need a clearer order.

When you revise for *organization,* you make sure your beginning and ending work together and your middle paragraphs are in the best possible order. The rubric strip above can guide your revision.

▪ Do my beginning and ending work together?

Your beginning and ending work together if they use the same persuasive strategy to convince the reader. Here are three strategies to make your beginning and ending work as a team:

1. Begin with a **problem** and end with your **solution**.
2. Begin with a **question** and end with your **answer**.
3. Begin with a **common belief** and end with your **specific position**.

Exercise

For each beginning and ending, indicate which strategy (1, 2, or 3) is used.

1. **Beginning:** Aside from diet, exercise, and lifestyle, what other factor most affects longevity?
   Ending: The other factor that affects longevity is money—and the access it provides to health care. This situation is unfair, and it needs to change.
2. **Beginning:** Every person in the United States has a heart, a stomach, and a brain, but over 45 million of those people do not have health care coverage.
   Ending: Government of the people, by the people, and for the people must make sure that all the people receive adequate health care.
3. **Beginning:** Health insurance companies, in order to protect their profitability, are free to deny coverage to those who most need it.
   Ending: A government-sponsored health care program is a more equitable way to ensure adequate health care for everyone.

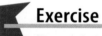
Revise

Check your beginning and ending. Make sure they work together persuasively. If they do not, revise using one of the strategies above.

3 My beginning and ending should work together better, and my middle paragraphs should be rearranged.

2 I need to create an effective beginning and ending and organize the middle paragraphs.

1 I need help understanding how to organize a persuasive essay.

■ Are my middle paragraphs in the best order?

Your middle paragraphs are in the best order if your reasons are organized by importance. Here are three strategies for organizing your middle paragraphs:

1. **Start strong.** Place your most important reason first, give other reasons next, and end with your answer to an objection.
2. **End strong.** Begin with your least important reason and build to the most important reason. Then answer an objection.
3. **Try 2-3-1.** Begin with your second most important reason, provide your least important reason, and finish with your strongest reason. Then answer an objection.

Exercise

Read the following four reasons for universal health care and decide on an order for them. Indicate which strategy you chose and why.

1. Lack of universal health care harms children most.
2. Though some people point to higher taxes for socialized medicine, U.S. citizens already pay exorbitant amounts for medical insurance.
3. Citizens of western nations with socialized medicine live an average of five years longer than citizens of the United States.
4. Universal health care would reduce infant mortality rates.

Revise

Check the order of your reasons. If your reasons do not have a clear order, use one of the strategies above to reorganize them.

Organization
Changes ensure that the beginning and ending work together.

The best way to reverse the current trend is to make
∧Random drug testing of high school athletes ~~should be~~ ^ℓ
mandatory. Testing can be done in a way that protects . . .

Persuasive

Revising ■ for Voice

6 My persuasive voice creates total confidence in my position.

5 My level of language is appropriate, and I use an anecdote to connect with my reader.

4 In most places, my level of language is appropriate, but I could use a more engaging anecdote.

When you revise for *voice,* you make sure you have used the correct level of language and have connected with your reader. Follow the rubric strip above.

■ Have I used the correct level of language?

You have used the correct level of language if you use a semiformal voice. Here are three levels of voice:

- **Formal voice** avoids contractions, humor, colloquial expressions, slang, and personal references to the writer.
- **Semiformal voice** occasionally uses contractions and appropriate humor, colloquial expressions, and personal references to the writer. A semiformal voice avoids slang.
- **Informal voice** is full of contractions, humor, colloquial expressions, slang, and many personal references to the writer.

Exercise

Read each sentence below and decide whether the level of language is formal, semiformal, or informal. Rewrite formal or informal sentences to create an appropriate level of language.

1. Governmental interventions into the privacy of citizens through such means as non-court-ordered wiretaps should be eliminated.
2. Those Washington bigwigs maybe got it in their brains they can do whatever they want, but they got a big-time wake-up call coming.
3. Private phone lines are called private for a reason, and the government doesn't have the right to listen in on every call I make to Aunt Millie.
4. I say it's time to toss the fat cats from Capitol Hill.

Revise

Check your level of language. Read your draft, making sure that you have used a semiformal level of language. Revise parts that sound too formal or informal.

3 In a number of places, my writing sounds too formal or informal, and I need to add an anecdote.

 2 My language level varies wildly, and I should find an anecdote to include.

 1 I need help understanding how to create an appropriate writing voice.

■ How can I connect with my audience?

One powerful way to connect with your audience is to use an anecdote. An anecdote is a little story that demonstrates a point. Anecdotes give the reader specific examples of the controversy's effects. To find an anecdote to include, ask yourself the following questions:

1. What experiences have I had that demonstrate the problem?

2. What experiences have people in my school or community had that show the effects of the controversy?

3. What stories in the news media provide examples that support my position?

Revise

Think of anecdotes. Consider adding a story to demonstrate your point in a way that connects with the reader.

Voice
An anecdote is added to connect with the reader.

In 2005, scandal rocked the world of professional baseball as allegations of the use of steroids and other performance-enhancing drugs hit the headlines. Responding to pressure by Congress, Major League Baseball instituted standards for testing players for the use of these drugs ("Baseball Battles"). However, the controversy extends far beyond the baseball diamond.

∧ Steroids and other drugs that quickly build muscle mass and make athletes stronger and faster have permeated virtually all major sports. For example, in the last five years, . . .

Persuasive

Revising ■ for Word Choice

6 My word choice makes a powerful case for my position.

5 I have used only the best modifiers, and I have avoided overusing words.

4 I have a few unnecessary modifiers, and I may overuse a word or two.

When you revise for *word choice,* you check to make sure you have used only the best modifiers and have avoided repeating certain words too often. The rubric strip above can help you revise.

■ Have I used only the best modifiers?

You have used only the best modifiers if you have cut those that do not help to clarify your meaning. Here are types of modifiers that you should remove from your writing:

- ■ "Waffle words" are modifiers that make your voice sound uncertain.
  It's kind of sad that government doesn't care very much about homelessness.

- ■ Redundant modifiers are words that aren't needed.
  The desperate plight of the indigent homeless is terribly depressing.

- ■ Strings of modifiers should be replaced with one strong modifier.
  The number of young, inexperienced, teenaged people who are homeless is rising.

Exercise

Rewrite each sentence below, removing the unnecessary modifiers.

1. Congressional legislators passed legal legislation mandating the "least restrictive" environment for mental psychiatric patients.
2. The law sort of emptied the nation's asylums since the least restrictive environment for people taking prescription mental-health medications was not within the walls of an asylum.
3. However, once the medicine ran out, the patients had a rough, difficult, troubling time surviving homeless on the streets.
4. Though some institutional asylums have gotten a bad, negative, unpleasant reputation, others are well run and kind of necessary.
5. Homelessness sometimes maybe results from a psychological mental condition, so the state should provide a home.

Revise

Check your modifiers. Read your essay, watching for "waffle words," redundant modifiers, and strings of modifiers. Cut any you find.

3 I need to cut many unnecessary modifiers and remove repeated words.

2 My modifiers do not make my ideas clear, and I have repeated many words.

1 I need help understanding how to improve word choice.

■ How can I avoid repeating the same word too often?

You can avoid repeating the same word over and over by using one of the following strategies:

- ■ Replace the word with an appropriate synonym.

  medicine   **prescription**   **pharmaceuticals**   **controlled substance**

- ■ Replace the word with a pronoun, making sure the antecedent is clear.

  it   **they**   **he**   **she**   **one**   **some**   **many**   **few**

- ■ Rewrite sentences to avoid the word.

  Instead of . . .   **When there's no money to buy** medications, **people will stop taking their** medications.

  Write . . .   **Without money to refill prescriptions, people will discontinue their medications.**

Write

Replace overused words. Read your work, watching for overused words. Replace them with synonyms or pronouns, or rewrite the sentence to eliminate the repetition.

Word Choice
Sentences are reworked to avoid repetition.

Also, because ~~student athletes know that~~ steroids and

other performance-enhancing drugs are illegal, most student

athletes realize that getting caught with ~~performance-~~ them

~~enhancing drugs~~ would mean immediate expulsion from

sports. As a result, student � athletes will do everything they

can to cover up their use. Peer pressure only reinforces . . .

Persuasive

Revising ▪ for Sentence Fluency

 6 My sentences spark the reader's interest in my position.

 5 I have effectively used long and short sentences in my essay.

4 I have used some short sentences for effect, but I should expand some sentences.

When you revise for *sentence fluency*, you check to see whether you have used long and short sentences effectively. The rubric strip above can guide your revision.

▪ When should I use long sentences?

You should use long sentences to convey a wealth of information about a complex issue. Consider this short sentence:

Stem-cell researchers conduct experiments.

This sentence answers *who* (stem-cell researchers) and *what* (conduct experiments), but it does not provide other details the reader needs, such as *where, why,* and *how:*

1. *Where?* in states where it is allowed (prepositional phrase and subordinate clause)
2. *How?* by injecting undifferentiated cells into damaged areas (prepositional phrases)
3. *Why?* to reconstruct tissues (infinitive phrase)

These answers can be added to the original sentence to create a cumulative sentence that is full of detail. (For more about cumulative sentences, see page **750**.)

In states where it is allowed, stem-cell researchers conduct experiments by injecting undifferentiated cells into damaged areas to reconstruct tissues.

Revise

Create cumulative sentences. Read your writing and watch for short sentences that do not provide enough detail. For each sentence, answer the following questions, using prepositional phrases, infinitive phrases, and subordinate clauses.

1. Where? 3. How?
2. When? 4. Why?

Combine some of your answers with the original question to create a cumulative sentence.

3 I need to expand a number of sentences and use short sentences to punctuate my ideas.

2 My sentences have little rhythm, and I need to use long and short sentences more effectively.

1 I need help understanding how to create sentence fluency.

■ When should I use short sentences?

You should use short sentences to make an important point. When constructed carefully, short sentences pack a punch—and improve sentence rhythm. Note the power of the short sentences in the following paragraph.

> Both sides of the stem-cell research controversy believe they hold the moral high ground. Those who oppose stem-cell research feel they are advocating for the tens of thousands of frozen embryos that scientists may use in their research. Those who favor stem-cell research feel they are advocating for the millions of people living with neuromuscular diseases. Both sides are correct. Albert Schweitzer once said, "It is good to maintain and further life; it is bad to damage and destroy life." These are wise words. The best use of stem-cell research maintains and furthers life on both ends of the scale—using adult instead of embryonic stem cells.

Revise

Employ short sentences. Read your work, carefully, looking for places where you want to make a strong point. Insert a short sentence that makes the point.

Sentence Fluency
A cumulative sentence and a short sentence improve flow.

, causing unprovoked rage and violence among users
In addition, these drugs can affect mental health.

Sometimes the mood swings lead to depression and
That fact makes these drugs doubly deadly.
even suicide. Fortunately, if treatment is provided soon

enough, most of these health issues can be avoided or

reversed—another reason for supporting mandatory testing

("Anabolic").

    Of course, some civil rights advocates believe that

random drug testing for performance-enhancing drugs . . .

Persuasive

Revising ■ Improve your writing.

Revise

Check your revising. On a piece of paper, write the numbers 1 to 12. If you answer "yes" to a question below, put a check mark next to that number. If not, continue to work on that part of your essay.

Revising Checklist

Ideas

_____ 1. Do I state my position clearly?

_____ 2. Have I effectively supported each topic sentence?

_____ 3. Have I fairly presented my position and avoided logical fallacies?

Organization

_____ 4. Do my beginning and ending work together well?

_____ 5. Have I chosen the best order for my middle paragraphs?

_____ 6. Are my reasons connected logically?

Voice

_____ 7. Have I used the right level of language?

_____ 8. Does my voice connect with my audience?

Word Choice

_____ 9. Have I used the best modifiers?

_____ 10. Have I avoided repeating words too often?

Sentence Fluency

_____ 11. Have I used longer sentences to provide a wealth of information?

_____ 12. Have I used shorter sentences to deliver precise points?

Revise

Make a clean copy. When you are finished with your revision, make a clean copy of your article for editing.

Editing

Now that you have finished revising your essay of argumentation, you are ready to edit for conventions: punctuation, capitalization, spelling, and grammar.

Keys to Effective Editing

1. Use a dictionary, a thesaurus, and the "Proofreader's Guide" in the back of this book to check your writing.

2. Mark corrections using the editing and proofreading marks on the inside back cover.

3. Edit on a clean revised copy of your essay.

4. Check for words or phrases that may be confusing to the reader. Replace them to improve your essay's clarity.

5. Check for errors in punctuation, capitalization, spelling, and grammar. Then either enter the changes on your computer file or write a new handwritten copy that includes the changes.

Persuasive

Editing ■ for Conventions

When you edit for *conventions,* you correct punctuation, capitalization, spelling, and grammar errors. The rubric strip above can guide your editing.

■ How can I check subject-verb agreement?

Check subject-verb agreement by making sure subjects and verbs have the same number. If the subject is singular, the verb must be singular. If the subject is plural, the verb must be plural.

> The **doctrine** of preemptive war **has** many detractors.
> **Critics argue** that preemptive war is like punishing a person before any crime has been committed.

Compound Subjects

If the compound subjects are joined by *and,* use a plural verb.

> The **president *and* the secretary** of defense **contend** that it is better to preempt an attack than retaliate after one has taken place.

If the subjects are joined by *or* or *nor,* match the verb to the nearest subject.

> Even so, neither **diplomacy *nor* war has eliminated** terrorism.

Indefinite Pronouns

Some indefinite pronouns are singular: *each, either, neither, one, everybody, another, anybody, everyone, nobody, everything, somebody,* and *someone.*

> **Nobody wants** war.

Some indefinite pronouns are plural: *both, few, many,* and *several.*

> **Many believe** that war is necessary to stop tyranny.

Some indefinite pronouns are singular or plural, depending on the object in the prepositional phrase that follows the pronoun: *all, any, most, none,* and *some.*

> **Most** of the **world participates** in the war on terrorism.
> **Most** of the **nations,** however, **oppose** the doctrine of preemptive war.

Edit

Check agreement. Read your position essay and check for the agreement of your subjects and verbs. Make any necessary corrections.

3 I need to correct several errors in my paper because they confuse the reader.

2 I need to correct many errors because they make my essay difficult to read.

1 I need help finding errors and making corrections.

■ How can I check pronoun-antecedent agreement?

To check pronoun-antecedent agreement, make sure pronouns have the same number and gender as the nouns they replace.

Incorrect: Each politician **should make** their **position clear.**
(*Politician* is singular, but *their* is plural.)

Incorrect: Each politician **should make** his **position clear.**
(The word *his* makes a sexist assumption about the gender of the politician.)

Correct: Each politician **should make** his or her **position clear.**
(The singular *politician* needs singular male and female pronouns.)

Correct: Politicians **should make** their **positions clear.**
(*Politicians* and *their* are both plural.)

Exercise

Rewrite each sentence below, correcting the pronoun-antecedent errors.

1. Every member of Congress must vote his conscience.
2. Each voter must cherish their right to vote.
3. The representative from each district should tell where they stand.

Edit

Check pronoun-antecedent agreement. Read your essay carefully, checking to make sure that pronouns and antecedents agree in number and gender. Make any necessary corrections.

Conventions
Pronoun-antecedent errors are corrected.

Random drug testing is a way of publicly telling athletes that adults care about what students do in ~~his or her~~ *their* private lives and want to see ~~him or her~~ *them* make good decisions.

Editing ■ Check for conventions.

Edit

Check your editing. On a piece of paper, write the numbers 1 to 10. If you can answer "yes," to a question below, put a check mark after that number. If you can't, continue to edit for that convention.

Editing Checklist

Conventions

PUNCTUATION

_____ **1.** Do I use end punctuation after all my sentences?

_____ **2.** Do I use commas after long introductory phrases and clauses?

_____ **3.** Have I correctly punctuated quotations?

CAPITALIZATION

_____ **4.** Do I start all my sentences with capital letters?

_____ **5.** Do I capitalize all proper nouns and adjectives?

SPELLING

_____ **6.** Have I spelled all words correctly?

_____ **7.** Have I checked for commonly misused pairs?

GRAMMAR

_____ **8.** Do my subjects and verbs agree in number?

_____ **9.** Do my pronouns and antecedents agree in number and gender?

_____ **10.** Have I avoided double subjects?

■ Add a title.

After your editing is complete, add a title that engages your reader and sums up the content of your essay. Here are a few ways to create an effective essay title.

- Call the reader to action: **Test for Performance Drugs Now**
- Take a position: **Performance Drug Testing Just Makes Sense**
- Be creative: **Stop Steroids Cold**

Publishing ■ Share your essay.

The purpose of an essay of argumentation is to take a position on a controversial issue and defend the position using ideas and details. Once you've done this, it's time to share what you've written.

Publish

Format your final copy. To format a handwritten essay, use the guidelines below or follow your teacher's instructions. (If you are using a computer, see pages **91–95**.) Make a clean copy and carefully proofread it.

■ Focus on presentation.

- Write neatly using blue or black ink.
- Place your name in the upper left corner of page 1.
- Skip a line and center your title; skip another line and start your essay.
- Indent every paragraph and leave a one-inch margin on all four sides.
- Write your last name and the page number in the upper right corner of every page after page 1.

Publish Your Essay

Check the guidelines of local newspapers to see which ones might be interested in your essay. Format your paper according to the guidelines, write a cover letter (or an e-mail message) introducing yourself, and send in your essay.

Self-Publish Your Work

Use a personal computer to format your essay. Add photographs or illustrations. Work with the layout and design until you feel your essay is clear and compelling. Then print copies of your work and mail them to relatives or post copies on school or library bulletin boards. (Get permission first.)

Stage a Debate

Find a classmate who takes the position opposite to the one expressed in your essay. Invite him or her to prepare an essay stating this position. Then stage a debate by reading your essays publicly. Invite a panel of students and teachers to judge which essay makes its point most effectively.

Persuasive

Rubric for Persuasive Writing

Use this rubric to assess your persuasive writing using the six traits.

6	**5**	**4**
Ideas		
The position is convincingly presented and supported; it compels the reader to act.	The position is supported with logical reasons; an important objection is countered.	Most of the reasons support the writer's position. An objection is addressed.
Organization		
All parts of the essay work together to build a very thoughtful, convincing position.	The opening states the position, the middle provides clear support, and the ending reinforces the position.	Most parts of the essay are organized adequately except for one part.
Voice		
The writer's voice is completely confident, knowledgeable, and convincing.	The writer's voice is persuasive, knowledgeable, and respectful.	The writer respects the audience but needs to sound more persuasive or knowledgeable.
Word Choice		
The writer's choice of words makes a powerful case.	The writer's word choice helps persuade the reader.	The writer avoids unneeded modifiers but needs to remove some repetition.
Sentence Fluency		
The sentences flow smoothly throughout the strong essay.	Variety is seen in the types of sentences used and in their beginnings.	Variety is seen in most of the sentences.
Conventions		
The writing is error free.	Grammar and punctuation errors are few. The reader is not distracted by the errors.	Distracting grammar and punctuation errors are seen in a few sentences.

3	**2**	**1**
More supporting reasons and a more convincing response to an objection are needed.	A clearer position statement is needed. Better support for the position must be provided.	A new position statement and reasons are needed.
Some parts of the essay need to be reorganized.	The beginning, middle, and ending run together.	The organization is unclear and incomplete.
The writer's voice needs to be more persuasive and respectful.	The writer's voice sounds too emotional and unconvincing.	The writer needs to learn about voice in persuasive writing.
The writer needs to change modifiers and remove some repetition.	The words do not create a clear message. Some words are repeated.	Word choice for persuasive writing has not been considered.
More variety is needed in the beginnings or kinds of sentences used.	Too many sentences are worded in the same way.	Sentence fluency has not been considered.
There are a number of errors that will confuse the reader.	Frequent errors make the essay difficult to read.	Nearly every sentence contains errors.

Persuasive

Evaluating an Essay of Argumentation

Read the essay of argumentation below and focus on its strengths and weaknesses. Then read the student self-assessment on the next page. (**The student essay below contains some errors.**)

A Free Media Helps Us—Even in War Time

During recent years, the U.S. Government limited the ability of the media to report freely from the war zone. Instead, reporters were embedded, or placed within selected military units, where their movements were controlled. Free speech advocates decried the move to limit the reporters' access, but the government insisted that the efforts were necessary both to protect reporters' safety and to avoid leaking information that might be valuable to the enemy. However, even during wartime, the benefits of a free media outweigh the risks.

At a time of national crisis, people need to be able to trust the government. If government manipulates the media, then this trust can be lost. Any number of military secrets must be kept during war time, but the release of general news information does not compromise military intelligence. Denying citizens basic information about the conduct of the war not only denies them a right to information that directly affects them but creates a suspicion of the government that can weaken the country.

In addition, a free media helps deliver the information the citizens need to make decisions about the conduct of the war. While the war itself is prosecuted by our armed forces, those very forces are drawn from the ranks of citizens. And while the decision to go to war and even continue to fight is made by government, the government acts at the will of the people. If the people are denied the information they need, the input they provide to their representatives about the war will be inaccurate, and the government will not be able to express the people's will.

Most critically, the freedom of the media is one on which our system of government was founded. The media of colonial American helped create the uprising against tyranny that led to the formation of our free nation, and the Constitution guaranteed the free press in the First Amendment. Even today, media freedom helps protect the people against a government that may act in the best interests of a few instead of that of the vast majority.

Some might argue that during wartime, we must allow the government to decide what information we can see and hear, and that the free flow of information compromises our battlefield plans.

However, there has been little evidence that the media has ever compromised a military operation. In fact, media has often informed the public of the results of military operations, providing the public with critical information about the conduct of the war.

Our soldiers fight to defend our freedoms, including freedom of the press. A free press during wartime gives citizens valuable information without compromising military secrecy. Free reporting on the war might even enable our nation to avoid some costly political and military mistakes. So support a free media during wartime—your actions might even save a soldier's life.

Student Self-Assessment

Persuasive Rubric Checklist

Title: A Free Media Helps Us—Even in War Time
Writer: Cole Margolis

4 **Ideas**
- Does my essay include a clear position statement?
- Do I support my position with reasons and details?
- Do I avoid logic errors?

5 **Organization**
- Does the beginning introduce the topic and state the position?
- Does the middle support my position?
- Does my ending restate the position and offer a final thought?

5 **Voice**
- Do I use the right level of language?
- Do I connect with the reader?

4 **Word Choice**
- Have I used only necessary modifiers?
- Have I avoided repeating words too often?

4 **Sentence Fluency**
- Do I use long sentences effectively?
- Do I use short sentences effectively?

4 **Conventions**
- Have I avoided most errors in punctuation, capitalization, spelling, and grammar?

OVERALL COMMENTS:

I think my essay does a good job of explaining the controversy and arguing for my position.

I use the right language level and engage my reader. I should have included some synonyms for the word "media" and used more sentence variety.

I guess I used an appeal to ignorance in the last middle paragraph.

My essay includes a few errors, so I should have proofread one more time.

Persuasive

Review your essay. Rate your essay and write comments that explain why you gave yourself the scores you did.

Reflecting on Your Writing

Now that you have completed your essay of argumentation, take some time to reflect on your writing experience. On a separate sheet of paper, complete each sentence below.

My Essay of Argumentation

1. The strongest part of my essay is . . .

2. The part that still needs work is . . .

3. The prewriting activity that worked best for me was . . .

4. The main thing I learned about writing an essay of argumentation is . . .

5. In my next essay of argumentation, I would like to . . .

6. One question I still have about writing an essay of argumentation is . . .

Persuasive Writing
Writing an Essay of Evaluation

In popular magazines, you're sure to find articles that explore current trends, new products, businesses, organizations, and so on. An article in one magazine may explore a new trend in health and fitness. An article in another magazine may assess the effectiveness of a nonprofit group. These articles usually evaluate the topic's value and significance, its strengths and weaknesses, and its overall place in the scheme of things.

In this chapter, you will read a sample essay in which a student evaluates a particular elective class. Then you will write your own essay of evaluation. Remember to look at both the pros and cons of the topic so you can develop a thoughtful, convincing piece of writing.

Writing Guidelines

Subject: A current trend, product, or group
Form: Essay of evaluation
Purpose: To present a thoughtful assessment
Audience: Classmates

"Whatever is popular deserves attention."
—James Mackintosh

Essay of Evaluation

An essay of evaluation tells the value of something. It describes the subject and gives an opinion about its worth, providing details to support the opinion. The following essay evaluates a senior-level class.

Beginning
The beginning introduces the topic and provides a thesis statement (underlined).

Middle
Each middle paragraph describes part of the topic and tells what is good (and bad) about it.

To Act or Not to Act

Only one class at Greendale High School lets students dress up like singing candlesticks, carve rocks from foam, and play double-blind freeze. The class is Drama and Theater, which is taught by Mr. Maclay. But it isn't all fun and games. The course also includes a serious study of plays throughout time and analysis of how plays are put together. <u>Drama and Theater begins by pouring knowledge into students' heads and ends by requiring students to pour out that knowledge onstage.</u>

The first half of the course is devoted to drama, which is the study of the history, variety, and structure of plays. The course covers plays that range from ancient to modern, from classics by playwrights like Shakespeare and O'Neill to obscure and experimental plays. Students learn to interpret drama, which is an essential skill for anyone in theater. Actors and directors must interpret drama to give an authentic performance; technical people must interpret drama to design effective sets, lighting, and sound; and theater managers and promoters must interpret drama to schedule shows and attract audiences.

The second half of the course focuses on theater—which is the art of putting on a play. Students must complete projects in many areas of theater production: lighting, set and costume design, makeup, stage management, directing, and acting. This requirement means that everyone learns what it is like for the other people involved in a production. Often, actors and crews hang together and exclude other groups. Mr. Maclay told us some great horror stories about techie-actor wars from shows he was in. By the time of our final production, our class was a close-knit theater group that worked well together under stress.

The best feature of the class, though, is Mr. Maclay himself, whose philosophy of teaching and acting is expressed in the words of Polonius: "To thine own self be true" (*Hamlet* 1.3.78). Mr. Maclay has appeared in famous regional theaters like the Guthrie in Minneapolis and has performed with prestigious theater companies such as Steppenwolf in Chicago. He has a wealth of knowledge and stories that he uses as he teaches. For instance, instead of simply saying that mistakes happen onstage, Mr. Maclay tells how he once tripped on his coat and almost knocked Nicole Parker of *MAD TV* off the stage when they were in a summer production of *The Sound of Music*. His stories are educational, entertaining, and inspirational. Mr. Maclay expects a great deal out of himself and his students, and he inspires everyone to rise to the challenge.

Sometimes, however, Mr. Maclay's ambitions exceed his students' abilities. For example, he places too much emphasis on advanced acting techniques. Chekhov, Meisner, and Stanislavsky may have wonderful methods for acting, but, to rephrase Polonius: "Though this be method, yet there is madness in it" (*Hamlet* 2.2.206). Mr. Maclay requires each student to memorize a Shakespearean soliloquy and recite it for the class. After the students nervously deliver their speeches, Mr. Maclay calls them up again to redeliver the soliloquies in different ways: as fast as possible, as loud as possible, sarcastically, with gestures for each word, like cartoon characters. Few students can rise to this challenge.

Overall, Drama and Theater is a terrific, fascinating course. Mr. Maclay expects great things out of his students, and most often students surprise themselves by meeting or exceeding his expectations. Even when Mr. Maclay pushes students beyond their abilities, they realize how much more they need to learn. He teaches his students that "We are such stuff as dreams are made on" (*The Tempest* 4.1.156).

Ending
The ending sums up the evaluation and leaves the reader with a final thought.

Persuasive

 Respond to the Reading. Answer the following questions.

Ideas (1) What is the difference between drama and theater? (2) What sorts of details does the writer include to make the difference obvious?

Organization (3) Which paragraphs deal with the positive aspects of the class? (4) Which paragraph deals with the negative aspects?

Voice & Word Choice (5) How do examples, anecdotes, and quotations affect the writer's voice?

Prewriting ▪ Select a topic.

The purpose of an essay of evaluation is to assess the value or worth of a timely topic. Sam began by listing potential topics that interested him.

Topics List

School
- student council
- community service requirements
- drama skills class *
- language lab

Community
- Harbor Fest
- crime watch program
- Gritty Coffeehouse
- new supercenter

Popular Trends
- latest MP3 player
- blogging
- American Idol
- energy drinks

At first Sam thought he would assess the impact of the new supercenter in his community, but he wasn't sure that his classmates would be interested in this topic. So, instead, he decided to focus on a school-related topic—the drama skills class in his school.

Prewrite

Choose your topic. List possible topics related to school, community, and popular trends. (Try to list at least three topics under each category.) Then put an asterisk next to the topic that you want to write about.

▪ Focus on the traits.

Ideas The goal of an essay of evaluation is to present an insightful assessment of a topic. To be insightful, you will need to consider all aspects of your topic (significance, strengths, weaknesses, and so on).

■ Gather and organize details.

Once you have chosen the topic, you need to gather and organize information for your essay. To plan his essay, Sam used a pro-con chart, listing the strengths (pluses) and weaknesses (minuses) of the Drama and Theater class.

Pro-Con Chart

Pro	Con
Learning about great plays throughout history	Too many methods of acting
Working in all areas of play production	Too challenging sometimes
Mr. Maclay's skills, stories, and challenges	

Collect your information. Use a pro-con chart to collect information for your essay. Try to include at least two or three main points under each label.

■ Write a position statement.

A thesis states the focus of your essay and guides your writing. An effective thesis statement usually takes a stand or expresses a specific feeling about or feature of your topic. Use the following formula to form your thesis.

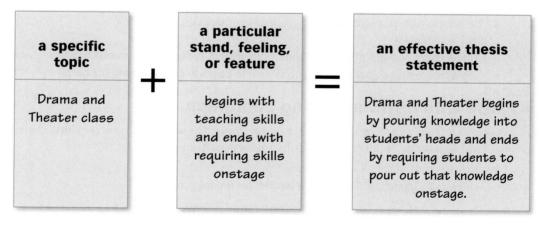

a specific topic		a particular stand, feeling, or feature		an effective thesis statement
Drama and Theater class	**+**	begins with teaching skills and ends with requiring skills onstage	**=**	Drama and Theater begins by pouring knowledge into students' heads and ends by requiring students to pour out that knowledge onstage.

Write your thesis statement. Use the information above as a guide to create your thesis.

Persuasive

Writing ■ Create your first draft.

As you write your essay, use your planning from the previous page and refer to the following guidelines.

■ Write your beginning paragraph.

Your beginning paragraph should introduce your topic in an interesting way and state your thesis.

- ■ Capture your reader's attention in the first sentence.

  Only one class at Greendale High School lets students dress up like singing candlesticks, carve rocks from foam, and play double-blind freeze.

- ■ Provide background information and end with your thesis statement.

  Drama and Theater begins by pouring knowledge into students' heads and ends by requiring students to pour out that knowledge onstage.

■ Write your middle paragraphs.

The middle paragraphs should develop the main points in your evaluation. (See your pro-con chart.) Devote a separate paragraph to each main point. Organize these paragraphs in a logical way—perhaps starting with the "pros" and ending with the "cons."

- ■ Provide a topic sentence for each paragraph.

  The first half of the course is devoted to drama, which is the study of the history, variety, and structure of plays.

- ■ Develop each paragraph with supporting details, examples, and anecdotes.

  The course covers plays that range from ancient to modern, from classics by playwrights like Shakespeare and O'Neill to obscure and experimental plays.

■ Finish with a strong ending paragraph.

Your ending paragraph should restate your thesis, summarize your main points, and leave the reader with a final important thought.

- ■ Summarize your evaluation.

  Overall, Drama and Theater is a terrific, fascinating course.

- ■ Provide a closing thought that will remain with the reader.

  He teaches his students "We are such stuff as dreams are made on"
  (The Tempest 4.1.156).

Write

Write your first draft. Use the guidelines above and your prewriting work to help you complete your first draft.

Revising ■ Improve your first draft.

When you revise your first draft, you clarify your ideas, check your organization, and improve your voice. The guidelines below can help you revise.

Revising Checklist

Ideas

_____ **1.** Do I clearly introduce my topic?
_____ **2.** Have I stated a thesis about the topic?
_____ **3.** Have I effectively evaluated the topic?

Organization

_____ **4.** Does my essay have a strong beginning, middle, and ending?
_____ **5.** Have I presented my points in a logical order?

Voice

_____ **6.** Is my voice confident and convincing?
_____ **7.** Do I avoid being overly emotional?

Word Choice

_____ **8.** Do I clearly explain unfamiliar terms and concepts?

Sentence Fluency

_____ **9.** Do I use a variety of sentence lengths and beginnings?

Revise

Revise your first draft. Carefully review your essay using the checklist above. Make the necessary improvements.

■ Add a title.

A good title introduces your topic and catches the reader's interest. Here are some different ways to approach writing a title.

■ Use a line from the evaluation: **Pouring In and Pouring Out**
■ Be clever: **To Act or Not to Act**
■ Create an interesting rhythm: **Fun and Games and More**

Persuasive

Editing ▪ Check for conventions.

After revising your essay, you'll need to edit it for conventions: punctuation, capitalization, spelling, and grammar. If your conventions are correct, the reader will be more likely to respect your evaluation.

Editing Checklist

Conventions

PUNCTUATION

_____ **1.** Have I ended my sentences with the correct punctuation?

_____ **2.** Have I used commas, semicolons, and colons correctly?

_____ **3.** Have I punctuated quotations correctly?

CAPITALIZATION

_____ **4.** Did I capitalize the first word in every sentence?

_____ **5.** Did I capitalize all proper nouns and adjectives?

SPELLING

_____ **6.** Did I spell all my words correctly?

_____ **7.** Did I double-check for words that my spell-checker might miss?

GRAMMAR

_____ **8.** Did I use the correct forms of verbs (*he saw,* not *he seen*)?

_____ **9.** Do my subjects and verbs agree in number?

_____ **10.** Do my pronouns agree with their antecedents?

Edit

Edit your essay. Use the checklist above to edit for conventions. Then prepare a final copy of your essay of evaluation and proofread it.

Publishing ▪ Share your work.

It's time to make your ideas public—by sharing them. Encourage readers to respond to your ideas.

Publish

Publish your essay of evaluation. Choose one of these methods.

▪ Submit your essay to your school or local newspaper.

▪ Post your essay on a Web site.

Writing for Assessment
Responding to Persuasive Prompts

Sometimes it's necessary to create and present a persuasive argument quickly. For example, imagine that you're trying to convince your parents to let your borrow their car to drive to the home of a friend in another town. Your parents are reluctant, but you feel you have good reasons to support your argument. Creating an organized argument quickly may mean the difference between visiting your friend and staying home for the evening.

Writing tests are another situation in which you must organize and present an argument in a relatively short period of time. After reading a prompt, you'll need to choose a position; structure your argument; and write, revise, and edit your response—all within a predetermined time limit. This chapter will show you how to respond to a persuasive writing prompt quickly and effectively.

Writing Guidelines

Subject: A persuasive prompt
Form: Response essay
Purpose: To demonstrate competence
Audience: Instructor

"Opinions cannot survive if one
has no chance to fight for them."

—Thomas Mann

Prewriting ■ Analyze a persuasive prompt.

To respond to a persuasive prompt, begin by analyzing the prompt. A thorough analysis of the prompt will give you your topic, the form of your response, your role in writing, your expected audience, and your purpose for writing. To analyze a prompt quickly and effectively, use the STRAP questions:

<u>S</u>ubject: What topic should I write about (policy, proposal, decision)?

<u>T</u>ype: What form of writing should I create (essay, letter, editorial, article, report)?

<u>R</u>ole: What role should I assume as the writer (student, son or daughter, friend, employee, citizen)?

<u>A</u>udience: To whom am I writing (teacher, parents, classmates, employer, official)?

<u>P</u>urpose: What is the goal of my writing (persuade, respond, evaluate, tell, describe)?

Subject
Type
Role
Audience
Purpose

In response to problems with traffic on the roads in your community, a council member has proposed assessing a $50 fee on each car. The money collected will be used to reduce the cost of local bus service. As an ***automobile owner who commutes to work by bus,*** write a letter to the city council to persuade them to vote for or against this new fee.

Note: The following key words are often found in persuasive prompts: *convince. argue, defend, persuade.*

Try It!

Analyze this prompt by answering the STRAP questions.

A group of legislators in your state has proposed a new law that would require all children under the age of 12 to wear helmets while cycling. As someone with siblings or neighbors of that age, write an editorial for your local newspaper encouraging other legislators to support or oppose the law.

Prewriting ▪ Plan your response.

After answering the STRAP questions, you need to begin planning your persuasive response. One of the following graphic organizers can help you to plan your response quickly.

T-Bar

Pro	Con

Quick List

1. First Point
   —Detail
   —Example
2. Second Point
   —Detail
   —Example
3. Third Point
   —Detail
   —Example

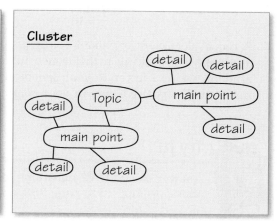

Cluster

▪ Choose a side.

Persuasive prompts often ask you to choose one side or the other of an argument. In order to do this, you'll need to consider the ideas on both sides first, and then choose the side with the strongest reasons behind it.

One way to thoroughly examine both sides of an argument is to use a graphic organizer. Placing the "pros" and "cons" side by side will make it easier for you to determine the stronger side.

Considering both sides of an argument will also help you to find an important objection to respond to. By explaining how the objection is wrong or weak, you will demonstrate that you have considered both sides of the issue; this can strengthen your argument.

Prewrite

Use a graphic organizer. Reread the persuasive prompts on page 268. Choose one and use a graphic organizer to plan your response to the prompt.

Tip

One secret to success with writing prompts is careful time management. For example, if you have 45 minutes to respond, use the first 5 minutes to analyze the prompt and plan your response, the last 5 minutes to revise and edit your response, and the 35 minutes in between for writing your response.

Persuasive

Writing ■ Respond to a prompt.

Once you have answered the STRAP questions and planned your response using a graphic organizer, you can begin writing.

Sample Persuasive Prompt

A recent documentary about young people highlighted ways that high school students are making a difference in their communities. As a high school student, write a letter to your school newspaper that invites students to get involved in a positive way in your community.

Try It!

Answer the STRAP questions for the above prompt. (See page **268**.)

Sample Response

Dear Editor:

Beginning
The beginning paragraph draws the reader in to the letter.

How would you like to help save lives without spending years training to be a doctor, a nurse, or a firefighter? You can make a life-changing difference, and it won't take much of your time. I'm talking about giving blood.

While surgery, accidents, and illness can all bring someone to the point of death, a transfusion can change that outcome. In addition, modern medicine is able to separate blood into its components: platelets, plasma, stem cells, and so on. So someone who is a hemophiliac (a person whose blood lacks enough clotting potential) and a person being treated for cancer can both be helped. Stem-cell therapies are being used to treat a variety of illnesses. One donation of blood may actually save a number of lives because of the many ways blood can be used.

Middle
The first middle paragraphs express reasons for supporting the position.

The process of giving blood only takes about 20 minutes. Snacks and juice are provided at the donation site. You need a valid ID and a parental permission slip if you are under 18. Students must be at least 16 years old, weigh at least 110 pounds, and be in good health.

James Loclin, a senior, said, "I would like to give blood, but I am on medication." There are both tests and restrictions in place to keep the nation's blood supply safe. Those who have had a tattoo or a body piercing (not including ears) are not allowed to give blood for one year owing to the risk of blood infections with those activities. Those on medication or those who have traveled abroad should talk to the technicians to find out if they can safely donate blood.

The final middle paragraph cites objections and responds to them.

You may be someone who would like to give blood, but you fear the process. You may worry about getting AIDS or just hate needles. You may think you'll feel faint or be at risk until your blood supply is back to normal. The donor program has anticipated all these concerns. The needles used are new and sterile, so you won't contract AIDS or any other blood-borne disease. The needles are also extremely sharp and generally cause little discomfort. Finally, about one pint of blood is taken, so your blood supply is not drastically reduced. Just remember, your discomfort will be outweighed by a lifesaving gift.

Ending
The ending restates the writer's position and makes a call to action.

The student council supports the annual blood drive. Let's all turn out to surpass the goal of 150 pints. The donation center will be in the school gym on Friday, September 20, from 8:00 a.m. to 2:00 p.m. I gave last year. It felt great to help someone I didn't even know. Get in line early to give the gift of life.

Sincerely,

Veronica Heath

Persuasive

Write

Respond to a persuasive prompt. Use the prompt you chose on page 268, your answers to the STRAP questions, and your graphic organizer to write a response. Finish your response in the time allotted by your teacher.

Revising ■ Improve your response.

Before you begin a writing test, find out if you are allowed to make changes to your draft copy. If changes are allowed, make them as clear and neat as possible. Use the STRAP questions to guide your revisions.

> **Subject:** Have I responded to the topic of the prompt? Do all my main points support my position?
>
> **Type:** Have I responded in the form requested (essay, letter, editorial, article, report)?
>
> **Role:** Have I assumed the role called for in the prompt?
>
> **Audience:** Have I addressed the audience identified in the prompt?
>
> **Purpose:** Does my response accomplish the goal indicated in the prompt?

Revise

Improve your work. Carefully review your response, using the STRAP questions above as your guide. Within the time allowed, make changes to revise your response.

Editing ■ Check your response.

After revising, be sure to read through your response one final time. Correct any errors in conventions: punctuation, capitalization, spelling, and grammar.

Editing Checklist

Conventions

_____ **1.** Have I used end punctuation for every sentence?

_____ **2.** Have I capitalized all proper nouns and the first word of every sentence?

_____ **3.** Have I spelled all words correctly?

_____ **4.** Have I made sure my subjects and verbs agree?

_____ **5.** Have I used the right words (*to/too/two, there/their/they're*)?

Edit

Check your conventions. Read through your response one final time. In the time allowed, neatly correct any errors in punctuation, capitalization, spelling, and grammar.

Persuasive Writing on Tests

Before you write . . .

- **Analyze the prompt.**
  Use the STRAP questions. Remember that a persuasive prompt asks you to use facts and logical reasons to persuade or convince.

- **Plan your response.**
  Carefully allot the time you will spend on planning, writing, revising, and checking conventions. Use a graphic organizer to gather your details and organize your response.

As you write . . .

- **Stay focused.**
  Keep your main idea or argument in mind as you write. All your reasons should clearly support your argument.

- **Answer a significant objection.**
  Make your argument stronger by responding to a likely objection.

- **Summarize your argument.**
  In the final paragraph, summarize your opinion and supporting reasons to make a final plea to the reader.

After you have written a first draft . . .

- **Revise and edit.**
  Use the STRAP questions to revise your response. Correct any errors in punctuation, capitalization, spelling, and grammar.

Try It!

Choose one of the prompts below. First, analyze it using the STRAP questions. Then use a graphic organizer to gather details and plan. Finally, write, revise, and edit your response.

- Swordfish populations are declining due to overfishing. Local restaurants are campaigning for people to give swordfish a break by choosing other fish on the menu. Write a letter to the local newspaper editor asking people to support or oppose this campaign.

- Many people in this country do not get enough exercise. Yet exercise is known to help maintain an appropriate weight, reduce the risk of heart disease, and improve general health. As a health-care professional, write an essay for a fitness Web site that seeks to convince people to exercise more.

Response to Literature

Response to Literature
Analyzing a Theme

Plays are among the earliest forms of art. Before television and film, before theaters and amphitheaters, before writing itself, plays fired the imagination of ancient people. The same cave dwellers who created charcoal murals of great hunts probably acted out those hunts around the campfire. Some plays entertained. Others enlightened. But almost all plays helped people to explain the meaning of life and how their world worked.

Plays have always had a profound effect on viewers. The ancient Greeks said that plays create *catharsis*—literally washing the soul. Tragedies allow audiences to experience terrible events without being destroyed, and comedies allow audiences to laugh and forget their troubles. People keep going to plays because they make life better.

In this chapter, you will learn how to analyze a play, beginning with the characters, setting, and plot. Through these basic elements, you will discover the meaning—or theme—of the play. Then you will write an analysis that will deepen your understanding of this ancient art form.

Writing Guidelines

Subject: A play
Form: Literary analysis
Purpose: To analyze a main theme
Audience: Classmates

"A good drama critic is one who perceives what is happening in the theater of his time. A great drama critic also perceives what is not happening."

—Kenneth Tynan

Writing Warm-Up ■ Think about drama.

Almost all plays contain the same elements: characters, conflict, action, dialogue, plot, and theme. Even TV dramas have these elements. To better understand the basic elements of one particular play, a student named Sa'id filled out a play map.

Play Map

Title:	Party at the End of the World
Playwright:	Dedra Runningcloud
Characters:	Jonas Jenkins (a drifter prophet), Sheriff Smith, Lyndsey Peck (owner of the Eel Creek General Store)
Setting:	Eel Creek, Alaska, a remote village above the Arctic Circle
Conflict:	Jonas Jenkins says the world will end, but most people won't believe him.
Plot:	
Event 1:	Sheriff Smith tries but fails to run Jonas off.
Event 2:	Jonas meets Lindsey in the general store.
Event 3:	Jonas's dire predictions start to come true.
Climax:	Lyndsey holds an "End of the World Party" on the rooftop of the general store, and Jonas and the others who attend see a spectacular meteor shower. It seems the world is really coming to an end.
Resolution:	The sun rises on a new day, proving Jonas wrong, except that he had passed away during the party. He had predicted the end of the world for himself.
Theme:	Look at life through a wide-angle lens.

Write

Fill out a play map. Think of a play (or a TV drama—if your teacher allows it) you have recently seen or read and fill out a play map. Do your best to remember each element of the play.

Writing an Analysis Paragraph

Using his play map, Sa'id wrote a one-paragraph analysis of the play. Note that his analysis has the following parts:

- A **topic sentence** naming the play and playwright and summarizing the analysis
- **Body sentences** describing the characters, setting, and plot and indicating the theme
- A **closing sentence** providing a thoughtful conclusion

Sample Analysis Paragraph

The **opening sentence** names the play and the playwright and summarizes the analysis.

The **body sentences** describe the key elements and indicate the theme.

The **closing sentence** provides a thoughtful ending.

Look Out for Jonas

In *Party at the End of the World*, playwright Dedra Runningcloud explores how different points of view bring people together—and drive them apart. The play centers on Jonas Jenkins, a "drifter prophet" who arrives in the small town of Eel Creek, Alaska, and proclaims that the world will end that night. Jenkins's predictions startle the people of the town. "Look out for Jonas!" a child cries. Sheriff Smith arrives to run Jonas out of town but can't find the prophet, who has wandered into the Eel Creek General Store. There, Jonas meets the storekeeper, Lyndsey Peck, and tells her the world will end that night. Instead of fearing him, Lyndsey joins in the fantasy and declares an "End of the World Party" on the store roof. Lyndsey hosts the celebration, and Jonas and an eclectic group of townsfolk lie in lawn chairs and watch a spectacular meteor shower. When the sun rises the next day, those who were partying discover that the world didn't end, but Jonas has had a heart attack. From his point of view, it really was the end of the world. Runningcloud contrasts the close-minded suspicion of Sheriff Smith with the open-minded acceptance of Lyndsey Peck. Both agree with the child— "Look out for Jonas!"—but in opposite ways. By accepting and even celebrating Jonas's point of view, Lyndsey brings the community together.

Literature

Write

Write an analysis paragraph. Use the play map you created on page **276** to create a one-paragraph analysis of the play and its main theme.

"You need three things in the theater—the play, the actors, and the audience—and each must give something."

—Kenneth Haigh

Understanding Your Goal

Your goal in this chapter is to write an essay that analyzes an important theme of a play. The chart below lists the key traits of a play analysis, with specific suggestions for this assignment.

Traits of a Play Analysis

- ### Ideas
  Write a thesis statement that names the play and focuses on a main theme. Then analyze that theme by connecting it to the characters, setting, and plot. Include textual evidence from the play.

- ### Organization
  Create a beginning that introduces the play and the thesis, a middle that logically analyzes the theme, and a closing that puts the play in perspective.

- ### Voice
  Show your knowledge and understanding of the play while also creating a narrative flow, allowing the reader to experience the play's action.

- ### Word Choice
  Correctly use play terminology in your analysis and choose words that capture a precise meaning.

- ### Sentence Fluency
  Write sentences that flow smoothly and have a variety of lengths and beginnings.

- ### Conventions
  Check your writing for punctuation, capitalization, spelling, and grammar errors.

Get the big picture. Review the rubric on pages 310–311 before you begin writing. This rubric will guide you throughout the revising and editing steps in the writing process.

Response Essay

In the following essay, Joelle analyzes *Sisters*—a play by Marsha A. Jackson.

Beginning
The beginning catches the reader's interest, introduces the play, and states the thesis (underlined).

Middle
The first middle paragraph sets the scene.

Stuck with Each Other

In the dark theater, children sing a haunting tune: "Don't Play with the Alley Children." It's a singsong chant that young Olivia Williams and her friends would sing in their upper-middle-class apartments while young Cassie Charles and her friends played among the garbage cans below. Though both girls are African Americans, they are divided by their social class, their experience, and their strategies for living in a white world. Then, one New Year's Eve, the grown-up Olivia is stranded in her ad-agency office along with the grown-up Cassie, a cleaning woman. In her play *Sisters,* Marsha A. Jackson contrasts the two women's lives, showing how color and gender make two very different women into true sisters.

The action of the play begins on New Year's Eve in Olivia's office at Peat, Montgriff, and Simon, an ad agency in Atlanta, Georgia. Olivia kneels on the floor among boxes and is packing up her office when Cassie arrives singing "I'm Every Woman" at the top of her lungs. The two women could not be more different. Olivia is 30, single, stiff, proper, and sad, listening to MUZAK as she packs up her life. Cassie is 40, a mom, loose and happy, listening to Whitney Houston. As Jackson points out in her notes before the play, "Both characters are intentionally broadly drawn in Act I, such that the laughter is the medium of entry into the complexity of each character and situation" (104). These two women begin as stereotypes, but when they get stuck together, both characters start to unfold.

A storm begins outside, lightning strikes, and the power in the building goes out. Olivia and Cassie, alone in the building, must rely on each other. They walk down twenty flights of stairs so that Olivia can drive Cassie home, but Olivia has forgotten her car keys, and the storm has turned to a blizzard. All traffic is stopped, and the trains that Cassie would ride aren't running because of the blackout.

The women climb back up the stairs, and Cassie reluctantly helps Olivia pack up her office while the two women unpack their lives. Olivia reveals that she is leaving because she has hit the "glass ceiling" and, despite her hard

Literature

work, is getting passed over for promotions. Cassie says that Olivia's ambition is a curse: "Being ungrateful for what you got, and wishing for things you can't have. If that ain't a curse, I ain't seen one" (134). Cassie has her own hang-ups. She has taken care of others her whole life: first her grandmother and now her son. Olivia points out, "Who's taking care of you, Cassie? You've been so busy working, trying to convince yourself you don't deserve a life, you didn't even feel it when you gave up" (144). As they talk, Olivia and Cassie grow to understand each other.

Jackson seems to be showing that the things that keep people apart—walls and alleys, work and money—aren't as powerful as the forces that draw them together. Simply by setting these two women in the same space, Jackson undoes the years and dollars that had kept them apart. Stuck with each other on New Year's Eve, Olivia and Cassie create their own celebration. They trade stories, listen to music, dance, and even make resolutions. Olivia resolves to find her way in a "white man's world" and have fun doing it. Cassie resolves to start her own cleaning business and move up in the world.

Ending
The ending paragraph reflects on the main theme of the play.

By the end of their time together, Olivia and Cassie are more than friends: They are sisters. Their theme song no longer is "Don't Play with the Alley Children" but "Blest Be the Tie That Binds." Marsha Jackson has brought two very different women together—two different aspects of the playwright herself. Jackson not only wrote the play but starred as Olivia during its run. As a classically trained playwright and a leading light in the theater scenes of Atlanta and Houston, Jackson is very much like Olivia. But the loving way in which she writes Cassie's part—and her own experience of being an "alley child" in a white world—show that part of Jackson is and always will be Cassie.

Respond to the reading. Answer the following questions about the essay:

Ideas (1) What theme does Joelle focus on in her analysis? (2) How do the characters, the setting, and the plot demonstrate the theme?

Organization (3) How are the middle paragraphs organized?

Voice & Word Choice (4) Where does the writer's voice sound most analytical? Explain. (5) Where does the writer's voice sound most narrative? Explain.

Prewriting

To get started on your analysis, you need to unlock the secrets of a play. The keys to prewriting can help you do so. Once you finish the activities on the next pages, you'll be ready to write.

Keys to Effective Prewriting

1. Select a play that interests you and contains a main theme to explore.

2. Reread the play and (if possible) see a performance of it.

3. Research the background of the play and the playwright.

4. Write a clear thesis statement that identifies the theme you will analyze. Develop topic sentences for the main points of your analysis.

5. Plan your essay using an outline or organized list.

Prewriting ■ Select a play.

You may already know what play you would like to analyze. If not, follow the instructions on this page.

Think about plays you have read and plays that you have seen performed—in or out of school. Also, consider famous plays that have been made into movies. To select a play, Julius created a topics list.

Topics List

Plays I've Read	Plays I've Seen	Plays Made into Movies
Romeo and Juliet	The Fantasticks	The Night of the Iguana
Julius Caesar	Godspell	Death of a Salesman
Inherit the Wind	The Lion King	Chicago
The Glass Menagerie *		

Prewrite

Brainstorm a topics list. Write "Plays I've Read," "Plays I've Seen," and "Plays Made into Movies" at the top of a piece of paper. Underneath, list topic ideas. Place an asterisk (*) next to the play you'd like to write about.

■ Focus on the traits.

Ideas To create a thorough analysis, try to select a play that you can both read and see onstage. If you've read but haven't seen a certain play, find the video of a performance. Also consider getting the script for a play you've seen performed locally.

■ Write down main events.

After you have selected a play to write about, you need to read (or reread) it and, if possible, view it. Then consider the play's basic elements. Julius created the following play map for *The Glass Menagerie*.

Play Map

Title: The Glass Menagerie

Playwright: Tennessee Williams

Characters: Amanda Wingfield (the mother), Laura Wingfield (the shy daughter), Tom Wingfield (the son), and Jim O'Connor (the gentleman caller)

Setting: The Wingfield apartment in an overcrowded city tenement

Conflict: Laura has withdrawn from life, and her mother and brother want to bring her out.

Plot:

Event 1: Amanda reminisces about her gentleman callers.

Event 2: Amanda learns Laura has quit business school.

Event 3: Tom arranges for a friend to come to dinner.

Climax: The gentleman caller, Jim O'Connor, kisses Laura, but then reveals that he is already "going steady" with someone else.

Resolution: Laura is left desolate, and Tom, tired of working to support his mother and sister, runs away, chasing his military dreams.

Theme: Life may be fragile, but it can't be lived in a glass case, without risk.

Prewrite

Create a play map. Fill in the main elements of the play you have chosen to write about.

Literature

Prewriting ▪ Consider themes.

To fully understand a play, you need to understand the playwright and the background of the play. Often this information appears in the introduction, preface, or appendix of the published play. (You can also do some research at the library or online.) Julius formed a set of questions to investigate the background of *The Glass Menagerie*.

Background Questions

Who is the playwright, and when and where did the playwright live?
Tennessee Williams was born on March 26, 1914, in Columbus, Ohio. His real name was Thomas Lanier Williams.

What was the playwright's first produced play, and when was it performed?
Williams's first play was Battle of Angels, performed in 1940.

What are the playwright's most famous plays and awards?
Williams also wrote A Streetcar Named Desire and Cat on a Hot Tin Roof, both of which won the Pulitzer Prize and the Drama Critics Award.

When was the play first performed and where?
The Glass Menagerie was first performed at the Civic Theatre in Chicago, opening December 24, 1944.

What did audiences and critics think of the play?
Audiences and critics loved The Glass Menagerie, and its success made Tennessee Williams an overnight star. He talked about the success being a "catastrophe" for him because it was so sudden.

What did the playwright think of this play?
Tennessee Williams called The Glass Menagerie a "memory play," one that portrays life not with stark realism, but with "a closer approach, a more penetrating and vivid expression of things as they are."

Prewrite

Research the background of the play. Read the material printed with the play or do your own research. Write down answers to the questions above.

Note: If you are writing about an older play, such as a work by Shakespeare or Sophocles, you may not be able to answer all of the background questions. Answer those you can and add any others that occur to you.

■ Write a thesis statement.

Your thesis statement should name the play and playwright and focus on the theme you plan to explore. The following formula can help you.

play and playwright		theme		thesis statement
The Glass Menagerie by Tennessee Williams	**+**	Life is fragile, but it can't be lived without risk.	**=**	In The Glass Menagerie, Tennessee Williams shows that though life is fragile, it can't be lived without risk.

Prewrite

Write your thesis statement. Use the formula above as you develop a thesis statement for your essay. Try two or three versions until you are satisfied.

■ Organize the middle of your essay.

The middle of your essay should set the scene, highlight key actions in the plot, give insights into the characters' actions, and discuss the theme. Here are Julius's topic sentences.

Topic Sentence 1 (setting the scene)

> Each of the Wingfields—mother Amanda, son Tom, and daughter Laura—lives physically in the apartment but psychologically very far from it.

Topic Sentence 2 (plot and characters)

> Soon after the characters are introduced, Amanda is shocked to learn about the secret lives her two children are leading.

Topic Sentence 3 (plot and characters)

> When the "gentleman caller," Jim O'Connor, arrives at the Wingfield apartment, he brings life to the whole place.

Topic Sentence 4 (theme)

> Jim O'Connor seems to be everything the Wingfields need—romance, adventure, confidence, and risk.

Prewrite

Create topic sentences. Follow the pattern that Julius used above, or create your own pattern. Write a topic sentence for each middle paragraph, focusing on the basic elements of the play (page 283).

Prewriting ■ Plan your essay.

Julius planned his essay with a sentence outline, but if your teacher prefers, you can create a topic outline, or even a simple list.

Sentence Outline

Thesis Statement: In The Glass Menagerie, Tennessee Williams shows that though life is fragile, it can't be lived without risk.

I. Each of the Wingfields—mother Amanda, son Tom, and daughter Laura—lives physically in the apartment but psychologically very far from it.
   A. Amanda grew up with Southern gentility.
   B. Tom works at a factory to support the family but wants to be a poet.
   C. Laura collects glass animals and "attends" a business college.
II. Soon after the characters are introduced, Amanda is shocked to learn about the secret lives her two children are leading.
   A. Laura has dropped out of business college.
   B. Tom goes to movies, dreaming of adventure.
   C. Amanda gets Tom to invite a "gentleman caller" to meet Laura.
III. When the "gentleman caller," Jim O'Connor, arrives at the Wingfield apartment, he brings life to the whole place.
   A. He believes in adventure, just as Tom does.
   B. Jim represents the genteel past to Amanda.
   C. He is the boy Laura had a crush on in high school.
IV. Jim O'Connor seems to be everything the Wingfields need—romance, adventure, confidence, and risk.
   A. Jim remembers Laura as "Blue Roses."
   B. Jim accidentally breaks her glass unicorn.
   C. He kisses her, but then tells her he is "going steady" with another girl.

Prewrite

Plan your essay. Use your thesis statement and topic sentences to create an outline or list to plan your essay. Add details to support each topic sentence.

Writing

After thinking carefully about the elements of the play and planning your analysis, you are ready to start writing. By following your plan, you can get all of your ideas on paper.

Keys to Effective Writing

1. Write on every other line so that you have room to make changes.

2. Use your outline or organized list to guide your writing.

3. Create a beginning that introduces the play and playwright and states your thesis.

4. Support your topic sentences with evidence quoted and paraphrased from the play.

5. Analyze the theme, focusing on characters, setting, and plot.

6. Write an ending that connects the theme to the playwright.

Literature

Writing ▪ Get the big picture.

Your analysis should include three parts: a beginning, a middle, and an ending. The chart below shows how the three parts of a play analysis fit together. The examples are from the essay on pages **289–292**.

BEGINNING

The **beginning** captures the reader's interest, names the play and playwright, and states the thesis.

Thesis Statement
In The Glass Menagerie, Tennessee Williams shows that though life is fragile, it can't be lived without risk.

MIDDLE

The **middle** paragraphs analyze the theme by focusing on character, setting, and plot.

Topic Sentences
Each of the Wingfields—mother Amanda, son Tom, and daughter Laura—lives physically in the apartment but psychologically very far from it.

Soon after the characters are introduced, Amanda is shocked to learn about the secret lives her two children are leading.

When the "gentleman caller," Jim O'Connor, arrives at the Wingfield apartment, he brings life to the whole place.

Jim O'Connor seems to be everything the Wingfields need—romance, adventure, confidence, and risk.

ENDING

The **ending** connects the main theme to the playwright.

Closing Sentences
When Jim O'Connor leaves the apartment, he takes the newfound hope away with him. That's because he can't live life for the Wingfields. Everyone must take his or her own fragile soul out into the world and risk it—as Jim does.

■ Start your essay.

The opening of your analysis should capture the reader's interest, introduce the play and playwright, and state your thesis. Here are some strategies for capturing your reader's interest:

- ■ **Start with a strong image.**
  Aside from her mother and brother, Laura Wingfield's only companions in life are tiny, fragile glass creatures—her "glass menagerie."

- ■ **Use a quotation from the play.**
  "The Wingfield apartment is in the rear of the building, one of those vast hive-like conglomerations of cellular living-units that flower as warty growths in overcrowded urban centers of lower middle-class population" (27). It's a location most people can imagine, a location many people can simply look around and see. . . .

- ■ **Begin with an intriguing idea.**
  From the moment the curtain opens, the audience wonders about the smiling portrait of the sailor—the one Wingfield who no longer remains in the cramped apartment. . . .

Beginning Paragraph

Julius begins his essay with an intriguing idea and then provides background information before stating his thesis.

> The first paragraph catches the reader's interest and delivers the thesis statement (underlined).

From the moment the curtain opens, the audience wonders about the smiling portrait of the sailor—the one Wingfield who no longer remains in the cramped apartment. The father has escaped the claustrophobic world where the mother and her two grown children still live. The whole play takes place in this small space, with an occasional breath of fresh air out on the fire escape in the alley. The family has withdrawn to this apartment as if it is a safe haven from the world, but their unhappiness demonstrates that the apartment is anything but safe. The Wingfields aren't really living. In The Glass Menagerie, Tennessee Williams shows that though life is fragile, it can't be lived without risk.

Write your beginning. Use one of the strategies above to capture the reader's interest. Then provide background information and present your thesis.

Literature

Writing ■ Develop the middle part.

In the middle part of your essay, you systematically analyze the theme. First, focus on major elements of the play—characters, setting, and plot—and show how each contributes to the theme. Then discuss the theme itself.

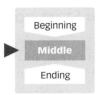

Beginning

Middle

Ending

Middle Paragraphs

The first middle paragraph uses characters and setting to analyze the theme.

> Each of the Wingfields—mother Amanda, son Tom, and daughter Laura—lives physically in the apartment but psychologically very far from it. Amanda is an older woman brought up in the genteel traditions of the Old South, with lemonade on verandas and gentlemen callers. She lives in this bygone age and discusses her glory days of dating, even though they resulted in a broken marriage and single motherhood. Tom also feels trapped, working in a shoe factory, though he wishes to be a poet. Coworkers call him "Shakespeare" (92). Tom works simply to make money to support his mother and sister, though he spends nights at the movies, wishing for adventure. Laura is the most lost and fragile of them all. She had been a shy girl in high school, with a crippled leg and lungs weakened by "pleurosis." Laura has withdrawn from the world, spending her time with a collection of animal statues, her "glass menagerie." Her favorite is also the oldest, a unicorn that tries to fit in with a shelf full of horses. This unicorn symbolizes Laura, who doesn't fit in and is so very fragile.

The next middle paragraphs use plot to analyze the theme.

> Soon after the characters are introduced, Amanda is shocked to learn about the secret lives her two children are leading. When Amanda stops at Rubicam's Business College, where her daughter is supposed to be taking classes, she learns that Laura became so nervous in the first week of class that she threw up and dropped out of school. She has been going to the library and wandering around town instead of going to class. Shortly afterward, Amanda learns of Tom's dreams of adventure and his plans to join the military. "Man is by instinct a lover, a hunter, a fighter, and none of those

instincts are given much play at the warehouse," Tom tells his mother (64). Frustrated with both of her children, Amanda asks Tom to help Laura find a man. Tom at first says no, but then arranges for a gentleman caller.

When the "gentleman caller," Jim O'Connor, arrives at the Wingfield apartment, he brings life to the whole place. Jim is Tom's only friend and confidant at the factory, and he understands Tom's desire for adventure. Jim also enlivens Amanda, who redecorates the apartment to make ready for him. To Amanda, Jim represents the return of the gracious past. But Jim's strongest effect is on Laura, who has secretly loved him since his glory days in high school. Back then, she had been absent for a while, and Jim asked why. When Laura said "pleurosis," Jim heard "blue roses," and called her that name (112). The name is another symbol of Laura's odd and fragile beauty.

Jim O'Connor seems to be everything the Wingfields need—romance, adventure, confidence, and risk. Perhaps Amanda has found a way back to bygone days; perhaps Tom has found a coconspirator to help him escape the factory; perhaps Laura has found a gentleman who would lift her out of her fragile glass world and into life. Laura trusts Jim with the unicorn, and he gently sets it on a table. Later, as he tries to teach Laura to dance, they knock the unicorn off the table, and its horn is broken away. Jim is sorry, but Laura says, "I'll just imagine he had an operation. The horn was removed to make him feel less—freakish! . . . Now he will feel more at home with the other horses, the ones that don't have horns" (125). Jim steals a kiss from Laura, but calls himself "stumblejohn" for doing it, given that he has a steady girlfriend already. This is just what Laura needs—to take risks, even possibly to get broken, if only to fit in better with the rest of the world. The problem is that she isn't like her unicorn—she doesn't lose her horn or learn to fit in with the other horses.

> The last middle paragraph focuses directly on the theme.

Literature

Write

Write your middle paragraphs. Use your topic sentences and outline (pages 285–286) as a guide. Add quotations from the play for support.

Writing ■ End your essay.

The ending of your analysis should expand on the main theme of the play. Here are strategies you can try:

- **Connect the theme to life in general.**
  When Jim O'Connor leaves the apartment, he takes the newfound hope away with him. That's because he can't live life for the Wingfields. Everyone must take his or her own fragile soul out into the world and risk it—as Jim does.

- **Relate the theme of the play to the playwright's life.**
  When Tom Wingfield leaves home, abandoning his job at the shoe warehouse, Tennessee Williams is reliving his own escape from the shoe warehouse where he worked before becoming a successful playwright.

- **Provide a powerful quotation from the play.**
  After leaving home, Tom is haunted by thoughts of his sister and her glass menagerie: "The window is filled with pieces of colored glass . . . like bits of a shattered rainbow. . . . Oh, Laura, Laura, I tried to leave you behind me, but I am more faithful than I intended to be!" (137).

Ending Paragraph

In his final paragraph, Julius connects the play to life in general.

> The ending paragraph expands upon the theme.

When Jim O'Connor leaves the apartment, he takes the newfound hope away with him. That's because he can't live life for the Wingfields. Everyone must take his or her own fragile soul out into the world and risk it—as Jim does. Amanda's hope that a gentleman caller would make her life perfect was dashed when her husband left, and now Laura's hope for a similar knight in shining armor is also dashed. Such rescuers don't exist. Only Tom escapes the apartment, but he can't be free either, because he knows his mother and sister are still there, waiting for their lives to begin.

Write

Write your ending and form a complete first draft. Develop the last paragraph of your essay, using one or more of the suggestions listed above. Make a complete copy of your essay, double-spacing or writing on every other line to leave room for revising.

Revising

When you write, you allow your thoughts to pour out onto the page. When you revise, you re-examine those thoughts to improve your paper, deciding what to add, delete, move, or rework. The points below give you an overview of the revision process.

Keys to Effective Revising

1. Read your essay aloud to see whether it makes sense from start to finish.

2. Check your beginning and ending. To start, you must capture the reader's interest, introduce the play and playwright, and present the theme. To end, you must expand on the theme.

3. Review each middle paragraph for unity and organization.

4. Check your voice. It should be analytical and, when necessary, narrative.

5. Review your word choice and sentence fluency.

6. Use the editing and proofreading marks on the inside back cover of this book.

Literature

Revising ▪ for Ideas

 6 My ideas provide a complete and careful analysis of the play.

 5 I have effectively summarized material and included appropriate quotations.

4 Most of my summaries are effective, but I should make better use of quotations.

When you revise for *ideas,* you check your thesis statement, topic sentences, and details. These two pages will also help you revise your summaries and include effective quotations. The rubric strip above will guide you as you revise for ideas.

▪ Have I created effective summaries?

You have created effective summaries if you have included only the information the reader needs—but *all* the information the reader needs. Some summaries are puffed up with unnecessary details. Others are confusing because of missing details. Ask yourself the following questions:

1. What does my reader know about the play?

2. What does my reader need to know about the play?

Exercise

Read the summary that follows. Find two details that are not necessary and should be deleted. Also indicate which detail is missing. (Ask yourself: What do I still need to know?)

1   In *Dear World,* the madwomen of Paris battle rampant capitalism to save the
2 city they love. A prospector has discovered that a great deposit of oil stretches
3 beneath Café Francis in Paris, and so he, a lawyer, and a politician plot to blow
4 up the café. A deaf-mute hangs out there. The sinister plot is foiled when the
5 politician's servant drops the bomb in the Seine instead of placing it in the café's
6 flower box. The café patrons—led by the madwomen—band together to stop the
7 conspiracy. They sing and dance, talking about good garbage and ugly garbage. In
8 the end, the madwomen defeat the evil trio by faking uranium.

Revise

Check your summaries. Be sure you have included only the information the reader needs, but *all* the information the reader needs. Ask yourself the following questions:

1. What does my reader know about the play?

2. What does my reader need to know about the play?

3 I need to improve my summaries and provide more helpful quotations.

2 My summaries are unclear or confusing, and I need to quote from the play.

1 I need help to understand how to summarize and quote from a play.

■ Have I used effective quotations?

You have used effective quotations if you have quoted only those passages that make a strong, clear point. An analysis with too many quotations becomes cumbersome, while one with too few quotations gives the reader little insight into the play.

Exercise

In the following paragraph, decide which quotation should remain and which should be deleted. Give reasons for your decision.

1   The madwomen enlist the aid of the Sewerman who poles around the sewers
2   of Paris on a gondola. The Sewerman seems to have the same madness as the
3   ladies, reveling in garbage: "It used to be if garbage smelled a little strange, it was
4   only because it was a little confused. Everything was there: sardines, cologne,
5   iodine, roses. Ah! The feast you found floating by" (43). The Sewerman's madness
6   allows him to see beauty in everything, even garbage. A stark contrast is drawn
7   between the Sewerman's madness and the madness of rampant capitalism, which
8   sees beauty in nothing. As the politician sings: "There will be a sweet taste in the
9   air, of industrial waste in the air" (32).

Revise

Check your quotations. Be sure that each one strongly supports your point and that you have not used too many or too few quotations.

Ideas
An ineffective quotation is deleted.

When Laura said "pleurosis," Jim heard "blue roses," and called her that name (112). The name is another symbol of Laura's odd and fragile beauty. ~~Jim apologizes about the nickname, saying, "I hope you didn't mind" (113).~~

Literature

Revising ■ for Organization

 6 All the parts of my essay work together to create an insightful analysis.

 5 I use transitions to connect my paragraphs and key words to connect my sentences.

 4 I use transitions to connect my paragraphs, but I should use more key words to connect my sentences.

When you revise for *organization,* you check the overall structure of your essay and the unity of each paragraph. The rubric strip above can guide your revision.

■ Have I clearly connected my paragraphs?

You have clearly connected your paragraphs if you have used transitions. Different types of organization use different transitional words and phrases.

Time Order	Point by Point	Logical Order
First	Considering the characters,	To begin with,
Soon	As to the plot,	Furthermore,
In the end	In the climactic scene,	As a result,

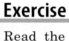

Exercise

Read the following thesis statement and topic sentences. Identify the transitional words and phrases used in the topic sentences and indicate the organizational pattern.

Thesis statement: In *The Final Adventure,* playwright Stephen Dietz explores the uses of deception.

1. By focusing on two great deceivers—Sherlock Holmes and Professor Moriarty—Dietz differentiates between "good" and "bad" deception.
2. In terms of plot, the play is one grand spiderweb woven by Holmes.
3. At the climax, Dietz pits his two deceivers in a battle to the death atop Reichenbach Falls in Switzerland.
4. Looking at the theme in a larger context, Dietz himself is a "good deceiver," using actors, costumes, and sets to fool the audience.
5. The theme of deception expands, taking in the whole play and its many costumes, sets, and sound effects.

Revise

 Review your paragraphs. Have you connected them with transitions that show the overall structure of the analysis? If not, consider adding transitional words and phrases to your topic sentences to make the structure clear.

3 I need clearer transitions to connect my paragraphs and should use key words to connect my sentences.

2 My paragraphs and sentences show no connection, and I need to use transitions and key words.

1 I need to learn how to organize an analysis of a play.

■ Have I used key words to connect my sentences?

You have used key words if an important term from one sentence is repeated in another. Key words connect your ideas like the pieces of a jigsaw puzzle.

Watson himself is often the unwitting but **willing** victim of Holmes's deceptions.	The doctor's **willingness** comes from trust in his friend, which shows that deceivers can be **heroic**.	Holmes's **heroism,** despite his deceptions, is strongly contrasted with the villainy of the deceitful Moriarty.

Exercise

Identify the key words that connect the sentences below.

1   Holmes and Moriarty each weave webs of deception in *The Final Adventure.*
2   Holmes's web is, in fact, the larger of the two, constructed to slowly contract around
3   his prey. That prey, Moriarty, escapes the outer strands of the web only to be caught
4   in the center. He cannot escape the central strand because it is not a deception but
5   the truth—evidence to convict the crime boss and destroy his syndicate.

Revise

Check your sentences. Have you connected them with keywords? If not, add some to clarify and improve the flow of your ideas.

Literature

Organization
Key words help connect the ideas in sentences.

Tom also feels trapped, working in a shoe factory, though he
wishes to be a poet. ~~Friends~~ Coworkers call him "Shakespeare" (92).
works simply to
Tom makes money to support his mother and sister, though

he spends nights at the movies, wishing for adventure. . . .

Revising ▪ for Voice

 6 My writing voice sounds distinctive and engaging from start to finish.

5 I narrate events in a compelling way and create an effective analysis of the play.

 4 I narrate the events of the play well, but my analysis of the theme does not sound effective.

When you revise your play analysis for *voice,* make sure you effectively narrate the plot and analyze the theme. The rubric strip above will guide your revision for voice.

▪ Have I used a compelling narrative voice?

You have used a compelling narrative voice if your summary of the plot is vivid and inviting and your character descriptions are revealing. A compelling narrative voice does the following things:

1. Describes people, places, and things using sensory details.

2. Shows important action with vivid verbs.

3. Provides dialogue that reveals personalities.

Exercise

For each pair of sentences, indicate which sentence has a better narrative voice and why.

1. a. The game show host, Brad Bowers, doesn't seem very genuine.
   b. The game show host, Brad Bowers, wears a perpetual plastic smile and an obvious toupee.

2. a. Brad Bowers bursts through the curtain opening, leaps down from the stage, and grabs audience members to join in the game show, *King of the Mountain.*
   b. Brad Bowers comes out on stage and then goes down in the audience and asks questions to see who knows the answers.

3. a. Bowers is so vain that he refuses to wear glasses, though he needs them.
   b. Bowers declares, "There's nothing wrong with my eyes," just before he runs into a couch and tumbles headlong.

Revise

Refine your narrative voice. Review the part of your essay that focuses on the plot and characters. Make sure you provide clear descriptions, use vivid verbs to describe action, and provide dialogue that reveals personality.

My narration of events should be more compelling, and my analysis should be more effective.

 Throughout my essay, my voice is flat and needs to be made effective.

 I need help understanding how to create an effective voice for my play analysis.

■ Have I used an effective analytical voice?

You have used an effective analytical voice if your writing does the following things:

1. Divides a topic into parts.
2. Defines each part.
3. Shows how the parts relate to each other and to the whole.

Exercise

Read the paragraph below and identify how the writer divides the topic into parts, defines each part, and shows the relationship between the parts.

1   **All of the contestants in Game Show hope for a shot at the American Dream.**
2 **Ethel Tinsley wants to win enough money to publish her book. Dolly Perkins hopes**
3 **to be able to move out of the "retirement villa" where she lives. Kathy Burns and**
4 **Steve Nystrom both want to advance their film careers—and perhaps rekindle their**
5 **romance. Most of the contestants are destined not for the American Dream but for the**
6 **American Reality: that competition results in one winner and many losers.**

Revise

Review your analytical voice. Read the part of your essay that analyzes the theme. Be sure you have divided the theme into parts and shown how the parts relate to each other.

Voice
The writer divides the topic into parts and defines each.

Jim O'Connor seems to be everything the Wingfields

need—romance, adventure, confidence, and risk.

Perhaps Amanda has found a way back to bygone days; perhaps Tom has found a coconspirator to help him escape the factory; perhaps Laura has found a gentleman who would lift her out of her fragile glass world and into life.

Literature

Revising ■ for Word Choice

6 My writing voice sounds distinctive and engaging from start to finish.

5 I have correctly used theater terminology and have referred to symbols in the play.

4 I have used most terminology correctly, but I should refer to symbols in the play.

When you revise for *word choice,* be sure you have used play terminology correctly and referred to symbols in the play. Use the rubric strip above to help you revise for word choice.

■ How can I check my use of play terminology?

You can check your play terminology by reviewing these basic terms:

Act: A main part of a play; a group of scenes

Character: A person or an animal in a play

Climax: The moment when the main character confronts the conflict

Comedy: A play in which the hero is redeemed despite flaws

Conflict: The problem or clash between forces in a play

Dialogue: Characters speaking to each other

Drama: The study of plays and playwriting; a play that deals with serious themes

Monologue: One character speaking to the audience

Narrator: A person who speaks directly to the audience and connects the scenes

Plot: The series of events that intensify conflict and lead to a climax

Prop: A small item actors use and manipulate onstage

Scene: Part of an act happening in one place and time

Set: The arrangement of the stage to represent a specific place

Setting: The place and time where the action of the play occurs

Soliloquy: A speech delivered by one character

Stage: The main area of action for the play

Symbol: A person, a place, a thing, or an idea that stands for something else

Theme: The playwright's message about life or human nature

Tone: The playwright's attitude toward the subject

Tragedy: A play in which the hero's flaws cause his or her undoing

Revise

Check your theater terminology. Read through your essay and make sure you use correct and precise terminology when discussing your play.

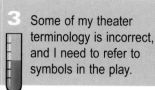

3 Some of my theater terminology is incorrect, and I need to refer to symbols in the play.

2 I need to use theater terminology, and I need to refer to symbols in the play.

1 I need help understanding word choice in a play analysis.

■ How can I discover symbols in the play?

You can discover symbols in a play by paying close attention to words that the author gives special treatment to. Watch especially for these types of words:

■ **Words Used in Titles**
The title *The Glass Menagerie* hints at two symbols: glass, which stands for fragility and beauty (Laura), and menagerie, a collection of living things representing the Wingfields and people in general.

■ **Words Used Repeatedly**
In *The Glass Menagerie,* the character Tom is often associated with the word *movie,* which symbolizes adventure.

■ **Words That Describe Important Props**
In *The Glass Menagerie,* the unicorn is Laura's favorite glass animal, the one that doesn't fit in and is "freakish." It is a symbol of Laura herself.

Note: A symbol is a person, a place, a thing, or an idea that stands for something else. Symbols are keys to unlocking a play's themes.

Revise

Check your symbolism. Consider words that appear in the title of the play, words that are repeated in connection with one character or situation, and words that describe important props. Refer to these symbols in your analysis and show how they demonstrate the theme.

Word Choice
A symbol is explained.

This is just what she needs—to take risks, even possibly to get broken, if only to fit in better with the rest of the world.

The problem is that Laura isn't like her unicorn—she doesn't lose her horn or learn to fit in with the other horses.

Revising ▪ for Sentence Fluency

6 The sentences in my analysis are deftly written and a pleasure to read.

5 I have smoothly integrated quotations in my analysis, and I have created an effective sentence rhythm.

4 Most of my quotations are smoothly included, but I should vary my sentence lengths to create a better rhythm.

When you revise for *sentence fluency,* be sure that you have smoothly integrated quotations in your analysis and that you have created an effective sentence rhythm. The rubric strip above will guide your revision for sentence fluency.

▪ Have I smoothly integrated quotations?

You have smoothly integrated quotations if they fit naturally in the flow of your analysis. Here are three strategies for integrating quotations into your analysis:

- Make **short quotations** part of the sentence.
  Daniel begins the three-man play by pledging to "capture, in a single theatrical experience, the genius of *The Complete Works of William Shakespeare*" (8).

Shakespeare's Globe Theatre

- Introduce **medium-length quotations** as you would dialogue.
  During the show, Adam often butchers famous lines, for example, reciting the following: "What's in a name, anyway? That which we call a nose / By any other name would still smell" (18).

- When **quoting four or more lines,** indent the material as an excerpt.
  Adam even turns an audience member into an actor, coaching her how to play the part of Ophelia from Hamlet:

  > Now your job as an actress is to take all of these elements, synthesize them within your soul, then, at that moment of truth, we're going to build everyone into a mighty frenzy, stop everything, all attention goes to you, and you let out with that scream that epitomizes Ophelia. (63)

Revise

Check your quotations. If a quotation breaks the flow of thought, revise using one of the strategies above.

3 Some of my quotations stop the flow of the analysis, and I need to vary my sentences.

 2 I haven't smoothly integrated any quotations, and I need sentence rhythm.

 1 I need help understanding how to quote from a play and how to create sentence rhythm.

■ Have I created an effective sentence rhythm?

You have created an effective rhythm if you have done the following:

- Used **medium sentences** (about 20 words) for most of your writing
- Used **long sentences** (30 words or more) to express complex ideas
- Used **short sentences** (10 words or fewer) to make a strong point

Exercise

Count the number of words in each sentence below and label them medium, long, or short. What effect does the sentence length in this passage have on the rhythm?

> After the three-man troupe acts out a 20-minute version of *Hamlet*—complete with Hamlet's soliloquy, Ophelia's drowning, and the deaths of Gertrude, Claudias, and Hamlet himself—they notice they have some time left to do *Hamlet* "One more time" (72). They proceed to compact the whole play into two gory minutes that end with everyone dead onstage. Jess then suggests that they do the play "faster" (74). The three actors simply walk onstage and die. Lastly, Daniel suggests that they do the play "backwards," a crazy spectacle of characters coming back to life, reciting lines backward, and even depicting Ophelia's drowning. These four versions of *Hamlet* bring the crowd to its feet.

Revise

Check your sentence lengths. Be sure to vary your sentences effectively, using different lengths for different purposes.

Literature

Sentence Fluency
Sentence variety is improved.

Amanda's hope that a gentleman caller would make her life perfect was dashed when her husband left. *and* Now Laura's hope for a similar knight in shining armor is also dashed. Such rescuers don't exist, and only Tom escapes the apartment, but he can't be free . . .

Revising ■ Improve your writing.

Revise

Check your revising. On a piece of paper, write the numbers 1 to 13. If you can answer "yes" to a question, put a check mark after that number. If not, continue to work with that part of your essay.

Revising Checklist

Ideas

_____ **1.** Does my thesis statement focus on a major theme of the play?
_____ **2.** Have I analyzed the theme using character, setting, and plot?
_____ **3.** Have I created effective summaries and used appropriate quotations?

Organization

_____ **4.** Does my beginning catch the reader's attention and introduce the thesis?
_____ **5.** Are my middle paragraphs connected with transitions?
_____ **6.** Are the ideas in my sentences connected with key words?
_____ **7.** Does the ending expand upon the theme?

Voice

_____ **8.** Have I used an engaging narrative voice to summarize the play?
_____ **9.** Have I used a strong analytical voice to explain the theme?

Word Choice

_____ **10.** Do I use theater terminology correctly?
_____ **11.** Have I identified symbols in the play?

Sentence Fluency

_____ **12.** Have I integrated quotations smoothly?
_____ **13.** Have I varied the length of my sentences?

Revise

Make a clean copy. When you finish revising your essay, make a clean copy for editing.

Editing

Once you have finished revising your work for its content, you need to edit it for punctuation, capitalization, spelling, and grammar.

Keys to Effective Editing

1. Use a dictionary, a thesaurus, and the "Proofreader's Guide" in the back of this book (pages 604–763).

2. Check your use of any comparative and superlative modifiers.

3. Check your writing for punctuation, capitalization, spelling, and grammar errors.

4. If you use a computer, edit on a printed copy and enter your changes on the computer.

5. Use the editing and proofreading marks on the inside back cover of this book.

Literature

Editing ■ for Conventions

6 My grammar and punctuation are correct, and the copy is free of spelling errors.

5 I have one or two errors in grammar, spelling, or punctuation, but they won't distract the reader.

4 I need to correct a few errors in punctuation, spelling, or grammar, which may distract the reader.

When you revise for *conventions,* you check punctuation, capitalization, spelling, and grammar. The rubric strip above can guide you.

■ How can I avoid the most common comma errors?

You can avoid the most common comma errors by following these rules:

1. Place a comma after long introductory word groups.
   In *Cat on a Hot Tin Roof,* a wealthy Southern family deals with many crises.

2. Put a comma before a coordinating conjunction in a compound sentence.
   Maggie longs for her husband, but Brick is consumed with grief over the death of his best friend from high school.

3. Place a comma after each item in a series (except the last).
   Neither Brick, Maggie, nor Big Daddy himself realizes how little time he has.

4. Use a comma to separate equal adjectives.
   Big Daddy is a forceful, proud man.

5. Use commas to set off nonrestrictive word groups.
   But neither pride nor force can save him from cancer, which silently eats him away.

Exercise

Correct the comma errors in the following paragraph.

> Much of the conflict in *Cat on a Hot Tin Roof* comes from the fact that Brick cannot be the man he needs to be. An injury keeps him from playing football and the death of his friend haunts every moment of every day. Maggie wants her husband to be a husband and Big Daddy wants his son to be a son. While Big Daddy lives Brick doesn't have to stop wallowing. When Big Daddy discovers he is dying Brick has to crawl out of the bottle and take his father's place. It is a daunting difficult job and Brick has never before shown an interest in doing it. Once the shadow of Big Daddy has left his life Brick is ready to come into the light.

Edit

Check your commas. Make sure you have followed the five comma rules shown above.

3 I need to correct a number of errors that will probably confuse the reader.

2 I need to fix many errors that make my writing hard to read and understand.

1 I need help making corrections.

■ Have I correctly punctuated citations from the play?

You have correctly punctuated citations if you follow these rules.

1. Place the page number in parentheses before the end punctuation.

Brick says he is disgusted with "mendacity," or lying (79).

2. Do not use a period, but do use a question mark or an exclamation point in a quotation that ends the sentence.

Big Daddy asks about the word *mendacity*: "Don't it mean lying and liars?" (79).

3. When quoting from a verse play, show line breaks with a space, a slash, and a space; use Arabic numerals to indicate act, scene, and line; and separate these numbers with periods.

Perhaps the most famous line from *The Tempest* is spoken by Prospero after Caliban interrupts his fanciful masque: "We are such stuff / As dreams are made on, and our little life / Is rounded with a sleep" (4.1.156–158).

4. Show deletions from a quotation by using an ellipsis (three periods with a space before and after each one).

Big Daddy tells his wife, Ida, "You thought I was dying and you started taking over, well, . . . I'm not gonna die" (57).

Edit

Check the punctuation of your citations. Follow the rules above, making sure each citation is clear but unobtrusive.

Conventions
A comma is inserted and punctuation of a citation is corrected.

Jim is sorry‸ but Laura says, "I'll just imagine he had an operation. The horn was removed to make him feel less— freakish! . . . Now he will feel more at home with the other horses, the ones that don't have horns." (125)₎ Jim steals a kiss from Laura, but calls himself "stumblejohn" for . . .

Literature

Editing ■ Check for conventions.

Check your editing. On a piece of paper, write the numbers 1 to 12. Put a check by the number if you can answer "yes" to that question. If not, continue to edit your essay for that convention.

Editing Checklist

Conventions

PUNCTUATION

_____ **1.** Does each sentence have correct end punctuation?

_____ **2.** Have I used quotation marks and correctly cited direct quotations?

_____ **3.** Have I correctly hyphenated compound adjectives?

_____ **4.** Have I used parentheses to set off page numbers?

_____ **5.** Have I avoided comma errors?

CAPITALIZATION

_____ **6.** Do I start all my sentences with capital letters?

_____ **7.** Have I capitalized all proper nouns?

SPELLING

_____ **8.** Have I spelled all my words correctly?

_____ **9.** Have I double-checked the spelling of names and terms from the play?

GRAMMAR

_____ **10.** Have I used correct verb tenses throughout?

_____ **11.** Have I used the correct comparative and superlative forms?

_____ **12.** Have I used the right words *(its, it's)*?

■ Add a title.

Be sure to give your analysis a title that attracts the reader's attention and represents your essay well. Try one of these strategies:

■ Create a play on words: **Glass People**
■ Use a common expression: **Those Who Live in Glass Apartments**
■ Take a line from the essay: **Broken to Fit In**

Publishing ■ Share your essay.

You're nearly done! You've selected a topic, gathered and organized details, written a first draft, revised it, and edited it. Now it's time to share your analysis with others.

Make a final copy. Follow your teacher's instructions or use the guidelines below to format your paper. (If you are using a computer, see pages 91–95.) Prepare a final copy of your essay and proofread it for errors.

■ Focus on presentation.

- ■ Use blue or black ink and write neatly.
- ■ Write your name in the upper left corner of page 1.
- ■ Skip a line and center your title; skip another line and start your essay.
- ■ Indent every paragraph and leave a one-inch margin on all four sides.
- ■ Write your last name and the page number in the upper right-hand corner of every page after page 1.

Preform a Dramatic Reading

Present your analysis as a speech. Use props that represent important symbols or ideas in the play. If you have access to a video performance of the play, show short excerpts to make a point.

Post Online

Search online for the title of the play, looking for sites that include chat rooms or bulletin boards. Post your essay where others interested in the play can see it and read it.

Stage a Scene

Choose your favorite scene from the play and perform it with fellow classmates. Either read the scene dramatically (this is called "reader's theater"), or perform it—memorizing lines, blocking the action, and devising costumes, sets, props, and lighting.

Rubric for a Response to Literature

Use this rubric to guide and assess your writing. Refer to it whenever you want to improve your writing using the six traits.

6 Ideas	5	4
The ideas show a complete understanding of the reading.	The essay has a clear focus statement and necessary supporting details.	The essay has a clear focus statement. Unnecessary details need to be cut.

Organization		
All the parts work together to create an insightful essay.	The organization pattern fits the topic and purpose. All parts of the essay are well developed.	The organization pattern fits the topic and purpose. A part of the essay needs better development.

Voice		
The voice expresses interest and complete understanding. It engages the reader.	The voice expresses interest in and understanding of the topic.	The voice expresses interest but needs to show more understanding.

Word Choice		
The word choice reflects a thorough understanding of the reading.	The word choice, including the use of quotations, creates a clear message.	The word choice is clear, but better quotations would improve the essay.

Sentence Fluency		
The sentences in the essay create a clear flow of ideas.	The sentences are skillfully written and keep the reader's interest.	No sentence problems exist. More sentence variety is needed.

Conventions		
Grammar and punctuation are correct, and the copy is free of all errors.	The essay has one or two errors that do not interfere with the reader's understanding.	The essay has a few careless errors in punctuation and grammar.

3	2	1
The focus statement is too broad. A variety of details are needed.	The focus statement is unclear. More details are needed.	The essay needs a focus statement and details.
The organization fits the essay's purpose. Some parts need more development.	The organization doesn't fit the purpose.	A plan needs to be followed.
The voice needs to be more interesting and express more understanding.	The voice does not show interest in or an understanding of the topic.	The writer needs to understand how to create voice.
The word choice is too general, and quotations are needed.	Little attention is given to word choice.	The writer needs help with word choice.
A few sentence problems need to be corrected.	The essay has many sentence problems.	The writer needs to learn how to construct sentences.
The errors in the essay confuse the reader.	The number of errors makes the essay hard to read.	Help is needed to make corrections.

Literature

Evaluating a Response to Literature

Read the following analysis of Shakespeare's *The Tempest*. Then read the self-evaluation on the next page. **(There may be errors in the essay below.)**

Good Dreams and Evil Realities

Long before *The Poseidon Adventure, The Perfect Storm,* or *Titanic,* William Shakespeare wrote of another great shipwreck in *The Tempest*. A raging storm at sea batters the ship that carries King Alonso of Naples, Duke Antonio of Milan, and their retinue. These nobles and the ship's crew are "wracked" upon a strange and magical island. There, they all fall under the grand spell of Prospero, the rightful duke of Milan. In *The Tempest,* Shakespeare shows how good fantasies can transform evil realities.

Prospero's spell is meant to purge the bad blood in his family. Prospero's brother Antonio stole the throne of Milan from him and, with the help of the king of Naples, exiled Prospero and his young daughter, Miranda, to a desert island. There, Prospero discovered two strangely magical beings: Caliban, the monstrous man-fish, and Ariel, an airy spirit. Prospero takes charge of the brutish Caliban and the spiritual Ariel, using one to tame the island physically and the other to prepare his great spell.

The illusions begin with the tempest itself. Ariel and his spirit kin churn the sea and sky and make the ship seem to wreck on the shore. The usurping Antonio and the conniving Alonso stagger out of the ship along with their company. They have barely been on shore half an hour before Antonio and the brother to the king try to murder King Alonso and usurp his throne. Their plot, though, is broken up by Ariel, who sings to startle the conspirators and awaken the king. Throughout *The Tempest,* the illusions and magic that Prospero creates through Ariel perform this function—not destroying but saving.

As the play progresses, the shipwreck "survivors" split up and wander the island, each group experiencing illusions that suit their crimes. King Alonso thinks his son Ferdinand is dead—when in fact he is falling in love with Prospero's daughter, Miranda. Their marriage in the end will allow Prospero's daughter to gently "usurp" the rule of Naples. Meanwhile, Caliban falls in with the jester Trinculo and the drunken butler Stephano, and the three hatch a ridiculous plot to kill Prospero and take over his island. They end up hopelessly mired in mud and horse manure. Even Antonio must face up to what he has done. After presenting the usurper with an ethereal banquet, Ariel withdraws it before Antonio can eat and confronts him with his evil: "I and my fellows are ministers of fate," Ariel says, "But remember / (For that is my business to you) that you three from Milan / Did supplant good Prospero; . . . Upon your heads is nothing but heart's sorrow" (3.3.60-61, 68-70, 81).

Though Prospero might seem to be taking revenge, the purpose of these illusions isn't simply to punish, but to correct an evil reality. Alonso's son Ferdinand isn't truly dead. Nor is Antonio killed for his treason against his brother. In the end, a right relationship is created among them all. Prospero's wisdom, compassion, and maturity seem to reflect Shakespeare's own. *The Tempest* was one of the last plays Shakespeare ever wrote, and it has the feeling of a man putting his affairs in order. Prospero breaks his wand at the end of *The Tempest,* saying he will create no more illusions, and Shakespeare puts down his pen with the same result. In that way, *The Tempest* shows how Shakespeare believed that the good dream of theater has the power to correct the evil realities of the world outside.

Student Self-Assessment

Response Rubric Checklist

Title: <u>Good Dreams and Evil Realities</u>
Writer: <u>Dave Denoon</u>

4   **Ideas**
- Do I have a clear thesis statement?
- Do I use effective details?

4   **Organization**
- Does the beginning state the thesis?
- Does the middle focus on major elements?
- Does the ending expand the theme?

5   **Voice**
- Is my voice suitably analytical?
- Is my voice compelling as I narrate the plot?

4   **Word Choice**
- Have I used correct theater terminology?
- Have I focused on symbols?

5   **Sentence Fluency**
- Do my sentences read smoothly?

5   **Conventions**
- Have I followed the rules of English?

OVERALL COMMENTS:

I love <u>The Tempest</u>, and I did a good job exploring the play.

I should have gone into more depth analyzing the theme, and I should have used more quotations.

I mentioned the wand, but I should have talked about other symbols.

Use the rubric. Rate your essay using the rubric on pages 310–311. Write comments about your scores.

Reflecting on Your Writing

Take a few moments to think back on your experience of analyzing a play. Reflection helps you to retain what you have learned and prepare for future writing assignments.

My Play Analysis

1. The strongest part of my analysis is . . .

2. The part that most needs to be changed is . . .

3. The main thing I learned about analyzing a play is . . .

4. Next time I analyze a play or another work of literature, I would like to . . .

5. One question I still have about analyzing a play is . . .

6. Right now, I would describe my writing ability as (excellent, good, fair, poor) because . . .

Response to Literature
Analyzing a Novel

In a personal response, you explore your thoughts and feelings about a piece of literature. In a review, you discuss the merits of a particular literary work. In an analysis, you present your understanding or interpretation of a novel or a series of stories. Writing an effective literary analysis requires a high level of critical thinking on your part.

In this chapter, you will read a sample analysis of the novel *The Curious Incident of the Dog in the Night-Time* by Mark Haddon, tracing the theme of mystery that runs through the story. Then you will write your own analysis of a novel, focusing on a main theme or another key feature.

Base your literary analysis on a close and careful reading of the novel. Then present your ideas in a carefully planned essay, connecting all of your main points with specific references to the text.

Writing Guidelines

Subject: **A novel**
Form: **Literary analysis**
Purpose: **To analyze a main theme**
Audience: **Classmates**

"A good novel tells us the truth about its hero; but a bad novel tells us the truth about its author."

—G. K. Chesterton

Novel Analysis

In the following analysis, Andrew examines a main theme in the novel *The Curious Incident of the Dog in the Night-Time*. The side notes highlight important features in the analysis.

The Limits of Being Normal

Beginning
The beginning includes a quotation, background information, and the thesis statement (underlined).

Sherlock Holmes once asked Dr. Watson about "the curious incident of the dog in the night-time." When Watson pointed out that the dog did nothing in the night-time, Holmes responded, "That was the curious incident." In *The Curious Incident of the Dog in the Night-Time*, Mark Haddon introduces another detective obsessed with discovering the truth. Christopher John Francis Boone is a 15-year-old autistic savant who has trouble understanding other people but knows every prime number up to 7,057. As Christopher investigates the mysterious death of a neighborhood dog, Haddon uses the theme of mystery to explore the complexities of human interaction.

Middle
The main characters, situations, and conflicts are summarized.

The story begins when Christopher discovers a crime scene across the street. A large black poodle named Wellington lies dead, and Christopher kneels to cradle the dog. When the dog's owner discovers him there, Christopher says he did not kill the dog, but he gets in a scuffle with the police and lands in jail. After his father comes to get him out, Christopher pledges to solve the mystery of Wellington's death.

As Christopher investigates the killing, Haddon brings him into direct confrontation with a deeper mystery: other human beings. Like most people with autism, Christopher has trouble reading even simple facial expressions. At one point, he says that people look at him when they speak, trying to see what he is thinking, but he can't see what they are thinking. People are confusing to Christopher.

The writer analyzes the theme of mystery in the novel.

By contrast, he likes dogs because he can always tell what they are thinking; they have only four moods —"happy, sad, cross and concentrating"—and they don't lie since they can't talk (4). All these facts make Christopher alone in his social world and demonstrate the very meaning of the word *autism*. In fact, Christopher has a recurrent, favorite dream: "And in the dream nearly everyone on the earth is dead . . . and eventually there is no one left in the world" except people with autism (198).

Another elaboration on the theme is provided.

Haddon deepens the theme of mystery by exploring the complexities of human language. For example, Christopher never lies. A lie means saying something happened that didn't happen, and Christopher cannot see the point of it. For him, the only things worth speaking about are facts and mathematics. Christopher also doesn't understand jokes and metaphors, such as "apple of my eye." He writes, "When I try and make a picture of the phrase in my head, it just confuses me because imagining an apple in someone's eye doesn't have anything to do with liking someone a lot . . . " (15).

The writer outlines the climactic part of the book.

Christopher's quest for truth leads him inevitably to discover even deeper mysteries. Two years before the beginning of the story, Christopher's mother died of a sudden heart attack. At that time, Mrs. Shears, the neighbor woman who owned Wellington, became a family friend who helped them deal with their grief. Her friendship with the Boones ended on the night that Wellington was killed—but the question is whether the friendship ended because of the dog's death, or the dog died because the friendship ended. As Christopher investigates, he strips away years' worth of lies and discovers the truth.

Ending
The ending gives the theme its final interpretation.

At the beginning of the book, Christopher writes, "This is a murder mystery novel" (4), but it is much more than that. Haddon uses the theme of mystery to show how deeply mysterious human expressions, language, and relationships are to a person with autism. At first, the book seems to show the limitations of being autistic, but in the end, it shows the limits of being normal. Christopher himself describes it best in the final sentence of the book: "And I know I can do this because I went to London on my own, and because I solved the mystery of Who Killed Wellington? . . . and I was brave and I wrote a book and that means I can do anything" (221).

Respond to the reading. Answer the following questions.

Ideas (1) What theme does the analysis explore? (2) What does the analysis reveal about people with autism? Name two things.

Organization (3) How is the analysis organized?

Voice & Word Choice (4) What section of the analysis shows the essay writer at his analytical best? Explain your choice.

Literature

Prewriting ▪ Consider the elements of a novel.

Novels are complex, so if you try to consider a whole novel at once, you may feel overwhelmed. Instead, start your analysis by thinking about the novel's different elements. Andrew answered questions about the elements of *The Curious Incident of the Dog in the Night-Time* to clarify the book's complexities for himself.

Questions About Elements

Characters

—**Who is the main character?** Christopher Boone, a 15-year-old with autism

—**What other characters are in the novel?** Christopher's father, his counselor, the next-door neighbor, and Wellington, a black poodle

Setting

—**Where does the action take place?** Swindon and London, England

—**When does the action take place?** modern day

Conflict

—**What does the main character want?** to find out who killed Wellington

—**What obstacles does the character face?** his trouble understanding people

Plot

—**What happens at the beginning?** Christopher discovers that Wellington has been killed and pledges to find the killer.

—**What happens in the middle?** Christopher investigates and discovers a terrible secret, then runs away to London.

—**What happens in the ending?** Christopher solves the mystery of Wellington's death and determines to solve other deep mysteries about his own life.

Theme

—**What important idea about life is the author trying to convey?** the mystery of understanding other people and what it is like to be alone

—**What symbols represent the theme?** the dead dog, the drawer full of letters, red cars in a row, brown things, math problems

Prewrite

Consider the elements. Choose a novel to analyze. Then answer the questions above about it. Consider your book's major themes and how they are demonstrated through the characters, setting, conflict, and so on.

Prewriting ■ Write the thesis statement.

Once you have analyzed the elements of your novel, write a thesis statement about the theme you wish to focus on. Andrew used the following formula to focus on one theme of *The Curious Incident of the Dog in the Night-Time.*

main action		**idea about theme**		**a strong thesis statement**
Christopher investigates the mysterious death of a neighborhood dog.	**+**	Haddon uses the theme of mystery to explore the complexities of human interactions.	**=**	As Christopher investigates the mysterious death of a neighborhood dog, Haddon uses the theme of mystery to explore the complexities of human interactions.

Prewrite

Write your thesis statement. Use the model above to meld the story and theme of your novel into a strong thesis statement. Try two or three versions if necessary.

■ Gather support.

You should analyze the theme by showing how it is demonstrated through other elements of the story: characters, conflicts, and plot. Andrew used a gathering chart to list the ways these elements supported the theme of mystery.

Gathering Chart

Theme: The mystery of other people

Characters	Conflicts	Plot
Christopher has autism and doesn't understand others.	Christopher wants to solve the crime.	The police arrive and arrest Christopher.
The police officer doesn't understand Christopher's intentions.	When the police officer touches Christopher, he strikes back.	His father has to pick him up from lockup.

Prewrite

Support the theme. Create a chart like the one above, listing how characters, conflicts, and plot support the theme you have chosen to write about. Decide which details you would like to include in your analysis.

Literature

Writing ■ Write the first draft.

A first draft is your chance to put all your ideas on paper. Start by reading through your prewriting in order to have your main ideas firmly in mind. Then begin your draft. If new ideas come to you as you write, go ahead and add them. Below is a brief guide to writing your first draft.

■ Beginning

- ■ Write your introductory paragraph.
- ■ Include your thesis statement.

Tip

In your opening paragraph, include the name of the novel and the author.

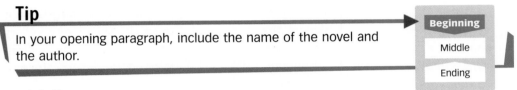

■ Middle

- ■ Use a separate paragraph for each of your main points.
- ■ Support your main points with details, including quoted words and phrases and specific examples from the novel.

Tip

Include whatever background is needed, but don't just retell the story. Explain how key elements present the theme.

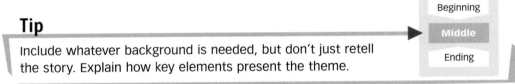

■ Ending

- ■ Restate your thesis statement and sum up your main points.
- ■ Offer your personal insights into the novel's theme.

Tip

End your analysis with something new. Delve into your topic and leave the reader with something to think about.

Write

Develop your first draft. Using your prewriting materials as a guide, write the first draft of your analysis.

Revising

After you have written a first draft, put it aside for a while to get a fresh perspective. Then revise your work for the first five traits.

Revise

Revise your analysis. Use the checklist below to guide your revision. Number a piece of paper from 1 to 12. If you can answer "yes" to a question, place a check mark beside the number. Keep revising until all questions are checked.

Revising Checklist

Ideas

_____ **1.** Have I clearly stated the thesis for my analysis?

_____ **2.** Do I include all the main ideas along with supporting details?

Organization

_____ **3.** Is my thinking reasonable and understandable?

_____ **4.** Does my analysis include a beginning, a middle, and an ending?

_____ **5.** Does each main point have its own paragraph with a focused topic sentence?

_____ **6.** Does my ending include a personal insight?

Voice

_____ **7.** Do I sound authoritative?

_____ **8.** Do I use quotations effectively to demonstrate the author's voice and the voice of different characters?

Word Choice

_____ **9.** Do I use words that clearly show my understanding?

_____ **10.** Do I avoid "loaded" words that make me sound biased in my interpretation?

Sentence Fluency

_____ **11.** Do my sentences move naturally from one point to the next?

_____ **12.** Do I use logical transitions?

Literature

Editing ▪ Check for conventions.

After you have made the necessary improvements in your analysis, you should edit your work for punctuation, capitalization, spelling, and grammar errors.

Edit

Edit for conventions. Use the following conventions checklist to guide your editing. Write the numbers 1 to 7 on a piece of paper. When you can answer "yes" to a question, place a check mark beside the number. Keep editing until you can answer "yes" to all the questions.

Editing Checklist

Conventions

_____ **1.** Have I used correct end punctuation after each sentence?

_____ **2.** Have I used commas correctly?

_____ **3.** Have I spelled all words correctly and checked any that I question?

_____ **4.** Do my subjects and verbs agree in number?

_____ **5.** Do my pronouns refer to clear antecedents and agree with them in number and gender?

_____ **6.** Have I placed quotation marks around exact words quoted from the novel?

_____ **7.** Have I included page numbers in parentheses after quoted material?

Publishing ▪ Share your analysis.

When you complete your analysis, it's time to share your ideas. Here are a number of options:

- **Send your analysis to a newspaper or magazine.** Check the submission guidelines and format the work as a review of a book.
- **Post your analysis at a library.** Ask your school or local librarian for permission.
- **E-mail your analysis to the publisher or author.** Search the Internet for a "contact us" link. Publishers and authors appreciate hearing from readers—especially those who like their books!

Publish

Publish your analysis. Choose one of the methods above, format your analysis accordingly, and share your work with others.

Writing for Assessment
Responding to Prompts About Literature

Many assessment tests now include writing about literature. The test will typically include a prompt asking you to respond to one or two specific aspects of a given literary selection. For instance, you may be asked to focus on the plot of a novel, the theme of a poem, or a character in a story. Your writing will show how well you understand these elements of literature.

In this chapter, you are reminded of the value of using the writing process—even in a timed test situation. You'll read examples of effective fiction and nonfiction responses, and you'll get a chance to respond to some prompts on your own.

Writing Guidelines

Subject:	**Literature prompt**
Form:	**Response to a prompt**
Purpose:	**To demonstrate competence**
Audience:	**Instructor**

"To understand a literary style, consider what it omits."

—Mason Cooley

"Surely that's the whole point about literature—that for a body of fiction to constitute literature, it must rise above its origins, its setting, even its language, to render accessible to a reader anywhere some insight into the human condition."

—Shashi Tharoor

Prewriting ■ Analyze a literature prompt.

A prompt about literature asks you to respond to specific characteristics of a story, a poem, a novel, or a nonfiction selection. As you read a prompt, look for key words that tell you exactly what the prompt requires (such as *explain, describe,* or *compare*). In the sample prompt below, key words and phrases are underlined. The word *discuss* gives the main direction or focus for the response.

Sample Prompt

John Milton's *Paradise Lost* follows <u>Adam and Eve's defiance</u> and fall from grace. In an essay, <u>discuss</u> how Milton uses <u>images of light and darkness to express other opposites</u> appearing throughout the poem. How does this <u>pattern</u> lead to your understanding of the epic poem's major theme? Support your thesis with examples from the text.

Try It!

Copy the following sample prompts on a sheet of paper. Underline key words and phrases for each prompt and make notes about the kinds of supporting information that you would need for a response.

1. *Go Tell It on the Mountain* is James Baldwin's account of a Southern family's move to Harlem and young John's struggle with his identity. Write an essay that compares John's feelings about white people to those of Gabriel (his stepfather) and to those of Richard (his natural father). Quote the characters in your response.

2. In Sylvia Plath's *The Ball Jar,* Esther, a smart, ambitious young woman, searches for values in 1950s America but eventually suffers a nervous breakdown. In an essay, describe the role that Esther's mother—and Esther's attitude toward her—plays in the main character's breakdown.

■ Plan your response.

Once you analyze and understand a prompt, you are ready to plan your response. If a reading selection is provided, read it with the prompt in mind, picking out the information you need for your response. Then form your topic sentence and organize the details.

Sample Prompt and Selection

This excerpt from Thoreau's *Walden* focuses on the author's surroundings. In a paragraph, describe the feeling or mood created in this passage.

My <u>nearest neighbor is</u> a mile <u>distant</u>, and <u>no house is visible</u> from any place but the hill-tops within half a mile of my own. I have my <u>horizon bounded by woods</u> all to myself; a distant view of the railroad where it touches the pond on the one hand, and of the fence which skirts the woodland road on the other. But for the most part it is <u>as solitary where I live as on the prairies</u>. . . . I have, as it were, my own sun and moon and stars, and <u>a little world all to myself</u>.

> The underlined words connote solitude.

■ Write a topic sentence.

After reading the prompt and selection, one student wrote this topic sentence.

> **Thoreau's description of his surroundings** (specific topic) **creates a feeling of pleasing solitude** (focus related to the prompt).

■ Create a graphic organizer.

The student also used a graphic organizer to gather details.

Author's terms	Feeling created
nearest neighbor is distant	privacy
horizon bounded by woods	security
solitary as the prairies	isolation
little world all to myself	satisfaction

Literature

Writing ▪ Respond to a literature prompt.

Note below how one student underlined key phrases and added side notes on a copy of the selection to address the focus of the prompt.

Sample Prompt and Selection

The excerpt below is from F. Scott Fitzgerald's short story "The Diamond as Big as the Ritz," a tale about the Washingtons, a ridiculously wealthy family, who think they are entirely above the law and general social customs. In a brief essay, discuss how Fitzgerald portrays the family and their vision of reality.

The awestruck young visitor learns that the owner had workers kidnapped for his personal use and yet ended up disappointed in their conventionalism.

John was enchanted by the wonders of the château and the valley. Braddock Washington, so Percy told him, had caused to be kidnapped a landscape gardener, an architect, a designer of state settings, and a French decadent poet left over from the last century. He . . . left them to work out some ideas of their own. But one by one they had shown their uselessness. . . . And as for the architect and the landscape gardener, they thought only in terms of convention. They must make this like this and that like that.

But . . . they all went mad early one morning . . . and were now confined comfortably in an insane asylum at Westport, Connecticut.

"But," inquired John curiously, "who did plan all your wonderful reception rooms and halls, and approaches and bathrooms—?"

"Well," answered Percy, "I blush to tell you, but it was a moving-picture fella. He was the only man we found who was used to playing with an unlimited amount of money, though he did tuck his napkin in his collar and couldn't read or write."

Even someone who met their standards in terms of being able to spend enough money comes up short in other ways.

As August drew to a close John began to regret that he must soon go back to school. He and Kismine had decided to elope the following June.

"It would be nicer to be married here," Kismine confessed, "but of course I could never get father's permission to marry you at all. Next to that I'd rather elope. It's terrible for wealthy people to be married in America at present—they always have to send out bulletins to the press saying that they're going to be married in remnants, when what they mean is just a peck of old second-hand pearls and some used lace worn once by the Empress Eugenie."

The dialogue reveals how the speakers feel about what they see as the "struggle" of wealthy people.

"I know," agreed John fervently. ". . . Gwendolyn married a man whose father owns half of West Virginia. She wrote home saying what a tough struggle she was carrying on on his salary as a bank clerk—and then she ended up by saying that 'Thank God, I have four good maids anyhow, and that helps a little.' "

"It's absurd," commented Kismine. "Think of the millions and millions of people in the world, labourers and all, who get along with only two maids."

■ Write a thesis statement.

After reading the excerpt and making notes, the student wrote the following thesis statement for his response essay.

> **The perception of life held by the Washingtons** (specific topic) **shows that these people are, in fact, out of touch with reality** (particular focus related to the prompt).

■ Create a graphic organizer.

The student writer used a line diagram to organize the main points and supporting details for an essay response.

the Washingtons

"real" struggle

employing gardners, architects, and poets

need workers used to "playing" with real money

condescension toward others

no idea how ordinary wealthy people live

belittles sending out press bulletins

"tough struggle" to have four maids

Writing ▪ Student Response

In this student response to the excerpt from "The Diamond as Big as the Ritz," note how the writer used details from the story to support the thesis statement.

Beginning
The first paragraph leads up to the thesis statement (underlined).

Whose Reality?

This excerpt from F. Scott Fitzgerald's story "The Diamond as Big as the Ritz" elicits an ironic feeling about "poor rich people." Most individuals strive to improve their lives, but most people can only wish for what the Washingtons see as a burden or strain. <u>The perception of life held by the Washingtons shows that these people are, in fact, out of touch with reality.</u>

Middle
One paragraph focuses on the Washingtons' "struggles."

The characters in this story come off as somewhat pathetic as they describe what they perceive as real struggles in their lives. In the realm of extreme wealth portrayed here, there are chateaus and villas in which to employ gardeners and architects—and poets! It seems, however, such a burden for Braddock Washington to locate the workers, only to find that they think "only in terms of convention." Their uselessness evident, he finds someone "used to playing with an unlimited amount of money"—obviously an important attribute. Braddock seems unaware of the fact that inhabitants of the average household, by contrast, maintain a comfortable home all by themselves. In doing so, they deal with more immediate and pressing struggles, both financial and physical.

Fitzgerald reveals how condescending the Washingtons are toward those who aren't like them.

The other middle paragraph focuses on how condescending they are toward others.

The Washingtons don't have any idea how ordinary wealthy people live. Toward the end of the excerpt, Kismine relates how wealthy people feel obligated to "send out bulletins to the press" about their valuable wedding clothes, but then she goes on to belittle this practice: "what they mean is just a peck of old second-hand pearls and some used lace." And then John agrees with her, scoffing at the "tough struggle" of a wealthy family with four maids. Again, Kismine demeans such suffering as "absurd"; but then she betrays her ignorance by commenting on how well most people, "labourers and all," do with only two!

Ending
The closing restates the thesis and provides a final thought.

Fitzgerald does not say that wealthy people's perception of struggling is invalid. He acknowledges that wealthy people suffer, too, in their own little worlds, but he implies that their struggles are so far from the reality of most people as to make them almost laughable. This excerpt seems to add just one more aspect to a phrase famously attributed to Fitzgerald: "The very rich are different from you and me."

Respond to the reading. Answer the following questions about the student response. Explain your answers.

Ideas (1) What is the focus of the student writer's thesis statement? (2) Does each middle paragraph clearly support the thesis statement? Explain.

Organization (3) Does the ending connect with the beginning? Explain.

Voice & Word Choice (4) Which verbs used by the student writer seem most effective? List three or four.

Practice Literary Prompt

Whenever you respond to a writing prompt, especially in a timed situation, begin by studying the prompt. Find the key word that indicates what you are to do in the response: *compare, explain, describe,* and so on.

In addition, be sure that you understand any specific points you need to address in your response before you read the selection. Of course, it is important to quote examples and specific details from the selection to support your thesis. However, it is equally important to share your own insights about the selection.

Practice Prompt and Selection

In the following poem, William Butler Yeats reacts to the state of humanity following World War I. Explain how Yeats portrays the world, paying careful attention to the disturbing images throughout the poem.

The Second Coming

by William Butler Yeats

Turning and turning in the widening gyre[1]
The falcon cannot hear the falconer;
Things fall apart; the centre cannot hold;
Mere anarchy is loosed upon the world,
The blood-dimmed tide is loosed, and everywhere
The ceremony of innocence is drowned;
The best lack all conviction, while the worst
Are full of passionate intensity.

Surely some revelation is at hand;
Surely the Second Coming is at hand.
The Second Coming! Hardly are those words out
When a vast image out of Spiritus Mundi[2]
Troubles my sight: somewhere in sands of the desert
A shape with lion body and the head of a man,

A gaze blank and pitiless as the sun,
Is moving its slow thighs, while all about it
Reel shadows of the indignant desert birds.
The darkness drops again; but now I know
That twenty centuries of stony sleep
Were vexed to nightmare by a rocking cradle,
And what rough beast, its hour come round at last,
Slouches towards Bethlehem to be born?

[1] gyre: spiral
[2] Spiritus Mundi: the collective
   spirit of mankind

Respond to a fiction prompt. Read Yeats's poem (above). After reading through everything once, read the prompt again to make sure you understand its focus. Then carefully reread the poem. Next, form a thesis statement; quickly arrange your main supporting details in a graphic organizer; and write your essay. When you're through, check your work for spelling, mechanics, and punctuation errors.

Literature

Writing ■ Respond to a nonfiction prompt.

The following prompt deals with a nonfiction selection. A student has underlined key words and phrases in the selection and added notes in the margin.

Prompt and Selection

While very young, Helen Keller lost her sight and hearing. In this excerpt from her autobiography, *The Story of My Life,* Keller describes several episodes from her early life. Explain in an essay why you think Ms. Keller shared these particular memories. What do they say about the youngster's resourcefulness?

These memories, for different reasons, made impressions on Helen.

Many incidents of those early years are fixed in my memory, isolated, but clear and distinct, making the sense of that silent, aimless, dayless life all the more intense.

At five I learned to fold and put away the clean clothes when they were brought in from the laundry, and I distinguished my own from the rest. I knew by the way my mother and aunt dressed when they were going out, and I invariably begged to go with them. I was always sent for when there was company, and when the guests took their leave, I waved my hand to them, I think with a vague remembrance of the meaning of the gesture.

In one memory, she learns something the hard way.

One day I happened to spill water on my apron, and I spread it out to dry before the fire which was flickering on the sitting-room hearth. The apron did not dry quickly enough to suit me, so I drew nearer and threw it right over the hot ashes. The fire leaped into life; the flames encircled me so that in a moment my clothes were blazing. I made a terrified noise that brought Viny, my old nurse, to the rescue. Throwing a blanket over me, she almost suffocated me, but she put out the fire. Except for my hands and hair, I was not badly burned.

In this memory, she learns to her great satisfaction that she can have power over others.

About this time I found out the use of a key. One morning I locked my mother up in the pantry, where she . . . kept pounding on the door, while I sat outside on the porch steps and laughed with glee as I felt the jar of the pounding. This most naughty prank of mine convinced my parents that I must be taught as soon as possible. After my teacher, Miss Sullivan, came to me, I sought an early opportunity to lock her in her room. I went upstairs with something which my mother made me understand

I was to give to Miss Sullivan; but no sooner had I given it to her than I slammed the door, locked it, and hid the key under the wardrobe in the hall. I could not be induced to tell where the key was. My father was obliged to get a ladder and take Miss Sullivan out through the window— much to my delight. Months after I produced the key.

Despite trying, she does not learn the reason for a mystery.

When I was about five years old we moved. . . . My earliest distinct recollection of my father is making my way through great drifts of newspapers to his side and finding him alone, holding a sheet of paper before his face. I was greatly puzzled to know what he was doing. I imitated this action, even wearing his spectacles, thinking they might help solve the mystery. But I did not find out the secret for several years. Then I learned what those papers were, and that my father edited one of them.

■ Write a thesis statement.

After reading the excerpt and making notes, the student wrote the following thesis statement for her essay.

> **Sharing these particular memories** (specific topic) **demonstrates that Ms. Keller didn't let her disabilities prevent her from trying to discover some things on her own** (focus related to the prompt).

■ Create a graphic organizer.

The student writer organized her details using a collection grid.

Memory	What she learned from it
Placing damp apron on fire	Getting too close to fire means you get burned.
Discovery of what a key does	She could lock people up, gaining control for a brief time.
Father with paper in front of his face	Sometimes you don't learn the reason for an action just by imitating it.

■ Student Response

Having completed her planning, the student wrote the following essay in response to the prompt and excerpt from *The Story of My Life*.

Beginning
The first paragraph identifies the subject of the prompt and leads up to the thesis statement (underlined).

Middle
The middle paragraphs focus on the different memories.

Rising Above

This excerpt from Helen Keller's autobiography, The Story of My Life, focuses on a few key memories from her very early life, after she lost her ability to see or hear. It would be easy to believe that a child without these abilities would have no incentive to learn, living a "silent, aimless, dayless life." But by sharing these particular memories, Ms. Keller demonstrates that she didn't let her disabilities prevent her from trying to discover some things on her own.

She relates how she learned to use her sense of touch to distinguish her clothes from others in the laundry and to determine how her mother and aunt were dressed when they went out. She also recalls being summoned to wave to guests when they would leave, but with only "a vague remembrance of the meaning of the gesture." But from each of three specific memories, she appears to have learned something distinctly important.

First, she remembers placing a damp apron near the fire to dry. Her impatience leads her to draw closer to the hearth to put the apron directly on the hot ashes, where it promptly catches fire. Helen makes "a terrified noise" that brings help, preventing her from serious injury. The lesson learned from this encounter was a rather simple one about physical danger.

The next memory she describes illustrates a more complex lesson. Helen not only learns how to use a key but also finds that this knowledge gives her a modicum of control over others. She locks up both her mother and her teacher and—despite her awareness that it's a "most naughty prank"—takes delight from it. She experiences the thrill of having power.

In the final memory, Ms. Keller admits to a degree of defeat in her effort to unravel a certain mystery. Imagine her frustration at finding her father "alone, holding a sheet of paper before his face" and not having a clue as to the reason for such an action! Of course, imitation doesn't reveal his motive. The child learns that she won't always be able to puzzle things out on her own; in this case, she doesn't uncover "the secret" until several years later.

Helen Keller's remarkable resourcefulness eventually led her to rise above her disabilities. Her innate intelligence and spirit come through in this excerpt as she relates these memories and what she learned from them. Sharing them is inspirational, giving hope to others who feel somehow limited.

Respond to the reading. Answer the following questions about the student response.

Ideas (1) What is the thesis of the student's response? (2) What details does the student use to support her thesis? Name three.

Organization (3) How does the writer organize her response? (4) Does each middle paragraph clearly support the thesis statement? Explain.

Voice & Word Choice (5) Which words or phrases quoted from the story are most effective? Name two.

Practice Nonfiction Prompt

Whether you are reading and responding to fiction or nonfiction, remember that the author of the selection carefully chose the words to describe a person, establish a setting, share information, arouse an emotion, and so on. In a response, be just as careful when choosing your words.

Practice Prompt and Selection

The following excerpt is from Diane Eickhoff's *Revolutionary Heart*, a biography of Clarina Nichols, a pioneer in the women's rights movement. In an essay, describe how Clarina's parents shaped her beliefs. How did they instill in her the idea of equality?

Clarina Irene Howard was born January 25, 1810, in West Townshend, a small farming village tucked into the Green Mountains of southern Vermont. If she were alive today, she would easily recognize the countryside where she grew up—the bend in the river, the valley, the mountains that wrap themselves around the little town like a giant's protective arm.

Clarina Howard's earliest American ancestor was William Hayward, a young Puritan who at eighteen set sail from England in the mid-1630s, married an adventurous shipmate two years his senior, fathered four sons, and died at sea in 1653. In fact, both sides of her family had pedigrees intertwined with the farmers, merchants, soldiers and statesmen who formed New England in its early days. After her grandfathers fought in the Revolutionary War, they "packed their brides on horseback, with feather beds strapped on behind and blazed tracks from Connecticut, Massachusetts, and Rhode Island to the green hills and fertile valleys of the Green Mountain State." Though Vermont was an isolated, uncultivated wilderness at that time, there were opportunities for people willing to work hard for the chance to improve their fortunes—which Clarina's grandparents did to a remarkable degree.

Chapin Howard, her father, operated the town's tannery, a business that turned raw animal skins into leather for sturdy shoes and stout harnesses. An ambitious, public-spirited, likable man, Chapin later owned a hotel, served three terms in the state legislature, helped organize and finance a Baptist seminary in Townshend, and made a fortune with his son Aurelius buying and selling land in territorial Michigan. By the time Clarina Howard was grown, her father was one of the wealthiest men in town, but because he was generous, tactful, and didn't put on airs, Mr.

Howard was respected by rich and poor alike.

Her mother, Birsha Smith Howard, expected her daughters to work hard, even though the family was wealthy enough to employ servants. Mrs. Howard wanted to make sure her five daughters could run their own households, with or without servants. As she grew up, young Clarina learned how to cook delicate pastries and roast gourmet cuts of beef, but she also learned how to milk cows, churn butter, and take care of vegetables from planting to pickling. Though every female was expected to develop some level of proficiency in the sewing arts, Mrs. Howard's eldest daughter excelled at any type of handwork. After she had solved a vexing sewing problem with a bit of collar ribbon, her mother declared, "That is Clarina all over—so ingenious!" She became expert at fine embroidery, could spin and weave, sew and knit, and construct every article of clothing from dainty bonnets to thick wool stockings. She was especially apt at knitting, which would become a trademark occupation for her later in life. "We always knit while we read," she would one day tell the reformer Amelia Bloomer, "and can think so much better to the click of the needles."

Despite being well-to-do, the Howards were not extravagant and didn't spend money unnecessarily. Clarina Nichols recalled having "a handsome suit for summer and another for winter." The following year her Sunday dress became her everyday dress, and her everyday dress became her petticoat. Old petticoats were used for quilts and hooked rugs. After that they could still be used for patches and rags. She liked to quote her grandmother Smith's words: "There is nothing like economy in a family."

Mrs. Howard was a good republican mother who understood the need for an educated citizenry. All her children—the five girls as well as the three boys—received good basic educations. She expected them to do well in school, and she meant business. Clarina Nichols recalled being spanked once because she was unable to spell the word "cider." She needed little incentive after that: "I took to learning like a duck to water."

Respond to a nonfiction prompt. Read the practice prompt on the previous page again to be sure that you understand its focus. Then carefully reread the selection. Next, form a thesis statement; quickly arrange your main supporting details in a graphic organizer; and write your essay. Use the revising and editing tips on the next page to check your response before turning it in.

Literature

Revising ▪ Improve your response.

Always review your response at the end of a writing test. Make any changes and corrections as neatly as possible. Use the following questions to help you revise your response.

- ▪ **Ideas** Does my thesis statement address the focus of the prompt? Do the details support the thesis?

- ▪ **Organization** Have I included a beginning, a middle, and an ending? Does each paragraph have a focus? Did I conclude with an insight about the literature selection?

- ▪ **Voice** Do I sound knowledgeable and confident?

- ▪ **Word Choice** Do the words that I use reflect a thorough understanding of the literature selection? Have I avoided any unnecessary repetition?

- ▪ **Sentence Fluency** Are all of my sentences complete? Do my sentences flow smoothly from one to the next?

Revise

Improve your work. Reread your practice response, asking yourself the questions above. Make any necessary changes neatly.

Editing ▪ Check your response.

In your final read-through, check your punctuation, capitalization, spelling, and grammar.

Editing Checklist

Conventions

_____ **1.** Have I used end punctuation for every sentence?

_____ **2.** Have I capitalized all proper nouns and first words of sentences?

_____ **3.** Have I checked the spelling in my work?

_____ **4.** Have I made sure my subjects and verbs agree?

_____ **5.** Have I put quotation marks around the exact words that I quoted from the selection?

Edit

Check your response. Read over your work, looking for errors in punctuation, capitalization, spelling, and grammar. Make corrections neatly.

Responding to Literature on Tests

Use the following tips as a guide whenever you respond to a prompt about literature. These tips will help you respond to both fiction and nonfiction selections.

Before You Write . . .

- **Be clear about the time limit.**
  Plan enough time for prewriting, writing, and revising.
- **Understand the prompt.**
  Be sure that you know what the prompt requires. Pay special attention to the key word that tells you what you need to do.
- **Read the selection with the focus of the prompt in mind.**
  Take notes that will help you form your thesis. If you're working on a copy of the selection, underline important details.
- **Form your thesis statement.**
  The thesis statement should identify the specific topic plus the focus of the prompt.
- **Fill in a graphic organizer.**
  Jot down main points and possible quotations for your essay.

As You Write . . .

- **Maintain the focus of your essay.**
  Keep your thesis in mind as you write.
- **Be selective.** Use examples from your graphic organizer and the selection to support your thesis.
- **End in a meaningful way.**
  Start by revisiting the thesis. Then try to share a final insight about the topic with the reader.

After You Have Written a First Draft . . .

- **Check for completeness and correctness.**
  Use the questions on page **338** to revise your essay. Then check for errors in punctuation, capitalization, spelling, and grammar.

Try It!

Read and analyze a prompt and literary selection your teacher supplies. Form a thesis statement that reflects the focus of the prompt, list supporting ideas in a graphic organizer, and write your essay. Then revise and edit your response.

Literature

Creative Writing

Writing Stories

Stories can do many things. They can take us to faraway places and let us experience cultures other than our own. They can make us laugh or cry through exciting plots that keep us reading. But stories can offer more than just excitement or inventiveness. They also explore a character's inner feelings, sharing with us moments that can be very familiar, very similar to our own experiences. They allow us to examine those feelings and maybe understand ourselves a little better.

In this chapter, you will be writing a story that explores a character's inner feelings. You will establish a situation that tests a character's beliefs and examine the way that situation affects the person. You will also explore how to use a symbol to represent important characters or items in the story.

Writing Guidelines

Subject: A character's inner feelings
Form: Short story
Purpose: To engage and entertain
Audience: Classmates

"The American imagination releases itself very easily in the short story—and has done so since the beginning of our national history."
—Henry Seidel Canby

The Shape of Stories

Most stories create dramatic tension by establishing a conflict, introducing complications, building to a climax, and so on. The graphic that follows shows the basic pattern that most fiction follows.

Plot Line

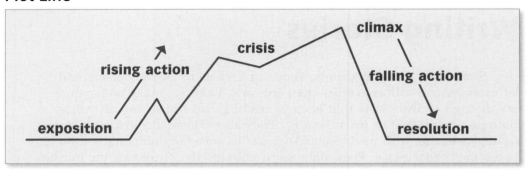

The **exposition** introduces the main character(s), the settings, and the conflict. It gives background information the reader needs to understand the story.

The **rising action** is a series of events, called *complications,* that build suspense. Each event develops the story line. During the rising action, the drama builds as the character faces complications that block his or her way.

The **crisis** is a moment of realization for the main character, when he or she comes to some decision or does something that will determine the outcome of the story. The crisis is not the climax but will lead to it.

The **climax** is the moment of truth, or the emotional high point of the story, when the main character either triumphs or fails. The climax should also somehow cause a change, either obvious or subtle, in the main character.

The **falling action** shows how the main character adjusts to the change.

The **resolution,** also called the *denouement,* is the ending. The falling action and resolution should be short, bringing the story to a satisfying close.

Try It!

Think about a story you read recently and answer these questions.

1. Who was the main character, and what was the setting? (exposition)
2. What challenges did the main character face? (rising action)
3. When did the main character make a difficult decision? (crisis)
4. What was the high point of the story? (climax)
5. What happened afterward? (falling action and resolution)

Sample Story

Every story has conflict, but sometimes that conflict is subtle. Some stories revolve around characters and the forces that motivate and change them. Jordan decided to write about how a single moment can change someone's life.

Soaking

Marcus pulled into his driveway, shut off the engine, and sank back, exhausted. Football practice had been brutal, and every fiber of his being was calling out for a hot, soaking bath. Of course, Mom would have other ideas. She always wanted him to do homework before anything else—before watching TV or talking on the phone or even taking a bath. But tonight was different. It had to be. Marcus felt like one big bruise. *I'm going to take that bath,* Marcus thought, *no matter what.*

He dragged himself up to the back door and was surprised to find it locked. Odd. His mother usually left the door open. Digging around in the garden, he found the "secret" rock that hid the spare key and let himself in. The house was unusually quiet.

"Mom?" he called out, but got no answer. He shrugged. Strange. She always made it a point of being there when he and his sister Chelsea got home.

This is my golden opportunity. As long as Mom's not home, there won't be any nagging about homework.

Marcus went to the kitchen, opened the fridge, and crouched down, staring in. On the bottom shelf sat a plastic container with baby carrots in water, what Mom called the perfect after-school snack. She had a strange idea of perfection. If she were here, Marcus would be crunching carrots—but since she wasn't . . . He reached to the cupboard above the fridge and pulled out some snack cakes and chips. Mom once kidded that she weighed the junk food to make sure nobody cheated, but Marcus doubted it. *She won't notice a little grazing. Besides, I've probably burned ten thousand calories at practice. It's not a problem.* Finishing his snack, Marcus hauled himself upstairs for a long, hot soak.

He stepped into the bathroom, leaned down to the tub, and grasped the porcelain handle. Twisting it brought out a gurgling column of water. Once it was hot, Marcus plugged the tub, pulled Mom's Epsom salts from the closet,

The **exposition** presents the central symbol—the bath—and the first step in the rising action.

The **rising action** adds complications and develops the central symbol.

and poured some in. *This is going to be good,* he thought, anticipating the joy of the warm water enveloping his body.

As the tub filled, Marcus went to his room to get some clean clothes. A pile of clean laundry waited on the bed. *I guess I'm supposed to fold these and put them away. Yeah, right. I've got my own system.* Marcus scooped up the pile of clothes, carried it to a big chair by the window, and dumped it atop last week's pile. Then he plucked a wrinkled T-shirt, sweats, underwear, and mismatched socks from the mess and carried them with him toward the bathroom.

Halfway there, his eye snagged on the books stacked on his desk. He could almost hear his mother say, "Homework first!" but the thought just made him snort. *Homework last. First a bath, and then the Packers, and then algebra—cramming for the test tomorrow. I can't do it right now anyway. I need Mom's help.*

The telephone rang. Marcus startled. "It's probably her, making sure I'm doing my homework." He went out into the hallway, grabbed the cordless, and went in to check on the bathwater.

"Marcus?" It was his father's voice.

"Hey, Dad! You gonna be home soon? The Packers are on TV tonight."

"Marcus, listen!" His father's sharp voice cut him off.

"Dad? What's wrong?" Marcus asked, quickly turning off the water.

"I'm at the hospital, son. You mother's been in an accident. A drunk driver . . . " Marcus sat on the side of the tub, suddenly unable to breathe, as though he'd been dunked in a tank of ice water.

"Is she—okay?" he heard himself say.

"The doctors said she'll pull through, but she's pretty well banged up. Her leg's broken, she's got some cracked ribs, and her shoulder was crushed. She'll be in the hospital for a while, and then she'll have a long recovery period."

"I'll be right there," Marcus said.

"No, don't. She'll be asleep for a while. Besides, I need you to wait for Chelsea. When she gets home from her Scout meeting, you'll have to tell her. You can bring her here with you then."

Marcus couldn't speak, but finally managed to squeak out a sound. "Okay. Tell her I love her, will you?"

New complications are presented through dialogue, leading up to a **crisis** for the main character.

"I will," his father said, and then he started to cry. Marcus had never heard his father cry before.

"Dad? I love you, too," Marcus said. It was quiet on the other end.

"I love you, son." *How long has it been since he said that to me?*

The cooling bathwater reflects a key change in the story line.

He hung up, and Marcus sat numbly, phone in hand, for a long time. When he finally looked at his tub, the water had cooled. He opened the drain and went back into his room to change into clean clothes. Afterward, he sat down, feeling out of breath.

The **climax** comes when Marcus realizes his life has changed.

Sitting on his unmade bed, Marcus gazed around the room, so familiar and suddenly so strange. Clothes and books were everywhere—his hockey skates sitting in a corner, papers and junk cluttering the top of his dresser, CD cases everywhere but in their rack. His mother was always after him to pick up, and she usually just got disgusted and cleaned it for him. He'd never even thought about it, or the million other little things she was always doing for him and his sister. Now it would be his turn to take care of her as she recovered. It would be different, but he would handle it. He had to.

The **final metaphor** represents the change in the character's life.

Marcus sat down on the floor by the big chair and slowly began folding his laundry. *After I finish this, I'll clean the rest of this dump. Then it'll be algebra until Chelsea gets home, and I'll make sure Chelsea brings her homework to the hospital, too. . . .* Marcus continued folding clothes, letting the eerie quiet of the empty house rise up around him. The only sound was the gentle gurgle of bathwater spiraling down the drain.

Respond to the reading. Answer the following questions.

Ideas (1) What is the conflict? (2) What is the significance of Marcus's room in the story?

Organization (3) How does the story build in suspense?

Voice (4) How does the writer show us the character's thoughts? (5) How does the dialogue help create a feeling?

Prewriting ■ Find your focus.

You can develop a story idea by listing possibilities for the three basic elements: character, conflict, and setting. *Remember:* Your story will focus on a character whose views are tested and changed. Jordan generated this story-elements chart:

Story-Elements Chart

Characters	Conflicts	Settings
a track star	trying to find a job	a highway
the new kid	losing a game or contest	a rundown park
a linebacker	adopting a pet	a fast-food restaurant
the preacher's son	dealing with an injury	a car wash

By mixing and matching the different entries in the columns, Jordan came up with the following list of possible stories. He starred the one he decided to use.

> – A track star adopts a pet greyhound and trains it in a rundown park.
> – The preacher's son loses a fund-raising contest at a car wash.
> – A linebacker deals with his mother's injury in a crash on the highway. *

Prewrite

Create a story-elements chart. List characters, conflicts, and settings. Then mix and match them to develop three story ideas and choose one.

■ Build complications.

Next, Jordan listed complications—events that would increase the conflict, leading toward the climax of the story.

> First . . . the player's mom isn't home.
> Then . . . he's glad she's not there to boss him around.
> Next . . . he gets a phone call to say she's been in a car wreck.
> After . . . he feels bad he took her for granted.

Prewrite

List complications. Write "First," "Then," "Next," and "After" on a piece of paper. Then write down how the conflict begins. Continue by writing events or details that make the conflict more serious, leading to a climax.

■ Develop a symbol.

A symbol is a person, a place, a thing, or an event that represents something else. You can use a symbol to make ideas concrete and to unify action. Jordan used a thought map to think about symbols. He wrote important characters and ideas in the center, and then thought of concrete symbols to represent them.

Thought Map

 Prewrite

Create a thought map. Write down important characters and ideas for your story. Then write possible symbols of each, connecting them. Choose one main symbol for your story, but also keep the other symbols in mind.

■ Use dialogue.

Dialogue lets characters speak for themselves. Jordan's story uses regular dialogue, set off with quotation marks (" "), and internal dialogue, indicated with *italics*, which lets the reader hear the conflict inside the main character.

"I love you, son." *How long has it been since he said that to me?*

Note: Use internal dialogue only with the main character so that your point of view does not shift.

Try It!

Experiment with dialogue. Answer each of the following questions the way your main character would. Use regular dialogue to let the person speak and use internal dialogue to show what the person is thinking.

1. What's your least favorite thing to do?

Example answer: "Algebra homework," Marcus said. *Though cleaning my room would be a close second.*

2. What's your favorite thing to do?
3. What's the biggest challenge that you face?
4. Do you think you'll overcome the challenge? Why or why not?

Writing ▪ Develop the first draft.

Your story should include a beginning, a middle, and an ending that work together to show how the character changes.

▪ Start strong.

In your beginning, you should capture your reader's interest and introduce the main character, setting, and conflict. Here are strategies for capturing your reader's attention.

- **Present your symbol.**
  As he drove from football practice, Marcus could think only of a steaming bathtub, the water hot enough to boil away his bruises.

- **Begin with action.**
  Crunch! Marcus collapsed beneath a pile of jerseys and shoulder pads. It was the last tackle in the last skirmish of practice, and it made every bone and bruise ache.

- **Begin with dialogue.**
  "Hey, Mom," Marcus said, walking through the front door. "You home?"

- **Set the scene.**
  Marcus pulled into his driveway, shut off the engine, and sank back, exhausted.

▪ Build the action.

In the middle of your story, provide complications that lead to the climax. Follow these tips:

- Use **action** that shows what the main character is experiencing.
- Use **dialogue** to let characters speak, and use **internal dialogue** to show the thoughts of your main character.
- Unify the middle of your story using a **symbol** for an important idea.
- Intensify the **conflict** as the character approaches the climax.

▪ Bring the story to a close.

Show how the character is changed by the climax. Then, in the falling action and resolution, indicate how life will be different for him or her.

Write your first draft. Use your planning from pages 346–347 and the information above to guide your writing.

Revising ■ Improve your writing.

Use the following checklists as you revise and edit your story.

Revising Checklist

Ideas

_____ **1.** Is my main character believable?
_____ **2.** Is the conflict clear, and is the change obvious?
_____ **3.** Have I described the setting (place and time) clearly?

Organization

_____ **4.** Does my beginning capture the reader's interest and introduce the main character, setting, and conflict?
_____ **5.** Does my middle provide complications that lead to the climax?
_____ **6.** Does my ending resolve the conflict and show how the character changed?

Voice

_____ **7.** Does my dialogue (regular and internal) sound natural?

Word Choice

_____ **8.** Have I used specific nouns and active verbs?

Sentence Fluency

_____ **9.** Do I vary my sentence types to create an effective rhythm?

Editing ■ Check for conventions.

When you edit, check your *punctuation, capitalization, spelling,* and *grammar.*

Editing Checklist

Conventions

_____ **1.** Have I checked for easily confused words (*there, their,* and *they're*)?
_____ **2.** Have I correctly punctuated dialogue (regular and internal)?

Elements of Fiction

The following terms will help you write about and discuss literature.

Antagonist The person or force that works against the hero of the story (See *protagonist*.)

Character A person or an animal in a story

Climax The moment of change when the protagonist either succeeds or fails and is somehow changed by the action

Conflict A problem or clash between two forces in a story
- **Person vs. person** A problem between characters
- **Person vs. self** A problem within a character's own mind
- **Person vs. society** A problem between a character and society, the law, or some tradition
- **Person vs. nature** A problem with an element of nature, such as a blizzard or a hurricane
- **Person vs. destiny** A problem or struggle that appears to be beyond a character's control

Narrator The person or character who tells the story, gives background information, and fills in details between dialogue

Plot, Plot Line See page **342**.

Point of View The angle from which a story is told
- In **first-person point of view,** one character is telling the story.
- In **third-person point of view,** someone outside the story, a narrator, is telling it.
- In **omniscient point of view,** the narrator tells the thoughts and feelings of all the characters.
- In **limited omniscient point of view,** the narrator tells the thoughts of only one character.
- In **camera view** (objective), the narrator records the action from his or her own point of view, without any of the characters' thoughts.

Protagonist The main character or hero in a story (See *antagonist.*)

Rising Action A series of events that propel the story to the climax

Setting The place and time period in which a story takes place

Theme The author's message about life or human nature

Tone The writer's attitude toward her or his subject (*angry, humorous,* and so on)

Writing Plays

A play is an exciting writing challenge. Because a play is intended to be watched rather than read, its story is told with action and speech rather than with long sections of description. Even so, the script must be clearly written, giving the reader an understanding of the characters and what happens to them.

In terms of plot, writing a play is like writing any other narrative. The main character desires something and meets with opposition before finally succeeding or failing. At the climax, the character changes in some way, realizing a universal truth about the world or about him- or herself.

In this chapter you will read a short play about a character who, faced with a personal dilemma, finally makes a decision. You will then write your own short play, creating a character who wants something or faces an obstacle, and then comes to a decision to overcome the problem. You will also use stage directions to explain your characters' actions on stage.

Writing Guidelines

Subject: **Facing a personal dilemma**
Form: **Brief play**
Purpose: **To entertain and enlighten**
Audience: **Classmates**

"The structure of a play is always the story of how the birds came home to roost."

—Arthur Miller

Sample Play

Deanna wrote the following play in which a character must make an important personal decision.

Exchange Rate

Characters: **Jori,** who wants to be an exchange student
Tess, her friend
Mikyl, Jori's boyfriend

(The stage is bare. The lights come up on Jori, Center, as Tess rushes in to her.)

TESS: Jori, I can't believe you're going to France for a whole year!

JORI: Isn't it awesome! A whole year of traveling, learning a new culture, meeting new people . . .

TESS: Especially those French boys! Oo la la!

JORI: I don't care about that! After all, I have Mikyl.

TESS: Um, yeah, but you won't have him for a whole year! Aren't you worried about that?

JORI: We'll be okay. We can write and e-mail.

TESS: He can't take an e-mail to homecoming, the Holiday Ball, prom, or games. Come on, Jori. Mikyl, all alone, for a year? I don't think so!

JORI: I never thought of that. I mean, Mikyl and I—we're forever!

TESS: Jori, senior year is longer than forever.

JORI: Maybe I shouldn't leave! This is a hard decision.

TESS: *(Gently)* I know.

(The lights on the two go down, and Jori moves Down Right, where the lights come up on Mikyl, who is sitting on the floor pantomiming changing a tire. Jori crouches next to him.)

MIKYL: Wow. What an amazing opportunity for you.

JORI: Yeah, but I'm thinking maybe I shouldn't go.

MIKYL: Are you nuts? Why not?

JORI: Mikyl, it's a whole year. I'll miss you so much!

MIKYL: And I'll miss you, but we can write and e-mail each other.

JORI: Well . . .

MIKYL: We can handle it, Jori. We can handle anything.

Background information is given and the conflict is suggested.

A third character is introduced.

(The lights go down and Jori moves Stage Left, where the lights come up on Tess.)

JORI: See? He's fine with it.

TESS: Well, sure! He loves you and wants you to be happy. But don't you want the best for him?

JORI: Of course I do.

TESS: So you want him to put his life on hold for you?

JORI: I don't want Mikyl to suffer, Tess! I really want to go, but I don't want to lose him!

TESS: *(Gently)* I know.

(Their light goes down and Jori moves Center, where the lights come up on Mikyl, who is examining a fishing reel.)

JORI: I'll be back in June. It's not so bad. You'll hardly know I'm gone. *(Casually)* And you'll be going out with other girls . . .

MIKYL: Why would I do that?

JORI: It's your senior year. You should have fun.

MIKYL: You're wearing my ring. We're exclusive.

JORI: Mikyl, I'm going to be gone a whole year. I don't want you to just freeze-dry yourself until I get back.

MIKYL: Jori, I don't want to date anyone else.

JORI: Oh. *(Hesitantly she walks away, thinking.)* Well . . . maybe I do.

MIKYL: Huh?

JORI: I mean, I'll be in Paris, Mikyl. Think of it! I'll be going to museums and the theater and parties . . .

MIKYL: Jori, are you breaking up with me?

JORI: *(It's painful for her to say this.)* I just thought, maybe we should take a little time off. See what's what.

MIKYL: You ARE breaking up with me!

JORI: Mikyl . . .

MIKYL: Jori, I thought you loved me! We planned . . .

JORI: *(Weakly)* People change.

MIKYL: Yeah, so I see.

JORI: I mean, *(Forcing a casual attitude)* I'm going to be traveling, changing, becoming worldly.

MIKYL: Oh, I'll just be stagnating in the home pond, huh?

JORI: Oh, I'm sure you'll be moving right along, too.

A complication is presented.

A new approach is used to solve the conflict.

Stage directions in parentheses reveal the character's feelings.

Creative Writing

MIKYL: Darn right I will! Listen, why don't you just give me back my ring right now, before you depart for your new, better life.

JORI: Oh! Oh. Sure. *(Turns away and slowly slips off the ring. Stares at it a minute before plastering a smile on her face and turning back.)* Here! I feel lighter already.

MIKYL: I'll bet. Sorry it was weighing you down for so long. *(Softly)* It's still warm. *(Jori makes a move toward him, then checks herself.)*

JORI: Well! I guess that's that.

MIKYL: Yeah. Have fun in France, and don't waste a minute thinking about me. I'll be having a great life!

JORI: *(Softly)* That's all I ever wanted for you. *(Pause)*

MIKYL: You really are amazing, you know.

JORI: I don't have to go, Mikyl.

MIKYL: Yes, you do.

JORI: I can say no. I can stay here, with you. We'd have the best senior year . . .

MIKYL: You can't do that, Jori. You really want this. Maybe this will be a good test for us. If we can stand this, we're meant to be.

JORI: We are. I'm sure of it.

MIKYL: What about my ring? *(Holds it out to her.)*

JORI: Maybe you'll want to give it to someone else.

MIKYL: Maybe I'll hold onto it until June.

JORI: Maybe you will. *(Looks at him.)* Maybe you won't. Mikyl, I'm going to go to France. I have to go. *(Turns, then looks back.)* But I really do love you.

MIKYL: *(Softly)* I know.

(She runs to him, and they hug.)

The decision is made, the conflict overcome, and the play ends.

Respond to the Reading. Answer the following questions about the play.

Ideas (1) What does Jori want? (2) What is her obstacle?

Organization (3) How does the author build the suspense?

Voice & Word Choice (4) Find three stage directions that help you understand how the actor should say the line. (5) Why do you think the author repeats the phrase "I know"?

Prewriting ■ Invent a main character.

One way to start planning a play is to select a main character who wants something. That something is called the character's **objective**, and the reason the character wants it is called the **motivation**. Deanna wanted to write about a teenage girl, so she made a list of things her character might want.

- To have a car
- To host a surprise party for a friend
- To be an exchange student
- To be admitted to a prestigious college

Deanna decided to explore the idea of becoming an exchange student.

Prewrite

Invent your main character. Think about a possible character. Then explore potential objectives before deciding on your character's objective.

■ Choose a conflict.

Conflict is the heart of drama. To write a good play, you must include an **obstacle** that prevents your character from achieving his or her goal. There are two types of conflict.

- **Internal conflict**: The main character struggles to make a decision.
- **External conflict**: The main character struggles against an outside force, either another person, society, an idea, or an element of nature.

Deanna made the following chart to look at the possible conflicts her character could face. She starred the one she decided to use.

Conflict Chart

External Conflicts	Internal Conflicts
– Her boyfriend/parents/gymnastics coach/friends ask her not to go.	– She doesn't want to leave her friends.
– She has to come up with money to pay for the trip.	* – She doesn't want to lose her boyfriend; neither does she want him to be unhappy.
– Her host family sounds unfriendly.	
– She will probably have to repeat her senior year when she returns.	– She knows she will be homesick.
	– She is afraid of flying.

Prewrite

Choose your character's conflict. Make a list of possible obstacles to your character's objective and select the one you would like to write about.

Prewriting ■ Plan your resolution.

In the sample play, Jori's obstacle to becoming an exchange student is her desire both to keep her boyfriend and to see him happy. To overcome her internal conflict, Jori tries several strategies.

Resolution Chart

Character	Option
Jori	do not go to avoid separation stay "together" but see other people break up wait and see what the future brings

■ Develop secondary characters.

Secondary characters should be used selectively—especially in a short play. Each should have a specific role. Secondary characters can play the following roles.

- Give background information.
- Provide a sounding board for the main character.
- Introduce complications that block the main character's goal.

Prewrite

Create your secondary characters. Invent a few secondary characters and determine the purpose for each.

■ Consider using irony.

Irony is the use of words to express something other than what is really meant. There are three kinds of dramatic irony:

- **Verbal:** A character says one thing but means another.
  "Oh, sure, I just love making a fool of myself in front of others!"

- **Dramatic:** The audience knows something the character does not.
  In *Romeo and Juliet,* Romeo thinks Juliet is dead so he kills himself, but we know Juliet is alive.

- **Situational:** What is expected to happen and what does happen are very different things.
  Willy Loman thinks his life insurance money will make his family happy, but his death just brings them sorrow.

In her play, Deanna utilizes dramatic irony when she has Jori tell Mikyl she wants to date others. The readers know that's not so, but Mikyl does not know it.

Writing ▪ Write your first draft.

Remember to let your characters tell the story and reveal their personalities through what they say and do. Keep in mind the interplay of action and dialogue.

Beginning

1. **Give the opening stage directions.** Include any information that will help the reader visualize the scene.
2. **Introduce your characters and conflict.** Include enough background information to explain to the audience how the characters arrived at this opening situation.

Middle

3. **Use dialogue and action to move the play along.** Include complications to add suspense and keep the audience interested. Write stage directions that convey the subtext.
4. **Divide into scenes if necessary.** Use separate scenes to condense time or present a new development.
5. **Present the climax.** Bring the main character to a point where the conflict is resolved.

Ending

6. **Bring your play to a close.** Show how the character has changed and wrap up the action with a definite ending.

▪ Build scenes.

A scene is like a mini-play with its own beginning, middle, and ending. Each scene should advance the action, build upon the character's objective, create complications, and move toward the resolution.

In the sample play, each of the scenes has a specific purpose:

Scene 1: To present background information and provide the conflict

Scene 2: To introduce Mikyl and provide one solution: that he and Jori "stay together" while she is gone

Scene 3: To build suspense as Tess suggests that Jori shouldn't try to tie Mikyl to a commitment

Scene 4: To present the final confrontation, the climax, and the end of the play

Write

Write your play. Write your play, using your prewriting as a guide. Use at least two scenes and work in new ideas that occur to you as you write.

Creative Writing

Writing ▪ Create subtext.

Subtext is the unspoken emotions of your characters—what they really think and feel, even while their actions suggest something else. Sometimes the playwright will include stage directions to help actors understand their character's motivation.

In the sample play, the subtext of the action is suggested through the stage directions. For example, when Jori removes Mikyl's ring, the dialogue suggests she is happy to break up. However, the stage directions present the subtext.

> JORI: Oh! Oh. Sure. *(Turns away and slowly slips off the ring. Stares at it a minute before plastering a smile on her face and turning back.)* Here! I feel lighter already.

These stage directions help the reader see that Jori does not want to give Mikyl his ring. We know that she is trying to make it easier for him when she leaves. That she still cares is further emphasized by the later stage directions.

> *(Jori makes a move toward him, then checks herself.)*

▪ Think about stage directions.

As you write stage directions, consider using stage shorthand to indicate the acting areas. The diagram below identifies the shorthand.

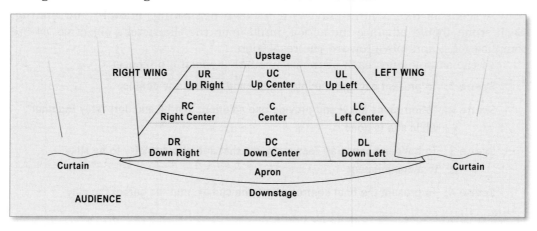

Revising ■ Improve your writing.

Read your play out loud or have someone else read it to you. Change any lines that sound forced or unnatural. Use these questions to guide your revisions.

Revising Checklist

Ideas

_____ **1.** Is the conflict believable?

_____ **2.** Have I included complications?

_____ **3.** Do the characters seem real?

Organization

_____ **4.** Does my play move logically from one scene to the next?

_____ **5.** Does my play build to a logical conclusion?

Voice

_____ **6.** Does the dialogue sound natural?

_____ **7.** Does the tone convey the intended meaning and purpose of the play?

Sentence Fluency

_____ **8.** Does the dialogue move smoothly?

_____ **9.** Do the stage directions make sense?

Editing ■ Check for conventions.

Editing Checklist

_____ **1.** Does the play follow correct script form?

_____ **2.** Have I used parentheses for directions?

_____ **3.** Have I checked my punctuation?

_____ **4.** Have I checked for spelling errors?

Publishing ■ Present your play.

Share your play with an audience. Have some students act it out in class, or post it on your (or your school's) Web site.

Creative Writing

Writing a Radio Play

One of the best things about radio plays is that both the writer and the audience can really use their imaginations. The stories come to life entirely through the voices of the actors and the sound effects. With this in mind, Rahji developed a script.

Fireworks

(SCENE: A PARK, FOURTH OF JULY. WE HEAR FIREWORKS IN THE DISTANCE PUNCTUATED BY THE CROWD'S "OOOHS" AND "AAAHS.")

    LUC: Wow, Cher! These are the best Fourth of July fireworks.
CHER: They're nice, Luc.

(SOUND: A LOUD BOOM AND THE CROWD'S OOOOH!)

    LUC: Nice? They're spectacular!
CHER: Yes. Listen, Luc, we have to talk.

(SOUND: A CRACKLING NOISE AND THE CROWD'S AAAAH!)

    LUC: That one was really cool! Talk about what?
CHER: About us, Luc. I mean, I think we should see other people.

(SOUND: A POP FOLLOWED BY SMALLER POPS, AND THE SOUND OF LAUGHTER AND APPLAUSE.)

    LUC: Wow, that was—What?
CHER: I think we should break up.
    LUC: But, Cher, we had the whole summer planned! We were
            going to go on nature hikes, go bird-watching, . . .
CHER: YOU had the whole summer planned!
    LUC: I thought you'd like doing those things, too.
CHER: Listen, Luc, it's more than just the things we like to do.

(SOUND: BOOM AND AUDIENCE REACTION.)

    LUC: What else is it, then?
CHER: It's us, Luc. We don't click. There's just no magic between
            us, no—fireworks. I'm really sorry, Luc.
    LUC: But—
CHER: Goodbye, Luc.

(SOUND: A WHISTLING BUILDUP AND THEN A FIZZLE. AUDIENCE GROANS IN DISAPPOINTMENT.)

Try It!

Write a short radio play of your own, presenting a conflict between two people. Include important background noises or special sound effects.

Writing Poetry

Some people think poetry is just for literature books. Others think it's mainly for greeting cards. But the earliest poetry was used for public performance, and much of the best modern poetry is written by everyday people for other everyday people.

In essence, a poem is "heightened" language—carefully chosen words with sounds and rhythms that are fun to hear, and with imagery and ideas that surprise or delight. In this chapter, you will find various examples of poetic forms along with definitions and demonstrations of common poetic techniques. As the examples show, poetry is for everybody!

By following the instructions in this chapter, you will learn to write your own sonnets, free-verse poems, and cinquains. We hope that you will return to this chapter often, whenever you have an idea that deserves to be expressed in a poem.

Writing Guidelines

Subject: Man and machine
Form: Sonnet
Purpose: To entertain
Audience: Friends, family, and classmates

"The future masters of technology will have to be light-hearted and intelligent. The machine easily masters the grim and the dumb."

—Marshall McLuhan

Understanding Sonnets

The sonnet originated in Italy during the Middle Ages, then found its way into English poetry around the time of Shakespeare. A sonnet is 14 lines long, with a logical structure, a regular rhythm, and—usually—a rhyme scheme.

The English sonnet consists of three *quatrains* (four lines each) that present a theme, followed by a *couplet* (two lines) that responds to the theme. The Italian sonnet is an *octave* (eight lines—often as two quatrains) presenting the theme, followed by a *sestet* (six lines) of response.

The rhythm of sonnets in English is generally iambic pentameter (see pages **364** and **369**), and the most common rhyme scheme is *abab cdcd efef gg*. Common rhyme schemes for the Italian sonnet form are *abababab* or *abbaabba* for the octave and *cdecde* or *cdccdc* for the sestet. Other structures and rhyme schemes are possible. For an unrhymed sonnet, see W. H. Auden's "The Secret Agent."

A sonnet may be written about any topic. Boyce Pappan wrote about his car.

This sonnet follows the Italian form of octave and sestet.

The rhyme scheme is very loose *(abcbdefe ghihjh)*.

Most lines are iambic pentameter. Exceptions add emphasis to individual words and phrases.

Old Junker

My car is old as me—in car years, that's
middle-aged—an unappreciated
stretch of time between "brand new" and "classic"
when one's value is depreciated.
In other words, it's simply out of style,
so it doesn't get as much attention
as it once did. No one admires it. (I
never wash or wax it, I should mention.)

Still, I love this car and it's comfortable
as only an old car can be. No fear
of spilling something—the upholstery's
already stained. And you will never hear
me complain about gas mileage. Now if
I could only get the thing in gear!

Respond to the reading. On your own paper, reflect on the ideas, organization, and word choice of the sonnet above.

Ideas (1) Summarize the main idea of the poem in your own words.

Organization (2) What theme does the octave present?
(3) What response does the sestet provide?

Voice (4) What is the writer's attitude or tone in the poem?

Prewriting ▪ Choose a topic and a focus.

To decide on a topic, Boyce used freewriting. Here's part of what he wrote:

> What does "man and machine" mean to me? Machines are tools we use to enhance our abilities. Maybe I could write about a screwdriver or a hammer. Not a lot to say about something that simple. How about something more complex, like a car? Yeah! I could come up with lots of ideas about my car! I couldn't get by without my old . . .

Prewrite

Select a focus. Use freewriting to brainstorm for a topic related to "man and machine." Keep writing whatever comes to mind until you discover something exciting.

▪ Gather details.

Make a list of thoughts about your topic. List descriptive details as well as feelings or ideas you have. Your list may also include possible similes or metaphors to use in your poem. (See page **368**.) Here's part of Boyce's list about his car:

> It's as old as I am.
> Ugly and rusty outside, but comfortable inside
> I never wash it!
> Not very powerful, but great gas mileage
> At that awkward age between new and classic
> Tricky to start on cold days
> It's my one private spot on the planet.
> Like my locker, it's full of books, old papers, clothes, and junk!
> In its day, it was "stylish"; what happened?
> Don't have to worry about scratching it (like I would a new car)

▪ Organize details.

Next arrange the ideas in your list. Place similar ideas together. Think about what each section of your sonnet might cover. (Remember, most sonnets are either three quatrains and an answering couplet or an octave and an answering sestet.) Review Boyce's sonnet on page **362** to see how he used his details.

Prewrite

Gather details. Make a list of descriptive details, feelings, and ideas about your topic. Include similes and metaphors that occur to you.

Writing ■ Write your first draft.

Write a first draft of your poem. Watch for opportunities to use the various poetic techniques described below and on pages 368–369.

■ Use rhythm.

The standard rhythm for a sonnet is iambic pentameter. (See page 369.) As you write, let this rhythm guide your phrases. But remember, it's okay to vary the rhythm, especially for emphasis.

> ⏑ / ⏑ / ⏑ / ⏑ / ⏑ /
> My car is old as me. In car years, that's

■ Use rhyme.

While you are drafting your poem, a rhyme scheme may begin to suggest itself. If so, allow it to guide your word choice. However, don't work too hard at rhyming yet. Just focus on completing your first draft.

> In other words, it's simply out of style,
> so it doesn't get as much **attention**
> as it once did. No one admires it. (I
> never wash or wax it, I should **mention**.)

■ Use enjambment.

Poems with lines that always end on a rhyme can sometimes sound singsongy, like a nursery rhyme. When you use enjambment—carrying sentences from line to line and ending them inside a line—your poems will flow more naturally. Enjambment also makes rhyming simpler. (It's easier to fit a rhyme inside a sentence than at the end.)

> as only an old car can be. **No fear**
> of spilling something—the upholstery's
> already stained. And you will never hear

Write your first draft. Use your plan as a guide. Watch for opportunities to use poetic techniques such as rhythm, rhyme, and enjambment to make your sonnet read effectively.

Revising ■ Improve your poem.

After drafting a sonnet, let it sit for a while. Later, when you return to it with fresh eyes, you will notice which parts work and which parts could be improved. Also have a trusted friend respond to the poem. Then make any needed changes, based on the traits of good writing.

- ■ **Ideas** Do I use effective details? Does my poem show my feelings without telling the reader what to think?
- ■ **Organization** Does my poem follow a sonnet structure? Does it introduce an idea in the quatrains or octave and a response in the couplet or sestet?
- ■ **Voice** Does my poem show inventiveness and personality?
- ■ **Word Choice** Are my words precise and interesting? Do my rhymes work well? (See page **369**.)
- ■ **Sentence Fluency** Do my phrases and ideas flow smoothly? Are they—at least loosely—set in iambic pentameter?

Revise

Revise your poem. Using the questions above as a guide, keep revising until your poem is the best that it can be.

Editing ■ Check for errors.

Because poetry is a concise form, every word, every punctuation mark, is important. Careful editing is essential.

Edit

Edit your poem. Be sure that every element of your poem accomplishes the purpose you intend.

Publishing ■ Share your poem.

There are many ways in which you can share a sonnet. Here are a few ideas:

- ■ **Post it.** Put it on a bulletin board or a Web site.
- ■ **Submit it.** Send your poem to a contest or a magazine.
- ■ **Perform it**. Have an "open-mike" poetry reading in your class.
- ■ **Send it** to friends and family members in a card or by e-mail.

Publish

Publish your poem. Share your poem with others and discuss the ideas and feelings it presents. Ask your teacher for other publishing ideas.

Creative Writing

Sample Free Verse

At first glance, free verse may seem to follow no rules at all. Actually, each free-verse poem creates its own form—using traditional poetic elements such as consonance, assonance, repetition, and rhythm. (See pages **368–369**.) However, free verse almost never uses end rhymes.

Justine Fredrickson wrote the following free-verse poem about an old-fashioned typewriter. Notice the poetic techniques she used.

> ### "Dear Aunt Janie"
>
> My Aunt Janie
> left me a typewriter—
> a clunky machine
>
> with which she wrote letters
> starting, "Dear Niece"
> and spilling her thoughts
>
> It sat on my dresser for weeks
> near the window,
> just catching dust in the sun
>
> When friends asked,
> "Where'd you get
> that clackety old thing?"
>
> I'd shrug
> and change the subject
>
> This afternoon I came home
> to find a white sheet of paper
> waiting in the roller
>
> As I touched the keys,
> this poem spilled out

Consonance is used in the repeated "t" of line 2.

The words "Dear Niece" echo the poem's title. Assonance is used with the words "just," "dust," and "sun" in line 9.

Periods are left out to avoid abrupt pauses at the ends of sentences.

The ending recalls an earlier thought in the poem.

Tip

Notice how the sparseness of language in this poem invites readers to fill in the meaning for themselves. In creative writing, it's best not to tell your reader how to think.

Write

Write a free-verse poem. Follow the writing process to write a free-verse poem of your own. Use techniques such as consonance, assonance, repetition, and rhythm (see pages **368–369**) to make your poem a work of art.

Writing Cinquains

A cinquain (sometimes called a quintet) is a carefully structured poem of five lines. The first line has two syllables, the second has four, the third six, the fourth eight, and the final line just two again. Often the rhythm is iambic, although this is not a strict rule. Generally both syllables in the first and last lines are strongly accented. Most cinquains are unrhymed, although rhyme is sometimes used for humorous effect.

In a poem such as this, short, precise words are essential. It's important to make every syllable count—not just to fill the form. Also, a good cinquain delays its sense of closure until the very last line. Those final two syllables should feel like a climax to the poem.

Hammers

Hammers
are perfect for
driving nails or breaking
things: full piggy banks, geodes—and
silence.

—Avery Strattman

Mystery Machine

What does
this machine do?
I see levers and dials;
I hear gears whirring, smell something
burning!

— Marissa Troff

Write

Write a cinquain. Follow the prewriting activities on page 363 to generate a topic and gather details. Then write a cinquain in the form shown above.

Using Special Poetry Techniques

Poets use a variety of special techniques in their work. This page and the next define some of the most important ones.

Figures of Speech

- A **simile** *(sĭmˊə-lē)* compares two unlike things with the word *like* or *as*.

  The washing machine coughed
  like a dying stegosaurus.

- A **metaphor** *(mĕtˊə-fôr)* compares two unlike things without using *like* or *as*.

  That radio was more
  than tubes and speakers;
  it was the wide world come to visit
  in her parlor.

- **Personification** *(pər-sŏnˊə-fĭ-kāˊshən)* is a technique that gives human traits to something that is nonhuman.

  The mailbox gaped
  with open mouth,
  speechless.

- **Hyperbole** *(hī-pûrˊbə-lē)* is an exaggerated statement, often humorous.

  A bicycle sped past
  with a sonic boom!

Sounds of Poetry

- **Alliteration** *(ə-lĭtˊə-rāˊshən)* is the repetition of consonant sounds at the beginning of words.

  I never wash or wax it, I should mention.

- **Assonance** *(ăsˊə-nəns)* is the repetition of vowel sounds anywhere in words.

  just catching dust in the sun

- **Consonance** *(kŏnˊsə-nəns)* is the repetition of consonant sounds anywhere in words.

  No fear of spilling something—the upholstery's
  already stained.

- **Enjambment** (*ĕn-jăm´mənt*) is running a sentence across more than one line of verse or from one stanza to another.

  a clunky machine
  with which she wrote letters
  starting, "Dear Niece"

- **Line breaks** help control the rhythm of a poem. The reader naturally pauses at the end of a line, the last word of which receives added emphasis.

  Branches reaching out,
  stretching,
  as though fingers yearning
  to strum the wind.

- **Onomatopoeia** (*ŏn´ə-măt´ə-pē´ə*) is the use of words that sound like what they name.

  that clackety **old thing?**

- **Repetition** (*rĕp´i-tĭsh´ən*) uses the same word, phrase, or pattern of words more than once, for emphasis or for rhythm.

  What **flames shot** from the **tailpipes!**
  What **smoke rolled** from the **spinning tires!**
  What **gasps rose** from the **crowd!**

- **Rhyme** (*rīm*) means using words whose endings sound alike. *End rhyme* happens at the end of lines.

  so it doesn't get as much attention
  as it once did. No one admires it. (I
  never wash or wax it, I should mention**.)**

Internal rhyme happens within lines.

  Finding **her way in** blinding **snow.**

- **Rhythm** (*rĭth´əm*) is the pattern of accented and unaccented syllables in a poem.

  - **Iambic:** an unstressed followed by a stressed syllable (*ĭ am´*)
  - **Trochaic:** a stressed followed by an unstressed syllable (*la´-tĕr*)
  - **Anapestic:** two unstressed followed by a stressed syllable (*to the moon´*)
  - **Dactylic:** a stressed followed by two unstressed syllables (*stealth´-ĭ-lў*)

The rhythm of free-verse poetry tends to flow naturally, like speaking. Traditional poetry follows a more regular pattern, as in the following example.

  Moon´ on snow´
  Evén´ing glow´

Research Writing

Research Writing
Research Skills

Doing research will help you in more ways than you know. If you begin with a topic that's too broad, research can help you narrow it. If you don't know which side of an issue to write about, research can help you take a position. Anyone who has ever done research knows that it can provide not only answers, but also additional questions to consider in the thorough coverage of your topic.

That's why it's as important to know *how* to research as it is to know *what* to research. This chapter will serve as a guide to various kinds of information, where to find them, and how to gauge their reliability.

- **Primary vs. Secondary Sources**
- **Evaluating Sources of Information**
- **Using the Internet**
- **Using the Library**
- **Using Reference Books**

"The outcome of any serious research can only be to make two questions grow where only one grew before."

—Thorstein Veblen

Primary vs. Secondary Sources

Primary sources are original sources (diaries, people, events, surveys). They inform you directly, not through a second person's explanation or interpretation. Ideally, when you research a topic, you should find as much primary information as possible.

Primary sources include . . .

- **Diaries, journals, and letters:** You can often find these in museums, in libraries, or at historic sites.
- **Presentations:** A speaker at a museum or a historic site can give you firsthand information, but be aware of the presenter's own interpretation of events.
- **Interviews:** Talk to an expert on your research topic. You can do this by phone, e-mail, or letter.
- **Surveys and questionnaires:** These tools help you gather a great deal of data from many people.
- **Observation and participation:** Your own observations of a person, a place, or an event provide excellent firsthand information. Participating in an event can give you insights that cannot be discovered through the reports of others.

Secondary sources are third-person accounts found in research done by other people. Much of the news *(television, radio, Internet, books, magazines)* can be considered a secondary source of information. Keep in mind that, by their very nature, secondary sources represent filtered information that may contain biases or misunderstandings.

Primary Sources	Secondary Sources
1. Reading the journal of a travel guide	1. Exploring a Web site about being a travel guide
2. Listening to a presentation by a travel guide	2. Reading a magazine article about a travel guide
3. Interviewing a travel guide	3. Watching a TV documentary about a travel guide

Try It!

List two primary and two secondary sources you might use to learn about the era of your parents' adolescence. Be as specific as you can be.

Evaluating Sources of Information

You may find a lot of information about your research topic. But before you use any of it, decide whether or not the information is dependable. Use the following questions to help you decide about the reliability of your sources.

Is the source a primary source or a secondary source?

You can usually trust any information you've collected yourself, but be careful with secondary sources. Although many of them are reliable, others may contain outdated or incorrect information.

Is the source an expert?

An expert knows more about a subject than other people. Using an expert's thoughts and opinions can make your paper more believable. If you aren't sure about a source's authority, ask a teacher or librarian what he or she thinks.

Is the information accurate?

Sources that people respect are usually very accurate. Big-city newspapers (*New York Times* or *Chicago Tribune*) and well-known Web sites (CNN or ESPN) are reliable sources of information. Little-known sources that do not support their facts or that contain errors are not reliable.

Tip

Be especially cautious about the accuracy of information on the Internet. While there is an incredible amount of information available on the Net, there is also a lot of misinformation.

Is the information fair and complete?

A reliable source should provide information fairly, covering all sides of a subject. If a source presents only one side of a subject, its information may not be accurate. To make themselves sound better, politicians and advertisers often present just their side of a subject. Avoid sources that are one-sided; look for those that are balanced.

Is the information current?

Usually, you want to have the most up-to-date information about a subject. Sometimes information changes, and sources can become outdated quickly. Check the copyright page in a book, the issue date of a magazine, and the posting date of online information.

Using the Internet

Because you can access many resources by surfing the Web, the Internet is a valuable research aid. You can find government publications, encyclopedia entries, business reports, and firsthand observations on the Internet.

Remember these points.

- **Use the Internet wisely.** Sites that include *.edu, .org,* and *.gov* in the Web address are often reliable. These sites are from educational, nonprofit, or government agencies. If you have questions about the reliability of a site, talk to your teacher. (See also page **373**.) Remember to check the date of the Web site. Abandoned Web sites may contain outdated information.

- **Try several search engines.** When you type a term into a search engine's input box, the search engine scans its database for matching sites. Then the engine returns recommendations for you to explore. Because there is an enormous amount of information on the Web, no one search engine can handle it all. So employ at least two search engines when you surf the Web. Enter keywords to start your research or enter specific questions to zero in on your topic.

- **Take advantage of links.** When you read a page, watch for links to other sites. These may offer different perspectives or points of view on your topic.

- **Experiment with keywords.** Sometimes you must ask a number of different questions or use different keywords to find the information you need.

- **Ignore Web sites that advertise research papers for sale.** Using these sites is dishonest. Teachers and librarians can recognize and verify when a paper is someone else's work.

- **Learn your school's Internet policy.** Using the computer at school is a privilege. To maintain that privilege, follow your school's Internet policy and any guidelines your parents may have set.

Try It!

With a partner, make a list of all the search engines you know of. Then enter the keywords "search engine" into one of them and compare the results to your list. Is there one that you believe would yield the best results for a topic you are interested in?

Using the Library

The Internet may be a good place to initiate your research, but a library is often a more valuable place to continue your research. A library offers materials that are more in-depth and reliable than what you find on the Internet. Most libraries contain the following resources.

Books

- **Reference** books include encyclopedias, almanacs, dictionaries, atlases, and directories, plus other resources such as consumer information guides and car-repair manuals. Reference books provide a quick review or overview of research topics.

- **Nonfiction** texts are a good source of facts that can serve as a foundation for your research. Check the copyright dates to be sure you are reading reasonably up-to-date information. (Some libraries organize nonfiction using the Library of Congress system, but most use the Dewey decimal system as shown on page **377**.)

- **Fiction** can sometimes aid or enhance your research. For example, a historical novel can reveal people's feelings about a particular time in history. (Fiction books are grouped together in alphabetical order by the authors' last names.)

Periodicals

Periodicals *(newspapers* and *magazines)* are grouped together in a library. Use the *Readers' Guide to Periodical Literature* to find articles in periodicals. (See page **382**.) You will have to ask the librarian for older issues. Your library may subscribe to online databases of periodicals.

The Media Section

The media section of your library includes DVD's, CD-ROM's, CD's, cassettes, and videotapes. These resources can immerse you in an event. Keep in mind, however, that directors and screenwriters may present events in a way that accommodates their personal views.

Computers

Computers in most libraries are connected to the Internet, although there may be restrictions on their use.

Try It!

Practice using the online *Readers' Guide to Periodical Literature* or another online database of periodicals. Think of several broad topics and look them up. Notice how this resource can help you narrow a broad topic.

Use the computer catalog.

While some libraries still use a card catalog in a cabinet with drawers, most libraries keep their catalog on computer. Each system varies a bit, so ask for help if necessary. A **computer catalog** lists the books held in your library and affiliated systems. It lets you know if a book is available or if you must wait for it.

Use a variety of search methods.

When you are using a computer catalog, you can find information about a book with any of the following methods:

- If you know it, enter the **title** of the book.
- If you know the **author** of the book, enter the first and last names.
- A general search of your **subject** will also help you find books on your topic. Enter either the subject or a related keyword.

Sample Computer Catalog Screen

In the illustration below, the key to the right identifies the types of information provided for a particular resource, in this case, a book. Once you locate the book you need, make note of the call number. You will use this to find the book on the shelf.

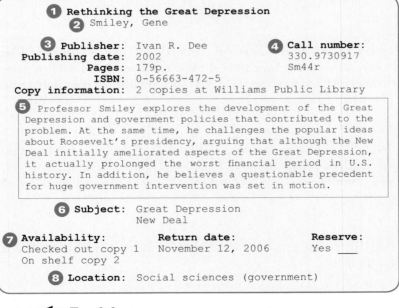

1. Title heading
2. Author's name
3. Publisher, copyright date, and other book information
4. Call number
5. Descriptive info
6. Subject heading(s)
7. Availability status
8. Location information

Try It!

Use the computer catalog to see what current newspapers your library subscribes to. Ask the librarian for help if necessary.

Understand call numbers.

All nonfiction books in the library have **call numbers**. The books are arranged on the shelves according to these numbers. Call numbers are usually based on the **Dewey decimal classification** system, which divides nonfiction books into 10 subject categories.

000–099	**General Works**	**500–599**	**Sciences**
100–199	**Philosophy**	**600–699**	**Technology**
200–299	**Religion**	**700–799**	**Arts and Recreation**
300–399	**Social Sciences**	**800–899**	**Literature**
400–499	**Languages**	**900–999**	**History and Geography**

A call number often has a decimal in it, followed by the first letter of an author's name. Note how the following call numbers are ordered on the shelves.

Try It!

Each subject category or class in the Dewey decimal classification system is divided into *divisions*. Identify the division for books listed in the 900's. **Note:** Each division is further divided into *sections* and *subsections*.

Identify the parts of a book.

Each part of a book provides valuable information. The **title page** includes the title of the book, the author's name, and the publisher's name and city. The **copyright page** follows with the year the book was published. The **preface, foreword, or introduction** comes before the table of contents and tells why the book was written. The **table of contents** lists the names and page numbers of sections and chapters in the book. At the end of the book, you may find at least one **appendix,** containing various maps, tables, and lists. Finally, the **index** is an alphabetical list of important topics and their page numbers in the book.

Using Reference Books

A reference book is a special kind of nonfiction book that contains specific facts or background information. The reference section includes encyclopedias, dictionaries, almanacs, and so on. Usually, reference books cannot be checked out, so you must use them in the library.

Refer to encyclopedias.

An encyclopedia is a set of books (or a CD-ROM) that contains basic information on topics from A to Z. Topics are arranged alphabetically.

Tips for Using Encyclopedias

- **At the end of an article, there is often a list of related articles.**
  You can read these other articles to learn more about your topic.

- **The index can help you find out more about your topic.**
  The index is usually in a separate volume or at the end of the last volume. It lists every article that contains information about a topic. For example, if you look up "newspapers" in the index, you would find a list of articles—"United States Media," "Freedom of the Press," and so on—that include information on that topic. (See below.)

- **Libraries usually have several sets of encyclopedias.**
  Review each set and decide which one best serves your needs. (Always check with your teacher first to see if you can use an encyclopedia as a source for your research.)

Sample Encyclopedia Index

Encyclopedia volume

The Great Depression D: 331–336 with pictures and illustrations

Herbert Hoover **H: 242**

Page numbers

The New Deal **V:** 311–312

Franklin Delano Roosevelt **V: 310–312**

See also the related topics in the Great Depression *article.*

Related topics

Government Policies **U: 332**

Public Works Projects **U: 333**

CCC **C: 135**

WPA and Parks **P: 299**

World War II **W: 276**

Consult other reference books.

Most libraries contain several types of reference books in addition to encyclopedias.

Almanacs

Almanacs are books filled with facts and statistics about many different subjects. *The World Almanac and Book of Facts* contains celebrity profiles; statistics about politics, business, and sports; plus consumer information.

Atlases

Atlases contain detailed maps of the world, continents, countries, and so on. They also contain statistics and related information. Specialized atlases cover topics like outer space and the oceans.

Dictionaries

Dictionaries contain definitions of words and their origins. Biographical dictionaries focus on famous people. Specialized dictionaries deal with science, history, medicine, and other subjects.

Directories

Directories list information about groups of people, businesses, and organizations. The most widely used directories are telephone books.

Periodical Indexes

Periodical indexes list articles in magazines and newspapers. These indexes are arranged alphabetically by subject.

- The *Readers' Guide to Periodical Literature* lists articles from many publications. (See page **382**.)
- The *New York Times Index* lists articles from the *New York Times* newspaper.

Other Reference Books

Some reference books do not fit into any one category but are recognized by their names:

- *Facts on File* includes thousands of short but informative facts about events, discoveries, people, and places.
- *Facts About the Presidents* presents information about all of the American presidents.
- *Bartlett's Familiar Quotations* lists thousands of quotations from famous people.

Check a dictionary.

A dictionary gives many types of information:

- **Guide words:** These are the first and last words on the page. Guide words show whether the word you are looking for will be found alphabetically on that page.
- **Entry words:** Each word defined in a dictionary is called an entry word. Entry words are listed alphabetically.
- **Etymology:** Many dictionaries give etymologies (word histories) for certain words. An etymology tells what language an English word came from, how the word entered our language, and when it was first used.
- **Syllable divisions:** A dictionary tells you where you may divide a word.
- **Pronunciation and accent marks:** A dictionary tells you how to pronounce a word and also provides a key to pronunciation symbols, usually at the bottom of each page.
- **Illustrations:** For some entries, an illustration, a photograph, or a drawing is provided.
- **Parts of speech:** A dictionary tells you what part(s) of speech a word is, using these abbreviations:

n.	**noun**	*tr. v.*	**transitive verb**
pron.	**pronoun**	*interj.*	**interjection**
intr. v.	**intransitive verb**	*conj.*	**conjunction**
adj.	**adjective**	*adv.*	**adverb**
prep.	**preposition**		

- **Spelling and capitalization:** The dictionary shows the acceptable spelling, as well as capitalization, for words. (For some words, more than one spelling is given.)
- **Definitions:** Some dictionaries are large enough to list all of the meanings for a word. Most standard-size dictionaries, however, will list only three or four of the most commonly accepted meanings. Take time to read all of the meanings to be sure that you are using the word correctly.

Try It!

Find a word in a dictionary that is totally unfamiliar to you. Look at its pronunciation and say it out loud. Use it correctly in a sentence.

Sample Dictionary Page

Guide words

Entry word

Etymology

Syllable divisions

Pronunciation and accent marks

Illustration

Parts of speech

Spelling

Definitions

Circle | Circularize   261

cir•cle (sûr′kəl) *n.* **1.** A plane curve everywhere equidistant from a given fixed point, the center. **2.** A planar region bounded by a circle. **3.** Something, such as a ring, shaped like such a plane curve. **4.** A circular course, circuit, or orbit. **5.** A traffic circle. **6.** A curved section or tier of seats in a theater. **7.** A series or process that finishes at its starting point or repeats itself; a cycle. **8.** A group of people sharing an interest, activity, or achievement. **9.** A territorial or administrative division, esp. of a province, in some European countries. **10.** A sphere of influence or interest; domain. **11.** *Logic* A vicious circle. ❖ *v.* **-cled, -cling, -cles** —*tr.* **1.** To make or form a circle around; enclose. **2.** To move in a circle around. —*intr.* To move in a circle. **—idiom: circle the wagons** To take a defensive position. [ME *cercle* < OFr. < Lat. *circulus,* dim. of *circus,* circle < Gk. *kirkos, krikos.*] —**cir′cler** (-klər) *n.*

circle graph *n.* See **pie chart.**

cir•clet (sûr′klĭt) *n.* A small circle, esp. a circular ornament. [ME *cerclet* < OFr., dim. of *cercle,* circle. See CIRCLE.]

cir•cuit (sûr′kĭt) *n.* **1a.** A closed, usu. circular line that goes around an object or area. **b.** The region enclosed by such a line. **2a.** A path or route that returns to its starting point. **b.** The act of following such a path or route. **c.** A journey made on such a path or route. **3.** *Electronics* **a.** A closed path followed by an electric current. **b.** A configuration of electrically or electromagnetically connected components or devices. **4a.** A regular or accustomed course from place to place; a round: *the lecture circuit.* **b.** The area or district thus covered, esp. a territory under the jurisdiction of a judge in which periodic court sessions are held. **5a.** An association of theaters among which plays, acts, or films move for presentation. **b.** A group of nightclubs, show halls, or resorts at which entertainers appear in turn. **c.** An association of teams or clubs. **d.** A series of competitions held in different places. ❖ *intr. & tr.v.* **-cuit•ed, -cuit•ing, -cuits** To make a circuit or circuit of. [ME, circumference < OFr. < Lat. *circuitus,* a going around < p. part. of *circumīre,* to go around : *circum-,* circum- + *īre,* to go; see **ei-** in App.]

circuit board *n.* *Computer Science* An insulated board on which interconnected circuits and components such as microchips are mounted or etched.

circuit breaker *n.* An automatic switch that stops the flow of electric current in an overloaded electric circuit.

circuit court *n.* A state court that holds sessions at several different places within a judicial district.

cir•cu•i•tous (sər-kyōō′ĭ-təs) *adj.* Being or taking a roundabout, lengthy course. [< Med.Lat. *circuitōsus* < Lat. *circuitus,* a going around. See CIRCUIT.] —**cir•cu′i•tous•ly** *adv.* —**cir•cu′i•ty, cir•cu′i•tous•ness** *n.*

circuit rider *n.* A cleric who travels from church to church.

cir•cuit•ry (sûr′kĭ-trē) *n., pl.* **-ries 1.** The design of or a detailed plan for an electric circuit. **2.** Electric circuits considered as a group.

cir•cu•lar (sûr′kyə-lər) *adj.* **1.** Of or relating to a circle. **2a.** Shaped like or nearly like a circle; round. **b.** Moving in or forming a circle. **3.** Circuitous; roundabout. **4.** Using a premise to prove a conclusion that in turn is used to prove the premise: *a circular argument.* **5.** Addressed or distributed to a large number of persons. ❖ *n.* A circular printed advertisement, directive, or notice. [ME *circuler* < AN < Lat. *circulāris* < *circulus,* circle. See CIRCLE.] —**cir•cu•lar′i•ty** (-lăr′ĭ-tē) *n.* —**cir′cu•lar•ly** *adv.*

circular function *n.* See **trigonometric function.**

cir•cu•lar•ize (sûr′kyə-lə-rīz′) *tr.v.* **-ized, -iz•ing, -iz•es 1.** To publicize with circulars. **2.** To canvass or poll using a questionnaire. —**cir′cu•lar•i•za′tion** (-lər-ĭ-zā′shən) *n.*

switch

battery

circuit
simple electrical circuit
system

ă pat	oi boy
ā pay	ou out
âr care	ōō took
ä father	ōō boot
ĕ pet	ŭ cut
ē be	ûr urge
ĭ pit	th thin
ī pie	th this
îr pier	hw which
ŏ pot	zh vision
ō toe	ə about,
ô paw	item

Stress marks:
′ (primary);
′ (secondary), as in
lexicon (lĕk′sĭ-kŏn′)

Use periodical guides.

Periodical guides are located in the reference or periodical section of the library. These guides alphabetically list topics and articles found in magazines, newspapers, and journals. Some guides are printed volumes, some are CD's, and some are on library Web sites. Ask your librarian for help.

Readers' Guide to Periodical Literature

The *Readers' Guide to Periodical Literature* is a well-known periodical reference source and is found in most libraries. The following tips will help you look up your topic in this resource:

- Articles are always listed alphabetically by author and topic.
- Some topics are subdivided, with each article listed under the appropriate subtopic.
- Cross-references refer to related topic entries where you may find more articles pertinent to your topic.

Sample *Readers' Guide* Format

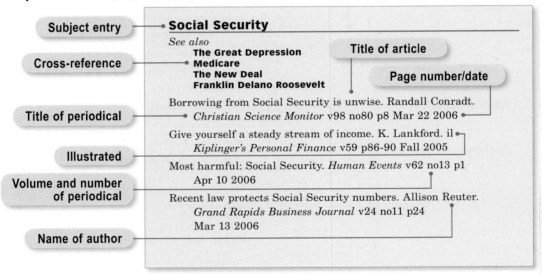

Subject entry	**Social Security**
	See also
	The Great Depression
Cross-reference	Medicare
	The New Deal
	Franklin Delano Roosevelt

Title of article

Page number/date

Borrowing from Social Security is unwise. Randall Conradt. *Christian Science Monitor* v98 no80 p8 Mar 22 2006

Give yourself a steady stream of income. K. Lankford. il *Kiplinger's Personal Finance* v59 p86-90 Fall 2005

Most harmful: Social Security. *Human Events* v62 no13 p1 Apr 10 2006

Recent law protects Social Security numbers. Allison Reuter. *Grand Rapids Business Journal* v24 no11 p24 Mar 13 2006

Title of periodical

Illustrated

Volume and number of periodical

Name of author

Tip

When you find a listing for your topic, write down the name and issue date of the magazine and the title and page numbers of the article. Your librarian may get the periodical for you, or you may need to find it yourself.

Research Writing
MLA Research Paper

Historians do more than tell what happened during a particular time period. Historians carry out careful research about a person, a place, or an event, and then attempt to put their findings into perspective.

Like a historian, when you write a research paper, you need to do more than present the information that you have gathered. You need to analyze the data and present your own interpretation of its impact or importance.

One important aspect of American history is presidential policy. Each presidential administration creates its own policies in a number of areas, from foreign relations to economics. Most of these policies tend to produce both positive and negative effects. In this chapter, you'll learn all the steps necessary to write a research paper that analyzes a particular policy enacted by a president of the United States.

Writing Guidelines

Subject: A presidential policy

Form: Research paper

Purpose: To research a presidential policy and analyze its effectiveness

Audience: Classmates

"Self-confidence is the first requisite to great undertakings."

—Samuel Johnson

Research Paper

While browsing a book of photographs from the Great Depression, Shawna Lopez became interested in this critical period in American history. She decided to write a paper about a presidential policy called the New Deal designed to help Americans get through this troubled time. You will find Shawna's paper on the next eight pages of this chapter. The margin notes point out important features of organization and formatting.

Title Page
Center the title about one-third of the way down the page. Center author information two-thirds of the way down.

Roosevelt's New Deal:

Success or Failure?

Shawna Lopez
Mr. Collins
Language Arts
March 9, 2006

Outline
Center the title one inch from the top of the page. Double-space throughout. Include the outline after the title page and before the first page of the paper.

Roosevelt's New Deal: Success or Failure?

Thesis statement: Although its success was incomplete, the New Deal saved the United States from collapsing into chaos and gave the nation's citizens the hope they needed to survive.

I. In the 1920s, the U.S. economy roared ahead like a powerful automobile, but beneath the shiny exterior, the economy was corroding.
  A. The value of stocks rose rapidly, and investors grew wealthy.
  B. Workers couldn't afford to buy consumer goods, so businesses cut back on production.
  C. Farm prices lagged, and many farmers lived in poverty.
II. In October 1929, the U.S. economy suddenly collapsed.
  A. The stock market dropped drastically, and investors rushed to sell their shares.
  B. Within weeks, the value of U.S. stocks had dropped by one-third.
  C. Banks had begun to fail, taking their customers' savings with them.
  D. President Herbert Hoover mistakenly believed that the economy would correct itself without government help.

Note: Not all teachers require a title page or an outline. If yours does, follow the guidelines above, or use specific instructions provided by your teacher.

Lopez 1

Shawna Lopez
Mr. Collins
Language Arts
March 9, 2006

The entire paper is double-spaced.

Roosevelt's New Deal: Success or Failure?

When he took office on March 4, 1933, President Franklin Delano Roosevelt assumed leadership of a nation mired in poverty and racked by hopelessness. Four years before, a stock market crash had set off the Great Depression, a collapse of the United States economy. Many factories, businesses, and banks closed down, and millions of U.S. citizens lost their jobs. Untold numbers of families had lost their savings and even their homes (Leuchtenburg 1).

Beginning A dramatic opening grabs the reader's attention.

As a candidate, Roosevelt had promised a "new deal for the American people" (Heale). As president, he began to dramatically restructure the U.S. economy with an economic program called the New Deal. The New Deal created jobs, changed banking practices, and prevented many people from losing their savings and their homes (Church). As much as it changed the economy, the New Deal did not end the Great Depression. Although its success was incomplete, the New Deal saved the United States from collapsing into chaos and gave the nation's citizens the hope they needed to survive.

The beginning part leads up to the thesis statement (underlined).

Lopez 2

An Economic Meltdown

In the 1920s, the U.S. economy roared ahead like a powerful automobile, but beneath the shiny exterior, the economy was corroding. According to Kennedy in <u>Freedom from Fear</u>, "Nearly three decades of barely punctuated economic growth, capped by seven years of unprecedented prosperity, gave to the entire country, an air of masterful confidence in the future" (11). The value of stocks rose rapidly, and investors grew wealthy (Kennedy 10–15). Unfortunately, businesspeople took too much of the profit from their businesses and paid workers too little. Workers couldn't afford to buy consumer goods, so businesses began cutting back on production. Farm prices also lagged, and many farmers lived in poverty (Hartford).

Then, in October 1929 the U.S. economy suddenly collapsed. The stock market dropped drastically, and investors rushed to sell their shares. Within weeks, the value of U.S. stocks had dropped by one-third. The Great Depression had begun (Hartford). Even before this time, banks had begun to fail, taking their customers' savings with them. After 1929, thousands more failed (Badger 31). President Herbert Hoover mistakenly believed that the economy would correct itself without much government help, but the economy only worsened. By 1932, 25 percent of U.S. citizens were unemployed. Many had lost their homes and didn't have the food they needed to survive (Heale). As time passed, the nation's depression became an economic and

Middle
The first middle section explains the need for the political policy.

The source of paraphrased information is cited in parentheses.

Research

Lopez 3

psychological problem. With national spirits at a new low, the country turned to Franklin Roosevelt for help. They put their faith in Roosevelt—and his New Deal.

The New Deal

In the first phase of the New Deal, Roosevelt addressed one of the nation's most pressing problems—the soundness of the banks. Panicked by bank failures, people had made "runs" on banks, pulling out their savings and draining the banks of needed funds. This caused even more failures (Badger 31). To stop this chain reaction, Roosevelt declared a "banking holiday" and closed all the banks. He then presented Congress with legislation to make banks stronger (Friedel 95). When the first banks reopened on March 13, people began to return their money (Hartford). The nation's psychology had begun to shift from despair to hope. Healing had begun.

Roosevelt understood that people needed financial relief, and that a flow of cash would jump-start the economy. In 1933, he introduced the National Industrial Recovery Act (NIRA). Congress approved giving him unprecedented legislative power to make laws to solve the nation's economic woes. With this act he authorized a number of new agencies that put people to work. The Tennessee Valley Authority hired workers to build electrical dams in the rural South. The Civilian Conservation Corps, or CCC, put people to work in forests, planting trees and building roads and shelters. The wages were low—just $30 per month in the CCC (Church), but as with the restructuring of the banks,

When a source has page numbers, the appropriate numbers are included in the citation.

Examples are included to clarify key points.

Lopez 4

the psychological effect was critical. People who had lost hope and self-esteem once again became breadwinners, and their confidence began to return.

The New Deal helped citizens in other ways, too. The Home Owners Loan Act and the Farm Credit Act helped Americans refinance their mortgages and save their homes and farms (Hartford). The Social Security Act established a system by which workers paid money into a government fund that would provide them with a pension when they retired (Leuchtenburg 133). This pension secured the future for senior citizens, among those most vulnerable to economic downturns. The importance of Social Security was more than its economic benefits. Providing a future for the nation's elderly helped promote a feeling of national security that was critical during a very uncertain time.

Bumps in the Road

The newfound hope was real, but NIRA's Title 1 was in trouble. Title 1 attempted to create jobs and increase salaries by regulating labor practices, wages, and prices. It set maximum work hours per week, which forced businesses to hire more workers. It also set minimum wages and guaranteed the right of workers to form unions. Although these were all noble goals, the process to achieve those goals was coercive and cumbersome, often unequally applied.

Each paragraph includes a topic sentence, followed by supporting details.

Headings guide the reader from section to section.

Lopez 5

Other aspects of the NIRA proved equally problematic. The board that administered the act, the National Recovery Administration (NRA), churned out so many regulations that they became impossible to enforce, and even to understand. Many business owners and labor groups manipulated the regulations to their favor whenever possible, while other businesses simply ignored them (Black 303). The massive regulatory machine also helped turn many businesspeople against the New Deal. In 1935, the Supreme Court ruled against the NIRA. Historian Frank Friedel stated, "Chief Justice Hughes was devastating. He held that Roosevelt's code-making [lawmaking] authority was indeed an 'unconstitutional delegation of legislative power' " (161).

The Agricultural Adjustment Act (AAA) met a similar fate. Created to help farmers, the AAA paid farmers to reduce production, which in theory would cause farm prices to rise. Farmers would then make more for the crops they sold. AAA payments came from taxes on companies that processed and sold agricultural products. In fact, the AAA only succeeded in raising farm prices temporarily, and farmers continued to struggle (Black 307–8). In addition, processors hated paying the tax required by the act. They filed suit, and in 1936, the Supreme Court declared the AAA unconstitutional, saying that the agency had no authority to make laws (Black 328–29).

> A quotation is integrated into the paper to create an authoritative voice.

> Smooth-reading sentences make the paper very "readable."

Lopez 6

The End of the New Deal

By 1937, the New Deal had begun to improve the U.S. economy. Unemployment fell to about 12 percent, the lowest in years. Impressed by the improvements, Roosevelt cut back on government spending for New Deal programs (Black 428). This turned out to be a big mistake. By early 1938, the economy was sinking again. The unemployment rate rose to 22.5 percent, and the stock market had taken a major slide. Quickly, Roosevelt reversed position, and the economy began to respond (Black 435–36). Employment rose, and so did industrial production. However, the Depression still gripped the United States, and it would take a bigger force than the New Deal to create an economic boom.

During the 1930s, a depression also gripped Europe. In Germany, the poor economic conditions helped fascist leader Adolph Hitler rise to power. In September 1939, Hitler's Germany initiated a world war by invading Poland. In December 1941, after being attacked by Japan, the United States entered the war. Soon U.S. factories converted to production of tanks, planes, bombs, and other war materials. By 1943, employment boomed, and factories were rolling again. The Depression was over, and the United States would enter one of its most productive periods ever (Hartford).

Conclusion

While the New Deal provided jobs for many people and allowed many families to keep their homes and farms,

---

Statistics help to paint a clear picture.

Dates help the reader follow the main points.

Lopez 7

it did not succeed in ending the Great Depression. Those who criticize the New Deal often fail to account for its major achievement: It saved the United States from complete collapse. In Europe, the German government lapsed into fascism, largely as a result of a depression there. In the United States, the same might have happened except for Roosevelt and the New Deal. The programs of the New Deal restored the citizens' faith that a democratic, capitalistic system could respond to their needs in the worst of economic times. This restored faith helped democracy and free enterprise to survive. The New Deal also created a new United States, one that would provide a safety net for the old, the infirm, and the suffering, and helped to prevent another economic and social tragedy from happening.

Perhaps just as important, the New Deal helped to convince people of the value of shared sacrifice and innovative vision. Both would prove critical in bringing the nation through another crisis—World War II. Conditioned by years of working together and following the leadership of Franklin Delano Roosevelt, U.S. citizens would meet the challenge of the war as a nation largely unified and willing to make the sacrifices necessary to defeat fascism. Once again, President Roosevelt would ask his nation to follow his creative leadership and make sacrifices for the common good. Once again, Roosevelt would help to kindle the faith and hope so critical to survival in a time of national crisis.

The conclusion includes the analysis and ideas of the writer.

Ending
Parallel ideas bring the paper to an effective close.

Lopez 8

Works Cited

Badger, Anthony J. The New Deal: The Depression Years,
1933–1940. Chicago: Dee, 1989.

Black, Conrad. Franklin Delano Roosevelt: Champion of
Freedom. New York: Public Affairs, 2003.

Church, George J. "Taking Care of Our Own: The New Deal
Probed the Limits of Government." Time. 9 Mar. 1998:
106.

Friedel, Frank. Franklin D. Roosevelt: A Rendezvous with
Destiny. New York: Back Bay, 1990.

Hartford, Colleen. "The Battle Over the New Deal."
American History Place. 2005. 1 Mar. 2006 <http://
www.americanhistoryplace/battle_over_new_deal.html>.

Heale, Michael. "The New Deal." Modern History Review
April 2001: 16–20.

Kennedy, David M. Freedom from Fear: The American
People in Depression and War, 1929–1945. Oxford:
Oxford UP, 1999.

Leuchtenburg, William E. Franklin D. Roosevelt and the
New Deal. New York: Harper, 1963.

A separate page alphabetically lists sources cited in the paper.

Lines that run over are indented five spaces.

Respond to the reading. Now that you have read the sample research paper, answer the following questions.

Ideas (1) Name two ways in which the New Deal was successful—and two ways in which it fell short. (2) Why does the writer think the New Deal was important?

Organization (3) In a general way, how is the paper organized?

Voice (4) Is the voice of the paper convincing? Why or why not?

Prewriting

In order to develop an effective research paper, you'll need to carry out a great deal of planning and research. During the prewriting stage, you will need to select an appropriate topic, gather facts and details about it, establish a thesis or focus, organize your data for writing, and so on.

Keys to Effective Prewriting

1. For your topic, choose a significant presidential policy to analyze.

2. Make a list of questions you want to answer about the policy.

3. Use a gathering grid to organize your research questions and answers. Use note cards to keep track of longer answers. (See pages 397–398.)

4. Cite the sources of any information you paraphrase or quote.

5. Keep track of the publication details of all your sources. (See page 399.)

6. Gather enough information to offer a clear and complete analysis of your topic.

Prewriting ▪ Select a topic.

To search for a topic, Shawna listed three U.S. presidents that she had studied, plus a significant policy that each one enacted. She also noted a few key points about each policy.

Topics List

Franklin Roosevelt
New Deal
  – response to the Depression
  – jump-started the economy
  – gave people hope

John F. Kennedy
Alliance for Progress
  – help for Latin America
  – growth of industry
  – land reform

Lyndon Johnson
Great Society
  – response to poverty
  – focused on civil rights
  – expanded Social Security

Prewrite

Make a topics list. Create a list like the one above identifying two or three presidents and a significant policy enacted by each one. If necessary, refer to a textbook, your classroom notes, or the Internet for ideas. Also note a few key points about each policy. Then choose the policy you find most interesting as the topic of your paper.

▪ Focus on the traits.

Ideas Choose a policy that truly interests you. Also consider the availability of information about your choice. You will need a thorough understanding of the policy in order to develop an effective analysis.

■ Size up your topic.

A paper analyzing a presidential policy should cover these main areas.

- ■ **The policy:** Identify the policy, its reason for being, and its goals.
- ■ **The successes:** Examine aspects of the policy that succeeded.
- ■ **The failures:** Explain the ways in which the policy fell short.
- ■ **Conclusion:** Summarize the main features of the policy. Then share your overall analysis of it.

Research Notes

To prepare for writing her paper on the New Deal, Shawna did some quick research about the policy. She took notes on what she found.

What was the New Deal?
- The New Deal was a far-reaching economic program created in response to the Great Depression.
- Its goals were to end the Depression and put the U.S. on a better economic footing.

What were some of its successes?
- Roosevelt's "banking holiday" kept many banks from failing.
- The Tennessee Valley Authority and the Civilian Conservation Corps used government funds to put people to work.
- The Home Owners Loan Act and the Farm Credit Act helped save people's homes and farms.

What were some of its failures?
- The National Industrial Recovery Act was too complicated.
- The Agricultural Adjustment Act only succeeded temporarily.

How effective was the New Deal?
- It was only partially successful in ending the Great Depression.
- It saved the U.S. democratic, capitalistic system.

Shawna's initial research convinced her that her topic would provide enough information to support a research paper. Further, she realized that the successes and failures of the New Deal would make it a compelling topic.

Prewrite

Size up your topic. Do some quick research on your topic using the Internet or another reliable basic resource. Can you find sufficient information to support a research paper? If not, consider another topic.

Prewriting ■ Use a gathering grid.

To help organize the information that you gather, use a graphic organizer such as a gathering grid. Shawna created a gathering grid to organize her research about the New Deal. In the left-hand column, she listed questions she wanted to answer. Across the top, she listed resources that answered those questions. For answers too long to fit in the grid, Shawna used note cards. (See page **397**.) A portion of Shawna's grid is shown below.

Gathering Grid

THE NEW DEAL	Franklin D. Roosevelt and the New Deal (book)	"The New Deal" (magazine article)	The New Deal: The Depression Years, 1933–1940 (book)
Why was the policy created?	See note card 1.		
What were its successes?	TVA built dams for flood control and electricity.	Civilian Conservation Corps	Banking holiday People putting money back in banks
What were its failures?	NIRA was declared unconstitutional.	AAA was struck down by Supreme Court in 1936.	

Prewrite

Create a gathering grid. List questions in the left-hand column of your grid. Across the top, list sources you will use. Fill in the grid with answers you find. Use note cards for longer, more detailed answers.

■ Create note cards.

A gathering grid works well for short answers, but when your answers are longer, it's better to use note cards. Number each note card and write a question at the top. Then answer the question with a list, a quotation, or a paraphrase. (See page **398**.) At the bottom, identify the source, including the page number if appropriate.

Note Cards

List

Question —— • Why was the policy created?   ①
Answer —— • The Great Depression ruined the economy.
   • stock market crash
   • banks failing
   • people losing jobs, homes, and farms
   • many living in shacks
   • many going hungry
                    Franklin D. Roosevelt and the New Deal
                                          pages 1 and 2

Paraphrase

What were its successes?   ②

The "banking holiday" was a success. When the first banks reopened on March 13, people began to return their money. By the end of April 1933, more than 2/3 of banks had reopened.
                    "The Battle Over the New Deal" •

Card number

Source

What were its failures?   ③
The National Industrial Recovery Act (NIRA) was ruled unconstitutional by the Supreme Court.

Quotation

Answer — • "Chief Justice Hughes was devastating. He held that
(quotation)   Roosevelt's code-making authority was indeed an
            'unconstitutional delegation of legislative power.'"
                Franklin D. Roosevelt: A Rendezvous with Destiny
                                          page 161

Prewrite

Create note cards. When your answers are too long to fit in a gathering grid, make note cards such as the ones above.

Prewriting ■ Avoid plagiarism.

Plagiarism means using someone else's words or ideas without giving them credit. Plagiarism is intellectual thievery and must always be avoided. As you write down facts and ideas during your research, take care to note their source and indicate whether the note is a paraphrase or a quotation.

- **Paraphrase:** When you paraphrase, you rewrite information in your own words. This is usually the best approach for including information in your paper. Don't forget—even when you paraphrase, you must give credit to the source of the paraphrased idea.

- **Quote exact words:** To add authority or color to your paper, you may wish to use the exact words from one of your sources. Be sure to include these words in quotation marks and to give credit to the source.

Paraphrasing

Why was the policy created?
Panicked by bank failures, people had made "runs" on banks, pulling out their savings and draining the banks of needed funds. This caused even more failures.

The New Deal
page 31

Quoting Exact Words

Why was the policy created?
"As banks ran into trouble, investors withdrew their assets. [. . .] Their withdrawals put more pressure on the banks. [. . .] As the economy worsened, the banks suffered once more. A total of 2,294 banks failed in 1931, and 1,453 in 1932."

The New Deal
page 31

Note: Use ellipses [. . .] in your quotations to show where words from the original source have been left out.

Try It!

Create two note cards for the same key passage from your research. On one card, *quote* a sentence from the passage. On the other card, *paraphrase* the passage. Give credit for the source on each card.

Research

■ Keep track of your sources.

As you conduct your research, keep careful track of the sources of information you find so that you can correctly cite those sources in your final paper. You'll need to record the following information:

- **Book:** Author's name. Title. Publisher and city. Copyright date.
- **Magazine:** Author's name. Article title. Magazine title. Date published. Page numbers.
- **Newspaper:** Author's name. Article title. Newspaper title. City. Date published. Section. Page numbers.
- **Internet:** Author's name (if listed). Page title. Site title. Date posted or copyright date (if listed). Site sponsor. Date visited. Electronic address.
- **Videocassette or DVD:** Title. Distributor. Release date. Medium.

Source Notes

Book

Black, Conrad. <u>Franklin Delano Roosevelt: Champion of Freedom</u>. New York: Public Affairs. 2003.

Magazine

Church, George J. "Taking Care of Our Own: The New Deal Probed the Limits of Government." <u>Time</u>. March 9, 1998. Page 106.

Internet

Hartford, Colleen. "The Battle Over the New Deal." <u>American History Place</u>. Posted in 2005. Visited March 1, 2006. <http://www.americanhistoryplace/battle_over_new_deal.html>

Newspaper

Ringle, Ken. "FDR's Monumental Place in History." <u>The Washington Post</u>. May 2, 1997. Section A. Page 1.

Television Program

"F.D.R." <u>The American Experience</u>. WGBH, Boston, MA. Viewed April 28, 2006.

Interview

James Lavelle. E-mail interview. March 25, 2006.

Prewrite

List sources. Keep a list of your sources, using the information above as your guide. Whenever you use a new source, add it to your list.

Prewriting ▪ Write your thesis statement.

Once you've completed your research, it's time to write a thesis statement. Your thesis statement expresses the main idea or focus of your research, and it helps guide your writing. All of the other ideas in your paper should support the thesis. You can use the formula below to help you write your thesis statement.

an interesting topic		special part to emphasize		a thesis statement
the New Deal	**+**	saved the United States from collapsing into chaos and gave the nation's citizens hope	**=**	The New Deal saved the United States from collapsing into chaos and gave the nation's citizens the hope they needed to survive.

Sample Thesis Statements

Wind power (an interesting topic) **provides a viable energy source in the Plains states** (a special part to emphasize).

A cell that functions abnormally (an interesting topic) **can initiate a process that results in cancer** (a special part to emphasize).

The marketing of high-profile professional athletes (an interesting topic) **has become big business** (a special part to emphasize).

Prewrite

Create your thesis statement. Carefully review your research notes and choose a main point you want to make about your topic. Using the formula above, write a thesis statement for that idea.

■ Outline your ideas.

An outline is a powerful tool for organizing and planning your research paper. The outline serves as a map or a blueprint to guide your writing. There are two main kinds of outlines: A topic outline lists ideas as words or phrases; a sentence outline lists the ideas as full sentences.

Below is the first part of a sentence outline for the paper on pages **385–392**. The outline begins with a thesis statement. Next, it lists the main point (topic sentence), marked by a Roman numeral, for each middle paragraph. Below each main point is a list of supporting details identified by capital letters.

Sentence Outline

In an outline, if you have a Roman numeral I, you must have at least a Roman numeral II. If you have a capital letter A, you must have at least a capital letter B.

Thesis Statement	Thesis Statement: Although its success was incomplete, the New Deal saved the United States from collapsing into chaos and gave the nation's citizens the hope they needed to survive.
Major Points (I., II.)	I. In the 1920s, the U.S. economy roared ahead like a powerful automobile, but beneath the shiny exterior, the economy was corroding.
Supporting Ideas (A., B., C., D.)	A. The value of stocks rose rapidly, and investors grew wealthy.
	B. Workers couldn't afford to buy consumer goods, so businesses cut back on production.
	C. Farm prices lagged, and many farmers lived in poverty.
Continue . . .	II. In October 1929, the U.S. economy suddenly collapsed.
	A. The stock market dropped drastically, and investors rushed to sell their shares.
	B. Within weeks, the value of U.S. stocks had dropped by one-third.
	C. Banks had begun to fail, taking their customers' savings with them.

Prewrite

Create your outline. Write a sentence outline for your paper, using the main points and details from your research. Be sure that each topic sentence (I., II., III., . . .) supports the thesis statement, and that each detail (A., B., C., . . .) supports its topic sentence. Use your outline as a guide for writing your first draft.

Writing

Now that you have organized your research and prepared an outline, it's time to write your first draft. Don't worry about getting everything perfect in the first draft; you'll have a chance to improve your writing later. For now, just get your ideas down on paper in a way that makes sense to you. The following points will help you.

Keys to Effective Writing

1. In the beginning part, grab your reader's attention, introduce your topic, and present your thesis statement.

2. In the next section, explain the presidential policy and why it was created.

3. Next explore the successes of the policy.

4. Follow with a discussion of the policy's failures.

5. In the final section, analyze the effectiveness of the policy.

6. Cite the sources of any ideas you paraphrase or quote and list those sources alphabetically on a works-cited page.

■ Start your research report.

The opening part of your paper should grab your reader's attention, introduce your topic, and present your thesis statement. Here are two ways to begin.

- ■ Open with a dramatic situation.

  When he took office on March 4, 1933, President Franklin Delano Roosevelt assumed leadership of a nation mired in poverty and racked by hopelessness.

- ■ Start with an interesting fact.

  By 1932, more than one-quarter of the population of the United States was unemployed.

Beginning Paragraphs

Beginning
The beginning paragraphs open with a dramatic situation.

When he took office on March 4, 1933, President Franklin Delano Roosevelt assumed leadership of a nation mired in poverty and racked by hopelessness. Four years before, a stock market crash had set off the Great Depression, a collapse of the United States economy. Many factories, businesses, and banks closed down, and millions of U.S. citizens lost their jobs. Untold numbers of families had lost their savings and even their homes (Leuchtenburg 1).

As a candidate, Roosevelt had promised a "new deal for the American people" (Heale). As president, he began to dramatically restructure the U.S. economy with an economic program called the New Deal. The New Deal created jobs, changed banking practices, and prevented many people from losing their savings and their homes (Church). As much as it changed the economy, the New Deal did not end the Great

The opening ends with a thesis statement (underlined).

Depression. <u>Although its success was incomplete, the New Deal saved the United States from collapsing into chaos and gave the nation's citizens the hope they needed to survive.</u>

Write

Write your beginning paragraphs. Using one of the approaches above, grab the reader's interest, introduce your topic, and state your thesis.

Writing ■ Develop the middle part.

The middle of your research paper should include ideas and details that support your thesis statement. Each middle paragraph should cover one main idea. Use your sentence outline to guide your writing.

Middle Paragraphs

Middle
The first middle section explains why the political policy was created.

The details in each paragraph support its topic sentence (underlined).

An Economic Meltdown

In the 1920s, the U.S. economy roared ahead like a powerful automobile, but beneath the shiny exterior, the economy was corroding. According to Kennedy in Freedom from Fear, "Nearly three decades of barely punctuated economic growth, capped by seven years of unprecedented prosperity, gave to the entire country, an air of masterful confidence in the future" (11). The value of stocks rose rapidly, and investors grew wealthy (Kennedy 10–15). Unfortunately. businesspeople took too much of the profit from their businesses and paid workers too little. Workers couldn't afford to buy consumer goods, so businesses began cutting back on production. Farm prices also lagged, and many farmers lived in poverty (Hartford).

Then, in October 1929, the U.S. economy suddenly collapsed. The stock market dropped drastically, and investors rushed to sell their shares. Within weeks, the value of U.S. stocks had dropped by one-third. The Great Depression had begun (Hartford). Even before this time, banks had begun to fail, taking their customers' savings with them. After 1929, thousands more failed (Badger 31). President Herbert Hoover mistakenly believed that the economy would correct itself without much government help, but the economy only worsened. By 1932, 25 percent of U.S. citizens were unemployed. Many had lost their homes and didn't have the food they needed to survive (Heale). As time passed, the nation's depression became an economic and psychological problem. With national spirits at a new low, the country turned to Franklin Roosevelt for help. They put their faith in Roosevelt—and his New Deal.

The New Deal

The next middle section describes the policy.

In the first phase of the New Deal, Roosevelt addressed one of the nation's most pressing problems—the soundness of the banks. Panicked by bank failures, people had made "runs" on banks, pulling out their savings and draining the banks of needed funds. This caused even more failures (Badger 31). To stop this chain reaction, Roosevelt declared a "banking holiday" and closed all the banks. He then presented Congress with legislation to make banks stronger (Friedel 95). When the first banks reopened on March 13, people began to return their money (Hartford). The nation's psychology had begun to shift from despair to hope. Healing had begun.

Sentences are arranged so the reader can easily follow the ideas.

Roosevelt understood that people needed financial relief, and that a flow of cash would jump-start the economy. In 1933, he introduced the National Industrial Recovery Act (NIRA). Congress approved giving him unprecedented legislative power to make laws to solve the nation's . . .

Write

Write your middle paragraphs. Keep these tips in mind as you write.

1. Use a topic sentence and supporting details in each paragraph.
2. Refer to your outline (page 401) and the keys on page 402 for direction.
3. Add parenthetical references to credit all sources. (See pages 426–428.)

Writing ▪ End your research paper.

Your ending should sum up your research and bring your paper to a thoughtful close. You should . . .

- remind the reader of the thesis of your paper.
- review your key points.
- leave the reader with something to think about.

Ending Paragraphs

Ending
The conclusion summarizes the paper's main points and shares the writer's views on the policy's effectiveness.

The writer considers how the policy may have prepared the nation for its next great challenge.

Conclusion

While the New Deal provided jobs for many people and allowed many families to keep their homes and farms, it did not succeed in ending the Great Depression. Those who criticize the New Deal often fail to account for its major achievement: It saved the United States from complete collapse. In Europe, the German government lapsed into fascism, largely as a result of a depression there. In the United States, the same might have happened except for Roosevelt and the New Deal. The programs of the New Deal restored the citizens' faith that a democratic, capitalistic system could respond to their needs in the worst of economic times. This restored faith helped democracy and free enterprise to survive. The New Deal also created a new United States, one that would provide a safety net for the old, the infirm, and the suffering, and helped to prevent another economic and social tragedy from happening.

Perhaps just as important, the New Deal helped to convince people of the value of shared sacrifice and innovative vision. Both would prove critical in bringing the nation . . .

Write

Write your ending. Draft your ending paragraph(s) using the guidelines above.

■ Create your works-cited page.

The purpose of a works-cited page is to let your reader find and read the sources you used. Creating a works-cited page isn't difficult. First, format the sources you used, using the information from your source notes (page **399**). Then list those sources in alphabetical order. The examples on this page show the standard MLA format for common types of sources.

Works-Cited Entries

Book

Black, Conrad. Franklin Delano Roosevelt: Champion of Freedom. New York: Public Affairs, 2003.

Magazine

Church, George J. "Taking Care of Our Own: The New Deal Probed the Limits of Government." Time 9 Mar. 1998: 106.

Internet

Hartford, Colleen. "The Battle Over the New Deal." American History Place. 2005. 1 Mar. 2006 <http://www.americanhistoryplace/battle_over_new_deal.html>.

Newspaper

Ringle, Ken. "FDR's Monumental Place in History." The Washington Post 2 May 1997: A1.

Television Program

"F.D.R." The American Experience. WGBH, Boston. 28 Apr. 2006.

Interview

Lavelle, James. E-mail interview. 25 Mar. 2006.

Write

Format your sources. Check your paper and your list of sources (page **399**) to see which sources you actually used. Then follow these directions.

1. Format your sources using the guidelines above. You can write them on a sheet of paper or on note cards.

2. List your sources in alphabetical order.

3. Create your works-cited page. (See the example on page **392**.)

Revising

In the first draft of your research paper, you connect all of your ideas. During revising, you make sure that the ideas are clear and well supported, the organization is logical, the voice sounds knowledgeable, the words are specific and accurate, and the sentences are varied and flow smoothly.

Keys to Effective Revising

1. Read your draft aloud to yourself or to a friend. Note any parts of the draft that sound unclear or unconvincing.

2. Review your thesis statement to be sure that it states the main point about your topic.

3. Be sure that your beginning engages the reader and that the ending includes your own analysis.

4. Check to see that the middle explains the need for the policy as well as its successes and failures.

5. Make sure your voice is knowledgeable and convincing.

6. Check for effective word choice and a smooth flow of sentences.

■ Improve your writing.

There are always ways to improve a first draft. Shawna made a number of important revisions to improve the ideas, organization, voice, word choice, and sentence fluency in her research paper.

Bumps in the Road

The newfound hope was real, but NIRA's Title 1 was in trouble. Title 1 attempted to create jobs and increase salaries by regulating labor practices, wages, and prices. ~~Title 1~~ It set maximum work hours per week, which forced businesses to hire more workers. It also set minimum wages and guaranteed the right of workers to form unions. Although These were all noble goals, ~~yet~~ the process to achieve those goals was coercive, cumbersome, and often unequally applied. Other aspects of the NIRA proved equally problematic. The board that administered the act, the National Recovery Administration (NRA), ~~made~~ churned out so many regulations that they became impossible to enforce, and even to understand. Many business owners and labor groups manipulated the regulations to their favor whenever possible, while Other businesses simply ignored them (Black 303). The massive regulatory machine also helped turn many businesspeople against the New Deal. In 1935, the Supreme Court ruled against the NIRA. Historian Frank Friedel stated, "Chief Justice Hughes was devastating. He held that Roosevelt's code-making [lawmaking] authority was indeed an 'unconstitutional delegation of legislative power' " (161).

A sentence beginning is varied.

A transition is inserted.

A transitional sentence improves clarity.

Word choice is strengthened.

Two sentences are combined for fluency.

A bracketed clarification is added.

Wording is changed to improve voice.

An idea is moved for better organization.

An important idea is added.

The Agricultural Adjustment Act (AAA) ~~was also bad~~ **met a similar fate.** ~~in ways,~~ Created to help farmers, the AAA paid farmers to reduce production, which in theory would cause farm prices to rise. Farmers would then make more for the crops they sold. In fact, the AAA only succeeded in raising farm prices temporarily, and farmers continued to struggle (Black 307–308). AAA payments came from taxes on companies that processed and sold agricultural products. In addition, processors hated paying the tax required by the act. They filed suit, and in 1936, the Supreme Court declared the AAA unconstitutional **, saying that the agency had no authority to make laws** (Black 328–329).

Revise

Revise your writing. Carefully review your first draft for ideas, organization, voice, word choice, and sentence fluency. Make any changes needed to improve your paper.

Revising ■ Use a checklist.

On a piece of paper, write the numbers 1 to 14. If you can answer "yes" to a question below, put a check mark next to that number. If not, continue to work on that part of your research paper.

Revising Checklist

Ideas

_____ **1.** Have I chosen an interesting presidential policy to write about?
_____ **2.** Do I state my thesis clearly?
_____ **3.** Have I included enough details to support my thesis?
_____ **4.** Do I give credit for ideas that I have paraphrased or quoted from other sources?

Organization

_____ **5.** Does my beginning paragraph capture the reader's interest and introduce my topic?
_____ **6.** Do my first middle paragraphs explain the need for the policy?
_____ **7.** Do my next middle paragraphs explore the successes and failures of the policy?
_____ **8.** Does my ending include a summary and my own analysis of the policy's effectiveness?

Voice

_____ **9.** Does my voice sound knowledgeable and engaging?
_____ **10.** Does my voice sound natural?

Word Choice

_____ **11.** Have I used specific nouns and active verbs?
_____ **12.** Do I avoid unnecessary modifiers?

Sentence Fluency

_____ **13.** Have I used a variety of sentence lengths and constructions?
_____ **14.** Do my sentences flow smoothly?

Editing

When you have finished revising your research paper, all that remains is to check it for conventions in spelling, punctuation, capitalization, and grammar.

Keys to Effective Editing

1. Read your paper aloud and listen for words or phrases that may be incorrect.

2. Use a dictionary, a thesaurus, your computer's spell-check function, and the "Proofreader's Guide" in the back of this book.

3. Look carefully for errors in punctuation, capitalization, spelling, and grammar.

4. Check your paper for proper formatting and for accuracy of citations. (See pages 384–392 and 407.)

5. If you use a computer, edit on a printed copy. Then enter your changes on the computer.

6. Use the editing and proofreading marks on the inside back cover of this book.

■ **Check for conventions.**

After revising the first draft of her paper, Shawna checked the new version for punctuation, capitalization, spelling, and grammar errors. She also asked a classmate to look it over.

The End of the New Deal

By 1937, the New Deal had begun to improve the U.S. economy. Unemployment fell to about 12 percent, the lowest in years. ~~Impresed~~ *Impressed* by the improvements, Roosevelt cut back on government spending for New Deal programs (Black, 428). This turned out to be a big mistake. By early 1938, the economy was sinking again. The unemployment rate rose to 22.5 percent, and the stock market had taken a major slide. Quickly, Roosevelt reversed position, and the economy ~~begun~~ *began* to respond (Black 435–436). Employment rose, and so did industrial production. However, the Depression still gripped the United States, and it would take a bigger force than the New Deal to create an economic boom.

During the 1930s, a depression also gripped Europe. In Germany, the poor economic conditions helped fascist leader Adolph Hitler rise to power. In September 1939, Hitler's Germany initiated a World War by invading Poland. In December 1941, after being attacked by Japan, the United States entered the war. Soon U.S. factories converted to production of tanks, planes, bombs, and other war

A spelling error is corrected.

An unnecessary punctuation mark is deleted.

An error in verb tense is corrected.

A capitalization error is marked.

An abbreviation is properly punctuated.

materials. By 1943, employment boomed, and factories were rolling again. The Depression was over, and the United States would enter one of its most productive ~~productve~~ periods ever (Hartford).

Another spelling error is corrected.

Conclusion

While the New Deal provided jobs for many people and allowed many families to keep their homes and farms, it did not succeed in ending the *G* great Depression. Those who

A capitalization error is marked.

criticize the New Deal often fail to account for its major achievement: It saved the United States from collapse. In Europe, the German government lapsed into fascism, largely as a result of a depression there. In the United States, the same might have happened except for Roosevelt and the New Deal. The programs of the New Deal restored the

An apostrophe is added to indicate possession.

citizens' faith that a democratic, capitalistic system could respond to their needs in the worst of economic times. This restored faith helped democracy and free enterprise to survive. The New Deal also created a new United States, one that would provide a safety net for the old, the infirm, and the suffering, and helped to prevent another economic and social tragedy from happening.

Edit

Check your work for conventions. To begin, use your computer's spell-checker and grammar-checker to search your work for errors. Then print a clean copy of your paper and read it again to catch any errors the computer may have missed. Also ask a classmate to check over your paper.

Editing ▪ Use a checklist.

On a piece of paper, write the numbers 1 to 12. If you can answer "yes" to a question, put a check mark next to that number. If not, continue editing for that convention.

Editing Checklist

Conventions

PUNCTUATION

_____ **1.** Do I correctly punctuate compound and complex sentences?

_____ **2.** Have I correctly cited sources in my research paper?

_____ **3.** Do I use quotation marks around all quoted words from my sources?

_____ **4.** Do I use underlining for all words that should be italicized?

_____ **5.** Have I correctly formatted a works-cited page?

CAPITALIZATION

_____ **6.** Have I capitalized proper nouns and adjectives?

_____ **7.** Do I begin each sentence with a capital letter?

SPELLING

_____ **8.** Have I spelled all words correctly?

_____ **9.** Have I double-checked words my spell-checker may have missed?

GRAMMAR

_____ **10.** Do I use the correct forms of verbs (*he saw*, not *he seen*)?

_____ **11.** Have I used the right words (*there, their, they're*)?

_____ **12.** Do my subjects and verbs agree?

Italics and Underlining in MLA Research Papers

Most high school research papers use the Modern Language Association (MLA) format. (See pages **426–436**.) The MLA format requires underlining instead of italics for titles and specialized words. However, be sure to follow your teacher's instructions.

Publishing ▪ Share your paper.

When your editing is finished, make a neat final copy of your research paper and proofread it again before sharing it. Make extra copies for family members and friends if you wish. A research paper can also serve as the basis for a speech, a multimedia presentation, or a Web page. (See pages **439–449**.) You worked hard on your paper, so find the best way to share your writing.

Publish

Make a final copy. To format your paper, use the following guidelines. (Also see pages **91–95** for instructions about designing on the computer.) Create a neat final copy to share.

▪ Focus on presentation.

- ▪ Use blue or black ink and double-space the entire paper.
- ▪ Write your name, your teacher's name, the class, and the date in the upper left corner of page 1.
- ▪ Skip a line and center your title; skip another line and start your writing.
- ▪ Indent every paragraph and leave a one-inch margin on all four sides.
- ▪ Write your name and the page number in the upper right corner of every page.
- ▪ If your teacher requires a title page and outline, follow his or her instructions. (See page **384**.)

▪ Add a Title

Give your paper a title that will attract the reader's attention and provide some information about the topic. Try one of these approaches.

- ▪ Ask a question:
  Roosevelt's New Deal: Success or Failure?
- ▪ Be creative:
  The Big Deal About the New Deal
- ▪ Use an idea from your paper:
  The Deal That Saved the Nation
- ▪ Use compelling words:
  The New Deal = Relief + Hope

Writing Responsibly

When you write a report based on research you've carried out, it's important to acknowledge your sources. Whether you use direct quotations or simply paraphrase another author's ideas, you commit plagiarism if you do not cite your source. The consequences of stealing copyrighted material vary, but in any case, plagiarism is wrong.

Citing your sources isn't difficult. Additionally, it shows that you've actually done your research, which adds authority to your writing. This chapter will answer your questions about using sources and avoiding plagiarism to produce a responsibly written research paper.

- Using Sources
- Avoiding Plagiarism
- Writing Paraphrases
- Using Quoted Material

"Next to the originator of a good sentence is the first quoter of it."

—Ralph Waldo Emerson

Using Sources

What does *research* mean? Research means "searching out answers to questions."

Begin your research.

- **Consider your topic.** What do you already know about your topic? If you had to write your paper right now, what would you write?
- **Begin with the basics.** An encyclopedia or a Web search will turn up basic information. Use these sources for an overview of the topic.
- **Ask questions.** What do you wonder about your topic? Make a list of questions; then consider what sources you will search to find answers.

Reflect on your research.

- **Think about what you have read.** How has your initial research affected your thinking about the topic? What new questions do you have as a result of your reading?
- **Refine your topic, if necessary.** What new questions and ideas have occurred to you? Should you broaden or narrow your topic?

Do further research.

- **Focus your efforts.** Look for answers to your new questions.
- **Use the best sources.** Use trustworthy books, periodicals, and Web sites to find answers to your questions. Also, consider conducting surveys and personal interviews, and writing letters to experts.

 ## Try It!

Whom could you interview for more information on your topic? Write three or four specific questions for this person, aiming for insight that you wouldn't find in other sources.

Present your results.

- **Make the topic your own.** Your research paper should not just repeat other people's ideas. First and foremost, it should present your own thoughts and understanding of the topic.
- **Paraphrase or quote appropriately.** To support your ideas, paraphrase or quote credible sources as needed. References to other sources should be used only to enhance or support your own thinking.
- **Credit your sources.** Let your reader know the source of each idea you summarize or quote.

Avoiding Plagiarism

You owe it to your sources and your reader to give credit for others' ideas in your research paper. If you don't, you may be guilty of *plagiarism*—the act of presenting someone else's ideas as your own. (See the following pages for examples.) Cite every piece of information you borrow unless you're sure that the information is common knowledge.

Forms of Plagiarism

- **Submitting another writer's paper:** The most blatant form of plagiarism is to put your name on someone else's work (another student's paper, an essay bought from a "paper mill," the text of an article from the Internet, and so on) and turn it in as your own.
- **Using copy-and-paste:** It is unethical to copy phrases, sentences, or larger sections from a source and paste them into your paper without giving credit for the material.
- **Neglecting necessary quotation marks:** Whether it's just a phrase or a larger section of text, if you use the exact words of a source, they must be put in quotation marks and identified with a citation.
- **Paraphrasing without citing a source:** Paraphrasing (rephrasing ideas in your own words) is an important research skill. However, paraphrased ideas must be credited to the source, even if you reword the material entirely.
- **Confusing borrowed material with your own ideas:** While taking research notes, it is important to identify the source of each idea you record. That way, you won't forget whom to credit as you write your paper.

Other Source Abuses

- **Using sources inaccurately:** Be certain that your quotation or paraphrase accurately reflects the meaning of the original. Do not misrepresent the original author's intent.
- **Overusing source material:** Your paper should be primarily your words and thoughts, supported by outside sources. If you simply string together quotations and paraphrases, your voice will be lost.
- **"Plunking" source material:** When you write, smoothly incorporate any information from an outside source. Dropping in or "plunking" a quotation or paraphrased idea without comment creates choppy, disconnected writing.
- **Relying too heavily on one source:** If your writing is dominated by one source, readers may doubt the depth and integrity of your research.

Original Article

The excerpt below is from an original article about peer-to-peer music sharing. Take note of the examples of plagiarism that follow on the next page.

"Face the Music" by Claire Baughn

. . . **Anyone who uses computer technology like peer-to-peer (P2P) networking to share copyrighted music faces being sued by the music industry.** What the industry is finding out, however, is that prosecuting people who use widely available technology isn't stopping the activity. Recording companies need to understand that **they cannot regulate file-sharing technology the way they regulate the sale of physical objects such as tapes and CD's.**

Members of the Recording Industry Association of America (RIAA) are recording companies trying to protect their financial interests. The RIAA terms P2P networking as "online piracy" even while admitting that the sharing enabled by digital technology has numerous advantages. Unfortunately, RIAA members think that more people sharing music means fewer people buying it, so they are targeting P2P services and their users with copyright infringement lawsuits.

There's no question that copyright is an important part of music; **those who write and perform music deserve to profit from their work.** But are musicians really being hurt by P2P's and other file-sharing devices? A recent study shows that the music industry is affected very little. Researchers from Harvard University have published a study showing that sharing music on P2P networks has no effect on CD sales. In fact, **not only does P2P sharing not *hurt* musicians—it actually *helps* some artists promote their music.** These musicians avoid the industry middleman, delivering their music directly to the consumer. They make music because they love it—not to become rich.

Money is an important factor, but the consumer's right to privacy may be the most emotional part of the issue. Privacy is guaranteed by implication in the Bill of Rights (protected by a number of amendments), and it should apply to Internet users as much as to anyone else. However, the RIAA's approach to discouraging the downloading of copyrighted material requires Internet service providers (ISP's) to identify individuals whose Internet addresses indicate music sharing. (In a number of cases, the ISP's are colleges and universities, drawing them into the fray, as well.) In one instance, Dawnell Leadbetter's ISP gave up her identity to RIAA, and the association threatened her with a lawsuit . . .

Examples of Plagiarism

Below are the three common types of plagiarism, sometimes committed on purpose and sometimes by accident. The plagiarized text is shown in bold type.

⊘ Using copy-and-paste

- In this sample, the writer pastes in two sentences from the original article without using quotation marks or a citation.

In the land of the free, it's ironic that **anyone who uses computer technology like peer-to-peer (P2P) networking to share copyrighted music faces being sued by the music industry.** These companies seem to forget who made them wealthy in the first place—and, too bad for them, but **they cannot regulate file-sharing technology the way they regulate the sale of physical objects such as tapes and CD's.**

⊘ Neglecting necessary quotation marks

- In the sample below, the writer cites the source of the exact words that she uses from the original article, but she doesn't enclose these words in quotation marks.

There are good reasons for musicians to copyright what they produce. In a recent article on P2P networking, Claire Baughn acknowledges this fact: **Those who write and perform music deserve to profit from their work** ("Face"). She goes on to say, however, that **not only does P2P sharing not *hurt* musicians—it actually *helps* some artists promote their music.** Why would the music industry have a problem with it?

⊘ Paraphrasing without citing a source

- Below the writer accurately paraphrases (restates) a passage from the original article, but she includes no citation.

Probably the most emotional part of the issue is that of privacy, which is protected by law. Apparently, the RIAA disputes that this protection extends to use of the Internet, for the group has been demanding that Internet service providers identify music sharers. It's an outrageous abuse of power.

Writing Paraphrases

There are two ways to share information from another source: (1) quote the source directly, or (2) paraphrase the source. When you quote directly, you include the exact words of the author and put quotation marks around them. When you paraphrase, you use your own words to restate someone else's ideas. In either case, you must cite your source. To paraphrase, follow the steps below.

1. **Skim the selection first** to get the overall meaning.

2. **Read the selection carefully**, paying attention to key words and phrases.

3. **List the main ideas** on a piece of paper.

4. **Review the selection** again.

5. **Write your paraphrase**; restate the author's ideas using your own words.

   ■ Stick to the essential information. Drop anecdotes and details.

   ■ Put quotation marks around key words or phrases taken directly from the source.

   ■ Arrange the ideas into a smooth, logical order.

6. **Check your paraphrase** for accuracy by asking these questions: *Did I keep the author's ideas and viewpoints clear in my paraphrase? Have I quoted where necessary? Have I cut out enough of the original? Too much? Could another person understand the author's main idea by reading my paraphrase?*

FYI

A *quotation,* a *paraphrase,* and a *summary* are all ways of referencing a source.

■ **Quoting:** A quotation states the words of a source exactly. Quoting should be used sparingly in a research paper so that your writing doesn't sound like a patchwork of other people's statements. Use a quotation only when the exact words of the source are essential.

■ **Paraphrasing:** In a paraphrase, you recast an idea from a source into your own words. Paraphrasing demonstrates that you understand the idea, and it maintains your voice within your paper. Paraphrasing is more commonly used than quoting or summarizing.

■ **Summarizing:** A summary is a condensed version of an entire source. In a research paper, there is seldom any need to summarize an entire work unless that work is the subject of the paper. For example, you might summarize the plot of *King Lear* in a research paper about that play.

Sample Paraphrases

The original passage below is from *Life in a Medieval City*, a book by Edwin Benson. Below it are two sample paraphrases, properly cited.

Original Passage

The rooms in the houses were quite small, with low ceilings. The small windows, fitted with wooden shutters or glazed with many small panes kept together with strips of lead, lighted the rooms but poorly. The interior walls were of timbering and plaster, often white- or colour-washed. The ventilation and hygienic conditions generally were far from good, as may be imagined from a consideration of the smallness of the houses, the compactness of the city, . . . and especially the primitive system of sanitation, which was content to use the front street as a main sewer. . . .

Rooms were furnished with chairs, tables, benches, chests, bedsteads, and, in some cases, tub-shaped baths. Carpets were to be found only in the houses of the very wealthy. The floors of ordinary houses were covered with rushes and straw. The spit was a much used cooking utensil. Table-cloths, knives, and spoons were in general use, but not the fork before the fifteenth century. At one time, food was manipulated by the fingers. York was advanced in table manners, for it is known that a fork was used in the house of a citizen family here in 1443. . . .

Basic Paraphrase with Quotation

According to Benson, houses had small rooms and small windows that offered little natural light. Dried straw covered the floors (only the very wealthy had carpets). Basic furniture occupied each room, and in the kitchen were tablecloths, knives, and spoons—"but not the fork before the fifteenth century," although in York "it is known that a fork was used in the house of a citizen family here in 1433." Sanitation at the time was practically nonexistent; the street also served as a sewer (32–33).

Basic Paraphrase

According to Benson, houses had small rooms and small windows that offered little natural light. Dried straw covered the floors (only the very wealthy had carpets). Basic furniture occupied each room, and in the kitchen were tablecloths, knives, and spoons (but no forks). Sanitation at the time was practically nonexistent; the street also served as a sewer (32–33).

Using Quoted Material

A quotation can be a single word or an entire paragraph. Choose quotations carefully, keep them as brief as possible, and use them only when they are necessary. When you do quote material directly, be sure that the capitalization, punctuation, and spelling are the same as that in the original work. Clearly mark changes for your readers: (1) changes within the quotation are enclosed in brackets [like this]; (2) explanations of sources are enclosed in parentheses after the closing quotation marks, but before the closing punctuation (like this).

Short Quotations

If a quotation is four typed lines or fewer, work it into the body of your paper and put quotation marks around it.

Long Quotations

Quotations of more than four typed lines (40 words in APA) should be set off from the rest of the writing by indenting each line 10 spaces and double-spacing the material. When quoting two or more paragraphs, indent the first line of each paragraph three additional spaces. Do not use quotation marks. (See **632.3**.)

Note: Place the parenthetical reference after the final punctuation mark of the quotation. Generally, a colon is used to introduce quotations set off from the text. (See **620.4**.)

Quoting Poetry

When quoting up to three lines of poetry (or lyrics), use quotation marks and work the lines into your writing. Use a diagonal (/) to show where each line of the poem ends. For quotations of four lines or more, indent each line 10 spaces (and double-space the same as the rest of the text). Do not use quotation marks.

Note: To show that you have left out a line or more of verse in a longer quotation, make a line of spaced periods the approximate length of a complete line of the poem.

Partial Quotations

If you want to leave out part of the quotation, use an ellipsis to signify the omission. An ellipsis (. . .) is three periods with a space before and after each one. (See page **642**.)

Note: Do not take out something that will change the author's original meaning.

Documenting Research

Most academic disciplines have their own manuals of style for research paper documentation. The style manual of the Modern Language Association *(MLA Handbook for Writers of Research Papers),* for example, is widely used in the humanities (literature, philosophy, history, and so on), making it the most popular manual in high school and college writing courses. (For complete information about MLA style, refer to the latest version of the *MLA Handbook.*) For papers in social sciences and social studies, the documentation style of the American Psychological Association (APA) is often used.

This chapter will provide you with guidelines for citing sources in both the MLA and APA styles. *Remember:* Always follow your teacher's directions, which may include special requirements or exceptions for the use of either documentation style. Because these styles continue to evolve, the Write Source Web site maintains the most up-to-date information about documenting electronic sources. You will also find a sample APA research paper at www.thewritesource.com/apa.htm.

- **Guidelines for In-Text Citations**
- **MLA Works-Cited List**
- **APA Reference List**

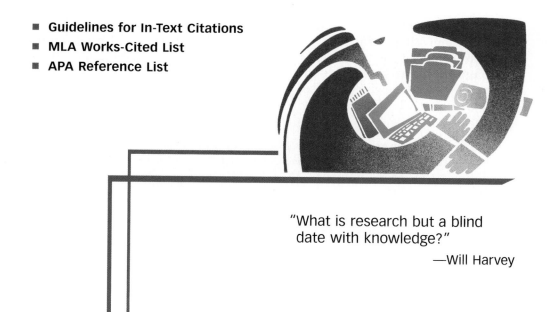

"What is research but a blind date with knowledge?"

—Will Harvey

Guidelines for In-Text Citations

The simplest way to credit a source is to insert the information in parentheses after the words or ideas taken from that source. These in-text citations (often called "parenthetical references") refer to the "Works Cited" page at the end of an MLA paper or the "References" page concluding an APA paper.

Points to Remember

- Make sure each in-text citation clearly points to an entry in your reference list or list of works cited. Use the word or words by which the entry is alphabetized.
- Keep citations brief and integrate them into your writing.
- When paraphrasing rather than quoting, make it clear where your borrowing begins and ends. Use stylistic cues to distinguish the source's thoughts ("Kalmbach points out . . . ") from your own ("However, I believe . . . ").
- Place your parenthetical citation, at the end of a sentence, before the end punctuation.
- Do not offer page numbers when citing complete works. If you cite a specific part, give the page number, chapter, or section, using the appropriate abbreviations (p. or pp., chap., or sec.). Do not, however, use p. and pp. in MLA parenthetical citations.

MLA	APA
• Place the **author's last name** (or, if unavailable, the first word or two of the title) and/or **page number** (if available) in parentheses following the cited text, except when these items have been included in the text.	• Place the **author** (or title), **date of the source,** and **page number** (if any), separated by commas, in parentheses, following the cited text, unless these items have been included in the text.
• For inclusive **page numbers** larger than 99, give only the two digits of the second number (113–14, not 113–114).	• **Titles** of books are italicized; place quotation marks around titles of articles.
• Underline **titles** of books; place quotation marks around titles of articles.	

Model In-Text Citations

MLA	**APA**

A Work by One Author

Genetic engineering was dubbed "eugenics" by a cousin of Darwin's, Sir Francis Galton, in 1885 (Bullough 5).	Bush's 2002 budget was based on revenue estimates that "now appear to have been far too optimistic" (Lemann, 2003, p. 48).

A Work by Two or Three Authors

Students learned more than a full year's Spanish in ten days using the complete supermemory method (Ostrander and Schroeder 51).	Love changes not just who we are, but who we can become, as well (Lewis, Amini, & Lannon, 2000).

Note: For APA, this format also applies to a work by up to five authors. After the first citation, list only the first author followed by *et al.* (meaning "and others").

A Work by Many Authors

This format applies to a work by four or more authors in MLA format or six or more authors in APA format. List only the first author followed by *et al.*

Communication on the job is more than talking; it is "inseparable from your total behavior" (Culligan et al. 111).	Among children 13 to 14 years old, a direct correlation can be shown between cigarette advertising and smoking (Lopez et al., 2004).

An Anonymous Work

When there is no author listed, give the title or a shortened version of the title as it appears on the works-cited or reference page.

Statistics indicate that drinking water can make up 20 percent of a person's total exposure to lead (Information 572).	. . . including a guide to low-impact exercise (*Staying Healthy,* 2004).

Personal Communications

For an MLA paper, this parenthetical reference is the same as that for a publication with one author. In an APA paper, cite letters, e-mail messages, phone conversations, and so on as "personal communication" with their full date.

MLA	APA
. . . concern for the wetland frog population (Barzinji).	. . . hiring this spring (R. Fouser, personal communication, December 14, 2004).

A Work Referred to in Another Work

In MLA, use the abbreviation *qtd. in* (quoted in) before the source in your reference. For APA, credit the source by adding *as cited in* within the parentheses.

Quoting Prose

In MLA format, when you are quoting any sort of prose that takes more than four typed lines, do not use quotation marks. Instead, indent each line of the quotation one inch (ten spaces), and put the parenthetical citation (the pages and any chapter or other numbers) outside the end punctuation mark of the quotation.

Allende describes the flying machine that Marcos has assembled:

> The contraption lay with its stomach on terra firma, heavy and sluggish and looking more like a wounded duck than like one of those newfangled airplanes they were starting to produce in the United States. There was nothing in its appearance to suggest that it could move, much less take flight. (12; ch. 1)

Note: In APA format, quotations of 40 or more words are handled similarly, although the block of lines is indented only 5 spaces, and the abbreviation p. or pp. is included in the parenthetical reference.

Try It!

Paraphrase the passage below and refer to the source in a parenthetical citation in both MLA and APA styles.

> "For two years Napoleon held (Europe) at bay, making up for his lack of soldiers by his marvelous military skill and by the enthusiasm which he never failed to arouse in his troops. In 1814, however, surrounded by the troops of Austria, Prussia, Russia, and England, he had to confess himself beaten."

Source: *The World War and What Was Behind It* by L. P. Benezet, published 1918; not paginated

MLA Works-Cited List

The works-cited section of your report lists all of the sources you have referred to in your text. It does not include sources you may have read but did not refer to in your paper. Begin your list on a new page.

List each entry alphabetically by author's last name. If there is no author, use the first word of the title (disregard *A, An, The*). Note that titles are underlined not italicized. Use a single space after all punctuation in a works-cited entry.

List only the city for the place of publication unless it is outside the United States. In that case, add an abbreviation of the country if necessary for clarity. If several cities are listed, give only the first.

Additionally, note that publishers' names should be shortened by omitting articles (*a, an, the*), business abbreviations (*Co., Inc.*), and descriptive words (*Books, Press*). Cite the surname alone if the publisher's name includes the name of one person. If it includes the names of more than one person, cite only the first of the surnames. Abbreviate "University Press" as UP. Also use standard abbreviations whenever possible.

Books

Basic Format

Author's last name, First name. Book Title. City: Publisher, date.

Opie, John. Ogallala: Water for a Dry Land. Lincoln: U of Nebraska P, 1993.

Add page numbers if the citation is to only a part of the work. In the rare instance that a book does not state publication information, use the following abbreviations in place of information you cannot supply:

n.p.	No place of publication given	n.p.	No publisher given
n.d.	No date of publication given	n. pag.	No pagination given

A Work by Two or Three Authors

Haynes, John Earl, and Harvey Klehr. In Denial: Historians, Communism, & Espionage. San Francisco: Encounter, 2003.

List the authors in the same order as they appear on the title page. Reverse only the name of the first author.

A Work by Four or More Authors

Schulte-Peevers, Andrea, et al. Germany. Victoria, Austral.: Lonely Planet, 2000.

Two or More Books by the Same Author

List the books alphabetically according to title. After the first entry, substitute three hyphens for the author's name.

Dershowitz, Alan M. Rights from Wrongs. New York: Basic, 2005.

---. Supreme Injustice: How the High Court Hijacked Election 2000. Oxford: Oxford UP, 2001.

An Anonymous Book

Chase's Calendar of Events 2002. Chicago: Contemporary, 2002.

A Single Work from an Anthology

Mitchell, Joseph. "The Bottom of the Harbor." American Sea Writing.
Ed. Peter Neill. New York: Library of America, 2000. 584–608.

An Article in a Familiar Reference Book

It is not necessary to give full publication information for familiar reference works (encyclopedias, dictionaries). List the edition and publication year. If an article is initialed, check the index of authors for the author's full name.

Lum, P. Andrea. "Computed Tomography." World Book. 2000 ed.

A Government Publication

State the name of the government (country, state, and so on) followed by the name of the agency. Most federal publications are published by the Government Printing Office (GPO).

United States. Dept. of Labor. Bureau of Labor Statistics. Occupational Outlook
Handbook 2000–2001. Washington: GPO, 2000.

When citing the *Congressional Record,* give only the date and page numbers.

Cong. Rec. 5 Feb. 2002: S311–15.

A Pamphlet, Brochure, Manual, or Other Workplace Document

Treat any such publication as you would a book.

Grayson, George W. The North American Free Trade Agreement. New York: Foreign
Policy Assn., 1993.

If publication information is missing, list the country of publication [in brackets] if known. Beyond that, use n.p. and n.d. as for a book.

Pedestrian Safety. [United States]: n.p., n.d.

Research

One Volume of a Multivolume Work

Cooke, Jacob Ernest, and Milton M. Klein, eds. <u>North America in Colonial Times</u>.
Vol. 2. New York: Scribner's, 1998.

Note: If you cite two or more volumes in a multivolume work, give the total number of volumes after each title. Offer specific references to volume and page numbers in the parenthetical reference in your text, like this: (8:112–14).

Salzman, Jack, David Lionel Smith, and Cornel West. <u>Encyclopedia of African-American Culture and History</u>. 5 vols. New York: Simon, 1996.

An Introduction, a Preface, a Foreword, or an Afterword

To cite the introduction, preface, foreword, or afterword of a book, list the author of the part first. Then identify the part by type, with no quotation marks or underlining, followed by the title of the book. Next, identify the author of the work, using the word *By.* (If the book author and the part's author are the same person, give just the last name after *By.*) For a book that gives cover credit to an editor instead of an author, identify the editor as usual. Finally, list any page numbers for the part being cited.

Barry, Anne. Afterword. <u>Making Room for Students</u>. By Celia Oyler. New York: Teachers College, 1996.

Lefebvre, Mark. Foreword. <u>The Journey Home</u>. Vol. 1. Ed. Jim Stephens. Madison: North Country, 1989. ix.

Second and Subsequent Edition

An edition refers to the particular publication you are citing, as in the third (3rd) edition.

Joss, Molly W. <u>Looking Good in Presentations</u>. 3rd ed. Scottsdale: Coriolis, 1999.

An Edition with Author and Editor

The term *edition* also refers to the work of one person that is prepared by another person, an editor.

Shakespeare, William. <u>A Midsummer Night's Dream</u>.
Ed. Jane Bachman. Lincolnwood: NTC, 1994.

Periodicals

Basic Format

Author's last name, First name. "Article Title." Periodical Title
date: page nos.

Stearns, Denise Heffernan. "Testing by Design." Middle Ground
Oct. 2000: 21–25.

An Article in a Weekly or Biweekly Magazine

List the author (if identified), article title (in quotation marks), publication
title (underlined), full date of publication, and page numbers for the article. Do not
include volume and issue numbers.

Goodell, Jeff. "The Uneasy Assimilation." Rolling Stone 6–13 Dec. 2001: 63–66.

An Article in a Monthly or Bimonthly Magazine

As for a weekly or biweekly magazine, list the author (if identified), article title
(in quotation marks), and publication title (underlined). Then identify the month(s)
and year of the issue, followed by page numbers for the article. However, do not give
volume and issue numbers.

"Patent Pamphleteer." Scientific American Dec. 2001: 33.

An Article in a Scholarly Journal Paginated by Issue

Rather than by month or the full date of publication, scholarly journals are
identified by volume number. If each issue is numbered from page 1, your works-
cited entry should identify the issue number, as well. List the volume number
immediately after the journal title, followed by a period and the issue number, the
year of publication (in parentheses), and the page numbers of the article.

Chu, Wujin. "Costs and Benefits of Hard-Sell." Journal of Marketing Research 32.2
(1995): 97–102.

An Article in a Scholarly Journal with Continuous Pagination

For scholarly journals that continue pagination from issue to issue, no issue
number is needed in the works-cited entry.

Tebble, Nicola J., David W. Thomas, and Patricia Price. "Anxiety and Self-
Consciousness in Patients with Minor Facial Lacerations." Journal of Advanced
Nursing 47 (2004): 417–26.

Note: For articles that are continued on a nonconsecutive page, whatever the
publication type, add a plus sign (+) after the first page number.

A Printed Interview

Begin with the name of the person interviewed.

Cantwell, Maria. "The New Technocrat." By Erika Rasmusson. <u>Working Woman</u> Apr.
   2001: 20–21.

If the interview is untitled, use *Interview* (no italics) in place of the title.

A Newspaper Article

Bleakley, Fred R. "Companies' Profits Grew 48% Despite Economy."
   <u>Wall Street Journal</u> 1 May 1995, Midwest ed.: 1.

If a local paper does not name the city, add it in brackets (not underlined).

To cite an article in a lettered section of the newspaper, list the section and the page number (A4). If the sections are numbered, however, use a comma after the year (or the edition); then indicate sec. 1, 2, 3, and so on, followed by a colon and the page number (sec. 1: 20). An unsigned newspaper article follows the same format:

"Bombs—Real and Threatened—Keep Northern Ireland Edgy." <u>Chicago Tribune</u> 6 Dec.
   2001, sec. 1: 20.

A Newspaper Editorial

If an article is an editorial, put *Editorial* (no italics) after the title.

"Hospital Power." Editorial. <u>Bangor Daily News</u> 14 Sept. 2004: A6.

A Review

Begin with the author (if identified) and title of the review. Use the notation *Rev. of* (no italics) between the title of the review and that of the original work. Identify the author of the original work with the word *by* (no italics). Then follow with publication data for the review.

Olsen, Jack. "Brains and Industry." Rev. of <u>Land of Opportunity</u>, by Sarah Marr. <u>New</u>
   <u>York Times</u> 23 Apr. 1995, sec. 3: 28.

Note: If you cite a review of a work by an editor or a translator, use *ed.* or *trans.* instead of *by.*

An Article with a Title or Quotation Within Its Title

Morgenstern, Joe. "Sleeper of the Year: <u>In the Bedroom</u> Is Rich Tale of Tragic Love."
   <u>Wall Street Journal</u> 23 Nov. 2001: W1.

Note: Use single quotation marks around the shorter title if it is a title normally punctuated with quotation marks.

Online Sources

The format for most online sources is the same as for other media, but with the addition of the electronic publication information.

Basic Format

Author's last name, First name. "Title." Site Title. Date of posting or last update. Site sponsor. Date accessed <address>.

Tenenbaum, David. "Dust Never Sleeps." The Why Files. 28 July 1999. U of Wisconsin, Board of Regents. 26 April 2005 <http://whyfiles.org/shorties/air_dust.html>.

Note: If certain details are not available, go on to the next item in the entry.

A Site with a Long URL

If you must include a line break in a URL, do so only after a slash, and do not add a hyphen. For a long and complicated address, give the URL of the site's search page instead.

MacLeod, Donald. "Shake-Up for Academic Publishing." EducationGuardian.co.uk. 10 Nov. 2004 <http://www.guardian.co.uk/Archive/>.

If no search page is available, give the home page URL and path of links to the document.

"Frederica: An 18th-Century Planned Community." National Register of Historic Places. National Parks Service. 27 Feb. 2004 <http://www.cr.nps.gov/nr/>. Path: Education; Hispanic Heritage Month; Frederica.

An Article in an Online Periodical

Begin with the author's name; the article title in quotation marks; and the underlined name of the periodical, its volume or issue number, and date of publication. Include page numbers (or other sections) if numbered. Close with the date of access and URL.

Dickerson, John. "Nailing Jello." Time.com 5 Nov. 2001. 9 Dec. 2001 <http://www.time.com/time/columnist/dickerson/>.

An Article in an Online Reference Work

Unless the author of the entry is identified, begin with the entry name in quotation marks. Follow with the usual online publication information.

"Eakins, Thomas." Britannica Concise Encyclopedia 2004. Encyclopædia Britannica. 26 Sept. 2004 <http://concise.britannica.com/ebc/article?tocId=9363299>.

An Article in an Online Service

When you use a library to access a subscription service, add the name of the database if known (underlined), the service, and the library. Then give the date of access followed by the Internet address for the home page of the service (if known). If no Internet address is given for an entry, add a keyword or path statement in its place, if appropriate.

> Davis, Jerome. "Massacre in Kiev." Washington Post 29 Nov. 1999, final ed.: C12.
> National Newspapers. ProQuest. Gateway Technical College Elkhorn Campus Library.
> 30 Nov. 1999 <http://proquest.umi.com/pqdweb>. Path: World Events; Conflict; Kiev.

An Online Governmental Publication

As with a governmental publication in print, begin with the name of the government (country, state, and so on) followed by the name of the agency. After the publication title, add the electronic publication information.

> United States. Dept. of Labor. Office of Disability Employment Policy. Emergency
> Preparedness for People with Disabilities. Apr. 2004. 12 Sept. 2004
> <http://www.dol.gov/odep/ep/eps.pdf>.

When citing the *Congressional Record,* only the date and page numbers are required.

> Cong. Rec. 5 Feb. 2002: S311–15.

An Online Multimedia Resource: Painting, Photograph, Musical Composition, Film or Film Clip, Etc.

After the usual information for the type of work being cited, add the electronic publication information.

> Goya, Francisco de. Saturn Devouring His Children. 1819–1823. Museo del Prado,
> Madrid. 13 Dec. 2003 <http://www.usc.edu/schools/annenberg/asc/projects/comm544/
> library/>.

An E-Mail Communication

Identify the author of the e-mail, then list the "Subject" line of the e-mail as a title, in quotation marks. Next, include a description—usually *E-mail to the author* (no italics), meaning the author of the paper. Finally, give the date of the message.

> Barzinji, Atman. "Re: Frog Populations in Wisconsin Wetlands." E-mail
> to the author. 1 Jan. 2002.

Research

Other Sources: Primary, Personal, and Multimedia

The following examples of works-cited entries illustrate how to cite sources such as television or radio programs, films, live performances, and other miscellaneous nonprint sources.

A Television or Radio Program

"Another Atlantis?" Deep Sea Detectives. The History Channel. 13 June 2005.

A Film

The director, distributor, and year of release follow the title. Other information may be included if pertinent.

The Aviator. Dir. Martin Scorsese. Perf. Leonardo DiCaprio. Miramax Films, 2004.

A Video Recording

Cite a filmstrip, slide program, videocassette, or DVD just as you would a film, but include the medium before the name of the distributor.

Beyond the Da Vinci Code. DVD. A&E Home Video, 2005.

An Audio Recording

If you are not citing a CD, indicate *LP, Audiocassette,* or *Audiotape* (no italics) before the name of the manufacturer. If you are citing a specific song on a musical recording, place its title in quotation marks before the title of the recording.

Welch, Jack. Winning. Harper Audio, 2005.

An Interview by the Author (Yourself)

Brooks, Sarah. Personal interview. 15 Oct. 2002.

A Cartoon or Comic Strip (in Print)

Luckovich, Mike. "The Drawing Board." Cartoon. Time 17 Sept. 2001: 18.

A Lecture, a Speech, an Address, or a Reading

If there is a title, use it. Otherwise, use the descriptive label (for example, Lecture).

Annan, Kofi. Lecture. Acceptance of Nobel Peace Prize. Oslo City Hall, Oslo, Norway. 10 Dec. 2001.

APA Reference List

The reference list begins on a separate page and includes all retrievable sources cited in a paper. List the entries alphabetically by author's last name. If no author is given, then list by title (disregarding *A, An,* or *The*).

Leave a single space after all end punctuation marks. Quotation marks are not used for article titles; italicize other titles. Capitalize the first word (and any proper nouns) of book and article titles, as well as the first word after a colon or dash within the title; capitalize the names of periodicals in the usual upper- and lowercase manner.

Books

Basic Format

Author's last name, Initials. (year). *Book title.* Location: Publisher.

> Guttman, J. (1999). *The gift wrapped in sorrow: A mother's quest for healing.* Palm Springs, CA: JMJ.

Note: Give the city or publication alone if it is well-known. Otherwise, include the state. Include the state or province and the country if outside the United States.

A Book by Two or More Authors

> Lynn, J., & Harrold, J. (1999). *Handbook for mortals: Guidance for people facing serious illness.* New York: Oxford UP.

List up to six authors; abbreviate subsequent authors as "et al." List all authors' names in reverse order. Separate authors' names with commas, and include an ampersand (&) before the last.

An Anonymous Book

If an author is listed as "Anonymous," treat it as the author's name. Otherwise, follow this format:

> *American Medical Association essential guide to asthma.* (2003). New York: American Medical Association.

A Single Work from an Anthology

> Nichols, J. (2005). Diversity and stability in language. In B. D. Joseph & R. D. Janda (Eds.), *The handbook of historical linguistics* (pp. 283–310). Malden, MA: Blackwell.

An Article in a Reference Book

> Lewer, N. (1999). Non-lethal weapons. In *World encyclopedia of peace* (pp. 279–280). Oxford: Pergamon.

Periodicals

Basic Format

Author's last name, Initials. (year, Month day). Article. Periodical, *vol.* (issue), pages.

Silberman, S. (2001, December). The geek syndrome. *Wired, 9*(12), 174–183.

A Journal Article, Two Authors

Newman, P. A., & Nash, E. R. (2005). The unusual southern hemisphere stratosphere winter of 2002. *Journal of the Atmospheric Sciences, 62*(3), 614–628.

A Journal Article, More Than Six Authors

Watanabe, T., Bihoreau, M-T., McCarthy, L., Kiguwa, S., Hishigaki, H., Tsaji, A., et al. (1999, May 1). A radiation hybrid map of the rat genome containing 5,255 markers. *Nature Genetics, 22*, 27–36.

A Journal Article, Paginated by Issue

When the page numbering of the issue starts with page 1, the issue number (not italicized) is placed in parentheses after the volume number.

Lewer, N. (1999, summer). Nonlethal weapons. *Forum, 14*(2), 39–45.

A Newspaper Article

For newspapers, use "p." or "pp." before the page numbers; if the article is not on continuous pages, give all the page numbers, separated by commas.

Stolberg, S. C. (2002, January 4). Breakthrough in pig cloning could aid organ transplants. *The New York Times*, pp. 1A, 17A.

Online Sources

Basic Format

Author's last name, Initials. (year, Month day). Article. Periodical, *vol.* (issue), pages if available. Retrieved Month day, year, from electronic address.

Volz, J. (2000, January). Successful aging: The second 50. *Monitor on Psychology, 31*(1). Retrieved Apr. 26, 2006, from http://www.apa.org/monitor/jan00/cs.html

Note: If you have read an exact duplicate of a print article online, simply use the basic journal reference, but add [Electronic version] after the title of the article.

Making Oral Presentations

The last time you heard a speech was probably . . . today! Teachers give oral presentations every day. Usually the purpose of their talks is to inform or to demonstrate, but other presentations may attempt to persuade. Whatever the purpose of an oral presentation, it succeeds because of three key factors: familiarity with the material, preparation, and practice.

This chapter offers guidelines and tips for oral presentations. You'll learn how to organize your material, how to bring it to life with visual aids, and how to practice your way to a smooth, effective delivery.

- **Planning Your Presentation**
- **Creating Note Cards**
- **Considering Visual Aids**
- **Practicing Your Speech**
- **Delivering Your Presentation**
- **Evaluating a Presentation**
- **Preparing a Multimedia Report**
- **Multimedia Report Traits Checklist**

"A speech is poetry: cadence, rhythm, imagery, sweep! A speech reminds us that words, like children, have the power to make dance the dullest beanbag of a heart."

—Peggy Noonan

Planning Your Presentation

To transform a research paper into an oral presentation, you need to consider your purpose, your audience, and the content of your paper.

Determine your purpose.

Your purpose is your reason for giving a presentation.

- **Informative** speeches educate by providing valuable information.
- **Persuasive** speeches argue for or against something.
- **Demonstration** speeches show how to do or make something.

Consider your audience.

As you think about your audience, keep the following points in mind.

- **Be clear.** Listeners should understand your main points immediately.
- **Anticipate questions** the audience might have and answer them. This helps keep the audience connected.
- **Engage your listeners** through thought-provoking questions, revealing anecdotes, interesting details, and effective visuals.

Review your research paper.

During an oral report, obviously your audience cannot go back and listen again to earlier statements, so you must be sure to share your ideas clearly from beginning to end. Review your paper to see how the different parts will work in an oral presentation. Use the following questions as a review guide.

- Will my opening grab the listeners' attention?
- What are the main points that listeners need to know?
- How many supporting details should I include for each main point?
- What visual aids can I use to create interest in my topic? (See page 444.)
- Will the ending have the proper impact on the listeners?

Try It!

Choose a research paper you've completed. Review it as if you were a member of an audience, hearing the ideas in a presentation. What questions might this audience have about the topic? List them on a sheet of paper and then provide an answer for each one.

Adapt your paper.

To create a more effective oral presentation, you may need to rewrite certain parts of your paper. The new beginning below grabs the listeners' attention by using short, punchy phrases. The new ending makes a more immediate connection with the beginning.

Written Introduction (page 385)

When he took office on March 4, 1933, President Franklin Delano Roosevelt assumed leadership of a nation mired in poverty and racked by hopelessness. Four years before, a stock market crash had set off the Great Depression, a collapse of the United States economy. Many factories, businesses, and banks closed down, and millions of U.S. citizens lost their jobs. . . .

Oral Introduction

Imagine the changed lives of so many people following the stock market crash of 1929. The Great Depression left families without jobs, savings, even homes. Now imagine the incredible responsibility of the new president four years later. When he took office on March 4, 1933, Franklin Delano Roosevelt . . .

Written Conclusion (pages 390–391)

While the New Deal provided jobs for many people and allowed many families to keep their homes and farms, it did not succeed in ending the Great Depression. Those who criticize the New Deal often fail to account for its major achievement: It saved the U.S. from complete collapse. . . .

Oral Conclusion

The New Deal did not halt the depression, but it improved the nation's morale for years to come. When the U.S. was drawn into World War II, the country met the challenge, largely because of the mind-set established by the New Deal. People knew the value of shared sacrifice and innovative vision and heeded Roosevelt's requests to benefit the common good. Ultimately, the New Deal fostered the recovery of a nation's hope—not once, but twice.

"Eloquence is in the assembly, not merely in the speaker."
—William Pitt

Creating Note Cards

If you are giving a prepared speech rather than an oral reading of your paper, you should use note cards to remind you of your main ideas. The guidelines below will help you make effective cards.

Follow these note-card guidelines.

Write out your entire introduction and conclusion on separate note cards. For the body of your speech, write one point per card, along with specific details.

- Place each main point at the top of a separate note card.
- Write supporting ideas on the lines below the main idea, using key words and phrases to help you remember specific details.
- Number each card.
- Highlight any ideas you want to emphasize.
- Mark the places that call for visual aids.

Consider the three main parts.

As you prepare your note cards, keep the following points in mind about the three parts of your oral presentation: the introduction, body, and conclusion.

- **The introduction** should grab the listeners' attention, identify the topic and the focus of your presentation, and provide any essential background information about the topic. (See pages **440–441**.)
- **The body** should contain the main points from your paper and present details that will hold your listeners' attention. Remember to note the visual aids that you plan to use.
- **The conclusion** should restate your focus and leave the listeners with a final thought about your topic. (See pages **440–441**.)

Try It!

Using one of your recent research papers, adapt the introduction and conclusion for an oral report. Write your complete beginning and ending on separate note cards.

Sample Note Cards

Below are the note cards Shawna used for her oral presentation about the New Deal.

Introduction 1

photo: depression-era suffering

Imagine the changed lives of so many people following the stock market crash of 1929. The Great Depression left families without jobs, savings, even homes. Now imagine the incredible responsibility of the new president four years later. When he took office on Mar...

The Great Depression 2

photo: another depression-era picture

− 1920s: U.S. economy out of control, in need of new political policy

− 25 percent of working population unemployed by 1932

− many without enough food or homes

The New Deal 3

photo: TVA workers

− Roosevelt's economic program to restructure economy

− banks being made stronger

− legislation to help people refinance mortgages, save homes

− Social Security to provide for retirement

Unsuccessful programs 4

− NIRA's attempt to regulate labor practices

− too much red tape with NRA; regulations manipulated

− AAA not helping farmers enough

Later years of New Deal 5

chart: unemployment statistics '37-'43

− economic recovery led to funding cut in 1937

− position reversed in '38 due to sinking economy

− economic boom created when U.S. entered WWII

Conclusion 6

The New Deal did not halt the depression, but it improved the nation's morale for years to come. When the U.S. was drawn into World War II, the country met the challenge, largely because of the mind-set established by the New Deal. People knew the value of shared sacrifice and innovative vision and heeded Roosevelt's . . .

Considering Visual Aids

Consider using visual aids during your speech. They can make your presentation clearer and more meaningful. Here are some examples.

Posters	can include words, pictures, or both.
Photographs	illustrate what you are talking about.
Charts	explain points, compare facts, or give statistics.
Maps	identify or locate specific places being discussed.
Objects	show important items related to your topic.
Computer slides	project your photographs, charts, and maps onto a screen and turn your speech into a multimedia presentation. (See pages **448–449**.)

Indicate when to present visuals.

Write notes on your note cards to indicate where a visual aid would be helpful. Shawna considered the following visuals for her presentation about the New Deal.

- **photo of depression-era unemployment lines**
- **photo of TVA workers on a dam project**
- **chart showing unemployment statistics 1937–1943**

Try It!

Identify two or three visual aids you could use in your presentation. Explain when and how you would use each one.

Tip

When creating visual aids, keep these points in mind.

- **Make them big.** Your visuals should be large enough for everyone in the audience to see.
- **Keep them simple.** Use labels and short phrases rather than full sentences.
- **Make them eye-catching.** Use color, bold lines, and simple shapes to make the contents clear and interesting.

Practicing Your Speech

Practice is the key to giving an effective oral presentation. Knowing what to say and how to say it will help eliminate those butterflies speakers often feel. Here are some hints for an effective practice session.

- **Arrange your note cards in the proper order.** This will eliminate any confusion as you practice.

- **Practice in front of a mirror.** Check your posture and eye contact and be sure your visual aids are easy to see.

- **Practice in front of others.** Friends and family can help you identify parts that need work.

- **Record or videotape a practice presentation.** Do you sound interested in your topic? Are your voice and message clear?

- **Time yourself.** If your teacher has set a time limit, practice staying within it.

- **Speak clearly.** Do not rush your words, especially later when you are in front of your audience.

- **Speak up.** Your voice will sound louder to you than it will to the audience. If you sound too loud to yourself, you are probably sounding just right to your audience.

- **Work on eye contact.** Look down only to glance at a card.

- **Look interested and confident.** This will help engage your listeners.

Practice Checklist

To review each practice session, ask yourself the following questions.

_____ **1.** Did I appear at ease?
_____ **2.** Could my voice be heard and my words understood?
_____ **3.** Did I sound as though I enjoyed and understood my topic?
_____ **4.** Were my visual aids interesting and used effectively?
_____ **5.** Did I avoid rushing through my speech?
_____ **6.** Did I include everything I wanted to say?

Try It!

Practice your presentation. Give your speech to family or friends. Also consider videotaping your speech.

Delivering Your Presentation

When you deliver a speech, concentrate on your voice quality and body language. They communicate as much as your words do.

Control your voice.

Volume, tone, and *pace* are three aspects of your formal speaking voice. If you can control these, your listeners will be able to follow your ideas.

- **Volume** is the loudness of your voice. Imagine that you are speaking to someone in the back of the room and adjust your volume accordingly.
- **Tone** expresses your feelings. Be enthusiastic about your topic and let your voice show that.
- **Pace** is the speed at which you speak. For the most part, speak at a relaxed pace.

Tip

You can make an important point by slowing down, by pausing, by increasing your volume, or by emphasizing individual words.

Consider your body language.

Your body language *(posture, gestures,* and *facial expressions)* plays an important role during a speech. Follow the suggestions given below in order to communicate effectively.

- **Assume a straight but relaxed posture.** This tells the audience that you are confident and prepared. If you are using a podium, let your hands rest lightly on the surface.
- **Pause before you begin.** Take a deep breath and relax.
- **Look at your audience.** Try to look toward every section of the room at least once during your speech.
- **Think about what you are saying** and let your facial expressions reflect your true feelings.
- **Point to your visual aids** or use natural gestures to make a point.

Try It!

Deliver your presentation. As you do, be sure to control your voice and exhibit the proper body language.

Evaluating a Presentation

You can use an evaluation sheet to rate a classmate's speech. Circle the best description for each trait. Then offer at least one positive comment and one helpful suggestion.

Peer Evaluation Sheet

Speaker _____ Evaluator _____

1. Vocal Presentation

Volume:

Clear and loud   Loud enough   A little soft   Mumbled

Pace:

Relaxed   A little rushed or slow   Rushed or slow   Hard to follow

Comments:

a. _____

b. _____

2. Physical Presentation

Posture:

Relaxed, straight   A bit stiff   Fidgeted a lot   Slumped

Eye contact:

Excellent contact   Some contact   Quick glances   None

Comments:

a. _____

b. _____

3. Information

Thought provoking   Interesting   A few points   Not informative

Comments:

a. _____

b. _____

4. Visual Aids

Well used   Easy to follow   Not clear   None

Comments:

a. _____

b. _____

Preparing a Multimedia Report

You can enhance an oral report by using electronic aids such as slides and sound. In order to use these effectively, you must plan exactly how each will fit into your speech.

Here is a planning script for a multimedia report on the New Deal. What will be *seen* appears in the "Video" column, and what will be *heard* appears in the "Audio" column. (Note that the speaker's directions are general, not the actual script.)

Planning Script

Video	Audio
1. **Title Screen:** "Roosevelt's New Deal: Success or Failure?"	SOUND: Music (fades and rises appropriately in subsequent slides)
2. **Slide 2:** Depression-era photo	SPEAKER: Introduction
3. **Slide 3:** Photo of unemployment lines	SPEAKER: Explanation of Great Depression
4. **Slide 4:** Photo of TVA workers on dam project	SPEAKER: Explanation of how the New Deal helped restructure economy
5. **Slide 5:** Acronyms (+ meanings) of failed programs	SPEAKER: Explanation of failed programs
6. **Slide 6:** Chart of unemployment statistics 1937–1943	SPEAKER: Explanation of New Deal's later years
7. **Slide 7:** Photo of people donating scrap metal to war effort	SOUND: Music up. Conclusion

Multimedia Report Traits Checklist

Use the following checklist to help you improve your multimedia report. When you can answer "yes" to all of the questions, your report is ready.

Revising Checklist

Ideas

_____ **1.** Have I included the main ideas of my research paper in my multimedia report?

_____ **2.** Have I effectively supported my main ideas?

_____ **3.** Does each slide or sound bite suit the audience and the purpose of the paper?

Organization

_____ **4.** Do I state the topic in my introduction?

_____ **5.** Do I include the main points in the body?

_____ **6.** Do I restate my focus in the conclusion?

Voice

_____ **7.** Do I sound interested and enthusiastic?

_____ **8.** Is my voice clear, relaxed, and expressive?

Media and Word Choice

_____ **9.** Are the words and pictures on each slide easy to see and read?

_____ **10.** Have I chosen the best audio and video clips?

Presentation Fluency

_____ **11.** Does my oral report flow smoothly from point to point?

Conventions

_____ **12.** Is each slide free of errors in grammar, spelling, capitalization, and punctuation?

Writing Across the Curriculum

Writing in Science

Writing is central to science. It allows scientists to express their hypotheses, to record their observations, and to communicate their conclusions. Writing gives structure to the scientific method and allows scientists to share what they've learned with others.

In science classes—biology, chemistry, physics, botany, geology, astronomy, and oceanography—you can make discoveries about the natural world and learn ways to explore it further. Writing about the practical applications of science in your everyday life requires research skills, accurate observations, and clear explanations.

This chapter covers the types of writing that will help you in your science classes and in applying scientific principles to everyday tasks. Research papers and responses to prompts allow you to share what you've learned with your teacher and others, while practical writing allows you to apply what you've learned to your life.

- ■ **Taking Classroom Notes**
- ■ **Taking Reading Notes**
- ■ **Keeping a Learning Log**
- ■ **Writing Guidelines: Cause-Effect Essay**
- ■ **Writing Guidelines: Directions**
- ■ **Writing Guidelines: Response to an Expository Prompt**

"Aerodynamically, the bumble bee shouldn't be able to fly, but the bumble bee doesn't know it so it goes on flying anyway."

—Mary Kay Ash

Taking Classroom Notes

Taking good notes helps you remember key lecture points, understand new material, and prepare for tests and writing assignments. Here are a few tips.

Before You Take Notes . . .

- **Set up your notes** in a three-ring binder so you can insert handouts. A spiral notebook with a pocket is another option.
- **Date each entry** in your notebook and write down the topic.
- **Organize each page.** A two-column format with lecture information on the left and questions on the right works well.

As You Take Notes . . .

- **Listen for key words.** Pay attention to information that comes after phrases like *for example*, *as a result*, or *most importantly*.
- **Use your own words** as much as possible.
- **Write down questions** as they occur to you.
- **Draw pictures** or quick sketches to capture complex ideas.

After You Take Notes . . .

- **Reread your notes** after class to add any information needed to make the notes clear.
- **Study your notes** to prepare for tests and exams.

The date and topic are noted.	**March 6, 2006 – First law of thermodynamics and conservation of energy** First law of thermodynamics: – Applies principle of conservation of energy – Conservation of Energy= Energy can be transferred from one system to another in many forms. However, it <u>cannot be created or destroyed</u>. Total energy of an isolated system remains constant.
Main points are underlined.	Key points: – Fundamental principle of all science, especially physics and chemistry – Change in internal energy is equal to heat transferred into the system minus energy used in work by the system. – Can also be stated positively if W (work) is defined as the work done <u>on</u> the system instead of work done <u>by</u> the system.
Dashes set off subpoints.	Formulas: – $\triangle U = Q - W$, with $\triangle U$ =changes in internal energy, Q = heat added <u>to</u> the system and W = work done <u>by</u> the system. – Einstein stated that energy and matter are interchangeable, the quantity of energy and matter in the universe being fixed. $E = MC^2$ – Energy (E) is equal to matter (M) times the square of a constant (C).

Taking Reading Notes

Note taking can increase your understanding of reading assignments. Here are some tips on taking reading notes.

Before You Take Notes . . .

- **Write the date, book title, chapter, and topic** before each entry.
- **Organize each page.** For a two-column format, put your notes on the left and your thoughts and questions on the right.
- **Quickly skim the assigned text.** Read the title, introduction, headings, and chapter summaries. Look at graphics, charts, and examples.

As You Take Notes . . .

- **Write down headings or subtopics** and key details under each.
- **Use your own words** to help you understand the material better.
- **Summarize graphics.** Write down or sketch out main ideas.
- **List vocabulary words** and look up definitions later.

After You Take Notes . . .

- **Review your notes.** When you're done reading, write down any other questions you have. Research the answers and add them to your notes.

Nov. 12, 2006: <u>Modern Physics</u>, Chapt. 12, Sec. 3 Radioactive Decay

Many nuclei are radioactive or unstable. They eventually decay—emit a particle, transform one nucleus into another, or change to a lower energy state—until a stable nucleus is reached.

– Nucleon number [r= total number of nucleons (neutrons + protons)] must be the same before and after a decay.

– <u>Alpha decay</u>: Nucleus with too many protons—excessive repulsion. Emit a helium nucleus to reduce the repulsion.

– <u>Beta decay</u>: Neutron/proton ratio too great in the nucleus—instability. Neutron turns into a proton and an electron, and electron is emitted.

– <u>Gamma decay</u>: Nucleus is at too high an energy. The nucleus falls down to a lower energy state, emitting a high-energy photon called a gamma particle.

In Beta decay, what if the neutron/proton ratio is too small?

1. positron emission
   A proton turns into a neutron and a positron—a positively charged electron. The positron is emitted.

2. electron capture
   The nucleus "captures" an electron, which turns a proton into a neutron.

Why is radioactive decay important?

When the unstable nuclei of atoms decay and release particles, the result is radiation. Some high-level radiation can cause tissue damage, cancers, and even death.

Questions and thoughts are listed in the second column.

Keeping a Learning Log

A learning log is a specialized journal you use to reflect on things you are learning in class. In a learning log, you write about new concepts by connecting them to previous learning or personal experience. Here are some tips for keeping a learning log.

Before You Make an Entry . . .

- **Set up your learning log** in a binder or notebook.
- **Write the topic and date of each entry** so that you can find it easily.
- **Leave wide margins** so you have room for your own thoughts and questions.

As You Make an Entry . . .

- **Summarize key concepts** and develop meaningful comparisons.
- **Apply new ideas** to things you already know.
- **Think about questions** you may have about the subject.
- **Predict how the new ideas may prove helpful** in the future.
- **Make personal connections** by explaining what the ideas mean to you.

After You Make an Entry . . .

- **Review your entries** periodically to see how your thoughts have been developing.
- **Research any questions** you have and write down the answers.
- **Continue your reflections** by writing new observations in the margins.

Tip

You can use an approach called "stop and write" in your learning log. Stop in the middle of your reading or at the end of a class discussion and write down your thoughts about what you've just learned. This can show how well you understand the science topics you are studying. Your learning-log entries can also help you prepare for exams by showing you which concepts are the most difficult for you.

Try It!

Follow the guidelines above to set up your own learning log. When you have a few minutes during class, stop and write, reflecting on what you are learning. Make personal connections with the ideas.

Sample Learning-Log Entries

Here are some sample learning-log entries made by a student taking a meteorology class. The student thinks about the ideas discussed in class, analyzes them, and applies the theories to current weather trends.

The date and topic are given, and ideas from the class are reviewed.

Sept. 28, 2006—El Niño

El Niño is the name for unusually warm ocean temperatures off the coast of Peru. It usually begins around the end of December and lasts several weeks. It has been known to last almost a year. Fish die in the warm waters and the jet stream shifts. El Niño causes warm winters in normally cold states and lots of rain in southern states. Now I understand why we sometimes have hardly any snow. In fact, we sometimes have more rain than snow. Of course, this means ice on the lakes is probably not safe.

Q. What impact does El Niño have on U.S. weather?

A. In El Niño winters, temperatures are usually warmer in the north central states and cooler than normal in the Southeast and Southwest.

Questions are listed, and answers from the teacher and other sources are added.

Sept. 29, 2006—El Niño

During an El Niño, normal trade winds weaken. Warmer western Pacific water then flows east to Peru. This is the fifth-largest fishing ground in the world. The cold, deep waters are rich in nutrients. This water does not cycle upward during an El Niño. I didn't know that the fish caught off Peru are ground up into meal for poultry. When there are fewer fish because of El Niño, feed prices go up and so does the price of chicken. I don't pay much attention to chicken prices. For me, the strange winter weather is disappointing because I enjoy winter sports.

Q. When was the last strong El Niño?

A. We looked this up online on the National Oceanic and Atmospheric Web site. A strong El Niño was visible as warm water spreading from the western Pacific to the eastern Pacific during 1997.

Writing Guidelines ■ Cause-Effect Essay

In your science classes, you may be called on to research the causes and effects of scientific phenomena. Your focus can be on one cause and one main effect, multiple causes and effects, one effect and its many causes, and so on. Follow these guidelines.

Prewriting

- **Select a topic.** If your teacher doesn't assign a specific topic, review your class notes, learning log, and textbook for ideas. Think about topics you have discussed in class. Choose a topic with a number of causes and/or effects.
- **Gather details.** Research your topic so that you understand it thoroughly. List the topic's cause and effects, or the central effect and its causes. (Consider using a graphic organizer. See page **64**.)
- **Outline your essay.** Write a thesis statement that names your topic. Then write down the cause and effects, in order of importance. Include important supporting details.

Writing

- **Connect your ideas.** Create a beginning that introduces the topic and leads to your thesis statement. Follow your outline as you write the middle of your essay. Include the details you gathered in your research. Conclude by explaining what you learned.

Revising

- **Review your writing.** Review your first draft for *ideas, organization* and *voice.* Ask yourself these questions: *Does my essay focus on the cause and its effects? Does it include plenty of scientifically valid details? Does my voice sound knowledgeable and appropriate?*
- **Improve your style.** Check your *word choice* and *sentence fluency,* asking these questions: *Have I correctly used and defined any scientific terms? Do my ideas flow smoothly?* Use the rubric on pages **198–199** as a final revising guide.

Editing

- **Check for conventions.** Read your revised essay, looking for errors in spelling, punctuation, and grammar.
- **Prepare a final copy.** Make a neat final copy of your cause-effect essay and proofread it one last time.

■ Sample Cause-Effect Essay

In this essay, Janet Ledman discusses the causes and effects of flu epidemics in human populations.

The **beginning** introduces the topic and leads to the thesis statement (underlined).

The **first middle** paragraph discusses the cause.

The **second middle** paragraph examines current effects.

Avian Influenza (Bird Flu)

Medical science has solved many riddles in the last 50 years, leading to the defeat of major diseases such as polio and smallpox. On the other hand, as the number of people and the ease of travel between countries increases, the threat of a pandemic (worldwide epidemic) is very real. Currently, health centers around the world are striving to head off such a crisis. Many are concerned that the world is heading for a catastrophic outbreak of avian influenza, often called bird flu.

In several countries, particularly in China, millions of people raise chickens, turkeys, and ducks. Unfortunately, these people often live surrounded by these birds. That means that any serious illness that affects the birds has access to the humans. The proximity of a human population that lacks sufficient hygiene raises the danger level. If mutation occurs, this bird virus could well move from simply infecting birds to infecting people, who then infect other people. This is what happened in the great flu epidemic of 1918 that killed an estimated 50 million people worldwide.

The effects of current strains of avian influenza are severe. For birds, a highly infectious form of the flu usually means death. The loss of these flocks impacts local economies. When humans are infected, fever, sore throat, pneumonia, and acute respiratory distress can easily overwhelm and kill. Young adults, normally able to fight flu, seem to be especially vulnerable. In Hong Kong, eighteen people were infected and six died. Authorities believe they halted the spread of the illness by killing 1.5 million domestic chickens and turkeys. Disease control centers around the world have sent out similar reports of people stricken with the bird flu. If the virus manages to mutate so that human-to-human transmission is possible, death will stalk the world.

Ledman 2

The last two middle paragraphs discuss the possible effects of a pandemic on families, communities, and nations around the world.

At first, an outbreak will mean quarantining individuals and whole families. In the United States, the emphasis on personal freedom and rights will make implementing such action more difficult. But if officials do not act soon enough, the flu will spread. If the local quarantines fail, communities and surrounding areas will be closed off, conceivably restricting travel throughout entire states. Imagine National Guard troops on patrol, preventing anyone from entering or leaving an area the size of a state! Schools and colleges will be closed. Large public gatherings will be banned. People will not go to movies or eat at restaurants. Should the contagion rage in spite of these efforts, nations may close their borders to protect themselves. Those needing help could end up isolated, left to die or recover on their own. Dealing with the millions of patients and deaths would be just the beginning.

Companies, both large and small, would be impacted. The fragile airline industry may cease to exist or be severely scaled back. Trade, particularly of agricultural products, would suffer. Some countries dependent on outside sources for goods and/or food could well collapse into anarchy. Of course, places that cater to tourists would be big losers. During the four months it takes to develop a vaccine to fight the spread of the virus, avian influenza could do untold damage.

The ending summarizes the dilemma for the medical community.

Health officials face a dilemma. Do they act now, spending valuable time and resources to prepare for a pandemic that may not happen, or do they wait? If the flu virus mutates and begins a human-to-human journey, the world will suffer. The risk is too great to ignore, so research concerning avian influenza and its successful treatment will continue.

Try It!

Write a cause-effect essay. Select a topic that interests you and follow the writing guidelines on page **456**.

Writing Guidelines ■ Directions

You may also have the opportunity to write about science outside of school. For example, you may be asked to write a set of how-to directions based on scientific knowledge you've learned in class. While this type of writing is more informal than academic writing, it still requires careful attention to detail. Follow these writing guidelines.

Prewriting

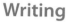

- **Focus on the purpose** of your writing task.
- **Jot down the key points** you want to make.
  Write out the steps in the process that need to be explained.

Writing

- **Keep your main purpose in mind** as you write.
- **Use examples and specific details** to support and explain each step.
- **Keep your audience in mind.** For example, if you are writing instructions for someone who's doing a project for the first time, you cannot assume anything. Fully explain the names and functions of various ingredients or tools, where supplies are kept, and basic safety precautions.
- **Sum up.** Give the reader tips about where to get additional information if needed.

Revising

- **Improve your writing.** Review your first draft for *ideas, organization,* and *voice.* Ask these questions: *Are my directions clear and complete? Do they follow a logical sequence? Have I included only important details?*
- **Improve your style.** Evaluate your *word choice* and *sentence fluency,* asking these questions: *Have I used specific nouns and active verbs? Are technical terms explained? Do my directions read smoothly?*

Editing

- **Check for conventions.** Proofread your writing for errors in punctuation, capitalization, spelling, and grammar. Remember, even a few errors affect the credibility of your information.
- **Prepare a final copy.** Make a neat final copy for your audience.

■ Sample Directions

Miguel entered a contest in which he was required to write directions for building a model bridge. He relied on the concepts he had learned in his physics class.

The beginning introduces the topic and lists the necessary materials.

The middle explains how to build the bridge and describes its strengths.

The ending gives final directions and recommends testing the finished project.

Building a Truss Bridge

A truss bridge is a type of bridge commonly used by railroads. The following materials are needed to construct a model truss bridge: quarter-inch and half-inch square pine sticks and sixteenth-inch-thick plywood. The necessary tools include a coping saw and woodworkers' glue.

To build the base, place two half-inch pine sticks, each 20 1/2 inches long, four inches apart. Attach them to each other on the ends with four-inch lengths of half-inch pine.

Next, to form the trusses, use the quarter-inch pine to build six equilateral triangles with four-inch sides, and four equilateral triangles with three-inch sides. Set one of the smaller triangles (point up) in front of you. Then place in a row three larger triangles (points up) next to the first one. Finish the row with another small triangle (point up). Now place a 3 1/2-inch piece of the smaller dimension pine from the top of the first small triangle to the top of the first large triangle and from the top of the third large triangle to the top of the second small triangle. Place a four-inch piece of pine from the top of the first large triangle to the top of the second large triangle and then from the top of the second to the top of the third large triangle.

Carefully glue the triangles together as they are now laid out. Glue small squares of the plywood on top of each of the connecting points. These mimic the plates used in real bridges to both connect and add strength to a joint. Now construct a second truss in the same way.

Finally, attach one truss to each side of the base structure built earlier. Connect the joint points on the tops of the two trusses using long enough pine pieces to form triangles. Allow the glue to dry on the model bridge and then test its strength. Constructed properly, the bridge should support a fair amount of weight. Trusses are an effective way to support the load that a roadbed must carry. The triangles, which cannot be pushed out of shape, make the trusses strong.

Writing Guidelines ■ Response to an Expository Prompt

On a science test, you may be asked to write a response to an expository prompt. This sort of test question is a great way to evaluate your knowledge and understanding of a scientific concept. Use the following tips to make the best of the limited time you will have to respond.

Before You Write . . .

- **Understand the prompt.** Review the STRAP questions listed on page **212**. Remember that an expository prompt asks you to explain something or to share information.
- **Use your time wisely.** Plan a few minutes for making notes or filling in a graphic organizer before you begin writing, the main portion of time for the actual writing, and another few minutes at the end to check over your response.

As You Write . . .

- **Decide on a focus or thesis for your essay.** Keep this main idea or purpose in mind during your writing.
- **Be selective.** Working from your notes, use examples and explanations that directly support your focus.
- **End in a meaningful way.** Close your essay by restating your main idea in a new way.

After You've Written Your Response . . .

- **Check for completeness.** Use the STRAP questions on page **216** as a guide to revision.
- **Check for correctness.** Correct any errors in punctuation, capitalization, spelling, and grammar.

Tip

Many students feel nervous when taking a test, and that is only natural. However, by taking time to plan your response before you begin writing, you can relax and write with confidence.

■ Sample Response to an Expository Prompt

Once you have answered the STRAP questions (page **212**) and planned your response, you can begin writing.

Prompt

Two identical pieces of steel are placed in the water. One is shaped like a boat and the other is flat. What happens to each piece of steel? Why did this happen? How can this knowledge be put to practical use? Explain.

The introduction proposes an answer to the first part of the prompt.

In the middle, the student supports his answer by explaining a scientific principle.

The ending explains the practical use of the principle.

Displacement

Steel has a density greater than water. What this means is that a flat piece of steel placed in the water will sink. Shape that same piece of steel into a large enough boat, and it will float.

More than 2,200 years ago, Archimedes, a Greek mathematician, noticed that a liquid pushes up on an object placed in it with a force equal to the weight of the liquid displaced by the object. Since the density of a flat piece of steel is greater than the water it displaces, which means it weighs more, the steel will sink.

If a shipbuilder, on the other hand, uses that same amount of steel to build a boat shape of the right size, the density of the boat will be less than the water it displaces. The reason this happens is that a boat is mostly air with a steel skin. The boat will settle into the water, pushing the liquid out of the way until the amount of water moved weighs as much as the boat. The boat will then float.

A liquid denser than water, like mercury, would need less volume displaced for the ship to float. A lighter liquid, like alcohol, would need a much greater volume displaced to float the ship.

With this knowledge, shipbuilders can determine the best materials to use in a ship, and how much volume displacement is necessary to float that ship in either freshwater or seawater.

Writing in Social Studies

When you write in social studies, you may be asked to create an essay or other response based on information found in a variety of documents—texts, charts, graphs, maps, photos, and so on. In order to accomplish such a task, you'll need to quickly analyze the documents and summarize important information. You'll also need to organize your information carefully and write a response that satisfies the assignment's criteria.

This chapter models several types of writing you may be asked to do in your social studies classes, including an informative essay, responding to an editorial cartoon, and responding to a series of documents. You'll also find helpful tips for taking notes; keeping a learning log; and planning, writing, and editing a social studies response.

- Taking Classroom Notes
- Keeping a Learning Log
- Writing Guidelines: Informative Essay
- Writing Guidelines: Response to an Editorial Cartoon
- Writing Guidelines: Document-Based Essay

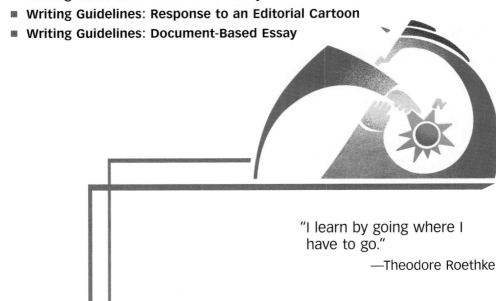

"I learn by going where I have to go."

—Theodore Roethke

Taking Classroom Notes

Good note taking is a skill worth learning. Effective notes can help you understand a topic better, prepare for tests, and do better on writing assignments. Here are some tips for taking effective notes in class.

Before You Take Notes . . .

- **Write the topic and date** at the top of each page.
- **Do any assigned reading** before coming to class.

As You Take Notes . . .

- **Listen carefully and write down** the main ideas.
- **Copy what the teacher writes** on the board or on an overhead.
- **Condense information.** Write phrases and lists, not full sentences.
- **Use your own words** as much as possible.
- **Note new or unfamiliar terms** and add a definition later.

After You Take Notes . . .

- **Review your notes** as soon as possible.
- **Find answers to any questions** you still have.

Classroom Notes

The date and topic are noted.

Underlined headings organize notes.

Dashes set off facts and details.

> May 12, 2006
> **Student Activism During the 1960s and 1970s**
> <u>Reasons for Activism</u>
> — Protests against Vietnam War
> — Civil rights for African Americans, Latinos, and Native Americans
> — Campaign to win right to vote at age 18
> — Concerns about the environment
> <u>Results</u>
> — Helped end Vietnam War
> — Helped win civil rights
> — Gave 18-year-olds the vote
> — Started Earth Day
>
> activism:
>   campaigning
>   for political or
>   social change

Try It!

Follow the tips and sample above the next time you take notes in class.

Keeping a Learning Log

A learning log is a specialized notebook in which you can reflect on the facts, ideas, and social studies themes you learn about in the classroom. Writing in your learning log can help you clarify your understanding of a topic. It can also help you connect what you've learned in class to your everyday life.

Before You Make an Entry . . .

- **Write the date and topic** on the page each time you make an entry.

As You Make an Entry . . .

- **Summarize key concepts** and compare them to more familiar ideas.
- **Connect to the material** by explaining what it means to you.

After You Make an Entry . . .

- **Review your entries** to see how well you understand the class material.

Sample Learning Log

The writer makes a personal connection to the topic.

> May 12, 2006
> Student Activism in the 1960s and '70s
>
> Today we talked about student activism in the 1960s and '70s. I had heard a bit about student protests against the Vietnam War, but I wasn't aware of their extent. Today I also learned more about student activism in other areas, such as civil rights and the environment.
>
> Our classroom discussion about student activism made me think about the Friends of the North Branch Watershed group at our school. They are a group of students who are working to help clean up the North Branch River. Saturday they are holding their annual river cleanup. I think I will go to the event and use it as the topic of my descriptive social studies essay.

Try It!

Keep a learning log for one of your classes. Concentrate on understanding topics and making a personal connection to what you learned.

Writing Guidelines ■ Informative Essay

Prewriting

- **Select a topic.** Your teacher will often assign a topic. If not, choose a topic you would personally like to learn more about—a specific event, person, place, or issue that relates to your course work.
- **Gather details.** Learn all you can about your topic. Get some background information from books and Web site articles. Study maps, graphs, and charts. This background information will help you write a clear and interesting description.
- **Outline your essay.** Organize your notes carefully, keeping related details together. If you are recalling an event, consider organizing your details in chronological order. If you are providing information about a place, a person, or an issue, consider organizing your details by order of location, order of importance, or by some other logical order.

Writing

- **Connect your ideas.** Start by introducing your topic. Engage the reader with an anecdote or interesting detail. In the middle paragraphs, develop the topic using a clear and effective method of organization. Write an ending that sums up your essay.

Revising

- **Improve your writing.** Review your first draft for *ideas*, *organization*, and *voice*. Then revise to make your ideas clear and your voice engaging and informative.
- **Improve your style.** Check for *word choice* and *sentence fluency*. Make sure your sentences flow smoothly and unfamiliar terms are explained.

Editing

- **Check for conventions.** Proofread your essay carefully. You may also wish to ask a friend to read it. Correct all errors in punctuation, capitalization, spelling, and grammar.
- **Prepare a final copy.** Make a neat final copy of your informative essay. Proofread this copy again before sharing it.

Sample Informative Essay

In this essay, a student writes about an environmental issue after personally taking part in a cleanup event and interviewing a few of the participants.

Cleaning Up a "Tired" River

Seventeen-year-old Janice Hart spent last Saturday morning doing something she'd never imagined she'd do: hauling discarded tires and other debris out of the North Branch River. "I never thought of myself as an environmentalist," she said. When students clean up a river, they make a difference, and when they bring the problem to public attention, they can inspire change.

Hart, a senior at Ridgefield's Hamilton High School, was taking part in the annual cleanup sponsored by the Friends of the North Branch Watershed. The group, which was founded by Hamilton High students, is dedicated to cleaning up the river—and keeping it that way. More than thirty group members showed up on Saturday and spent eight hours making the river cleaner.

The history of human damage to the North Branch is a long one. In the early 1900s, William Hamilton's paper mill spewed waste into the river. Later, other factories moved in and dumped more pollutants. But by the 1970s, most of the factories had closed down, and new antipollution laws forced the remaining ones to clean up their act. Today, the river is cleaner than it's been in years, but it's still far from perfect.

According to Elena Redmond, president of Friends of the North Branch, the group hauls tons of trash out of the river each year. And most of that, she says, comes from one source—discarded tires. "It's a big problem," Redmond said Saturday, pointing to a growing heap of tires on the bank of the river. "Landfills charge a fee for disposal. Rather than pay the fee, people dump tires in the river."

That may be about to change. For the past year, Redmond said, the group has been lobbying the state legislature to create a new tire-deposit law. Under the proposed law, tire buyers would put down a $5 deposit for every tire they buy, and they'd get their deposit back by returning the tires for recycling.

In just a few weeks, the Friends' bill will be voted on by the legislature. That's just more evidence, Redmond said, of the power of student activism. "Maybe someday," she said, pointing at the heap of tires, "these will become an endangered species."

Writing Guidelines ■ Response to an Editorial Cartoon

Editorial cartoons use a powerful combination of words and images to comment on important, timely issues. Often, these cartoons employ exaggerated representations called caricatures to help make their point. Editorial cartoons may also include symbols, labels, and brief captions. The following guidelines can help you to interpret and respond to an editorial cartoon.

Prewriting

- **Analyze the cartoon.** Review both the visual and text elements of the cartoon carefully. If you are not sure what a particular element means, ask for help.
- **Gathering details.** On a separate piece of paper, list the different elements of the cartoon. Write a brief description next to the element. (The two examples below relate to the cartoon on the next page.)

Amounts of money: The CEO has much more money than the employee.
Faces: The CEO is smiling; the employee is not.

- **Plan your response.** After identifying the cartoon's main point, include that idea in a topic sentence. Then decide which details of the cartoon you will use to support your topic sentence.

Writing

- **Connect your ideas.** Start with your topic sentence. Then write body sentences that include supporting details from the cartoon. End with a sentence that restates the main point of the cartoon.

Revising

- **Improve your writing.** Review what you've written. Ask yourself if you have clearly explained the point of the cartoon. If necessary, revise to make your explanation clearer.
- **Improve your style.** Check for *word choice* and *sentence fluency.*

Editing

- **Check for conventions.** Review your response and correct any errors in punctuation, capitalization, spelling, and grammar.
- **Prepare a final copy.** Make a clean final copy of your response.

■ Sample Editorial Cartoon

"Big Business, 2006: Isn't it nice to share?"

Sample Response

A student named Ellie Jacobs wrote the following paragraph after taking some time to analyze the editorial cartoon above.

Isn't It Nice to Share?

This editorial cartoon makes a clear point about today's large corporations: The CEO's receive an unfairly large share of the profit compared to the average employee. In the cartoon, a well-dressed CEO sits on a huge pile of money. This is his share, and he is dressed to prove it. In contrast, a ragged worker holds his share—a tiny fraction of the CEO's. The fact that the CEO is smiling and the worker frowning only adds impact to the point—one is happy with the situation, the other unhappy. The sarcastically toned caption reads, "Isn't it nice to share?" This implies, of course, that sharing in this fashion is neither nice nor right. The CEO gets far more than a fair share.

Try It!

Find an editorial cartoon in a national or local newspaper. Use the guidelines on page **468** and the sample above to help you write a response to the cartoon.

Writing Guidelines ▪ Document-Based Essay

In social studies class, you may be asked to analyze and respond to a series of documents. The documents may include excerpts from books, magazines, Web pages, diaries, or other text sources. Visual documents, such as photographs, maps, editorial cartoons, tables, graphs, or time lines, may also be included.

Often, you will be asked to analyze the documents and write an essay based on them. On some occasions you may be asked to gather information from a document and present it in a new form, such as a graph or table. In either situation, you must quickly and accurately analyze the documents and prepare your response. Here are some guidelines that will help you.

Prewriting

- **Read all the information thoroughly.** In addition to the documents, review the introduction to the topic and your responses to any questions about each document.
- **Be sure you understand the prompt.** Focus on cue words such as *compare*, *explain*, and *define* that indicate the type of thinking and writing that is expected.
- **Analyze each document.** Consider how the documents relate to any questions you must answer—and to each other. Be aware of documents that present opposing views.
- **Organize your facts.** Use a graphic organizer to plan your response. Create an outline that gathers information from all the documents and your own prior knowledge.

Writing

- **Write your introductory paragraph.** Restate the question as a thesis statement.
- **Write the body of your essay.** Use each main point as the topic sentence of a paragraph that explains one main idea. Be sure to follow your outline.
- **Write a concluding paragraph.** Briefly restate your position.

Revising

- **Improve your style.** Check for *word choice* and *sentence fluency*.

Editing

- **Check for conventions.** Proofread your essay carefully. Then correct any errors in punctuation, capitalization, spelling, and grammar.
- **Prepare a final copy.** Make a neat final copy of your essay.

■ Sample Documents

Introduction: Activist students played an important role in the politics of the 1960s and 1970s. One important issue was the campaign to lower the minimum voting age from 21 to 18. In 1971, the states ratified an amendment to the Constitution, giving Americans 18 years of age and older the right to vote.

Document One

We Want the Vote!

For more than five years, the United States has been fighting a war in Vietnam. Thousands of American soldiers have been wounded or died there. Yet many of us who are asked to sacrifice our lives for our country are unable to participate in its political system. That's because while we 18-year-olds can be drafted into the military, we cannot legally vote in elections. That's one thing we intend to change. We want the vote, and we won't stop asking until we get it.

By the time they have reached the age of 18, many young Americans are serving their country not only in the military, but by participating in politics. We are on the front lines, fighting for civil rights and the environment, and fighting against the war. And we feel that if we are old enough to participate in the political battles at home and the military battles in Vietnam, we are old enough to vote. Deny us the vote, and you'll stop us from changing the world for the better.

Source: "We Want the Vote!"
pamphlet by members of VOTE NOW!, 1970

Task: Summarize the main reasons 18-year-olds felt they were entitled to vote.

Only the most important information is included in the summary.

In 1970, 18-year-olds were very involved in American politics. Many were also being sent to fight in Vietnam. Some young people felt that because they served their country in these ways, they deserved the right to vote. They believed they could make the country better if given a chance.

Document Two

Poster: Old Enough to Die. Old Enough to Vote.

Task: Explain how this poster might be an effective way to support the campaign for voting rights for people 18 and over.

_____ The poster would be effective because it states the case simply and powerfully. Putting a human face on the argument helps to build support for young people who want to vote. _____

Source: Voting Rights Archive

Document Three

Americans Age 18–21 Voting for President, 1972–1996

Year	% Who Registered	% Who Voted	% of Total Voters
1996	45.6	31	3.21
1992	44.9	33.2	3.29
1988	44.9	33.2	3.49
1984	47	36.7	4.05
1980	44.7	35.7	4.71
1976	47.1	38	5.3
1972	36.4	20.8	3.81

Source: Federal Elections Commission

Task: Explain the trend in young people's voting patterns from 1972 to 1996. Use fractions and ratios in your explanation.

_____ From 1972 to 1996, the participation of young voters generally declined. At the peak in 1976, almost half of those 18-21 registered to vote, and the group that did go to the polls represented 1 out of 20 voters for that election. But after that, participation dropped off. In 1996, fewer than one-third of those 18–21 voted, representing 1 out of 30 votes cast. _____

Document Four

Margin of Victory in U.S. Presidential Elections, 1972–1996

Year	% Voting Republican	% Voting Democratic	Winning Party
1996	40.72	49.23	Democratic
1992	37.45	43.01	Democratic
1988	53.77	45.65	Republican
1984	58.77	40.56	Republican
1980	50.75	41.01	Republican
1976	48.02	50.08	Democratic
1972	60.67	37.52	Republican

Source: Federal Elections Commission

Task: Calculate the greatest and smallest margins of victory for presidential elections between 1972–1996.

Statistics are used to make some generalizations.

> The greatest margin of victory was in 1972, with the Republican camp defeating the Democrats by 23.15 percent of the total vote. The smallest margin was in 1976, with the Democrats defeating the Republicans by only 2.08 percent.

Document Five

"Bad politicians are sent to Washington by good people who don't vote."
—William E. Simon, former secretary of the United States Treasury

Task: How does this quotation relate to the argument over lowering the voting age?

Inference is used to make the connection.

> There are two ways to connect this to the debate: (1) When very few of the informed young people vote, bad politicians may be voted into office. (2) If more informed young people voted, better politicians may get elected.

Document Six

Excerpt 1

In 1996, there were 24,650,000 18- to 24-year-olds in the United States. Of these, 7,996,000 voted. That means that only 32.4 percent of the 18-to-24-year-olds voted in that presidential election year! In 1998, only 18 percent of that population voted! Why are these numbers so low? What can YOU do to change these statistics? Read on to find out why your vote is so important and what you can do to get involved in changing history.

Excerpt 2

WHY VOTE?

Your vote is your voice. Our elected officials make decisions that affect your life in innumerable ways. If you want your opinions to count when those decisions are made, then you must elect people who share your beliefs. If you want your voice to be heard, you have to vote. In many cases, your vote is the only chance you get to tell the government what you want it to do. And if you don't like the way the government is spending your tax dollars, or you don't agree with the laws that tell you what you can or cannot do, voting is one of the most important ways you can change things.

Source: League of Women Voters: Youth Vote, 2006
http://www.lwvcef.org/youthvote/index.htm

Task: What does this document tell you about young people's interest and participation in politics today, more than 30 years after they won the right to vote?

Thirty years after winning the right to vote, the number of young people who vote is lower than ever. Although people try to convince this age group to vote, not many are listening, which limits young people's potential to change the world.

■ Sample Document-Based Essay

In this essay, a student writes an essay that draws on information presented in the six original documents.

Task: Extended Essay

Using all six documents and your own knowledge about this topic, write an essay explaining why young people thought they should be able to vote and how they worked to win their campaign. Be sure to express your opinion about progress toward the goal of "changing the world for the better."

Documents 1, 2, and 5
The opening provides background about winning the vote and states the thesis.

Documents 1 and 2
The main issues surrounding the campaign for the vote are explained.

Fighting for the Right to Vote

In the 1960s, America's young people faced a dilemma. Spurred by the Vietnam War, the civil rights movement, and concerns over the environment, many young people became involved in politics. However, because the minimum voting age was 21, the influence these people could have over the political direction of the United States was limited. Young people could—and did—publicly state their position on the issues, but they could not vote to elect politicians who shared their views. Working together and using aggressive campaign strategies, young activists lowered the voting age to 18. Since then, their poor turnout at the polls has limited their goal of "changing the world" by voting.

Perhaps no issue drove the campaign for the vote more directly than the Vietnam War. During the war, thousands of Americans age 18–20 served in the military, and thousands were wounded or killed. Some of these soldiers volunteered to serve in the military, but many were drafted into the military and legally required to serve. Many young people resented the fact that while 18- to 20-year-olds could be required to fight and die for their country, they did not have the right to vote. So they began a campaign to lower the minimum voting age to 18.

The campaign to win the vote featured appeals to other Americans to recognize the sacrifices young people were making for their country and the potential contributions young voters could make to the political system. Young campaigners used pamphlets, posters, and other printed materials to plead their case. The tone of these materials was aggressive, and even dramatic. One pamphlet announced, "We want the vote, and we won't stop asking until we get it." A poster used a stark picture of a soldier to put a human face on the sacrifice being made by young American soldiers.

The campaign to win the vote was successful, with the voting age lowered in 1971 to age 18. Off to a slow start in the 1972 election, the young voters did arrive at the polls in 1976 and made a difference. That year, the Democratic candidate won by a slim 2.08 percent margin. Some believe that the young people's vote made this victory possible. Their voting record since shows that the potential promised during the suffrage campaign has not been realized. Overall, in presidential elections from 1972 to 1996, fewer than half of eligible 18- to 21-year-olds have voted. More ominously, the number of 18- to 21-year-olds going to the polls has steadily declined. In the 1998 congressional and gubernatorial elections, only 18 percent of young people bothered to vote.

The lack of participation among young voters harms efforts to make America a better place. As former secretary of the United States Treasury William E. Simon once remarked, "Bad politicians are sent to Washington by good people who don't vote." Those who hope that young people can revitalize the American political system have not given up. Campaigns such as Rock the Vote and Youth Vote are working to encourage young people to vote. If these new campaigns succeed, the potential for young voters to change the world may be realized.

Essay Checklist

_____ 1. Do all the ideas in my essay relate to my thesis statement?
_____ 2. Do I cover all the requirements outlined in the task?
_____ 3. Do I summarize my main points in the conclusion?
_____ 4. Do I refer to information from all my documents?
_____ 5. Do I include some of my own knowledge about this topic?
_____ 6. Have I checked my punctuation, grammar, and spelling?

Writing in Math

When it comes to math, writing is one of the most valuable learning tools you have at your disposal. And as the math becomes more challenging—trigonometry, calculus, advanced algebra—the more essential and helpful writing becomes. Writing, in fact, helps you clarify your thinking and gain mastery over your math course work.

Keeping a learning log, writing summaries, forming statistical arguments—all of these forms of writing will sharpen your ability to distill the meaning of mathematical concepts. When you write in a learning log, you should write freely, sorting out your thoughts about new topics. When you write summaries or arguments, you should be more analytical, carefully displaying your understanding. This chapter will help you with all of your writing in math, from learning log entries to responding to math prompts.

- **Taking Classroom Notes**
- **Keeping a Learning Log**
- **Writing Guidelines: Article Summary**
- **Writing Guidelines: Statistical Argument**
- **Response to a Math Prompt**
- **Other Forms of Writing in Math**

"It is impossible to be a mathematician without being a poet in soul."

—Sophia Kovalevskaya

Taking Classroom Notes

Using your own words to write down math steps and formulas can help you understand and remember them. Here are some note-taking tips.

Before You Take Notes . . .

- **Use a three-ring binder to store your notes** so that you can add handouts, work sheets, tests, and so on.
- **Write the date, textbook pages, and topic** at the beginning of each entry.

As You Take Notes . . .

- **Write down what your teacher puts on the board or overhead.** This information often contains math concepts, definitions, math terms, formulas, and important examples.
- **Put concepts in your own words.** Also write down questions you have about the material.
- **Draw pictures.** Use diagrams to help you visualize the problem.

After You Take Notes . . .

- **Find the answers** to your questions.
- **Study your notes** before the next class and again before exams.

Notes

January 16, 2007

Definition Logarithm (log): $\log_b b^x = x$

A logarithm indicates a relationship with exponents. Once the pattern is recognized, problems become much easier to handle.

Example 1: $\log_7 z = 2$
This would be the same as $7^2 = z$.
Since $7^2 = 49$, then $z = 49$.

Example 2: $\log_y 81 = 4$
This would be the same as $y^4 = 81$.
Since $3^4 = 81$, then $y = 3$.

Example 3: $\log_2 8 = x$
This would be the same as $2^x = 8$.
Since $2^3 = 8$, then $x = 3$.

Keeping a Learning Log

A learning log allows you to write about what you are learning, think through new concepts, ask questions, and find answers.

Before You Write . . .

- **Set up the log.** Use a section of your three-ring binder so you have your learning log together with your notes.
- **Write the date and topic** at the beginning of each entry.
- **Leave wide margins** for writing questions and answers.

As You Write . . .

- **Reflect on what you learn** by writing about what you understand and what is still confusing to you.
- **Summarize key concepts** and think about how they connect to your own experiences and to other ideas you have learned in math.

After You Write . . .

- **Answer any questions** you may still have about the topic.
- **Review your log** before a test or when you study a new topic.

Learning Log

January 16, 2007

Some Properties of Logarithms

1. $\log(ab) = \log a + \log b$
Example:
$\log(12) = \log(3 \cdot 4) = \log 3 + \log 4$

2. $\log\left(\dfrac{a}{b}\right) = \log a - \log b$
Example:
$\log 4 = \log\left(\dfrac{20}{5}\right) = \log 20 - \log 5$

Logarithms and exponents are related. Logarithm properties actually come from exponent properties.

How to remember properties:

1. When multiplying the same variable, add the exponents: $a^m \cdot a^n = a^{m+n}$. Taking the log of a product is the same as adding the log of each factor.

2. To divide the same variables, subtract the exponents:

$\dfrac{a^m}{a^n} = a^{m-n}$. Taking the log of a quotient is the same as subtracting the log of each part.

In any base, the following rules apply: $\log(ab) = \log a + \log b$; $\log(a/b) = \log a - \log b$; $\log(1/a) = -\log a$; $\log a^b = b \log a$; $\log 1 = 0$ and $\log 0$ is undefined.

Writing Guidelines ▪ Article Summary

Many magazine articles and news stories include statistics and mathematical concepts. Use the following guidelines when summarizing a math-related article.

Prewriting

- **Select an article.** Find an article that presents figures and statistics to support the story.
- **Read the article.** Try to get an overall feeling for the topic. Then reread it carefully, paying attention to the details.
- **Find the focus.** Write down the main idea of the article.
- **Gather details, including math-related points.** Select only the most important details that support the main idea of the article.

Writing

- **Write your first draft.** State the main point of the article in your topic sentence. Then provide supporting details. End with a sentence that summarizes your thoughts.

Revising

- **Improve your writing.** Review your first draft for *ideas, organization,* and *voice.* Ask yourself the following questions: *Have I clearly presented the focus of the article? Have I included the most important supporting details? Have I explained any use of mathematical concepts in the article? Is my summary clear?*
- **Improve your style.** Check your *word choice* and *sentence fluency.* Ask yourself the following questions: *Have I used specific nouns and verbs? Does my summary read smoothly?*

Editing

- **Check for conventions.** Edit your revised draft, correcting any errors in punctuation, capitalization, spelling, and grammar.
- **Prepare a final copy.** Make all corrections and write a neat final draft.

Try It!

Find an article containing statistics and figures. Using the guidelines above and the sample on the next page, write a summary and create a graph to illustrate the data.

■ Math Article and Sample Summary

A student read the following article and wrote a brief summary, including a graph to illustrate the statistics in the article.

Employment Increase Misleading

A look at the 2006 employment picture of Grange County shows good news and bad news.

According to figures from the State Department of Revenue, employment in Grange County increased .86 percent, from 106,972 in December of 2005 to 107,895 in December of 2006. Most of the growth was due to new businesses located in new malls in the towns of Terrell, Point Leon, and Jasper. At first glance, this appears to be a positive trend; however, other factors make the picture less than perfect.

First, it must be noted that most of the new businesses are retail outlets or fast-food chains. Nearly half of workers at these businesses earn no more than minimum wage, many working less than full-time, with no benefits.

Next, while many new jobs have been introduced, many have been lost, due to businesses either moving or closing. The most significant impact was felt by the loss of Yarrow Graphics, accounting for a loss of 297 jobs.

In addition, some local companies closed in the face of new competition. Among them was Point Leon's Main Street Grocery. Owner Jim Hawkins cited an inability to compete with the Mega Bite discount grocery that opened in the town's new mall. Of Main Street's 92 employees, 51 found jobs at the new store, earning significantly less at Mega Bite.

In December of 2005, only 20,774 workers in Grange County were earning minimum wage, while the next year that group rose a startling 47 percent to 30,448. The number of workers earning between $6 and $10 per hour saw a smaller increase of 4 percent, from 32,369 to 33,620. Meanwhile, the number of workers earning higher wages dropped. The largest decrease came in workers earning between $10 and $20 per hour. Their numbers fell from 41,649 in 2005 to 33,804 in 2006—a staggering 19 percent drop. Numbers of those earning more than $20 per hour also fell, a less startling but still significant 18 percent, from 12,180 to 10,023 jobs.

While the county has enjoyed a rise in employment, taxable income has not enjoyed a proportionate rise, tempering any economic celebration.

Sample Summary

More Jobs, Not Better Jobs

The article "Employment Increase Misleading" reports on the current employment picture in Grange County. While the number of jobs has increased, salaries have decreased. Both the increase and decrease can be blamed on the types of new businesses in the area. Companies offering high-paying jobs have either relocated or closed down, while new businesses offering low-paying or minimum-wage jobs have proliferated. (See the graph.) Local workers have had to settle for lower pay than they had been earning. So while more people are working, they are earning less.

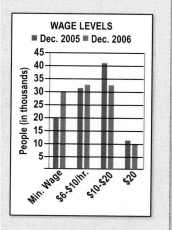

WAGE LEVELS
■ Dec. 2005 ■ Dec. 2006

People (in thousands): Min. Wage, $6-$10/hr., $10-$20, $20

Writing Guidelines ▪ Statistical Argument

Use the guidelines below to help you write a persuasive essay containing statistical supporting evidence.

Prewriting

- **Select a topic.** Think about a timely, statistic-driven topic related to your school or community: student dropout rate, state test scores, sports statistics, student volunteer activity, and so on. Choose a topic that interests you and will interest your readers.
- **Gather information.** Research your topic, using reliable sources of information. Take notes on key facts and figures.
- **Form an opinion.** State an opinion about the topic after reviewing your notes.

Writing

- **Write your first draft.** Introduce your topic and state your opinion. In your middle paragraphs, use your facts and statistics to support your position. Write an ending that restates your opinion.

Revising

- **Improve your argument.** Consider your *ideas*, *organization*, and *voice*. Ask these questions: *Is my position clear? Have I developed a convincing argument using statistics? Is my argument well organized? Does my voice sound confident?*
- **Improve your style.** Check your *word choice* and *sentence fluency*. Ask these questions: *Have I defined any unfamiliar terms? Do my sentences read smoothly?*

Editing

- **Check for conventions.** Correct any errors in punctuation, capitalization, spelling, and grammar.
- **Prepare a final copy.** Make a neat final copy of your argument and proofread it.

Try It!

Select and research a timely, statistic-driven topic to write about. Gather information and form an opinion about the topic. Then write your argument, using statistics to make your point.

■ Sample Statistical Argument

The student writing the following persuasive essay uses statistics to emphasize the need for after-school programs.

The **beginning** includes statistics to introduce the topic.

The opinion statement is underlined.

In the **middle** part, statistics help support the opinion.

The **ending** restates the opinion.

Happily Ever After

According to the U.S. Department of Labor, of the more than 28 million kids whose parents work outside the home, as many as 15 million have no prearranged supervision after school. Further, Child Trends Research reports that more than 4 million kids—10 percent of children between the ages of 6 and 12—are totally on their own until their parents get home from work. After-school programs are necessary for the safety of the entire community and the future of this country.

After-school programs have been proven to decrease crime and violence. According to studies by the organization Fight Crime: Invest in Kids, the time period between 3:00 p.m. and 6:00 p.m. is considered a "danger zone," with higher rates of violent crimes committed by children. After instituting an after-school program in the San Diego Public Schools, authorities noted a 13.1 percent reduction in after-school arrests, as well as an 11.7 percent reduction in juvenile violent crime.

Students who participate in after-school programs do better in school and are less likely to drop out. They are also more likely to continue their education after high school. In addition, research shows they are less likely to engage in risky activities such as drinking, drugs, sex, and violent acts.

Finally, after-school programs save money. Research shows that every dollar invested in an after-school program saves taxpayers $3 in truancy and court costs, as well as the expense of students repeating a grade. A Brandeis University study reported that parents of unsupervised children miss an average of eight days of work per year and make more errors due to situations involving their children. After-school programs help eliminate these situations.

After-school activity programs are crucial to protecting not only children, but society in general. When people realize the importance of such programs, they may begin shaping a new world.

Writing Guidelines ▪ Response to a Math Prompt

Math prompts propose word problems. You are asked to respond in writing in addition to showing your mathematical calculations and your answers. First you must analyze the prompt and decide what you are supposed to do. Then you respond one step at a time. Follow these guidelines.

Before You Write . . .

- **Read the prompt.** Read carefully and watch for key words such as *find, solve, justify, demonstrate,* or *compare.* Then carry out the requested actions only. Be aware that some prompts have more than one part.
- **Gather details and data.** Write down any values, assumptions, or variables provided in the prompt.

As You Write . . .

- **Build your solution.** Respond to each part of the prompt. Jot down formulas or equations and sketch brief diagrams if they will help solve the problem. Make the necessary calculations to get an answer and show all of your work.

After You've Written a First Draft . . .

- **Improve your response.** Reread the prompt after you do your calculations. If the problem has more than one part, be sure you have answered every part. Work the problem in another way to check that your solution is correct.
- **Check for conventions.** Check your solution for errors in punctuation, capitalization, spelling, and grammar.
- **Prepare a final copy.** Make a neat copy of your solution.

■ Sample Response to a Math Prompt

The following math prompt contains more than one part. The writer provides a solution using words, numbers, and a diagram.

> What is the probability of getting a sum of seven on two dice? First explain what is meant by probability and then solve the problem.

Student Response

Probability

Probability refers to the number of times the desired result occurs out of the total number of possible outcomes. This problem asks for the number of ways to get a sum of seven on two dice out of all of the possibilities when we roll two dice.

To solve this problem, I need to know the total possible results when throwing two dice (first number indicates result on first die and second number is result on second die):

1,1	1,2	1,3	1,4	1,5	(1,6)
2,1	2,2	2,3	2,4	(2,5)	2,6
3,1	3,2	3,3	(3,4)	3,5	3,6
4,1	4,2	(4,3)	4,4	4,5	4,6
5,1	(5,2)	5,3	5,4	5,5	5,6
(6,1)	6,2	6,3	6,4	6,5	6,6

This gives thirty-six possible results when throwing two dice. Looking at all of the possibilities, there are only six ways to get a sum of seven: 1+6, 2+5, 3+4, 4+3, 5+2, and 6+1. Therefore, the probability of getting a sum of seven would be 1 to 6: $\dfrac{sum}{total} = \dfrac{6}{36} = \dfrac{1}{6}$.

Try It!

Find a math prompt and write a response. Choose a practice prompt from your textbook or one recommended by your teacher. Follow the guidelines on page **484**.

Other Forms of Writing in Math

Definition

Calculus—Write a detailed expository paragraph defining a vector and explaining its function in math.

Narrative

Any Math—Tell about a time you couldn't understand a mathematical principle, and how you finally found a way to make it clear.

Compare-Contrast

Algebra—Compare and contrast real numbers and imaginary numbers. Include descriptions, properties, and functions.

Position Paper

Any Math—Defend or oppose the requirement of three years of math to get into college.

Process

Geometry—Explain the process you would use to figure the number of bricks you would need to build a wall around your backyard.

Research

Statistics—Calculate the probability of your favorite baseball team going to the World Series this year. Figure in the statistics of past seasons and each player's performance numbers, along with variables such as injuries, possible trades, and so on.

Writing in the Applied Sciences

Thoughtful logic is at the heart of all scientific thinking and writing. Let's say you need to replace a light switch. You ask questions about what you need to do, and then you search for answers. Whether you go online, read a manual, or ask for advice, in the hands-on world of applied science, it is critical to know every step. Your safety may be at stake. Whenever you are asked to explain something, focus on being clear and complete.

In this chapter, you will learn about writing directions, essays of explanation, and even letters of complaint. Apply the solid logic of science and the clarity of good research to all your writing.

- **Taking Classroom Notes**
- **Keeping a Learning Log**
- **Writing Guidelines: Explanatory Essay**
- **Writing Guidelines: Career Review**
- **Writing Guidelines: Response to a Prompt**
- **Other Forms of Practical Writing**

"Don't rule out working with your hands. It does not preclude using your head."

—Andy Rooney

Taking Classroom Notes

Note taking can help you keep your projects organized and on track.

Before You Take Notes . . .

- **Keep a separate notebook for each class,** or use a three-ring binder with tabbed dividers for separate sections.
- **Divide your paper into two columns.** Use one for notes, and the other for questions or drawings.

As You Take Notes . . .

- **Date each entry** and keep the pages in order.
- **Briefly jot down teacher instructions** as they are given in class.
- **Draw diagrams** and use graphics to organize details.

After You Take Notes . . .

- **Review your notes** with a partner and highlight main ideas.
- **Study your notes** before beginning a project or before a test.

January 9, 2007   Replacing a Switch

Shut off power to the circuit at the fuse box by removing the fuse or pushing the circuit breaker switch to off. Use a current tester at the light switch to be sure the power is off.

- Remove switch plate.
- Remove switch from the wall box.
- Loosen screws and remove wires keeping track of which wire is attached to the top screw.
- Attach wires to the new switch. Be sure each wire is underneath each screw head and tighten the screws.
- Fold the wires into the wall box and tighten screws that hold the switch in the box.
- Attach switch plate.

Turn the power back on at the fuse box and test the light.

To light

From power

Try It!

Take notes in an applied sciences class. Try to include a sketch or diagram in your notes.

Keeping a Learning Log

A learning log is a journal for recording what you learn in a class. The log lets you reflect on ideas, make drawings, and comment on projects.

Before You Write . . .

- **Use a separate section in your notes** or a separate notebook.
- **Leave space** for writing questions and answers later on.

As You Write . . .

- **Date each entry** and keep the pages in order.
- **Write about what you experienced,** what you learned, what worked and what didn't, and ask questions.
- **Consider your next steps.** Write about how the material connects with other things you have learned, and where it might lead.

After You Write . . .

- **Use your log as a supplement** to your notes to review for a test.
- **Write the answers to questions** you had in class or during a project.

October 6, 2006   Cooking Class

The five basic ingredients you need for making bread are flour, yeast, water, shortening, and salt. The flour's protein is called gluten, which traps air bubbles. The gluten combines with the flour's starch to create the texture of the bread. Some recipes add sugar to help get the yeast working, but there's some sugar in the flour that activates the yeast. Fat coats the gluten molecules, makes the finished bread softer, and helps it brown. Water or other liquids react with the gluten and the starch and create steam that makes the bread soft and high. Salt adds flavor and also strengthens the gluten.

Some breads call for eggs, which give a light texture, and sugar, which contributes to browning and flavor. Other ingredients can add nutrients and flavor.

My aunt told me to put a pan of water in the oven as the bread bakes so the crust doesn't get hard.

The more times the bread is punched down and allowed to rise, the higher and softer the bread will be.

Try It!

Set up a learning log in a notebook. Be sure to date each entry.

Writing Guidelines ■ Explanatory Essay

An explanatory essay states a thesis and then provides details that clarify and explain the position given.

Prewriting

- **Select a topic.** If your teacher does not assign a specific topic, review your notes, manual, or textbook for ideas. For example, in a metals fabrication class you might explain why it is important to prevent electrode contamination.
- **Gather details.** Use a graphic organizer to help you arrange your supporting details. Include facts, examples, and anecdotes to support your claims.
- **Plan and organize.** Decide in which order to present your support points. How are they related? Decide on a pattern for moving smoothly from one topic to the next.

Writing

- **Connect your ideas.** Introduce your points and their connection in the beginning paragraph. Then present each point, covering one completely before moving on to the next.

Revising

- **Improve your writing.** Examine your work for *ideas, organization,* and *voice.* Rework any ideas that are unclear or incomplete.
- **Improve your style.** Look at your *word choice* and *sentence fluency* and make any changes necessary to improve clarity and flow.

Editing

- **Check for conventions.** Look for errors in spelling, punctuation, and grammar.
- **Make a neat final copy.**

Applied Sciences

■ Sample Explanatory Essay

For her nutrition class, Hanae explained the dangers of a high-protein diet.

The beginning introduces the topic and leads to the thesis statement (underlined).

The middle gives reasons that support the thesis.

The ending wraps up and makes a final statement.

More Than Weight Loss with High-Protein Diets

High-protein diets, which emphasize meat, eggs, seafood, and cheese, have become popular. <u>However, while this type of diet produces quick weight loss, research shows its dangers far outweigh the benefits.</u>

A 1988 publication called "Nutrition and Health in the United States" was published by the Surgeon General, and it discouraged high-protein diets because of the high levels of protein and saturated fat consumed. When carbohydrates needed for complete synthesis of fat are eliminated from the diet, the body faces a challenge: how to burn excess amounts of fat.

Fewer carbohydrates create problems. Fewer high-fiber plant foods combined with an increase in high-fat foods means increased cholesterol levels. Without the high-fiber plant foods, potassium, calcium, and magnesium are reduced and sodium levels rise, increasing the risk of high blood pressure that can lead to heart disease or a stroke. With fewer carbohydrates to help retain body fluids, the body risks dehydration. That strains the kidneys, When excess protein accumulates in the kidneys and is not adequately diluted, a person may develop kidney stones, kidney failure, or gallbladder disease.

The American Heart Association links high-protein diets and osteoporosis, rheumatoid arthritis, and even multiple sclerosis. Most high-protein foods are acidic. The body tries to maintain its alkaline pH balance. To do so, it dissolves bone into phosphorus and calcium to counteract the acid. This bone degeneration is the first step to osteoporosis. The kidneys excrete this bone material, potentially resulting in kidney stones.

Stay healthy when you need to lose weight. Your best diet strategy is to eat a healthy diet, balance protein and carbohydrates, and increase your physical activity.

Try It!

Write an essay of explanation. Select and explain one aspect of a topic.

Writing Guidelines ▪ Career Review

A career review is a specific type of essay of analysis. It includes the job's requirements, such as education or physical stamina, future advancement possibilities, benefits, and salary.

Prewriting

- **Present your topic.** Explain which job you are analyzing. Remember your purpose. What important factors do you need to consider?
- **Gather details.** A career analysis should include details about the requirements, benefits, and future of the job. Include anything that makes the career stand out or fall short.
- **Plan and organize.** A good way to write a career analysis is point by point, covering each area of the career before moving on to the next.

Writing

- **Include a clear beginning.** Explain why you are examining this topic.
- **Write the middle.** Analyze the different areas of the topic, point by point.
- **End with a final comment.** Wrap up by sharing one final insight about the topic.

Revising

- **Improve your writing.** Look for *ideas, organization,* and *voice.* Consider all aspects of the topic.
- **Improve your style.** Look for smooth sentences. Let your interest in the topic show through.

Editing

- **Check for conventions.** Look for and correct any errors in spelling, punctuation, or grammar.
- **Make a clean final copy.**

■ Sample Career Review

Leon's careers class explores the duties and requirements of different careers. Here is his review of the job of radiological technician.

The beginning explains the topic.

The middle covers different aspects of the job.

The ending offers a summary and a final insight.

Becoming a Radiology Technician

With the aging population in this country, the number of health-related jobs is growing. A top job of the future is that of a radiology technician who handles X-ray equipment.

Radiology technicians, or radiographers, have a variety of duties. First of all, they need people skills, as they prepare people for X-rays and explain procedures. If diagnostic dye is used, sometimes technicians must mix the contrast medium as well as administer it to the patient. To administer X-rays, technicians set the level of radiation and the right distance between the machine and the area to be X-rayed. Fine adjustments create the correct angle, density, and contrast for the film to show clear images that allow doctors to make exact diagnoses.

Technical training is required. High school courses in science and computers are a good start. Specialized training is offered in technical schools, colleges, hospitals, and the military. Two-year associate degrees and bachelor's degrees are favored by hospitals. Teaching and administrative positions require four-year degrees.

Most jobs are in hospitals, although positions are also available in doctors' offices, diagnostic imaging centers, and outpatient care centers. People work around 40 hours per week. In 2004, salaries for radiographers varied with about half earning from $36,000 to $53,000 and others more than $60,000. Those trained in more complex radiological imaging, such as CT scans and MRI's, find the highest paying jobs.

In summary, the job of radiology technician appears to be interesting, challenging, and important. It's clear that this is a promising career that can make a difference.

Try It!

Select a job or career area and write an analysis of it. Include as much detail as you can, and give an opinion about the job.

Writing Guidelines ▪ Response to a Prompt

Before You Write . . .

- **Know your time limit.** Set time limits for yourself to allow time for prewriting, writing, and revising.
- **Examine the prompt.** Look for key words that will help you determine the following elements:
  - **Subject** What is the topic of your writing?
  - **Purpose** Will you explain, inform, analyze, or persuade?
  - **Focus** What aspect of the subject should you examine?
  - **Form** Are you to write an essay? A letter? A poem? A story? Be clear as to how your response is to be formatted.
- **Plan your response.** Write your thesis or opinion statement and use a brief outline or graphic organizer.

As You Write . . .

- **Write an effective opening paragraph.** Use a hook to grab your reader's attention. Then introduce your topic and include your thesis statement.
- **Develop the middle.** Develop a clear topic sentence for each paragraph. Support each main point with details, including examples and paraphrases. If you are allowed to look at notes or texts, include quotations and statistics.
- **Write a strong closing paragraph.** Restate your thesis and offer a final thought. If you are writing a persuasive piece, include a call to action.

After You've Written a First Draft . . .

- **Read through your work.** Add, cut, or move your details to make your work stronger. Be aware of your time as you work, making as many changes as time allows.
- **Check for conventions.** Correct any errors you find.

■ Sample Response to a Prompt

Teresa wrote a response to the following prompt in her life-skills class.

> Your landlord has neglected to repair a leaky faucet, a running toilet, and a broken light fixture in your apartment. Write a letter of complaint convincing the landlord to take care of the problems.

The beginning opens with a positive statement and the thesis (underlined).

The middle gives the main points as topic sentences.

The ending restates the thesis (underlined) and adds a final statement.

Dear Mr. Miller:

First of all, I want to tell you I enjoy my apartment. It's so spacious, and the neighbors are great. However, I still have the leaking faucet and running toilet in the bathroom and the broken light fixture in the kitchen. Although I mentioned them when I first moved in last month, nothing has been done to fix them. <u>I must complain about the slow response and ask you again to please repair these problems.</u>

The water situation is most serious. The constant dripping is annoying and expensive. I checked my bill with my neighbors, and neither of their bills is as high as mine. They don't have leaks.

The broken kitchen light fixture is also a problem. Without a window in the kitchen, the main fixture is my only light except the stove hood, and it does not light the sink area.

<u>Please take care of these problems.</u> They represent both cost and possible safety issues. Because they were noted as needing fixing on my initial move-in sheet, I ask you to fix them as soon as possible. I do not want to have to contact the Tenants' Union for assistance.

Thank you for your attention to this matter.

Sincerely,

Teresa Hernandez

Try It!

Write a letter of complaint for a real or fictitious situation.

Other Forms of Practical Writing

Process Essay

Architectural Drafting—Explain how to measure a kitchen for new cabinets and countertops.

Essay of Classification

Textile Arts—Explain the different types of needlework and give an example of each.

Essay of Analysis

Auto Mechanics—Analyze the pros and cons of a hydrogen-powered engine and consider its current feasibility for the mass market.

Essay of Explanation

Home Decorating—Explain the various uses of ceramic tile in the home and how to choose the right type of tile for each situation.

Problem-Solution Essay

Advanced Metals Fabrication—Explain the problems encountered by using a contaminated electrode in welding and explain how to repair it.

Persuasive Essay

Health—Write a paper persuading people not to be afraid of or avoid someone who has been diagnosed HIV positive.

Comparison-Contrast Essay

Classic Cooking—Compare the cuisines of Italy and Greece and explain reasons for the differences and similarities.

Writing in the Arts

Archaeologists have found that even before there was language, there was art, with cave paintings telling stories and relating experiences. But art is more than a basic means of communication. Mahatma Gandhi once said, "True art takes note not merely of form but also of what lies behind." That means that art is not just visual or aural; it is cerebral, stirring great thoughts as well as deep emotions—thoughts and emotions you can explore and write about.

When you write about art, you can examine your own reactions and analyze exactly why a piece affects you the way it does. You can examine the effect some aspect of art may have had on history, or its reflection of a particular time period. This chapter will help you write learning logs, essays, and reports about the arts. You will also learn to respond to an art prompt, using your thoughts and emotions to analyze and critique art. In writing about art, you can understand yourself and others a little better.

- **Taking Classroom Notes**
- **Keeping a Learning Log**
- **Writing Guidelines: Research Report**
- **Writing Guidelines: Performance Review**
- **Writing Guidelines: Response to an Art Prompt**

"I try to apply colors like words that shape poems, like notes that shape music."

—Joan Miro

Taking Classroom Notes

In art and music classes, you usually work with a variety of art materials or practice for instrumental or vocal performances. However, it may occasionally be necessary to take notes in class. (See pages **528–530** for more information.)

Take notes when . . .

- **your teacher writes information on the board or overhead.**
  Taking notes helps make important information part of your own thinking. Be sure to write down new vocabulary words as well as names, dates, and key phrases.

- **you have a demonstration in class.**
  Your class may view slides of art pieces or listen to recordings of various musical styles. Taking notes will help you organize and remember the various works.

- **you have a guest speaker or performer.**
  Professional artists may visit your class and demonstrate or discuss their work. Your notes can help you think about the presentation. You may want to jot down questions you'd like to ask after the presentation.

Tip

- Date each entry and give it a topic heading so you can find it quickly when reviewing.

- List new vocabulary words. Leave room for adding definitions or examples later.

- Write down hints or examples to help jog your memory about a name, a term, or a concept.

- Draw sketches that may help you remember artworks.

- Mark a spot in your notes with a question mark if something confuses you and ask about it later.

- Divide note pages into two columns with one side wider than the other, so you can put notes on one side and questions on the other.

- Work with a "study buddy." You can compare notes, go over questions, and review for tests together.

Keeping a Learning Log

In project-based classes such as art, dance, theater, and music, a learning log can help you keep track of, and reflect on, your progress. Andre wrote the following entries for a beginning class in watercolor painting. On the left side, he made notes about what the teacher talked about. On the right side, he added comments.

Sample Entry

April 3, 2006

In watercolor painting, what is left out can be as important as what is put on the paper. White paper showing through is often part of the composition. Different brushstrokes and washes create different effects.

Mr. Kirke showed us watercolor paintings of flowers that incorporated white space and used different types of washes.

April 4, 2006

A flat wash is an important basic technique.
1. Clip a sheet of paper on a board.
2. Have plenty of clean water in jars.
3. Brush a band of color across the top.
4. Brush a second band in the opposite direction, picking up the fluid paint at the base of the previous stroke.
5. Continue laying in bands of the same color, working quickly and tilting the board to keep the leading edge wet.
6. Use a dry brush to pick up the excess color along the bottom of the wash.

Mr. Kirke let us experiment with using watercolors. I found out why it is important to let the one layer dry before applying more paint. When I started doing a tree on top of a flat wash for the sky, the painting got muddy because the blue wash wasn't quite dry. Unlike oil paints, you can't slather on watercolors over wet paint because the colors will run together.

April 10, 2006

Use this technique on paper that is already wet with a background color. The color will spread more slowly as the paper dries.
1. First dampen the paper.
2. Touch the color onto the paper with the tip of a large brush.
3. Clean brush carefully between colors.

We worked on wet-on-wet techniques. I started with gray, giving the effect of a stormy sky.
The technique is more complicated and interesting when applying two colors. I tried blending green and yellow to make a distant, hazy, yellow-green woods.

Try It!

Set up a learning log for your drama, art, or music class. Keep one side for notes or instructions and the other side for your own comments.

Writing Guidelines ▪ Research Report

You may be asked to write a research report in your art or music class. You may decide to write about a famous painter or analyze a trend in music. The following guidelines will help you create a research report.

Prewriting

- **Choose a subject.** If your teacher doesn't provide a specific subject, list artworks, artists, musical trends, or other ideas that interest you.
- **List what you already know** about the subject, jotting down questions that you have.
- **Conduct research** about the subject. Check school or public library catalogs for books, look through magazines, and explore Web sites.
- **Write a thesis statement.** Review your research notes. Then write a thesis statement that clearly identifies the specific topic and focus for your research paper.
- **Plan and organize.** Outline your paper, putting details in the most appropriate order—for example, you may put key points in spatial order, chronological order, or order of importance.

Writing

- **Connect your ideas.** Introduce your topic, give background information, and state your thesis.
- **In the middle paragraphs,** support the thesis statement with specific details. Finally, summarize what you have learned or what you have to say about the topic.

Revising

- **Improve your writing.** Check your *ideas, organization,* and *voice.* Ask these questions: *Have I created a clear thesis? Have I supported it with a variety of details? Are my details in the best order? Do I sound knowledgeable?*
- **Improve your style.** Check your *word choice* and *sentence fluency.* Ask these questions: *Have I explained any technical terms? Do my sentences flow smoothly?*

Editing

- **Check for conventions.** Look for errors in spelling, punctuation, and grammar.
- **Prepare your final copy.** Proofread your research paper before turning it in.

■ Sample Research Report

You can learn about the arts by studying how different artistic expressions reflect different periods and events throughout history. Tamika Sanders had been studying the migration of African Americans to the northern United States in her history class. She discovered that African American painter Jacob Lawrence had created a series of paintings called *The Great Migration,* and she decided, with permission from both teachers, to make that the topic of a report for her art and history classes.

Tamika Sanders
Mrs. Southwell
History
May 15, 2006

The Great Migration

The beginning presents the thesis statement of the report (underlined).

Painter Jacob Lawrence used art to tell stories— usually through a series of paintings on panels. <u>In the Migration series, which he started in 1940, Lawrence used the technique to capture the story of African Americans moving north after the turn of the century.</u>

Lawrence began his career as an artist during the Depression in the Works Progress Administration's federal arts program. He said his style of telling stories through a series of paintings was influenced by African storytelling traditions, Mexican mural painters, and American cartoon strips (Black Genius). He often laid out his designs like a modern storyboard (Whitney). Before the *Migration* series, he had created historical painting series on Harriet Tubman, John Brown, and Frederick Douglass.

The middle of the report discusses Lawrence's background and the influences that affected his art.

The *Migration* series was inspired by the people Lawrence grew up with. Although he had never been to the South before beginning his work, almost everyone in his neighborhood and family had moved north during the previous 50 years. His parents were part of the migration, with his mother settling in Harlem, where Lawrence grew up (Washington).

Arriving in the North, many blacks found new education opportunities and more jobs, but often experienced new forms of discrimination and injustice as well. To tell this story in paintings, Lawrence used bold colors, the geometric forms and shapes of his urban home, and intentionally distorted figures to illustrate the universal nature of the migrants' experiences.

The paintings cover all aspects of the move north. The first panel shows a crowd of stylized figures moving forward toward abstract railroad departure gates labeled "Chicago," "New York," and "St. Louis." Another painting in the series shows a quick, vivid arc of railroad track reflecting the industry where many of the immigrants found employment. Yet another shows well-dressed, haughty, long-time northern black residents, who often looked down on the poorly dressed, new rural immigrants.

As in many of his other series paintings, Lawrence repeated motifs, shapes, and words. In the *Migration* series, he repeated the images of a single large spike, chain links, hands, and a hammer to show the continuity in the lives, experiences, and struggles of the immigrants (Whitney).

The **ending** concludes with a summary of the impact of Lawrence's work.

The *Migration* series made Lawrence commercially successful, but to him, telling the story and the history was most important. "We have a tremendous history," he told a writer, "and I'm not just talking about the black, but the American people. . . . It's all one story. Exploring the American experience is a beautiful thing" (Black Genius).

Note: Tamika also included a works-cited page to list the sources she cites in her report. (See pages **392** and **407**).

Writing Guidelines ■ Performance Review

You may be asked to write about the arts by reviewing a specific performance. On the other hand, you may enjoy a performance so much that you want to share your thoughts with others through a blog, on your own Web site, or in a letter to someone.

While this type of writing is more informal, or personal, than most academic writing, you should follow basic writing guidelines. Readers will respect your evaluation if your writing shows clarity and insight, so be sure to maintain your focus throughout the review.

Prewriting

- **Focus on what you want to say.**
- **Make notes** on your impressions of an art show or a concert.
- **Write a thesis statement.** Review your notes and state your focus.
- **Plan and organize.** Outline key points you want to make in your review.

Writing

- **Write freely,** always keeping your main idea in mind. Use your outline as a basic writing guide.
- **Use examples to support your points.** Whether readers agree with you or not, they will appreciate what you've written if you support your point of view with solid evidence.
- **Keep your audience in mind** in terms of what you need to explain.
- **Write a strong ending.** Sum up why the topic was important enough for you to write about.

Revising

- **Improve your writing.** Check your *ideas, organization,* and *voice.* Ask these questions: *Have I created a clear thesis? Have I supported it with a variety of details? Are my details in the best order? Do I sound knowledgeable?*
- **Improve your style.** Check your *word choice* and *sentence fluency.* Ask these questions: *Have I explained any technical terms? Do my sentences flow smoothly?*

Editing

- **Check for conventions.** Look for errors in spelling, punctuation, and grammar.
- **Prepare your final copy.** Proofread your review before sharing it.

■ Sample Performance Review

Greg's school newspaper asked him to write a review about an African dance and drum troupe for the print edition of the paper and for the Web site. Greg took notes at the concert and then wrote about what he learned and about his reaction to the performance itself.

The **beginning** explains who the group is and gives the writer's reaction to the performance.

The **middle** describes the performers, the drums, and the sounds of the event.

The **ending** invites others to discover the group and learn about the special drums.

Feel the Rhythm

Now I know exactly what people mean when they say "you have to feel the rhythm." The pounding rhythm of beating drums and stomping feet went right down to my bones at the performance by African Steps. This dance and drum troupe from King High School shook the rafters in our auditorium during their Black History Month appearance on February 15.

African Steps weaves music and dance together seamlessly. The dancers wear ankle bells and shell bracelets so their movements become part of the pounding rhythm. The drummers' hands dance across the skins, flowing into the choreography.

If you think of drums as simple instruments, you would change your mind after hearing the complex interplay of the many different styles of drums African Steps uses—from pounding bass rhythms to more subtle, almost melodic tones. In introducing themselves, the drummers explained each drum's role. The djembe, for example, has a wide range of sound. It's a hollow drum made from a tree trunk and covered with goatskin. The drum hangs on straps from the musician's shoulders. It's played with the hands only. The kpanlogo gives a smooth but earthy tone.

The powerful, joyful rhythms had even the teachers in the back of the auditorium tapping their feet and swaying. This performance, and the explanations the dancers and drummers gave about the different pieces they performed, helped me appreciate African culture through music and dance. Don't miss the chance to share the experience.

Writing Guidelines ▪ Response to an Art Prompt

You may be asked to write a short essay in response to a prompt about art or music as a class assignment or as part of a test. Responding to a prompt allows you to express what you have learned about a specific work of art or style of music. Here are guidelines for responding to an art prompt.

Before You Write . . .

- **Understand the prompt.** Read the prompt and focus on what you are asked to do. Should you explain, compare, describe, or persuade?

- **Gather your details.** If permitted, review your notes and research materials. Highlight or jot down important details. Note sources for quotations or facts. If you aren't permitted to use notes or research materials, jot down key facts that you remember about the topic.

- **Organize your details.** Check the prompt for clues that will help you organize your response. For example, if the prompt asks you to describe the jazz classic *Take Five* and discuss how improvisation reshapes the music, you might begin with a general description of the piece and then discuss specific musical themes that serve as springboards for improvisation. You could mention how specific instruments and performers develop the basic themes in creative variations.

As You Write . . .

- **Write freely.** Use your notes as a guide and try to include all your main ideas. Many short responses are just one paragraph long. If your prompt calls for an essay, use a new paragraph for each main point.

After You've Written a First Draft . . .

- **Improve your writing.** Read your draft and cut any details that don't fit the prompt. Add information that will clarify your ideas or help answer the prompt. Make your response as complete as possible.

- **Improve your style.** Check your *word choice* and *sentence fluency* so that your response reads smoothly.

- **Check for conventions.** Look for errors in spelling, punctuation, and grammar.

■ Sample Response to an Art Prompt

In a two-part response, Jasmine discusses the style of artist Paul Cezanne.

> Answer the following questions in one or more paragraphs: (1) Why did some consider Cezanne's work primitive? (2) Is the term appropriate in referring to Cezanne's work?

First, the writer explains who Cezanne was and what factors led some to define his work as primitive.

Then the writer gives specific examples.

Response #1

Paul Cezanne, a nineteenth-century French painter, is sometimes called the father of modern art. At the time, both his critics and his supporters often used the term "primitive" to refer to his work.

Cezanne's use of pure color with simple brushstrokes and heavy, fluid pigments led many to underestimate his technical skills as an artist and compare his works to those of untutored "primitive" artists. In addition, his figures were often distorted as he experimented with ways to put down on canvas what his eye was seeing. This approach was often misinterpreted as that of an artist lacking in basic drawing skills. He was obsessed with form and technique rather than with subject. As a result, the public often didn't understand his paintings.

Next, the writer argues that the term "primitive" isn't appropriate for most of the artist's work.

Response #2

Cezanne's early experimental paintings may be called primitive in technique, but as he came closer and closer to putting down on canvas what he saw in nature, he began to use space, mass, and color in a very sophisticated way. Some of his early works, full of emotional intensity, laid the groundwork for the expressionist movement. By the late 1900s, his paintings became more abstract, with buildings and figures evolving into geometric forms. These works set the stage for cubism.

Try It!

Respond to a short-essay prompt your teacher will supply about a topic you are studying. Write a one- or two-paragraph answer.

Writing in the Workplace

In the workplace, every bit of correspondence reflects the business and the professionalism of the people working there. Despite the changing landscape of business communication, good writing skills remain the bedrock for career success. Whatever the task—writing an e-mail message, a memo, a report, a presentation, or a proposal—it's important to communicate clearly and quickly in this environment.

Even if you remain a student for several more years, you'll find yourself using forms of workplace communication. You'll write letters and e-mail messages; you'll develop multimedia presentations; you'll create your résumé. In this chapter, some of the many forms of business writing are covered, along with tips and techniques to strengthen your skills.

- Business Letter
- Writing Guidelines: Résumé
- Writing Guidelines: Proposal
- Writing Guidelines: Memo
- Writing Guidelines: E-Mail Message
- Writing Guidelines: News Release

"In business you get what you want by giving other people what they want."

—Alice Foote MacDougall

Parts of a Business Letter

Writers use business letters to request information, apply for a job, or file a complaint. The basic format of an effective letter is similar whether it is sent through the regular mail or delivered via e-mail.

- The **heading** includes the writer's complete address, either on company stationery, in a computer template, or typed out manually. The heading also includes the day, month, and year. If the address is part of the letterhead, place only the date in the upper left corner.

- The **inside address** includes the recipient's name and complete address. If you're not sure who should receive the letter or how to correctly spell someone's name, you can call the company to ask. If a person's title is a single word or very short, include it on the same line as the name, preceded by a comma. If the title is longer, put it on a separate line under the name.

- The **salutation** is the greeting. For business letters, use a colon following the recipient's name, not a comma. Use *Mr.* or *Ms.* followed by the person's last name, unless you happen to be well acquainted with the person. Do not guess at whether a woman prefers *Miss* or *Mrs.* If the person's gender is not obvious from the name, one acceptable solution is to use the full name in the salutation. For example, *Dear Pat Johnson.* If you don't know the name of the person who will read your letter, use a salutation such as one of these:

  - Dear Manager:
  - Dear Sir or Madam:
  - Attention: Human Resources Department
  - Attention: Personnel Director

- The **body** is the main part of the letter. It is organized into three parts. The beginning states why you are writing, the middle provides the needed details, and the ending focuses on what should happen next. In a business letter, double-space between the paragraphs; do not indent. If the letter is longer than one page, on subsequent pages put the reader's name at the top left, the page number in the center, and the date at the right margin.

- The **complimentary closing** ends the message. Use *Sincerely* or *Yours truly*—followed by a comma. Capitalize only the first word.

- The **signature** makes the letter official. Leave four blank lines between the complimentary closing and your typed name. Write your signature in that space.

- The **notes** tell who authored the letter (uppercase initials and a colon), who typed the letter (lowercase initials), who received a copy (after *cc:*), and what enclosures are included (after *Enclosure* or *Encl.:*).

Letter of Inquiry or Request

Plains Union High School offers advertising space in the programs they produce for the school's concerts and plays. Mandisa Kwafume, student liaison for the parents' Band Boosters Club, wrote this letter to solicit more advertising revenue from the business community. (The inside address would change depending on the business owner being contacted.)

Heading

Plains Union High School Band Boosters Club
676 Highway R
Dry Plains, TX 78112
October 3, 2007

Four to Seven Spaces

Inside address

Rex Neinheus
Area Aquatics
1322 Main Street
Dry Plains, TX 78113

Double Space

Salutation

Dear Mr. Neinheus:

Double Space

Body
The writer explains why she is writing, provides needed details, and suggests a next step.

I am writing on behalf of the Plains Union High School Band Boosters Club. Perhaps you are aware that the high school presents several concerts and plays throughout the year. Did you also know that many local businesses advertise in the programs for these events? Here is your opportunity to join them.

Purchasing an ad in one or more of the programs is a smart business move. The performers' family and friends—most of whom live in the area—read the programs and notice the businesses advertising in them. They'll make an effort to patronize a business that supports the school through advertising.

Enclosed you will find an insertion order for any size advertisement you care to place. You may provide camera-ready copy, or we will be happy to design something for you. Please be sure to indicate which program(s) you prefer for your ad; a checklist is provided.

Complimentary closing

Thank you for supporting the arts at Plains Union High School.

Double Space

Sincerely,

Signature

Mandisa Kwafume   Four Spaces

Mandisa Kwafume, Student Liaison

Double Space

**Initials
Copies
Enclosure**

MK: jb
cc: Ms. Felicia Goodman, President
Encl: insertion order

Letter of Application

Lou Roberts wrote the following letter to apply for a summer science research internship position.

24 Hampshire Street
Skones, MT 59781
February 2, 2007

Brian Allman, Director
Office of Biomedical Studies
Medical College of Butte
540 Kings Row
Butte, MT 59702

Dear Mr. Allman:

The opening introduces the writer as well as the purpose of the letter.

Please find enclosed my official application for your High School Summer Research Internship Program, as well as the names and contact information for two references. I believe I am qualified for this internship and would love the opportunity to work with the mentors at the Medical College of Butte. Allow me to outline my research interests and career goals.

The middle paragraphs discuss background, qualifications, and long-range goals.

I developed my interest in biochemistry and cell biology in my high school science classes this past year. In these classes, we planned and executed several research experiments related to allergic reactions, and I would like to continue to investigate the physiology behind these "overreactions" of the immune system.

I hope this internship will be the first step in my ultimate goal of becoming an immunologist. I look forward to helping people who suffer from allergies (myself included) to manage and treat their conditions. I realize how intensive the training for such a career is, and I can't think of a better introduction to it than this internship.

The closing adds information and thanks the reader.

If you have any specific questions for me, please e-mail me at lrbts@email.net or call me at (406) 555-0515. Thank you for your consideration, and I hope to hear from you soon.

Sincerely,

Lou Roberts

Lou Roberts

Encl: application, references

Preparing a Letter for Mailing

Letters sent through the mail will get to their destinations faster if they are properly addressed and stamped. Always include a ZIP code.

Address the envelope.

Place the return address in the upper left corner, the destination address in the center, and the correct postage in the upper right corner. Some word processing programs will automatically format the return and destination addresses.

LOU ROBERTS
24 HAMPSHIRE STREET
SKONES MT 59781

MR BRIAN ALLMAN
OFFICE OF BIOMEDICAL STUDIES
MEDICAL COLLEGE OF BUTTE
540 KINGS ROW
BUTTE MT 59702

There are two acceptable forms for addressing the envelope: the traditional form and the form preferred by the postal service.

Traditional Form	**Postal Service Form**
Liam O'Donnell	LIAM O'DONNELL
Macalester College	MACALESTER COLLEGE
Admissions Office	ADMISSIONS OFFICE
1600 N. Grand Ave.	1600 N GRAND AVE
St. Paul, MN 55105-1801	ST PAUL MN 55105-1801

Follow U.S. Postal Service guidelines.

The official United States Postal Service guidelines are available at any post office or online at www.usps.org.

- Capitalize everything in the address and leave out commas and periods.
- Use the list of common state and street abbreviations found in the *National ZIP Code Directory* or on page **660** of this book.
- Use numbers rather than words for numbered streets (for example, 42ND AVE or 9TH AVE NW).
- If you know the ZIP + 4 code, use it.

Writing Guidelines ▪ Résumé

The purpose of a résumé is to interest an employer so he or she will call you for an interview. Instead of simply telling about yourself in a letter, use a special résumé format to highlight your skills, knowledge, work experience, and education, especially as they relate to the position for which you're applying. Prepare a basic version of your résumé. Then, depending upon the requirements of each position, customize your objective and your abilities to match the employer's expectations.

Prewriting

- **Think about your abilities,** experiences, and accomplishments.
- **Gather details** that will create a complete picture of you. Include classes or training taken outside of school, achievements, and other experience such as volunteer work, club duties, and so on.

Writing

- **Use a traditional résumé format** and organize the information into these parts:
  - Personal contact information
  - Objective
  - Qualifications
  - Specific work experience
  - Education
  - References (Be sure to get permission from each person you wish to use as a reference. It's a good idea to let them know each time you apply for a job so they will be prepared for a phone call.)

Revising

- **Improve your writing** by asking yourself these questions: *Have I included specific, accurate, and complete information? Have I given the most important information first? Have I used a business-like writing style? Have I used words appropriate to the reader? Have I defined any unfamiliar technical terms?*

Editing

- **Check for errors** in punctuation, mechanics, and grammar.
- **Ask someone else** to look over your résumé as well.

Publishing

- **Use text features** such as boldface, columns, bullets, and white space to make your résumé attractive and readable.

■ Sample Résumé

A strong résumé isn't generic. Here is how one student presented himself in his search for summer employment on a landscaping crew.

> The **beginning** provides contact information and the objective.

> The **middle** lists key details.

> The **ending** notes that references are available.

Delmer Sobodian

250 Lowe Avenue • Sherwood Heights, MI 49065
Phone 517-555-1662   E-mail delsob@themailstop.com

Objective:	Seeking full-time summer employment on a landscaping crew.
Qualifications:	• Experienced with landscaping materials and plants • Team worker • Fast learner • Good physical condition
Experience:	*May–October and winter holiday season 2006* Garcia's Gardens & Gifts Part-time yard worker and cashier. Became familiar with different kinds of plants, trees, and shrubs and their care. *October 2005 – March 2006* Shop A Lot supermarket Part-time stocker and cashier. Often worked with heavy loads.
Education:	Will graduate from Cayman High School in June; plan to attend Tuyo Community College this fall to work on a degree in horticulture. Member of my school's chapter of the National FFA Organization; assisted in yearly sale of native-species plants to raise funds for our chapter.
References:	Available upon request.

Writing Guidelines ▪ Proposal

People write proposals to fix problems, address specific needs, or make improvements. A proposal may be a simple letter suggesting the addition of a new microwave to the lunchroom or a complex report recommending establishment of a company day-care center.

Prewriting

- **Consider your audience** by thinking about who will receive your proposal and what you want that person to understand.
- **Determine your purpose** and jot down what you want your proposal to accomplish. What action are you proposing?
- **Gather details** based on what your reader needs to know in order to make a decision. Gather necessary supporting information.

Writing

- **Prepare a heading** that includes the following information:

    To: The reader's name
    From: Your first and last name
    Date: The month, day, and year
    Subject: A concise summary of the proposal

- **Organize the body** into three parts:

    Beginning: State what you are proposing and why.
    Middle: Provide details such as financial costs and other required resources. Write out key points and information supporting them. Show how the action will benefit the organization.
    Ending: Summarize what actions need to be taken next or what recommendations you are making.

Revising

- **Improve your writing.** Ask yourself these questions: *Is my proposal clear and logical? Is my purpose obvious? Have I provided sufficient information and detail to convince the reader that action is needed? Do I have an effective beginning, middle, and ending? Do I provide information to support my recommendations? Have I used a positive, persuasive tone? Have I explained any unfamiliar terms? Does my proposal read smoothly?*

Editing

- **Check for conventions.** Be sure punctuation, grammar, and mechanics are correct.
- **Prepare a final copy.** Proofread the final copy of your proposal.

Workplace

■ Sample Proposal

Alec Guiterrez works part-time for Roccoco's, a local restaurant. He drafted this proposal to create a Web site for the restaurant.

To: Juliet Barnes

From: Alec Guiterrez

Date: May 22, 2007

Subject: Web site for Roccoco's

The beginning states the rationale.

Rationale:
More and more, people who need information about a place of business turn to the Internet. Without a Web site, a restaurant like Roccoco's is missing out on business. People looking on the Net for a place to eat won't find out about us. People who see our ad in the papers don't have a Web address for more information.

The middle provides important details.

We can boost our credibility—and our business—with a Web site that I am willing to create. The restaurant's financial outlay will be minimal. I ask only that you pay me my normal wage for the time I spend on it. Other than that expense, there will be an annual charge for a domain name and a monthly charge for an Internet service provider to host the site. The following are approximate costs:

Initial outlay
Site creation: 8 hours @ $6.75		$54
Domain name registration:		12
		$66 total

Monthly maintenance
Site maintenance: 1.5 hours @ $6.75		$10
ISP hosting:		10
		$20 total

The ending makes recommendations.

Recommendations:
As you can see, this is a very reasonable cost for the benefits. With a presence on the Web, Roccoco's can easily inform customers of our location, highlight specials, and offer coupons.

Ms. Barnes, I am sure this is the right direction for Roccoco's. I designed my own Web site and would like the opportunity to create one for Roccoco's. I am happy to answer any questions you may have.

Writing Guidelines ▪ Memo

Memos are short messages in which you ask and answer questions, describe procedures, give short reports, and remind others about deadlines and meetings. Memos are important to the flow of information within any organization. Many routine memos in schools and workplaces are distributed electronically, with hard copies posted on bulletin boards or sent by interoffice mail.

Prewriting

- **Consider your audience** by thinking about who will receive your memo and why.
- **Determine your purpose** and jot down your reason for writing the memo.
- **Gather necessary details** based on what your reader needs to know.

Writing

- **Prepare the heading** by typing "Memo" and centering it. Use a preprinted memo form or include a heading that contains the following information:

Date:	The month, day, and year
To:	The reader's name
From:	Your first and last name (You may initial it before sending.)
Subject:	The memo's topic in a clear, simple statement

- **Organize the body** into three parts:

Beginning:	State why you are writing the memo.
Middle:	Provide all the necessary details. Consider putting the most important points in a list rather than writing them out.
Ending:	Focus on what happens next—the action or response you would like from the reader or readers.

Revising

- **Improve your writing** by asking yourself these questions related to *ideas, organization, voice, word choice,* and *sentence fluency: Is my topic clear? Is my purpose obvious? Do I have an effective beginning, middle, and ending? Have I used a positive, friendly tone? Have I explained any unfamiliar terms? Does my memo read smoothly?*

Editing

- **Check for conventions.** Correct any errors in punctuation, grammar, and mechanics.
- **Prepare a final copy** of your memo and proofread it before distributing it.

■ Sample Workplace Memo

Ben Braun, an assistant to the personnel director, typed up this memo about the company's monthly staff improvement meetings.

The **heading** identifies the date, recipients, sender, and subject.

The **beginning** states why you are writing.

The **middle** shares the necessary details.

The **ending** makes a call for action.

Memo

Date: October 22, 2007

To: Inter-Tech Staff

From: Ben Braun, Assistant to the Personnel Director

Subject: New Technology

Our next staff meeting will be held on Thursday, November 8, at 9:00 a.m. in the new training center.

The guest at that meeting will be Dr. G. F. Hollis, a professor at City Technical College. She will speak on the latest technology and how we can expect it to affect us and our work.

Dr. Hollis is planning a winter-term training program that will cover all facets of office technology and communication. Those attending the meeting will receive additional information on the program.

Please sign up with me before the end of the day on Tuesday, November 6, if you plan to attend the meeting.

Try It!

Draft a memo to a group of which you are a member. Follow the guidelines on the previous page and the model above.

Writing Guidelines ▪ E-Mail Message

Electronic mail is a fast, convenient way to communicate in the workplace. It saves paper and allows many people to share information simultaneously. Increasingly, e-mail is used not only within the office, but also to communicate with customers and business partners.

Prewriting

- **Consider your audience** and your purpose for sending the message.
- **Gather details** based on what the reader needs to know.

Writing

- **Organize the body** into three parts:

  Beginning: Complete your e-mail header, making sure your subject line is clear. Expand on the subject in the first sentences of your message. Get right to the point.

  Middle: Supply all the details of your message while keeping your paragraphs short. Double-space between paragraphs. Try to limit your message to one or two screens and use numbers, lists, and headings to organize your thoughts.

  Ending: Let your reader know what follow-up action is needed and when; then end politely.

Revising

- **Improve your writing** by asking yourself these questions: *Is my message accurate, complete, and clear? Do I have an effective beginning, middle, and ending? Is my tone appropriate for the topic and the reader?*
- **Improve your style.** Ask yourself these questions related to *word choice* and *sentence fluency*: *Have I used clear, everyday language? Does my message read smoothly?*

Editing

- **Check for conventions.** Correct any errors in grammar, punctuation, and mechanics before sending your e-mail.

Tip

- Never use all capital letters in an e-mail message; people feel you are shouting at them.
- Follow grammar conventions.
- Proofread. Because e-mail is so fast, it's easy to dash off a message and overlook a typo or a missing word.

■ Sample E-Mail Message

Following an unpleasant experience at a local automobile dealership, Emiko Tikaram decided to contact the manufacturer directly to voice her concerns. She copied the general manager of the dealership, as well.

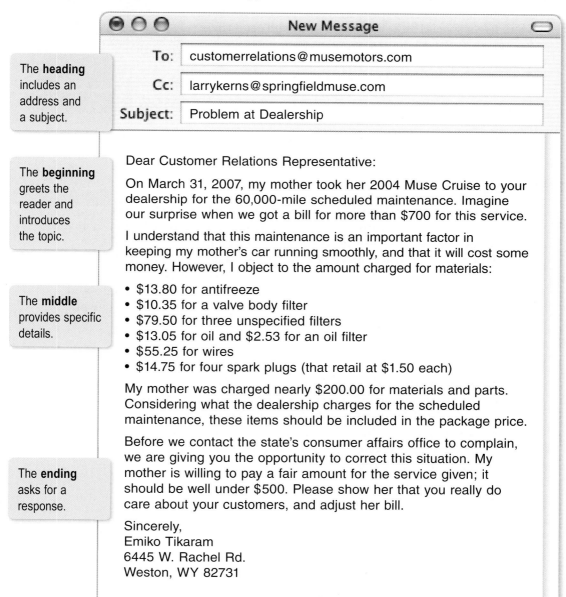

The **heading** includes an address and a subject.

New Message

To: customerrelations@musemotors.com

Cc: larrykerns@springfieldmuse.com

Subject: Problem at Dealership

The **beginning** greets the reader and introduces the topic.

Dear Customer Relations Representative:

On March 31, 2007, my mother took her 2004 Muse Cruise to your dealership for the 60,000-mile scheduled maintenance. Imagine our surprise when we got a bill for more than $700 for this service.

I understand that this maintenance is an important factor in keeping my mother's car running smoothly, and that it will cost some money. However, I object to the amount charged for materials:

The **middle** provides specific details.

- $13.80 for antifreeze
- $10.35 for a valve body filter
- $79.50 for three unspecified filters
- $13.05 for oil and $2.53 for an oil filter
- $55.25 for wires
- $14.75 for four spark plugs (that retail at $1.50 each)

My mother was charged nearly $200.00 for materials and parts. Considering what the dealership charges for the scheduled maintenance, these items should be included in the package price.

The **ending** asks for a response.

Before we contact the state's consumer affairs office to complain, we are giving you the opportunity to correct this situation. My mother is willing to pay a fair amount for the service given; it should be well under $500. Please show her that you really do care about your customers, and adjust her bill.

Sincerely,
Emiko Tikaram
6445 W. Rachel Rd.
Weston, WY 82731

Writing Guidelines ▪ News Release

A business may want to provide information to potential clients and an organization may want to inform the general public. Because it isn't practical to send out hundreds of personal letters, public-relations writers use a special news release format and send their information to the media (radio, television, newspapers, or business magazines). The media, in turn, publish the information for their readers or listeners.

Prewriting

- **Collect the facts** you wish to communicate—who, what, where, when, why, and how. You may also collect quotations and testimonials.

Writing

- **Organize your details** from the most important to the least important so the initial reader can quickly determine whether or not to include your release in the next publication.
- **Write in a simple, business-like style,** using short to medium-length sentences, active voice, and appropriate words.
- **Follow a traditional news release format** including the date and your contact information. A magazine or newspaper editor may want more information before writing a story.

Revising

- **Improve your writing** by asking yourself these questions about *ideas, organization, voice,* and *word choice*: *Have I included specific, accurate, and complete facts? Are they organized from most important to least important? Have I followed a conventional press release format? Do I sound professional and knowledgeable? Have I defined any technical or unfamiliar terms?*

Editing

- **Check for conventions.** Correct any errors in punctuation, mechanics, and grammar.

Publishing

- **Prepare a final copy** for distribution using your company or school letterhead. Proofread carefully before you send it.

■ Sample News Release

Andy Frick prepared this news release to inform area readers and listeners of his high school's spring jazz concert featuring a special guest.

The **heading** identifies key information.

Orleans High School
4500 East Field Drive • Hunt, NV 89035
(705) 555-8876   Fax (705) 555-8880

For Immediate Release   Contact:
February 24, 2007   Andy Frick, (705) 555-2560

The **beginning** identifies the topic.

HUNT, NV—Orleans High School presents its annual spring jazz concert on March 17 with a special guest appearance by renowned recording artist Lucy Kane. The concert at the school's auditorium, 4500 East Field Drive, will also feature the Voices of Jazz choral group and the Orleans Jazz Band. The theme of the concert will be "Fresh as a Spring Daisy."

The **middle** provides additional details.

Saxophonist Lucy Kane has performed nationally as a solo artist and as a member of several jazz ensembles for nine years. She states, "Whenever I am approached to perform at a high school, I make a special effort to appear. It's so important for students to see what a career in music can be."

Art Rankin, head of the music department at Orleans, says, "We were thrilled when Ms. Kane indicated she was available. Jazz fans throughout the region always enjoy her shows."

The **ending** gives purchasing information.

Tickets for the concert are available at the school; ticket prices are $10.00 in advance and $12.00 the day of the show. Proceeds will go toward the Orleans High School music department's efforts to purchase a new grand piano.

END

The Tools of Learning

Listening and Speaking

Strong listening and speaking skills are the essence of effective communication. As you mature, you probably find these skills gaining importance in your everyday life. Good speaking skills allow you to communicate clearly with teachers, classmates, bosses, and co-workers. Solid listening skills help you understand lectures and take good notes.

The groundwork of learning is listening. It requires you to synthesize a speaker's main ideas and to evaluate and organize information. Speaking is vital, too. With it, you can convey ideas and feelings, explain, argue, persuade, inform, and even entertain. In this chapter, you will learn to improve your listening and speaking skills. As they improve, so will your ability to communicate effectively.

- **Listening in Class**
- **Speaking in Class**
- **A Closer Look at Listening and Speaking**

"I like to listen. I have learned a great deal from listening carefully. Most people never listen."

—Ernest Hemingway

Listening in Class

To listen well, you need to go beyond just "hearing" what a speaker says. Listening takes practice and effort. These tips will help you become a better listener.

- **Know why you're listening.** What is the speaker's message? Will there be an exam? Are you being asked to complete an assignment?
- **Listen for facts.** The 5W and H questions—*who? what? when? where? why?* and *how?*—will help you identify the most important information.
- **Take notes.** As you hear important information, write it in your notebook. Also write down questions and comments in the margins. Review and complete your notes as soon after class as possible.
- **Put the speaker's ideas into your own words.** Paraphrase the speaker's key points when you take notes. Add your own comments.

Try It!

Practice your listening skills by taking notes in class or while viewing a documentary on television. Put the speaker's ideas into your own words. Use the margins in your notebook to add your questions and comments.

Multiple Intelligences

- Theory created by Harvard Prof. Howard Gardner
- A person's intelligence is made up of multiple <u>faculties</u> that can work alone or together.
- Faculties= inherent powers & abilities.
- Gardner's 8 Faculties (a.k.a. "Intelligences"): Musical, Bodily-Kinesthetic, Logical-Mathematical, Linguistic, Spatial, Interpersonal, Intrapersonal, Naturalist.
- They provide 8 different pathways to teaching and learning.

Are there more faculties than just these 8?

Does everyone have all 8 faculties?

See handout for definitions and examples of faculties.

Speaking in Class

Speaking in a group discussion is an important skill to master. A meaningful discussion depends on cooperation. These basic strategies will help you and your classmates become better speakers.

Before You Speak . . .

- **Listen** carefully and take notes.
- **Think** about what others are saying.
- **Wait** until it's your turn to speak.
- **Plan** how you can add something positive to the discussion.

As You Speak . . .

- **Use a loud, clear voice.**
- **Avoid repeating** what's already been said.
- **Support your ideas** with examples, facts, or anecdotes.
- **Maintain eye contact** with others in the group or class.

Tip

- Focus your comments on ideas, not on personalities.
- Ask meaningful questions.
- When necessary, summarize specific ideas brought up in the discussion.
- Mention another person's comments and expand on them constructively.

Try It!

Exercise your group discussion skills by taking part in the following "panel discussion" activity.

1. As a class, brainstorm discussion topics from current events or as directed by your teacher. Make a list of the topics.
2. Divide into groups (panels) of four or five. Each panel chooses one topic from the list and takes a turn discussing the topic for 10 to 15 minutes with the class acting as an audience. There is no preparation time; participants should speak spontaneously about the issue.
3. Following each discussion, the audience analyzes the discussion based on the strategies on this page.

A Closer Look at Listening and Speaking

Improving your listening and speaking skills will help you increase your confidence and effectiveness as a communicator. Follow these basic guidelines to carry on productive conversations and discussions.

Good Listeners	Good Speakers
<ul><li>think about what the speaker is saying</li><li>stay focused so that they are prepared to respond thoughtfully</li><li>pay attention to the speaker's tone of voice, gestures, and facial expressions</li><li>interrupt only when necessary to ask questions</li></ul>	<ul><li>speak loudly and clearly</li><li>maintain eye contact with their listeners</li><li>emphasize their main ideas by changing the tone and volume of their voice</li><li>respect their audience by explaining and clarifying information that may be confusing</li><li>use gestures and body language effectively to enhance their message</li></ul>

Try It!

Role-playing is an excellent way to practice listening and speaking skills. Try role-playing using this "read-question-answer" activity.

1. Imagine that you are a well-known author speaking to a group of students. Choose an excerpt from a book or a poem you have written. Read it to the group.
2. Have listeners take notes, jotting down questions and comments about "your" writing and the content of the excerpt.
3. Following the reading, role-play a question-answer session in which listeners ask questions and you answer extemporaneously (unrehearsed).

Taking Notes

Think of the volume of information your brain takes in each day. In this age of technology, information comes at you at a record pace. If you don't jot down the important things, you run the risk of not remembering them at all. This is why good note-taking skills are so important. Notes allow you to sort, organize, and process information.

Active listening and purposeful note taking are critical skills for students to master. Taking good notes can help you learn more efficiently, prepare for exams, and save time. In this chapter, you will learn how to sharpen your note-taking skills while listening to a lecture, reading a text, and attending a meeting.

- **Taking Classroom Notes**
- **Taking Reading Notes**
- **Taking Meeting Minutes**

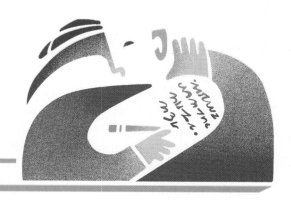

"The pen is the tongue of the mind."

—Miguel de Cervantes

Taking Classroom Notes

Your teacher may give a lecture to explain an important subject, introduce a new topic, or help the class review for a test. The following tips will help you take clear, organized lecture notes.

Guidelines for Class Notes

1. **Write the topic and date at the top of each page.** If you use loose-leaf paper, number each page as well.

2. **Listen carefully.** This is the key to taking good notes. If you are busy writing, you may miss important clues. For example, if a teacher says, "There are five steps you need to follow," listen for the five steps. Also listen for key words such as *first, second, next,* or *most importantly.*

3. **Use your own words.** You can't write down everything your teacher says. Instead, try to put the main points into your own words. You can fill in the details later.

4. **Begin taking notes right away** or you may miss something important. It's hard to catch up while taking notes.

5. **Write quickly, but neatly.** Your notes won't be helpful if you can't read them.

6. **Condense information.**
   - Use lists, phrases, and abbreviations *(p=page, ex=for example).*
   - Skip the small, unnecessary words, such as articles *(a, an, the).*
   - Shorten some words *(intro* for *introduction, chap* for *chapter).*
   - Use numbers and symbols *(1st, 2nd, +, =).*
   - Develop a personal shorthand *(w=with, w/o=without).*

7. **Draw sketches and diagrams** to explain a concept quickly.

8. **Copy important information** your teacher writes on the board.

9. **Ask your teacher** to explain something you don't understand, to repeat something, or to please slow down.

 Try It!

Review some of your recent class notes while thinking of the guidelines above. How could you improve your note-taking skills? Explain.

Set up your notes.

Keep your notes in a notebook, preferably one for each subject. You can also take notes on loose-leaf paper kept in a three-ring binder, which lets you add and remove pages as needed. Write only on one side of the paper. This makes it easier to read and find portions of your notes.

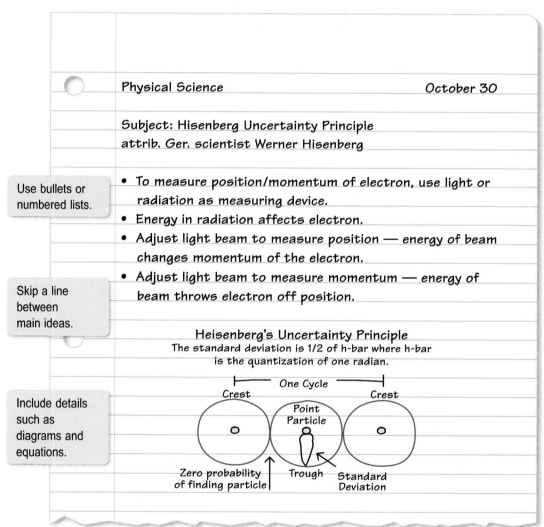

Physical Science   October 30

Subject: Hisenberg Uncertainty Principle
attrib. Ger. scientist Werner Hisenberg

Use bullets or numbered lists.

- To measure position/momentum of electron, use light or radiation as measuring device.
- Energy in radiation affects electron.
- Adjust light beam to measure position — energy of beam changes momentum of the electron.
- Adjust light beam to measure momentum — energy of beam throws electron off position.

Skip a line between main ideas.

Heisenberg's Uncertainty Principle
The standard deviation is 1/2 of h-bar where h-bar is the quantization of one radian.

Include details such as diagrams and equations.

One Cycle
Crest   Crest
Point Particle
Zero probability of finding particle   Trough   Standard Deviation

FYI

Note taking helps you listen better in class, organize your ideas more effectively, and remember more of what you hear.

Review your notes.

As you read over your notes, do the following:

1. **Circle and correct spelling errors.**
2. **Underline unfamiliar terms.** Look them up in a dictionary or glossary and write the words and their meanings in the margin.
3. **Write your questions in the margin.** Look for answers on your own first, ask a teacher or classmate for help next, then jot down answers.
4. **Use a highlighter to mark the most important notes,** a different-colored pen to circle or underline key ideas.
5. **Rewrite your notes.** Take this chance to learn the material.
6. **Review your notes.** Look over your notes before the next class, especially if you are having a test or class discussion.

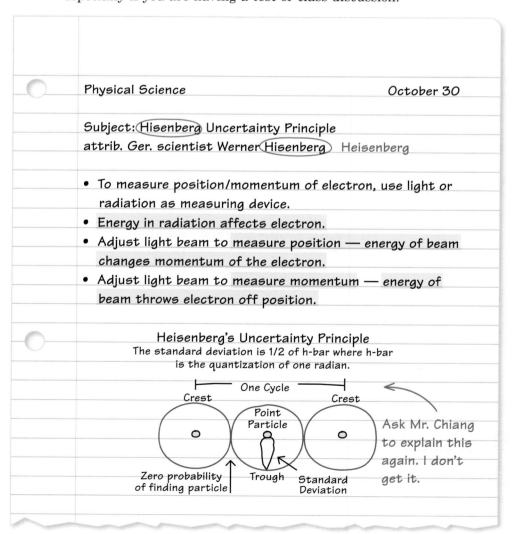

Physical Science   October 30

Subject: (Hisenberg) Uncertainty Principle
attrib. Ger. scientist Werner (Hisenberg) Heisenberg

- To measure position/momentum of electron, use light or radiation as measuring device.
- Energy in radiation affects electron.
- Adjust light beam to measure position — energy of beam changes momentum of the electron.
- Adjust light beam to measure momentum — energy of beam throws electron off position.

Heisenberg's Uncertainty Principle
The standard deviation is 1/2 of h-bar where h-bar
is the quantization of one radian.

|—— One Cycle ——|
Crest   Crest

Point
Particle

Ask Mr. Chiang
to explain this
again. I don't
get it.

Zero probability   Trough
of finding particle   Standard
                            Deviation

Taking Reading Notes

Taking notes while you read an assignment is easier than taking notes during a lecture. You can stop to write at any time, which means you can write more neatly and carefully. Here are some tips for taking reading notes.

Guidelines for Reading Notes

1. **Preview the assignment.** Look through your assignment to see what your reading is about. Look at the title, introduction, headings, and chapter summary. Also look at any pictures, maps, or graphics. (See page **95**.)

2. **Quickly read the entire assignment** once before taking notes. This gives you an overview of the material and allows you to pick out the main ideas.

3. **Take notes while reading a second time.** Read the material slowly, taking notes as you go along. Stop at new ideas or words.

   - **Write down the important information.**

   - **Put notes in your own words.** Don't just copy passages from the book. You learn more when you rewrite ideas in your words. (See pages **543–550** for more information on summaries and paraphrases.)

   - **Use headings or subtitles.** Headings and subtitles help to organize your notes. Write down the important information under each heading or subtitle.

   - **Include notes about pictures, charts, and illustrations.** You can also make quick sketches of these visual elements.

   - **Use graphic organizers.** (See pages **64–65**.)

   - **List and define any new words.** Look up each word in the glossary or in a dictionary. Write down the appropriate meaning in your notes. Also write down the number of the page where the word is located. This way you can easily find it again.

4. **Learn more.** See "Critical Reading" on pages **533–542** for more information on taking reading notes.

Try It!

For your next reading assignment, take notes using the tips above.

Taking Meeting Minutes

Recording the minutes of a meeting is another form of note taking. Minutes must be well organized and include everything from who is present to what is discussed and decided. Always report minutes in an objective (impersonal) voice. To record minutes during a meeting, you must listen carefully and write down information accurately. The following guidelines will help.

Guidelines for Taking Minutes

- Begin with the organization's name, the date, location, and topic of the meeting.

- Record what time the meeting begins.

- List those present (or absent). Indicate who led the meeting and who recorded the minutes.

- Note "old business" (from a previous meeting) that is discussed or resolved.

- Note "new business" (plans or decisions to be handled in the current meeting).

- Record any votes taken and their results.

- Record when the meeting is adjourned.

Longview High School Spanish Club Minutes
> **Date:** January 26, 2006
> **Location:** Room 221 (Señor Ares, Faculty Advisor)
> **Topic:** Spring Trip
> **Meeting Time:** 2:15 P.M.–3:15 P.M.

Attending
Aslea Barron, Mary Canady, Chad Cooling, Megan Dilley (chair), Sheree Hewerdine, Raina Hawkins (recording), Tom Garcia

Absent
Taresha Young

Old Business
Mr. Machado, president and CEO of CityCorp Printing, visited our club last Monday. We gave him a plaque to thank his company for funding our spring trip to Mexico.

Señor Ares reported that all travel arrangements have been made. He announced that we will visit Mexico City, Taxco, and Acapulco.

A meeting for Spanish Club members and their parents was scheduled for February 9, 2006, at 7:00 PM in the school cafeteria.

New Business
At our next meeting on February 2, Tom will share his research about Mexico's City Museo Nacional de Antropologia.

At the February 9 meeting, Ruth Phillips, RN, will speak to students and parents about health requirements for the trip.

All signed permission slips must be returned to Señor Ares by February 15. We will take a field trip on March 6 to have our passport photos taken.

Tip

When you take minutes to tell what was discussed and decided upon by a group, record only the main points, not all the details. Be sure to accurately record any votes or official action taken.

Critical Reading

Many assignments require you to understand and interpret printed material and apply what you read. This is called *critical reading*. It means looking beyond the actual words to examine, question, and test the content. Successful critical reading enhances clarity and comprehension, allowing you to better understand the writer's message.

Critical reading requires several important steps. These include *surveying* an assigned reading, *questioning* what you read, *taking notes* about the text, and *reviewing* what you've read. In this chapter, you will learn to read critically to gain a clearer understanding of your reading assignments, as well as any reading that you must do on tests.

- **Critical Reading: SQ3R**
- **Before You Read**
- **As You Read**
- **After You Read**
- **Reading Fiction**
- **Reading Poetry**

"Reading is to the mind what exercise is to the body. It is wholesome and bracing for the mind to have its faculties kept on the stretch."

—August Hare

Critical Reading: SQ3R

An effective reading technique for all types of nonfiction is the SQ3R method. SQ3R stands for the five steps in this reading process: *survey, question, read, recite,* and *review.* These five steps are explained below and on the following pages.

Before You Read . . .

- **Survey** Preview the reading assignment for its general content. Begin by reading the first and last paragraphs. Then read titles, subtitles, headings, and subheadings to see what is being covered. Take note of illustrations and any terms in bold or italic type.

- **Question** Ask yourself what you already know about the topic of the reading. Write down questions you still need answered. To get started, you could turn the text's titles, subtitles, headings, and subheadings into questions. Asking questions keeps you actively involved while reading.

As You Read . . .

- **Read** Read slowly and carefully. Look for the main idea in each paragraph, section, or chapter. Try to answer questions you have already identified. At different points, also ask these questions: *What does this mean? How does it connect with previous material? What will come next?* Take notes as you go along. Take the time to read difficult parts slowly. Reread them if necessary.

- **Recite** Test your comprehension of the material by summarizing the main points out loud. Summarizing (reciting) in this way is one of the most valuable parts of SQ3R. After you read a page, section, or chapter, try to answer the 5 W and H questions (*who? what? where? when? why?* and *how?*) about that part. Reread any parts as needed.

After You Read . . .

- **Review** Assess your knowledge by reviewing your notes. See how well you understand the entire reading assignment. Ask yourself these questions: *Have all my questions been answered? Can I summarize each main section? Can I summarize or outline the whole assignment?* Consider outlining the material (or using another type of graphic organizer) to help you remember what you have read.

Note: Critical reading means looking beyond surface details and thinking carefully about the information that is presented.

Before You Read

Try to get the big picture of each assignment as you begin to read. The tips that follow will help you get started.

Survey the reading.

To begin, survey the text for a general understanding of the main points.

- **Scan** chapter titles, subtitles, headings, and boldfaced type.
- **Identify the purpose of the material:** to inform, to persuade, to entertain.
- **Read** the first and last paragraphs.
- **List** the topic and the main points as best you can.

Sample Survey Notes

Below, Samantha surveys the beginning of an article about "senior slump." She writes her notes on a copy of the article.

Are You Suffering from Senior Slump?

You've made it to your senior year, and your plans for next year are in place. Now you can just relax and coast. If you believe this, you may be suffering from "senior slump"—a belief that your education is nearly over and you can relax. Many high school seniors suffer from this condition and pay a high price.

Senior slump can be harmful because the final months before graduation can impact your future. If a college has accepted you, it can request and review your grades at any time during your senior year. If your grades slip, you may be asked to explain why. Poor grades in your senior year can mean entering college on probation, or not entering at all.

Another symptom of senior slump is loading up on electives instead of taking challenging honors classes. Whether your plans include college, work, or the military, much is expected of a high school graduate. If you slack off, it will probably come back to haunt you.

While a senior slump is inadvisable, so is crashing and burning. Try to balance your senior year. Challenge yourself to keep your grades up, spend quiet periods planning for next year, and find some time to relax and have fun.

Purpose:
To inform

Topic:
Senior slump

Key Points:
- Seniors can fall into a slump.
- Grades may drop, so don't slack off.
- Poor grades can keep you from getting into college or force you to enter on probation.
- Taking easy courses won't prepare you for the future.
- Balance is the key.

Question the material.

After you have surveyed the entire text, ask questions about the reading. Use the following guidelines:

- **List what you already know about the topic.**
- **List questions that you still want answered.** Also ask the 5 W and H questions.
- **Turn headings and main points into questions.** For example, you may reword a chapter titled "Defining and Pursuing a Liberal Education" into *"What is a liberal education? Do I want to pursue a liberal education?"*

Below, Samantha formed questions about the main points of the sample article. Next to her questions she noted things she already knew about the topic.

Already know:

1. Am I in a senior slump?
2. Will the college penalize me if my grades slip from A's to B's?
3. When is it all right to choose some fun electives?
4. How can I keep myself challenged?
5. What can I do to balance my senior year?
6. Whom can I talk to about the way I feel?

Senior slump can lead to poor grades.

It can affect my college acceptance and my performance during freshman year.

I need to keep my brain in shape.

Balancing learning and relaxation is key.

Try It!

Choose a reading assignment you've been given recently. Survey the text and write down any questions you have about the material.

As You Read

Once you have surveyed the assignment and formed questions about it, you are ready to read carefully. Try to turn your reading into a conversation with the text. Respect what the writer has to say, even as you question certain parts, and stay open to the unexpected.

Read (and take notes).

Always have a goal in mind when you read. Follow these guidelines as you read the material and answer the questions you listed.

- **Read slowly** so that you don't miss anything.
- **Reread parts** that seem challenging.
- **Write down key concepts.** (These are often in bold.)
- **Define key concepts** using context or a dictionary.
- **Record any additional questions** you may have.
- **Keep the following questions in mind** as you read: *What does this mean? How does it connect with what I already know about the topic? What will probably come next?*

Try It!

Read your chosen assignment critically. Take careful notes as you go along, using the guidelines above.

Recite material out loud.

After you complete the entire reading, it's time to reinforce what you have learned. Repeating information out loud is an effective way to evaluate how well you understand it. Use the following guidelines:

- **Recite the key points** without looking at your notes.
- **Answer the 5 W and H questions** *(Who? What? Where? When? Why? and How?)* about the material.
- **Ask (and answer) your other questions** about the topic.
- **Identify any new questions** that occur to you.

Try It!

Recite what you have learned from your reading assignment. Use the guidelines above to help you complete this step.

After You Read

Having completed the first four steps in the SQ3R method, you should review the reading. Reviewing will help you see how well you understand the material.

Review the material.

A final review of your reading will make the information part of your own thinking. Use the following guidelines:

- **Go over your notes** one section at a time.
- **Keep searching for answers** if you have any unanswered questions.
- **Ask for help** if you cannot figure something out on your own.
- **Add illustrations or graphic organizers** to your notes to make complex ideas clearer.
- **Summarize the reading** at the end of your notes.

In the example below, Samantha wrote a summary paragraph for the article about senior slump. She also wrote some final thoughts about the material in the margin.

Sample Summary

"Are You Suffering from Senior Slump?"—Summary

This article defines "senior slump" as the belief that your education is nearly over so you can relax. The symptoms of senior slump are letting your grades slip and not challenging your mind. The cure is a balanced senior year that includes equal parts learning, thinking, and relaxation.

I need more information about senior slump and what to do about it.

I know that I'm not taking my senior year seriously.

This article made me aware that I need to make some changes.

Try It!

Review your reading assignment. Go over your notes and summarize the assignment. Be sure to include the main ideas and write any final thoughts in the margin.

Reading Fiction

Fiction uses imagined characters and events to reveal what is very often authentic or true about real life. This makes fiction a notable way to learn. Here are some tips for reading fiction.

Before You Read . . .

- **Learn something about the author** and his or her other works.
- **React thoughtfully** to the title and opening pages.

As You Read . . .

- **Identify** the following story elements: *setting, tone, main characters, central conflict,* and *theme.*
- **Predict** what will happen next.
- **Write** your reactions to the short story or novel in a reading journal as you go along.
- **Think** about the characters and what they do. *What motivates the characters? Have you encountered people similar to these characters? Have you faced situations similar to the ones faced by the main characters? Would you have reacted in the same way?*
- **Consider** how the author's life may have influenced the story.
- **Notice** the author's style and word choice. *How effectively has the author used literary devices? Did the author use particular words or phrases to suit a certain audience?*
- **Discuss** the story with others who are reading it.

After You Read . . .

- **Consider** how the main character changes during the course of the story. Often, this is the key to understanding a work of fiction.
- **Determine** the story's main message or theme; then decide how effectively this message is communicated.

Try It!

Use the information above as a guide to help you better understand and enjoy the next short story or novel you read.

React to fiction.

The excerpt below is from Mary Shelley's classic novel *Frankenstein*. The margin notes reveal one student's reactions, which he wrote on a photocopy of the story. He makes observations, asks questions, and attempts to define a confusing term.

I'm not sure what "Prometheus" means. The best definition I found is "a Titan who stole fire from Olympus and gave it to mankind."

Why did he hold back and not destroy the cottage and its people?

Great descriptive writing

I feel sorry for the monster. The anger he feels toward his creator and all mankind comes through the strongest in this paragraph.

Frankenstein, or *The Modern* Prometheus
by Mary Wollstonecraft (Godwin) Shelley

Cursed, cursed creator! Why did I live? Why, in that instant, did I not extinguish the spark of existence which you had so wantonly bestowed? I know not; despair had not yet taken possession of me; my feelings were those of rage and revenge. I could with pleasure have destroyed the cottage and its inhabitants and have glutted myself with their shrieks and misery.

When night came I quitted my retreat and wandered in the wood; and now, no longer restrained by the fear of discovery, I gave vent to my anguish in fearful howlings. I was like a wild beast that had broken the toils, destroying the objects that obstructed me and ranging through the wood with a stag-like swiftness. Oh! What a miserable night I passed! The cold stars shone in mockery, and the bare trees waved their branches above me; now and then the sweet voice of a bird burst forth amidst the universal stillness. All, save I, were at rest or in enjoyment; I, like the arch-fiend, bore a hell within me, and finding myself unsympathized with, wished to tear up the trees, spread havoc and destruction around me, and then to have sat down and enjoyed the ruin.

But this was a luxury of sensation that could not endure; I became fatigued with excess of bodily exertion and sank on the damp grass in the sick impotence of despair. There was none among the myriads of men that existed who would pity or assist me; and should I feel kindness towards my enemies? No; from that moment I declared everlasting war against the species, and more than all, against him who had formed me and sent me forth to this insupportable misery.

The sun rose; I heard the voices of men and knew that it was impossible to return to my retreat during that day. Accordingly I hid myself in some thick underwood, determining to devote the ensuing hours to reflection on my situation.

Reading Poetry

You may not understand a poem completely in one reading, especially if it is lengthy or complex. In fact, each time you read a poem, you will probably discover something new about it. Reacting to poetry in a reading journal will help you to appreciate it more. Here are some strategies for reading poetry.

First Reading

- **Read the poem** at your normal reading speed to gain an overall first impression.
- **Jot down brief notes** about your immediate reaction to the poem.

Second Reading

- **Read the poem again**—out loud, if possible. Pay attention to the sound of the poem.
- **Note examples of sound devices** in the poem—alliteration, assonance, rhyme (see pages **368–369**). Finding a poem's phrasing and rhythm can help you discover its meaning.
- **Observe** the punctuation, spacing, and special treatment of words and lines.
- **Think** about the theme of the poem.

Third Reading

- **Identify** the type of poem you're reading. Does this poem follow the usual pattern of that particular type? If not, why not?
- **Determine** the literal sense or meaning of the poem. What is the poem about? What does it seem to say about its topic?
- **Look** for figurative language in the poem. How does this language— metaphors, similes, personification, symbols—support or add to the meaning of the poem? (See pages **600–601** and **368–369**.)

Try It!

Use the strategies above the next time you read a poem, especially one you need to write about as an assignment.

React to poetry.

"Sonnet 18" is a poem by William Shakespeare. The notes on the copy of the poem below show one student's reaction to it. The student makes observations, asks questions, reacts to word choice, and so forth. Whenever you read a challenging poem, try to react to it in several different ways.

Sonnet 18
by William Shakespeare

Theme:
the stability
of love

Shall I compare thee to a summer's day?
Thou art more lovely and more temperate:
Rough winds do shake the darling buds of May,
And summer's lease hath all too short a date:

This is an English sonnet:
14 lines
3 quatrains
1 final rhyming couplet

Everything changes. Summer always comes to an end.

Sometime too hot the eye of heaven shines,
And often is his gold complexion dimm'd;
And every fair from fair sometime declines,
By chance, or nature's changing course untrimm'd;

But thy eternal summer shall not fade,
Nor lose possession of that fair thou ow'st;
Nor shall Death brag thou wander'st in his shade,
When in eternal lines to time thou grow'st:

The last quatrain and couplet mean that, unlike summer, this person's beauty won't fade. It lives on because of this sonnet.

I wonder what this poem would sound like written in modern language?

So long as men can breathe, or eyes can see,
So long lives this, and this gives life to thee.

Try It!

Write freely for 5 to 10 minutes when you finish reading a poem. Include any thoughts or feelings you have about the poem. Relate it to other poems you have read.

Summarizing and Paraphrasing

Summarizing and paraphrasing are useful writing techniques. Using your own words to reduce and restate another writer's thoughts forces you to pull out the essentials from the reading—the main points, the key details, or the thread of the argument. It also stretches your ability to comprehend, analyze, and synthesize information—all important thinking skills.

Reports, term papers, and other types of academic writing often require you to summarize and paraphrase. As you apply these important writing skills, you will find that they help you to understand even the most challenging reading material. In this chapter, you will read examples of both kinds of writing and have an opportunity to practice writing your own summaries and paraphrases.

- **Sample Article and Summary**
- **Guidelines for Summarizing**
- **Strategies for Paraphrasing**
- **Sample Paragraphs and Paraphrases**
- **Paraphrasing a Paragraph**

"The most valuable of all talents is that of never using two words when one will do."

—Thomas Jefferson

Sample Article and Summary

The following article is about the counterculture movement in the United States that took place in the 1960s.

The Antiwar Movement—Counterculture of the '60s

"All we are asking is give peace a chance." This mantra was chanted and sung in countless antiwar rallies in the 1960s. In a nation divided by the Vietnam War, thousands of American youth protested the war through rallies, demonstrations, and concerts for peace. They were soundly opposed to the conflict in southeast Asia, and the strength of their conviction created a rising counterculture in the United States.

This new culture rebelled against the traditional values of middle-class society. It exhibited its rebellion through long hair, rock music, and peaceful resistance. "Hippies" and "flower children" formed a community in the Haight-Ashbury neighborhood in San Francisco. Fed up with what they called "the establishment," they adopted the slogan "turn on, tune in, and drop out."

In the 1960s, young adults in the United States were more outspoken than at any other time in the nation's history. They took their protests to college campuses in major U.S. cities. They demonstrated at the Capitol in Washington, D.C., and near the White House. They gathered in San Francisco, with numbers exceeding fifty thousand, to participate in what they called the "Summer of Love," urging peace and nonconformity.

Before long, radical counterculture subgroups formed across the country. These groups planned and participated in more and more demonstrations in protest to the war, the bombing of Cambodia, and the draft. Their politics were described as the "new left," and it was common for police, and even the National Guard, to break up their demonstrations using riot gear and tear gas.

Peaceful protests against the war declined as more overt civil disobedience entered into the picture in an attempt to gain national attention. The counterculture movement of the sixties had fallen victim to more violence in its resolution for peace.

Sample Summary

The following is a student summary of the preceding article. Pay close attention to the three main points: the topic sentence, the body, and the closing sentence. (See side notes.)

The **topic sentence** expresses the main idea.

Each sentence in the **body** summarizes one or even two paragraphs from the article.

The **closing sentence** shares the article's concluding thoughts.

The Antiwar Movement—Counterculture of the '60s

In the 1960s, thousands of youth in the United States protested the Vietnam War. They formed a counterculture that rebelled against the war and traditional middle-class values. Their protests included peaceful demonstrations on college campuses and at the Capitol and the White House in Washington, D.C. Later, radical subgroups formed and engaged in more demonstrative protests as a way to get attention. Police often used riot gear and tear gas to break up the demonstrations. Ironically, the counterculture movement of the 1960s had turned more violent in its quest for peace.

Respond to the reading. Answer the following questions.

Ideas (1) What details from the original article are included in the summary? (2) What kinds of details are not included?

Organization (3) How is the summary paragraph organized?

Voice & Word Choice (4) Compare the first sentence of the summary with the first paragraph of the original. Which is simpler? Which offers more detail?

Guidelines for Summarizing

Follow these guidelines whenever you are asked to write a summary.

Prewriting

- **Select an article on a topic that interests you** or relates to a subject you are currently studying. Make a photocopy of the article if possible.
- **Read the article once,** quickly. Then read it again, underlining passages (if working with a photocopy) or taking notes on the key details.
- **Think about the article.** Identify and write down the main idea. For example, here is the main idea of the sample article:

   In the 1960s, youth in the United States shaped a counterculture in response to the Vietnam War.

Writing

- **Write a topic sentence** that states the main idea of the article.
- **Write body sentences** that communicate the most important ideas of the article in your own words.
- **Conclude** by reminding your reader of the main point of the article. (Remember: A summary should not contain your personal opinions.)

Revising **and** Editing

Read and revise your summary and make necessary changes. Also edit for conventions. Ask yourself the following questions:

Ideas	*Do I correctly identify the article's main idea in my topic sentence? Do my body sentences contain only the most important details from the article?*
Organization	*Are the ideas in my paragraph arranged in the same order as the original article?*
Voice	*Does my voice sound informed and interested?*
Word Choice	*Have I used my own words for the most part? Are there terms that need to be defined?*
Sentence Fluency	*Have I varied sentence structures and lengths?*
Conventions	*Have I eliminated all errors in punctuation, spelling, and grammar?*

Summarizing

Summarize an article.

The following article is about creating content for the Internet.

Content Creators

If you create something of your own and share it on the Internet, you are a content creator. Half of all teens who use the Internet (about 12 million between the ages of 12 and 17) are content creators. They regularly produce Web pages and blogs and post their original artwork, stories, and videos online.

The possibilities for creating digital content have increased dramatically with advancing technology. High-speed Internet connections combined with digital publishing software make it easy to create, remix, and share content. These tools allow teens to manipulate text, images, video, and audio files and share them on Web pages that they create for themselves and others.

Blogs are the most popular way for teens to share content. A blog is a Web log, a kind of Web page that serves as an online journal where thoughts and ideas are exchanged. One in five online teens (about 4 million) has created a personal blog. And thirty-eight percent of all online teens read them. Most teen blog creators are very Internet savvy, and approximately 9 out of 10 report creating content to help adults do something online that the adults could not do themselves.

Web pages and blogs are just the beginning. Technology and teens go hand in hand. Today's teen content creators will be tomorrow's digital inventors. The possibilities for creating and sharing on the Internet are endless.

Try It!

Summarize the article above. Write a summary paragraph about this article, using the guidelines provided on page **546**.

Strategies for Paraphrasing

A paraphrase is a type of summary. It is effective for clarifying or explaining the meaning of an important passage that you would like to use in your research. While a summary is shorter than the original text and condenses the text's meaning, a paraphrase can be longer than the original material. A paraphrase *interprets* the key point of the original. Use the following strategies as a guide when you paraphrase.

Follow a plan: In order to complete an effective paraphrase, you must follow a series of important steps. There are no shortcuts.

- **Review the entire passage.** This will help you identify the main point and purpose of the material.
- **Carefully read the passage.** If necessary, reread parts that seem especially important or challenging.
- **Write your paraphrase.** Be sure your interpretation is clear and complete. For the most part, use your own words. (See below.)
- **Check your paraphrase.** Be sure that you have captured the tone and meaning of the passage.

Use your own words: Avoid the original writer's words as much as possible. Exceptions include key words such as *critical* and *perfection,* or proper nouns such as Arrowhead High School. (See the paraphrases on page **549**.)

- **Consult a dictionary.** Refer to a dictionary to help you think of new ways to express certain terms or ideas.
- **Refer to a thesaurus.** When needed for clarification, use synonyms in place of words in the original text. For example, if the writer is describing a *realm,* a thesaurus will suggest synonyms such as *empire,* and *kingdom.* Pick the synonym that fits the context of the passage.

Capture the original voice: In a paraphrase, you should try to communicate the original writer's opinions and feelings. Read the examples that follow.

> The National Zoo has acquired a rare snow leopard, scheduled to arrive in March. It will be on display in the Big Cats exhibit beginning April 16th.

Original News Report

- **Paraphrase with inappropriate voice:** National Zoo roars into March with the addition of a snow leopard.
- **Paraphrase with proper voice:** In March, the National Zoo will add a rare snow leopard to its Big Cats exhibit.

Sample Paragraphs and Paraphrases

The following expository paragraph discusses the author Edgar Allan Poe.

Poe was a tireless critic of his own work, and both his standards of workmanship and his critical precepts have been of great service to his careless countrymen. He turned out between four and five short stories a year, was poorly paid for them, and indeed found difficulty in selling them at all. Yet he was constantly correcting them for the better. His best poems were likewise his latest. He was tantalized with the desire for artistic perfection. He became the pathbreaker for a long file of men in France, Italy, England, and America. He found the way and they brought back the glory and the cash.

Bliss Perry, *The American Spirit in Literature*

A student shows her understanding of the paragraph.

Poe wrote several stories a year, but he had a hard time selling them. He was paid poorly for the ones that he did sell. Poe was perpetually critical of his own works, and he worked tirelessly toward perfection. His hard work paid off with his last poems, which were his best. Other writers imitated Poe's style, and they were the ones who earned more money and fame.

The following text is part of a sports review in a high school newspaper.

This school year, Phillips Rey High School, located in Phelps, entered District Six in the South-State Interschool Athletic Association, allowing its teams to compete in district and state playoffs. Phillips Rey has been in Eagle Township for more than 50 years, establishing a solid athletic presence. The strength of its girls' basketball team was proven last Wednesday when the team beat our Arrowhead girls' team 48-37. The Arrowhead team easily won first place in last year's SSIAA playoffs, but with Phillips Rey in District Six, our girls will have to fight hard to hang on to the traveling trophy.

A student reflects the writer's enthusiasm in her paraphrase of the review.

This year, Phillips Rey High School joined the District Six South-State Interschool Athletic Association. Phillips Rey's teams will now compete with our Arrowhead High School teams. Phillips Rey has a long history of athletic excellence. Last Wednesday, its girls' basketball team beat our Arrowhead girls' team 48-37. The Arrowhead girls had no problem taking first place in last year's SSIAA playoffs, but to hang on to their traveling trophy, they will have to play hard to beat Phillips Rey.

Paraphrase a paragraph.

Each sample paragraph below has a main idea and a distinct author's voice.

It was plain that unless Lincoln could unite the various classes of the North, his utter failure would be a foregone conclusion. He saw this clearly. His first move was selecting his cabinet. He chose not only from various geographical divisions of the country but also from diverse political divisions of the party. It was not his purpose to have secretaries that would mimic himself, but able and representative men of various political opinions. At the outset, this did not meet with approval. Later, its wisdom was apparent. In the more than 100 years of United States administration history, there has never been an abler or a purer cabinet.

The system of democracy is not unique to the United States. The freedom to choose leaders is an important part of human rights and democracy around the world. It is so important that the U.S. government has made supporting human rights and democracy a major part of its relationships with other countries. The State Department works directly to help countries have free and fair elections. Sometimes the State Department also works with the United Nations to aid the voting process. By supporting democracies around the world, the United States makes the world safer and more prosperous. We are all better off when the world's people have the freedom to make their own choices, to work for a better life, and to live without fear.

On January 29, 1863, General Grant took command of the army intended to operate against Vicksburg, Mississippi, the last place held by the rebels on the Mississippi, and the only point at which they could cross the river and keep up communication with their armies in the southwest. It was the first high ground below Memphis, was very strongly fortified, and was held by a large army under General Pemberton. The complete possession of the Mississippi was essential to the federal government because the control of that great river would cut the Confederacy in two.

Try It!

Using the guidelines on page **548**, paraphrase one of the paragraphs above. Include the main idea and the author's point of view in your own words.

Taking Tests

Tests are a part of school life. They help instructors see how well you understand a subject and where you need more work. Unfortunately, tests are stressful because they are usually connected with grades, and that stress can work against you. However, if you know how to take a test, you can ease that stress, perform better, and give a more accurate picture of your knowledge and understanding.

Taking a test is like any other challenge in life: If you are prepared, you will do well. This chapter will help you understand the different kinds of tests and the best way to prepare for each. Once you understand that tests are not meant to trick you, but rather to evaluate your understanding, you will be better able to prepare for them.

- **Preparing for a Test**
- **Test-Taking Tips**
- **Taking Objective Tests**
- **Taking Essay Tests**
- **Taking Standardized Tests**

"I loved tests because it was another form of competing, a healthy competition."

—Suzanne Farrell

Preparing for a Test

When preparing for a test, you should anticipate its content. Usually, you can expect a test to cover what you've learned in class. Take good notes during lectures and review them often. Also keep your graded assignments so you can look them over later. Following the cycle below will help you improve your test scores.

Test-Prep Cycle

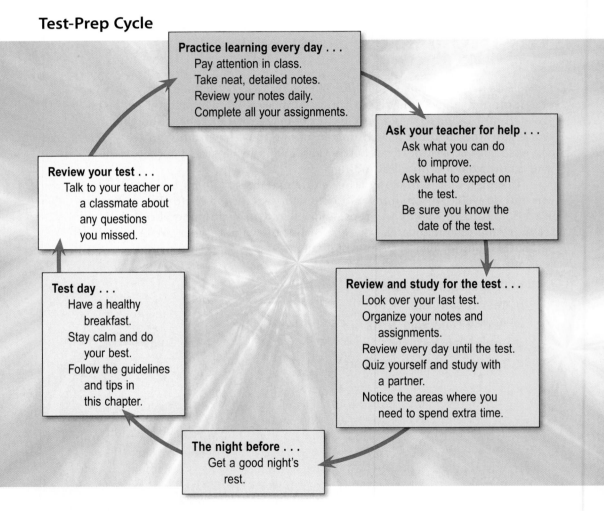

Practice learning every day . . .
Pay attention in class.
Take neat, detailed notes.
Review your notes daily.
Complete all your assignments.

Ask your teacher for help . . .
Ask what you can do
to improve.
Ask what to expect on
the test.
Be sure you know the
date of the test.

Review your test . . .
Talk to your teacher or
a classmate about
any questions
you missed.

Review and study for the test . . .
Look over your last test.
Organize your notes and
assignments.
Review every day until the test.
Quiz yourself and study with
a partner.
Notice the areas where you
need to spend extra time.

Test day . . .
Have a healthy
breakfast.
Stay calm and do
your best.
Follow the guidelines
and tips in
this chapter.

The night before . . .
Get a good night's
rest.

Try It!

Think of the ways you prepared for your last test. Did you leave out any of the above steps? See if you can improve your test scores by following this test-prep cycle.

Test-Taking Tips

- **Listen carefully** as your teacher gives directions, makes any corrections, or provides other information. Stay focused while your teacher is talking; otherwise, you might miss important comments such as these:

"Make this change in number three."

"You have 30 minutes to finish the test."

"Write your answer to the final question on the back of the test sheet."

- **Put your name on the test right away.**
- **Take a quick look at the entire test.** This will help you decide how much time to spend on each section or question.
- **Begin the test.** Read the instructions before answering each set of questions. Do exactly what they tell you to do.
- **Read each question carefully.** Be sure you understand the question completely before answering it.
- **Answer all of the questions you are sure of first.** Then go back to the other questions and do your best to answer each one. Keep track of the time as you work on the more difficult questions.
- **Check over your answers when you finish the test.** If you skipped any really difficult questions, try to answer them now.

Try It!

Review these tips right before your next test and then put them into practice. Upon completion of the test, determine how closely you followed this advice.

Taking Objective Tests

Tests often have four different types of objective questions: true/false, matching, multiple-choice, and fill-in-the-blanks.

True/False

In a true/false test, you decide if a statement is correct or incorrect. Most true/false questions focus on the details, so read each statement carefully.

- **Look for absolutes and qualifiers.** Statements with absolutes such as *always, never, all,* and *none* are often false. Statements that use qualifiers such as *often, rarely,* and *seldom* are more likely to be true.

  False   Nearsightedness is *always* hereditary in nature.
  (Nearsightedness is *often* hereditary in nature.)

  True   As weather conditions change, warm, moist air associated with the Gulf Stream *often* provides a source of moisture for rainfall.

- **Test each part.** If even a single word or phrase in a statement is false, then the entire statement is false.

  False   The Gulf Stream is a warm, rapid, relatively narrow ocean current that flows along the west coast of the United States.
  (The Gulf Stream flows along the *east* coast of the United States.)

- **Watch for statements that contain more than one negative word.** Words such as *don't, can't, doesn't,* and *wasn't* can confuse, so be sure you know what the statement means.

  True   It is unlikely ice will not melt when the temperature rises above 32 degrees F.

Matching

In matching tests, you match items in one column to those in another column.

- **Read both columns before answering any questions.** This helps you find the best match for each item.
- **Match the items you know first.** If each answer is used only once, cross out the letter or number after you've used it.
- **Find grammar clues.** For example, plural subjects need plural verbs.

  Match each word with its meaning.

  1. animus   __2__   a lack of oxygen in the lungs

  2. asphyxia   ____   those who argue in defense of a doctrine

  3. apologists   __1__   a motivating force

Tests

Multiple-Choice

In multiple-choice questions, you choose the right answer from several possibilities.

- **Read each question carefully.** Usually, you will be asked to choose the best answer. Sometimes your choices may include "all of the above" or "none of the above."

    1. In *Frankenstein,* who is accused of murdering Victor's younger brother?
        A. Victor
        B. Alphonse
        C. Justine
        D. none of the above

- **Anticipate the answer.** Before reading the choices, try to answer the question or complete the sentence.
- **Read all the choices before you answer.** It's tempting to choose the first answer that seems close, but there may be another choice that is better.
- **Consider "all of the above" and "none of the above" answers carefully.** If there is even one choice that you know to be incorrect, do not choose "all of the above." If there is one choice you know to be correct, do not choose "none of the above."
- **Eliminate the wrong or unlikely choices first.**

    2. The first telegraph signal was successfully sent in _____.
        A. 1866
        B. 1940 *(too late)*
        C. 1799 *(too early)*
        D. 1902 *(first radio signal across the Atlantic)*

Fill-in-the-Blanks

Fill-in-the-blanks questions require you to complete the missing parts of a statement.

- **Check the number of blanks.** Often, there is one for each word.

    1. The "backbone" of the North American continent is the continental   divide .

- **Check for grammar clues.** If there is an *a* before the blank, the answer should begin with a consonant. If there is an *an* before the blank, the answer should begin with a vowel.

    2. A polygon of eight sides and eight angles is an octagon .

Try It!

Which types of objective questions are the most difficult for you? Use these tips to help you on your next test.

Taking Essay Tests

Many students feel that essay questions are the hardest type because, unlike other questions, possible answers are not given. Essay-test prompts require you to show how facts and supporting details are connected. The next few pages offer tips for taking an essay test.

Understand and restate the prompt.

- **Read the question carefully.**
- **Underline the key words** that explain what you are being asked to do. Here are some key words and their explanations.

Compare . . . . . Tell how things are alike.

Contrast . . . . . Tell how things are different.

Cause . . . . Describe how one thing has affected another.

Define . . . . Give a clear, specific meaning for a word or an idea.

Describe . . . . . Use sensory details to explain how something looks, sounds, and so on.

Evaluate . . . . . Make a value judgment supported by facts or examples.

Explain . . . . Use details and facts to tell what something means or how it works, or give reasons that tell why.

Identify . . . . . . Answer the question using one or more of the 5 W's.

Illustrate . . . . . Use examples to show how something works or why it's important.

Prove . . . . Use facts and details to tell why something is true.

Review . . . . Create an overall picture of the topic.

Summarize . . . Tell the main idea and key points about the topic.

- **Rephrase the prompt into a thesis statement.** It often works well to drop the key word from your thesis statement.

Prompt: Explain why Macbeth plans to have Banquo and his son, Fleance, murdered.

Thesis statement: Macbeth plans to murder Banquo and Fleance because he doesn't want Fleance to become king.

Try It!

Turn each essay-test prompt below into a thesis statement.

1. Explain what makes Macbeth a tragic hero.

2. Describe the vision Macbeth sees before he kills Duncan.

Plan a one-paragraph response.

Tests may include one or more prompts that call for a paragraph response rather than a full-length essay. The following guidelines will help you write an effective one-paragraph response to a prompt.

- **Read the prompt carefully.** Underline the key words and phrases.
- **Identify what you are asked to do** (explain, compare, prove, define).
- **Plan your response.**
  1. Turn the prompt into a topic sentence.
  2. Include at least three supporting details. Keep your topic sentence in mind as you select supporting details.

Prompt

Define and give an example of mutualism.

Planning Notes

<u>Topic sentence:</u> Mutualism is the relationship between two different species of interdependent organisms in which each benefits from the other.

Supporting details:
1. Example: relationship between fruit-bearing plants and fruit-eating birds
2. Fruit provides nutrition for birds
3. Fruit contains seeds that pass through bird's digestive system
4. Bird distributes seeds in waste so plant can reproduce

Response

Mutualism

Mutualism is the relationship between two different species of interdependent organisms in which each benefits from the other. A good example of mutualism is the relationship between the fruit of plants and fruit-eating birds. When a bird eats fruit, it receives nutrition. The fruit contains seeds that pass through the bird's digestive system. The seeds are distributed in the bird's waste, allowing the fruit-bearing plant to reproduce.

Plan an essay response.

Some essay prompts require you to respond with a full-length essay. The following tips will help you write a clear, well-organized response essay.

- **Read the prompt** and restate it as a thesis statement.
- **Plan your response** by outlining details that support your thesis.
- **Write your essay answer.** Include your thesis statement in your opening paragraph. Each main point of your outline becomes the topic sentence for a body paragraph. In the final paragraph, write a meaningful conclusion that shows you truly understand the topic.

Prompt

Contrast how a writer might use dramatic monologue and soliloquy.

Planning Notes

Thesis statement: Although both techniques involve a single speaker, soliloquy and dramatic monologue have different purposes and effects in literature.

I. A soliloquy and a monologue are both spoken by single characters.
   A. In a soliloquy, the speaker thinks out loud and is usually alone.
   B. An example of a soliloquy is Juliet's balcony speech from Romeo and Juliet.
   C. In a dramatic monologue, the speaker speaks to someone who remains silent.
   D. An example of a dramatic monologue is the duke's speech in the Robert Browning poem "My Last Duchess."
II. Soliloquies and dramatic monologues have specific purposes.
   A. Writers often use soliloquies to reveal a character's thoughts.
      1. Juliet reveals her feelings for Romeo.
      2. When Romeo learns Juliet's feelings, the plot can be advanced.
   B. A dramatic monologue shows how a character relates to others.
      1. The duke tries to prove he would be a good husband. . . .

■ Sample Essay Response

The following essay response follows the outline on the previous page. The thesis statement appears at the beginning of the response. The final paragraph is a meaningful conclusion that shows that the writer clearly understands the topic.

Speaking All Alone

Although both techniques involve a single speaker, soliloquy and dramatic monologue have different purposes and effects in literature.

A soliloquy and a dramatic monologue are both spoken by single characters. In a soliloquy, the speaker thinks out loud and is usually alone. One of the most famous soliloquies occurs in <u>Romeo and Juliet</u> when Juliet speaks from her heart near the start of the balcony scene. During a dramatic monologue, a character speaks to someone who remains silent. In Robert Browning's poem "My Last Duchess," the duke talks about his former wife to another man, whose reactions we do not hear.

Soliloquies and dramatic monologues have specific purposes. Writers often use soliloquies to reveal a character's thoughts. In the balcony scene, Juliet says things to herself that she would not tell anyone else. She is embarrassed when Romeo speaks and reveals his presence. We (and Romeo) know her true thoughts, and the romance picks up speed.

A dramatic monologue shows how a character relates to others. The duke in "My Last Duchess" is talking to a man who has been sent to find out whether the duke would be a good husband. Instead of showing himself to be a considerate man, the duke brags about how he dominated his first wife. His words reveal a totally unlikable character.

Literary characters can be interesting for what they say. Soliloquy and dramatic monologue are two methods that writers use to tell the reader what their characters are really like. Even though only one character is speaking in both cases, the effects can be critical to the plot.

Try It!

Plan and respond to the following prompt: Aldous Huxley said, "Technological progress has merely provided us with more efficient means for going backward." Do you agree or disagree? Support your opinion with two examples from history or from your own observations or experiences.

Taking Standardized Tests

At certain times throughout your formal education, you will be required to take standardized tests. The guidelines below will help you take these tests.

Before the Test . . .

- **Know what to expect.** Ask your teacher what subjects will be covered on the standardized test, what format will be used, and what day the test will be given.
- **Get a good night's rest.** Also be sure to eat breakfast before any test.
- **Be prepared.** Bring extra pens, pencils, and erasers. Make sure to have enough blank paper for notes, outlines, or numerical calculations.

During the Test . . .

- **Listen to the instructions and carefully follow directions.** Standardized tests follow strict guidelines. You will be given exact instructions on how to fill in information and supply answers.
- **Pace yourself.** In general, don't spend more than one minute on an objective question; move on and come back to it later.
- **Keep your eyes on your own work.** Don't worry if others finish before you.
- **Match question numbers to answer numbers.** If you skip a question in the question booklet, be sure to skip the corresponding number on your answer sheet. Every few questions, double-check the question number against your answer sheet.
- **Answer every question.** As long as there is no penalty for incorrect answers, you should always answer every question. First eliminate all the choices that are obviously incorrect and then use logic to make your best educated guess.
- **Review your answers.** If you have time left, be sure that you've answered all the questions and haven't made any accidental mistakes. In general, don't change an answer unless you are sure that it's wrong. If you need to change an answer, erase the original answer completely.

After the Test . . .

- **Be sure you have filled in all information correctly.**
- **Erase any unnecessary marks before turning in your test.**

Taking Exit and Entrance Exams

Teachers and administrators use exit and entrance exams to assess your ability to use skills and strategies in a subject area such as English or mathematics. Many school districts use exit exams to determine if students are qualified to graduate from high school. Scores on entrance exams such as the SAT and ACT help college admissions departments determine whether a student meets a school's admission standards.

Most exit and entrance exams include components designed to test your writing skills. When you take an entrance or exit exam, you may be asked to respond to writing prompts and answer objective questions that test your revising and editing skills. In this chapter, you'll learn strategies and skills that will help you succeed on the writing portion of exit and entrance exams.

- **Questions About Conventions**
- **Sentence-Revision Questions**
- **Paragraph-Revision Questions**
- **Editing Questions**
- **Responding to Writing Prompts**
- **Budgeting Time for On-Demand Writing**

"Beware the man who knows the answer before he understands the question."

—C. M. Manasco

Questions About Conventions

Some questions on exit and entrance exams ask you to edit sentences for conventions: punctuation, capitalization, spelling, and grammar. Read each question and its possible answers carefully. The following examples are typical conventions questions.

Exercise

Read the text in *italics* and follow the directions in bold. (Answers appear on the bottom of page **563**.)

1. *Dover High School starts the last week in* <u>August and</u> *Seth Jones High School begins the first week in September.*
The best punctuation for the underlined section is

   A. August, and
   B. August and
   C. August. and
   D. NO CHANGE

2. *Charise says that her three* <u>brothers-in-law</u> *hope to start a Web-based company that will market their ideas.*
The correct spelling for the underlined noun is

   A. brother-in-laws
   B. brothers'-in-law
   C. brothers-in-laws
   D. NO CHANGE

3. *The customs agent looked at the passport and asked the man,* <u>How long will you be staying in New York?</u>
The correct punctuation for the underlined section is

   A. "How . . . New York"?
   B. "how . . . New York"?
   C. "How . . . New York?"
   D. NO CHANGE

4. *The decision to change the import* <u>tariff</u> *on wool products was not* <u>spontaneus,</u> *for it came after five months of* <u>extensive</u> *research and debate.*
Which underlined word is spelled incorrectly?

   A. tariff
   B. spontaneus
   C. extensive
   D. All three are correct.

5. *None of the 85 people on the boat <u>were</u> willing to get into the water once the shark was sighted.*

The correct choice for the underlined word is

A. was

B. are

C. is

D. NO CHANGE

6. *After hiking more than four miles out of the way due to a washed-out trail, the tired group of campers <u>couldn't hardly</u> take another step.*

The correct way to write the underlined section is

A. could hardly

B. couldn't take

C. Both A and B

D. NO CHANGE

Tip

When you answer multiple-choice questions, be sure you . . .

- **Read the question completely.** Do not try to answer a question until you understand all of its parts.

- **Read all answers.** Sometimes answers are remarkably similar. The right answer might be "All of the above," "None of the above," or "A and B."

- **Eliminate obviously wrong answers.** Cross out answers you know are incorrect before making your choice.

- **Don't guess.** Most entrance exams will penalize incorrect answers as a way to discourage guessing.

Answer Key

1. The focus is punctuation (compound sentences), and the answer is **A**.

2. The focus is spelling, and the answer is **D**.

3. The focus is punctuation (dialogue), and the answer is **C**.

4. The focus is spelling, and the answer is **B**.

5. The focus is grammar (verb tense and subject-verb agreement), and the answer is **D**.

6. The focus is grammar (double negatives), and the answer is **C**.

Sentence-Revision Questions

Some sentence-revision questions test your ability to revise, combine, clarify, and correct sentences.

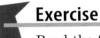

Exercise

Read the following sentences and choose the best revision or NO CHANGE. (Answers are on the bottom of page **565**.)

1. *Demonstrating a new out-of-bounds play, we sat on the bleachers to watch the basketball coach.*
   - **A.** To watch the basketball coach, we sat on the bleachers demonstrating a new out-of-bounds play.
   - **B.** We sat on the bleachers to watch the basketball coach demonstrating a new out-of-bounds play.
   - **C.** Watching the basketball coach demonstrating a new out-of-bounds play, we sat on the bleachers.
   - **D.** NO CHANGE

2. *On Saturday morning, Thomas ate breakfast and then he put the finishing touches on his science project and then he walked to Dunn's Hardware to start his new job.*
   - **A.** Thomas ate breakfast . . . his science project. Then he walked . . . job.
   - **B.** Thomas ate breakfast. Then he put . . . project. He walked . . . job.
   - **C.** Thomas ate breakfast, put the . . . project, and then walked . . . job.
   - **D.** NO CHANGE

3. *Before we started our workout. We jogged around the track.*
   - **A.** Before we started our workout, we jogged around the track.
   - **B.** We jogged around the track, before we started our workout.
   - **C.** We jogged around the track before we started our workout.
   - **D.** Both A and C

4. *Caroline won more trophies than any other team member.*
   - **A.** Caroline won the most trophies.
   - **B.** Caroline won more trophies than any other team member won.
   - **C.** Caroline won even more trophies than any other team member.
   - **D.** NO CHANGE

5. *The thunderstorm roared through town, <u>soaking the clothes on the line</u>* <u>*and leaving them dripping wet*</u>.

    A. soaking the clothes on the line and leaving them dripping.
    B. soaking the dripping wet clothes on the line.
    C. leaving the clothes on the line dripping.
    D. NO CHANGE

6. *<u>The girls' soccer team happy to have new uniforms will play in the post-</u>* <u>*season tournament*</u>.

    A. The girls' soccer team, happy to have new uniforms will play . . . tournament.
    B. The girls' soccer team happy to have new uniforms, will . . . tournament.
    C. The girls' soccer team, happy to have new uniforms, will . . . tournament.

7. <u>*The new passenger plane is huge. The plane has two levels for*</u> <u>*passengers. It can hold as many as 850 people*</u>.

    A. The huge new passenger plane has two levels for passengers and can hold as many as 850 people.
    B. The new passenger plane is huge and has two levels for passengers. It can hold as many as 850 people.
    C. The new passenger plane is huge. It has two levels for passengers and can hold as many as 850 people.
    D. NO CHANGE

Answer Key

    1. The focus is misplaced modifiers, and the answer is **B**.
    2. The focus is rambling sentences, and the answer is **C**.
    3. The focus is fragments and combining, and the answer is **D**.
    4. The focus is incomplete comparisons, and the answer is **B**.
    5. The focus is avoiding redundancy, and the answer is **C**.
    6. The focus is restrictive and nonrestrictive clauses and phrases, and the answer is **C**.
    7. The focus is combining sentences, and the answer is **A**.

Paragraph-Revision Questions

Some questions test paragraph-revising skills. The key to success is to carefully read and reread the sample paragraph.

Exercise

Read the following text and answer the questions on page **567**. (Answers are on the bottom of page **567**.)

(1) After World War II, the United States and the Soviet Union engaged in the cold war, the cold war was a protracted political struggle over who would become the dominant world power. *(2)* The two countries competed in a variety of venues. *(3)* Their most dramatic competition was the so-called "space race," the battle to see who could attain supremacy in the exploration of outer space.

(4) In 1957, Russia's launch of *Sputnik 1,* the world's first artificial satellite, shocked the world. *(5)* Suddenly the launch of *Sputnik* created fears that the Soviet Union would develop space weaponry that would give it a military edge. *(6)* These weapons have rarely been used. *(7)* The launch also shook the United States to its core. As the first nation to develop nuclear weapons, the United States had enjoyed military superiority because of nuclear weapons.

(8) The United States developed its own space program. *(9)* Soon, the program began to focus on an almost unbelievable goal— taking human passengers to the moon and bringing them back. *(10)* The program developed to reach the moon was known as *Apollo.* *(11)* The first Apollo mission ended in tragedy during a test when the rocket caught fire on the launchpad, killing all three members of the crew. *(12)* Subsequent tests proved more successful, and in 1969, *Apollo 11* landed two U.S. astronauts on the moon. *(13)* Around the world, millions watched the event live on television.

(14) Several lunar landings gave the United States a key victory in the space race, but another program helped maintain U.S. dominance. *(15)* In 1981, the United States launched the first reusable space shuttle, signaling the next phase in space exploration. *(16)* More importantly, the United States and the Soviet Union finally began to cooperate on space exploration.

1. *Which part of sentence 1 should be deleted?*

    A. After World War II
    B. engaged in the cold war
    C. the cold war was
    D. NO CHANGE

2. *Which of the following would make the best addition to the beginning of sentence 8?*

    A. In response to *Sputnik,*
    B. The Soviets fought back,
    C. First of all,
    D. In conclusion,

3. *Which of the following sentences should be deleted?*

    A. Sentence 2.
    B. Sentence 6.
    C. Sentence 11.
    D. Sentence 15.

4. *Which revision would improve this essay?*

    A. Switch sentence 5 with sentence group 7.
    B. Switch sentence 1 with sentence 3.
    C. Switch sentence 11 with sentence 15.
    D. Switch sentence 15 with sentence 16.

5. *Which sentence would make the best conclusion to this passage?*

    A. The moon would never again be explored.
    B. Space exploration was no longer important.
    C. The *Apollo* program was no longer significant.
    D. The space race was over, but the exploration of space would continue.

Answer Key

1. The focus is on unnecessary repetition in an appositive, and the answer is **C**.
2. The focus is on effective use of transitions, and the answer is **A**.
3. The focus is on details appropriate to the topic sentence, and the answer is **B**.
4. The focus is on moving text, and the answer is **A**.
5. The focus is on closings, and the answer is **D**.

Editing Questions

Some tests assess your editing skills by asking you to spot problems in writing. (See the tip on page **563**.)

Exercise

Choose the underlined word or words that should be edited or choose LEAVE AS IS. (Answers appear at the bottom of the page.)

1. *Jerome, Baker, or Steve* <u>are</u> *not ready* <u>to board</u> *the train* <u>for</u> *New York.*
                                A   **B**   **C**
    D. LEAVE AS IS

2. *Jumping* <u>off the fence</u>, *Kale* <u>he</u> *landed badly* <u>and</u> *twisted his ankle.*
                    A   **B**   **C**
    D. LEAVE AS IS

3. *The massive size of the* <u>huge</u> *volcanic cloud* <u>blotted</u> *out the sun for* <u>three</u> *days.*
                             A   **B**   **C**
    D. LEAVE AS IS

4. <u>After</u> *practice, Bill* <u>timidly</u> *asked the director if he found* <u>his</u> *playbook.*
    A   **B**   **C**
    D. LEAVE AS IS

5. <u>For the summer</u>, *Jim plans to play baseball,* <u>movies</u>, *and go* <u>swimming</u>.
           A   **B**   **C**
    D. LEAVE AS IS

6. *After his friends described the roof at the new ballpark,* <u>Mr. Abar</u>
                                                     A
    <u>decided</u> *he* <u>should probably go watch the opening of the roof himself.</u>
    B   **C**
    D. LEAVE AS IS

Answer Key

   1. The focus is subject-verb agreement, and the answer is **A**.
   2. The focus is double subjects, and the answer is **B**.
   3. The focus is wordiness or redundancy, and the answer is **A**.
   4. The focus is indefinite references, and the answer is **C**.
   5. The focus is parallel structure, and the answer is **B**.
   6. The focus is ineffective writing, and the answer is **C**.

Responding to Writing Prompts

Some state and district exit exams require you to respond to a writing prompt in the form of an essay, a narrative, or a letter. You may be prompted to write from your own experience, or you may be asked to read one or two short passages and respond to them. These exams are usually timed, but some states and districts give students as much time as they need.

College entrance tests such as the ACT and SAT also include a timed writing section. The prompts on these tests ask you to support your point of view on a topic. The essays are evaluated on clarity, consistency, level of detail, and appropriateness. While correctness is important, evaluators understand that you are working within a limited time frame.

When you respond to a prompt, start by analyzing the prompt so that you know exactly what the test requires you to write. One way to analyze a prompt is to answer the following **STRAP questions** about it.

Subject: What topic (career, service, community) should I write about?

Type: What form (essay, letter, editorial, article, report) of writing should I create?

Role: What position (student, son or daughter, friend, employee) should I assume as the writer?

Audience: Who (teacher, parents, friends, community members, employer) is the intended reader?

Purpose: What is the goal (persuade, respond, evaluate, explain, tell, describe) of my writing?

Exercise

Analyze the following prompts by answering each STRAP question. (Note: If a prompt does not answer a question specifically, use your best judgment to answer.)

1. You have just learned that you can graduate in December. You have the option of taking additional classes and graduating in June or graduating early and beginning course work in a trade school or college. Which would you choose? Write a letter to the faculty and principal explaining your decision and asking for their support.

2. The school's budget has to be cut due to a revenue shortfall. As part of a student-faculty committee, your job is to propose the possible elimination of several sports. Write an essay explaining which sports should be cut and why. Use sound logic.

Review a prompt and response.

The following prompt is similar to what you would find on an entrance or exit exam. Review it and the student response.

Sample Prompt

Former Green Bay Packers coach Vince Lombardi knew a lot about teamwork. According to Lombardi, "People who work together will win, whether it be against complex football defenses, or the problems of modern society." Drawing on your own experience, write an essay for your classmates explaining how a project you worked on benefited from teamwork.

Sample STRAP Answers and Quick List

The student writer analyzed the prompt using the STRAP questions, wrote his position, and created a quick list. Other graphic organizers can help plan a response.

Subject: Value of teamwork
Type: Essay of exposition
Role: Student
Audience: Classmates
Purpose: Explain a personal experience.

Position: Teamwork makes a big project go smoothly.

– The benefit concert demanded more than I could handle alone.
– I needed volunteers for the many tasks.
– A dedicated group got the job done.

Sample Response

Next, the student developed his response. He paid as much attention to each part—the beginning, the middle, and the ending—as time permitted.

Teamwork at Work

The **opening** leads to a position statement (underlined).

After volunteering at the Mendon Brook Food Bank last summer, I decided to organize a classical concert to benefit the facility. I thought it would be something I could accomplish on my own, but doing the project taught me a valuable lesson: sometimes it takes more than one person to get the job done. <u>The food bank benefit concert succeeded because a talented group of people combined their skills and worked as a team.</u>

At first, I thought that I could easily organize the benefit concert by myself. As a member of the school orchestra, I had played violin in concerts for six years. I felt confident playing in public and had even performed in several benefit concerts. In addition, I knew other musicians who could help me realize my plan.

Middle paragraphs share examples of teamwork to support the main idea.

As I began to work, I realized the project was too big for just one person. It takes more than music to make a concert happen. I was able to put together a group of musicians and choose selections to perform, but I needed to find a venue, generate publicity, and even provide catering for people who attended. I quickly became overwhelmed and asked some friends and relatives for help.

My friend Carla, who is a fantastic writer and artist, handled the publicity like a professional. James, who had a summer job at a local college, found a hall we could use for free. Anna and her mother, who both love to cook, took charge of the catering. My dad found volunteers from work to serve as ushers. As the project progressed, we all ended up pitching in to do a little of everything.

The **closing** restates the lesson learned through this experience.

In the end, the benefit concert was a great success, raising $700 for the Mendon Brook Food Bank. I also benefited because I learned the value of teamwork. The next time I need to tackle a project, I'll try the team approach. When it comes to doing a big job, the skills and energy of a group of people accomplish more than one person could ever accomplish alone.

Exercise

Use the STRAP questions to analyze the following prompt. Then create a position statement and quick list and begin your response. Finish writing, revising, and editing in the time your teacher provides.

Imagine that the senate wants to require that all people serve their country prior to pursuing college or a career. Would you support compulsory two-year service to the country for graduating seniors? The service could be community- or military-based. Write a letter to your senator supporting your position.

Respond to prompts about literature.

Prompts may be based on literature that you have read prior to the exam or on selections that you read during the test. Here are some tips on writing responses to literature.

- **Write a thesis (focus) statement.** Reword the prompt so that it applies to the literature you're writing about.
- **Briefly outline your main points.** Support your thesis statement with convincing details.
- **Avoid summarizing the literature.** Follow your outline; don't simply retell a story or paraphrase a poem.
- **Include comments on the author's techniques.** Point out literary devices (symbols, repetition, metaphors, word choice) that reveal the author's purpose.
- **Make direct references to the text.** Quote or paraphrase important excerpts to support your analysis.

Sample Prompt and Response

Time and mortality are common themes in literature. The two poems that follow both deal with these themes, and each also says something about art itself. In "When I Have Fears That I May Cease to Be," John Keats writes about a poet's anxiousness to capture his thoughts on paper. In "Languages," Carl Sandburg describes how all languages change with time. Discuss what these two poems, taken together, have to say about time and human expression.

When I Have Fears That I May Cease to Be

When I have fears that I may cease to be
Before my pen has glean'd my teeming brain,
Before high piled books, in charact'ry,
Hold like rich garners the full-ripen'd grain;
When I behold, upon the night's starr'd face,
Huge cloudy symbols of a high romance,
And think that I may never live to trace
Their shadows, with the magic hand of chance;
And when I feel, fair creature of an hour!
That I shall never look upon thee more,
Never have relish in the faery power
Of unreflecting love!—then on the shore
Of the wide world I stand alone, and think
Till Love and Fame to nothingness do sink.

—John Keats (1795–1821)

Languages

There are no handles upon a language
Whereby men take hold of it
And mark it with signs for its remembrance.
It is a river, this language,
Once in a thousand years
Breaking a new course
Changing its way to the ocean.
It is mountain effluvia
Moving to valleys
And from nation to nation
Crossing borders and mixing.
Languages die like rivers.
Words wrapped round your tongue today
And broken to shape of thought
Between your teeth and lips speaking
Now and today
Shall be faded hieroglyphics
Ten thousand years from now.
Sing—and singing—remember
Your song dies and changes
And is not here to-morrow
Any more than the wind
Blowing ten thousand years ago.

—**Carl Sandburg (1878–1967)**

Sample STRAP Answers and Quick List

<u>S</u>ubject: Time and human
expression in
"When I Have
Fears . . ." and
"Languages"
<u>T</u>ype: Essay
<u>R</u>ole: Reader
<u>A</u>udience: Testers
<u>P</u>urpose: Analyze

Position: Both poems are positive
statements about eternity.
  1. Keats feels the tension of limited time.
     – Too many ideas, eternal "symbols,"
       mortal love
     – He takes comfort in eternity.
  2. Sandburg describes continual change.
     – Languages change and die like rivers.
     – Sing because today will soon be gone.

■ Sample Response

Following his quick list, the student wrote a response that quoted and paraphrased passages from the two poems.

The opening introduces both poems and ends with a thesis statement (underlined).

The first middle paragraph discusses one poem.

The next middle paragraph discusses the other poem.

The ending revisits the thesis statement.

Inevitable Change

John Keats' famous sonnet "When I Have Fears That I May Cease to Be" is often described as extremely dark and pessimistic. To many readers, it seems to end on an especially negative note about the pointlessness of effort in the face of eternity. Likewise, Carl Sandburg's "Languages" might be interpreted as a depressing recognition of mortality in the face of endless change. Upon careful reading, however, these two works reveal something different. Both poems are actually positive statements about life and eternity.

Keats' opening line "When I have fears . . . " begins in tension. The first three quatrains reveal fear that there won't be time to write all the thoughts of his "teeming brain," to explore "huge . . . symbols of a high romance," and to enjoy simple, "unreflecting love." In the final couplet, Keats' answer to these fears is to "stand alone" on the "shore of the wide world" until all tension fades. The suggestion is that it fades in the face of eternity.

Similarly, Sandburg's poem ends with a statement that some may take as bleak. He says, "Your song . . . / . . . is not here tomorrow" and compares it to "the wind / Blowing ten thousand years ago." Within the context of the whole poem, however, we can see that Sandburg celebrates life. He describes language as a living river, unable to be controlled. He says, "Sing—and singing—remember." What we are to remember is that life itself is change.

Together, these two poems reveal that eternity need not frighten us. It is only when we fear our mortality that we either grow tense at the shortness of time—as in Keats' poem—or try to resist change—as in Sandburg's. By accepting our mortality, the authors suggest, we become free to sing and love and explore and grow—to enjoy to the fullest our time on earth.

Budgeting Time for On-Demand Writing

Responding to a prompt in an "on-demand" writing environment requires a special set of skills. The following tips can help you create your best response.

Before You Write . . .

- **Know how much time you have.** Structure your response according to the clock. Use an accelerated approach for a 30-minute response, but take more time with prewriting and revising if you have 60 or 90 minutes.

- **Analyze the prompt.** Answer the STRAP questions so that you know exactly how to respond. Here are a sample prompt and one student's analysis:

What does it mean to be a humble person? What kind of person is humble? Write an essay defining humility and how it relates to the life of a student.

Subject: Humility
Type: Essay of definition
Role: Student
Audience: Tester
Purpose: To define

- **Plan your response.** Write your thesis or opinion statement and use a brief outline or graphic organizer to plan your writing.

During Your Writing . . .

- **Write an effective opening paragraph.** Capture your reader's attention, introduce the topic, and state your thesis.

- **Develop the middle part.** Begin each paragraph with a topic sentence (main point) that supports your thesis. Each topic sentence should pertain to and explain your thesis. Use a variety of details, including quotations, paraphrases, and analyses. For persuasive writing, answer a major objection to your opinion.

- **Write a strong closing paragraph.** Complete your writing by providing a final thought or by restating your thesis. For persuasive writing, consider a call to action.

After You've Written a First Draft . . .

- **Read your work.** Watch for places where adding, cutting, or moving details will make your work stronger.

- **Check for conventions.** Correct any errors you find.

A Writer's Resource

Basic Paragraph Skills

When it comes to writing well, you must remember these two words: support and organization. You need to select details that support your main point, and you need to organize those details effectively. That's where the simple, time-honored tradition of paragraphing comes into play. Paragraphs help you organize your thoughts and make it easier for readers to follow your line of thinking.

In this chapter, you will examine the four basic types of paragraphs. Each has a specific purpose, and each requires a particular type of thinking. Then you will look at examples of different ways you can organize your paragraphs to make them most effective. Learning how to write effective paragraphs will give you control of all your academic writing—from essays to research papers.

- **The Parts of a Paragraph**
- **Types of Paragraphs: Narrative, Descriptive, Expository, and Persuasive**
- **Patterns of Organization: Classification, Comparison-Contrast, Cause-and-Effect, Process, and Climax**

"I often have to write a hundred pages or more before there's a paragraph that's alive."

—Philip Roth

The Parts of a Paragraph

A basic paragraph contains three parts: a topic sentence, body sentences, and a closing sentence. Each detail in the body supports the topic sentence. The following expository paragraph provides information about hot-air ballooning.

Topic Sentence

Body

Closing Sentence

Hot-Air Ballooning

Based on the simple scientific principle that hot air rises, hot-air ballooning has been a popular pastime for more than two centuries. While the idea of a lighter-than-air vehicle had been around since Archimedes, the first functional balloon was created in France in 1783 by brothers Joseph and Etienne Montgolfier, who sent a duck, a chicken, and a sheep into the air for a brief but historical ride. Later that year, the first manned trip was taken by physicist Pilatre de Rozier and the Marquis Francois d'Arlandes, who glided over Paris for 28 minutes. Today's balloons have changed little from those early models, with the balloon envelope designed to trap hot air and lift the structure into the air. The envelope is formed from many strips, called *gores*, pieced together to create a rounded shape. Montgolfiers' envelope was made of paper, but later balloons were created of silk, and today's models are usually made of ripstop nylon. The tapered bottom edge is open, with a fireproof skirt attached. Early balloons were kept aloft by burning a mixture of straw and manure, but today, propane tanks are used, suspended just below the skirt. Beneath the tanks hangs a basket, usually made of wicker, and large enough for passengers and extra propane tanks. Hot-air ballooning fell out of favor in the nineteenth century with the advent of gas balloons, which could travel farther. Then, in the mid-twentieth century, traditional ballooning had a renaissance. Today people enjoy peaceful scenic rides as well as the sport of balloon racing. Whatever the purpose, balloon enthusiasts throughout the world enjoy gliding on air.

 Respond to the reading. What is the main idea of this paragraph? What specific details in the body support this idea? Name two or three of them.

A Closer Look at the Parts

Every paragraph, whether written to stand alone or to be part of a longer piece of writing, has three parts.

The Topic Sentence

Every topic sentence should do two things: (1) give the specific topic of the paragraph and (2) present a specific feature or feeling about the topic. When writing your topic sentence, you could use the following formula as a guide.

a specific topic *(hot-air ballooning)*

+ a particular feature or feeling about the topic *(has been a popular pastime for more than two centuries)*

= **an effective topic sentence** *(Hot-air ballooning has been a popular pastime for more than two centuries.)*

Tip

You can add phrases or clauses to your topic sentence as long as the basic sentence contains the main point your paragraph will explore.

Based on the simple scientific principle that hot air rises, **hot-air ballooning has been a popular pastime for more than two centuries.**

The Body

Each sentence in the body of the paragraph should support the topic sentence while adding new details about the topic.

- Use specific details to make your paragraph interesting.
  Early balloons were kept aloft by burning a mixture of straw and manure.

- Use the method of organization that best suits your topic: classification, order of importance, chronological order, and so on.

The Closing Sentence

The closing sentence ends the paragraph. It may restate the topic, summarize the paragraph, or provide a link to the next paragraph.

Whatever the purpose, balloon enthusiasts throughout the world enjoy gliding on air.

Resource

Types of Paragraphs

There are four basic types of paragraphs: *narrative, descriptive, expository,* and *persuasive*.

Narrative Paragraph

A **narrative paragraph** tells a story. It may draw from the writer's personal experience or from other sources of information. A narrative paragraph is almost always organized chronologically, or according to time.

Topic Sentence

Body

Closing Sentence

A Good Start

Working in a day care center wasn't my idea of an ideal job, but it was the only one I had been offered, so I steeled myself for a summer surrounded by crazy kids. I was surprised to find the basement was relatively quiet. About eighteen kids of varying ages filled various areas of the main room. Some were building small projects, some were reading, and others were softly practicing musical instruments. I was taken to a back room with high, sunny windows. There, nine little kids were busy around a long table, engrossed in planting a minigarden in long wooden trays. I was an assistant supervisor, and soon we were giggling away, "hoeing" rows with our fingers and carefully planting tiny tomato and pepper seeds. One little girl shyly pulled on my shirt. Her neatly cornrowed hair sparkled in the sunlight as she softly asked me to help her plant some beans. I held a little jar over some newspaper as she carefully poured in some dirt. Then we selected some beans from a small pile. As she gently wriggled them down between the glass and the dirt, she explained that this way we could watch them grow. When we were finished, she gave me a smile and a hug. As we admired our work, I said to myself that this summer might be fun.

Respond to the reading. What is the tone of the story (sad, humorous, angry, and so on)? What details help make the story interesting? Amusing?

Write a narrative paragraph. Write a narrative paragraph in which you share your first job interview or your first tryout for an activity.

Descriptive Paragraph

A **descriptive paragraph** gives the reader a detailed picture of a person, a place, an object, or an event. This type of paragraph should contain a variety of sensory details—specific sights, sounds, smells, tastes, and textures.

The Garden on the Balcony

Topic Sentence

In the middle of the city, high above the traffic and pollution, my mother has created a little bit of country on our apartment's balcony. When you step out through the sliding door, you feel as though you have been transported to a secret garden. The sounds of traffic are muffled, creating a soft background that mingles with the lively Tejano music my mom plays. On the left, a wall divides our balcony from our neighbor's. There, my mother has leaned a trellis and planted pots of climbing vines. In the summer, purple and pink trumpet-shaped flowers create a gorgeous cascade of color. In the fall, the leaves glow red. My dad

Body

built a slender table that hugs part of the safety wall along the front of the balcony, and there my mother has her herb garden, unusual pots containing lacy-leafed plants that fill the air with savory smells of basil and chive. Along the floor are large and small planters my sister created in her pottery class at the Y. Some overflow with bushy greenery; others contain bright geraniums. On the right, along our other wall, huddles our small gas barbecue. My father hung a board on that wall to hold garden tools and barbecue utensils. Nearby, two small lawn chairs flank a tiny, round

Closing Sentence

wooden table. Two more chairs are folded against the wall, ready for a family dinner. On a stifling summer day, our balcony is our garden in the sky.

Resource

 Respond to the reading. Does this description create a clear picture of the place being described? Which two or three details are particularly effective?

 Write a descriptive paragraph. Describe someone you see in public. Use sensory details to let the reader know exactly how this person "appears" to you.

Expository Paragraph

An **expository paragraph** shares information about a specific topic. It presents facts, gives directions, defines terms, explains a process, and so on. An expository paragraph may use classification, comparison-contrast, cause-effect, problem-solution, or chronological organization.

Hadrian's Wall

Topic Sentence

Hadrian's Wall was a monumental undertaking, a stone border that stretched across the northern part of England. Roman emperor Hadrian initiated the building of the wall in 122 C.E. The brick and turf wall ran 75 miles from east to west and took 10 years to complete. The wall varied from 8 to 10 feet in depth and from 13 to 16 feet in height. A turret used for signaling was placed each mile along the wall. Fourteen full-sized forts were eventually added along the wall, each housing up to 1,000 troops and employing gates to allow passage to the other side. The importance of the wall changed after Hadrian's death in 138 C.E. when the new emperor, Antoninus Pius, built his own wall—the Antonine Wall—about 100 miles north. In 164 C.E., emperor Marcus Aurelius once again

Body

utilized Hadrian's Wall, and it remained in use until the Roman withdrawal from Britain around the fourth century. Although some might argue the wall was built to separate Scotland from England, in fact, the wall is south of the Scottish border. Actually, the wall marked the northern border of the Roman Empire at the time and had several other practical purposes as well. For one, it was an effective warning to northern barbarians not to challenge Rome. It also kept soldiers occupied and provided trade opportunities for the locals. Through the years, stones were taken to

Closing Sentence

build other structures, and today the wall is in disrepair. However, Hadrian's Wall is still a tourist destination, an impressive reminder of an ancient, changing Britain.

Respond to the reading. What is the main point of the above paragraph? Give three examples of details used to support that idea.

Write an expository paragraph. Write a paragraph that gives information about a topic. Include plenty of details to support your topic sentence.

Persuasive Paragraph

A **persuasive paragraph** expresses an opinion and tries to convince the reader that the opinion is valid. To be persuasive, a writer must include effective supporting reasons and facts.

Pet Population

Topic Sentence

Spaying or neutering is a humane way to treat the growing problem of unwanted animals in the United States. These simple operations can eliminate aggressive behavior and roaming, reducing the risk that a pet may be hit by a car or injured in a fight with another animal. While "fixing" a pet may make it gentler, it will not eliminate the protective behavior desired of watchdogs. Some say that fixing a cat or dog will make it fat and lazy, but it doesn't—overfeeding and lack of exercise do that. Spaying or neutering a pet may actually protect the animal's health, reducing or eliminating the risk of various cancers. Altered pets, in fact, live long, healthy lives. Perhaps the most compelling reason for altering a pet is to reduce the number of unwanted animals that fill pounds and humane societies. According to the American Humane Society, one dog or cat can be responsible for thousands of puppies or kittens born within a seven-year period. Controlling the pet population can reduce the numbers of homeless dogs and cats that roam city streets and the countryside, just trying to survive. These abandoned animals often revert to the wild, posing a threat or nuisance similar to the one posed by coyotes. It's cruel and even dangerous to allow animals to continue having unwanted litters. If people spay or neuter their pets, we can create a healthier, safer world for domestic animals.

Body

Closing Sentence

Resource

Respond to the reading. What are three main reasons offered for the writer's opinion? Which of these reasons is the most important?

Write a persuasive paragraph. Write a paragraph presenting your opinion. Include at least three strong reasons to support your argument.

Patterns of Organization

On the next five pages, sample paragraphs show basic patterns of organization. Reviewing these samples can help you organize your own writing.

Classification Order

Classification is used when you need to divide or break down a topic into categories. The line diagram below helps to organize the topic of plastics.

Line Diagram

Topic Sentence

Body

Closing Sentence

Plastics

Since the first plastic, cellulose nitrate, was developed more than 100 years ago, this durable material has become an integral part of daily life. Three structurally different plastics are created by chemically changing natural materials or by synthesizing raw materials. The three types are characterized by their molecular structure, which determines how each type reacts to heat. *Thermoplastics* have a branched molecular structure that forms the weakest bond. Pliable at normal temperatures, they melt into a sticky mess with high heat (packaging). Durable *elastomers* have a crosslink structure that allows for flexibility. Once shaped through heating, however, they cannot be reshaped but retain flexibility (tires). *Thermosets,* the most tightly structured plastics, are very hard, with a tightly woven molecular structure that resists reshaping once they are cured. This type of plastic is used to make everything from outlet covers to computer shelves. Different types of plastics, each designed to meet different needs, all play key roles in today's world.

 Respond to the reading. How is the topic classified in this paragraph? What are two things that you learned about the topic?

Comparison-Contrast Order

Organizing by **comparison** allows you to show the similarities or differences between two subjects. A Venn diagram effectively organizes this type of paragraph.

Venn Diagram

Marsupials	Both	Monotremes
Suckle young	Have a marsupium bone	Secrete milk on fur
Permanent pouch	One baby per year	Temporary pouch
Have live babies	Give babies milk	Lay eggs
More mammal-like		Some reptilian characteristics
More than 200 species		Only three species

Topic Sentence

Body

Closing Sentence

Marsupials and Monotremes

Australia's marsupials and monotremes are very different from each other. Both types of mammals give birth to one baby per year and possess a marsupium bone that supports a pouch. However, the similarities end there. The monotreme does not possess a permanent pouch, nor does it suckle its young the way marsupials do. It secretes the milk onto its fur, and the baby laps it up. Marsupials give birth to live, undeveloped babies that grow within the mother's pouch; monotremes lay eggs. Physically, monotremes are reptilian-like with horizontal limb orientation, outward-turned rear feet, and the ability to regulate their body temperature. Marsupials have a more vertical bone structure and are warm-blooded. There are only three species of monotremes—the platypus and the long- and short-nosed echidna—and they are found only in Australia and New Guinea. There are more than 200 species of marsupials, some of which are found in South America. One species, the opossum, is native to North America. Marsupials and monotremes are amazing and unusual mammals that are very different from each other.

 Respond to the reading. How many differences between the two topics are identified? Name them.

Resource

Cause-and-Effect Order

The **cause-and-effect** organizational pattern allows you to discuss the effects of a particular event or happening (the cause). The paragraph below discusses one cause (laughter) and its effects.

Cause-Effect Organizer

Laughter
mind
- reduces stress
- relaxes a person
- reduces depression

bodies
- stimulates immune system
- lowers blood pressure
- boosts the heart
- tones muscles

Topic Sentence

Body

Closing Sentence

The Effects of Laughter

A sense of humor can be one of the most powerful forces in our lives, affecting both the mind and the body. Laughter perks up brain function by stimulating the release of chemicals called *endorphins*. These chemicals relax a person, alleviate stress, reduce depression, and provide an overall sense of well-being. Endorphins do more than just make people feel good. Research shows that these chemicals, stimulated by laughter, have an even more important effect on the body. They can help the body deal with pain and even stimulate the immune system. Patients with a positive attitude and a well-developed sense of humor actually get well faster than those who flounder in pain and self-pity. Laughter can positively affect a person in other ways as well, lowering blood pressure and improving heart health. Laughing can even tone muscles. Did you ever laugh till your sides ached? That's because laughing actually stimulates your muscles. Although not a substitute for a real workout, belly laughs provide healthy exercise. So that old saying, "Laughter is the best medicine," may be true.

 Respond to the reading. What are two ways laughter can affect us? Give two supporting details for each.

Process Organization

Process organization uses a step-by-step approach to explain a process. You start by introducing the topic and then follow with an appropriate series of steps.

Process Diagram

<u>The Process of Cheese Making</u>

Step 1: bacteria culture added to milk to produce lactic acid
Step 2: milk separates and rennet stirred in
Step 3: curds cut and drained, solids heated
Step 4: curd salted and put in press
Step 5: cheese coated with wax

Topic Sentence

Body

Closing Sentence

Cheese Making

Cheese making was a chore for pioneers, but today many people enjoy making cheese. Although the process has been modernized, cheese is still made by souring and curdling milk, then separating liquids from the solids. To begin, warm milk is "ripened" by the addition of a bacterial culture. This starter culture produces lactic acid in the milk, which facilitates the separation of the milk into curds (solids) and whey (liquid). Then rennet, a chemical derived from either an animal or vegetable source, is stirred into the mixture to further coagulate the milk solids. Once the curds are set, they are cut into smaller pieces and drained, and the solids are heated gradually until firm. The curds are drained again, then salted and put into a cheese press to squeeze out the remaining whey. During the pressing process, the cheese is turned regularly to facilitate drying. Once the cheese has dried, it may be coated with a special wax to preserve it. Some cheeses can be eaten right away while others are best left to age for better flavor. With a little effort and know-how anyone can make delicious homemade cheese.

Respond to the reading. What transitional words or phrases are used to connect ideas? Name three.

Climax Organization

Climax (specific to general) is a method of organization in which the specific details lead up to an important summary statement. (If a topic sentence is used, it is placed at the end.) The following paragraph shows the excitement building as the writer waits for a concert to begin.

Details List

Leading up to a concert

- house lights dimmed
- multicolored spotlights begin
- sound builds
- feet stamping, hand clapping, whistling
- guitar blasts
- flash of light, shower of sparks

Anxiously Waiting

Opening Sentence

As the lights dimmed in the amphitheater, multicolored spotlights began to circle overhead, bouncing off the ceiling and swirling over the heads of the crowd. The sound began to build. At first, it sounded like thunder rumbling in the distance, but soon it grew to a deafening roar. People all around were stamping their feet, clapping

Body

their hands, and whistling through their fingers to show that they were ready for the show to begin. The crowd noise was soon drowned out by a blast of bass guitar and drums that seemed to come out of nowhere. Behind a blinding flash of light and a shower of glittering sparks, the band

Summary Topic Sentence

appeared on stage and began to play. At last, the concert had begun.

 Respond to the reading. What types of details does the writer use to build to the climax? Give two examples of effective details.

Basic Essay Skills

As you take more advanced classes, you will find that most of your writing assignments are in the form of essays—from essay tests to responses to literature. In these essays, you will explain, argue, or describe your thinking on a particular topic. The approach you take in each essay will depend on the guidelines established by your instructor and on your own judgment about how the topic should be presented. You may decide a traditional, straightforward approach works best, or you may find a more creative approach effective.

No matter which approach you take, developing an essay can be a challenge. You must have a good understanding of your topic and confidence in your position on that topic. Then you must develop your ideas so that your reader can clearly understand your thinking. The information in this chapter serves as a basic guide to essay writing.

- **Understanding the Basic Parts**
- **Outlining Your ideas**
- **Writing Thesis Statements**
- **Creating Great Beginnings**
- **Developing the Middle Part**
- **Using Transitions**
- **Shaping Great Endings**
- **Key Terms, Techniques, and Forms**

"Writing is the best way to talk without being interrupted."

—Jules Renard

Understanding the Basic Parts

Each part of an essay—the beginning, middle, and ending—plays an important role. To develop your writing, refer to the suggestions below and to the sample essays earlier in this book.

Beginning **Your opening paragraph should capture the reader's attention and state your thesis.** Here are some ways to capture your reader's attention:

- Tell a dramatic or exciting story (anecdote) about the topic.
- Ask an intriguing question or two.
- Provide a few surprising facts or statistics.
- Provide an interesting quotation.
- Explain your personal experience or involvement with the topic.

> **Beginning**
> Middle
> Ending

Middle **The middle paragraphs should support your thesis statement.** They provide information that fully explains the thesis statement. For example, in an essay about the changes in the cartoon animation industry, each middle paragraph could focus on one main trend in that industry. Follow your own outline while writing this section.

> Beginning
> **Middle**
> Ending

Ending **Your closing paragraph should summarize your thesis and leave the reader with something to think about.** Here are some strategies for creating a strong closing:

- Review your main points.
- Emphasize the special importance of one main point.
- Answer any questions the reader may still have.
- Draw a conclusion and put the information in perspective.
- Provide a significant final thought for the reader.

> Beginning
> Middle
> **Ending**

Outlining Your Ideas

Once you've established a general pattern of development, you're ready to organize the main points and supporting details that you will cover in your essay. To help you organize this information, it may be wise to use a list, a topic outline, or a sentence outline.

Topic Outline

An outline is an orderly listing of related ideas. In a **topic outline**, each new idea is stated as a word or phrase rather than in complete sentence. Before you start, write your working thesis statement at the top of your paper to keep you focused on the subject of your essay. Do not attempt to outline your opening and closing paragraphs unless specifically asked to do so.

Introduction

I. Effects of malnutrition on the body
   A. Extreme weight loss and stunted growth
   B. Frequent infections
   C. Less resistance to diseases
II. Extreme forms of malnutrition
   A. Marasmus
   B. Kwashiorkor
III. Effects of malnutrition on development
   A. Limited ability to walk and to talk
   B. Stunted intellectual development
   C. Effects continuing into adulthood

Conclusion

Resource

Sentence Outline

A **sentence outline** contains more detail than a topic outline, and each new idea is expressed as a complete sentence. A sentence outline is often required for longer essays or research papers.

Introduction

I. Genetic engineering is a form of biotechnology.
   A. Scientists can manipulate genes.
   B. Genes can be copied and moved to cells in other species.
   C. Scientists can recombine genes and clone entire organisms.
II. Genetic engineering affects animal and plant breeding.
   A. Past species-improvement efforts proved unpredictable.
   B. Now development time is cut dramatically with better results.
   C. Animals are potential chemical factories, and new animals can be created and patented.
III. Genetic engineering is feared by some.
   A. Dangerous organisms could be released.
   B. Public confidence in scientists has been undermined.

Conclusion

Writing Thesis Statements

In most cases, a thesis statement takes a stand or expresses a specific feature or feeling about your topic. An effective thesis statement gives you the necessary direction to develop your essay.

Use a formula.

a specific topic *(multicultural education)*
+ **a particular feature or feeling about the topic** *(is vital to a society made up of many different peoples)*

= **an effective topic sentence** *(Multicultural education is vital to a society made up of many different peoples.)*

Sample Thesis Statements

Writing Assignment: Examine a psychological theme in a novel.
Specific Topic: *Animal Dreams*
Thesis Statement: In *Animal Dreams* by Barbara Kingsolver (**topic**), a woman's search for personal identity is juxtaposed with her father's identity loss to Alzheimer's (**particular feature**).

Writing Assignment: Defend a strongly held principle.
Specific Topic: The use of chemicals in food production
Thesis Statement: The use of chemicals in food production (**topic**) needs to be more stringently regulated (**particular stand**).

Writing Assignment: Review a music concert.
Specific Topic: The rap group Word
Thesis Statement: The rap group "Word" (**topic**) combines a powerful message with an infectious rhythm (**particular feeling**).

Thesis Checklist

Be sure that your thesis statement . . .

_____ identifies a limited, specific topic,
_____ focuses on a particular feature or feeling about the topic,
_____ can be supported with convincing facts and details, and
_____ meets the requirements of the assignment.

Creating Great Beginnings

Beginning
Middle
Ending

The opening paragraph of an essay should grab the reader's attention, introduce your topic, and present your thesis. Try one of these approaches to start an opening paragraph:

- **Start with an interesting fact.**
  Recently, the question has come up about whether astronauts ever really did walk on the moon.

- **Ask an interesting question.**
  How would you feel if you knew the government had set up an elaborate hoax to make you think astronauts had landed on the moon?

- **Start with a quotation.**
  "The body of physical evidence that humans did walk on the moon is simply overwhelming." So says Dr. Robert Park, Director of the Washington office of the American Physical Society and a known critic of NASA's manned space program.

Try a beginning strategy.

If you have trouble coming up with a good opening paragraph, follow the step-by-step example below.

First sentence Grab the reader's attention with an opening sentence (see approaches above).

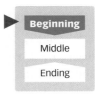

> Recently, the question has come up about whether astronauts ever really did walk on the moon.

Second sentence Give some background information about the topic.

> The creators of a television "expose" show suggest that the whole moon landing was really staged in a movie studio.

Third sentence Introduce the specific topic of the essay in a way that builds up to the thesis statement.

> However, this criticism has not gone unchallenged by NASA scientists.

Fourth sentence Give the thesis statement of the paper (see page 592).

> The fact is, there is overwhelming evidence to support our country's claims that our astronauts have in fact walked on the moon.

Resource

Developing the Middle Part

The middle part of an essay is where you do most of the work. In this part, you develop the main points that support your thesis statement.

Use your outline or other planning notes as a guide when you write this section. However, new ideas may pop into your head as you go along. You may incorporate these ideas into your draft or make a note to further research the ideas later.

Advance your thesis.

Keep these points in mind as you explain and develop your thesis statement.

- **Cover your main points.** Develop each main point in a paragraph or series of paragraphs.
- **Give background information.** If necessary, provide some history to put the topic in context.
- **Define terms.** Clarify any terms that your reader is not likely to know.
- **Order the main points.** Present the main ideas in a logical order (according to your outline).

Test your ideas.

When you write the middle part of an essay, you're testing your first thoughts about your topic. Here are some ways to test your line of thinking as you write.

- **Raise questions.** Anticipate any questions the reader may have about your topic.
- **Consider alternative ideas.** Take inventory of your thesis as you go along: Do you need to strengthen or rethink it? Also look at your main points from different angles.
- **Answer objections.** Address different points of view about your topic.

Build a coherent structure.

Each middle paragraph should include main points and details that logically develop your thesis.

- **Develop one paragraph at a time.** Start a new paragraph whenever you shift to another main idea about the topic.
- **Connect your main points.** Use transitional phrases to link each new paragraph with the preceding one. (See page **595**.)

Using Transitions

Transitions can be used to connect one sentence to another sentence within a paragraph, or to connect one paragraph to another within a longer essay or report. The lists that follow show a number of transitions and how they are used. Each colored list is a group of transitions that could work well together in a piece of writing.

Words used to show location

above	around	between	inside	outside
across	behind	by	into	over
against	below	down	near	throughout
along	beneath	in back of	next to	to the right
among	beside	in front of	on top of	under

Above	In front of	On top of
Below	Beside	Next to
To the left	In back of	Beneath
To the right		

Words used to show time

about	during	yesterday	until	finally
after	first	meanwhile	next	then
at	second	today	soon	as soon as
before	to begin	tomorrow	later	in the end

First	To begin	Now	First	Before
Second	To continue	Soon	Then	During
Third	To conclude	Eventually	Next	After
Finally			In the end	

Words used to compare things

likewise	as	in the same way	one way
like	also	similarly	both

In the same way	One way
Also	Another way
Similarly	Both

Words used to contrast (show differences)

but	still	although	on the other hand
however	yet	otherwise	even though

On the other hand   Although
Even though   Yet
Still   Nevertheless

Words used to emphasize a point

again	truly	especially	for this reason
to repeat	in fact	to emphasize	

For this reason   Truly   In fact
Especially   To emphasize   To repeat

Words used to conclude or summarize

finally	as a result	to sum it up	in conclusion
lastly	therefore	all in all	because

Because   As a result   To sum it up   Therefore
In conclusion   All in all   Because   Finally

Words used to add information

again	another	for instance	for example
also	and	moreover	additionally
as well	besides	along with	other
next	finally	in addition	

For example   For instance   Next   Another
Additionally   Besides   Moreover   Along with
Finally   Next   Also   As well

Words used to clarify

in other words	for instance	that is	for example

For instance   For example
In other words   Equally important

Shaping Great Endings

Beginning

Middle

Ending

The closing paragraph of a paper should summarize your thesis and leave the reader with something to think about. When writing your closing paragraph, use two or more of the following approaches:

- **Review** your main points.
- **Emphasize** the special importance of one main point.
- **Answer any questions** the reader may still have.
- **Draw a conclusion** and put the information in perspective.
- **Provide a significant final thought** for the reader.

Try an ending strategy.

If you have trouble coming up with an effective closing paragraph, follow the step-by-step example below.

First sentence Reflect on the topic. Start by reflecting on the material presented previously about the topic.

> The moon landing was real and was an important milestone in the history of the United States space program.

Second sentence Add another point. Include a final point of interest that you didn't mention before.

> If the landing had been merely a hoax, other countries such as Russia and China could have easily prepared their own "moon landing" to rival ours, but they didn't.

Third sentence Emphasize the most important point. Stress the importance of one or more key points that support the thesis.

> The information gathered by the moon astronauts, along with the rocks they brought home, proved invaluable to modern technology.

Fourth sentence Wrap up the topic or draw a conclusion. Add one final thought about the topic or draw a conclusion from the points you've presented in the writing.

> The moon walk was real—as real as the new industries and materials developed during its planning, and as real as the pride we still feel when we remember those remarkable astronauts who took that first "giant leap for mankind."

Learning Key Writing Terms

The next two pages include important terms related to writing. Refer to these pages whenever you have a question about the vocabulary associated with any part of the writing process.

Balance	Arranging words or phrases in a way that gives them equal importance
Body	The main part of a piece of writing, containing details that support or develop the thesis statement
Brainstorming	Collecting ideas by thinking freely about all the possibilities; used most often in groups
Central idea	The main point of a piece of writing, often stated in a thesis statement or a topic sentence
Closing sentence	The summary or final sentence in a piece of writing
Coherence	The logical arrangement of ideas that makes them clear and easy to follow
Dialogue	Written conversation between two or more people
Emphasis	Giving great importance to a specific idea in a piece of writing
Exposition	Writing that explains and informs
Figurative language	Language that goes beyond the normal meaning of the words used, often called "figures of speech"
Focus (thesis)	The specific part of a topic that is written about in an essay
Generalization	A general statement that gives an overall view rather than focusing on specific details
Grammar	The rules that govern the standard structure and features of a language
Idiom	A phrase or an expression that means something different from what the words actually say
	The answer was really out in left field. (This means the answer was not even close to being correct.)
	Next year you'll sing a different tune. (This means you'll think differently.)
Jargon	The special language of a certain group or occupation
	The weaver pointed out the fabric's unique warp **and** woof.
	Computer jargon: byte icon server virus

Limiting the subject	Narrowing a general subject to a more specific one
Literal	The actual dictionary meaning of a word; language that means exactly what it appears to mean
Loaded words	Words slanted for or against the subject **The new tax bill** helps the rich **and** hurts the poor.
Logic	Correctly using facts, examples, and reasons to support a point
Modifiers	Words, phrases, or clauses that limit or describe another word or group of words
Objective	Writing that gives factual information without adding feelings or opinions (See *subjective*.)
Poetic license	A writer's freedom to bend the rules of writing to achieve a certain effect
Point of view	The position or angle from which a story is told (See page **350**.)
Prose	Writing in standard sentence form
Purpose	The specific goal of the writing
Style	The author's unique choice of words and sentences
Subjective	Writing that includes the writer's feelings, attitudes, and opinions (See *objective*.)
Supporting details	Facts or ideas used to sustain the main point
Syntax	The order and relationship of words in a sentence
Theme	The main point or unifying idea of a piece of writing
Thesis statement	A statement of the purpose, or main idea, of an essay
Tone	The writer's attitude toward the subject
Topic	The specific subject of a piece of writing
Topic sentence	The sentence that carries the main idea of a paragraph
Transitions	Words or phrases that connect or tie ideas together
Unity	A sense of solidarity in writing in which each sentence helps to develop the main idea
Usage	The way in which people use language (*Standard* language follows the rules; *nonstandard* language does not.)
Voice	A writer's personal tone or feeling that comes across in a piece of writing

Resource

Using Writing Techniques

Experiment with some of these techniques in your own essays and stories.

Allusion	A reference to a familiar person, place, thing, or event **Mario threw me my mitt. "Hey, Babe Ruth, you forgot this!"**
Analogy	A comparison of similar ideas or objects to help clarify one of them **The mind of a bigot is like the pupil of the eye: The more light you shine on it, the more it will contract.** —Oliver Wendell Holmes, Jr.
Anecdote	A brief story used to illustrate or make a point **It is said that the last words John Adams uttered were "Thomas Jefferson survives." Ironically, Jefferson had died just a few hours earlier. Both deaths occurred on July 4, 1826—the 50th anniversary of the Declaration of Independence shepherded by the two great men.** (This ironic anecdote intensifies the importance of both men in our nation's history.)
Colloquialism	A common word or phrase suitable for everyday conversation but not for formal speech or writing **"Cool" and "rad" are colloquialisms suggesting approval.**
Exaggeration	An overstatement or a stretching of the truth to emphasize a point (See *hyperbole* and *overstatement*.) **We opened up the boat's engine and sped along at a million miles an hour.**
Flashback	A technique in which a writer interrupts a story to go back and relive an earlier time or event **I stopped at the gate, panting.** Suddenly I was seven years old again, and my brother was there, calling me "chicken" from the edge of the stone well. **Then I opened my eyes and heard only the crickets chirping. The years, the well, and my brother were gone. I turned back to the road, determined to get home before nightfall.**
Foreshadowing	Hints about what will happen next in a story **As Mai explained why she had to break their date, she noticed Luke looking past her.** Turning, she saw Meg smiling—at Luke.
Hyperbole	(hi-púr-bə-lē) Exaggeration used to emphasize a point **The music was** loud enough to make your ears bleed.
Irony	An expression in which the author says one thing but means just the opposite **As we all know,** there's nothing students love more than homework.

Resource

Juxtaposition	Putting two words or ideas close together to create a contrasting of ideas or an ironic meaning **Ah, the** sweet smell **of** fuel emissions!
Local color	The use of details that are common in a certain place
Metaphor	A figure of speech that compares two things without using the words *like* or *as* **The sheep were** dense, dancing clouds **scuttling across the road.**
Overstatement	An exaggeration or a stretching of the truth (See *exaggeration* and *hyperbole*.) **If I eat one more piece of turkey,** I will burst!
Oxymoron	Connecting two words with opposite meanings **small fortune cruel kindness original copy**
Paradox	A true statement that says two opposite things **As I crossed the finish line dead last, I felt a surge of triumph.**
Parallelism	Repeating similar grammatical structures (words, phrases, or sentences) to give writing rhythm We cannot undo, we will not forget, **and** we should not ignore **the pain of the past.**
Personification	A figure of speech in which a nonhuman thing is given human characteristics **The computer spit out my disk.**
Pun	A phrase that uses words that sound the same in a way that gives them a funny effect **I call my dog Trousers because he** pants **so much.**
Simile	A figure of speech that compares two things using *like* or *as* **Her silent anger was** like a rock wall, **hard and impenetrable.**
Slang	Informal words or phrases used by a particular group of people **cool it hang out shoot the curl**
Symbol	A concrete object used to represent an idea
Understatement	The opposite of exaggeration; using very calm language to call attention to an object or an idea **" . . . except for an interruption caused by my wife falling out of the car, the journey went very well."** —E. B. White

Knowing the Different Forms

Finding the right form for your writing is just as important as finding the right topic. When you are selecting a form, be sure to ask yourself whom you're writing for (your *audience*) and why you're writing (your *purpose*).

Anecdote	A brief story that helps to make a point
Autobiography	A writer's story of his or her own life
Biography	A writer's story of someone else's life
Book review	An essay offering an opinion about a book (not to be confused with *literary analysis*)
Cause and effect	An examination of an event, the forces leading up to that event, and the effects following the event
Character sketch	A brief description of a specific character showing some aspect of that character's personality
Descriptive writing	Writing with sensory details that allow the reader to clearly visualize a person, a place, a thing, or an idea
Editorial	A letter or an article offering an opinion, an idea, or a solution
Essay	A thoughtful piece of writing in which ideas are explained, analyzed, or evaluated
Expository writing	Writing that explains something by presenting its steps, causes, or kinds
Eyewitness account	A report giving specific details of an event
Fable	A short story that teaches a lesson or moral, often using talking animals as the main characters
Fantasy	A story set in an imaginary world in which the characters usually have supernatural powers or abilities
Freewriting	Spontaneous, rapid writing to explore your thoughts about a topic of interest
Historical fiction	An invented story based on an actual historical event
Interview	Writing based on facts and details obtained through speaking with another person
Journal writing	Writing regularly to record personal observations, thoughts, and ideas

Literary analysis	A careful examination or interpretation of some aspect of a piece of literature
Myth	A traditional story intended to explain a mystery of nature, religion, or culture
Novel	A book-length story with several characters and a well-developed plot, usually with one or more subplots
Personal narrative	Writing that shares an event or experience from the writer's personal life
Persuasive writing	Writing intended to persuade the reader to follow the writer's way of thinking about something
Play	A form that uses dialogue to tell a story, usually meant to be performed in front of an audience
Poem	A creative expression that may use rhyme, rhythm, and imagery
Problem-solution	Writing that presents a problem followed by a proposed solution
Process paper	Writing that explains how a process works, or how to do or make something
Profile	An essay that describes an individual or re-creates a time period
Proposal	Writing that includes specific information about an idea or a project that is being considered for approval
Research report	An essay that shares information about a topic that has been thoroughly researched
Response to literature	Writing that is a reaction to something the writer has read
Science fiction	Writing based on real or imaginary science and often set in the future
Short story	A short fictional piece with only a few characters and one conflict or problem
Summary	Writing that presents the most important ideas from a longer piece of writing
Tall tale	A humorous, exaggerated story about a character or an animal that does impossible things
Tragedy	Literature in which the hero fails or is destroyed because of a serious character flaw

Proofreader's Guide

Marking Punctuation

Period

605.1 At the End of a Sentence

Use a **period** at the end of a sentence that makes a statement, requests something, or gives a mild command.

(Statement) **The man who does not read good books has no advantage over the man who can't read them.**

—Mark Twain

(Request) **Please bring your folders and notebooks to class.**

(Mild command) **Listen carefully so that you understand these instructions.**

Note: It is not necessary to place a period after a statement that has parentheses around it and is part of another sentence.

My dog Bobot (I don't quite remember how he acquired this name) **is a Chesapeake Bay retriever—a hunting dog—who is afraid of loud noises.**

605.2 After an Initial or an Abbreviation

Place a period after an initial or an abbreviation (in American English).

Ms.   Sen.   D.D.S.   M.F.A.   M.D.   Jr.   U.S.   p.m.   a.m.
Edna St. Vincent Millay   Booker T. Washington   D. H. Lawrence

Note: When an abbreviation is the last word in a sentence, use only one period at the end of the sentence.

Jaleesa eyed each door until she found the name Fletcher B. Gale, M.D.

605.3 As a Decimal Point

A period is used as a decimal point.

New York City has a budget of $46.9 billion to serve its 8.1 million people.

Exclamation Point

605.4 To Express Strong Feeling

Use the **exclamation point** (sparingly) to express strong feeling. You may place it after a word, a phrase, or a sentence.

"That's not the point," said Wangero. "These are all pieces of dresses Grandma used to wear. She did all this stitching by hand. Imagine!"

—Alice Walker, "Everyday Use"

Punctuation

Question Mark

606.1 Direct Question

Place a **question mark** at the end of a direct question.

> **Now what? I wondered. Do I go out and buy a jar of honey and stand around waving it? How in the world am I supposed to catch a bear?**
> —Ken Taylor, "The Case of the Grizzly on the Greens"
> **Where did my body end and the crystal and white world begin?**
> —Ralph Ellison, *Invisible Man*

When a question ends with a quotation that is also a question, use only one question mark, and place it within the quotation marks.

> **On road trips, do you remember driving your parents crazy by asking, "Are we there yet?"**

Note: Do not use a question mark after an indirect question.

> **Out on the street, I picked out a friendly looking old man and asked him where the depot was.**
> —Wilson Rawls, *Where the Red Fern Grows*
> **Marta asked me if I finished my calculus homework yet.**

606.2 To Show Uncertainty

Use a question mark within parentheses to show uncertainty.

> **This summer marks the 20th season (?) of the American Players Theatre.**

606.3 Short Question Within a Sentence

Use a question mark for a short question within parentheses.

> **We crept so quietly** (had they heard us?) **past the kitchen door and back to our room.**

Use a question mark for a short question within dashes.

> **Maybe somewhere in the pasts of these humbled people, there were cases of bad mothering or absent fathering or emotional neglect**—what family surviving the '50s was exempt?—**but I couldn't believe these human errors brought the physical changes in Frank.**
> —Mary Kay Blakely, *Wake Me When It's Over*

Periods, Exclamation Points, and Question Marks

For each line in the paragraphs below, write where periods, exclamation points, or question marks are needed. Write the word preceding each mark. (Write "none" if no marks are needed.)

1   Herme was persistent about going after the job that he wanted

2   "A wildland firefighter" his mother exclaimed "Why did you choose a

3 job like that"

4   "Actually, Ma," Herme answered, "someday I want to be a smoke

5 jumper, like T J Brookes"

6   His mother got that "I'm going to win this argument" look on her face

7 "A smoke jumper" she cried out "I don't think so Mrs Wagero, down at the

8 church, she told me all about Terrance, Jr, the smoke jumper He still almost

9 gives his mama a heart attack every time he fights one of those wildfires No

10 You will *not* be a smoke jumper"

11   Herme picked up his backpack, kissed his mother good-bye, and headed

12 for the door The state employment office opened at eight The starting pay

13 for a tech trainee was just $700 an hour, but to Herme the low wage was

14 worth it—just to train as a wildland

15 firefighter, that was enough

Model

Model the following sentences to practice punctuating a sentence with a tag question (a short question at the end of a statement) correctly.

That's the Russian faith all over, isn't it? . . . Surely that's Russian, isn't it?
—Fyodor M. Dostoevsky, *The Brothers Karamazov*

Comma

608.1 Between Two Independent Clauses

Use a **comma** between two independent clauses that are joined by a coordinating conjunction *(and, but, or, nor, for, yet, so)*.

> I wanted to knock on the glass to attract attention, but I couldn't move.
>
> —Ralph Ellison, *Invisible Man*

Note: Do not confuse a sentence containing a compound verb for a compound sentence.

> I had to burn her trash and then sweep up her porches and halls.
>
> —Anne Moody, *Coming of Age in Mississippi*

608.2 To Separate Adjectives

Use commas to separate two or more adjectives that *equally* modify the same noun. (Note: Do not use a comma between the last adjective and the noun.)

> Bao's eyes met the hard, bright lights hanging directly above her.
>
> —Julie Ament, student writer

A Closer Look

To determine whether adjectives modify equally—and should, therefore, be separated by commas—use these two tests:

1. Shift the order of the adjectives; if the sentence is clear, the adjectives modify equally. (In the example below, *hot* and *smelly* can be shifted and the sentence is still clear; *usual* and *morning* cannot.)

2. Insert *and* between the adjectives; if the sentence reads well, use a comma when the *and* is omitted. (The word *and* can be inserted between *hot* and *smelly*, but *and* does not make sense between *usual* and *morning*.)

> Matty was tired of working in the hot, smelly kitchen and decided to take her usual morning walk.

608.3 To Separate Contrasted Elements

Use commas to separate contrasted elements within a sentence. Often the word or phrase that is set off is preceded by *not*.

> Since the stereotypes were about Asians, and not African Americans, no such reaction occurred.
>
> —Emmeline Chen, "Eliminating the Lighter Shades of Stereotyping"

Commas 1

- Between Independent Clauses
- To Separate Adjectives
- To Separate Contrasted Elements

 Indicate where commas are needed in the following sentences by writing the commas along with the words that surround them.

1. The newspaper printed a correction that Dr. Ellen Ochoa is Hispanic not Hawaiian.

2. Ellen was the first Hispanic female astronaut and she was also the inventor of optical analysis systems.

3. Her mother was a determined hardworking single parent who earned a college degree while raising five children.

4. Ellen possesses a powerful never-ending commitment to learn.

5. She is most often recognized as an astronaut not as an inventor.

6. Ellen completed a brief vigorous training program before her first shuttle ride.

7. "Usually it takes quite a bit longer but I got lucky," she said.

8. Ellen was accepted into the space program in 1991 and in 1993 she completed her first shuttle mission.

9. Few people know that she is also a talented experienced flutist.

10. Ochoa says, "Many doors opened for me when I completed college and I encourage all Latinas to seek out interesting challenging careers."

Model

Model the following sentence to practice using commas to separate adjectives.

She had a quiet, unthreatening way about her that made older, uglier, fatter people take to her despite her beauty.

—Maeve Binchy, *Scarlet Feather*

Comma *(continued)*

610.1 To Set Off Appositives

A specific kind of explanatory word or phrase called an **appositive** identifies or renames a preceding noun or pronoun.

> **Benson,** our uninhibited and enthusiastic Yorkshire terrier, **joined our family on my sister's fifteenth birthday.**
>
> —Chad Hockerman, student writer

Note: Do not use commas with *restrictive appositives*. A restrictive appositive is essential to the basic meaning of the sentence.

> **Sixteen-year-old student** Ray Perez **was awarded an athletic scholarship.**

610.2 Between Items in a Series

Use commas to separate individual words, phrases, or clauses in a series. (A series contains at least three items.)

> **Dad likes** meat, vegetables, and a salad **for dinner.** (words)
>
> **I** took her for walks, read her stories, and made up games **for her to play.** (phrases)
>
> —Anne Moody, *Coming of Age in Mississippi*

Note: Do not use commas when all the words in a series are connected with *or, nor,* or *and.*

> **Her fingernails are pointed** and **manicured** and **painted a shiny red.**
>
> —Carson McCullers, "Sucker"

610.3 After Introductory Phrases and Clauses

Use a comma after an introductory participial phrase.

> **Determined to finish the sweater by Friday, my grandmother knit night and day.**

Use a comma after a long introductory prepositional phrase or after two or more short ones.

> In the oddest places and at the strangest times, **my grandmother can be found knitting madly away.**

Note: You may omit the comma if the introductory phrase is short.

> Before breakfast **my grandmother knits.**

Use a comma after an introductory adverb (subordinate) clause.

> After the practice was over, **Tina walked home.**

Note: A comma is not used if an adverb clause *follows* the main clause and is needed to complete the meaning of the sentence.

> **Tina practiced hard** because she feared losing.

However, a comma is used if the adverb clause following the main clause begins with *although, even though, while,* or another conjunction expressing a contrast.

> **Tina walked home,** even though it was raining very hard.

Commas 2

- ■ **To Set Off Appositives**
- ■ **Between Items in a Series**
- ■ **After Introductory Phrases and Clauses**

 Indicate where commas are needed in the following sentences by writing the commas along with the words that surround them. If no commas are needed, write "none needed."

1. The idea of contact lenses the common substitute for glasses has been around for hundreds of years.

2. Leonardo da Vinci the Italian artist inventor and scientist sketched ideas for contacts in 1508.

3. More than a hundred years later Rene Descartes the French mathematician suggested placing a lens directly on the eye.

4. Though the idea had been around for centuries it was 1887 before the first contact lenses were produced.

5. The first glass lenses were made by F. A. Muller a German glassblower.

6. After centuries of ideas and experimentation today's contact wearers have their choice of hard soft or gas-permeable lenses.

7. Today about 90 percent of contacts sold in the United States are soft lenses.

8. Remi has a pair each of blue green and hazel lenses to suit her varying moods.

 ## Model

Model the following sentences to practice using commas between items in a series, after introductory phrases, and to set off appositives.

> **Bill Post ran forward, gathered his little family in his arms for a moment, and then quickly ushered them toward the safety of the house.**
> —Thomas Steinbeck, "The Night Guide"

> **A few days before the shooting, Director Yu, a lecturer at a cinema school in Shanghai, gave Huping a small book to read.**
> —Ha Jin, "A Tiger-Fighter Is Hard to Find"

Punctuation

Comma *(continued)*

612.1 To Enclose Parenthetical Elements

Use commas to separate parenthetical elements, such as an explanatory word or phrase, within a sentence.

> **They stood together**, away from the pile of stones in the corner, **and their jokes were quiet, and they smiled rather than laughed.**
>
> —Shirley Jackson, "The Lottery"
>
> **Allison meandered into class**, late as usual, **and sat down.**

612.2 To Set Off Nonrestrictive Phrases and Clauses

Use commas to set off **nonrestrictive** (unnecessary) clauses and participial phrases. A nonrestrictive clause or participial phrase adds information that is not necessary to the basic meaning of the sentence. For example, if the clause or phrase (in red) were left out in the two examples below, the meaning of the sentences would remain clear. Therefore, commas are used to set them off.

> **The Altena Fitness Center and Visker Gymnasium**, which were built last year, **are busy every day.** (nonrestrictive clause)
>
> **Students and faculty**, improving their health through exercise, **use both facilities throughout the week.** (nonrestrictive phrase)

Do not use commas to set off a **restrictive** (necessary) clause or participial phrase, which helps to define a noun or pronoun. It adds information that the reader needs to know in order to understand the sentence. For example, if the clause and phrase (in red) were dropped from the examples below, the meaning wouldn't be the same. Therefore, commas are *not* used.

> **The handball court** that has a sign-up sheet by the door **must be reserved.**
> The clause identifies which handball court must be reserved.
> (restrictive clause)
>
> **Individuals** wanting to use this court **must sign up a day in advance.**
> (restrictive phrase)

A Closer Look

Use *that* to introduce restrictive (necessary) clauses; use *which* to introduce nonrestrictive (unnecessary) clauses. When the two words are used in this way, the reader can quickly distinguish necessary and unnecessary information.

> **The treadmill** that monitors heart rate **is the one you must use.**
> (The reader needs the information to find the right treadmill.)
>
> **This treadmill**, which we got last year, **is required for your program.** (The main clause tells the reader which treadmill to use; the other clause gives additional, unnecessary information.)

Commas 3

- ■ **To Enclose Parenthetical Elements**
- ■ **To Set Off Nonrestrictive Phrases and Clauses**

 Indicate where commas are needed in the following sentences by writing the commas along with the words that surround them. If no commas are needed, write "none needed."

1. The classic *Star Trek* series the one with Kirk and Spock was on television for only three seasons.

2. The show which was created by Gene Roddenbery was canceled because of low ratings.

3. Fans called "Trekkies" wanting the show to return waged a letter-writing campaign.

4. The show returned in syndicated reruns and became very popular.

5. *Star Trek* movies some great and others not so great led to a new television series: *Star Trek: The Next Generation.*

6. The new show known for its Shakespearean references starred Patrick Stewart as Captain Jean-Luc Picard.

7. The series that stars William Shatner and Leonard Nimoy remains popular with *Star Trek* fans.

8. Vendors sell merchandise everything you can think of with a *Star Trek* logo at conventions.

Model

Model the following sentence to practice using commas to set off nonrestrictive clauses.

> I . . . developed a very practiced smile, which I call my "Noh smile" because it resembles a Noh mask whose features are frozen.
>
> —Arthur Golden, *Memoirs of a Geisha*

Comma *(continued)*

614.1 To Set Off Dates

Use commas to set off items in a date.

> **On September 30, 1997, my little sister entered our lives.**
> **He began working out on December 1, 2005, but quit by May 1, 2006.**

However, when only the month and year are given, no commas are needed.

> **He began working out in December 2005 but quit by May 2006.**

When a full date appears in the middle of a sentence, a comma follows the year.

> **On June 7, 1924, my great-grandfather met his future wife.**

614.2 To Set Off Items in Addresses

Use commas to set off items in an address. (No comma is placed between the state and ZIP code.)

> **Mail the box to Friends of Wildlife, Box 402, Spokane, Washington 20077.**

When a city and state (or country) appear in the middle of a sentence, a comma follows the last item in the address.

> **Several charitable organizations in Juneau, Alaska, pool their funds.**

614.3 In Numbers

Use commas to separate numerals in large numbers in order to distinguish hundreds, thousands, millions, and so forth.

> **1,101   25,000   7,642,020**

614.4 To Enclose Titles or Initials

Use commas to enclose a title or initials and names that follow a surname (a last name).

> **Letitia O'Reilly, M.D., is our family physician.**
> **Hickok, J. B., and Cody, William F., are two popular Western heroes.**

614.5 Before Tags

Use a comma before a tag, which is a short statement or question at the end of a sentence.

> **He's the candidate who lost the election, isn't he?**
> **You're not going to like this casserole, I know.**

614.6 Following Conjunctive Adverbs and Transitional Phrases

Use a comma following conjunctive adverbs such as *however, instead,* and *nevertheless,* and transitional phrases such as *for example, in fact,* and *as a result.* (Also see **618.2**.)

> **Jaleel is bright and studies hard; however, he suffers from test anxiety.**
> **Pablo was born in the Andes; as a result, he loves mountains.**

Commas 4

- ■ **To Set Off Dates**
- ■ **To Enclose Titles**
- ■ **Before Tags**
- ■ **Following Conjunctive Adverbs and Transitional Phrases**

 Indicate where commas are needed in the following sentences by writing the commas along with the words that surround them. If no commas are needed, write "none needed."

1. Cori Ramos is planning to attend USC this fall right?

2. I'm looking forward to graduation; however I'll miss high school and my friends.

3. The article written by Sanjay Singh M.D. is about fibromyalgia treatments.

4. On March 20 2003 the United States attacked Iraq.

5. Whether the attack was justified is under debate; in fact a majority of people did not believe so three years later.

6. Special-effects technology is improving all the time; furthermore there is a need for specialists in this field.

7. Maya Angelou Ph.D. will speak at my sister's graduation ceremony.

8. My cousin started biking competitively in April 2000.

9. He didn't expect to lose did he?

10. He looked forward to winning at least second place; after all he had trained so long and hard.

 ## Model

Model the following sentence to practice using a comma before a tag.

> **Though both sentences have a certain on-the-money ring to them, the first one sounds better, doesn't it?**
> —June Casagrande, *Grammar Snobs Are Great Big Meanies*

Comma *(continued)*

616.1 To Set Off Dialogue

Use commas to set off the speaker's exact words from the rest of the sentence. (It may be helpful to remember that the comma is always to the left of the quotation mark.)

"It's like we have our own government," adds Tanya, a 17-year-old squatter.
—Kyung Sun Yu and Nell Bernstein, "Street Teens Forge a Home"

616.2 To Set Off Interjections

Use a comma to separate an interjection or a weak exclamation from the rest of the sentence.

Hey, how am I to know that a minute's passed?
—Nathan Slaughter and Jim Schweitzer, *When Time Dies*

Wow, I had no idea that she wears contacts.

616.3 To Set Off Interruptions

Use commas to set off a word, a phrase, or a clause that interrupts the movement of a sentence. Such expressions usually can be identified through the following tests: (1) They may be omitted without changing the meaning of a sentence. (2) They may be placed nearly anywhere in the sentence without changing its meaning.

For me, well, **it's just a good job gone!**
—Langston Hughes

The safest way to cross this street, as a general rule, **is with the light.**

616.4 In Direct Address

Use commas to separate a noun of direct address from the rest of the sentence. A *noun of direct address* is the noun that names the person(s) spoken to.

"You wouldn't understand yet, son, **but your daddy's gonna make a transaction. . . . "**
—Lorraine Hansberry, *A Raisin in the Sun*

Quineisha, why aren't you answering your phone?

616.5 For Clarity or Emphasis

You may use a comma for clarity or for emphasis. There will be times when none of the traditional rules call for a comma, but one will be needed to prevent confusion or to emphasize an important idea.

It may be that those who do most, dream most. (emphasis)
—Stephen Leacock

What the crew does, does **affect our voyage.** (clarity)

Commas 5

- ■ To Set Off Dialogue
- ■ To Set Off Interjections
- ■ To Set Off Interruptions
- ■ In Direct Address
- ■ For Clarity or Emphasis

 Indicate where commas are needed in the following sentences by writing the commas along with the words that surround them.

1. What now dear reader shall we make of our telescope?

—Johannes Kepler

2. The world as a rule does not live on beaches and in country clubs.

—F. Scott Fitzgerald

3. Whatever you do do with all your might.

—Marcus Tullius Cicero

4. As the poet said "Only God can make a tree."

—Woody Allen

5. Don't criticize what you don't understand son.

—Elvis Presley

6. "Now I have asked you a question my friend" said Mr. Jaggers.

—Charles Dickens, *Great Expectations*

7. Well all I know is what I read in the papers.

—Will Rogers

Model

Model the following sentences to practice using a comma to set off an interruption, to set off dialogue, and in direct address.

> On the Web, right now, Clark was hunting for someplace to buy roofing.
> —Alice Munro, "The Runaway"

> "General, sir," Mortenson shouted, "I think we're heading the wrong way."
> —Greg Mortenson and David O. Relin, *Three Cups of Tea*

Punctuation

Semicolon

618.1 To Join Two Independent Clauses

Use a **semicolon** to join two or more closely related independent clauses that are not connected with a coordinating conjunction. (Independent clauses can stand alone as separate sentences.)

> I did not call myself a poet; I told people I wrote poems.
> —Terry McMillan, "Breaking Ice"

> Silence coated the room like a layer of tar; not even the breathing of the 11 Gehad made any sound.
> —Gann Bierner, "The Leap"

Note: When independent clauses are especially long or contain commas, a semicolon may punctuate the sentence, even though a coordinating conjunction connects the clauses.

> We waited all day in that wide line, tired travelers pressing in from all sides; and when we needed drinks or sandwiches, I would squeeze my way to the cafeteria and back.

618.2 With Conjunctive Adverbs and Transitional Phrases

A semicolon is used *before* a conjunctive adverb or transitional phrase (with a comma after it) when the word connects two independent clauses in a compound sentence.

> "I am faced with my imminent demise; therefore, life becomes a very precious thing."
> —Amy Taylor, "AIDS Can Happen Here!"

Common Conjunctive Adverbs

also, besides, finally, however, indeed, instead, meanwhile, moreover, nevertheless, next, still, then, therefore, thus

Common Transitional Phrases

after all, as a matter of fact, as a result, at any rate, at the same time, even so, for example, for instance, in addition, in conclusion, in fact, in other words, in the first place, on the contrary, on the other hand

---

618.3 To Separate Groups That Contain Commas

A semicolon is used to separate groups of words that already contain commas.

> Every Saturday night my little brother gathers up his things—goggles, shower cap, and snorkel; bubble bath, soap, and shampoo; tapes, stereo, and rubber duck—and heads for the tub.

Semicolons

- **To Join Two Independent Clauses**
- **With Conjunctive Adverbs**
- **To Separate Groups That Contain Commas**

 Indicate where a semicolon is needed in the following sentences by writing the semicolon along with the words that surround it.

1. Everyone is talking about the weather they wonder why significant weather events are happening more frequently.

2. Weather is news these days—hurricanes, cyclones, and tornadoes flash floods, droughts, and tsunamis even snow in the deep South.

3. Unusual weather events go back several decades consider January 1997, when snow fell near the bridge between Florida's mainland and the Keys.

4. In 1997 and 1998, El Niño raised water temperatures in the Pacific Ocean moveover, it had a worldwide effect.

5. Wetter conditions than normal affect Chile, Peru, and Ecuador southern Brazil and northern Argentina and Mexico's northwest states.

6. Earth is rapidly warming this is the reason many scientists use to explain unusual weather events.

7. As the climate grows warmer, evaporation will increase therefore, there will be heavier rainfalls and more erosion.

8. Higher ocean temperatures might change the path of hurricanes look for them to track more often through the Caribbean or to make landfall along the east coast of the United States.

Model

Model the following sentence to practice using a semicolon to join two independent clauses.

The trees echoed with birdsong; a warm southeasterly breeze carried the sweetness of lime blossom.

—Michelle Paver, *Spirit Walker*

Colon

620.1 After a Salutation

Use a **colon** after the salutation of a business letter.

Dear Judge Parker: **Dear Governor Whitman:**

620.2 Between Numerals Indicating Time

Use a colon between the hours, minutes, and seconds of a number indicating time.

8:30 p.m.   **9:45 a.m.**   **10:24:55**

620.3 For Emphasis

Use a colon to emphasize a word, a phrase, a clause, or a sentence that explains or adds impact to the main clause (also see **650.3**).

His guest lecturers are local chefs who learn a lesson themselves: Homeless people are worth employing.

—Beth Brophy, "Feeding Those Who Are Hungry"

620.4 To Introduce a Quotation

Use a colon to formally introduce a quotation, a sentence, or a question.

Directly a voice in the corner rang out wild and clear: "I've got him! I've got him!"

—Mark Twain, *Roughing It*

620.5 To Introduce a List

A colon is used to introduce a list.

I got all the proper equipment: scissors, a bucket of water to keep things clean, some cotton for the stuffing, and needle and thread to sew it up.

—Joan Baez, *Daybreak*

A Closer Look

Do not use a colon between a verb and its object or complement, or between a preposition and its object.

Incorrect: Min has: a snowmobile, an ATV, and a canoe.
Correct: Min has plenty of toys: a snowmobile, an ATV, and a canoe.
Incorrect: I watch a TV show about: cooking wild game.
Correct: I watch a TV show about a new subject: cooking wild game.

620.6 Between a Title and a Subtitle

Use a colon to distinguish between a title and a subtitle, volume and page, and chapter and verse in literature.

Encyclopedia Americana IV: 211   Psalm 23:1–6

Colons

- After a Salutation
- Between Numerals Indicating Time
- For Emphasis
- To Introduce a Quotation
- To Introduce a List
- Between a Title and Subtitle

 Indicate where a colon is needed in the following sentences by writing the colon along with the words or numbers that surround it.

1. Darnell found the following items in his backpack two notebooks, some dirty socks, his cell phone charger, a comb, and a twenty-dollar bill.

2. Last weekend, Salli bought the DVD of *The Chronicles of Narnia The Lion, the Witch, and the Wardrobe.*

3. Dad reminded me of the inevitable "Real life begins after graduation."

4. The letter began, "Dear Mr. Parker Welcome to Lingston University!"

5. Tanisha plans to take the 813 a.m. train to Chicago; she'll arrive home tonight at 745.

6. Malcolm Gladwell's book *The Tipping Point How Little Things Can Make A Big Difference* is about sudden, unexpected changes in our society.

7. I have a lot to do on Saturday attend my brother's softball game, help Mom clean the basement, and install some new software on my computer.

8. Kennedy couldn't stop herself from thinking about Juan Was he just using "work" as an excuse to not see her?

 ## Model

Model the following sentence to practice using colons to introduce a list.

It's more than just the way I look: refugee-skinny with absolutely no chest to speak of, hair the color of dirt, connect-the-dot freckles on my cheeks that, let me tell you, do not fade with lemon juice or sunscreen or even, sadly, sandpaper.

—Jodi Picoult, *My Sister's Keeper*

Test Prep

Read the following paragraphs. Write the letter of the correct way to punctuate each underlined part from the choices given on the next page. If it is already correct, choose "D."

<u>My best friend, Ty</u>, asked me if I wanted to try my hand at <u>filmmaking? It</u>
     1   **2**
seemed like such a monumental task. It takes years to make <u>a film, doesn't it</u>?
                                                                 3
Following some wheedling <u>on his part</u> Ty convinced me to join his filmmaking
                                              4
club.

The first thing I discovered was that short films can take <u>various forms</u>
                                                       5
<u>documentaries</u>, narrative fiction, music videos, narrative <u>poetry and</u> even political
                                                        6
campaign ads. I decided that making a short film is a lot like writing a short story
or an <u>essay the</u> principles even follow the traits of writing. First, you sort through
      7
all your <u>amazing creative ideas</u>, and then you choose one as the subject of your
                    8
film. You write a script, organize your ideas, and find the appropriate voice;
then you revise and edit. <u>Hey;</u> I can do that!
                 9

Ty and I came up with an idea that required a day trip to the nation's <u>capital
Washington D.C.</u> We would interview our U.S. <u>senator and</u> the topic would be the
   10   **11**
importance of teen voting. Our plan was to emphasize that <u>teens not just older
voting Americans</u> play an important role in all elections.
                                             12

On <u>April 11 2006</u> we conducted the interview. We had planned everything
     13
ahead of <u>time, as a result</u> the filmmaking went even better than we had expected.
        14
The senator helped our script by improvising the <u>ending</u>: "In just five minutes, one
                                       15
person can change the country—even the world." He liked our film <u>so much, that</u> he
                                                   16
plans to use it in his next election campaign!

<u>Filmmaking, which I thought would be hard</u> turned out to be one of the most
                       17
enjoyable experiences of my senior year. In fact, I plan to take some filmmaking
classes in college this fall. Perhaps I'll even choose it as <u>my major</u>!
                                                          18

1. **A** My best friend Ty
   B My best friend, Ty
   C My best friend Ty,
   D correct as is

2. **A** filmmaking; It
   B filmmaking. It
   C filmmaking, it
   D correct as is

3. **A** a film doesn't it?
   B a film, doesn't it.
   C a film doesn't it.
   D correct as is

4. **A** on his part,
   B on his part.
   C on his part;
   D correct as is

5. **A** various forms, documentaries,
   B various forms; documentaries
   C various forms: documentaries,
   D correct as is

6. **A** poetry and,
   B poetry, and
   C poetry, and,
   D correct as is

7. **A** essay, the
   B essay the,
   C essay; the
   D correct as is

8. **A** amazing, creative ideas
   B amazing, creative ideas,
   C amazing creative ideas
   D correct as is

9. **A** Hey,
   B Hey:
   C Hey?
   D correct as is

10. **A** capital, Washington D.C.
    B capital Washington, D.C.
    C capital, Washington, D.C.
    D correct as is

11. **A** senator, and
    B senator, and,
    C senator and,
    D correct as is

12. **A** teens, not just older voting Americans
    B teens, not just older voting Americans,
    C teens not just older voting Americans,
    D correct as is

13. **A** April 11, 2006
    B April 11 2006,
    C April 11, 2006,
    D correct as is

14. **A** time, as a result,
    B time; as a result,
    C time; as a result
    D correct as is

15. **A** ending;
    B ending
    C ending,
    D correct as is

16. **A** so much that
    B so much that,
    C so much, that,
    D correct as is

17. **A** Filmmaking which I thought would be hard
    B Filmmaking which I thought would be hard,
    C Filmmaking, which I thought would be hard,
    D correct as is

18. **A** my major?
    B my major;
    C my major,
    D correct as is

Hyphen

624.1 In Compound Words

Use the **hyphen** to make some compound words.

great-great-grandfather   **maid-in-waiting**   **three-year-old**

624.2 To Create New Words

Use a hyphen to form new words beginning with the prefixes *self-, ex-, all-,* and *half-*. Also use a hyphen to join any prefix to a proper noun, a proper adjective, or the official name of an office. Use a hyphen before the suffix *-elect.*

self-**contained**   ex-**governor**   all-**inclusive**   half-**painted**
pre-**Cambrian**   mid-**December**   president-**elect**

Use a hyphen to join the prefix *great-* only to the names of relatives.

great-**aunt,** great-**grandfather** (correct)   **great-hall** (incorrect)

624.3 To Form an Adjective

Use a hyphen to join two or more words that serve as a single adjective (a single-thought adjective) before a noun.

In real life I am a large, big-boned **woman with rough,** man-working **hands.**

—Alice Walker, "Everyday Use"

Use common sense to determine whether a compound adjective might be misread if it is not hyphenated. Generally, hyphenate a compound adjective that is composed of . . .

- a phrase   heat-and-serve **meal**   off-and-on **relationship**
- a noun + adjective   oven-safe **handles**   book-smart **student**
- a noun + participle (*ing* or *ed* form of a verb)   bone-chilling **story**

624.4 To Join Letters and Words

Use a hyphen to join a capital letter or lowercase letter to a noun or participle. (Check your dictionary if you're not sure of the hyphenation.)

T-**shirt**   Y-**turn**   G-**rated**   x-**axis**

A Closer Look

When words forming the adjective come after the noun, do not hyphenate them.

In real life I am large and big boned.

When the first of these words is an adverb ending in *-ly,* do not use a hyphen.

delicately prepared **pastry**

Also, do not use a hyphen when a number or a letter is the final element in a single-thought adjective.

class B **movie**

Hyphens 1

- In Compound Words
- To Create New Words
- To Form an Adjective
- To Join Letters and Words

For each sentence below, correctly write the words that should be hyphenated. Some sentences contain more than one hyphenated word.

1. The three year old Detroit based store is going out of business.

2. Our second quarter exam will cover chapters 12 through 14.

3. Some thought provoking arguments were raised in this award winning film.

4. My brother in law got a small business loan to open his restaurant.

5. Senator elect Ricchio spoke last night at the Italian American club.

6. The race car driver approached the S curve at an unsafe speed.

7. Dana's great grandpa is a self sufficient, fun loving person.

8. He decided to take Web based lessons to learn how to play the banjo.

9. Saied has a ten dollar credit on his prepaid phone card.

10. Tovah bought a yellow V neck T shirt at the mall.

Model

Model the following sentences to practice using hyphens to form adjectives and to create new words.

> The stones which Deucalion threw sprang up as full-grown men, strong, and handsome, and brave. —James Baldwin, "The Flood"

> He did look cautiously behind it first, as if he half-expected to be terrified with the sight of Marley's pigtail sticking out into the hall. —Charles Dickens, *A Christmas Carol*

Hyphen *(continued)*

626.1 Between Numbers and Fractions

Use a hyphen to join the words in compound numbers from *twenty-one* to *ninety-nine* when it is necessary to write them out (see **658.3**).

Use a hyphen between the numerator and denominator of a fraction, but not when one or both of those elements are already hyphenated.

four-tenths   five-sixteenths   (7/32) seven thirty-seconds

626.2 In a Special Series

Use hyphens when two or more words have a common element that is omitted in all but the last term.

The ship has lovely two-, four-, or six-person cabins.

626.3 To Join Numbers

Use a hyphen to join numbers indicating the life span of a person or the score in a contest or a vote.

We can thank Louis Pasteur (1822–1895) for pasteurized milk.

In the 2000 Rose Bowl, Wisconsin defeated Stanford 17–9.

626.4 To Prevent Confusion

Use a hyphen with prefixes or suffixes to avoid confusion or awkward spelling.

re-create (not *recreate*) the image   re-cover (not *recover*) the sofa

626.5 To Divide a Word

Use a hyphen to divide a word, only between its syllables, at the end of a line of print. Always place the hyphen after the syllable at the end of the line—never before a syllable at the beginning of the following line.

Guidelines for Dividing with Hyphens

1. Always divide a compound word between its basic units: **sister-in-law,** not **sis-ter-in-law.**

2. Avoid dividing a word of five or fewer letters: **paper, study, July.**

3. Avoid dividing the last word in a paragraph.

4. Never divide a one-syllable word: **rained, skills, through.**

5. Never divide a one-letter syllable from the rest of the word: **omit-ted,** not **o-mitted.**

6. When a vowel is a syllable by itself, divide the word after the vowel: **epi-sode,** not **ep-isode.**

7. Never divide abbreviations or contractions: **shouldn't,** not **should-n't.**

8. Never divide the last word in more than two lines in a row.

Hyphens 2

- ■ **Between Numbers and Fractions**
- ■ **In a Special Series**
- ■ **To Join Numbers**
- ■ **To Prevent Confusion**
- ■ **To Divide a Word**

 For each sentence below, correctly write the word(s) that should be hyphenated or are incorrectly hyphenated.

1. The unusual foliage has a shelllike coating.

2. Your assignment is to write an 800 to 1,000 word persuasive essay.

3. Say what you will, but I believe these arguments about money have stra-ined our relationship.

4. Even one thirty second of an inch error in measurement will result in an inaccurate reading.

5. Cut the board into two, four, and six inch lengths.

6. Dr. Mahan's degree is in chemistry, but he is always ready with one histo-rical fact or another to explain his lessons.

7. Two thirds of the crowd left when the score was 33 10 in the fourth quarter.

8. My boss asked me to resign the form after rereading sections 5 7.

9. Prior to the exam, the proctor gave this instruction: "You will need to o-mit question number six from your answers due to a printing error."

10. Sergei wrote of yesterday's Moscowwide electrical outage in his e-mail.

11. By 2015, more than one half of the world's population will live in urban areas.

12. Ramona created six and eight sided paper snowflakes.

 ## Model

Model the following sentence to practice using hyphens in a special series.

Two-, three-, and four-column notebooks are available at the bookstore.

Apostrophe

628.1 In Contractions

Use an **apostrophe** to show that one or more letters have been left out of a word group to form a contraction.

> hadn't – *o* is left out   they'd – *woul* is left out   it's – *i* is left out

Note: Use an apostrophe to show that one or more numerals or letters have been left out of numbers or words in order to show special pronunciation.

> class of '99 – *19* is left out   g'day – *ood* is left out

628.2 To Form Singular Possessives

Add an apostrophe and *s* to form the possessive of most singular nouns.

> Spock's **ears**   Captain Kirk's **singing**   the ship's **escape plan**

Note: When a singular noun ends with an *s* or a *z* sound, you may form the possessive by adding just an apostrophe. When the singular noun is a one-syllable word, however, you usually add both an apostrophe and an *s* to form the possessive.

> San Carlos' **government** (or) San Carlos's **government** (two-syllable word)
>
> Ross's **essay** (one-syllable word)   the class's **field trip** (one-syllable word)

628.3 To Form Plural Possessives

The possessive form of plural nouns ending in *s* is usually made by adding just an apostrophe.

> students' **homework**   bosses' **orders**

For plural nouns not ending in *s,* an apostrophe and *s* must be added.

> children's **book**   men's **department**

A Closer Look

It will help you punctuate correctly if you remember that the word immediately before the apostrophe is the owner.

> girl's **guitar** (*girl* is the owner)   boss's **order** (*boss* is the owner)
>
> girls' **guitars** (*girls* are the owners)   bosses' **order** (*bosses* are the owners)

628.4 To Show Shared Possession

When possession is shared by more than one noun, use the possessive form for the last noun in the series.

> Hoshi, Linda, and Nakiva's **water skis** (All three own the same skis.)
>
> Hoshi's, Linda's, and Nakiva's **water skis** (Each owns her own skis.)

Apostrophes 1

- In Contractions
- To Form Singular Possessives
- To Form Plural Possessives
- To Show Shared Possession

 For each sentence, write the contraction for or the possessive form of the word or words in parentheses.

1. *(Ravi, Simone, and Lucas)* biology classes went on a field trip together.

2. They had to take two buses because everyone *(would not)* fit on one.

3. *(Mount Ranier)* Sunrise Area was the destination for the *(students)* trip.

4. Simone said, "*(I have)* never been here before. I hope *(it will)* be fun!"

5. The *(classes)* assignment was to observe and investigate an *(alpine ecosystem)* fragility.

6. The *(teachers)* lesson plans provided excellent insight into the *(mountain)* ecological systems.

7. *(Ravi and Simone)* shoes *(were not)* appropriate for a three-mile hike.

8. Ravi wished *(he had)* worn hiking boots.

9. *(Mr. Sullivan and Mrs. Ling)* first-aid kit was put to good use.

10. *(It is)* a good thing that *(they are)* always prepared; the kids *(would have)* suffered without bandages for their blisters.

◤ Model

Model the following sentences to practice using apostrophes to form singular and plural possessives.

> **Take each man's censure, but reserve thy judgment.**
> —William Shakespeare, *Hamlet*

> **The notion that nutmeg could ward off the plague survived longer than many another old wives' tales.**
> —Simon Winchester, *Krakatoa*

Punctuation

Apostrophe *(continued)*

630.1 To Show Possession with Indefinite Pronouns

Form the possessive of an indefinite pronoun by placing an apostrophe and an *s* on the last word (see **704.1** and **706.3**).

> everyone's   anyone's   somebody's
>
> **It is** everybody's **responsibility to keep his or her locker orderly.**

In expressions using *else,* add the apostrophe and *s* after the last word.

> **This is** somebody else's **mess, not mine.**

630.2 To Show Possession in Compound Nouns

Form the possessive of a compound noun by placing the possessive ending after the last word.

> **the** secretary of the interior's (singular) **agenda**
> **her** lady-in-waiting's (singular) **day off**

If forming a possessive of a plural compound noun creates an awkward construction, you may replace the possessive with an *of* phrase. (All four forms below are correct.)

> **their** fathers-in-law's (plural) **birthdays**
> or **the birthdays of their fathers-in-law** (plural)
>
> **the** ambassadors-at-large's (plural) **plans**
> or **the plans of the ambassadors-at-large** (plural)

630.3 To Express Time or Amount

Use an apostrophe and an *s* with an adjective that is part of an expression indicating time or amount.

> **a penny's worth**   **two cents' worth**   **this morning's meeting**
> **yesterday's news**   **a day's wage**   **six months' pay**

630.4 To Form Certain Plurals

Use an apostrophe and *s* to form the plural of a letter, a number, a sign, or a word discussed as a word.

> **B – B's   C – C's   8 – 8's   + – +'s   *and* – *and*'s**
>
> **Ms. D'Aquisto says our conversations contain too many** *like's* **and** *no way's.*

Note: If two apostrophes are called for in the same word, omit the second one.

> **Follow closely the** *do's* **and** *don'ts* **(not** *don't's***) on the checklist.**

Apostrophes 2

- To Show Possession with Indefinite Pronouns
- To Show Possession in Compound Nouns
- To Express Time or Amount
- To Form Certain Plurals

Write each underlined word in the following paragraphs with the apostrophe placed correctly.

Each day, I drink about five **(1)** <u>dollars</u> worth of coffee. You might share **(2)** <u>everyone elses</u> opinion that I drink too much coffee, but that's not true—no **(3)** <u>*ifs, ands* or *buts*</u> about it! I buy only one cup of coffee a day, and it's always one of the **(4)** <u>Super 20s</u> at Sergio's Coffee Shop. (Each specialty cup of coffee holds 20 ounces.)

The shop is staffed by Sergio's family members, and these **(5)** <u>Italian Americans</u> cooking is superb. Sergio uses his **(6)** <u>sister-in-laws</u> recipes for the special coffee drinks, and she works in the shop as a barista. Her Almond Joy Super 20 (I love it!) is a flavored latte that's **(7)** <u>everybodys</u> favorite. Some of the other Super 20 flavors are **(8)** <u>Cs in 3s</u> (cappuccino with chocolate and caramel syrups) and **(9)** <u>Anyones</u> Guess, which is **(10)** <u>todays</u> flavor of the day.

Model

Model the following sentences to practice using apostrophes to express time or amount and to show possession with indefinite pronouns.

I never did a day's work in my life. It was all fun.

—Thomas Edison

Everybody's business is nobody's business, and nobody's business is my business.

—Clara Barton

Quotation Marks

632.1 To Set Off Direct Quotations

Place **quotation marks** before and after the words in direct quotations.

> **"Just come to a game,"** he pleads. **"You'll change your mind."**
>
> —Sandra Lampe, "Batter UP!"

In a quoted passage, put brackets around any word or punctuation mark that is not part of the original quotation. (See **644.1**.)

If you quote only part of the original passage, be sure to construct a sentence that is both accurate and grammatically correct.

> **Much of the restructuring of the Postal Service has involved "turning over large parts of its work to the private sector."**

632.2 Placement of Punctuation

Always place periods and commas inside quotation marks.

> **"Dr. Slaughter wants you to have liquids, Will,"** Mama said anxiously. **"He said not to give you any solid food tonight."**
>
> —Olive Ann Burns, *Cold Sassy Tree*

Place an exclamation point or a question mark *inside* quotation marks when it punctuates the quotation and *outside* when it punctuates the main sentence.

> **"Am I dreaming?"**   **Had she heard him say, "Here's the key to your new car"?**

Always place semicolons or colons outside quotation marks.

> **I wrote about James Joyce's "The Dead"; I found it thought provoking.**

632.3 For Long Quotations

If you quote more than one paragraph, place quotation marks before each paragraph and at the end of the last paragraph (Example A). If a quotation has more than four lines on a page, you may set it off from the text by indenting 10 spaces from the left margin (block form). Do not use quotation marks either before or after the quoted material, unless they appear in the original (Example B).

Example A

Example B

Quotation Marks 1

- **To Set Off Direct Quotations**
- **Placement of Punctuation**
- **For Long Quotations**

 Indicate where quotation marks are needed in the following paragraphs by writing the quotation marks along with the words and other punctuation after or before them. (Use ellipses to show omitted words in your answers.)

1   I couldn't believe what I held in my hands. It was a yellowed letter
2   that I'd discovered tucked among the pages of an old scrapbook in our attic.
3   Mom, look at this, I said. It's a love letter. I handed her the fragile page
4   filled with the following almost illegible scrawl.

5   This letter brings the same old theme, which instead of growing
6   old by telling only grows brighter. This proves that my love for
7   you is stronger with each passing day. My happiness can not be
8   any greater than since I met you, my darling Ella. Being apart
9   from you, far across the sea, seems like an eternity to me. I long
10   to see your smile again, to hold your hands, and to look into your
11   beautiful eyes.

12   Mom sighed. This letter is from your great-grandfather to his wife,
13   Ella, she said. Grandma told me once that Grandpa Doty had written her
14   some wonderful letters. She also told me how they fell in love.

15   It really was a love-at-first-sight story. Ella and William, a soldier,
16   met a few weeks before he was scheduled to leave for England. It was
17   during World War I, and many soldiers were dying in the war overseas.
18   The day before he shipped out, they ran off and got married against their
19   parents' wishes.

20   William wrote to Ella almost every day, and I wouldn't be surprised
21   if we find more letters up here. Now I can't wait to go through all this old
22   stuff! Mom said.

23   I can't either, I answered. All of a sudden, cleaning the attic was a
24   treasure hunt instead of a chore.

Model

Model the following sentence to practice correct placement of punctuation with quotation marks.

It is not a lucky word, this name "impossible"; no good comes of those who have it so often in their mouths.

—Thomas Carlyle

Quotation Marks *(continued)*

634.1 Quotation Marks Within Quotations

Use single quotation marks to punctuate a quotation within a quotation. Use double quotation marks if you need to distinguish a quotation within a quotation within a quotation.

> **"For tomorrow," said Mr. Botts, "read 'Unlighted Lamps.'"**
>
> **Sue asked, "Did you hear Mr. Botts say, 'Read "Unlighted Lamps"'?"**

634.2 For Special Words

You may use quotation marks (1) to distinguish a word that is being discussed, (2) to indicate that a word is unfamiliar slang, or (3) to point out that a word is being used in a special way.

> **(1) A commentary on the times is that the word "honesty" is now preceded by "old-fashioned."**
> —Larry Wolters
>
> **(2) I . . . asked the bartender where I could hear "chanky-chank," as Cajuns called their music.**
> —William Least Heat-Moon, *Blue Highways*
>
> **(3) Tom pushed the wheelchair across the street, showed the lady his "honest" smile . . . and stole her purse.**

Note: You may use italics (underlining) in place of quotation marks in each of these three situations. (See **636.3**.)

634.3 To Punctuate Titles

Use **quotation marks** to punctuate titles of songs, poems, short stories, one-act plays, lectures, episodes of radio or television programs, chapters of books, unpublished works, electronic files, and articles found in magazines, newspapers, encyclopedias, or online sources. (For punctuation of other titles, see **636.2**.)

> **"Santa Lucia"** (song)
> **"The Chameleon"** (short story)
> **"Twentieth-Century Memories"** (lecture)
> **"Affordable Adventures"** (magazine article)
> **"Dire Prophecy of the Howling Dog"** (chapter in a book)
> **"Dancing with Debra"** (television episode)
> **"Miss Julie"** (one-act play)

Note: Punctuate one title within another title as follows:

> **"Clarkson's 'Breakaway' Hits the Waves"**
> (title of a song in title of an article)

Quotation Marks 2

- Quotation Marks Within Quotations
- For Special Words
- To Punctuate Titles

 Write the word or words that should be enclosed in quotation marks in the following sentences.

1. Parker's poem entitled North to Midnight was accepted for publication in the national magazine *Know It!*

2. Tremain said, Did you see that ridiculous *Enquirer* article, Pterodactyls Found Alive in Tanzanian Cave?

3. The real estate agent used words like spacious, open, and airy to describe the home's sunroom.

4. Dad says that I should check out the drum solo in the song Away by an old rock group called Rain Sign.

5. Melissa's essay was titled The Natural State and told of the clear lakes, streams, and abundance of natural wildlife in Arkansas.

6. Rob asked, Have you read *Walden Pond* for English class?

7. His favorite episode of *Deadliest Catch* is Race Against the Ice.

8. Employees at the soda bottling company are subject to pop quizzes.

Model

Model the following sentence to practice using quotation marks within quotations.

> In a BBC review, Talia Kraines discusses the Black Eyed Peas CD *Monkey Business*: "The most immediate track is the incredibly silly 'My Humps.' Sounding like a cross between Paula Abdul's 'Opposites Attract' and Nenah Cherry's 'Buffalo Stance,' it wouldn't sound out of place on a Gwen Stefani album."

Italics (Underlining)

636.1 Handwritten and Printed Material

Italics is a printer's term for a style of type that is slightly slanted. In this sentence, the word *happiness* is printed in italics. In material that is handwritten or typed on a machine that cannot print in italics, underline each word or letter that should be in italics.

> *My Ántonia* is the story of a strong and determined pioneer woman.

> (printed)

> Willa Cather's <u>My Ántonia</u> describes pioneer life in America.

> (typed or handwritten)

636.2 In Titles

Use italics to indicate the titles of magazines, newspapers, pamphlets, books, full-length plays, films, videos, radio and television programs, book-length poems, ballets, operas, paintings, lengthy musical compositions, sculptures, cassettes, CD's, legal cases, and the names of ships and aircraft. (For punctuation of other titles, see **634.3**.)

> *Newsweek* (magazine)
> *Shakespeare in Love* (film)
> *Caring for Your Kitten* (pamphlet)
> *Chicago Tribune* (newspaper)

> *Cold Sassy Tree* (book)
> *Law & Order* (television program)
> *Hedda Gabler* (full-length play)
> *The Thinker* (sculpture)

636.3 For Special Uses

Use italics for a number, letter, or word that is being discussed or used in a special way. (Sometimes quotation marks are used for this reason. See **634.2**.)

> I hope that this letter *I* on my report card stands for *incredible* and not *incomplete*.

636.4 For Foreign Words

Use italics for foreign words that have not been adopted into the English language; also use italics for scientific names.

> The voyageurs—tough men with natural *bonhomie*—discovered the shy *Castor canadensis*, or North American beaver.

636.5 For Emphasis

Use italics for words that require particular emphasis.

> I guess it really *was* worth it to put in extra study time.

italic

Italics (Underlining)

- ■ **In Titles**
- ■ **For Special Uses**
- ■ **For Foreign Words**
- ■ **For Emphasis**

 Write and underline the word or words that should be italicized in the following sentences.

1. In algebra, we use the letters Z, Q, R, and C respectively to represent integers, rational, real, and complex numbers.

2. Giana hugged the queen—quite a faux pas, she later learned.

3. I enjoy planning trips to places I read about in National Geographic magazine.

4. Vinny did say that he would be late, remember?

5. Robin wrote a humorous opera called Diary of a Soccer Mom's Daughter.

6. Did you mix up the words bring and take?

7. "Not now!" Amber cried when her computer froze in the middle of a message.

8. She would have to call her cousin in New York about some tickets for the show Rent.

 ## Model

Model the following sentence to practice using italics (underlining) for emphasis.

> **"As yet," cried the stranger—his cheek glowing and his eye flashing with enthusiasm—"as yet, I have done *nothing*."**
>
> —Nathaniel Hawthorne, "The Ambitious Guest"

Punctuation

Parentheses

638.1 To Set Off Explanatory Material

You may use **parentheses** to set off explanatory or added material that interrupts the normal sentence structure.

> **Benson** (our dog) **sits in on our piano lessons** (on the piano bench), **much to the teacher's surprise and amusement.**
> > —Chad Hockerman, student writer

Note: Place question marks and exclamation points within the parentheses when they mark the added material.

> **Ivan at once concluded** (the rascal!) **that I had a passion for dances, and . . . wanted to drag me off to a dancing class.**
> > —Fyodor Dostoyevsky, "A Novel in Nine Letters"

638.2 With Full Sentences

When using a full sentence within another sentence, do not capitalize it or use a period inside the parentheses.

> **And, since your friend won't have the assignment** (he was just thinking about calling you), **you'll have to make a couple more calls to actually get it.**
> > —Ken Taylor, "The Art and Practice of Avoiding Homework"

When the parenthetical sentence comes after the period of the main sentence, capitalize and punctuate it the same way you would any other complete sentence.

> **They kiss and hug when they say "hello," and I love this.** (In Korea, people are much more formal; they just shake hands and bow to each other.)
> > —Sue Chong, "He Said I Was Too American"

Note: For unavoidable parentheses within parentheses (. . . [. . .] . . .), use brackets. Avoid overuse of parentheses by using commas instead.

Diagonal

638.3 To Show a Choice

Use a **diagonal** (also called a *slash* or forward *slash*) between two words, as in *and/or*, to indicate that either is acceptable.

> **Press the** load/eject **button.**
> **Don't worry; this is** indoor/outdoor **carpet.**

638.4 When Quoting Poetry

When quoting more than one line of poetry, use a diagonal to show where each line of poetry ends. (Insert a space on each side of the diagonal.)

> **I have learned not to worry about love;** / **but to honor its coming** / **with all my heart.**
> > —Alice Walker, "New Face"

Parentheses and Diagonals

- To Set Off Explanatory Material
- With Full Sentences
- To Show a Choice
- When Quoting Poetry

 For the following sentences, write the word or words that should be enclosed in parentheses or divided by a diagonal. (Include parentheses or diagonals.)

1. Thai food have you tried it? is gaining popularity.

2. Old-style Thai cooking features the foods of a "waterborne lifestyle." This means ingredients like aquatic animals, plants, and herbs.

3. Americanized Thai food a unique blend of flavors is influenced by centuries-old Eastern and Western cultures.

4. Choose a curry dish and or a spiced salad to begin your meal.

5. Thai food everything is served in bite-sized pieces never needs a knife.

6. The server provides his her patrons with just a fork and a spoon.

7. You might want to try Khao Phat and Phat Thai one of the popular rice and noodle dishes when you visit a Thai restaurant.

 Rewrite the haiku poem below as if you were quoting it in the text of an essay.

8. Moored to the heavens
The wistful moon and bound stars
Dream about dancing.

Model

Model the following sentence to practice parentheses to set off explanatory material.

We asked people in the street (outside the Palladium Theatre, as it happens, at about 5 p.m.) if they used proper punctuation when sending text messages.
—Lynne Truss, *Eats, Shoots and Leaves*

Dash

640.1 To Indicate a Sudden Break

Use a **dash** to indicate a sudden break or change in the sentence.

Near the semester's end—and this is not always due to poor planning—**some students may find themselves in a real crunch.**

Note: Dashes are often used in place of commas. Use dashes when you want to give special emphasis; use commas when there is no need for emphasis.

640.2 To Set Off an Introductory Series

Use a dash to set off an introductory series from the clause that explains the series.

A good book, a cup of tea, a comfortable chair—**these things always saved my mother's sanity.**

640.3 To Set Off Parenthetical Material

You may use a dash to set off parenthetical material—material that explains or clarifies a word or a phrase.

A single incident—a tornado that came without warning—**changed the face of the small town forever.**

640.4 To Indicate Interrupted Speech

Use a dash to show interrupted or faltering speech in dialogue.

Sojourner: Mama, why are you—

Mama: Isabelle, do as I say!

—Sandy Asher, *A Woman Called Truth*

640.5 For Emphasis

Use a dash to emphasize a word, a series, a phrase, or a clause.

After several hours of hearing the high-pitched yipping, Petra finally realized what it was—coyote pups.

After years of trial and error, Belther made history with his invention—the unicycle.

Dashes

- To Indicate a Sudden Break
- To Set Off an Introductory Series
- To Set Off Parenthetical Material
- For Emphasis

 A word, a phrase, or a clause follows each sentence below. Rewrite the sentences to include those words, set off by one or two dashes.

1. The strange sound came from Old Ike's cornfield; I couldn't tell if it was human, or not. (*a low, guttural groaning*)

2. One would never guess that this colorful bird is considered a pest in Australia. (*the Rainbow Lorikeet*)

3. The members of Lemuel's band, Elixer K8, finally reached their long sought-after goal. (*hearing their song played on the radio*)

4. That's all I need for a relaxing day on the beach. (*a cold drink, sunscreen, my MP3 player, and a good book*)

5. At 8:00 p.m. Saul arrived to take Trina to the prom. (*almost two hours late*)

6. Tony Akgulian spoke out in favor of a citywide graduation party sponsored by the Downtown Association. (*fifth-district alderman*)

7. Jarvis borrowed his brother's leather jacket to wear at the audition. (*the "lucky" jacket*)

8. Edward had applied to these prestigious schools. (*Princeton, Harvard, and Yale*)

Model

Model the following sentence to practice using dashes to set off parenthetical material.

> **When I first beheld this apparition—for I could scarcely regard it as less—my wonder and my terror were extreme.**
>
> —Edgar Allan Poe, "The Black Cat"

Ellipsis

642.1 To Show Omitted Words

Use an **ellipsis** (three periods with one space before and after each period) to show that one or more words have been omitted in a quotation.

(Original)

We the people of the United States, in order to form a more perfect Union, establish justice, insure domestic tranquility, provide for the common defense, promote the general welfare, and secure the blessings of liberty to ourselves and our posterity, do ordain and establish this Constitution for the United States of America.

—Preamble, U.S. Constitution

(Quotation)

"We the people . . . in order to form a more perfect Union . . . establish this Constitution for the United States of America."

642.2 At the End of a Sentence

If words from a quotation are omitted at the end of a sentence, place the ellipsis after the period that marks the conclusion of the sentence.

"Five score years ago, a great American, in whose symbolic shadow we stand, signed the Emancipation Proclamation. . . . But one hundred years later, we must face the tragic fact that the Negro is still not free."
—Martin Luther King, Jr., "I Have a Dream"

Note: If the quoted material is a complete sentence (even if it was not complete in the original), use a period, then an ellipsis.

(Original)

I am tired; my heart is sick and sad. From where the sun now stands I will fight no more forever.

—Chief Joseph of the Nez Percé

(Quotation)

"I am tired. . . . From where the sun now stands I will fight no more forever."

or

"I am tired. . . . I will fight no more. . . . "

642.3 To Show a Pause

Use an ellipsis to indicate a pause.

I brought my trembling hand to my focusing eyes. It was oozing, it was red, it was . . . it was . . . a tomato!
—Laura Baginski, student writer

Ellipses

- **To Show Omitted Words**
- **At the End of a Sentence**
- **To Show a Pause**

 For the following paragraph, select the least important information to replace with ellipses. Write the shortened paragraph on your paper.

1   Have you ever tried making a tasty, cheesy, wonderful, homemade
2 pizza from scratch? Making a pizza is easy to achieve, especially if you use
3 a bread machine. Combine the following easy-to-find ingredients in the pan
4 of the bread machine: 3 1/2 cups flour, 1 cup warm water, 2 tablespoons
5 dry yeast, 2 tablespoons honey (you can leave this ingredient out if you
6 want to; it's entirely up to you), 1/4 cup olive oil, and about 1/2 teaspoon of
7 salt (more or less, to your preferred taste). Set the machine to the "dough
8 only" setting and push the start button. When it is ready, place the dough
9 on a wood cutting board or another flat surface. Throw some flour on the
10 surface and flatten the dough with your hands or a sturdy rolling pin. Work
11 it until it's the size of the pan you plan to cook it on (a round pizza pan or
12 a cookie sheet works well). Rub a little olive oil onto the pan and then press
13 the dough evenly into the pan. Prick some small holes in the crust with a
14 fork. This will help to keep it from bubbling up while cooking, and it also
15 helps to hold the sauce, as well. Top the crust with pizza sauce, a lot of
16 tasty mozzarella cheese, and whatever other kinds of toppings that you like
17 on your pizza. Bake the pizza in a 400-degree oven until the crust is light
18 brown. Enjoy eating your pizza!

Exercise

For each of the following situations, write a sentence or two in which you use an ellipsis to show a pause.

Your best friend has asked a special person to the prom dance. You want to know if the answer was "yes."

You are surprised by the contents of a letter that you've just read.

Brackets

644.1 To Set Off Clarifying Information

Use **brackets** before and after words that are added to clarify what another person has said or written.

> **"They'd [the sweat bees] get into your mouth, ears, eyes, nose. You'd feel them all over you."**
> —Marilyn Johnson and Sasha Nyary,
> "Roosevelts in the Amazon"

Note: The brackets indicate that the words *the sweat bees* are not part of the quotation but were added for clarification.

644.2 Around an Editorial Correction

Place brackets around an editorial correction inserted within quoted material.

> **"Brooklyn alone has 8 percent of lead poisoning [victims] nationwide," said Marjorie Moore.**
> —Donna Actie, student writer

Note: The brackets indicate that the word *victims* replaced the author's original word.

Place brackets around the letters *sic* (Latin for "as such"); the letters indicate that an error appearing in the material being quoted was made by the original speaker or writer.

> **"When I'm queen," mused Lucy, "I'll show these blockheads whose [sic] got beauty and brains."**

644.3 To Set Off Added Words

Place brackets around comments that have been added to a quotation.

> **"Congratulations to the astronomy club's softball team, which put in, shall we say, a 'stellar' performance." [groans]**

Punctuation Marks

´	Accent, acute	,	Comma	( )	Parentheses
`	Accent, grave	†	Dagger	.	Period
'	Apostrophe	—	Dash	?	Question mark
*	Asterisk	/	Diagonal/Slash	" "	Quotation marks
{ }	Brace	¨ (ü)	Dieresis	§	Section
[ ]	Brackets	. . .	Ellipsis	;	Semicolon
^	Caret	!	Exclamation point	~	Tilde
(ç)	Cedilla	-	Hyphen	___	Underscore
^	Circumflex	...	Leaders		
:	Colon	¶	Paragraph		

Brackets

- ■ **To Set Off Clarifying Information**
- ■ **Around Editorial Corrections**
- ■ **To Set Off Added Words**

 Follow the directions for each activity below.

1. In the following quotation, the speaker is talking about solar flares. Rewrite the quotation, using that word in brackets to clarify the quotation.

> **"Early records indicate that the sun went through a period of inactivity in the late seventeenth century," Dr. Johnson explained. "Very few were seen from about 1645 to 1715."**

2. Quote the following statement and show that the error was made by the original author, Jean le Fleur.

> **Many belief that the "Kennedy curse" began with the death of Joseph Kennedy during World War II.**

3. In the following quotation, replace the speaker's use of the word *motorsport* with the words *auto racing*. Place brackets around your editorial correction.

> **According to David Carls, a local race-car enthusiast, "Motorsport is probably the world's most popular spectator sport because everybody dreams of being able to drive a car that fast—legally."**

4. Use brackets to add the writer's comment, a yawn, to these sentences.

> **All of this endless talk about a referendum is getting old. Put it on a ballot and take it to the people!**

 # Model

Model the following sentence to practice using brackets to set off clarifying information.

> **He [a physicist] is an atom's way of knowing about atoms.**
>
> —George Wald

Test Prep

From the choices given on the next page, write the letter of the correct way to punctuate each underlined part of the following essay. If it is already correct, write "D."

Ms. Hoffman, my art history teacher, said, "The origin of stained glass is a mystery." "Most likely, the technique came from making jewelry and mosaics.
1
For 50 years, 1050 1100 C.E., a monk wrote instructions for making stained
2
glass windows".
3
I couldn't wait to hear the monks' instructions. I've always been fascinated
4
by how adding just a little bit of metallic salts or oxides to liquid glass creates the beautiful colors. I had read a book called *Stained Glass Basics* and learned that go-
5 **6**
ld makes a brilliant cranberry color, cobalt makes blue, silver makes yellows-golds,
7
and copper makes green and, surprisingly, brick red. Yet I didn't know how to put it
8
together to create a piece of art. What would I learn from this monk about his 'new'
art form—a stained glass window?
9
"These old instructions are still followed today," Ms. Hoffman continued.
"Here is what they say; "To assemble these windows, first mark their leng-
10
ths and breadths on a wooden board. Then draw scrollwork, or anything else that pleases you, and select colors to add. Cut the glass with a grozing iron (a tool with a
12
hardened steel point—and fit the pieces together. Enclose them with cames [narrow
13
lead strips,] and solder them on both sides. Surround the window with a wooden frame strengthened with nails and set it up in the place you wish.' "
14
At this point, Ms. Hoffman asked, "Have you ever seen real stained glass in anyones' home? It can increase the value of a house dramatically." I volunteered that
15
I had seen a recreation of Van Gogh's painting "Irises" in a house in Rome, Virginia.
16 **17**
(The house had become a museum in the 1970s). Stained glass can add not only
18
beauty but also value to windows in any building.

1. **A** mystery." Most
    B mystery. Most
    C mystery. "Most
    D correct as is

2. **A** 1050—1100 C.E.
    B 1050 / 1100 C.E.
    C 1050-1100 C.E.
    D correct as is

3. **A** windows."
    B windows'.
    C windows.'
    D correct as is

4. **A** cound'nt wait to hear the monks'
    B could'nt wait to hear the monk's
    C couldn't wait to hear the monk's
    D correct as is

5. **A** "Stained Glass Basics"
    B 'Stained Glass Basics'
    C "Stained Glass Basics,"
    D correct as is

6. **A** gol-d
    B g-old
    C This word should not be divided.
    D correct as is

7. **A** yellows golds
    B yellows—golds
    C yellows/golds
    D correct as is

8. **A** Yet I di'dnt
    B Yet I did'nt
    C Yet: I didn't
    D correct as is

9. **A** "new" art form—a
    B "new" art form [a
    C 'new' art form (a
    D correct as is

10. **A** they say: 'To
    B they say: "To
    C they say; 'To
    D correct as is

11. **A** len-gths
    B le-ngths
    C This word should not be divided.
    D correct as is

12. **A** (a tool with a hardened steel point)
    B —a tool with a hardened steel point—
    C Either "A" or "B" is correct.
    D correct as is

13. **A** (narrow lead strips,)
    B (narrow lead strips)
    C [narrow lead strips),
    D correct as is

14. **A** wish."
    B wish'."
    C wish".
    D correct as is

15. **A** anyones's home
    B anyone's home
    C anyones home
    D correct as is

16. **A** recreation of Van Goghs'
    B re-creation of Van Goghs'
    C re-creation of Van Gogh's
    D correct as is

17. **A** Irises
    B 'Irises'
    C *Irises*
    D correct as is

18. **A** 1970s.
    B 1970s.)
    C [1970s].
    D correct as is

Checking Mechanics

Capitalization

648.1 Proper Nouns and Adjectives

Capitalize proper nouns and proper adjectives (those derived from proper nouns). The chart below provides a quick overview of capitalization rules. The pages following explain some specific rules of capitalization.

Capitalization at a Glance

Names of people	**Alice Walker, Matilda, Jim, Mr. Roker**
Days of the week, months	**Sunday, Tuesday, June, August**
Holidays, holy days	**Thanksgiving, Easter, Hanukkah**
Periods, events in history	**Middle Ages, the Battle of Bunker Hill**
Official documents	**Declaration of Independence**
Special events	**Elgin Community Spring Gala**
Languages, nationalities, religions	**French, Canadian, Islam**
Political parties	**Republican Party, Socialist Party**
Trade names	**Oscar Mayer hot dogs, Pontiac Sunbird**
Official titles used with names	**Mayor John Spitzer, Senator Feinstein**
Formal epithets	**Alexander the Great**

Geographical names

Planets, heavenly bodies	**Earth, Jupiter, the Milky Way**
Continents	**Australia, South America**
Countries	**Ireland, Grenada, Sri Lanka**
States, provinces	**Ohio, Utah, Nova Scotia**
Cities, towns, villages	**El Paso, Burlington, Wonewoc**
Streets, roads, highways	**Park Avenue, Route 66, Interstate 90**
Landforms	**the Rocky Mountains, the Sahara Desert**
Bodies of water	**Yellowstone Lake, Pumpkin Creek**
Buildings, monuments	**Elkhorn High School, Gateway Arch**
Public areas	**Times Square, Sequoia National Park**

Capitalization 1

■ **Proper Nouns and Adjectives**

For each sentence below, write the word or words that should be capitalized.

1. Charles the bald was the youngest son of louis the pious, emperor and king of the franks.

2. The fugitive slave law of 1793 provided the return of runaway slaves to their owners.

3. Swahili, also known as "kiswahili," is a complex language spoken in east africa.

4. To avoid using the word "crock-pot," a registered trademark, use "slow cooker" instead.

5. The swallows day parade is an annual event in orange county, california.

6. The dixie highway stretched as far north as ontario, canada, and reached as far south as florida city, florida.

7. Lake powell, lake mead, and lake nassar are all man-made lakes.

8. In which u.s. city can you find the united nations secretariat building?

9. It is located in the turtle bay neighborhood (in the borough of manhattan) in new york city.

10. The building was featured in the movies *the pink panther strikes again* and *the interpreter.*

Model

Model the following sentence to practice capitalizing proper nouns and adjectives.

It was early February, in the middle of the peaceful lull that settles over Venice every year between New Year's Day and Carnival.

—John Berendt, *The City of Fallen Angels*

Mechanics

Capitalization (continued)

650.1 First Words

Capitalize the first word of every sentence, including the first word of a full-sentence direct quotation.

> **The crowd was quiet. A girl whispered, "I hope it's not Nancy," and the sound of her whisper reached the edges of the crowd.**
> —Shirley Jackson, "The Lottery"

650.2 Sentences in Parentheses

Capitalize the first word in a sentence enclosed in parentheses, but do not capitalize the first word if the parenthetical appears within another sentence.

> **Shamelessly she winked at me and grinned again. (That grin! She could have taken it off her face and put it on the table.)**
> —Jean Stafford, "Bad Characters"

> **Damien's aunt (she's a wild woman) plays bingo every Saturday night.**

650.3 Sentences Following Colons

Capitalize the first word in a complete sentence that follows a colon when (1) you want to emphasize the sentence or (2) the sentence is a quotation.

> **When we quarreled and made horrible faces at one another, Mother knew what to say: "Your faces will stay that way, and no one will marry you."**

650.4 Sections of the Country

Capitalize words that indicate particular sections of the country; do not capitalize words that simply indicate direction.

> **Mr. Johnson is from the Southwest.** (section of the country)

> **After moving north to Montana, he had to buy winter clothes.** (direction)

650.5 Certain Religious Words

Capitalize nouns that refer to the Supreme Being, the word *Bible,* the books of the Bible, and the names for other holy books.

> **God   Jehovah   the Lord   the Savior   Allah   Bible   Genesis**

650.6 Titles

Capitalize the first word of a title, the last word, and every word in between except articles (*a, an, the*), short prepositions, and coordinating conjunctions. Follow this rule for titles of books, newspapers, magazines, poems, plays, songs, articles, films, works of art, photographs, and stories.

> *Washington Post*   "The Diary of a Madman"   *Nights of Rain and Stars*

Capitalization 2

- First Words
- Sentences in Parentheses
- Sentences Following Colons
- Sections of the Country
- Certain Religious Words
- Titles

 Find the word or word groups that are not correctly capitalized in the following paragraphs. Write the line number in which each error appears, followed by the corrected word(s).

1   There was a cavernous rumble. Reed said, "over there!" He was

2   pointing at a giant supercell. (these rotating thunderstorms can spawn

3   tornadoes.) I felt a huge adrenaline rush as we watched the storm ramble

4   toward us from the Southwest.

5   Soon enough, the expected happened: a black rope slithered down

6   from the wall cloud. I shouted, "we have a tornado!" Reed, a seasoned storm

7   chaser from the midwest, grabbed my arm, and we bolted for his truck.

8   I thanked god that I was assigned to chase with Reed. as a

9   filmmaker, I was excited to see his photogrammetric analysis of the

10 storm. (Tornado photogrammetry is the use of film or video to

11 determine wind speed.) Some of his weather photography was featured

12 in a recent edition of *national geographic* magazine.

13 The tornado was gone as abruptly as it had appeared. the wind had

14 died down, and an eerie green atmosphere blanketed the Area. Reed started

15 his truck, ready to pursue the next storm to hit this area of the deep south.

Model

Model the following sentence to practice capitalizing sections of the country.

The Avalon Peninsula is the easternmost prow of North America—a vaguely H-shaped chunk of land that is very nearly an island itself.

—Scott Weidensaul, *Return to Wild America*

Capitalization *(continued)*

652.1 Words Used as Names

Capitalize words like *father, mother, uncle,* and *senator* when they are used as titles with a personal name or when they are substituted for proper nouns (especially in direct address).

> **We've missed you, Aunt Lucinda!** (*Aunt* is part of the name.)
>
> **I hope Mayor Bates arrives soon.** (*Mayor* is part of the name.)

A Closer Look

To test whether a word is being substituted for a proper noun, simply read the sentence with a proper noun in place of the word. If the proper noun fits in the sentence, the word being tested should be capitalized; otherwise, the word should not be capitalized.

> **Did Mom (Sue) say we could go?** (*Sue* works in this sentence.)
>
> **Did your mom (Sue) say you could go?** (*Sue* does not work here.)

Note: Usually the word is not capitalized if it follows a possessive —*my, his, your*—as it does in the second sentence above.

652.2 Letters

Capitalize the letters used to indicate form or shape.

> **U-turn   I-beam   S-curve   T-shirt   V-shaped**

652.3 Organizations

Capitalize the name of an organization, an association, or a team.

> **Lake Ontario Sailors   American Indian Movement   Democratic Party**

652.4 Abbreviations

Capitalize abbreviations of titles and organizations. (Some other abbreviations are also capitalized. See pages **660–662**.)

> **AAA   CEO   NAACP   M.D.   Ph.D.**

652.5 Titles of Courses

Capitalize words like *sociology* and *history* when they are used as titles of specific courses; do not capitalize these words when they name a field of study.

> **Who teaches History 202?** (title of a specific course)
>
> **It's the same professor who teaches my sociology course.** (a field of study)

Note: The words *freshman, sophomore, junior,* and *senior* are not capitalized unless they are part of an official title.

> **Rosa is a senior this year and is in charge of the Senior Class Banquet.**

Capitalization 3

- Words Used as Names
- Letters
- Organizations
- Abbreviations
- Titles of Courses

 Find the words that are incorrectly lowercased in the following memo. Write the line number along with the words that should be capitalized.

1   **Date:**   December 11, 2006

2   **To:**   senator Robert Flanagan

3   **From:**   Mayor Dana Stepanski of Rockdale

4   **Subject:**   Update on Rerouting r.r. 27

5   Representatives from madd (mothers against drunk driving) have

6   gathered 2,500 signatures in support of rerouting the s-curve on Rural

7   Route 27. Monica Curtis, ph.d, president of the Rockdale chapter of MADD

8   and chairperson of the environmental and safety department at McKay

9   College, presented our city council with the petition.

10   Professor Curtis teaches the highway traffic safety course at the

11   college. She pointed out that r.r. 27 has had more accidents than any other

12   state highway in River Rock County. The petition addresses the issue of

13   accidents on the S-curve in 2005-2006. As you know, there have been six

14   fatalities on the curve, and the highway investigation committee reports

15   seventeen accidents there in 2005-2006.

16   This issue needs to be addressed. Please let me know when you are

17   available to meet with me to develop a proposal to present to governor

18   Billingsly.

Model

Model the following sentence to practice capitalizing titles of courses.

> **We happened to walk out of Professor Thomas Emerson's Political and Civil Rights course at the same time.** —Hilary Rodham Clinton, *Living History*

Mechanics

Plurals

654.1 Most Nouns

Form the **plurals** of most nouns by adding *s* to the singular.
    cheerleader – cheerleaders
    sign – signs
    crate – crates

654.2 Nouns Ending in *sh, ch, x, s,* and *z*

Form the plurals of nouns ending in *sh, ch, x, s,* and *z* by adding *es* to the singular.
    lunch – lunches   dish – dishes   mess – messes   fox – foxes

Exception: When the final *ch* sounds like *k*, add an *s* (*monarchs*).

654.3 Nouns Ending in *y*

The plurals of common nouns that end in *y*—preceded by a consonant—are formed by changing the *y* to *i* and adding *es*.
    fly – flies   jalopy – jalopies

Form the plurals of nouns that end in *y*—preceded by a vowel—by adding only an *s*.
    donkey – donkeys   monkey – monkeys

Note: Form the plurals of all proper nouns ending in *y* by adding *s* (*Kathys*).

654.4 Nouns Ending in *o*

The plurals of nouns ending in *o*—preceded by a vowel—are formed by adding an *s*.
    radio – radios   rodeo – rodeos   studio – studios   duo – duos

The plurals of most nouns ending in *o*—preceded by a consonant—are formed by adding *es*.
    echo – echoes   hero – heroes   tomato – tomatoes

Exception: Musical terms always form plurals by adding *s*.
    alto – altos   banjo – banjos   solo – solos   piano – pianos

654.5 Nouns Ending in *ful*

Form the plurals of nouns that end in *ful* by adding an *s* at the end of the word.
    two tankfuls   three pailfuls   four mouthfuls

Note: Do not confuse these examples with *three pails full* (when you are referring to three separate pails full of something) or *two tanks full.*

654.6 Compound Nouns

Form the plurals of most compound nouns by adding *s* or *es* to the important word in the compound.
    brothers-in-law   maids of honor   secretaries of state

Plurals 1

- Most Nouns
- Nouns Ending in *sh, ch, x, s,* and *z*
- Nouns Ending in *y*
- Nouns Ending in *o*
- Nouns Ending in *ful*
- Compound Nouns

Write the correct plurals of the underlined word or words in each sentence.

1. Ten local <u>artist</u> will present their renderings of <u>church</u> at Gallery One.

2. The <u>Knight of Columbus</u> are sponsoring the exhibit.

3. Two husband-wife <u>duo</u> will show their joint <u>work</u> of art.

4. The <u>Buchinsky</u> will exhibit their sculptures called "The Three <u>Faithful</u>."

5. These works feature <u>mystery</u> associated with historical <u>mosque</u>.

6. Carol and Franco Diaz will show religious folk art created from Mexican <u>box</u>.

7. <u>*Echo in Time*</u> and other paintings by Margaret Cliffton can be found in the <u>hallway</u> of the gallery.

8. Visitors can view a demonstration of fabric art using <u>chintz</u>.

9. They will also be able to sign up for art <u>class</u> at the gallery.

10. A highlight of the exhibit will be Fr. Anthony Spinozza's pen-and-ink <u>drawing</u> of Roman <u>church</u> from early <u>century</u>.

11. Several art <u>studio</u> will be open for tours Sunday afternoon.

12. Jacob Barr will entertain at the event with his original piano <u>solo</u>.

Model

Model the following sentences to practice using the plurals of nouns ending in *sh* and *ch*.

We would often be sorry if our wishes were gratified.
—Aesop

It is just the little touches after the average man would quit that make the master's fame.
—Orison Swett Marden

Mechanics

Plurals *(continued)*

656.1 Nouns Ending in *f* or *fe*

Form the plurals of nouns that end in *f* or *fe* in one of two ways: If the final *f* sound is still heard in the plural form of the word, simply add *s;* but if the final *f* sound becomes a *v* sound, change the *f* to *ve* and add *s.*

Plural ends with *f* sound: roof – roofs; chief – chiefs
Plural ends with *v* sound: wife – wives; loaf – loaves

Note: Several words are correct with either ending.

Plural ends with either sound: hoof – hooves/hoofs

656.2 Irregular Spelling

A number of words form a plural by taking on an irregular spelling.

crisis – crises	**child – children**	**radius – radii**
criterion – criteria	**goose – geese**	**die – dice**

Note: Some of these words are acceptable with the commonly used *s* or *es* ending.

index   indices/indexes   cactus – cacti/cactuses

Some nouns remain unchanged when used as plurals.

deer   sheep   salmon   aircraft   series

656.3 Words Discussed as Words

The plurals of symbols, letters, numbers, and words being discussed as words are formed by adding an apostrophe and an *s.*

Dad yelled a lot of *wow's* and *yippee's* when he saw my A's and B's.

Note: You may omit the apostrophe if it does not cause any confusion.

the three R's or Rs   YMCA's or YMCAs

656.4 Collective Nouns

A collective noun may be singular or plural depending upon how it's used. A collective noun is singular when it refers to a group considered as one unit; it is plural when it refers to the individuals in the group.

The class was on its best behavior. (group as a unit)
The class are preparing for their final exams. (individuals in the group)

If it seems awkward to use a plural verb with a collective noun, add a clearly plural noun such as *members* to the sentence (changing the noun to an adjective), or make the collective noun the object of a preposition that follows the plural noun.

The class members are preparing for their final exams.
The students in the class are preparing for their final exams.

Plurals 2

- Nouns Ending in *f* or *fe*
- Irregular Spellings
- Words Discussed as Words
- Collective Nouns

 Write the correct plurals of the underlined word or words in each sentence.

1. Football is a game of four quarters and two <u>half</u>.

2. Early colonists shouted *<u>huzzah</u>* instead of *<u>hurray</u>*.

3. <u>Chef</u> sometimes use bay <u>leaf</u> to season soups and stews.

4. Scientists found <u>fungus</u> and <u>bacterium</u> in the samples.

5. How many English words contain two <u>u</u> in a row?

6. *And Out Come the <u>Wolf</u>* is one of my sister's favorite punk-rock albums.

7. I determine if I want to read certain books by first reading <u>synopsis</u>.

8. On our drive through the country, we saw <u>deer</u>, <u>sheep</u>, and <u>sheaf</u> of wheat.

9. "All the <u>*and*</u> and <u>*but*</u> in this sentence should give you a clue, Dave," said the teacher, "that it's a run-on."

10. Have you ever wondered why <u>goose</u> have no <u>tooth</u>?

 For each sentence below, choose the correct pronoun (in parentheses).

11. The committee gathered *(their, its)* luggage at the airport.

12. The committee presented *(their, its)* findings at the convention.

 ## Exercise

Write one or two sentences using the plurals of all the following words.

index, phenomenon, thief, life, offspring

Mechanics

Numbers

658.1 Numerals or Words

Numbers from one to nine are usually written as words; numbers 10 and over are usually written as numerals. However, numbers being compared or contrasted should be kept in the same style.

8 to 11 years old   eight to eleven years old

You may use a combination of numerals and words for very large numbers.

1.5 million   3 billion to 3.2 billion   6 trillion

If numbers are used infrequently in a piece of writing, you may spell out those that can be written in no more than two words.

ten   twenty-five   two hundred   ten thousand

658.2 Numerals Only

Use numerals for the following forms: decimals, percentages, chapters, pages, addresses, phone numbers, identification numbers, and statistics.

26.2	**8 percent**	**Highway 36**	**chapter 7**
pages 287-89	**July 6, 1945**	**44 B.C.E.**	**a vote of 23 to 4**

Always use numerals with abbreviations and symbols.

8%   10 mm   3 cc   8 oz   90° C   24 mph   6' 3"

658.3 Words Only

Use words to express numbers that begin a sentence.

Fourteen students "forgot" their assignments.

Note: Change the sentence structure if this rule creates a clumsy construction.

Clumsy: *Six hundred thirty-nine* teachers were laid off this year.

Better: This year, 639 teachers were laid off.

Use words for numbers that come before a compound modifier if that modifier includes a numeral.

They made twelve 10-foot sub sandwiches for the picnic.

658.4 Time and Money

If time is expressed with an abbreviation, use numerals; if it is expressed in words, spell out the number.

4:00 A.M. (or) four o'clock

4:00 a.m.

If an amount of money is spelled out, so is the currency; use a numeral if a symbol is used.

twenty dollars (or) $20

Numbers

- Numerals or Words
- Numerals Only
- Words Only
- Time and Money

 For each sentence below, write the underlined numbers the correct way. If a number is already correctly presented, write "correct."

1. The <u>two-thousand-and-four</u> tsunami was the deadliest in history.

2. It struck at <u>seven-fifty-three</u> a.m. local time on December 26.

3. Initial estimates of the death toll neared <u>300,000</u> people.

4. The earthquake that caused it registered <u>nine-point-one</u> on the Richter scale.

5. The quake lasted between <u>500</u> and <u>six hundred</u> seconds.

6. The tsunami created waves up to <u>thirty</u> meters (<u>100</u> feet).

7. <u>Sixty-six</u> percent of the fishing fleet was destroyed in coastal areas.

8. Energy released by the quake equaled about as much as the United States typically uses in <u>11</u> days.

9. The quake caused the earth to wobble on its axis about <u>1</u> inch in the direction of <u>one-hundred forty-five</u> degrees east longitude.

10. <u>16</u> coral-reef atolls crushed by sea waves could be uninhabitable for decades.

11. <u>Three billion dollars</u> in aid was provided by world countries.

12. Many children aged <u>six to 18</u> contributed aid to victims.

 ## Model

Model the following sentences to practice using numbers and numerals correctly.

> **In the future, everyone will be famous for 15 minutes.**
> —Andy Warhol

> **Fifteen years ago, Congress took a significant step in implementing national health insurance for the aged with the establishment of medicare.**
> —Select Committee on Aging, "Medicare: A Fifteen-Year Perspective"

Abbreviations

660.1 Formal and Informal Abbreviations

An **abbreviation** is the shortened form of a word or phrase. Some abbreviations are always acceptable in both formal and informal writing:

Mr. Mrs. Jr. Ms. Dr. a.m. (A.M.) p.m. (P.M.)

Note: In most of your writing, you do not abbreviate the names of states, countries, months, days, or units of measure. However, you may use the abbreviation *U.S.* after it has been spelled out once. Do not abbreviate the words *Street, Company,* and similar words, especially when they are part of a proper name. Also, do not use signs or symbols (%, &, #, @) in place of words. The dollar sign, however, is appropriate with numerals ($325).

660.2 Correspondence Abbreviations

United States

	Standard	Postal
Alabama	Ala.	AL
Alaska	Alaska	AK
Arizona	Ariz.	AZ
Arkansas	Ark.	AR
California	Calif.	CA
Colorado	Colo.	CO
Connecticut	Conn.	CT
Delaware	Del.	DE
District of Columbia	D.C.	DC
Florida	Fla.	FL
Georgia	Ga.	GA
Guam	Guam	GU
Hawaii	Hawaii	HI
Idaho	Idaho	ID
Illinois	Ill.	IL
Indiana	Ind.	IN
Iowa	Iowa	IA
Kansas	Kan.	KS
Kentucky	Ky.	KY
Louisiana	La.	LA
Maine	Maine	ME
Maryland	Md.	MD
Massachusetts	Mass.	MA
Michigan	Mich.	MI
Minnesota	Minn.	MN
Mississippi	Miss.	MS
Missouri	Mo.	MO
Montana	Mont.	MT
Nebraska	Neb.	NE
Nevada	Nev.	NV
New Hampshire	N.H.	NH
New Jersey	N.J.	NJ
New Mexico	N.M.	NM
New York	N.Y.	NY
North Carolina	N.C.	NC
North Dakota	N.D.	ND
Ohio	Ohio	OH
Oklahoma	Okla.	OK
Oregon	Ore.	OR
Pennsylvania	Pa.	PA
Puerto Rico	P.R.	PR
Rhode Island	R.I.	RI
South Carolina	S.C.	SC
South Dakota	S.D.	SD
Tennessee	Tenn.	TN
Texas	Texas	TX
Utah	Utah	UT
Vermont	Vt.	VT
Virginia	Va.	VA
Virgin Islands	V.I.	VI
Washington	Wash.	WA
West Virginia	W.Va.	WV
Wisconsin	Wis.	WI
Wyoming	Wyo.	WY

Canadian Provinces

	Standard	Postal
Alberta	Alta.	AB
British Columbia	B.C.	BC
Labrador	Lab.	NL
Manitoba	Man.	MB
New Brunswick	N.B.	NB
Newfoundland	N.F.	NL
Northwest Territories	N.W.T.	NT
Nova Scotia	N.S.	NS
Nunavut		NU
Ontario	Ont.	ON
Prince Edward Island	P.E.I.	PE
Quebec	Que.	QC
Saskatchewan	Sask.	SK
Yukon Territory	Y.T.	YT

Addresses

	Standard	Postal
Apartment	Apt.	APT
Avenue	Ave.	AVE
Boulevard	Blvd.	BLVD
Circle	Cir.	CIR
Court	Ct.	CT
Drive	Dr.	DR
East	E.	E
Expressway	Expy.	EXPY
Freeway	Fwy.	FWY
Heights	Hts.	HTS
Highway	Hwy.	HWY
Hospital	Hosp.	HOSP
Junction	Junc.	JCT
Lake	L.	LK
Lakes	Ls.	LKS
Lane	Ln.	LN
Meadows	Mdws.	MDWS
North	N.	N
Palms	Palms	PLMS
Park	Pk.	PK
Parkway	Pky.	PKY
Place	Pl.	PL
Plaza	Plaza	PLZ
Post Office Box	P.O. Box	PO BOX
Ridge	Rdg.	RDG
River	R.	RV
Road	Rd.	RD
Room	Rm.	RM
Rural	R.	R
Rural Route	R.R.	RR
Shore	Sh.	SH
South	S.	S
Square	Sq.	SQ
Station	Sta.	STA
Street	St.	ST
Suite	Ste.	STE
Terrace	Ter.	TER
Turnpike	Tpke.	TPKE
Union	Un.	UN
View	View	VW
Village	Vil.	VLG
West	W.	W

661.1 Other Common Abbreviations

abr. abridged; abridgment
AC, ac alternating current
ack. acknowledge; acknowledgment
acv actual cash value
A.D. in the year of the Lord (Latin *anno Domini*)
AM amplitude modulation
A.M., a.m. before noon (Latin *ante meridiem*)
ASAP as soon as possible
avg., av. average
BBB Better Business Bureau
B.C. before Christ
B.C.E. before the Common Era
bibliog. bibliographer; bibliography
biog. biographer; biographical; biography
C 1. Celsius 2. centigrade 3. coulomb
c. 1. circa (about) 2. cup
cc 1. cubic centimeter 2. carbon copy
CDT, C.D.T. central daylight time
C.E. of the Common Era
chap. chapter
cm centimeter
c.o., c/o care of
COD, C.O.D 1. cash on delivery 2. collect on delivery
co-op. cooperative
CST, C.S.T. central standard time
cu., c cubic
D.A. district attorney
d.b.a. doing business as
DC, dc direct current
dec. deceased
dept. department
DST, D.S.T. daylight saving time
dup. duplicate
DVD digital video disc
ea. each
ed. edition; editor
EDT, E.D.T. eastern daylight time
e.g. for example (Latin *exempli gratia*)
EST, E.S.T. eastern standard time
etc. and so forth (Latin *et cetera*)
ex. example
F Fahrenheit
FM frequency modulation
F.O.B., f.o.b. free on board
ft foot
g 1. gram 2. gravity
gal. gallon
gloss. glossary
GNP gross national product
hdqrs, HQ headquarters
HIV human immunodeficiency virus

Hon. Honorable (title)
hp horsepower
HTML hypertext markup language
Hz hertz
ibid. in the same place (Latin *ibidem*)
id. the same (Latin *idem*)
i.e. that is (Latin *id est*)
illus. illustration
inc. incorporated
IQ, I.Q. intelligence quotient
IRS Internal Revenue Service
ISBN International Standard Book Number
Jr., jr. junior
K 1. kelvin (temperature unit) 2. Kelvin (temperature scale)
kc kilocycle
kg kilogram
km kilometer
kn knot
kW kilowatt
l liter
lat. latitude
lb, lb. pound (Latin *libra*)
l.c. lowercase
lit. literary; literature
log logarithm
long. longitude
Ltd., ltd. limited
m meter
M.A. master of arts (Latin *Magister Artium*)
Mc, mc megacycle
M.C., m.c. master of ceremonies
M.D. doctor of medicine (Latin *medicinae doctor*)
mdse. merchandise
mfg. manufacturing
mg milligram
mi. 1. mile 2. mill (monetary unit)
misc. miscellaneous
ml milliliter
mm millimeter
mpg, m.p.g. miles per gallon
mph, m.p.h. miles per hour
MS 1. manuscript 2. Mississippi 3. multiple sclerosis
Ms., Ms title of courtesy for a woman
MST, M.S.T. mountain standard time
neg. negative
N.S.F., n.s.f. not sufficient funds
oz, oz. ounce
PA 1. public-address system 2. Pennsylvania
pct. percent
pd. paid

PDT, P.D.T. Pacific daylight time
PFC, Pfc. private first class
pg., p. page
P.M., p.m. after noon (Latin *post meridiem*)
P.O. 1. personnel officer 2. purchase order 3. postal order; post office 4. (also **p.o.**) petty officer
pop. population
POW, P.O.W. prisoner of war
pp. pages
ppd. 1. postpaid 2. prepaid
PR, P.R. 1. public relations 2. Puerto Rico
P.S. post script
psi, p.s.i. pounds per square inch
PST, P.S.T. Pacific standard time
PTA, P.T.A. Parent Teacher Association
qt. quart
RF radio frequency
RN registered nurse
R.P.M., rpm revolutions per minute
R.S.V.P., r.s.v.p. please reply (French *répondez s'il vous plaît*)
SASE self-addressed stamped envelope
SCSI small computer system interface
SOS 1. international distress signal 2. any call for help
Sr. 1. senior (after surname) 2. sister (religious)
ST standard time
St. 1. saint 2. strait 3. street
std. standard
syn. synonymous; synonym
TBA to be announced
tbs, tbsp tablespoon
TM trademark
tsp teaspoon
UHF, uhf ultra high frequency
UPC universal product code
UV ultraviolet
V 1. *Physics:* velocity 2. *Electricity:* volt 3. volume
V.A., VA Veterans Administration
VHF, vhf very high frequency
VIP *Informal:* very important person
vol. 1. volume 2. volunteer
vs. versus
W 1. *Electricity:* watt 2. *Physics:* (also **w**) work 3. west
whse., whs. warehouse
wkly. weekly
w/o without
wt. weight
yd yard (measurement)

Mechanics

Acronyms and Initialisms

662.1 Acronyms

An **acronym** is a word formed from the first (or first few) letters of words in a phrase. Even though acronyms are abbreviations, they require no periods.

radar radio detecting and ranging
CARE Cooperative for American Relief Everywhere
NASA National Aeronautics and Space Administration
VISTA Volunteers in Service to America
LAN local area network

662.2 Initialisms

An **initialism** is similar to an acronym except that the initials used to form this abbreviation are pronounced individually.

CIA Central Intelligence Agency
FBI Federal Bureau of Investigation
FHA Federal Housing Administration

662.3 Common Acronyms and Initialisms

ADD	attention deficit disorder		**LLC**	limited liability company
AIDS	acquired immunodeficiency syndrome		**MADD**	Mothers Against Drunk Driving
AKA	also known as		**MRI**	magnetic resonance imaging
ATM	automatic teller machine		**NASA**	National Aeronautics and Space Administration
BMI	body mass index		**NATO**	North Atlantic Treaty Organization
CD	compact disc; certificate of deposit		**OPEC**	Organization of Petroleum-Exporting Countries
DMV	Department of Motor Vehicles		**OSHA**	Occupational Safety and Health Administration
ETA	estimated time of arrival			
FAA	Federal Aviation Administration		**PAC**	political action committee
FCC	Federal Communications Commission		**PDF**	portable document format
FDA	Food and Drug Administration		**PETA**	People for the Ethical Treatment of Animals
FDIC	Federal Deposit Insurance Corporation		**PIN**	personal identification number
FEMA	Federal Emergency Management Agency		**PSA**	public service announcement
FTC	Federal Trade Commission		**ROTC**	Reserve Officers' Training Corps
FYI	for your information			
GPS	global positioning system		**SADD**	Students Against Destructive Decisions
HDTV	high-definition television		**SUV**	sport utility vehicle
IRS	Internal Revenue Service		**SWAT**	special weapons and tactics
IT	information technology		**TDD**	telecommunications device for the deaf
JPEG	Joint Photographic Experts Group			
LCD	liquid crystal display			

Abbreviations, Acronyms, and Initialisms

 Write the correct abbreviation for the underlined word or words.

1. Find the <u>universal product code</u> on this <u>digital video disc</u>.

2. Luis lives at 1279 <u>North</u> Bethesda <u>Circle</u>, Watch Hill, <u>Rhode Island</u>.

3. During the awards ceremony, the <u>master of ceremonies</u> introduced the <u>very important persons</u>.

4. The program begins at 8:00 <u>ante meridiem, eastern daylight time</u>.

5. The National 4-H <u>headquarters</u> is in Washington, <u>District of Columbia</u>.

6. All books have an <u>international standard book number</u>.

7. <u>Mister</u> Jenkins took a class to learn <u>hypertext markup language</u>.

8. My grandfather is in a <u>Veterans Administration</u> hospital in <u>Iowa</u>.

9. Anwar Singh, <u>doctor of medicine</u>, spoke about the <u>human immunodeficiency virus</u>.

10. Under "time" for next week's meeting, someone had written "<u>to be announced</u>."

11. Look for a maximum <u>pounds per square inch</u> stamp on your tires before adding air.

12. The <u>longitude</u> of Tuscaloosa, <u>Alabama</u>, is 87.62 degrees; the <u>latitude</u> is 33.23 degrees.

 ## Model

Model the following acronyms and initialisms to come up with your own abbreviations. (Write at least one acronym and one initialism.)

BOYS — Bradford Orchid and Yam Society
JUSTICE — Jesuit University Students Together in Concerned Empowerment
ZFF — Zephyr Flower Flats
DHS — Department of Homeland Security

Mechanics

Spelling Rules

664.1 Write *i* before *e*

Write *i* before *e* except after *c*, or when sounded like *a* as in *neighbor* and *weigh*.

relief   receive   perceive   reign   freight   beige

Exceptions: There are a number of exceptions to this rule, including these: *neither, leisure, seize, weird, species, science.*

664.2 Words with Consonant Endings

When a one-syllable word *(bat)* ends in a consonant *(t)* preceded by one vowel *(a)*, double the final consonant before adding a suffix that begins with a vowel *(batting)*.

sum—summary   god—goddess

Note: When a multisyllabic word *(control)* ends in a consonant *(l)* preceded by one vowel *(o)*, the accent is on the last syllable *(con trol´)*, and the suffix begins with a vowel *(ing)*—the same rule holds true: Double the final consonant *(controlling)*.

prefer—preferred   begin—beginning
forget—forgettable   admit—admittance

664.3 Words with a Silent *e*

If a word ends with a silent *e*, drop the *e* before adding a suffix that begins with a vowel. Do not drop the *e* when the suffix begins with a consonant.

state—stating—statement   like—liking—likeness
use—using—useful   nine—ninety—nineteen

Exceptions: *judgment, truly, argument, ninth*

664.4 Words Ending in *y*

When *y* is the last letter in a word and the *y* is preceded by a consonant, change the *y* to *i* before adding any suffix except those beginning with *i*.

fry—fries—frying   hurry—hurried—hurrying   lady—ladies
ply—pliable   happy—happiness   beauty—beautiful

When *y* is the last letter in a word and the *y* is preceded by a vowel, do not change the *y* to *i* before adding a suffix.

play—plays—playful   stay—stays—staying
employ—employed

Important reminder: Never trust your spelling even to the best spell-checker. Use a dictionary for words your spell-checker does not cover.

Spelling 1

Find the 12 words that are misspelled in the following paragraph and write them correctly. (Each misspelled word is in the "Commonly Misspelled Words" list on pages 666–667.)

1   A playright is a person who writes dramatic literture. Sophocles
2   and Euripides, ancient Greeks, created some of the earleist plays around
3   the fifth century B.C.E. The dramatic forms of comedy and traggedy are
4   usualy studied in asociation with the life of William Shakespeare. He was
5   a brillient writer during England's Elizabethan period. Shakespeare's
6   works have withstood the test of time. Performances of his plays are still
7   presented by modern-day proffesional theater groups in America and
8   abroad. Undoutably, the works of these early authors were instramental in
9   influencing the creation of modern drama.

Model

Model the following sentences to practice using the spelling rules that deal with adding a suffix.

> A playwright lives in an occupied country. And if you can't live that way, you don't stay.
> —Arthur Miller

> It's discouraging to think how many people are shocked by honesty and how few by deceit.
> —Noel Coward

Commonly Misspelled Words

A

abbreviate
abrupt
absence
absolute (ly)
absurd
abundance
academic
accelerate
accept (ance)
accessible
accessory
accidentally
accommodate
accompany
accomplish
accumulate
accurate
accustom (ed)
ache
achieve (ment)
acknowledge
acquaintance
acquired
across
address
adequate
adjustment
admissible
admittance
adolescent
advantageous
advertisement
advisable
aggravate
aggression
alcohol
alleviate
almost
alternative
although
aluminum
amateur
analysis
analyze
anarchy
ancient
anecdote
anesthetic

annihilate
announce
annual
anonymous
answer
anxious
apologize
apparatus
apparent (ly)
appearance
appetite
applies
appreciate
appropriate
approximately
architect
arctic
argument
arithmetic
arrangement
artificial
ascend
assistance
association
athlete
attendance
attire
attitude
audience
authority
available

B

balance
balloon
bargain
basically
beautiful
beginning
believe
benefit (ed)
biscuit
bought
boycott
brevity
brilliant
Britain
bureau
business

C

cafeteria
caffeine
calculator
calendar
campaign
canceled
candidate
catastrophe
category
caught
cavalry
celebration
cemetery
certificate
changeable
chief
chocolate
circuit
circumstance
civilization
colonel
colossal
column
commercial
commitment
committed
committee
comparative
comparison
competitively
conceivable
condemn
condescend
conference
conferred
confidential
congratulate
conscience
conscientious
conscious
consequence
consumer
contaminate
convenience
cooperate
correspondence
cough
coupon

courageous
courteous
creditor
criticism
criticize
curiosity
curious
cylinder

D

dealt
deceitful
deceive
decision
defense
deferred
definite (ly)
definition
delicious
descend
describe
description
despair
desperate
destruction
development
diameter
diaphragm
diarrhea
dictionary
dining
disagreeable
disappear
disappoint
disastrous
discipline
discrimination
discuss
dismissal
dissatisfied
dissect
distinctly
dormitory
doubt
drought
duplicate
dyeing
dying

E

earliest
efficiency
eighth
elaborate
eligible
eliminate
ellipse
embarrass
emphasize
employee
enclosure
encourage
endeavor
English
enormous
enough
enrichment
enthusiastic
entirely
entrance
environment
equipment
equipped
equivalent
especially
essential
eventually
exaggerate
examination
exceed
excellent
excessive
excite
executive
exercise
exhaust (ed)
exhibition
exhilaration
existence
expensive
experience
explanation
exquisite
extinguish
extraordinary
extremely

F–G

facilities
familiar
fascinate
fashion
fatigue (d)
feature
February
fiery
financially
flourish
forcible
foreign
forfeit
fortunate
forty
fourth
freight
friend
fulfill
gauge
generally
generous
genuine
glimpse
gnarled
gnaw
government
gradual
grammar
gratitude
grievous
grocery
guard
guidance

H

happiness
harass
harmonize
height
hemorrhage
hereditary
hindrance
hoping
hopping
hospitable
humorous

hygiene
hymn
hypocrisy

I-J

ignorance
illiterate
illustrate
imaginary
immediately
immense
incidentally
inconvenience
incredible
indefinitely
independence
indispensable
industrial
industrious
inevitable
infinite
inflation
innocence
inoculation
inquiry
installation
instrumental
intelligence
interesting
interfere
interrupt
investigate
irregular
irresistible
issuing
itinerary
jealous (y)
jewelry
journal
judgment

K-L

knowledge
laboratory
laugh
lawyer
league
legacy
legalize
legitimate
leisure

liaison
license
lightning
likable
liquid
literature
loneliness

M-N

maintenance
maneuver
manufacture
marriage
mathematics
medieval
memento
menagerie
merchandise
merely
mileage
miniature
miscellaneous
mischievous
misspell
moat
mobile
mortgage
multiplied
muscle
musician
mustache
mutual
mysterious
naive
nauseous
necessary
neither
neurotic
nevertheless
ninety
nighttime
noticeable
nuclear
nuisance

O-P

obstacle
obvious
occasion
occupant
occupation

occurred
occurrence
official
often
omitted
opinion
opponent
opportunity
opposite
optimism
ordinarily
organization
original
outrageous
pamphlet
parallel
paralyze
partial
particularly
pastime
patience
peculiar
pedestal
performance
permanent
permissible
perseverance
personal (ly)
personality
perspiration
persuade
petition
phenomenon
physical
physician
picnicking
planned
playwright
plead
pneumonia
politician
ponder
positively
possession
practically
precede
precious
preference
prejudice
preparation
presence
prevalent
primitive

privilege
probably
proceed
professional
professor
prominent
pronounce
pronunciation
protein
psychology
puny
purchase
pursuing

Q-R

qualified
quality
quantity
questionnaire
quiet
quite
quizzes
recede
receipt
receive
recipe
recognize
recommend
reference
referred
regard
regimen
religious
repel
repetition
residue
responsibility
restaurant
rheumatism
rhythm
ridiculous
robot
roommate

S

sacrifice
salary
sandwich
satisfactory
scarcely
scenic

schedule
scholar
science
secretary
seize
separate
sergeant
several
severely
sheriff
shrubbery
siege
signature
signify
silhouette
similar
simultaneous
sincerely
skiing
skunk
society
solar
sophomore
souvenir
spaghetti
specific
specimen
statue
stomach
stopped
strength
strictly
submission
substitute
subtle
succeed
success
sufficient
supersede
suppose
surprise
suspicious
symbolism
sympathy
synthetic

T-U

tariff
technique
temperature
temporary
tendency

thermostat
thorough (ly)
though
throughout
tongue
tornado
tortoise
tragedy
transferred
tremendous
tried
trite
truly
unanimous
undoubtedly
unfortunately
unique
unnecessary
until
urgent
usable
usher
usually

vacuum
vague
valuable
variety
vengeance
versatile
vicinity
villain
visibility
visual

waif
Wednesday
weird
wholly
width
women
wrath
wreckage

yesterday
yield
yolk

Mechanics

Steps to Becoming a Better Speller

1. **Be patient.**
   Becoming a good speller takes time.

2. **Check the correct pronunciation of each word you are attempting to spell.**
   Knowing the correct pronunciation of a word can help you remember its spelling.

3. **Note the meaning and history of each word as you are checking the dictionary for pronunciation.**
   Knowing the meaning and history of a word provides you with a better notion of how the word is properly used, and this can help you remember its spelling.

4. **Before you close the dictionary, practice spelling the word.**
   Look away from the page and try to "see" the word in your mind. Then write it on a piece of paper. Check your spelling in the dictionary; repeat the process until you are able to spell the word correctly.

5. **Learn some spelling rules.**
   For four of the most useful rules, see page 664.

6. **Make a list of the words that you often misspell.**
   Select the first 10 and practice spelling them.

   STEP A: Read each word carefully; then write it on a piece of paper. Check to see that you've spelled it correctly. Repeat this step for the words that you misspelled.

   STEP B: When you have finished your first 10 words, ask someone to read them to you as you write them again. Then check for misspellings. If you find none, congratulations! (Repeat both steps with your next 10 words, and so on.)

7. **Write often.**

"There is little point in learning to spell if you have little intention of writing."
—Frank Smith

Spelling 2

For each quotation below, fill in the blank with the correct word from the list of "Commonly Misspelled Words" (pages 666–667).

1. Television is instantaneous and s____u_t_____s: Everyone gets the message at the same time.

—William J. Donnelly

2. It takes time to p_____e men to do even what is for their own good.

—Thomas Jefferson

3. The g____r l____ stump has as tender a bud as the sapling.

—Henry David Thoreau

4. Only strong personalities can endure history, the weak ones are
e_t____g_____d by it.

—Friedrich Nietzsche

5. The day is but a Scandinavian night; the winter is an a _ c ____ c summer.

—Henry David Thoreau

6. I have noted that persons with bad j____g_____t are most insistent that we do what they think best.

—Lionel Abel

7. R____e_____n is tedious.

—Mason Cooley

8. No l_g__c_ is so rich as honesty.

—William Shakespeare

9. S_____ is counted sweetest by those who ne'er succeed.

—Emily Dickinson

10. No guest is so welcome in a friend's house that he will not become a
n_____a_____ after three days.

—Titus Maccius Plautus

Model

Model the following sentence to practice using the spelling rule for writing *i* before *e.*

Time folded in on itself then. What is left lies in clear yet disjointed pieces in my head.

—Sue Monk Kidd, *The Secret Life of Bees*

Test Prep

Write the letter of the correct way to express each underlined part from the choices given on the next page. If it is already correct, choose "D."

See if you can form any <u>theorys</u> about what these <u>peoples</u>, events, and things
1 **2**
have in common: Elvis Presley, wildflowers, rock 'n' roll, the Civil War, <u>legendes of</u>
3
<u>the west</u>, the <u>nineteen ninety-two</u> Summer Olympics, and dinosaurs. If you can't
4
make a connection, don't <u>despair</u>. The answer is that all of them are on the <u>united</u>
5
<u>states postal service (USPS)</u> list of the 10 most popular commemorative postage
6
stamps in U.S. history.

In 1893, <u>postmaster General John Wanamaker</u> was reprimanded for <u>issueing</u>
7 **8**
the first commemorative stamps. Congress protested that the stamps, celebrating

the <u>world columbian exposition</u>, were <u>unneccessary</u>. Though he <u>recieved</u> criticism,
9 **10** **11**
Wanamaker believed that the stamps would be popular. He was <u>right: people</u>
12
(<u>hundreds</u> of them) stood in line to buy the stamps. Collectors came with <u>handfuls</u>
13
of cash to purchase the stamps as an investment. Two billion of the Columbian

stamps were sold for <u>$40 million dollars</u>. Today, one of these <u>4-¢</u> stamps is worth up
14 **15**
to $88. Commemorative stamp collection remains one of the most popular collection

<u>hobby</u> in the world.
16

1. **A** theoreys
   B theories
   C theoryes
   D correct as is

2. **A** people
   B persones
   C people's
   D correct as is

3. **A** Legendes of the West
   B legends of the west
   C legends of the West
   D correct as is

4. **A** nineteen 92
   B 19 ninety-two
   C 1992
   D correct as is

5. **A** dispair
   B dispare
   C despare
   D correct as is

6. **A** United States postal service (USPS)
   B United States Postal Service (U.S.P.S.)
   C United States Postal Service (USPS)
   D correct as is

7. **A** Postmaster General John Wanamaker
   B Postmaster general John Wanamaker
   C postmaster general John Wanamaker
   D correct as is

8. **A** ishuing
   B issuing
   C isueing
   D correct as is

9. **A** world Columbian exposition
   B world Columbian Exposition
   C World Columbian Exposition
   D correct as is

10. **A** unnecessary
    B uneccessary
    C unecesary
    D correct as is

11. **A** receivied
    B received
    C resieved
    D correct as is

12. **A** right: people (100's
    B right: People (100's
    C right: People (hundreds
    D correct as is

13. **A** handsful
    B handsfuls
    C handfulls
    D correct as is

14. **A** $40 million
    B 40 million $
    C 40,000,000 $
    D correct as is

15. **A** four-¢
    B four-cent
    C 4-cent
    D correct as is

16. **A** hobbeys
    B hobbys
    C hobbies
    D correct as is

Mechanics

Understanding Idioms

Idioms are phrases that are used in a special way. You can't understand an idiom just by knowing the meaning of each word in the phrase. You must learn it as a whole. For example, the idiom *bury the hatchet* means "to settle an argument," even though the individual words in the phrase mean something much different. This section will help you learn some of the common idioms in American English.

apple of his eye	**Eagle Lake is the** apple of his eye. (something he likes very much)
as plain as day	**The mistake in the ad was** as plain as day. (very clear)
as the crow flies	**New London is 200 miles from here** as the crow flies. (in a straight line)
at a snail's pace	**My last hour at work passes** at a snail's pace. (very, very slowly)
axe to grind	**The manager has an** axe to grind **with that umpire.** (disagreement to settle)
bad apple	**There are no** bad apples **in this class.** (bad influences)
beat around the bush	**Don't** beat around the bush; **answer the question.** (avoid getting to the point)
benefit of the doubt	**Everyone has been given the** benefit of the doubt **at least once.** (another chance)
beyond the shadow of a doubt	Beyond the shadow of a doubt, **this is my best science project.** (for certain)
blew my top	**When I saw the broken statue, I** blew my top. (showed great anger)
bone to pick	**Alison had a** bone to pick **with the student who copied her paper.** (problem to settle)
brain drain	Brain drain **is a serious problem in some states.** (the best students moving elsewhere)
break the ice	**The nervous ninth graders were afraid to** break the ice. (start a conversation)
burn the midnight oil	**Devon had to** burn the midnight oil **to finish his report.** (work late into the night)

bury the hatchet	My sisters were told to bury the hatchet **immediately.** (settle an argument)
by the skin of her teeth	Sumey avoided an accident by the skin of her teeth. (just barely)
champing at the bit	The skiers were champing at the bit **to get on the slopes.** (eager, excited)
chicken feed	The prize was chicken feed to some people. (not worth much money)
chip off the old block	Frank's just like his father. He's a chip off the old block. (just like someone else)
clean as a whistle	My boss told me to make sure the place was as clean as a whistle **before I left.** (very clean)
cold shoulder	I wanted to fit in with that group, but they gave me the cold shoulder. (ignored me)
crack of dawn	Ali delivers his papers at the crack of dawn. (first light of day, early morning)
cry wolf	If you cry wolf too often, no one will believe you. (say you are in trouble when you aren't)
dead of night	Hearing a loud noise in the dead of night frightened Bill. (middle of the night)
dirt cheap	A lot of clothes at that store are dirt cheap. (inexpensive, costing very little money)
doesn't hold a candle to	That award doesn't hold a candle to **a gold medal.** (is not as good as)
drop in the bucket	The contributions were a drop in the bucket. (a small amount compared to what's needed)
everything from A to Z	That catalog lists everything from A to Z. (a lot of different things)
face the music	Todd had to face the music **when he broke the window.** (deal with the punishment)
fish out of water	He felt like a fish out of water **in the new math class.** (someone in an unfamiliar place)
fit for a king	The food at the athletic banquet was fit for a king. (very special)

Idioms

flew off the handle	Bill flew off the handle **when he saw a reckless driver near the school.** (became very angry)
floating on air	Celine was floating on air **at the prom.** (feeling very happy)
food for thought	**The boys' foolish and dangerous prank gave us** food for thought. (something to think about)
get down to business	**After sharing several jokes, Mr. Sell said we should** get down to business. (start working)
get the upper hand	**The wrestler moved quickly on his opponent in order to** get the upper hand. (gain the advantage)
give their all	**Student volunteers** give their all **to help others.** (work as hard as they can)
go fly a kite	**Charlene stared at her nosy brother and said, "Go fly a kite."** (go away)
has a green thumb	**Talk to Mrs. Smith about your sick plant. She** has a green thumb. (is good at growing plants)
has a heart of gold	**Joe** has a heart of gold. (is very kind and generous)
hit a home run	**Rhonda** hit a home run **with her speech.** (succeeded, or did well)
hit the ceiling	**When my parents saw my grades, they** hit the ceiling. (were very angry)
hit the hay	**Exhausted from the hike, Jamal** hit the hay **without eating supper.** (went to bed)
in a nutshell	**Can you,** in a nutshell, **tell us your goals for this year?** (in summary)
in one ear and out the other	**Sharl, concerned about her pet, let the lecture go** in one ear and out the other. (without really listening)
in the black	**My aunt's gift shop is finally** in the black. (making money)
in the nick of time	**Janelle caught the falling vase** in the nick of time. (just in time)
in the red	**Many businesses start out** in the red. (in debt)
in the same boat	**The new tax bill meant everyone would be** in the same boat. (in a similar situation)

iron out	Joe will meet with the work crew to iron out their complaints. (solve, work out)
it goes without saying	It goes without saying that saving money is a good idea. (it is clear)
it stands to reason	It stands to reason that your stamina will increase if you run every day. (it makes sense)
keep a stiff upper lip	Keep a stiff upper lip when you visit the doctor. (be brave)
keep it under your hat	Keep it under your hat about the pop quiz. (don't tell anyone)
knock on wood	My uncle knocked on wood after he said he had never had the flu. (did something for good luck)
knuckle down	After wasting half the day, we were told to knuckle down. (work hard)
learn the ropes	It takes every new employee a few months to learn the ropes. (get to know how things are done)
leave no stone unturned	The police plan to leave no stone unturned at the crime scene. (check everything)
lend someone a hand	You will feel good if you lend someone a hand. (help someone)
let the cat out of the bag	Tom let the cat out of the bag during lunch. (told a secret)
let's face it	Let's face it. You don't like rap. (let's admit it)
look high and low	We looked high and low for Jan's dog. (looked everywhere)
lose face	In some cultures, it is very bad to lose face. (be embarrassed)
needle in a haystack	Trying to find a person in New York is like trying to find a needle in a haystack. (something impossible to find)
nose to the grindstone	With all of these assignments, I have to keep my nose to the grindstone. (work hard)
on cloud nine	After talking to my girlfriend, I was on cloud nine. (feeling very happy)
on pins and needles	Emiko was on pins and needles during the championship game. (feeling nervous)

out the window	**Once the rain started, our plans were** out the window. (ruined)
over and above	Over and above **the required work, Will cleaned up the lab.** (in addition to)
pain in the neck	**Franklin knew the report would be a** pain in the neck. (very annoying)
pull your leg	**Cary was only** pulling your leg. (telling you a little lie as a joke)
put his foot in his mouth	**Lane** put his foot in his mouth **when he answered the question.** (said something embarrassing)
put the cart before the horse	**Tonya** put the cart before the horse **when she sealed the envelope before inserting the letter.** (did something in the wrong order)
put your best foot forward	**When applying for a job, you should** put your best foot forward. (do the best that you can do)
red-letter day	**Sovann had a** red-letter day **because she did so well on her math test.** (very good day)
rock the boat	**I was told not to** rock the boat. (cause trouble)
rude awakening	**Jake will have a** rude awakening **when he sees the bill for his computer.** (sudden, unpleasant surprise)
save face	**His gift was clearly an attempt to** save face. (fix an embarrassing situation)
see eye to eye	**We** see eye to eye **about the need for a new school.** (are in agreement)
shake a leg	**I told Mako to** shake a leg **so that we wouldn't be late.** (hurry)
shift into high gear	**Greg had to** shift into high gear **to finish the test in time.** (speed up, hurry)
sight for sore eyes	**My grandmother's smiling face was a** sight for sore eyes. (good to see)
sight unseen	**Liz bought the coat** sight unseen. (without seeing it first)
sink or swim	**Whether you** sink or swim **in school depends on your study habits.** (fail or succeed)

spilled the beans	Suddenly, Kesia realized that she had spilled the beans. (revealed a secret)
spring chicken	Although Mr. Gordon isn't a spring chicken, he sure knows how to talk to kids. (young person)
stick to your guns	Know what you believe, and stick to your guns. (don't change your mind)
sweet tooth	Chocolate is often the candy of choice for those with a sweet tooth. (a love for sweets, like candy and cake)
take a dim view	My sister will take a dim view of that movie. (disapprove)
take it with a grain of salt	When you read that advertisement, take it with a grain of salt. (don't believe everything)
take the bull by the horns	It's time to take the bull by the horns so the project gets done on time. (take control)
through thick and thin	Those two girls have remained friends through thick and thin. (in good times and in bad times)
time flies	Time flies as you grow older. (time passes quickly)
time to kill	Grace had time to kill, so she read a book. (extra time)
to go overboard	The class was told not to go overboard. A $50.00 donation was fine. (to do too much)
toe the line	The new teacher made everyone toe the line. (follow the rules)
tongue-tied	He can talk easily with friends, but in class he is usually tongue-tied. (not knowing what to say)
turn over a new leaf	He decided to turn over a new leaf in school. (make a new start)
two peas in a pod	Ever since kindergarten, Lil and Eve have been like two peas in a pod. (very much alike)
under the weather	Guy was feeling under the weather this morning. (sick)
wallflower	Cho knew the other girls thought she was a wallflower. (a shy person)
word of mouth	Joseph learns a lot about his favorite team by word of mouth. (talking with other people)

Using the Right Word

a lot ■ *A lot* (always two words) is a vague descriptive phrase that should be used sparingly.

"You can observe a lot just by watching."

—Yogi Berra

accept, except ■ The verb *accept* means "to receive" or "to believe"; the preposition *except* means "other than."

The principal accepted the boy's story about the broken window, but she asked why no one except him saw the ball accidentally slip from his hand.

adapt, adopt ■ *Adapt* means "to adjust or change to fit"; *adopt* means "to choose and treat as your own" (a child, an idea).

After a lengthy period of study, Malcolm X adopted the Islamic faith and adapted to its lifestyle.

affect, effect ■ The verb *affect* means "to influence"; the verb *effect* means "to produce, accomplish, complete."

Ming's hard work effected an A on the test, which positively affected her semester grade.

The noun *effect* means the "result."

Good grades have a calming effect on parents.

aisle, isle ■ An *aisle* is a passage between seats; an *isle* is a small island.

Many airline passengers on their way to the Isle of Capri prefer an aisle seat.

all right ■ *All right* is always two words (not *alright*).

allusion, illusion ■ *Allusion* is an indirect reference to someone or something; *illusion* is a false picture or idea.

My little sister, under the illusion that she's movie-star material, makes frequent allusions to her future fans.

already, all ready ■ *Already* is an adverb meaning "before this time" or "by this time." *All ready* is an adjective meaning "fully prepared."

Note: Use *all ready* if you can substitute *ready* alone in the sentence.

Although I've already had some dessert, I am all ready for some ice cream from the street vendor.

Using the Right Word 1

accept, except; affect, effect; aisle, isle; already, all ready

 Find the words that are used incorrectly. Write the line number followed by the right word.

1   Parnel, feeling a bit depressed, is watching TV: an ancient movie

2 from the 1950s in which the wealthy escape to the Isle of Capri. Here's the

3 dashing Cary Grant, breakfasting on a veranda overlooking a lush valley.

4 There's his lovely lady Audrey Hepburn, all ready growing restless with the

5 relaxation. Cary knows, of course, it is up to him to effect a change in her

6 attitude, and sets about doing so. Getting Audrey to except this life of leisure

7 won't be easy, but, darn it, he's determined!

8   Obviously, the movie has a big affect on Parnel. He dreams he is Cary,

9 except with better-looking hair. He is making his way down the isle of a

10 small jet, which is all first class. He finds himself at the open door, all ready

11 to jump out. Cary/Parnel checks to make sure his parachute is secure; even

12 dreaming, he does not want to think about

13 how skydiving without a parachute will affect

14 his looks. He jumps . . . he falls gently . . . he

15 screams as he . . . hears his alarm clock.

 ## Model

Model the following sentences to practice using the verbs *affect* and *effect* correctly.

If we dreamed the same thing every night, it would affect us as much as the objects we see every day.
—Blaise Pascal

Frankly, I do not know how to effect a permanency in American foreign policy.
—Franklin D. Roosevelt

altogether, all together ■ *Altogether* means "entirely." The phrase *all together* means "in a group" or "all at once."

"There is altogether too much gridlock," complained the Democrats. All together, the Republicans yelled, "No way!"

among, between ■ *Among* is used when speaking of more than two persons or things. *Between* is used when speaking of only two.

The three of us talked among ourselves to decide between going out or eating in.

amount, number ■ *Amount* is used for bulk measurement. *Number* is used to count separate units. (See also *fewer, less*.)

A substantial amount of honey spilled all over a number of my CD's.

annual, biannual, semiannual, biennial, perennial ■ An *annual* event happens once every year. A *biannual* or *semiannual* event happens twice a year. A *biennial* event happens every two years. A *perennial* event is one that is persistent or constant.

Dad's annual family reunion gets bigger every year.
We're going shopping at the department store's semiannual white sale.
Due to dwindling attendance, the county fair is now a biennial celebration.
A perennial plant persists for several years.

anyway ■ Do not add an *s* to *anyway*.

ascent, assent ■ *Ascent* is the act of rising or climbing; *assent* is "to agree to something after some consideration" (or such an agreement).

We completed our ascent of the butte with the assent of the landowner.

bad, badly ■ *Bad* is an adjective. *Badly* is an adverb.

This apple is bad, but one bad apple doesn't always ruin the whole bushel.
In today's game, Sumey passed badly.

base, bass ■ *Base* is the foundation or the lower part of something. *Bass* (pronounced like *base*) is a deep sound or a musical instrument. *Bass* (pronounced like *class*) is a fish.

A car's wheel base is the distance between the centers of the front and rear wheels.
Luther is the bass player in his bluegrass band.

beside, besides ■ *Beside* means "by the side of." *Besides* means "in addition to."

Mother always grew roses beside the trash bin. Besides looking nice, they also gave off a sweet smell that masked odors.

Using the Right Word 2

among, between; amount, number; annual, biannual, semiannual, biennial, perennial; ascent, assent; beside, besides

In each paragraph below, find the word or words that are used incorrectly. Then write the right word(s) correctly. If there are no incorrect words, write "none."

1.　Among serious gardeners here in Watertown, the biennial sale at Garden Emporium—every March and October—is anticipated most. It offers the widest assortment of spring and fall perennials in the area, including a good amount of jonquils and hostas. Besides that, they also offer volume discounts.

2.　When it comes to choosing among one automaker's model and another manufacturer's car, buyers have their work cut out for them. Some makes are so similar that it's hard to tell them apart, even when they're right beside each other. In such a case, though, it's the dollar amount on the window sticker that will help the car shopper decide.

3.　It was getting difficult to organize the pinecone collectors' convention each year, so we decided to make it a biennial event instead. We were sure the members of the Cone Collectors of America would assent to this change; they had been "pining" for it for years!

4.　Jorge's assent in the amateur golf rankings is the result of consistent practice. He is now positioned between Dave Vasquez, the regional leader, and Marty White, winner of last year's Daily Cup tournament. Jorge's goal is to make it to the Jetar-Bettim Annual Tourney, to be held in Carson, Nevada, this year.

Model

Model the following sentences to practice using the words *amount* and *number* correctly.

> Talent isn't genius, and no amount of energy can make it so.
> —Louisa May Alcott

> Civilization is built on a number of ultimate principles . . . respect for human life, the punishment of crimes against property and persons, the equality of all good citizens before the law . . . or, in a word, justice.
> —Max Nordau

board, bored ■ *Board* is a piece of wood. *Board* is also an administrative group or council.

> **The school board approved the purchase of fifty 1- by 6-inch pine boards.**

Bored is the past tense of the verb "bore," which may mean "to make a hole by drilling" or "to become weary out of dullness."

> **Watching television bored Joe, so he took his drill and bored a hole in the wall where he could hang his new clock.**

brake, break ■ *Brake* is a device used to stop a vehicle. *Break* means "to separate or to destroy."

> **I hope the brakes on my car never break.**

bring, take ■ *Bring* suggests the action is directed toward the speaker; *take* suggests the action is directed away from the speaker.

> **Bring home some garbage bags so I can take the trash outside.**

can, may ■ *Can* suggests ability while *may* suggests permission.

> **"Can I go to the mall?" means "Am I physically able to go to the mall?"**
> **"May I go to the mall?" asks permission to go.**

capital, capitol ■ The noun *capital* refers to a city or to money. The adjective *capital* means "major or important." *Capitol* refers to a building.

> **The state capital is home to the capitol building for a capital reason. The state government contributed capital for its construction.**

cent, sent, scent ■ *Cent* is a coin; *sent* is the past tense of the verb "send"; *scent* is an odor or a smell.

> **For thirty-seven cents, I sent my girlfriend a mushy love poem in a perfumed envelope. She adored the scent but hated the poem.**

cereal, serial ■ *Cereal* is a grain, often made into breakfast food. *Serial* relates to something in a series.

> **Mohammed enjoys reading serial novels while he eats a bowl of cereal.**

chord, cord ■ *Chord* may mean "an emotion" or "a combination of musical tones sounded at the same time." A *cord* is a string or a rope.

> **The guitar player strummed the opening chord to the group's hit song, which struck a responsive chord with the audience.**

chose, choose ■ *Chose* (choz) is the past tense of the verb *choose* (chooz).

> **Last quarter I chose to read Chitra Divakaruni's *The Unknown Errors of Our Lives*—a fascinating book about Indian immigrants.**

Using the Right Word 3

brake, break; cereal, serial; chord, cord; chose, choose

 Write the correct choice from those given in parentheses.

1. Ms. Alford drove to the dealership to have her *(brake, break)* system inspected.

2. During a service call, most computer manufacturers require that you state the *(cereal, serial)* number of your product before they will answer any questions.

3. It is now possible for new parents to save the blood from the umbilical *(chord, cord)* that once connected their baby to his or her mother.

4. Aunt Margaret gave me two options for dinner; then she told me to *(choose, chose)* the one I'd like to make!

5. Nasim is going to *(brake, break)* a leg if he continues to snowboard without the proper equipment.

6. *(Cereal, Serial)* is an important ingredient in dog food, but it should not be the first in the list of ingredients.

7. The power *(chord, cord)* is commonly used in rock music.

8. Mae *(choose, chose)* from among dozens of fresh fruits and vegetables at the farmers' market.

9. *(Cereal, Serial)* dramas became known as "soaps" because detergent manufacturers often sponsored them.

10. You can *(brake, break)* the record for consecutive pogo-stick jumps by bouncing 177,738 times.

 ## Model

Model the following sentences to practice using the words *chord* and *cord* correctly.

> [A] chord in music is analogous to a word in language.
> —Sigmund Spaeth

> No cord or cable can draw so forcibly, or bind so fast, as love can do with a single thread.
> —Robert Burton

coarse, course ■ *Coarse* means "rough or crude"; *course* means "a path or direction taken." *Course* also means "a class or a series of studies."

> Fletcher, known for using coarse language, was barred from the golf course until he took an etiquette course.

complement, compliment ■ *Complement* refers to that which completes or fulfills. *Compliment* is an expression of admiration or praise.

> Kimberly smiled, thinking she had received a compliment when Carlos said that her new Chihuahua complemented her personality.

continual, continuous ■ *Continual* refers to something that happens again and again with some breaks or pauses; *continuous* refers to something that keeps happening, uninterrupted.

> Sunlight hits Iowa on a continual basis; sunlight hits Earth continuously.

counsel, council ■ When used as a noun, *counsel* means "advice"; when used as a verb, it means "to advise." *Council* refers to a group that advises.

> The student council counseled all freshmen to join a school club. That's good counsel.

desert, dessert ■ The noun *desert* (dĕz´ərt) refers to barren wilderness. *Dessert* (dǐ zûrt´) is food served at the end of a meal.

> The scorpion tiptoed through the moonlit desert, searching for dessert.

The verb *desert* (dǐ zûrt´) means "to abandon"; the noun *desert* (dǐ zûrt´) means "deserved reward or punishment."

> The burglar's hiding place deserted him when the spotlight swung his way; his subsequent arrest was his just desert.

die, dye ■ *Die* (dying) means "to stop living." *Dye* (dyeing) is used to change the color of something.

different from, different than ■ Use *different from* in a comparison of two things. *Different than* should be used only when followed by a clause.

> Carlos is quite different from his brother.
> Both are different than they were as children.

farther, further ■ *Farther* refers to a physical distance; *further* refers to additional time, quantity, or degree.

> Alaska extends farther north than Iceland does.
> Further information can be obtained in an atlas.

fewer, less ■ *Fewer* refers to the number of separate units; *less* refers to bulk quantity.

> Because we have fewer orders for cakes, we'll buy less sugar and flour.

Using the Right Word 4

complement, compliment; continual, continuous; desert, dessert;
different from, different than; fewer, less

 Write the correct choice from those given in parentheses.

1. *(Continually, Continuously)* rising at 5:30 a.m. to get to school by 7:00 is not my ideal way of life.

2. The stray dog would *(desert, dessert)* us after we fed him a few times.

3. How are tostadas *(different from, different than)* sopes?

4. Not all women consider being whistled at a *(complement, compliment)*.

5. Aunt Lulu would always let me eat *(desert, dessert)* first.

6. Generally speaking, a hybrid vehicle burns *(fewer, less)* gallons of gas over the same distance than a gas-only vehicle does.

7. Min braids cornrows *(different from, different than)* Rae Lin does.

8. We've had *(fewer, less)* sunshine this month than in any other this year.

9. Mr. Allen's neighbors began to worry about the *(continual, continuous)* music—the same CD—blaring from his apartment.

10. The hoodia plant grows wild only in the Kalahari *(Desert, Dessert)* of Africa.

11. My red jacket would be the perfect *(complement, compliment)* to your outfit!

12. Is a medal a fair *(desert, dessert)* for breaking a record in the Olympics?

 ## Model

Model the following sentences to practice using the words *complement* and *compliment* correctly.

> There may be as much nobility in being last as in being first, because the two positions are equally necessary in the world, the one to complement the other.
>
> —José Ortega Y Gasset

> We were told our campaign wasn't sufficiently slick. We regard that as a compliment.
>
> —Margaret Thatcher

flair, flare ■ *Flair* refers to style or natural talent; *flare* means "to light up quickly" or "burst out" (or an object that does so).

> Ronni was thrilled with Jorge's flair for decorating—until one of his strategically placed candles flared, marring the wall.

good, well ■ *Good* is an adjective; *well* is nearly always an adverb. (When *well* is used to describe a state of health, it is an adjective: He was happy to be *well* again.)

> The CD player works well.
>
> Our team looks good this season.

heal, heel ■ *Heal* means "to mend or restore to health." A *heel* is the back part of a foot.

> Achilles died because a poison arrow pierced his heel and caused a wound that would not heal.

healthful, healthy ■ *Healthful* means "causing or improving health"; *healthy* means "possessing health."

> Healthful foods build healthy bodies.

hear, here ■ You *hear* with your ears. *Here* means "the area close by."

heard, herd ■ *Heard* is the past tense of the verb "hear"; *herd* is a large group of animals.

hole, whole ■ A *hole* is a cavity or hollow place. *Whole* means "complete."

idle, idol ■ *Idle* means "not working." An *idol* is someone or something that is worshipped.

> The once-popular actress, who had been idle lately, wistfully recalled her days as an idol.

immigrate, emigrate ■ *Immigrate* means "to come into a new country or environment." *Emigrate* means "to go out of one country to live in another."

> Martin Ulferts immigrated to this country in 1882. He was only three years old when he emigrated from Germany.

imply, infer ■ *Imply* means "to suggest or express indirectly"; *infer* means "to draw a conclusion from facts." (A writer or speaker implies; a reader or listener infers.)

> Dad implied by his comment that I should drive more carefully, and I inferred that he was concerned for both me and his new car.

Using the Right Word 5

flair, flare; good, well; idle, idol; imply, infer

 Write the correct choice from those given in parentheses.

1. The groupings of pampas grass definitely add *(flair, flare)* to Jacinda's flower garden.

2. Tempers *(flaired, flared)* as it became evident that the "contest" was a hoax and there would be no winners.

3. After five months of winterlike conditions, it felt *(good, well)* to soak up some sun in the park.

4. I didn't sleep so *(good, well)* last night; nightmares plagued me.

5. Uncle Isaac's old jalopy has sat *(idle, idol)* in the barn for 15 years.

6. A dozen candles surrounded the *(idle, idol)* on the small altar.

7. Does wearing torn jeans *(imply, infer)* a lack of funds to purchase nicer clothing?

8. Satish *(implied, inferred)* from his boss's cold stare that he was in trouble.

9. Because Mia wasn't feeling *(good, well)*, she opted out of going to the mall with her friends.

10. The group stranded on a pleasure boat shot a *(flair, flare)* into the sky in hopes that rescuers would come.

 ## Model

Model the following sentences to practice using the words *idle* and *idol* correctly.

> There is one piece of advice, in a life of study, which I think no one will object to; and that is, every now and then to be completely idle—to do nothing at all.
> —Sydney Smith

> There is a strange and mighty race of people called the Americans, who are rapidly becoming the coldest in the world because of this cruel, man-eating idol, lucre.
> —Edward Dahlberg

insure, ensure ■ *Insure* means "to secure from financial harm or loss." *Ensure* means "to make certain of something."

> To ensure that you can legally drive that new car, you'll have to insure it.

it's, its ■ *It's* is the contraction of "it is." *Its* is the possessive form of "it."

> It's hard to believe, but the movie *Shrek* still holds its appeal for many kids.

later, latter ■ *Later* means "after a period of time." *Latter* refers to the second of two things mentioned.

> Later that year we had our second baby and adopted a stray kitten. The latter
> was far more welcomed by our toddler.

lay, lie ■ *Lay* means "to place." *Lay* is a transitive verb. (See **716.1**.)

> Lay your books on the big table.

Lie means "to recline," and *lay* is the past tense of *lie*. *Lie* is an intransitive verb. (See **716.1**.)

> In this heat, the children must lie down for a nap. Yesterday they lay down without one
> complaint. Sometimes they have lain in the hammocks to rest.

lead, led ■ *Lead* (lēd) is the present tense of the verb meaning "to guide." The past tense of the verb is *led* (lĕd). The noun *lead* (lĕd) is a metal.

> We were led along the path that leads to an abandoned lead mine.

learn, teach ■ *Learn* means "to acquire information." *Teach* means "to give information."

> I learn better when people teach with real-world examples.

leave, let ■ *Leave* means "to allow something to remain behind." *Let* means "to permit."

> Would you let me leave my bike at your house?

lend, borrow ■ *Lend* means "to give for temporary use." *Borrow* means "to receive for temporary use.

> I told Mom I needed to borrow $18 for a CD, but she said she could only lend money for
> school supplies.

like, as ■ When *like* is used as a preposition meaning "similar to," it can be followed only by a noun, pronoun, or noun phrase; when *as* is used as a subordinating conjunction, it introduces a subordinate clause.

> You could become a gymnast like her, as you work and practice hard.

medal, meddle ■ *Medal* is an award. *Meddle* means "to interfere."

> Some parents meddle in the awards process to be sure that their kids get medals.

Using the Right Word 6

insure, ensure; it's, its; lay, lie; lend, borrow; medal, meddle

Find the words that are used incorrectly. Write the line number followed by the right word.

1   Mr. and Mrs. Hartleson entered the bank together. They desperately

2   needed to borrow $10,000 to cover some overdue payments. They could no

3   longer lay low—they had to take action now to insure their stake in the new

4   condo development in which they had invested.

5   "Please let me handle this," said Mrs. Hartleson to her spouse. "You

6   can insure my success in this endeavor if you promise not to meddle."

7   If Mr. Hartleson was offended, he did not show it. "That's fair," he said.

8   "I know you are laying your professional reputation on the line here." Then

9   he added, "Its obvious that you'll deserve a medal if you pull this off." He

10   patted her on the back.

11   They were uneasy; if the bank would not borrow them the money, they

12 would be in serious financial trouble. Mr. Hartleson had recently been forced

13 to take a cut in pay, and although Mrs. Hartleson herself was a banker, this

14 time she was on the other side of the fence. *This* bank—and it's loan officers,

15 who looked decidedly unfriendly today—was going to sit in judgment.

16 Anxious sweat formed on the back of her neck.

Model

Model the following sentences to practice using the words *lend* and *borrow* correctly.

> **We don't inherit the earth from our ancestors; we borrow it from our children.**
> —David Brower

> **Parents lend children their experience and a vicarious memory; children endow their parents with a vicarious immortality.**
> —George Santayana

metal, mettle ■ *Metal* is a chemical element like iron or gold. *Mettle* is "strength of spirit."

Grandad's mettle during battle left him with some metal in his shoulder.

miner, minor ■ A *miner* digs for valuable ore. A *minor* is a person who is not legally an adult. A *minor* problem is one of no great importance.

moral, morale ■ A *moral* is a lesson drawn from a story; as an adjective, it relates to the principles of right and wrong. *Morale* refers to someone's attitude.

Ms. Ladue considers it her moral obligation to go to church every day.
The students' morale sank after their defeat in the forensics competition.

passed, past ■ *Passed* is a verb. *Past* can be used as a noun, an adjective, or a preposition.

That old pickup truck passed my sports car! (verb)
Many senior citizens hold dearly to the past. (noun)
Tilly's past life as a circus worker must have been . . . interesting. (adjective)
Who can walk past a bakery without looking in the window? (preposition)

peace, piece ■ *Peace* means "tranquility or freedom from war." *Piece* is a part or fragment.

Grandma sits in the peace and quiet of the parlor, enjoying a piece of pie.

peak, peek, pique ■ A *peak* is a high point. *Peek* means "brief look" (or "look briefly"). *Pique*, as a verb, means "to excite by challenging"; as a noun, it is a feeling of resentment.

The peak of Dr. Fedder's professional life was his ability to pique children's interest in his work. "Peek at this slide," he said to the eager students.

pedal, peddle, petal ■ A *pedal* is a foot lever; as a verb, it means "to ride a bike." *Peddle* means "to go from place to place selling something." A *petal* is part of a flower.

Don Miller paints beautiful petals on his homemade birdhouses. Then he pedals through the flea market every weekend to peddle them.

personal, personnel ■ *Personal* means "private." *Personnel* are people working at a particular job.

plain, plane ■ *Plain* means "an area of land that is flat or level"; it also means "clearly seen or clearly understood."

It's plain to see why settlers of the Great Plains had trouble moving west.
Plane means "flat, level"; it is also a tool used to smooth the surface of wood.

I used a plane to make the board plane and smooth.
Plane means "a level of existence or consciousness."

Using the Right Word 7

metal, mettle; peak, peek, pique; personal, personnel; plain, plane

 Write the correct choice from those given in parentheses.

1. "A *(plain, plane)* 'yes' or 'no' will suffice," admonished the defense attorney.

2. My illness is of a rather *(personal, personnel)* nature, and I'd rather not discuss it.

3. There is nothing that can *(peak, peek, pique)* my curiosity like an unfamiliar word.

4. It takes unusual *(metal, mettle)* to persevere despite harsh conditions.

5. As a child, Dale would *(peak, peek, pique)* down through the stairway railings, watching the people at his parents' parties.

6. Adding sand to paint transforms the wall from a *(plain, plane)* surface to a more interesting, texturized one.

7. Whereas many kitchen appliances used to be made of *(metal, mettle)*, today they are more likely to be plastic.

8. Just as Terry reached what he thought was the *(peak, peek, pique)* of his endurance, he got a second wind.

9. You must go to the *(personal, personnel)* office down the hall to report an on-the-job injury.

10. Abi left the meeting in a *(peak, peek, pique)* following Nathan's presentation of her idea as his own.

 ## Model

Model the following sentences to practice using the words *plain* and *plane* correctly.

Man cannot live on the human plane; he must be either above or below it.
—Eric Gill

Any woman who has brains and willing hands finds twenty remunerative occupations open to her where formerly she would have found merely the inevitable two—plain sewing, or the dull little boys.
—Clara Lanza

poor, pour, pore ■ *Poor* means "needy or pitiable." *Pour* means "to cause to flow in a stream." A *pore* is an opening in the skin.

> **Tough exams on late spring days make my poor pores pour sweat.**

principal, principle ■ As an adjective, *principal* means "primary." As a noun, it can mean "a school administrator" or "a sum of money." *Principle* means "idea or doctrine."

> **His principal concern is fitness. (adjective) The principal retired. (noun)**
> **During the first year of a loan, you pay more interest than principal. (noun)**
> **The principle of *caveat emptor* is "Let the buyer beware."**

quiet, quit, quite ■ *Quiet* is the opposite of "noisy." *Quit* means "to stop." *Quite* means "completely or entirely."

quote, quotation ■ *Quote* is a verb; *quotation* is a noun.

> **The quotation I used was from Woody Allen. You may quote me on that.**

real, really, very ■ Do not use *real* in place of the adverbs *very* or *really*.

> **Mother's cake is usually very (not *real*) tasty, but this one is really stale!**

right, write, wright, rite ■ *Right* means "correct or proper"; it also refers to that which a person has a legal claim to, as in copyright. *Write* means "to inscribe or record." A *wright* is a person who makes or builds something. *Rite* refers to a ritual or ceremonial act.

> **Write this down: It is the right of the shipwright to perform the rite of christening—breaking a bottle of champagne on the stern of the ship.**

ring, wring ■ *Ring* means "encircle" or "to sound by striking." *Wring* means "to squeeze or twist."

> **At the beach, Grandma would ring her head with a large scarf. Once, it blew into the sea, so she had me wring it out.**

scene, seen ■ *Scene* refers to the setting or location where something happens; it also may mean "sight or spectacle." *Seen* is a form of the verb "see."

> **Serena had seen her boyfriend making a scene; she cringed.**

seam, seem ■ *Seam* (noun) is a line formed by connecting two pieces. *Seem* (verb) means "to appear to exist."

> **The ragged seams in his old coat seem to match the creases in his face.**

set, sit ■ *Set* means "to place." *Sit* means "to put the body in a seated position." *Set* is transitive; *sit* is intransitive. (See **716.1**.)

> **How can you just sit there and watch as I set all these chairs in place?**

Using the Right Word 8

principal, principle; quote, quotation; real, really, very; right, write, wright, rite

In each paragraph below, find the word or words that are used incorrectly. Then write the right word(s) correctly. If there are no incorrect words, write "none."

1. Given the circumstances, uttering the quote from last night's *Daily Show* may not have been appropriate—but it *was* really funny. Unfortunately, it tends to lose its humor when you have to write it 50 times as a punishment from the principal.

2. Mario has had several real good stories published. Eventually he would like to be a well-known playwrite, but for now his principle concern is finishing a novel begun last year. He hopes to have it published by his twenty-first birthday.

3. Once a month, Jim performs a right of cleansing in which he drinks only water, rests, does yoga, and meditates for a full day. He says this ritual is based on the principle that regular "bathing" should apply not only to the outside of the body, but to its insides and to the mind, as well. He hasn't talked me into trying it myself, but it certainly hasn't seemed to do *him* any harm.

4. In any writing in which you quote another person's words, it is only right to acknowledge the source. To not do so is to steal—a real transgression in the world of publishing. Avoid plagiarism: Be sure to cite your quotations.

◀ Model

Model the following sentences to practice using the words *principal* and *principle* correctly.

I remember one dinner for which I had relied upon a form of ice as the principal feature of the dessert.

—Julia Ward Howe

The first principle of a free society is an untrammeled flow of words in an open forum.

—Adlai Stevenson

sight, cite, site ■ *Sight* means "the act of seeing"; a *sight* is what is seen. *Cite* means "to quote" or "to summon," as before a court. *Site* means "location."

> In her report, the general contractor cited several problems at the downtown job site. For one, the loading area was a chaotic sight.

sole, soul ■ *Sole* means "single, only one"; *sole* also refers to the bottom surface of the foot. *Soul* refers to the spiritual part of a person.

> As the sole inhabitant of the island, he put his heart and soul into his farming.

stationary, stationery ■ *Stationary* means "not movable"; *stationery* refers to the paper and envelopes used to write letters.

steal, steel ■ *Steal* means "to take something without permission"; *steel* is a type of metal.

> It takes nerves of steel to brazenly steal another's possessions in broad daylight.

than, then ■ *Than* is used in a comparison; *then* tells when.

> Abigail shouted that her big brother was bigger than my big brother. Then she ran away.

their, there, they're ■ *Their* is a possessive personal pronoun. *There* is an adverb used to point out location. *They're* is the contraction for "they are."

> They're a well-dressed couple. Do you see them there, with their matching jackets?

threw, through ■ *Threw* is the past tense of "throw." *Through* means "from beginning to end."

> Through seven innings, Danielle threw just seven strikes.

to, too, two ■ *To* is a preposition that can mean "in the direction of." *To* is also used to form an infinitive. (See **726.2**.) *Too* means "also" or "very." *Two* is a number.

vain, vane, vein ■ *Vain* means "valueless or fruitless"; it may also mean "holding a high regard for oneself." *Vane* is a flat piece of material set up to show which way the wind blows. *Vein* refers to a blood vessel or a mineral deposit.

> The vain prospector, boasting about the vein of silver he'd uncovered, paused to look up at the turning weather vane.

vary, very ■ *Vary* means "to change." *Very* means "to a high degree."

> Though the weather may vary from day to day, generally, it is very pleasant.

Using the Right Word 9

sight, cite, site; stationary, stationery; than, then; vain, vane, vein

 Select the correct word from the list above to complete each sentence.

1. With so many other means to send messages these days, is _____ obsolete?

2. A _____ from the leg is often used in heart bypass surgery.

3. A journalist may be out of a job if he or she does not _____ sources precisely.

4. The road curves around a large, _____ boulder.

5. According to the _____ atop the roof, the wind is coming from the north today.

6. Masafumi started to jack up the car, but _____ he remembered that he had to loosen the lug nuts first.

7. A person who accurately predicts future events is said to have "second _____."

8. Some might mistake someone with a high level of self-confidence for a _____ person.

9. An affordable _____ for a home is becoming increasingly hard to find.

10. Rather _____ taking the bus to school every day, Jasmine rides her bike when she can.

Model

Model the following sentences to practice using the words *sight* and *site* correctly.

> If the sight of the blue skies fills you with joy, if a blade of grass springing up in the fields has power to move you, if the simple things of nature have a message that you understand, rejoice, for your soul is alive. —Eleonora Duse

> Studying the mass of his manuscript was something like excavating the site of ancient Troy.
> —Edward Aswell

vial, vile ■ *A vial* is a small container for liquid. *Vile* is an adjective meaning "foul, despicable."

It's a vile job, but someone has to clean these lab vials.

waist, waste ■ *Waist* is the part of the body just above the hips. The verb *waste* means "to spend or use carelessly" or "to wear away or decay"; the noun *waste* refers to material that is unused or useless.

Her waist is small because she wastes no opportunity to exercise.

wait, weight ■ *Wait* means "to stay somewhere expecting something." *Weight* refers to a degree or unit of heaviness.

ware, wear, where ■ *Ware* refers to a product that is sold; *wear* means "to have on or to carry on one's body"; *where* asks "in what place?" or "in what situation?"

The designer boasted, "Where can anybody wear my ware? Anywhere."

way, weigh ■ *Way* means "path or route." *Weigh* means "to measure weight" or "to have a certain heaviness."

My dogs weigh too much. The best way to reduce is a daily run in the park.

weather, whether ■ *Weather* refers to the condition of the atmosphere. *Whether* refers to a possibility.

Due to the weather, the coach wondered whether he should cancel the meet.

which, that ■ Use *which* to refer to objects or animals in a nonrestrictive clause (set off with commas). Use *that* to refer to objects or animals in a restrictive clause. (For more information about these types of clauses, see **612.2**.)

The birds, which stay in the area all winter, know where the feeders are located.
The food that attracts the most birds is sunflower seed.

who, whom ■ Use *who* to refer to people. *Who* is used as the subject of a verb in an independent clause or in a relative clause. *Whom* is used as the object of a preposition or as a direct object.

To whom do we owe our thanks for these pizzas? And who ordered anchovies?

who's, whose ■ *Who's* is the contraction for "who is." *Whose* is a pronoun that can show possession or ownership.

Cody, whose car is new, will drive. Who's going to read the map?

your, you're ■ *Your* is a possessive pronoun. *You're* is the contraction for "you are."

Take your boots if you're going out in that snow.

Using the Right Word 10

waist, waste; which, that; who, whom; who's, whose; your, you're

For each numbered sentence, write the correct choice from the words given in parentheses.

(1) If *(your, you're)* like the average American, you generate about four pounds of garbage each day. **(2)** While some of it gets recycled or incinerated, most of the country's *(waist, waste)* ends up in landfills. **(3)** These burial sites for anything *(which, that)* can't be recycled are filling up fast as people produce more trash, and environmental problems sometimes follow.

(4) *(Who's, Whose)* the culprit? **(5)** It's not just one group of people *(who, whom)* share responsibility for America's growing trash predicament. Of course, individuals and organizations should try to reuse and recycle as much as they can. **(6)** A growing problem, however, is companies promoting disposable goods, *(which, that)* ultimately end up in a landfill. **(7)** It's *(your, you're)* choice whether to buy such items, so avoid them when possible.

(8) *(Who's, Whose)* job is it to make sure a landfill is safe? Although the federal Environmental Protection Agency's regulations must be met, each state has its own laws. Elected municipal officials also legislate actions related to landfills, so be sure to vote for those **(9)** *(who, whom)* you trust with the environment.

Model

Model the following sentences to practice using the words *who's* and *whose* correctly.

Show me a man who proposes on bended knee and I'll show you a man who's overcompensating.

—Laurien Berenson, *Hot Dog*

He felt that his whole life was some kind of dream, and he sometimes wondered whose it was and whether they were enjoying it.

—Douglas Adams, *The Hitchhiker's Guide to the Galaxy*

Test Prep

Write the letter of the line in which a word is used incorrectly. If all the words are correct, choose "D."

1. A Did you break this hammer? Perhaps Mr.
   B Schultz, who's a carpenter, would be kind
   C enough to borrow us one of his old ones.
   D All are used correctly.

2. A Though it's a bit scary to think about now,
   B Anna's fall was real funny when it
   C happened. I hope she's already feeling better.
   D All are used correctly.

3. A Rather than an impersonal e-mail, I prefer
   B a handwritten letter on pretty stationery.
   C It peaks my curiosity, and I tear it open to read!
   D All are used correctly.

4. A We hope our school's new principal will
   B affect a permanent change in the students'
   C attitudes, which are quite negative lately.
   D All are used correctly.

5. A With this product, in order to ensure the
   B the right result, apply it anytime
   C except when the ground is wet.
   D All are used correctly.

6. A I'm trying to eat less calories, but this
   B dessert looks fabulous—and it is the
   C perfect complement to your wonderful dinner!
   D All are used correctly.

7. A Yesterday Tim wasted no time in his
   B careful assent up the steep roof,
   C scrambling to the peak to repair the flapping shingles.
   D All are used correctly.

8. A My kindergarten teacher, who I adored,
   B had a flair for comforting little children.
   C She was different from the other adults at school.
   D All are used correctly.

9. A If your hoping to change my mind with
   B these compliments, I'm afraid they are
   C given in vain. I'm not changing my mind.
   D All are used correctly.

10. **A** Gene was glad he chose to give up his
   B isle seat on the airplane; there was
   C definitely less noise where he ended up.
   D All are used correctly.

11. **A** The amount of exercise you do directly
   B affects your health. Some people find this
   C known fact a bit difficult to accept.
   D All are used correctly.

12. **A** The box of cereal you are looking for is
   B among the Oaty-Os and the Weety-
   C Flakes. Those Ricey-Puffs sure taste good!
   D All are used correctly.

13. **A** Terell's car needed brake work. He told
   B the tow-truck driver, "It's by Bell's Diner
   C —the blue car which is parked nearest the door."
   D All are used correctly.

14. **A** Dad once demonstrated his metal by
   B rescuing a kid at a construction site.
   C That's why he's the only idol in my life.
   D All are used correctly.

15. **A** "What a sight!" Mr. Clayton said. "This
   B place is a real mess. You—" he said,
   C pointing at me. "Lie your books down and give me a hand."
   D All are used correctly.

16. **A** Must you continually refer to the
   B unusually high number of flamingos
   C here? After all, we're on an isle where they are common.
   D All are used correctly.

17. **A** Just because I do well in science and
   B math, do not imply that I want to be an
   C engineer. Besides, I'm actually looking into cosmetology.
   D All are used correctly.

18. **A** Are you familiar with the famous quote
   B about idle hands? Although I agree with
   C it in principle, I do admit to occasional laziness.
   D All are used correctly.

Parts of Speech

Words in the English language are used in eight different ways. For this reason, there are eight parts of speech.

700.1 Noun

A word that names a person, a place, a thing, or an idea
Governor Smith-Jones   Oregon   hospital   religion

700.2 Pronoun

A word used in place of a noun
I   you   she   him   who   everyone   these   neither theirs   themselves   which

700.3 Verb

A word that expresses an action or a state of being
float   sniff   discover   seem   were   was

700.4 Adjective

A word that describes a noun or a pronoun
young   big   grim   Canadian   longer

700.5 Adverb

A word that describes a verb, an adjective, or another adverb
briefly   forward   regally   slowly   better

700.6 Preposition

The first word or words in a prepositional phrase (which functions as an adjective or an adverb)
away from   under   before   with   for   out of

700.7 Conjunction

A word that connects other words or groups of words
and   but   although   because   either, or   so

700.8 Interjection

A word that shows strong emotion or surprise
Oh no!   Yipes!   Good grief!   Well, . . .

Parts of Speech

Noun

A **noun** is a word that names something: a person, a place, a thing, or an idea.

governor   Oregon   hospital   Buddhism   love

Classes of Nouns

The five classes of nouns are *proper, common, concrete, abstract,* and *collective*.

701.1 Proper Noun

A **proper noun** names a particular person, place, thing, or idea. Proper nouns are always capitalized.

Jackie Robinson   Brooklyn   World Series
Christianity   Ebbets Field   Hinduism

701.2 Common Noun

A **common noun** does not name a particular person, place, thing, or idea. Common nouns are not capitalized.

person   woman   president   park   baseball   government

701.3 Concrete Noun

A **concrete noun** names a thing that is tangible (can be seen, touched, heard, smelled, or tasted). Concrete nouns are either proper or common.

child   Grand Canyon   music
aroma   fireworks   Becky

701.4 Abstract Noun

An **abstract noun** names an idea, a condition, or a feeling—in other words, something that cannot be touched, smelled, tasted, seen, or heard.

New Deal   greed   poverty   progress   freedom   awe

701.5 Collective Noun

A **collective noun** names a group or a unit.

United States   Portland Cementers   team   crowd   community

Forms of Nouns

Nouns are grouped according to their *number, gender,* and *case.*

702.1 Number of a Noun

Number indicates whether the noun is singular or plural.

A **singular noun** refers to one person, place, thing, or idea.

actor   stadium   Canadian   bully   truth   child   person

A **plural noun** refers to more than one person, place, thing, or idea.

actors   stadiums   Canadians   bullies   truths   children   people

702.2 Gender of a Noun

Gender indicates whether a noun is masculine, feminine, neuter, or indefinite.

Masculine:

uncle   brother   men   bull   rooster   stallion

Feminine:

aunt   sister   women   cow   hen   filly

Neuter **(without gender):**

tree   cobweb   amoeba   closet

Indefinite (masculine or feminine): **president   plumber   doctor   parent**

702.3 Case of a Noun

Case tells how nouns are related to other words used with them. There are three cases: *nominative, possessive,* and *objective.*

■ A **nominative case** noun can be the subject of a clause.

> **Patsy's heart was beating very wildly beneath his jacket. . . . That black horse there owed something to the orphan he had made.**
> —Paul Dunbar, "The Finish of Patsy Barnes"

A nominative noun can also be a predicate noun (or predicate nominative), which follows a "be" verb *(am, is, are, was, were, be, being, been)* and renames the subject. In the sentence below, *type* renames *Mr. Cattanzara.*

> **Mr. Cattanzara was a different type than those in the neighborhood.**
> —Bernard Malamud, "A Summer's Reading"

■ A **possessive case** noun shows possession or ownership.

> **Like the spider's claw, a part of him touches a world he will never enter.**
> —Loren Eiseley, "The Hidden Teacher"

■ An **objective case** noun can be a direct object, an indirect object, or an object of the preposition.

> **Marna always gives Mylo science fiction books for his birthday.**

> (*Mylo* is the indirect object and *books* is the direct object of the verb "gives." *Birthday* is the object of the preposition "for.")

Nouns

- Classes of Nouns
- Number of a Noun
- Case of a Noun

 For each underlined noun, classify it as *proper* or *common* and *singular* or *plural*. Also indicate whether it is a *collective* noun and identify its case as *nominative*, *possessive*, or *objective*.

1. <u>Maddy</u>, my cat, is extremely overweight, but she is on a special <u>diet</u> now.

2. The life sciences <u>faculty</u> at Lee's school have judged our science <u>fair</u> for years.

3. Did your <u>father</u> ever see <u>Herb's</u> guitar?

4. We've had great <u>luck</u> to have six gorgeous <u>days</u> in a row!

5. This type of <u>iguana</u> is wild in <u>Mexico</u>.

6. My <u>niece</u> loves to see marching <u>bands</u> in city parades.

7. Juanita cooks <u>dinner</u> for her family on every <u>Thursday</u>.

8. <u>Ladybugs</u> must be squeezing in through cracks in the window <u>frame</u>.

9. His <u>computer's</u> hard drive is corrupt and needs replacing, according to the guy in the <u>Information Technology Department</u>.

10. Perhaps the <u>games</u> that his <u>son</u> installed caused the problem.

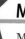 ## Model

Model the following sentences to practice using abstract nouns in the objective case.

Politics is made up largely of irrelevancies.

—Dalton Camp

She tells enough white lies to ice a wedding cake.

—Margot Asquith

Pronoun

A **pronoun** is a word used in place of a noun.

> **I, you, she, it, which, that, themselves, whoever, me, he, they, mine, ours**

The three types of pronouns are *simple, compound,* and *phrasal.*

> **Simple:** I, you, he, she, it, we, they, who, what
> **Compound:** myself, someone, anybody, everything, itself, whoever
> **Phrasal:** one another, each other

All pronouns have **antecedents**. An antecedent is the noun that the pronoun refers to or replaces.

> **Ambrosch** was considered the important person in the family. Mrs. Shimerda and Ántonia always deferred to **him**, though **he** was often surly with them and contemptuous toward **his** father.
> —Willa Cather, *My Ántonia*

(*Ambrosch* is the antecedent of *him, he,* and *his.*)

Note: Each pronoun must agree with its antecedent. (See page 756.)

704.1 Classes of Pronouns

The six classes of pronouns are *personal, reflexive and intensive, relative, indefinite, interrogative,* and *demonstrative.*

Personal
I, me, my, mine / we, us, our, ours
you, your, yours / they, them, their, theirs
he, him, his, she, her, hers, it, its

Reflexive and Intensive
myself, yourself, himself, herself, itself, ourselves, yourselves, themselves

Relative
what, who, whose, whom, which, that

Indefinite

all	both	everything	nobody	several
another	each	few	none	some
any	each one	many	no one	somebody
anybody	either	most	nothing	someone
anyone	everybody	much	one	something
anything	everyone	neither	other	such

Interrogative
who, whose, whom, which, what

Demonstrative
this, that, these, those

Pronouns 1

- ■ **Antecedents**

Find the pronoun in each sentence below. Write the pronoun—labeled as *simple, compound,* or *phrasal*—and its antecedent.

1. Dominique carefully chose the ingredients for her salad.

2. Bonita and Lora took down each other's phone number.

3. Gesturing at the pot of rice and beans, Claude said, "Is that for lunch?"

4. The toddlers—twins, by the look of things—grabbed the toy from the child-care provider and proclaimed, "Do ourselves!"

5. Uh-oh, the cell phone is displaying gibberish on its screen.

6. The honor-roll students lined up, and each one approached the stage to receive an award.

7. Dr. Lopez encouraged the crowd: "Everyone here has the potential to make a difference!"

8. Petra decided to change the tire herself.

9. Some of the lug nuts were rusty, and Petra had difficulty loosening them.

10. Petra positioned the jack and raised it up to the car's frame.

Model

Model the following sentences to practice using compound and phrasal pronouns.

The most important thing is to be whatever you are without shame.

—Rod Steiger

Hearing voices no one else can hear isn't a good sign, even in the wizarding world.
—J. K. Rowling, *Harry Potter and the Chamber of Secrets*

Pronoun *(continued)*

Personal Pronouns

A **personal pronoun** can take the place of any noun.

> Our coach made her point loud and clear when she raised her voice.

- A **reflexive pronoun** is formed by adding *-self* or *-selves* to a personal pronoun. A reflexive pronoun can be a direct object, an indirect object, an object of the preposition, or a predicate nominative.

  > Miss Sally Sunshine loves herself. (direct object of *loves*)
  >
  > Tomisha does not seem herself today. (predicate nominative)

- An **intensive pronoun** is a reflexive pronoun that intensifies, or emphasizes, the noun or pronoun it refers to.

  > Leo himself taught his children to invest their lives in others.

Relative Pronouns

A **relative pronoun** relates or connects an adjective clause to the noun or pronoun it modifies.

> Students who study regularly get the best grades. Surprise!
>
> The dance, which we had looked forward to for weeks, was canceled.

(The relative pronoun *who* relates the adjective clause to *students; which* relates the adjective clause to *dance*.)

Indefinite Pronouns

An **indefinite pronoun** refers to unnamed or unknown people or things.

> I don't know if you've known anybody from that far back; if you've loved anybody that long, first as an infant, then as a child, then as a man. . . . (The antecedent of *anybody* is unknown.)
> —James Baldwin, "My Dungeon Shook: Letter to My Nephew"

Interrogative Pronouns

An **interrogative pronoun** asks a question.

> "Then, who are you? Who could you be? What do you want from my husband?"
> —Elie Wiesel, "The Scrolls, Too, Are Mortal"

Demonstrative Pronouns

A **demonstrative pronoun** points out people, places, or things without naming them.

> This shouldn't be too hard   That looks about right.
>
> These are the best ones.   Those ought to be thrown out.

Note: When one of these words precedes a noun, it functions as an adjective, not a pronoun. (See **728.1**.)

> That movie bothers me. (*That* is an adjective.)

Pronouns 2

- Personal Pronouns
- Reflexive and Intensive Pronouns
- Relative Pronouns
- Indefinite Pronouns
- Interrogative Pronouns
- Demonstrative Pronouns

Write down the 12 pronouns in the paragraphs below and label their class.

1   In March 1989, a geomagnetic storm caused a malfunction in Quebec's
2   power grid. In only a minute and a half, a complete blackout that left 6
3   million people without power disrupted critical services (transportation, fire
4   and police protection)—and everything else—for nine hours.

5   What is a geomagnetic storm? You may have heard of it as a solar
6   storm. These storms are responsible for the incredible light displays
7   known as the auroras, but they also cause temporary disruptions of radio
8   transmissions, navigation systems, and, as evidenced above, power grids.
9   This is how it happens: A solar eruption causes an incredible solar wind
10 shock wave that strikes Earth's magnetic field a day or so later. The shock
11 waves change the electric currents in the atmosphere, which, in turn, are
12 attracted to electric transmission lines. The added current in the lines
13 overheats transformers, causing them to fail.

14 The utility companies themselves are not to blame since the storms
15 can't be prevented. Instead, they have plans to ride out the storms. That
16 may not be the best strategy, but the companies' only existing alternative is
17 installing complex, costly devices to block the extra current. With any luck,
18 nobody will have to cope with a solar storm causing a large-scale blackout.

 ## Model

Model the following sentences to practice using demonstrative pronouns.

I was thought to be 'stuck up.' I wasn't. I was just sure of myself. This is and always has been an unforgivable quality to the unsure.
—Bette Davis

Forms of Personal Pronouns

The form of a personal pronoun indicates its *number* (singular or plural), its *person* (first, second, third), its *case* (nominative, possessive, or objective), and its *gender* (masculine, feminine, or neuter).

708.1 Number of a Pronoun

Personal pronouns are singular or plural. The singular personal pronouns include *my, him, he, she, it.* The plural personal pronouns include *we, you, them, our.* (*You* can be singular or plural.) Notice in the caption below that the first you is singular and the second you is plural.

"Larry, you need to keep all four tires on the road when turning. Are you still with us back there?"

708.2 Person of a Pronoun

The **person** of a pronoun indicates whether the person, place, thing, or idea represented by the pronoun is speaking, is spoken to, or is spoken about.

- **First person** is used in place of the name of the speaker or speakers.

  "We don't do things like that," says Pa; "we're just and honest people. . . . I don't skip debts."
  —Jesse Stuart, "Split Cherry Tree"

- **Second person** pronouns name the person or persons spoken to.

  "If you hit your duck, you want me to go in after it?" Eugie said.
  —Gina Berriault, "The Stone Boy"

- **Third person** pronouns name the person or thing spoken about.

  She had hardly realized the news, further than to understand that she had been brought . . . face to face with something unexpected and final. It did not even occur to her to ask for any explanation.
  —Joseph Conrad, "The Idiots"

Pronouns 3

- Number of a Pronoun
- Person of a Pronoun

Identify the person and number of each underlined pronoun.

1. "<u>You</u> should rent the first season of *Friends* on DVD," Pasha said when <u>she</u> heard that <u>I</u> had never seen it.

2. <u>We</u> read *Things Fall Apart*, by Chinua Achebe, in <u>our</u> Contemporary Literature class.

3. <u>She</u> got to the gym just in time to see <u>her</u> boyfriend sink the winning basket.

4. "Will <u>you</u> call <u>us</u> if you're running late?" the parents asked the teens.

5. <u>I</u> am eager to try scuba diving in the ocean this summer.

6. Luisa, when are <u>you</u> picking <u>them</u> up at the airport?

7. Whether or not <u>they</u> called <u>him</u> to go to the movie, he was going to see <u>it</u>.

8. <u>I</u> can't believe that Li Ming didn't invite <u>them</u> to opening night.

9. "<u>You</u> have until Friday to complete <u>your</u> term papers," Mr. Weatherby told his students.

Model

Model the following sentence to practice using first- and third-person pronouns correctly.

I had been encouraged early on by my mother and my grandmother to be a high achiever, and I got hooked on the accolades they showered on me.
—Dana Buchman, *A Special Education*

710.1 Case of a Pronoun

The **case** of each pronoun tells how it is related to the other words used with it. There are three cases: *nominative, possessive,* and *objective.*

■ A **nominative case** pronoun can be the subject of a clause. The following are nominative forms: *I, you, he, she, it, we, they.*

> I like life when things go well. You must live life in order to love life.

A nominative pronoun is a *predicate nominative* if it follows a "be" verb (*am, is, are, was, were, be, being, been*) or another linking verb (*appear, become, feel,* etc.) and renames the subject.

> "Oh, it's only she who scared me just now," said Mama to Papa, glancing over her shoulder.
> "Yes, it is I," said Mai in a superior tone.

■ **Possessive case** pronouns show possession or ownership. Apostrophes, however, are not used with personal pronouns.

> But as I placed my hand upon his shoulder, there came a strong shudder over his whole person.
> —Edgar Allan Poe, "The Fall of the House of Usher"

■ An **objective case** pronoun can be a direct object, an indirect object, or an object of the preposition.

> The kids loved it! We lit a campfire for them and told them old ghost stories.
> (*It* is the direct object of the verb *loved. Them* is the object of the preposition *for* and the indirect object of the verb *told.*)

Number, Person, and Case of Personal Pronouns

	Nominative	Possessive	Objective
First Person Singular	I	my, mine	me
Second Person Singular	you	your, yours	you
Third Person Singular	he	his	him
	she	her, hers	her
	it	its	it
	Nominative	Possessive	Objective
First Person Plural	we	our, ours	us
Second Person Plural	you	your, yours	you
Third Person Plural	they	their, theirs	them

710.2 Gender of a Pronoun

Gender indicates whether a pronoun is masculine, feminine, or neuter.

Masculine: **he him his**   Feminine: **she her hers**
Neuter (without gender): **it its**

Pronouns 4

- Case of a Pronoun
- Gender of a Pronoun

 Identify each underlined pronoun as *nominative, possessive,* or *objective.* If the pronoun is gender-specific, write its gender, too.

(1) My sister-in-law Sookie and **(2)** I went shopping for my brother's birthday present. He's into snowboarding, and Sookie wanted to get **(3)** him a new board before **(4)** they went on **(5)** their vacation to the mountains. Snowboarding is a sport that Sookie knows **(6)** nothing about, so **(7)** she called **(8)** her amazing brother-in-law (that would be **(9)** me) to help her shop.

When **(10)** we got to the sporting goods store, I asked Sookie, "How much do **(11)** you want to spend?"

She said, "I want to get **(12)** your brother a good quality board, but **(13)** it should be one that really stands out."

Just then, I saw **(14)** it, and I pointed it out to Sookie. **(15)** Its jazzy, yellow design screamed at **(16)** us from across the aisle. (I wished that it were **(17)** mine.) Sookie looked at it closely and said, "**(18)** It is perfect! Let's get it for him."

◀ Model

Model the following sentences to practice using nominative- and objective-case pronouns.

Computers are useless. They can only give you answers.
—Pablo Picasso

There was a definite process by which one made people into friends, and it involved talking to them and listening to them for hours at a time.
—Rebecca West

Test Prep

For each underlined word (or words), write the letter of the part of speech from the choices given on the next page.

The world is becoming smaller as more people are able to reach faraway places
1
in a relatively short time. Air travel, once reserved for the "jet set," is now a ubiquitous

form of transportation, available to just about anyone, anywhere. Fortunately, air travel
2
is one of the safest modes of transportation, as well, thanks to air traffic controllers.
3   **4**

With the growing number of aircraft in the skies, the primary job of an air traffic
5   **6**
controller (ATC) is very important: He or she prevents planes from getting too close to
7
each other. With the assistance of computer software and radio contact with pilots, an

ATC keeps track of several aircraft simultaneously, thereby ensuring safe distances

between them. ATC's also provide weather information and navigation directions to
8
pilots when necessary.

What does it take to become an ATC? Excellent spatial perception is mandatory,
9   **10**
as are superior vision, hearing, and speaking skills. The position can involve a great

deal of stress, so having a healthy mind and body is a definite advantage. The Federal
11
Aviation Administration (FAA), the agency responsible for hiring and training ATC's,

administers physical and psychological tests to all applicants.

In the United States, there are only 12 colleges that offer ATC education.
12
Graduates of these programs receive 15 weeks of training at an FAA facility in
13
Oklahoma City, after which they get on-the-job training. Experienced controllers are
14   **15**
among the highest-paid federal employees, earning more than $100,000 annually.

The volume of air traffic today places a heavy demand on the air traffic control
16
system, and weather conditions play a big role in its smoothness. Being part of this
17
important service isn't for everyone. Those who thrive on challenge, however, will find
18
air traffic control a dream job.

1. **A**   proper noun, neuter gender
   B   common noun, neuter gender
   C   common noun, indefinite gender
   D   proper noun, indefinite gender

2. **A**   relative singular pronoun
   B   intensive third-person pronoun
   C   indefinite plural pronoun
   D   indefinite singular pronoun

3. **A**   indefinite neuter pronoun
   B   common noun, indefinite gender
   C   demonstrative pronoun, masculine gender
   D   common noun, neuter gender

4. **A**   proper noun, indefinite gender
   B   common noun, indefinite gender
   C   abstract plural noun
   D   concrete plural noun

5. **A**   abstract singular noun
   B   concrete singular noun
   C   abstract plural noun
   D   concrete plural noun

6. **A**   singular noun, indefinite gender
   B   plural noun, indefinite gender
   C   singular masculine noun
   D   singular feminine noun

7. **A**   objective case feminine pronoun
   B   nominative case pronoun, feminine gender
   C   indefinite feminine pronoun
   D   intensive feminine pronoun

8. **A**   plural first-person pronoun
   B   singular third-person pronoun
   C   plural pronoun, objective case
   D   plural pronoun, nominative case

9. **A**   interrogative pronoun, objective case
   B   singular third-person pronoun
   C   plural pronoun, objective case
   D   interrogative pronoun, possessive case

10. **A**   abstract noun, objective case
    B   abstract noun, nominative case
    C   concrete noun, objective case
    D   concrete noun, nominative case

11. **A**   proper singular noun
    B   proper plural noun
    C   concrete noun, objective case
    D   abstract noun, objective case

12. **A**   indefinite pronoun, nominative case
    B   relative pronoun, nominative case
    C   indefinite pronoun, objective case
    D   relative pronoun, objective case

13. **A**   concrete noun, possessive case
    B   collective noun, nominative case
    C   plural noun, antecedent of "they"
    D   abstract noun, antecedent of "these"

14. **A**   proper noun, objective case
    B   concrete noun, nominative case
    C   plural noun, antecedent of "they"
    D   abstract proper noun

15. **A**   personal pronoun, first person
    B   personal pronoun, third person
    C   intensive pronoun, third person
    D   relative neuter pronoun

16. **A**   concrete noun, nominative case
    B   concrete noun, objective case
    C   abstract noun, nominative case
    D   abstract noun, objective case

17. **A**   personal pronoun, objective case
    B   indefinite pronoun, possessive case
    C   personal pronoun, possessive case
    D   demonstrative pronoun, nominative case

18. **A**   personal pronoun, objective case
    B   indefinite pronoun, possessive case
    C   personal pronoun, possessive case
    D   demonstrative pronoun, nominative case

Verb

A **verb** is a word that expresses action (*run, carried, declared*) or state of being (*is, are, seemed*).

Classes of Verbs

714.1 Linking Verbs

A **linking verb** links the subject to a noun or an adjective in the predicate.

In the outfield, the boy felt confident.
He was the best fielder around.

Common Linking Verbs

is	are	was	were	be	been	am

Additional Linking Verbs

smell	seem	grow	become	appear	sound
taste	feel	get	remain	stay	look	turn

Note: The verbs listed as "additional linking verbs" function as linking verbs when they do not show actual action. An adjective usually follows these linking verbs. (When they do show action, an adverb or a direct object may follow them. In this case, they are action verbs.)

Linking: This fruit smells rotten.
Action: Maya always smells fruit carefully before eating it.

714.2 Auxiliary Verbs

Auxiliary verbs, or helping verbs, are used to form some of the **tenses (718.3),** the **mood (724.1),** and the **voice (722.2)** of the main verb. (In the example below, the auxiliary verbs are in red; the main verbs are in blue.)

The long procession was led by white-robed priests, their faces streaked with red and yellow and white ash. By this time the flames had stopped spurting, and the pit consisted of a red-hot mass of burning wood, which attendants were leveling with long branches.

—Leonard Feinberg, "Fire Walking in Ceylon"

Common Auxiliary Verbs

is	was	being	did	have	would	shall	might
am	were	been	does	had	could	can	must
are	be	do	has	should	will	may	

Verbs 1

- **Linking Verbs**
- **Auxiliary Verbs**

Label each underlined verb in the paragraph below as a *linking verb*, an *auxiliary verb*, or *neither*.

Laisha **(1)** is a real estate agent. She **(2)** has decided to have an addition to her house built. Although the addition **(3)** is going to cost a lot of money, Laisha **(4)** feels good about it. She **(5)** has no experience working with contractors, so she **(6)** will read as much as she can about it beforehand. She **(7)** does not want to seem like an easy target for unscrupulous businesses. She will **(8)** sound authoritative and **(9)** appear as though she's done this before. She will not **(10)** be weak in any negotiations. She **(11)** looks forward to the experience as one that **(12)** can improve her job skills.

Model

Model the following sentences to practice using linking and auxiliary verbs correctly.

The hallmark of creative people is their mental flexibility.
—Roger von Oech, *A Kick in the Seat of the Pants*

Our ability to delude ourselves may be an important survival tool.
—Jane Wagner

716.1 Action Verbs: Transitive and Intransitive

An **intransitive verb** communicates an action that is complete in itself. It does not need an object to receive the action.

> The boy flew on his skateboard. He jumped and flipped and twisted.

A **transitive verb** (red) is an action verb that needs an object (blue) to complete its meaning.

> The city council passed a strict noise ordinance.
>
> Raul takes pictures for the student paper.

While some action verbs are only transitive *or* intransitive, some can be either, depending on how they are used.

> He finally stopped to rest. (intransitive)
>
> He finally stopped the show. (transitive)

716.2 Objects with Transitive Verbs

- A **direct object** receives the action of a transitive verb directly from the subject. Without it, the transitive verb's meaning is incomplete.

    > The boy kicked his skateboard forward. (*Skateboard* is the direct object.)
    >
    > Then he put one foot on it and rode like a pro.

- An **indirect object** also receives the action of a transitive verb, but indirectly. An indirect object names the person *to whom* or *for whom* something is done. (An indirect object can also name the thing *to what* or *for what* something is done.)

    > Ms. Oakfield showed us pictures of the solar system.
    > (*Us* is the indirect object.)
    >
    > She gave Tony an A on his project.

Note: When the word naming the indirect receiver of the action is in a prepositional phrase, it is no longer considered an indirect object.

> Ms. Oakfield showed pictures of the solar system to us.
> (*Us* is the object of the preposition *to.*)

Verbs 2

- Transitive and Intransitive Verbs
- Direct and Indirect Objects

 For each underlined verb, indicate whether it is transitive or intransitive. For transitive verbs, write the direct object, too. If there is an indirect object, write and label it, as well.

For Dad's birthday, Mom and I **(1)** <u>are giving</u> him a gift he won't easily forget: a skydiving lesson. A small local airport **(2)** <u>offers</u> lessons from certified instructors. The plane **(3)** <u>will fly</u> at about 10,000 feet, and Dad will tandem-jump with the instructor. Then will come the scary part: free-falling! (Even though the free fall **(4)** <u>lasts</u> only about 45 seconds, I bet it will seem longer.) Once the instructor **(5)** <u>releases</u> the parachute, they will **(6)** <u>float</u> for about five minutes before reaching the ground.

If Dad **(7)** <u>likes</u> skydiving enough to do more jumps, he **(8)** <u>can jump</u> by himself eventually. For the first dozen or so jumps, however, an instructor **(9)** <u>must supervise</u> his efforts. He or she **(10)** <u>shows</u> students important things—such as the location of the pull cord for the reserve parachute.

▸ Model

Model the following sentences to practice using transitive verbs with direct and indirect objects.

> **Always acknowledge a fault. This will throw those in authority off their guard and give you an opportunity to commit more.**
> —Mark Twain

> **From the day I arrived until the day I left, she would tell me some pearl of wisdom that usually went in one ear and out the other.**
> —Patti LaBelle and Laura Randolph Lancaster,
> *Patti's Pearls: Lessons in Living Genuinely, Joyfully, Generously*

Forms of Verbs

A verb has different forms depending on its *number, person, tense, voice,* and *mood.*

718.1 Number of a Verb

Number indicates whether a verb is singular or plural. In a clause, the verb (in blue below) and its subject (in red) must both be singular or both be plural.

- **Singular**

    One large island floats off Italy's "toe."

    Italy's northern countryside includes the truly spectacular Alps.

- **Plural**

    Five small islands float inside Michigan's "thumb."

    The Porcupine Mountains rise above the shores of Lake Superior.

718.2 Person of a Verb

Person indicates whether the subject of the verb is first, second, or third person (is speaking, is spoken to, or is spoken about). The form of the verb usually changes only when a present-tense verb is used with a third-person singular subject.

	Singular	Plural
First Person	I sniff	we sniff
Second Person	you sniff	you sniff
Third Person	he/she/it sniffs	they sniff

718.3 Tense of a Verb

Tense indicates time. Each verb has three principal parts: the *present, past,* and *past participle.* All six tenses are formed from these principal parts. The past and past participle of regular verbs are formed by adding *ed* to the present form. For irregular verbs, the past and past participle are usually different words; however, a few have the same form in all three principal parts (see page **720.2**).

718.4 Simple Tenses

- **Present tense** expresses action that is happening at the present time, or action that happens continually, regularly.

    In September, sophomores smirk and joke about the "little freshies."

- **Past tense** expresses action that was completed at a particular time in the past.

    They forgot that just ninety days separated them from freshman status.

- **Future tense** expresses action that will take place in the future.

    They will recall this in three years when they will be freshmen again.

Verbs 3

- Number of a Verb
- Person of a Verb
- Simple Tenses of a Verb

 Find the verbs in the following sentences. Write each, followed by its person and number and its tense.

1. I think of Leonardo da Vinci as an artist, but he was quite an inventor, as well.

2. He created designs for a diving suit, a revolving bridge, and a helicopter.

3. Can you imagine such intelligence?

4. Flocks of starlings race after the lawn mower, seeking a meal of the bugs set loose by the blades.

5. Mahender attends Blakely School for the Blind.

6. The radio station will feature an interview with Ziggy Marley at 4:20 this afternoon.

7. You look as red as a ripe tomato!

8. Alfonso and Lela will call me when they are ready to go.

9. After I brushed my teeth, Rachelle offered me a warm brownie.

10. The British Virgin Islands attract tourists from around the world.

11. Jaime, please fold your clothes and put them away.

12. The summer solstice will occur at 11:59 p.m. on June 20, 2008.

 ## Model

Model the following sentences to practice using verbs of different number, person, and tense in the same sentence.

Home runs win a lot of games, but I never understood why fans are so obsessed with them.

—Hank Aaron

Always go to other people's funerals; otherwise, they won't come to yours.

—Yogi Berra

Forms of Verbs (continued)

720.1 Perfect Tenses

■ **Present perfect tense** expresses action that began in the past but continues in the present or is completed in the present.

Our boat **has weathered** worse storms than this one.

■ **Past perfect tense** expresses an action in the past that occurred before another past action.

They reported, wrongly, that the hurricane **had missed** the island.

■ **Future perfect tense** expresses action that will begin in the future and be completed by a specific time in the future.

By this time tomorrow, the hurricane **will have smashed** into the coast.

720.2 Irregular Verbs

Common Irregular Verbs and Their Principal Parts

Present Tense	Past Tense	Past Participle	Present Tense	Past Tense	Past Participle	Present Tense	Past Tense	Past Participle
am, be	was, were	been	go	went	gone	shrink	shrank	shrunk
begin	began	begun	grow	grew	grown	sing	sang, sung	sung
bite	bit	bitten	hang	hanged	hanged	sink	sank, sunk	sunk
blow	blew	blown	(execute)			sit	sat	sat
break	broke	broken	hang	hung	hung	slay	slew	slain
bring	brought	brought	(suspend)			speak	spoke	spoken
buy	bought	bought	hide	hid	hidden, hid	spring	sprang,	sprung
catch	caught	caught	know	knew	known		sprung	
choose	chose	chosen	lay	laid	laid	steal	stole	stolen
come	came	come	lead	led	led	strive	strove	striven
dive	dove	dived	leave	left	left	swear	swore	sworn
do	did	done	lie	lay	lain	swim	swam	swum
draw	drew	drawn	(recline)			swing	swung	swung
drink	drank	drunk	lie	lied	lied	take	took	taken
drive	drove	driven	(deceive)			teach	taught	taught
eat	ate	eaten	lose	lost	lost	tear	tore	torn
fall	fell	fallen	make	made	made	throw	threw	thrown
fight	fought	fought	ride	rode	ridden	wake	waked,	waked,
flee	fled	fled	ring	rang	rung		woke	woken
fly	flew	flown	rise	rose	risen	wear	wore	worn
forsake	forsook	forsaken	run	ran	run	weave	weaved,	weaved,
freeze	froze	frozen	see	saw	seen		wove	woven
get	got	gotten	shake	shook	shaken	wring	wrung	wrung
give	gave	given	show	showed	shown	write	wrote	written

These verbs are the same in all principal parts: *burst, cost, cut, hurt, let, put, set,* and *spread.*

Verbs 4

- Perfect Tense Verbs
- Irregular Verbs

 Write the past participle of the verb in parentheses to complete each sentence. Indicate whether the verb is *present perfect, past perfect,* or *future perfect.*

1. Melford hadn't *(see)* the cat in a while; he assumed that she had *(lie)* in a patch of sunlight for most of the afternoon.

2. I'm sure I have *(eat)* at this restaurant before, since I have never *(sit)* in a booth like this anywhere else!

3. By the time this batter will have *(swing)* at another pitch, the guy on second base will have *(run)* to third.

4. Colleen has *(lead)* her niece's scout troop for three years, and she's *(do)* a great job.

5. The vase, teetering on the edge of the shelf for so long, had finally *(fall)* and *(break)* into little pieces.

6. Odds are that Noney will have *(catch)* some serious tanning-booth rays before she heads to Florida this spring; she has *(grow)* rather fond of her skin's orangey glow.

7. D'Shawn had *(choose)* Melanie's watercolor painting over the others because he liked the way she had *(draw)* bare trees over the colors in dark ink.

8. Dad has *(lay)* his last brick; by tomorrow he will have *(throw)* out the trowel that he used for so many years.

Model

Model the following sentences to practice using irregular perfect tense verbs correctly.

A person who talks fast often says things she hasn't thought of yet.
—Caron Warner Lieber

The only ones among you who will be really happy are those who have sought and found how to serve.
—Albert Schweitzer

722.1 Continuous Tenses

- A **present continuous tense** verb expresses action that is not completed at the time of stating it. The present continuous tense is formed by adding *am, is,* or *are* to the *-ing* form of the main verb.

    Scientists are learning a great deal from their study of the sky.

- A **past continuous tense** verb expresses action that was happening at a certain time in the past. This tense is formed by adding *was* or *were* to the *-ing* form of the main verb.

    Astronomers were beginning their quest for knowledge hundreds of years ago.

- A **future continuous tense** verb expresses action that will take place at a certain time in the future. This tense is formed by adding *will be* to the *-ing* form of the main verb.

    Someday astronauts will be going to Mars.

    This tense can also be formed by adding a phrase noting the future *(are going to)* plus *be* to the *-ing* form of the main verb.

    They are going to be performing many experiments.

722.2 Voice of a Verb

Voice indicates whether the subject is acting or being acted upon.

- **Active voice** indicates that the subject of the verb is, has been, or will be doing something.

    For many years Lou Brock held the base-stealing record.

Active voice makes your writing more direct and lively.

- **Passive voice** indicates that the subject of the verb is being, has been, or will be acted upon.

    For many years the base-stealing record was held by Lou Brock.

Note: With a passive verb, the person or thing creating the action is not always stated.

The ordinance was overturned. (Who did the overturning?)

	Active Voice		**Passive Voice**	
Tense	Singular	Plural	Singular	Plural
Present	I see you see he/she/it sees	we see you see they see	I am seen you are seen he/she/it is seen	we are seen you are seen they are seen
Past	I/he saw you saw	we/they saw you saw	I/it was seen you were seen	we/they were seen you were seen
Future	I/you/he will see	we/you/they will see	I/you/it will be seen	we/you/they will be seen

Verbs 5

- **Continuous Tenses**
- **Voice of a Verb**

In each sentence below, identify the verb in the underlined group of words as *present continuous, past continuous,* or *future continuous.*

1. The students <u>are going to be creating their own Web page designs</u>.

2. Aliyya and her brother, Haani, <u>are working in their family's restaurant</u>.

3. <u>Construction workers were finally repaving</u> the pothole-filled road.

4. <u>Rufus and I are looking forward to</u> the first game of the season.

5. <u>You will be graduating soon</u>.

6. In my programming course, <u>I am learning</u> how to create lifelike animations.

7. <u>Darius was leaning against the wall</u>, waiting his turn in the long line.

8. Wolf <u>spiders were building an intricate web</u> on our front porch.

9. <u>Will they be laying their eggs</u> there soon?

10. Those <u>spiders aren't going to be catching many bugs</u> in that web.

Model

Model the following sentences, but change the passive voice to the active voice.

> [A] calm is not desirable in any situation in life. . . . Man was made for action and for bustle too, I believe.
> —Abigail Adams

> The wise are instructed by reason; ordinary minds by experience; the stupid, by necessity; and brutes by instinct.
> —Cicero

> I am prepared to meet my Maker. Whether my Maker is prepared for the great ordeal of meeting me is another matter.
> —Winston Churchill

724.1 Mood of a Verb

The **mood** of a verb indicates the tone or attitude with which a statement is made.

■ **Indicative mood** is used to state a fact or to ask a question.

> Sometimes I'd yell questions at the rocks and trees, and across gorges, or yodel, "What is the meaning of the void?" The answer was perfect silence, so I knew.

—Jack Kerouac, "Alone on a Mountain Top"

■ **Imperative mood** is used to give a command.

"Whatever you do, don't fly your kite during a storm."

—Mrs. Abiah Franklin

■ **Subjunctive mood** is no longer commonly used; however, careful writers may choose to use it to express the exact manner in which their statements are meant.

Use the subjunctive *were* to express a condition that is contrary to fact.

> If I were finished with my report, I could go to the movie.

Use the subjunctive *were* after *as though* or *as if* to express an unreal condition.

> Mrs. Young acted as if she were sixteen again.

Use the subjunctive *be* in "that" clauses to express necessity, legal decisions, or parliamentary motions.

> "It is moved and supported that no more than 6 million quad be used to explore the planet Earth."

> "Ridiculous! Knowing earthlings is bound to help us understand ourselves! Therefore, I move that the sum be amended to 12 million quad."

> "Stupidity! I move that all missions be postponed until we have living proof of life on Earth."

Verbs 6

- ### Mood of a Verb

 Write whether each statement shows *indicative,* *imperative,* **or** *subjunctive* **mood.**

1. If I were eighteen, I could vote in the November election.

2. Stop at my house after school and pick up Jana's homework.

3. Have you heard that Matthias got a job at Gordon's garage?

4. Be certain the air conditioning is operating by tomorrow!

5. Because someone else called in sick today, I'm working until ten tonight.

6. Pedro acts as if he were a shoo-in for the lead role.

7. Notice how Dot sands the table with fine-grain sandpaper.

8. Why do you like the idea of earlier start times for high schools?

9. I've decided to enroll in a technical college this fall.

10. Get off the freeway at the next exit.

11. The vice principal peered at the boys as though they were criminals.

12. Before you leave the house, make sure you empty the dishwasher and put the dishes away.

13. Tino proposed to his parents that he be permitted to be out until 1:00 a.m. on weekends.

14. Please take the garbage out.

 ## Model

Model the following sentences to practice using the imperative mood.

Do not try to fight a lion if you are not one yourself.

—African Proverb

Never chase a lie. Let it alone, and it will run itself to death.

—Lyman Beecher

Verbals

A **verbal** is a word that is derived from a verb but does not function as a verb in a sentence. Instead, a verbal acts as another part of speech—noun, adjective, or adverb. There are three types of verbals: *gerunds, infinitives,* and *participles.* Each is often part of a verbal phrase.

726.1 Gerunds

A **gerund** is a verb form that ends in *ing* and is used as a noun.

Swimming **is my favorite pastime.** (subject)

I began swimming **at the age of six months.**
(direct object)

The hardest part of swimming **is the resulting sore muscles.**
(object of the preposition *of*)

Swimming in chlorinated pools **makes my eyes red.**
(gerund phrase used as a subject)

726.2 Infinitives

An **infinitive** is a verb form that is usually introduced by *to*; the infinitive may be used as a noun, an adjective, or an adverb.

Most people find it easy to swim. (adverb modifying an adjective)

To swim the English Channel **must be a thrill.** (infinitive phrase as noun)

The urge to swim in tropical waters **is more common.** (infinitive phrase as adjective)

726.3 Participles

A **participle** is a verb form ending in *ing* or *ed* that acts as an adjective.

The workers raking leaves **are tired and hungry.**
(participial phrase modifying *workers*)

The bags full of raked **leaves are evidence of their hard work.**
(participle modifying *leaves*)

Smiling **faces greeted my father when he returned from a business trip.**
(participle modifying *faces*)

Note: The past participle of an irregular verb can also act as an adjective.

That rake is obviously broken.

It's a known **fact that leaves make good compost.**

Verbals

- Gerunds
- Infinitives
- Participles

Label each underlined phrase in the following paragraphs as a *gerund phrase*, a *participial phrase*, or an *infinitive phrase*. Also state the function of each infinitive phrase (*noun, adjective,* or *adverb*).

You may have heard the term "hijab" in the news lately. **(1)** <u>Derived from the Arabic word "hajaba,"</u> the word means "to hide from view." In the religion of Islam, passages in the holy book refer to the requirement for women **(2)** <u>to cover their heads and bodies.</u> Today, some people—**(3)** <u>Muslims included</u>—find hijab a controversial matter.

On one side of the issue are tradition and pride. Many women who observe hijab are comfortable with **(4)** <u>making the statement about their religious identity.</u> **(5)** <u>To maintain their religious beliefs</u> is more important than **(6)** <u>fitting in</u> to any other society. They are of the opinion that their way of dress forces others **(7)** <u>to judge them</u> for their intelligence and ability rather than for their looks and sexuality.

Some Muslim communities interpret hijab more loosely. Although **(8)** <u>covering the entire body</u> is not strictly enforced, families and the culture itself still expect women to dress modestly. Usually **(9)** <u>consisting of long-sleeved shirts or dresses,</u> long skirts or pants, and a scarf over the hair, this attire is acceptable to many **(10)** <u>working Muslim women.</u>

Model

Model the following sentences to practice using an infinitive as a noun.

> To fulfill a dream, to be allowed to sweat over lonely labor, to be given the chance to create is the meat and potatoes of life. The money is the gravy.
> —Bette Davis, *The Lonely Life*

> What would you attempt to do if you knew you could not fail?
> —Robert Schuller

Adjective

An **adjective** describes or modifies a noun or a pronoun. The articles *a, an,* and *the* are also adjectives.

> The young **driver peeked through** the big **steering wheel.**
>
> (*The* and *young* modify *driver;* the and *big* modify *steering wheel.*)

728.1 Types of Adjectives

A **proper adjective** is created from a proper noun and is capitalized.

> In Canada (proper noun), **you will find many cultures and climates.**
>
> Canadian (proper adjective) **winters can be harsh.**

A **predicate adjective** follows a form of the "be" verb (or other linking verb) and describes the subject.

> **Late autumn seems** grim **to those who love summer.** (*Grim* modifies *autumn.*)

Note: Some words can be either adjectives or pronouns (*that, these, all, each, both, many, some,* and so on). These words are adjectives when they come before the nouns they modify; they are pronouns when they stand alone.

> **Jiao made** both **goals.** (*Both* modifies *goals;* it is an adjective.)
>
> Both **were scored in the final period.** (*Both* stands alone; it is a pronoun.)

728.2 Forms of Adjectives

Adjectives have three forms: *positive, comparative,* and *superlative.*

- The **positive form** describes a noun or a pronoun without comparing it to anyone or anything else.

  > **The first game was** long and tiresome.

- The **comparative form** (*-er, more,* or *less*) compares two persons, places, things, or ideas.

  > **The second game was** longer and more tiresome **than the first.**

- The **superlative form** (*-est, most,* or *least*) compares three or more persons, places, things, or ideas.

  > **The third game was the** longest and most tiresome **of all.**

Note: Use *more* and *most* (or *less* and *least*)—instead of adding a suffix—with many adjectives of two or more syllables.

Positive	Comparative	Superlative
big	**bigger**	**biggest**
helpful	**more helpful**	**most helpful**
painful	**less painful**	**least painful**

Adjectives

- Types of Adjectives
- Forms of Adjectives

 Write the adjectives (not including articles) in each of the following sentences. Label *proper, predicate, comparative,* **and** *superlative* **adjectives. (Some adjectives will have two labels.)**

1. The new warehouse seems much larger than the old one.

2. I hope to scale Mt. Everest—the highest mountain in the world.

3. African sunsets on the Serengeti Plain are gorgeous.

4. Of all the bands, One Step Back was the least enjoyable.

5. Hunter looks handsome in his royal blue tuxedo.

6. Shineece's Chihuahua is smaller than any dog I have ever seen.

7. Olga crocheted long, multicolored scarves for both grandmothers.

8. Didn't second-hour geometry class seem longer than usual?

9. The Chinese culture was brought to life through Shaiming's amazing presentation.

10. The highway worker's bright orange vest really made her stand out against the gray-brown background of the bare trees lining the country road.

 ## Model

Model the following sentences to practice using adjectives well.

> His solid belly filled the stretched sack of his maroon cardigan sweater. . . .
> —Tom Bissell, *God Lives in St. Petersburg*

> Miss Bart was discerning enough to know that the inner vanity is generally in proportion to the outer self-depreciation.
> —Edith Wharton, *The House of Mirth*

Adverb

An **adverb** describes or modifies a verb, an adjective, or another adverb.

She sneezed loudly. (*Loudly* modifies the verb *sneezed*.)

Her sneezes are really **dramatic.** (*Really* modifies the adjective *dramatic*.)

The sneeze exploded very **noisily.** (*Very* modifies the adverb *noisily*.)

An adverb usually tells *when, where, how,* or *how much.*

730.1 Types of Adverbs

Adverbs can be cataloged in four basic ways: *time, place, manner,* and *degree.*

Time (These adverbs tell *when, how often,* and *how long.*)

today, yesterday   daily, weekly   briefly, eternally

Place (These adverbs tell *where, to where,* and *from where.*)

here, there   nearby, beyond   backward, forward

Manner (These adverbs often end in *ly* and tell *how* something is done.)

precisely   effectively   regally   smoothly   well

Degree (These adverbs tell *how much* or *how little.*)

substantially   greatly   entirely   partly   too

Note: Some adverbs can be written with or without the *ly* ending. When in doubt, use the *ly* form.

slow, slowly   loud, loudly   fair, fairly   tight, tightly   quick, quickly

730.2 Forms of Adverbs Adverbs of manner have three forms: *positive, comparative,* and *superlative.*

- The **positive form** describes a verb, an adjective, or another adverb without comparing it to anyone or anything else.

  Model X vacuum cleans well **and runs** quietly.

- The **comparative form** (*-er, more,* or *less*) compares how two things are done.

  Model Y vacuum cleans better **and runs** more quietly **than model X does.**

- The **superlative form** (*-est, most,* or *least*) compares how three or more things are done.

  Model Z vacuum cleans best **and runs** most quietly **of all.**

Positive	Comparative	Superlative
well	better	best
fast	faster	fastest
remorsefully	more remorsefully	most remorsefully

Adverbs

- **Types of Adverbs**
- **Forms of Adverbs**

 Write the adverbs in each of the following sentences (some sentences have more than one). Identify each as an adverb of *time, place, manner,* or *degree*. For an adverb of manner, also identify it as *positive, comparative,* or *superlative*.

1. Of all the board members, the mayor reacted most enthusiastically to our proposal.

2. P. J. sat there lazily while I foolishly hauled his boxes to the car alone.

3. Jason rode his motorbike clear across the course in minutes.

4. An immense cargo carrier roared deafeningly overhead.

5. Yesterday, my brother discovered that I'd accidentally dented his pickup truck.

6. I observed an affectionate side of Arnell when he spoke very gently to his nephew.

7. The speaker shared a very interesting anecdote.

8. His was one of the most finely planned science projects at the fair.

9. I performed well on last year's SAT's, but I slipped behind on my final exams.

10. Mr. and Mrs. O'Leary indulgently had their colorful tropical drinks delivered poolside.

Model

Model the following sentences to practice using comparative and superlative adverbs.

> **People always call it luck when you've acted more sensibly than they have.**
> —Anne Tyler, *Celestial Navigation*

> **Practice shows that those who speak the most knowingly and confidently often end up with the assignment to get the job done.**
> —Bill Swanson, *Swanson's Unwritten Rules of Management*

Preposition

A **preposition** is the first word (or group of words) in a prepositional phrase. It shows the relationship between its object (a noun or a pronoun that follows the preposition) and another word in the sentence. The first noun or pronoun following a preposition is its object.

> **To make a mustache, Natasha placed the hairy caterpillar under her nose.**
> (*Under* shows the relationship between the verb, *placed*, and the object of the preposition, *nose*.)
> **The drowsy insect clung obediently to the girl's upper lip.**
> (The first noun following the preposition *to* is *lip; lip* is the object of the preposition.)

732.1 Prepositional Phrases

A **prepositional phrase** includes the preposition, the object of the preposition, and the modifiers of the object. A prepositional phrase functions as an adverb or as an adjective.

> **Some people run away from caterpillars.**
> (The phrase functions as an adverb and modifies the verb *run*.)
> **However, little kids with inquisitive minds enjoy their company.**
> (The phrase functions as an adjective and modifies the noun *kids*.)

Note: A preposition is always followed by an object; if there is no object, the word is an adverb, not a preposition.

> **Natasha never played with caterpillars before.** (The word *before* is not followed by an object; therefore, it functions as an adverb that modifies *played*, a verb.)

Common Prepositions

aboard	before	from	of	save
about	behind	from among	off	since
above	below	from between	on	subsequent to
according to	beneath	from under	on account of	together with
across	beside	in	on behalf of	through
across from	besides	in addition to	onto	throughout
after	between	in back of	on top of	till
against	beyond	in behalf of	opposite	to
along	by	in front of	out	toward
alongside	by means of	in place of	out of	under
along with	concerning	in regard to	outside of	underneath
amid	considering	inside	over	until
among	despite	inside of	over to	unto
apart from	down	in spite of	owing to	up
around	down from	instead of	past	up to
aside from	during	into	prior to	upon
at	except	like	regarding	with
away from	except for	near	round	within
because of	for	near to	round about	without

Prepositions

■ **Prepositional Phrases**

For each underlined prepositional phrase, indicate whether it functions as an adjective or an adverb.

Nearly all my life, **(1)** <u>except the last three years</u>, was spent **(2)** <u>at home</u>. I never traveled much, and in fact, never expected to become a traveler, and above all an unwilling heroine **(3)** <u>in the North-West troubles</u>. I had several sisters and brothers. I was the eldest **(4)** <u>of the family</u>, and as such, **(5)** <u>for many years</u> had to devote my time **(6)** <u>to household cares</u>. My school days seem now the pleasantest period **(7)** <u>of my early life</u>.

From *Two Months in the Camp of Big Bear* by
Theresa Gowanlock and Theresa Delaney

If this journey had taken place **(8)** <u>during my days</u> **(9)** <u>of study and happiness</u>, it would have afforded me inexpressible pleasure. But a blight had come **(10)** <u>over my existence</u>, and I only visited these people **(11)** <u>for the sake of the information</u> they might give me **(12)** <u>on the subject</u> in which my interest was so terribly profound. Company was irksome to me; when alone, I could fill my mind **(13)** <u>with the sights</u> of heaven and earth; the voice of Henry soothed me, and I could thus cheat myself **(14)** <u>into a transitory peace</u>.

From *Frankenstein* by Mary Wollstonecraft Shelley

Model

Model the following sentence to practice using prepositional phrases effectively.

One minute you're pedaling along a highway, and the next minute, boom, you're face-down in the dirt. — Lance Armstrong, *It's Not About the Bike*

Conjunction

A **conjunction** connects individual words or groups of words. There are three kinds of conjunctions: *coordinating, correlative,* and *subordinating.*

734.1 Coordinating Conjunctions

Coordinating conjunctions usually connect a word to a word, a phrase to a phrase, or a clause to a clause. The words, phrases, or clauses joined by a coordinating conjunction are equal in importance or are of the same type.

> I could tell by my old man's eyes that he *was nervous* and *wanted to smooth things over,* but Syl didn't give him a chance.
> —Albert Halper, "Prelude"

(*And* connects the two parts of a compound predicate; *but* connects two independent clauses that could stand on their own.)

734.2 Correlative Conjunctions

Correlative conjunctions are conjunctions used in pairs.

> They were not only exhausted by the day's journey but also sunburned.

734.3 Subordinating Conjunctions

Subordinating conjunctions connect two clauses that are *not* equally important, thereby showing the relationship between them. A subordinating conjunction connects a dependent clause to an independent clause in order to complete the meaning of the dependent clause.

> A brown trout will study the bait before he eats it. (The clause *before he eats it* is dependent. It depends on the rest of the sentence to complete its meaning.)

Kinds of Conjunctions

Coordinating: **and, but, or, nor, for, yet, so**
Correlative: **either, or; neither, nor; not only, but also; both, and; whether, or**
Subordinating: **after, although, as, as if, as long as, as though, because, before, if, in order that, provided that, since, so that, that, though, till, unless, until, when, where, whereas, while**

Note: Relative pronouns (page **706.2**) and conjunctive adverbs (page **618.2**) can also connect clauses.

Interjection

An **interjection** communicates strong emotion or surprise. Punctuation—a comma or an exclamation point—sets off an interjection from the rest of the sentence.

> Oh no! The TV broke. Good grief! I have nothing to do! Yikes, I'll go mad!

Conjunctions

 Write the 16 conjunctions you find in the following paragraph and label them *coordinating,* *subordinating,* **or** *correlative.* **(Write both correlative conjunctions as one answer.)**

1   A very special baby was born on July 17, 1990. His given name was
2 Matthew Joseph Thaddeus Stepanek, but everyone knew him as "Mattie."
3 Mattie was special; not only was he born with a rare neuromuscular disease,
4 but he also was destined to become a well-known peacemaker and poet.
5 Mattie used a wheelchair to get around because he was unable to walk. He
6 also needed a ventilator so he could breathe. The pain and discomfort of his
7 illness never stopped him from writing and speaking about world peace.
8 Although he was often very ill in his short life (he died on June 22, 2004), he
9 neither complained nor wanted people to feel sorry for him. Before his death,
10 he published eight books of poetry, and five made it to the *New York Times*
11 best-seller list. Mattie also appeared on numerous talk shows to discuss his
12 philosophies about peace efforts and global tolerance. After he died, former
13 President Jimmy Carter delivered the eulogy at his funeral (the two had
14 been friends since 2002, bonding over their passion for peacemaking). Carter
15 said that he had known many kings and queens, but Mattie was the most
16 extraordinary person he had ever met. Matthew Joseph Thaddeus Stepanek
17 was indeed a remarkable young man, and he left us with these final
18 thought-provoking words: "Remember to play after every storm."

Model

Model the follow sentences to practice using interjections effectively.

> **Wow! Hey! What's this thing coming towards me very fast? Very, very fast.**
> — Douglas Adams, *The Hitchhiker's Guide to the Galaxy*

> **"This is fantastic!" Mr. Rumsfeld blurted. "I've got a laser pointer! Holy mackerel!"**
> —Eric Schmitt, *The New York Times*

Test Prep

For each underlined word or group of words, write the letter of the answer that best describes it from the choices given on the next page.

Each year, tens of thousands of <u>United States</u> citizens lose a limb or are born
1
without one. Until fairly recently, their choices <u>were</u> limited to getting by without
2
the limb <u>or</u> using a bulky, sometimes ugly artificial limb. Today, however, many
3
congenital or accidental amputees <u>experience</u> an improved quality of life <u>as a result</u>
4 **5**
of advances in the design of prosthetic limbs.

Someone who needs an artificial limb cannot <u>simply</u> go to the store and buy
6
one. The socket for each prosthetic—the part that fits onto the body—<u>must</u> be custom
7
made. A patient usually obtains a new <u>limb</u> through consultation with a doctor; a
8
prosthetist, who fits the limb; and a physical therapist, who helps the patient with
exercises that strengthen the specific muscles <u>used</u> to move the limb.
9

<u>Since</u> the weight of prosthetics is <u>important</u>, newer limbs <u>are made</u> mostly of
10 **11** **12**
plastic and lightweight metal. One of the greatest advances in prosthetic technology
is the use of myoelectricity, which allows electrical signals from the patient's muscles
<u>to move</u> the limb. Computerized components <u>further</u> enhance its range of motion and
13 **14**
responsiveness. <u>Offering</u> even greater freedom for amputees in the near future is the
15
goal of "biohybrid" limbs. Currently <u>in development</u>, these limbs will merge artificial
16
components with human tissue, permanently affixing the limb to the body.

Amputees—whether by birth, accident, or war—will <u>always</u> face obstacles in
17
their lives. But doctors, engineers (biomedical, chemical, electrical, and mechanical),
and prosthetic manufacturers have given these <u>people</u> a higher degree of normalcy.
18
They help people with limb loss avoid an additional loss: that of independence.

1. **A** abstract noun
   B proper noun
   C proper adjective
   D predicate adjective

2. **A** auxiliary verb
   B linking verb
   C intransitive verb
   D verbal

3. **A** correlative conjunction
   B coordinating conjunction
   C subordinating conjunction
   D interjection

4. **A** transitive verb
   B intransitive verb
   C participle
   D present perfect verb

5. **A** verbal
   B subordinating conjunction
   C prepositional phrase functioning as adjective
   D prepositional phrase functioning as adverb

6. **A** adjective
   B adverb of degree
   C adverb of manner
   D adverb of time

7. **A** auxiliary verb
   B linking verb
   C transitive verb
   D intransitive verb

8. **A** adverb of manner
   B abstract noun
   C indirect object
   D direct object

9. **A** transitive verb
   B auxiliary verb
   C participle
   D gerund

10. **A** subordinating conjunction
    B correlative conjunction
    C coordinating conjunction
    D preposition

11. **A** proper adjective
    B predicate adjective
    C adverb of manner
    D adverb of degree

12. **A** participial phrase
    B gerund phrase
    C active voice verb
    D passive voice verb

13. **A** intransitive verb
    B transitive verb
    C infinitive
    D participle

14. **A** adverb of manner
    B adverb of degree
    C adverb of time
    D adjective

15. **A** gerund
    B transitive verb
    C participle
    D auxiliary verb

16. **A** prepositional phrase functioning as adverb
    B prepositional phrase functioning as adjective
    C subordinating conjunction
    D interjection

17. **A** adverb of manner
    B adverb of place
    C adverb of degree
    D adverb of time

18. **A** adjective
    B direct object
    C indirect object
    D participle

Understanding Sentences

Constructing Sentences

A **sentence** is made up of one or more words that express a complete thought. Sentences begin with a capital letter; they end with a period, a question mark, or an exclamation point.

What should we do this afternoon? We could have a picnic. No, I hate the ants!

Using Subjects and Predicates

A sentence usually has a **subject** and a **predicate**. The subject is the part of the sentence about which something is said. The predicate, which contains the verb, is the part of the sentence that says something about the subject.

We write from aspiration and antagonism, as well as from experience.

—Ralph Waldo Emerson

738.1 The Subject

The **subject** is the part of the sentence about which something is said. The subject is always a noun; a pronoun; or a word, clause, or phrase that functions as a noun (such as a gerund or a gerund phrase or an infinitive).

Wolves **howl.** (noun)
They **howl for a variety of reasons.** (pronoun)
To establish their turf **may be one reason.** (infinitive phrase)
Searching for "lost" pack members **may be another.** (gerund phrase)
That wolves and dogs are similar animals **seems obvious.** (noun clause)

- A **simple subject** is the subject without its modifiers.
  Most wildlife biologists **disapprove of crossbreeding wolves and dogs.**

- A **complete subject** is the subject with all of its modifiers.
  Most wildlife biologists **disapprove of crossbreeding wolves and dogs.**

- A **compound subject** is composed of two or more simple subjects.
  Wise breeders and owners **know that wolf-dog puppies can display unexpected, destructive behaviors.**

738.2 Delayed Subject

In sentences that begin with *There* or *It* followed by a form of the "be" verb, the subject comes after the verb. The subject is also delayed in questions.

There was nothing in the refrigerator. (The subject is *nothing*; the verb is *was*.)
Where is my sandwich? (The subject is *sandwich*; the verb is *is*.)

Constructing Sentences 1

- Simple, Complete, and Compound Subjects
- Delayed Subjects

 Write the complete subject of each independent clause (and each dependent clause in a complex or compound-complex sentence). Circle the simple subject or subjects.

(1) In 1953, General Motors introduced an automobile destined to become one of the most popular cars in American history. **(2)** It was the Chevrolet Corvette. **(3)** It wasn't the Corvette's performance that was striking; the design sold the car. **(4)** You could only buy the '53 "Vettes" in white, and all were convertibles. **(5)** The red vinyl interior, soft black top, and red rims around the whitewall tires defined the design. **(6)** There was nothing else like it on the road. **(7)** The suggested retail price for the base model amounted to about $3,500.

(8) GM created only 300 of the '53 Corvettes, but the limited number was unintentional. **(9)** The powerful corporate giant got a late start building the cars. **(10)** A temporary manufacturing plant in Flint, Michigan, was the production site. **(11)** The plant and assembly line required time to set up, so workers were able to make just 300 cars before the start of the 1954 model year.

(12) About 225 of the '53 Corvettes still exist today, representing the rarest of all model-year Corvettes. **(13)** Whoever owns one of these automobiles holds a valuable collector's piece worth more than $105,000. **(14)** There is a nice little sum!

 ## Model

Model the following sentence to practice using a compound subject.

> **Junipero Serra, the Majorca-born missionary who headed the effort, and his small band of Franciscan followers built a chain of missions from San Diego in the south to San Rafael in the north.**
> — H. W. Brands, *The Age of Gold*

Sentences

740.1 Predicates

The **predicate** is the part of the sentence that shows action or says something about the subject.

> **Giant squid** do exist.

- A **simple predicate** is the verb without its modifiers.
  > **One giant squid** measured nearly 60 feet long.

- A **complete predicate** is the simple predicate with all its modifiers.
  > **One giant squid** measured nearly 60 feet long.
  > (*Measured* is the simple predicate; *nearly 60 feet long* modifies *measured*.)

- Compound and complex sentences have more than one predicate.
  > **The sperm whale** has an enormous head **that** is approximately a third of its entire length.
  > **A whale** is a mammal, **but a squid** is a mollusk.

- A **compound predicate** is composed of two or more simple predicates.
  > **A squid** grasps **its prey with tentacles and** bites **it with its beak.**

Note: A sentence can have a **compound subject** and a **compound predicate.**
  > **Both** sperm whales **and** giant squid live **and occasionally** clash **in the deep waters off New Zealand's South Island.**

- A **direct object** is part of the predicate and receives the action of the verb. (See **716.2.**)
  > **Sperm whales sometimes eat** giant squid.
  > (The direct object *giant squid* receives the action of the verb *eat* by answering the question *whales eat what?*)

Note: The **direct object** may be compound.
  > **In the past, whalers harvested** oil, spermaceti, **and** ambergris **from slain sperm whales.**

740.2 Understood Subjects and Predicates

Either the subject or the predicate may be "missing" from a sentence, but both must be clearly **understood.**

Who is in the hot-air balloon?
(*Who* is the subject; *is in the hot-air balloon* is the predicate.)

No one.
(*No one* is the subject; the predicate *is in the hot-air balloon* is understood.)

Get out of the way!
(The subject *you* is understood; *get out of the way* is the predicate.)

Constructing Sentences 2

- ■ Simple, Complete, and Compound Predicates

Write the complete predicate of each sentence. Circle the simple predicate or predicates. In sentences with a direct object, underline it.

1. Danica Patrick finished fourth in the 2005 Indianapolis 500.

2. She led for 19 laps and became the first woman driver ever to lead the race.

3. Her car stalled in the pits about halfway through the 500-mile race.

4. She restarted the car but dropped to the middle of the field.

5. Her fourth-place finish was the highest ever for a female driver.

6. Danica won the 2005 title of Rookie of the Year.

7. At 10 years old, Danica began racing go-carts.

8. Today Danica drives Indy cars for the Rahal-Letterman racing team.

9. In the 2006 Indy race, Danica could have taken first place.

10. Think about how exciting that would have been!

Model

Model the following sentence to practice using a compound predicate.

When I get bored, I drive downtown and get a great parking spot, then sit in my car and count how many people ask me if I'm leaving.
—Steven Wright

Using Phrases

A **phrase** is a group of related words that function as a single part of speech. The sentence below contains a number of phrases.

Finishing the race will require biking up some steep slopes.

finishing the race (This gerund phrase functions as a subject noun.)

will require (This phrase functions as a verb.)

biking up some steep slopes (This gerund phrase acts as an object noun.)

742.1 Types of Phrases

- An **appositive phrase,** which follows a noun or a pronoun and renames it, consists of a noun and its modifiers. An appositive adds new information about the noun or pronoun it follows.

    The Trans-Siberian Railroad, the world's longest railway, **stretches from Moscow to Vladivostok.** (The appositive phrase renames *Trans-Siberian Railroad* and provides new information.)

- A **verbal phrase** is a phrase based on one of the three types of verbals: *gerund, infinitive,* or *participle.* (See **726.1, 726.2,** and **726.3.**)

    - A **gerund phrase** consists of a gerund and its modifiers. The whole phrase functions as a noun.

        Spotting the tiny mouse **was easy for the hawk.**
        (The gerund phrase is used as the subject of the sentence.)

        Dinner escaped by ducking under a rock.
        (The gerund phrase is the object of the preposition *by.*)

    - An **infinitive phrase** consists of an infinitive and its modifiers. The whole phrase functions either as a noun, an adjective, or an adverb.

        To shake every voter's hand **was the candidate's goal.**
        (The infinitive phrase functions as a noun used as the subject.)

        Your efforts to clean the chalkboard **are appreciated.**
        (The infinitive phrase is used as an adjective modifying *efforts.*)

        Please watch carefully to see the difference.
        (The infinitive phrase is used as an adverb modifying *watch.*)

    - A **participial phrase** consists of a past or present participle and its modifiers. The whole phrase functions as an adjective.

        Following his nose, **the beagle took off like a jackrabbit.**
        (The participial phrase modifies the noun *beagle.*)

        The raccoons, warned by the rustling, **took cover.**
        (The participial phrase modifies the noun *raccoons.*)

Constructing Sentences 3

- ■ **Appositive Phrases**
- ■ **Verbal Phrases**

Identify each underlined phrase as an *appositive, gerund, infinitive,* or *participial* phrase. (One phrase below will have two correct answers.)

1. The citizens approved a referendum for <u>increasing library funds</u>.

2. Kai, <u>my best friend for ten years</u>, will be my college roommate.

3. Ping went to the mall <u>to buy a dress</u> for the prom.

4. James dreams about <u>becoming an ER doctor</u>.

5. <u>To avoid</u> <u>burning the burgers</u>, Ryan watched them closely.

6. Paul Anka, <u>the dog on the television show *Gilmore Girls*</u>, is named after a famous teen idol.

7. The student <u>chosen as valedictorian</u> will speak at the graduation ceremony.

8. <u>Camping in the woods</u> at this time of year is dangerous.

9. The camper <u>clearing the snow from the site</u> is building up a good appetite.

10. The best exercise, <u>walking every day</u>, costs only the price of a good pair of shoes.

Model

Model the following sentence to practice using a gerund phrase.

For me, singing sad songs often has a way of healing a situation.

—Reba McEntire

Using Phrases *(continued)*

■ A **verb phrase** consists of a main verb preceded by one or more helping verbs.

> **Snow** has been falling **for days.** (*Has been falling* is a verb phrase.)

■ A **prepositional phrase** is a group of words beginning with a preposition and ending with a noun or a pronoun. Prepositional phrases function mainly as adjectives and adverbs.

> **Reach for that catnip ball** behind the couch. (The prepositional phrase *behind the couch* is used as an adjective modifying *catnip ball.*)

> **Zach won the wheelchair race** in record time. (*In record time* is used as an adverb modifying the verb *won.*)

■ An **absolute phrase** consists of a noun and a participle (plus the participle's object, if there is one, and any modifiers). An absolute phrase functions as a modifier that adds information to the entire sentence. Absolute phrases are always set off with commas.

> Its wheels clattering rhythmically over the rails, **the train rolled into town.** (The noun *wheels* is modified by the present participle *clattering.* The entire phrase modifies the rest of the sentence.)

Using Clauses

A **clause** is a group of related words that has both a subject and a predicate.

744.1 | Independent and Dependent Clauses

An **independent clause** presents a complete thought and can stand alone as a sentence; a **dependent clause** (also called a *subordinate clause*) does not present a complete thought and cannot stand alone as a sentence.

> **Sparrows make nests in cattle barns** (independent clause) **so that they can stay warm during the winter** (dependent clause).

744.2 | Types of Dependent Clauses

There are three basic types of dependent clauses: *adverb, noun,* and *adjective.*

■ An **adverb clause** is used like an adverb to modify a verb, an adjective, or an adverb. Adverb clauses begin with a subordinating conjunction. (See **734.3.**)

> If I study hard, **I will pass this test.** (The adverb clause modifies the verb *will pass.*)

■ A **noun clause** is used in place of a noun.

> **However, the teacher said** that the essay questions are based only on the last two chapters. (The noun clause functions as a direct object.)

■ An **adjective clause** modifies a noun or a pronoun.

> **Tomorrow's test,** which covers the entire book, **is half essay and half short answers.** (The adjective clause modifies the noun *test.*)

Constructing Sentences 4

- **Verb Phrases**
- **Prepositional Phrases**
- **Absolute Phrases**
- **Dependent Clauses**
- **Independent Clauses**

For each underlined group of words, write whether it is a *verb phrase*, a *prepositional phrase*, or an *absolute phrase*.

1. Mara <u>did</u> not <u>find</u> the resources needed <u>for the assignment</u>.

2. <u>The school year nearly finished</u>, Hannah and Sally made plans <u>for the summer</u>.

3. My sister <u>will meet</u> us at the coffee shop <u>at three o'clock</u>.

4. <u>After the race</u>, Huan beelined for the water fountain, <u>his chest heaving</u>.

5. He <u>was having</u> difficulty breathing.

For each underlined group of words, write whether it is an *independent clause* or a *dependent clause*. If it is a dependent clause, also identify its type.

6. Nobody except Jaleesa knows <u>where the party will be</u>.

7. She took the job <u>so that she could pay her college tuition</u>.

8. <u>Ms. Klema has been giving me extra help</u>, and my grades are improving.

9. The house <u>that we used to live in</u> was sold.

10. <u>My back hurts so much</u> because I fell yesterday.

Model

Model the following sentence to practice using prepositional phrases effectively.

> **At the house, a small white gate opened from the lane into a country garden, which in summer would shine with bunched roses and morning glories and tresses of sweet pea.**
>
> —Frank Delaney, *Ireland*

Using Sentence Variety

A **sentence** may be classified according to the type of statement it makes, the way it is constructed, and its arrangement of words.

746.1 Kinds of Sentences

The five basic kinds of sentences are *declarative, interrogative, imperative, exclamatory,* and *conditional.*

- **Declarative sentences** make statements. They tell us something about a person, a place, a thing, or an idea. Although declarative sentences make up the bulk of most academic writing, there are overwhelmingly diverse ways in which to express them.

    The Statue of Liberty stands in New York Harbor.

    For over a century, it has greeted immigrants and visitors to America.

- **Interrogative sentences** ask questions.

    Did you know that the Statue of Liberty is made of copper and stands over 150 feet tall?

    Are we allowed to climb all the way to the top?

- **Imperative sentences** make commands.

    You must purchase a ticket.

    They often contain an understood subject *(you)* as in the examples below.

    Go see the Statue of Liberty.

    After a few weeks of physical conditioning, climb its 168 stairs.

- **Exclamatory sentences** communicate strong emotion or surprise.

    Climbing 168 stairs is not a dumb idea!

    Just muster some of that old pioneering spirit, that desire to try something new, that never-say-die attitude that made America great!

- **Conditional sentences** express wishes ("if . . . then" statements) or conditions contrary to fact.

    If I could design a country's flag, I would use six colors behind a sun, a star, and a moon.

    I would feel as if I were representing many cultures in my design.

Kinds of Statements

 Write the kind of statement each sentence makes: *declarative, interrogative, imperative, exclamatory,* or *conditional.*

1. A superstition is an illogical belief that comes from fear or ignorance.

2. You should hear some of these unusual, old superstitions!

3. If you carry a hoe into the house, you should carry it out walking backward to avoid bad luck.

4. Always close a front door with your face toward it.

5. Do you believe that an apple a day keeps the doctor away?

6. Seeing a single crow is unlucky, but seeing two means good luck.

7. Have you heard that a dead beetle tied around the neck is a cure for whooping cough?

8. When eating a fish, start at the tail and work toward the head.

9. We are what we believe ourselves to be.

10. If you believe in superstition, it will always follow you.

 ## Model

Model the following conditional statements.

> **Rome, after all, had more than half a dozen aqueducts: if one failed, the others could make up the deficit.**
> —Robert Harris, *Pompeii*

> **If you don't know where you are going, any road will get you there.**
> —Lewis Carroll

Sentences

748.1 Types of Sentence Constructions

A sentence may be *simple, compound, complex,* or *compound-complex.* It all depends on the relationship between independent and dependent clauses.

- A **simple sentence** can have a single subject or a compound subject. It can have a single predicate or a compound predicate. However, a simple sentence has only one independent clause, and it has no dependent clauses.

  My back aches.
  (single subject; single predicate)
  My teeth **and my** eyes hurt.
  (compound subject; single predicate)
  My throat **and nose feel** sore and look **red.**
  (compound subject; compound predicate)
  I must have caught the flu **from the sick kids in class.**
  (independent clause with two phrases: *from the sick kids* and *in class*)

- A **compound sentence** consists of two independent clauses. The clauses must be joined by a comma and a coordinating conjunction or by a semicolon.

  I usually don't mind missing school, but **this is not fun.**
  I feel too sick to watch TV; I feel too sick to eat.

Note: The comma can be omitted when the clauses are very short.

  I wept and **I wept.**

- A **complex sentence** contains one independent clause (in black) and one or more dependent clauses (in red).

  When I get back to school, **I'm actually going to appreciate it.**
  (dependent clause; independent clause)
  I won't even complain about math class, although I might be talking out of my head because I'm feverish.
  (independent clause; two dependent clauses)

- A **compound-complex sentence** contains two or more independent clauses (in black) and one or more dependent clauses (in red).

  Yes, I have a bad flu, and because I need to get well soon, **I won't think about school just yet.**
  (two independent clauses; one dependent clause)
  The best remedy for those who suffer with flu symptoms **is plenty of rest and fluids, but the chicken soup** that Grandma makes for me **always helps, too.**
  (two independent clauses; one dependent clauses)

Types of Sentence Constructions

Identify each of the following sentences as a *simple, compound, complex,* or *compound-complex* sentence.

1. The Tomb of the Unknowns is guarded 24 hours a day, 365 days a year, in all kinds of weather.

2. The Third United States Infantry is labeled "The Old Guard."

3. "The Old Guard" guards the tomb, and it follows strict rules.

4. Its procedure is precise.

5. A sentinel, man or woman, marches 21 paces past the tomb.

6. He makes a crisp 90-degree turn; he faces east for 21 seconds.

7. The sentinel makes another 90-degree turn, and then he faces north and stands for 21 seconds.

8. He quickly moves his rifle.

9. He places its barrel on his shoulder, facing away from the tomb, to show that he stands between the tomb and any threat.

10. After this procedure is completed, it is repeated, and this goes on 24 hours each day.

11. The Tomb of the Unknowns, located in Arlington National Cemetery, contains the remains of several unknown American soldiers.

12. The unknown soldiers were killed in both World Wars, the Korean War, and the Vietnam War.

Model

Model the following sentence to practice forming a compound sentence.

Windows rattled and floors shook; the sound was a giant hand shaking Lydia Kilkenny's sleeping shoulders.

—Myla Goldberg, *Wickett's Remedy*

750.1 Arrangements of Sentences

Depending on the arrangement of the words and the placement of emphasis, a sentence may also be classified as *loose, balanced, periodic,* or *cumulative.*

- A **loose sentence** expresses the main thought near the beginning and adds explanatory material as needed.

  > We hauled out the boxes of food and set up the camp stove, **all the time battling the hot wind that would not stop, even when we screamed into the sky.**

  > Memory performs the impossible for man—**holds together past and present, gives continuity and dignity to human life.**
  > —Mark Van Doren, *Liberal Education*

- A **balanced sentence** is constructed so that it emphasizes a similarity or a contrast between two or more of its parts (words, phrases, or clauses).

  > **The wind in our ears** drove us crazy **and** pushed us on.
  > (The similar wording emphasizes the main idea in this sentence.)

  > **Experience is not** what happens to you; **it is what you do with** what happens to you.
  > —Aldous Huxley

- A **periodic sentence** is one that postpones the crucial or most surprising idea until the end.

  > **Following my mother's repeated threats to ground me for life,** I decided it was time to propose a compromise.

  > **There is only one way to achieve happiness on this terrestrial ball—**and that is to have either a clear conscience or no conscience at all.
  > —Ogden Nash, *I'm a Stranger Here Myself*

- A **cumulative sentence** places the general idea in the middle of the sentence with modifying clauses and phrases coming before and after.

  > **With careful thought and extra attention to detail,** I wrote out my plan for being a model teenager, **a teen who cared about neatness and reliability.**

  > **Not too long ago,** architects who planned college classrooms and dormitories were advised against making the furnishings too pleasant or comfortable **lest the students become distracted or fall asleep.**
  > —Robert Sommer, "Hard Architecture"

Note: Writers often experiment with arrangement in order to have a variety of sentences in a particular piece of writing. Remember, however, that the arrangement of a sentence indicates the importance of the ideas within it. Don't rearrange sentences so much that your original emphasis is lost.

Arrangements of Sentences

Classify each of the following sentences as *loose, balanced, periodic,* or *cumulative.*

(1) Although she knew little about her ancestors, Soo Jin found genealogy intriguing. **(2)** Last summer, at a family reunion, she got a surprise. **(3)** A distant cousin presented her with her great-grandmother's diary, which was written in Korean. **(4)** Soo Jin was ecstatic, anticipating the family stories this book held.

(5) With great care, Soo Jin opened this heirloom from her ancestry, something she thought she would never do. **(6)** Until now, Soo Jin had not worried about learning Korean. **(7)** She hoped that someone at the reunion could read it, but she was disappointed. **(8)** She needed to find a translator, someone to unlock the diary's secrets.

(9) As it turned out, Mrs. Kim, a volunteer at the youth center, read Korean, and she helped Soo Jin. **(10)** Together, they enjoyed translating the diary.

Model

Model the following balanced and cumulative sentences.

> **The experience left me troubled; I knew there was something wrong but not quite what it was.**
> —Tim Flannery, *The Weather Makers*

> **While she watched, the snake nosed up into the exact corner between the cupboards and in an instant disappeared, as if it had been sucked up by vacuum tube.**
> —Christina Adam, *Any Small Thing Can Save You*

Sentences

Getting Sentence Parts to Agree

Agreement of Subject and Verb

A verb must agree in number (singular or plural) with its subject.

> The student was proud of her quarter grades.

Note: Do not be confused by words that come between the subject and verb.

> The manager, as well as the players, is required to display good sportsmanship. (*Manager*, not *players*, is the subject.)

752.1 Compound Subjects

Compound subjects joined by *or* or *nor* take a singular verb (when they are singular subjects).

> Neither Bev nor Kendra goes to the street dances.

Note: When one of the subjects joined by *or* or *nor* is singular and one is plural, the verb must agree with the subject nearer the verb.

> Neither Yoshi nor his friends sing in the band anymore. (The plural subject *friends* is nearer the verb, so the plural verb *sing* is correct.)

Compound subjects connected with *and* require a plural verb.

> Strength and balance are necessary for gymnastics.

752.2 Delayed Subjects

Delayed subjects occur when the verb comes before the subject in a sentence. In these inverted sentences, the delayed subject must agree with the verb.

> There are many hardworking students in our schools.
> There is present among many young people today a will to succeed.

(*Students* and *will* are the true subjects of these sentences, not *there*.)

752.3 "Be" Verbs

When a sentence contains a form of the "be" verb—and a noun comes before and after that verb—the verb must agree with the subject, not the *complement* (the noun coming after the verb).

> The cause of his problem was the bad brakes.
> The bad brakes were the cause of his problem.

752.4 Special Cases

Some nouns that are **plural in form but singular in meaning** take a singular verb: *mumps, measles, news, mathematics, economics, gallows, shambles.*

> Measles is still considered a serious disease in many parts of the world.

Some nouns that are plural in form but singular in meaning take a plural verb: *scissors, trousers, tidings.*

> The scissors disappear whenever I need them.

Agreement of Subject and Verb 1

For each sentence, write the correct verb from the choice given in parentheses.

1. Neither the school board nor the superintendent *(have, has)* made a decision.

2. On our flight to Italy *(was, were)* several athletes from Team USA.

3. There *(is, are)* too many abandoned animals at the shelter.

4. Someone who adopts one of these animals *(saves, save)* it from an uncertain fate.

5. *(Is, Are)* you interested in adopting a shelter dog?

6. Dwayne or his sisters *(is, are)* going to college in Montana.

7. Great—there *(go, goes)* our train to Chicago!

8. *(Were, Was)* Nina's parents asking about the trip?

9. The Downtown Committee *(is, are)* planning a fall harvest fair.

10. Kandi, Robyn, or Lyndsay *(have, has)* a laptop you might borrow.

11. I can't understand why the soda machines *(are, is)* gone.

12. My dad, as well as his golf partner, *(was, were)* asked to play in the tournament.

Model

Model the following sentences to practice correct subject-verb agreement.

Her cheekbones were still high and strong, but the skin was parched and ruddy.

— Jeannette Walls, *The Glass Castle: A Memoir*

Blue jeans are the most beautiful things since the gondola.

—Diana Vreeland

Agreement of Subject and Verb *(continued)*

754.1 Collective Nouns

Collective nouns *(faculty, committee, team, congress, species, crowd, army, pair, squad)* take a singular verb when they refer to a group as a unit; collective nouns take a plural verb when they refer to the individuals within the group.

> The favored team is losing, and the crowd is getting ugly. (Both *team* and *crowd* are considered units in this sentence, requiring the singular verb *is*.)

> The pair reunite after 20 years apart.
> (Here, *pair* refers to two individuals, so the plural verb *reunite* is required.)

754.2 Indefinite Pronouns

Some **indefinite pronouns** are singular: *each, either, neither, one, everybody, another, anybody, everyone, nobody, everything, somebody,* and *someone*. They require a singular verb.

> Everybody is invited to the cafeteria for refreshments.

Some **indefinite pronouns** are plural: *both, few, many,* and *several*.

> Several like chocolate cake. Many ask for ice cream, too.

Note: Do not be confused by words or phrases that come between the indefinite pronoun and the verb.

> One of the participants is (not *are*) going to have to stay late to clean up.

A Closer Look

> Some **indefinite pronouns** can be either singular or plural: *all, any, most, none,* and *some*. These pronouns are singular if the number of the noun in the prepositional phrase is singular; they are plural if the noun is plural.
>
> > Most of the food complaints are coming from the seniors.
> > (*Complaints* is plural, so *most* is plural.)
>
> > Most of the tabletop is sticky with melted ice cream.
> > (*Tabletop* is singular, so *most* is singular.)

754.3 Relative Pronouns

When a **relative pronoun** *(who, which, that)* is used as the subject of a clause, the number of the verb is determined by the antecedent of the pronoun. (The antecedent is the word to which the pronoun refers.)

> This is one of the books that are required for geography class.
> (The relative pronoun *that* requires the plural verb *are* because its antecedent, *books,* is plural.)

Note: To test this type of sentence for agreement, read the "of" phrase first.

> Of the books that are required for geography class, this is one.

Agreement of Subject and Verb 2

For each numbered sentence, write the correct verb from the choice given in parentheses.

(1) Imagine that you are a young person who *(live, lives)* in Florida during the first half of the twentieth century. **(2)** You are excited that one of your state's most famous athletes *(is, are)* Babe Didrikson. **(3)** Many girls your age *(credit, credits)* her as a role model. **(4)** Most of the local papers *(carry, carries)* stories about her versatile athletic abilities. **(5)** Because of Babe's basketball skills, her high school team *(play, plays)* in a women's national basketball championship. **(6)** Everyone *(is, are)* thrilled when she sets world records at the Olympics in the 80-yard dash and javelin throw.

(7) Babe's career *(don't, doesn't)* stop there. She pitches on a women's baseball team, and then she tries tennis. **(8)** This is one of the sports that *(is, are)* a problem for Babe. **(9)** The U.S. Lawn Tennis Association *(bar, bars)* her from the game because she plays too well. **(10)** By spring of 1934, Babe *(become, becomes)* famous as one of the top competitors on the professional golf circuit. **(11)** The Associated Press *(take, takes)* notice. **(12)** Its members *(vote, votes)* Babe Didrikson Zaharias the Top Woman Athlete of the Half Century (1900–1949).

Model

Model the following sentences to practice subject-verb agreement.

Everybody likes a compliment.

—Abraham Lincoln

Most of the luxuries and many of the so-called comforts of life are not only not indispensable, but positive hindrances to the elevation of mankind.

—Henry David Thoreau

Agreement of Pronoun and Antecedent

A pronoun must agree in number, person, and gender with its *antecedent*. (The *antecedent* is the word to which the pronoun refers.)

> Cal **brought** *his* **gerbil to school.** (The antecedent of *his* is *Cal*. Both the pronoun and its antecedent are singular, third person, and masculine; therefore, the pronoun is said to "agree" with its antecedent.)

756.1 Agreement in Number

Use a **singular pronoun** to refer to such antecedents as *each, either, neither, one, anyone, anybody, everyone, everybody, somebody, another, nobody,* and *a person.*

> **Neither of the brothers likes** *his* (not *their*) **room.**

Two or more singular antecedents joined by *or* or *nor* are also referred to by a **singular pronoun.**

> **Either** Connie **or** Sue **left** *her* **headset in the library.**

If one of the antecedents joined by *or* or *nor* is singular and one is plural, the pronoun should agree with the nearer antecedent.

> **Neither the** manager **nor the** players **were crazy about** *their* **new uniforms.**

Use a **plural pronoun** to refer to plural antecedents as well as compound subjects joined by *and.*

> Jared **and** Carlos **are finishing** *their* **assignments.**

756.2 Agreement in Gender

Use a **masculine** or **feminine pronoun** depending upon the gender of the antecedent.

> Tristan **would like to bring** *his* **dog along on the trip.**
> Claire **is always complaining that** *her* **feet are cold.**

Use a **neuter** pronoun when the antecedent has no gender.

> **The ancient** weeping willow **is losing many of** *its* **branches.**

When *a person* or *everyone* is used to refer to both sexes or either sex, you will have to choose whether to offer optional pronouns or rewrite the sentence.

> **A person** should be allowed to choose *her* or *his* own footwear. (optional pronouns)
> People **should be allowed to** choose *their* own footwear. (rewritten in plural form)

Agreement of Pronoun and Antecedent

 For each sentence, write the correct pronoun from the choice given in parentheses.

1. Leah and Abdul made plans to go to *(their, her)* senior prom.

2. Sidnie helped her brother fill out *(his, their)* income tax form.

3. Most of the wall had crayon marks all over *(it, them)*.

4. Each college-bound student should have received *(his or her, their)* application materials by now.

5. Francisco or Rory will babysit for *(their, his)* sister this Saturday night.

6. Chuck's new pants were too long, and he didn't know how to hem *(it, them)*.

7. Most of the team's shirts had commemorative patches on *(it, them)*.

8. Either Mr. Ramos or his son lost *(his, their)* drill at the work site.

9. My Princess Diana rosebush has black spots on *(its, her)* leaves.

10. I asked everyone to bring *(his or her, their)* ideas to the meeting.

11. Neither my motorcycle nor any bicycles had dents on *(it, them)* as a result of the hail.

12. Did anyone leave *(their, his or her)* cell phone at my house last night?

 ## Model

Model the following sentences to practice pronoun-antecedent agreement.

A good person will resist an evil system with his or her whole soul.
—Mohandas Karamchand Gandhi

Far away, there in the sunshine, are my highest aspirations. I may not reach them, but I can look up and see their beauty, believe in them, and try to follow where they lead.
—Louisa May Alcott

Test Prep

Write the letter or letters of the best answer or answers for each underlined part from the choices given on the next page.

Julian is a college student heading to the Gulf Coast, <u>the site of a devastating</u>
1
<u>hurricane.</u> <u>It's spring break, and instead of partying and tanning on the beach,</u>
2
<u>he decided to make a difference.</u> This is his first assignment <u>with the "alternative</u>
3
<u>break" movement.</u>

<u>Colleges and volunteer organizations across the nation</u> encourage students
4
to plan alternative breaks. Thousands of students <u>participate in the program each</u>
5
<u>year.</u> They volunteer <u>to build houses</u> for low-income families, care for AIDS patients,
6
tutor special-needs students, and more.

High school students <u>have been volunteering,</u> too. <u>If you read UCLA's survey</u>
7
<u>of 260,000 college freshmen, the results might surprise you.</u> <u>Desiring to aid their</u>
8   **9**
<u>communities,</u> 82 percent had volunteered during their senior year. <u>Volunteering</u>
                                                                       10
<u>weekly</u> was the goal of 70 percent of those surveyed. <u>Overall, teens volunteered with</u>

<u>an organization at nearly double the rate of adults.</u>
11
<u>If you were Julian, how would you be helping?</u> Mucking out damaged homes,
12
<u>clearing debris,</u> and putting tarps on roofs are just a few of the activities you might
13
do. <u>What a huge help you would be to the victims of a hurricane!</u>
14

1. **A** gerund phrase
   B infinitive phrase
   C participial phrase
   D appositive phrase

2. **A** simple sentence
   B compound-complex sentence
   C compound sentence
   D complex sentence

3. **A** dependent clause
   B independent clause
   C absolute phrase
   D prepositional phrase

4. **A** compound subject
   B delayed subject
   C simple subject
   D complete subject

5. **A** simple predicate
   B complete predicate
   C compound predicate
   D dependent clause

6. **A** gerund phrase
   B infinitive phrase
   C participial phrase
   D appositive phrase

7. **A** gerund phrase
   B participial phrase
   C complete predicate
   D verb phrase

8. **A** complex sentence
   B compound sentence
   C conditional sentence
   D periodic sentence

9. **A** gerund phrase
   B infinitive phrase
   C participial phrase
   D appositive phrase

10. **A** gerund phrase
    B infinitive phrase
    C participial phrase
    D appositive phrase

11. **A** cumulative sentence
    B balanced sentence
    C periodic sentence
    D loose sentence

12. **A** declarative sentence
    B interrogative sentence
    C exclamatory sentence
    D conditional sentence

13. **A** gerund phrase
    B infinitive phrase
    C participial phrase
    D appositive phrase

14. **A** declarative sentence
    B interrogative sentence
    C exclamatory sentence
    D conditional sentence

Diagramming Sentences

A **graphic diagram** of a sentence is a picture of how the words in that sentence are related and how they fit together to form a complete thought.

760.1 Simple Sentence with One Subject and One Verb

Chris fishes.

| Chris | fishes | | subject | verb |

760.2 Simple Sentence with a Predicate Adjective

Fish are delicious.

| Fish | are \ delicious | | subject | verb \ predicate adjective |

760.3 Simple Sentence with a Predicate Noun and Adjectives

Fishing is my favorite hobby.

Note: When possessive pronouns (*my, his, their,* etc.) are used as adjectives, they are placed on a diagonal line under the word they modify.

760.4 Simple Sentence with an Indirect and Direct Object

My grandpa gave us a trout.

Note: Articles (*a, an, the*) are adjectives and are placed on a diagonal line under the word they modify.

Sentence Diagramming 1

Diagram the following sentences.

1. Jerry MacDonald studies ancient fossils.

2. The New Mexico desert is his workplace.

3. His discoveries are incredible!

4. The Paleozoic Trackways Project was his best find.

5. Jerry dug.

6. He unearthed interesting tracks.

7. He showed some colleagues his discovery.

8. The tracks were prehistoric.

9. They gave us a new understanding.

10. Paleontology is exciting!

Half a truth is often a great lie.   —Benjamin Franklin

Model

Model the following proverbs to practice writing simple sentences with direct objects.

The early bird catches the worm.
The big thieves hang the little ones.

Diagramming Sentences *(continued)*

762.1 Simple Sentence with a Prepositional Phrase

I like fishing by myself.

762.2 Simple Sentence with a Compound Subject and Verb

The team and fans clapped and cheered.

762.3 Compound Sentence

The team scored, and the crowd cheered wildly.

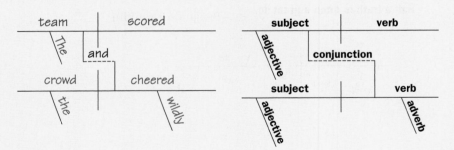

762.4 Complex Sentence with a Subordinate Clause

Before Erin scored, the crowd sat quietly.

Sentence Diagramming 2

Diagram the following sentences.

1. Jamar completed the first leg of the triathlon.

2. Landon and his dad explored caves with a guide.

3. In our high school, the principal has the toughest job.

4. The guard on duty at the mall always wears a uniform.

5. I will be tired when I get home from the game.

6. Geeta and Melissa went to the sale and bought some shoes.

7. You can grow awesome flowers, but it takes a "green thumb."

8. Some students are unprepared and so do not have control over their futures.

9. Hector went for a swim in the lake.

10. Lauren laughed, but her dad frowned.

Art knows no limit, and the artists will never achieve perfection.

—Bente Borsum

Model

Model the following sentences to practice writing compound and complex sentences.

If at first you don't succeed, you're running about average. —M. H. Alderson

I think, therefore I am.

—Rene Descartes

Credits

Page:

Page 381: Copyright © 2004 by Houghton Mifflin Company. Adapted and reproduced by permission from *The American Heritage College Dictionary,* Fourth Edition.

Photos:

Blend Images, LLC: p. 143

Getty Images: p. 55 Photodisc, p. 139 Photodisc, p. 114 Todd Davidson, p. 270 Digital Vision, p. 705 David De Lossy

iStockphoto: pages 165, 573, 613

© 2006 Jupiterimages Corporation: pages 20, 24, 26, 32, 37, 90, 118, 124, 157 (man), 367 (gears), 492, 494 (girl), 502, 525, 545, 593, 597, 615, 645, 658, 693, 697, 703, 715, 716, 756

Shutterstock: pages 2, 3, 4, 35, 75, 102, 104, 110, 120, 131, 135, 147, 157 (film strip), 166, 170, 171, 172, 180, 190, 191, 197, 205, 236, 253, 262, 282, 302, 309, 324, 331, 345, 356, 362, 365, 366, 367 (piggy bank), 368, 369, 378, 394, 396, 410 (field), 416, 426, 429, 431, 432, 434, 436, 440, 448, 455, 456, 458, 459, 461, 462, 464, 474, 484, 486, 490, 494 (faucet), 496, 498, 504, 505, 517, 520, 526, 528, 531, 536, 541, 542, 547, 552, 553, 566, 572, 579, 588, 607, 611, 619, 625, 629, 631, 635, 637, 639, 640, 645, 649, 662, 664, 665, 670, 679, 681, 682, 684, 686, 689, 694, 696, 700, 709, 711, 717, 723, 726, 729, 740, 741, 743, 744, 745, 746, 747, 749, 751, 753, 758

Icon images: various pages; Prewrite icon Electrique/ImageState; Write icon © Corbis; Revise icon/Photodisc/Getty Images

Acknowledgements

We're grateful to many people who helped bring *Write Source* to life. First, we must thank all the teachers and their students from across the country who contributed writing models and ideas.

In addition, we want to thank our Write Source/Great Source team for all their help:

Steven J. Augustyn, Laura Bachman, Ron Bachman, April Barrons, Heather Bazata, Colleen Belmont, Susan Boehm, Linne Bruskewitz, Evelyn Curley, Joanna Dupuis, Chris Erickson, Mark Fairweather, Jean Fischer, Hillary Gammons, Mariellen Hanrahan, Tammy Hintz, Kelly Kaiser, Judy Kerkhoff, Rob King, Lois Krenzke, Mark Lalumondier, Joyce Becker Lee, Ellen Leitheusser, Michele Order Litant, Dian Lynch, Colleen McCarthy, Gary Miller, Pat Moore, Kevin Nelson, Sue Paro, Linda Presto, Kathy Quirk, Betsy Rasmussen, Pat Reigel, Jason C. Reynolds, Christine Rieker, Susan Rogalski, Steve Schend, Janae Sebranek, Lester Smith, Richard Spencer, Stephen D. Sullivan, Jean Varley, and Claire Ziffer.

Index

The index will help you find specific information in this textbook. Entries in italics are words from the "Using the Right Word" section. The colored boxes contain information you will use often.